An Anthology of Philosophy in Persia

An Anthology of Philosophy in Persia

VOLUME I

From Zoroaster to ʿUmar Khayyām

SEYYED HOSSEIN NASR *with* MEHDI AMINRAZAVI

with the assistance of

M. R. JOZI

I.B.Tauris *Publishers*

LONDON • NEW YORK

in association with

The Institute of Ismaili Studies

LONDON

Published in 2008 by I.B.Tauris & Co Ltd
6 Salem Rd, London W2 4BU
175 Fifth Avenue, New York NY 10010
www.ibtauris.com

in association with The Institute of Ismaili Studies
42–44 Grosvenor Gardens, London SW1W 0EB
www.iis.ac.uk

In the United States of America and in Canada distributed by
St Martin's Press, 175 Fifth Avenue, New York NY 10010

First published in 1999 by Oxford University Press

ISBN 978 1 84511 541 8

A full CIP record for this book is available from the British Library
A full CIP record for this book is available from the Library of Congress

Library of Congress catalog card: available

Typeset in Minion Tra for The Institute of Ismaili Studies
Persian poem by Decotype, Amsterdam

Printed and bound in Great Britain by TJ International Ltd, Padstow, Cornwall

The Institute of Ismaili Studies

The Institute of Ismaili Studies was established in 1977 with the object of promoting scholarship and learning on Islam, in the historical as well as contemporary contexts, and a better understanding of its relationship with other societies and faiths.

The Institute's programmes encourage a perspective which is not confined to the theological and religious heritage of Islam, but seeks to explore the relationship of religious ideas to broader dimensions of society and culture. The programmes thus encourage an interdisciplinary approach to the materials of Islamic history and thought. Particular attention is also given to issues of modernity that arise as Muslims seek to relate their heritage to the contemporary situation.

Within the Islamic tradition, the Institute's programmes promote research on those areas which have, to date, received relatively little attention from scholars. These include the intellectual and literary expressions of Shiʿism in general, and Ismailism in particular.

In the context of Islamic societies, the Institute's programmes are informed by the full range and diversity of cultures in which Islam is practised today, from the Middle East, South and Central Asia, and Africa to the industrialized societies of the West, thus taking into consideration the variety of contexts which shape the ideals, beliefs and practices of the faith.

These objectives are realized through concrete programmes and activities organized and implemented by various departments of the Institute. The Institute also collaborates periodically, on a programme-specific basis, with other institutions of learning in the United Kingdom and abroad.

The Institute's academic publications fall into a number of interrelated categories:

1. Occasional papers or essays addressing broad themes of the relationship between religion and society, with special reference to Islam.
2. Monographs exploring specific aspects of Islamic faith and culture, or the contributions of individual Muslim thinkers or writers.
3. Editions or translations of significant primary or secondary texts.
4. Translations of poetic or literary texts which illustrate the rich heritage of spiritual, devotional and symbolic expressions in Muslim history.
5. Works on Ismaili history and thought, and the relationship of the Ismailis to other traditions, communities and schools of thought in Islam.
6. Proceedings of conferences and seminars sponsored by the Institute.
7. Bibliographical works and catalogues which document manuscripts, printed texts and other source materials.

This book falls into category two listed above.

In facilitating these and other publications, the Institute's sole aim is to encourage original research and analysis of relevant issues. While every effort is made to ensure that the publications are of a high academic standard, there is naturally bound to be a diversity of views, ideas and interpretations. As such, the opinions expressed in these publications must be understood as belonging to their authors alone.

دل گرچه در این بادیه بسیار شتافت   يك موی ندانست ولی موی شکافت
اندر دل من هزار خورشید بتافت   آخر به کمال ذره ای راه نیافت

Although my heart made much haste in this desert,
It did not know a single hair, but took to hair-splitting.
In my heart shone a thousand suns,
Yet it never discovered completely the nature of a single atom.

Ibn Sīnā (Avicenna)

Contents

Preface *M. Aminrazavi* xiii
List of Reprinted Works xvii
Note on Transliteration xix
List of Contributors xxi

Prolegomenon *S. H. Nasr* 1

PART I. EARLY PERSIAN PHILOSOPHY: ZOROASTRIAN THOUGHT

Introduction *M. Aminrazavi* 13

1. The Original Creation (from *Bundahišn*) 16
2. Greater Bundahišn 27
3. The Answers of Manūskihar (from *Dādistān-i Dīnīk*) 35
4. Opinions of the Spirit of Wisdom (from *Dīnā-i Maīnog-i Khirad*) 44
5. Selected Readings 53
6. Exegesis of the Good Religion (from *Dēnkard* VI) 88

PART II. EARLY PERSIAN PHILOSOPHY: MANICHAEISM

Introduction *M. Aminrazavi* 105

7. Central Principles (from the *Kephalaia*) 108

PART III. EARLY ISLAMIC PHILOSOPHY: THE PERIPATETICS

Introduction *S. H. Nasr* 127

8. Abu'l-ʿAbbās Muḥammad Īrānshahrī 130

Introduction *M. Aminrazavi* 130

The Ideas of Īrānshahrī (from *Zād al-musāfirīn*) 132

9. Abū Naṣr Fārābī 134

Introduction *S. H. Nasr* 134
A Paraphrase of Aristotle's *Analytica Posteriora* (from *Kitāb al-burhān*) 137
A Reconciliation of the Opinions of the Two Sages, Divine Plato and Aristotle (from *Kitāb al-jamʿ bayn ra'yay al-ḥakimayn Aflāṭūn al-ilāhī wa Arisṭū*) 155
The Perfect State (from *Mabādi' ārā' ahl al-madīnat al-fāḍilah*) 164

10. Abu'l-Ḥasan ʿĀmirī 180

Introduction *S. H. Nasr* 180
Knowledge and the Religious Sciences (from *al-Iʿlām bi manāqib al-Islām*) 182
On the Soul and its Fate (from *al-Amad ʿala'l-abad*) 207

11. Abū Sulaymān Sijistānī 216

Introduction *M. Aminrazavi* 216
Philosophical Treatises (*Muṣannafāt*) 218

12. Ibn Sīnā 243

Introduction *S. H. Nasr* 243
Metaphysics (from *Dānish-nāmah-yi ʿalā'ī*) 247
Creation *Ex-Nihilo* and Immediate Creation (from *al-Ishārāt wa'l-tanbīhāt*) 269
On Theodicy and Providence I (from *al-Shifā'*) 277
On Theodicy and Providence II (from *al-Ishārāt wa'l-tanbīhāt*) 289
On Time (from *al-Shifā'*) 292
The Stations of the Knowers (from *al-Ishārāt wa'l-tanbīhāt*) 303
Living Son of the Awake (from *Risālah Ḥayy ibn Yaqẓān*) 312
Introduction (from *Manṭiq al-mashraqiyyīn*) 321

13. Abū ʿAlī Aḥmad ibn Muḥammad Miskawayh 323

Introduction *S. H. Nasr* 323
Perennial Philosophy (Wisdom) (from *al-Ḥikmat al-khālidah* or *Jāwīdān-khirad*) 326
The Health of the Soul (from *Tahdhīb al-akhlāq*) 356

14. Bahmanyār ibn Marzbān 388

Introduction *M. Aminrazavi* 388
Author's Foreword (from *Kitāb al-taḥṣīl*) 390

PART IV. EARLY ISLAMIC PHILOSOPHY: THE INDEPENDENT PHILOSOPHERS

Introduction *S. H. Nasr* 409

15. Abū Bakr Muḥammad ibn Zakariyyā' Rāzī 411

Introduction *M. Aminrazavi* 411
Of the Excellence and Praise of Reason (from *al-Ṭibb al-rūḥānī*) 414
The Book of the Philosophic Life (from *al-Sīrat al-falsafiyyah*) 424

16. Abū Rayḥān Bīrūnī 434

Introduction *S. H. Nasr* 434
The Belief of the Hindus in God (from *Taḥqīq mā li'l-Hind*) 437
Questions and Answers (from *al-As'ilah wa'l-ajwibah*) 459

17. 'Umar Khayyām 474

Introduction *M. Aminrazavi* 474
The Necessity of Contradiction, Free Will and Determinism (*Ḍarūrat al-taḍādd fi'l-'ālam wa'l-jabr wa'l-baqā'*) 476
Universals of Existence (*Kulliyyāt-i wujūd*) 481

Select Bibliography 485
Index 496

Preface

In the 1970s, the Imperial Iranian Academy of Philosophy was established under the directorship of Professor Seyyed Hossein Nasr, with several goals including better introducing the rich philosophical traditions of Persia to the scholars and students of other cultures, in particular Europe and North America. At the time, UNESCO proposed that an anthology of Persian philosophers be edited by Professor Nasr. The anthology that UNESCO had proposed, however, was of a much more limited scale than the present work upon which the editors have embarked.

Owing to the political upheavals of the late 1970s in Iran, the plan to produce the anthology was postponed until 1992, when we began work based on Professor Nasr's original plan but on a much more extensive and elaborate scale, as developed by him with my help.

The first and foremost issue of importance was to decide upon the use of the word *philosophy* and the sense in which this term was to be applied in our selection process. Islamic civilization, like many other great civilizations, has produced an array of intellectual thought under the rubric of philosophy. In selecting the materials to be included in our anthology, we have used *philosophy* not only in its limited rationalistic sense but also in a wider sense to include certain aspects of theological debate, philosophical Sufism, philosophical narratives, and even philosophical hermeneutics (*ta'wīl*). We did, however, exclude pure Sufi texts and other materials that cannot be classified as philosophy in terms of both their content and their format.

In addition to our concern for the nature of the materials selected, we had to decide whether we should include the writings of certain figures whose Persian identity was dubious. In this regard, we excluded a number of such figures, but included those who were clearly under the influence of Persian theological and philosophical thought, such as ʿAllāf, Naẓẓām and Fārābī. Needless to say, the borders of Persia in the last two thousand years have changed frequently and a classical Persian thinker such as Bīrūnī may not, strictly speaking, be considered a Persian in a different time period if our criterion is solely the boundaries of modern nations. Clearly such geographical changes are of no consequence to the intellectual orientation of Persian philosophers.

The next problem to overcome was to secure the necessary funds to commission competent scholars to undertake the translations of the materials needed. With the assistance of several foundations whose contributions have been acknowledged, this became possible. Next, we had to complete the task of finding an ideal format that would present a balance in chronology and schools of thought. Whereas Western philosophical tradition consists of different eras—that is, Greek, medieval, modern, and contemporary—Islamic philosophy does not lend itself to such classifications. Nor can we divide precisely the Islamic philosophical tradition into well-defined philosophical paradigms and schools of thought, since they overlap and share much in common. Following considerable thought, we arranged the contents in such a way as to bring about a rapprochement between chronology and philosophical periods, as well as diverse schools of thought. The editors realize that there is no ideal order that can coherently and consistently bring together over 2,500 years of philosophical activity. For example, the often various work of a philosopher—for example, Ghazzālī—has had to be divided into several segments based on whether it is philosophical, theological, or philosophical Sufism; each part has had to be included in a different section of this anthology.

The next issue was to find scholars sufficiently competent both linguistically and philosophically to undertake the translation of dense philosophical treatises in Persian and Arabic. Though such scholars are available, they are scattered throughout the world, with a heavy concentration in North America. Coordinating our efforts with a large number of translators, while paying attention to the intricacies of such a major scholarly endeavour, proved to be both challenging and rewarding.

The editors have felt that since our contributors are well-established scholars, each of whom prefers to follow one of the standard systems of transliteration and bibliography, their work has been printed here in the style that the translators have desired. In our introductions, however, we have used the style preferable to us, which is different from some of our translators.

Throughout this work, bibliographical sources have been provided. Needless to say, the lists are not meant to be exhaustive; rather, they include some of the most important primary and secondary sources and are meant to be a guide for further research. Whenever possible, we have included in the bibliographies works that themselves are of a bibliographical nature, with exhaustive information concerning the writings of the author in question.

The result of several years' effort is this first volume of a multi-volume anthology that is inclusive of philosophical treatises of both pre-Islamic and early Islamic Persia. The anthology is expected to fill a gap in the field of Islamic philosophy and Persian thought, and to demonstrate that Islamic philosophy is a living tradition in Iran and did not come to an end in the seventh/thirteenth century after Ibn Rushd, as some have argued. Furthermore, the anthology provides a variety of writings to show that the edifices of Persian philosophy are diverse, in both content and format; it would be futile to consider only certain figures and their thoughts as seminal, and the rest devoid of any philosophical significance.

We would like to thank the foundations that have helped make publication of this volume possible, the Institut International de Philosophie (under the auspices of UNESCO) and especially its former president, Professor Raymond Klibansky, the Keyan Foundation, the Iranian Academic Society, The Centre for the Great Islamic Encyclopedia (Tehran), the Foundation for Traditional Studies as well as the numerous publishers who granted permission to use excerpts from their published materials.

Special thanks are due to The Institute of Ismaili Studies where Mr M. R. Jozi carefully edited each volume to prepare it in its final form for publication. We remain grateful to him as well as to Dr. Farhad Daftary and other members of the Institute along with I. B. Tauris for making the publication of this work possible.

Finally, we would like to express our gratitude and deep appreciation to our translators, whose arduous task has made possible this anthology. Their endeavours have helped to create a source book on Persian thought and Islamic philosophy that represents the contribution of Persia to this intellectual tradition.

May these volumes be an aid in bringing to light a hitherto neglected dimension of the rich culture of Persia and revealing the importance of the philosophical life of the land that until now has been known in the West primarily for its poetry, architecture, carpets and miniature paintings.

Mehdi Aminrazavi,
Manassas, Virginia
Bahman 1385 AA (s)
February 2007 AD

List of Reprinted Works

F. Max Müller, ed., *The Sacred Books of the East: Pahlavī Texts*. Delhi, 1977 (E. W. West tr., 'Bundahišn', vol. 5, pp. 3–20; 'Dādistān-i Dīnīk', vol. 18, pp. 11–25; 'Dīnā-i Maīnog-i Khirad', vol. 24, pp. 3–17).

R. C. Zaehner, *Zurvan: A Zoroastrian Dilemma*. Oxford, 1955 ('Greater Bundahišn', 'Zātspram', 'Dēnkart', 'Šikand Gumānī Vazār', 'Hormazyār', pp. 312–321, 341–343, 386–391, 394–396, 409–418).

M. Boyce, *Textual Sources for the Study of Zoroastrianism*. Manchester, 1984 ('Yasna', 'Greater Bundahišn', 'Vendidad', 'Hadhokht Nask', 'Maīnog-i Khirad', 'Dādistān-i Dīnīk', 'Arda Virāz', pp. 35–36, 45–53, 80–86).

Ārturpāt-ı Ēmetān, *The Wisdom of the Sāsaniān Sages* (Dēnkard VI), tr. Sh. Shaked, ed. Ehsan Yarshater. Boulder, CO, 1979, pp. 7–212 (selected passages).

I. Gardner, *The Kephalaia of the Teacher: The Edited Coptic Manichaean Texts in Translation with Commentary*. Leiden, 1995, pp. 27–28, 32–33, 49–50, 86–87, 133–134, 200–202, 209–216, 288–289.

al-Fārābī, *On the Perfect State* (Mabādi' ārā' ahl al-madīnat al-fāḍilah), ed. and tr. R. Walzer, Oxford, 1985, pp. 58–89, 229–259.

E. K. Rowson, *A Muslim Philosopher on the Soul and Its Fate: al-'Āmirī's* Kitāb al-amad 'ala'l-abad. New Haven, CT, 1988, pp. 59–87 (selected passages).

J. L. Kraemer, *Philosophy in the Renaissance of Islam: Abū Sulaymān al-Sijistānī and His Circle*. Leiden, 1986, pp. 279–304.

S. Inati, *A Study of Ibn Sīnā's Mysticism*, Albany, NY, 1996 (selected passages).

H. Corbin, *Avicenna and the Visionary Recital*, tr. from the French, W. R. Trask. Princeton, NJ, 1990, pp. 137–150.

Miskawayh, *The Refinement of Character* (Tahdhīb al-akhlāq), tr. C. K. Zurayk. Beirut, 1966, pp. 157–209.

A. J. Arberry, *The Spiritual Physick of Rhazes*. London, 1950, pp. 21–103.

al-Rāzi, 'The Book of the Philosophic Life', tr. and introduced C. E. Butterworth, *Interpretation*, 20:3 (1993), pp. 227–236.

E. C. Sachau, *Alberuni's India*. Lahore, 1962, vol. 1, pp. 32–39, 89–131.

R. Berjak and M. Iqbal, 'Ibn Sīnā–al-Bīrūnī Correspondence (*al-As'ilah wa'l ajwibah*)', *Islam and Science*, 49 (June, 2003), pp. 1–14.

M. W. Rahman, 'Ḍarūrat al-taḍādd fi'l-'ālam wa'l-jabr wa'l-baqā'' ('The Necessity of Contradiction, Free Will and Determinism') and 'Kulliyyāt-i wujūd' ('Universals of Existence'), in Swami Govinda Tirtha, *The Nectar of Grace: Omar Khayyām's Life and Works*. Allahabad, 1941, pp. 104–110; pp. 124–128.

Note on Transliteration

Arabic characters

ء	ʾ
ب	b
ت	t
ث	*th*
ج	j
ح	ḥ
خ	*kh*
د	d
ذ	*dh*
ر	r
ز	z
س	s
ش	*sh*
ص	ṣ
ض	ḍ
ط	ṭ
ظ	ẓ
ع	ʿ
غ	*gh*
ف	f
ق	q
ك	k
ل	l
م	m
ن	n
ه	h
و	w
ى	y
ة	ah; at (construct state)

long vowels	
ا	ā
و	ū
ي	ī
short vowels	
ـَ	a
ـُ	u
ـِ	i
diphthongs	
ـَو	aw
ـَى	ai (ay)
ـيّ	ayy (final form ī)
ـوّ	uww (final form ū)

Persian letters added to the Arabic alphabet

پ	p
چ	*ch*
ژ	*zh*
گ	g

List of Contributors*

SEYYED HOSSEIN NASR received his early education in Iran and completed his studies at The Massachusetts Institute of Technology and Harvard University. Nasr is the author of over three hundred articles and thirty books. He has taught at a number of universities, both in the Middle East, especially Tehran University, and in the United States; and he has lectured widely on Islamic philosophy. Nasr is currently the University Professor of Islamic Studies at The George Washington University.

MEHDI AMINRAZAVI received his early education in Iran and completed his master's degree in philosophy at the University of Washington and his doctorate in the philosophy of religion at Temple University. He is the author and editor of numerous articles and books, and is currently Professor of Philosophy and Religion at the University of Mary Washington and Director of the Middle Eastern Studies Program.

MAJID FAKHRY studied Islamic philosophy at the American University in Beirut and the University of Edinburgh. He is the author of numerous articles and books, including *History of Islamic Philosophy*. He is currently Emeritus Professor of Philosophy from the American University in Beirut and a research scholar at Georgetown University.

THOMAS GASKIL studied at the University of Massachusetts in Boston and Vanderbelt University, as well as in the School of Oriental Studies at the University of Arizona. He taught philosophy at Southern Illinois University; he has also written on non-Western philosophical thought.

ALMA GIESE completed her studies in Islamic studies at Freiburg and Giessen Universities. She has published extensively on Islamic philosophy and theology, and is an independent research scholar.

SHAMS INATI studied at the American University in Beirut and the State University of New York in Buffalo. She has written extensively on Islamic philosophy, in particular Ibn Sīnā, and is currently Professor of Islamic Studies at Villanova University.

EVERRET K. ROWSON studied at Princeton and Yale universities and is Professor of Middle Eastern and Islamic Studies at New York University. He has written extensively on Islamic philosophy and literature and is a specialist on ʿĀmirī.

YEGANE SHAYEGAN studied Islamic philosophy at Geneva and Harvard Universities and was a research scholar at University College London. Until her recent death she was a research fellow at the Iranian Academy of Philosophy in Tehran.

CHARLES BUTTERWORTH is Professor of Government and Politics at the University of Maryland. He specializes in medieval Islamic political philosophy; his publications include critical editions and translations of most of Averroes' Middle Commentaries and several treatises by Fārābī and Rāzī. He was the president of the American council for the study of Islamic Societies (ACSIS) as well as the Société Internationale pour l'Étude de l'Histoire de la Philosophie et la Science Arabe et Islamique.

*Contributors mentioned here are those who have translated new materials especially for this volume. The list of others whose translations have already appeared elsewhere and of which we have made use appears in the List of Reprinted Works.

Prolegomenon

In the Name of God – the All-Good, the Infinitely Compassionate

The name Persia conjures up in the mind of Western readers luxuriant gardens, delicately woven carpets, refined miniatures, and a rich poetry that combines the mystical with the sensuous. It also brings forth the image of a powerful and vast empire that vied with ancient Greece and Rome, as well as Byzantium, and that later became one of the major foci and a cradle of Islamic civilization. In ancient times, however, Persia was known to the Occident also as the land where the sun of philosophy shone so brightly that Plotinus entered the Roman army with the hope of going to Persia to encounter its philosophers. Moreover, when what remained of the Platonic Academy was closed by the Byzantines, the philosophers residing there took refuge in Persia. As far as Zoroaster, the prophet of ancient Persia, is concerned, he was known in the ancient world not only as a prophet but also as a philosopher. Furthermore, the three wise men present at the birth of Christ who represent Oriental wisdom hailed from 'the East', which at that time for Palestine would mean most likely no other place than Persia. As for Islamic philosophy, whose earlier schools influenced the West so greatly, most of its figures were either Persian or belonged to the Persianate zone of Islamic civilization.

Yet up to now there has been no anthology in any European language that has made available to the Western audience a selection of the major works from the long tradition of philosophy in Persia. The field of philosophy has not as yet witnessed the appearance of a work comparable to either the monumental *Survey of Persian Art* of Arthur Upham Pope or *L'Anthologie de la littérature persane* of Dh. Ṣafā. We hope to fill this vacuum to some extent with this work, which covers the entire tradition of philosophy in Persia from the time of Zoroaster to the last century.

Of course, the character of philosophy throughout its long history has not always been the same. During the pre-Islamic period, philosophy or wisdom (*sophia/*

khirad) was completely intertwined with religion, as is also observable in the other great civilizations of Asia such as the Indian and the Chinese. In contrast to the Greece of the sixth and fifth centuries BC, the Persian culture of the Achaemenian period did not produce texts of philosophy separated from religion. Rather, the two remained interwoven as one also observes in certain pre-Socratics such as Pythagoras, Parmenides and the real Empedocles, not as he was seen by Aristotle and Theophrastus. It is within the Persian religious texts of that period that one can find essential philosophical discussions of subjects ranging from metaphysics to cosmology to eschatology. This truth is to be observed already in the *Gathas*, as well as in later texts such as the *Dēnkard*. The most philosophical Zoroastrian texts appear, however, in the late Sasanid and early Islamic period, as can be seen in the *Bundahišn*. The Sasanid period also produced works on political philosophy and ethics, the so-called *tāj-nāmah* literature, which had considerable influence on practical philosophy during the Islamic period.

As for Manichaeism, the second major Iranian religion of the era preceding the coming of Islam, its rich cosmology and cosmogony were known to some authors of the Islamic period and its views of good and evil, theodicy, and ethics posed many philosophical and theological challenges to Islamic thinkers, as they did to Christian ones. Little is left of original Manichaean texts relating directly to philosophy, but many fragments and quotations have survived to this day remaining points of contention for centuries for Islamic as well as Christian thinkers. These fragments are also of much philosophical value irrespective of their later influence.

During the Islamic period, the School of Illumination (*ishrāq*) developed by Suhrawardī referred to a philosophical tradition in pre-Islamic Persia that was called the royal philosophy (*al-ḥikmat al-khusrawāniyyah*) and to which more recent Islamic philosophers have referred as the philosophy of the *fahlawiyyūn* or Pahlavis in consideration of the language, that is Pahlavi, in which Zoroastrian texts of the Sasanid period were written. This philosophical tradition was regarded as based upon the principle of unity and not the dualism for which the Iranian religions are usually known. This consciousness in the later philosophical tradition in Persia of a significant philosophical tradition in pre-Islamic Persia only confirms the views of the Graeco-Alexandrian authors of antiquity and points to a significant truth that is the reality of a philosophical tradition in ancient Persia—one which has been most often neglected in modern scholarship.

This close wedding of religion and philosophy continued into the next chapter of the history of Persia, when Persians embraced Islam and Persia became part of, and in fact a major part of, the intellectual tradition of Islamic civilization. A difference did, however, appear in that following the translation of Greek, Syriac, Pahlavi and Sanskrit texts into Arabic, Islamic philosophy began to manifest itself as a distinct discipline in the Islamic intellectual citadel, although still being deeply concerned with the questions posed by religion and revelation. By the third/ninth century, Islamic philosophy (*falsafah-ḥikmah*) was born as a distinct field of knowledge as seen in the writings of Abū Yaʿqūb al-Kindī, the first systematic Islamic philosopher who was, however, an Arab and not a Persian. But a majority of his most famous students, such as Aḥmad ibn Ṭayyib Sarakhsī and Abū Zayd Balkhī, were Persian as the centre of philosophical activity shifted within a century from Baghdad to Khurāsān. Henceforth, Persia became the main arena for philosophical activity in the Islamic world and has remained so to this day.

Of course, Islamic philosophy is a unity closely intertwined with the Islamic worldview and cannot be divided into Arabic and Persian so easily. Needless to say, it is easy to state that Islamic philosophy in Spain belongs to the Arabic zone of Islamic civilization and the School of Iṣfahān to the Persian. But some cases, especially in the early centuries, pose a problem, such as the early Muʿtazilites and the Ikhwān al-Ṣafāʾ (in the fourth/tenth century), in whose case it is not possible to distinguish the Arabic and Persian elements easily from each other. Problems are also posed by the fact that the borders of Persia have not been constant over the centuries and much of classical Persia lies outside of the borders of today's Iran, with the result that modern nationalisms of one kind or other have sought to lay claim to a common philosophical heritage. Therefore, in discussing philosophy in Persia during the Islamic period, it is important first of all to keep in mind the unity of Islamic philosophy that transcends ethnic and linguistic boundaries and, second, to remember that in speaking of Persia we have in mind a cultural world identified by many historians as the heart of the Persianate or Iranic zone of Islamic civilization and embracing not only present-day Iran but also Afghanistan, the rest of the greater Khurāsān in Central Asia, southern Caucasia, and at certain periods centres of Persianate culture in Iraq, Bahrain, and Anatolia, such as Najaf and Konya. It is also important to avoid all forms of chauvinism that is a fruit of modernism and alien to traditional philosophy in Persia and elsewhere.

In considering philosophy in Islamic Persia we must remember the fact that the Persians also wrote in Arabic and that in the field of philosophy, they wrote mostly but not by any means completely in Arabic, a practice that has continued to this day as one can see in the very popular works of the famous contemporary Persian philosopher ʿAllāmah Ṭabāṭabāʾī, *Bidāyat al-ḥikmah* and *Nihāyat al-ḥikmah*. The early Islamic philosophers all wrote in Arabic, Ibn Sīnā being the first person to write a work of Peripatetic philosophy in Persian. But in the fifth/eleventh century, other philosophers, especially the Ismailis, began to use Persian more and more as a vehicle for philosophical discourse to the extent that Nāṣir-i Khusraw, the greatest Ismaili philosopher, wrote his main philosophical works only in Persian. The use of Persian as a philosophical language continued to increase up to the eighth/fourteenth century, during which such notable figures as Suhrawardī, Afḍal al-Dīn Kāshānī, Naṣīr al-Dīn Ṭūsī, and Quṭb al-Dīn Shīrāzī wrote major works in Persian. In the tenth/sixteenth century, with the coming of the Safavids, who re-established Persia as a nation-state with Twelve-Imam Shiʿism as the state religion, paradoxically the use of Persian for philosophical discourse began to wane, to the extent that the greatest philosopher of that age, Mullā Ṣadrā, produced over forty prose works in Arabic but only one in Persian. The reason for this shift must be sought in the bringing of many Arab Shiʿi scholars to Persia but in any cast its causes are not our concern here. Many other philosophers, however, wrote a number of works in both languages. It was only during the Qājār period in the thirteenth/nineteenth century that Persian began to rise again as a philosophical language, commencing a trend that has continued to this day.

The use of both Arabic and Persian by the Persian philosophers of the Islamic period is of great philosophical interest in that, in contrast to the philosophers of Europe or the Arab world, the Persians could think in two types of languages, one Semitic and the other Iranian (related to the Indo-European family of languages), with completely different structures. In the whole domain of semantics and the relation between language and meaning, this situation provided opportunities of great value, as can be seen in the discussion of ontology by Mullā Ṣadrā.

This anthology, therefore, includes works translated from both Arabic and Persian, but it does not embrace the work of all philosophers who wrote in Persian, such as those of India (e.g., Shāh Walīallāh of Delhi), as well as some Ottoman philosophers. Despite their close link with the Islamic philosophical tradition in Persia, however, such figures have not been included in this anthology because Persia, even within its larger historical boundaries, does not include either world, although very close intellectual and cultural relations were kept between the Ottoman and Muslim Indian worlds and Persia.

In considering what constitutes 'philosophy' in Islamic Persia, we were forced to consider the current meaning of this term in English, as well as the meaning of *falsafah* and *ḥikmah* in Arabic and Persian and the richness of the Islamic intellectual tradition itself. The content of most of this anthology dealing with the Islamic period reflects this concern and especially our desire to present to the Western audience the diversity, variety, and wealth of the Islamic intellectual tradition in Persia. To this end we have sought to include all the different schools of thought that have a philosophical aspect or dimension, and have not limited ourselves simply to the early Peripatetic school, which, despite its inalienable link to the Islamic worldview and the fact that many of its major figures, including the most celebrated among them, namely Ibn Sīnā, were Persians, is still called Arabic philosophy in the West. We insist in fact that this philosophy is *Islamic philosophy*, and even when referring to Persia we consider it to be Islamic philosophy in

Persia rather than *Persian philosophy*. In any case, Islamic philosophy includes schools of thought not usually included in what the West has understood as Arabic philosophy in its treatments of Islamic philosophy. Also, needless to say, we have not set the termination of this philosophical tradition to correlate with the time when the West ceased to be interested in it. We have treated this philosophical tradition in an integral manner respecting its whole history to the present day. We have only limited it geographically by focusing upon what flourished in Persia and not in other Islamic lands, this task, as already mentioned, being difficult during certain periods because of the integral nature of the Islamic philosophical tradition and interactions and influences across geographical borders.

The roots of Islamic philosophical thought lie on the one hand in the Qur'ān, the *Ḥadīth*, and the sayings of certain Shiʿi Imams such as the *Nahj al-balāghah* of ʿAlī ibn Abī Ṭālib and on the other in the philosophical heritage of Persian and Greek Antiquity. This truth becomes apparent especially if this tradition is studied from within as it developed over the centuries in Persia. These roots grew into a tree that was nurtured primarily by the Graeco-Alexandrian philosophical tradition, much of which was integrated into the Islamic intellectual universe. From this integration, signs of which can be seen already in the circle of Imam Jaʿfar al-Ṣādiq and the meeting between Imam ʿAlī al-Riḍā and ʿImrān al-Ṣābī, the ground was prepared for the birth of the Islamic intellectual sciences (*al-ʿulūm al-ʿaqliyyah*), including philosophy with its centre in Baghdad. It was here that with al-Kindī, the 'philosopher of the Arabs', Islamic philosophy properly speaking was born in the third/ninth century. During the next century this school continued, with many Persians coming to study in this city of learning. One might say that the Persian members of the Baghdadi school of *mashshā'ī* or Peripatetic philosophy, as this school came to be known, include such stalwart later philosophers as Aḥmad ibn Ṭayyib Sarakhsī and the leader of this school in Baghdad in the fourth/tenth century, Abū Sulaymān Manṭiqī Sijistānī.

This school soon spread to Persia itself and by the fourth/tenth century Khurāsān became a second locus of activity of *mashshā'ī* philosophy soon surpassing Baghdad. The school of Khurāsān may be said to have begun with the mysterious Abu'l-ʿAbbās Īrānshahrī from whom only a few fragments survive. But its later members are well known. Abū Naṣr Fārābī, the second celebrated master of the *mashshā'ī* school after al-Kindī, studied philosophy in Khurāsān before coming to Baghdad and spending the last part of his life in Damascus. Abu'l-Ḥasan ʿĀmirī, the most famous philosophical figure between Fārābī and Ibn Sīnā who died in the fifth/eleventh century, also hailed from Khurāsān as did the most famous of all philosophers of Persia, Ibn Sīnā, who, however, spent most of his life in the western and central regions of Persia. With him *mashshā'ī* philosophy reached its peak, and he created a synthesis that has been a continuous source of philosophical discussion, inspiration, and criticism, but in any case always a living spring of philosophical thought for the past millennium in Persia as well as in many other Islamic lands.

Although Islamic philosophy has always been dominated by schools rather than individuals, there were also a number of important figures in the fourth/tenth century who cannot but be considered as independent philosophers. Among them the most important are Muḥammad ibn Zakariyyā' Rāzī and Abū Rayḥān Bīrūnī, both also among the greatest figures in the history of science. Rāzī, who criticized Aristotle and to some extent Plato, was influenced to a degree by the pre-Islamic philosophical thought of Persia and was deeply devoted to the 'philosophical life'. Bīrūnī, who was much interested in the thought of Rāzī, was drawn strongly to Indian thought and comparative religion while providing a philosophical criticism of *mashshā'ī* natural philosophy as expounded by Ibn Sīnā.

The development of *mashshā'ī* philosophy was also paralleled by other schools of thought of which, from the point of view of philosophy, the most important are theology (*kalām*) and Ismaili philosophy. Mu'tazilite *kalām*, which was dominant until the end of the third/ninth century, and many of whose practitioners were Persian, provided many challenges to philosophy although not as opposed to *falsafah* as the later school of Ash'arism whose founder was an Arab but many of whose later expositors, such as Imām al-Ḥaramayn Juwaynī and Abū Ḥāmid Muḥammad Ghazzālī, were Persians.

Ismaili thought, which developed alongside *mashshā'ī* philosophy, was itself of major philosophical significance. Drawn more to the Pythagorean, Hermetic, and Neoplatonic elements of Greek philosophy than to the Aristotelian, it produced major figures from the third/ninth century onward, such as Abū Ḥātam Rāzī, Abū Ya'qūb Sijistānī, Ḥamīd al-Dīn Kirmānī, and the most celebrated of the Ismaili philosophers, Nāṣir-i Khusraw, who died in the later fifth/eleventh century. The latter, although a Fāṭimid missionary (*dā'ī*) attached to the Fāṭimid court in Cairo, not only wrote all his works in Persian but also was a major poet of the Persian language. With him and Ibn Sīnā and his immediate students the first active period of Islamic philosophy in Persia came to an end and with changing political conditions for some time philosophy became eclipsed, opposed by both *kalām* and certain strands of Sufism.

With the advent of the Seljūqs, their defence of Ash'arite *kalām*, and opposition to *falsafah*, the last part of the fifth/eleventh century to the beginning of the seventh/thirteenth marks the eclipse in Persia of philosophy and especially the school of Ibn Sīnā. While *mashshā'ī* philosophy prospered in Andalusia, in Persia except for Khayyām and a few remaining students of Ibn Sīnā, no philosophers of any significance appeared on the horizon. This was the period of dominance of *kalām*; but by virtue of its embarking upon an intellectual battle against the *falāsifah*, this *kalām* itself became more philosophical and there developed what came to be known as 'later *kalām*' or philosophical *kalām* associated especially with one of the greatest religious thinkers of Persia, Abū Ḥāmid Muḥammad Ghazzālī (d. early sixth/twelfth century). Another major thinker, Fakhr al-Dīn Rāzī, was to follow soon after him. Both men wrote against Ibn Sīnā, but in doing so produced works of major philosophical importance and their thought influenced later schools of philosophy in Persia. Because of this fact and also the innate philosophical significance of their thought, they, as well as a number of later members of the school of Sunni *kalām*, are included in the present work and they belong in a sense to the tradition of philosophy in Persia despite their opposition to Ibn Sīnā and the Peripatetics.

The end of the sixth/twelfth century was witness to the rise of a new philosophical school associated with the name of Suhrawardī and known as the School of Illumination (*ishrāq*). Claiming to be a reviver of ancient Persian wisdom, as well as that of the ancient Greeks, Suhrawardī established a philosophy based upon illumination as well as ratiocination. Although put to death in Aleppo, his thought was revived by the two great commentators of his masterpiece, the *Ḥikmat al-ishrāq*, Muḥammad Shahrazūrī and Quṭb al-Dīn Shīrāzī, a generation after the death of the master. Henceforth *ishrāqī* thought became central to the development of philosophy in Persia and produced a number of important figures until the Safavid period, when it became a major influence upon and was integrated into the School of Iṣfahān in the eleventh/seventeenth century, especially the thought of its founder, Mīr Dāmād, and its most celebrated representative, Ṣadr al-Dīn Shīrāzī (Mullā Ṣadrā).

In the seventh /thirteenth century the thought of Ibn Sīnā, eclipsed by the attacks of the *mutakallimūn*, was also revived by one of the seminal figures of the intellectual history of Persia, Khwājah Naṣīr al-Dīn Ṭūsī, who was also the founder of Shi'i systematic theology or *kalām*. After Ṭūsī, the renewed *mashshā'ī* school produced many important figures, a number of whom were also interested in *ishrāqī* doctrines and philosophical Sufism, which was now establishing itself as a major intellectual perspective. The renewed *mashshā'ī* school continued into the Safavid period and despite the spread of the school of Mullā Ṣadrā has had followers in Persia to this day.

As for doctrinal or philosophical Sufism, its origin must be sought in some of the later works of Abū Ḥāmid Muḥammad Ghazzālī and 'Ayn al-Quḍāt Hamadānī. But the major impetus for this school came from the works of Ibn 'Arabī disseminated in the Persian world mostly through the writings of Ṣadr al-Dīn Qūnawī. Gradually these teachings also penetrated into Shi'i circles and doctrinal or philosophical Sufism became a major intellectual perspective in Persia, producing a number of important thinkers up to and within the Safavid period (in the tenth/sixteenth and eleventh/seventeenth centuries) when it also influenced deeply the works of Mullā Ṣadrā. Its expositors have in fact continued in Persia to the present day. Although members of this school did not consider themselves philosophers (*falasifah-ḥukamā'*) but gnostics (*'urafā'*), their teachings have the profoundest philosophical import if philosophy is understood in its traditional sense. For that very reason many of them can also be called theosophers in the original sense of the term, not to be mistaken with the nineteenth-century movement in England that became associated with the Theosophical Society. In fact the name given to later Islamic philosophers of Persia, especially from Mullā Ṣadrā onward—that is, *ḥakīm-i ilāhī*—means etymologically *theosophos* or theosopher.

The period from the seventh/thirteenth century to the tenth/sixteenth was also witness to the rise of systematic Shi'i *kalām* originated by Naṣīr al-Dīn Ṭūsī, whose *Kitāb al-tajrīd* is foundational to Shi'i theology. Commented upon by numerous writers over the centuries, this work marks the presence of a *kalām* that is also philosophically inclined and not opposed to *falsafah* as was Ash'arite *kalām*. This fact itself was instrumental, along with essential characteristics of Shi'ism itself, to facilitate the revival of Islamic philosophy in Shi'i circles in Persia preceding the Safavids and of course in the Safavid period itself. Shi'i *kalām* itself continued to survive as a living intellectual school into the Qajar period and even into the contemporary era.

The centuries separating Suhrawardī and Ṭūsī from the School of Iṣfahān and its founder Mīr Dāmād were witness to intense philosophical activity in Persia. This truth can be ascertained although our knowledge of this period is still incomplete. During those centuries, and in contrast to earlier Islamic history when various schools of thought were kept distinct from each other as we still see in the writings of Ṭūsī, the *mashshā'ī* and *ishrāqī* schools became intermingled with each other and also with *'irfān* and *kalām* of both Sunnism and Shi'ism. Different figures appeared at this time that cannot be classified uniquely within one school, such as Quṭb al-Dīn Shīrāzī, at once *mashshā'ī* and *ishraqī* philosopher, or Ibn Turkah Iṣfahānī, master of *mashshā'ī*, *ishrāqī*, and *'irfānī* wisdom. That is why it is difficult to classify the philosophers of this period under a single school, even if we have been forced to do so in this work for the sake of organization. The ground was being prepared at this time especially in Shiraz, where most of the philosophical activity of the two centuries preceding the Safavids took place and to whose philosophical life of this period one can refer as the School of Shīrāz, for the grand synthesis of Mullā Ṣadrā who in the eleventh/seventeenth century brought the School of Iṣfahān to its peak.

As for the School of Iṣfahān, it designates the philosophical school associated at its beginning with Mīr Dāmād, Mīr Findiriskī, and Bahā' al-Dīn 'Āmilī, all of whom lived in the Safavid capital Iṣfahān in the tenth/sixteenth century. This school reached its apogee with Mullā Ṣadrā and was continued by his major students, such as Mullā Muḥsin Fayḍ Kāshānī. But this period also included philosophers who did not follow Mullā Sadrā's 'transcendent theosophy' (*al-ḥikmat al-muta'āliyah*). Altogether the Safavid period was very rich in philosophical activity, and although opposed by some Shi'i scholars especially at the end of this period, philosophical activity continued into the Afshār and Zand periods and was revived again in Iṣfahān during the early Qajar period, before becoming transferred to the Qajar capital Tehran, which became the centre of philosophical activity in Persia during the thirteenth/nineteenth and fourteenth/twentieth centuries. The long tradition of philosophy in Persia thus reached the contemporary period and is in fact very much alive in Persia today, where it is undergoing another revival in Qum, the present religious centre of Persia, as well as in Tehran, Mashhad, and several other cities. The richness of the philosophical activity of the past four centuries is demonstrated by the major anthology of the philosophy of this period, in the original Arabic and Persian and not in translation, prepared by Henry Corbin and Sayyid Jalāl al-Dīn Āshtiyānī under the title *Anthologie des philosophes iraniens*, of which four volumes of some eight hundred pages each were published; the last three volumes, however, never saw the light of day as a result of the death of Corbin in 1978.

Constrained by numerous factors, human and material, this present anthology cannot be as detailed as that of Corbin and Āshtiyānī, who projected seven volumes for only four centuries. An anthology as detailed as theirs for twenty-five centuries of the history of philosophy in Persia would obviously necessitate some twenty to thirty volumes. Furthermore, ours is an anthology in English and theirs of texts in their original language. Consequently we have had to be more selective, concentrating on the most significant figures and also the most salient parts of their works. Needless to say, making a choice on both accounts was often very difficult and necessitated from time to time a painful omission of either a particular figure or works of a philosopher whose other writings were included in our selection. In any case we do not claim to be exhaustive but hope to be representative and to make available in English the actual thought, reasoning, and exposition of most of the major philosophical figures of Persia in matters that are either of general philosophical significance or of interest to an understanding of the philosophical world of the author in question.

In preparing this anthology we have depended first of all on reliable existing translations. Where these have not been available, we have invited the participation of expert translators from all over the world. We have also relied on printed Arabic and Persian texts for the most part but in some cases recourse has been had to manuscripts as well. Needless to say, the style of translation is not the same for every selection, and there are differences in the views of translators concerning the rendition of certain terms. We have not sought to impose uniformity here, seeing that all of the translators are established scholars in the field of Islamic thought. The diversity of styles of translation may in fact reveal something of the differences in approach to the study of Islamic and pre-Islamic philosophy today and also the general semantic questions of rendition and interpretation of a philosophical text from one language to another.

wa mā tawfīqī illā bi'Llāh
Seyyed Hossein Nasr
Bethesda, Maryland
Muharram 1428 AH (L.)
Bahman 1385 AA (S.)
February 2007 AD

Part I

Early Persian Philosophy: Zoroastrian Thought

Introduction

The Persian prophet Zoroaster (the name is the Greek form of the Persian Zarathustra) probably lived in the mid-late second millennium BC. Zarathustra is one of the first of the prophets of the world's major religions and while the place of his birth is subject to speculation—from Yazd, Kirmān, and today's Sīstān—most scholars believe he came from Central Asia and most likely from what is now called Kazakhistan.

What has survived of his direct teachings are seventeen hymns known as the *Gathas*. It is here that Zarathustra alludes to mythical stories without elaborating on them; but his 'genius' is not so much in creating new myths but in interpreting the old ones and drawing religious, metaphysical and moral conclusions from them. The Zoroastrian religion adheres fundamentally to a dualistic worldview even though in recent centuries a more monotheistic interpretation has become prevalent among most Zoroastrians. There is a strong presence of the view of the universe as alive in the Zoroastrian religion, which is perhaps why all things in the universe are divided into good and evil, helpful and harmful, and ultimately sacred and profane. While Zoroastrianism has undergone doctrinal changes such as a replacement of the early cyclical notion of time with a linear one, the core of its dualistic worldview has remained the same. Zoroastrianism soon spread through the Iranian plateau and came to be the religion of three major dynasties in Persia: the Achaemenians (550–330 BC), the Parthians (250 BC–AD 226) and the Sasanians (AD 226–651).

We have gathered in this chapter a set of writings from the core of the Zoroastrian sacred scriptures, the *Avesta* (Fundamental Utterance), which shed light on a variety of philosophical issues and themes in a religious and often mythical context. It bears witness to the fact that since ancient times an intellectual endeavour to understand the corporeal and the incorporeal world has been a salient feature of Persian culture. This intellectual engagement also may explain why so many philosophers, theologians and mystics of the Islamic world have come from

Greater Persia. Some of them, such as Marzbān ibn Bahmanyār, may have been first generation converts from the Zoroastrian religion.

The first section of the selections on Zoroastrian thought is from the *Bundahišn* in which the creation story, the character of Ahura Mazda, the wholly Good Lord, and the problem of theodicy are discussed. Omniscience, illumination and luminaries, and spiritual entities are also the subject of discussion here. In the second section, portions of the *Greater Bundahišn* dealing with the primal creation and the very process of it from the first spiritual beings who were created, such as Amahraspands, to the rest of the created order are presented. The notions of good and evil, their interaction, the coming of light from Ohrmazd and material darkness are among issues that are elaborated upon in this section. The third section is selected from *Dādistān-i Dīnīk* and addresses moral principles. The nature of justice, how goodness comes into existence, and how it is related to the notion of renovation are among issues discussed here. Zoroastrianism in Persia is known as a religion that emphasizes three precepts: good thoughts, good words, and good deeds. It is in *Dādistān-i Dīnīk* that we see an elaboration of these principles. Finally, the nature of righteousness and how it is that evil comes into the corporeal world are presented here.

Next, we have included a section of *Dīnā-i Maīnog-i Khirad* in which opinions of the spirit of wisdom are presented in the form of sixty-one pieces of advice. These sets of advice range from the moral and spiritual to how one can maintain bodily health.

The *Gathas* are the hymns in which the eternal struggle between Ahura Mazda (God or light) and his adversary Angra Mainyu, the source of darkness and the deceiver of men, are discussed. We have selected a section from the *Gathas* in which the manner of hostility of Angra Mainyu, the evil and destructive deity to Ahura Mazda the Good Lord and how Ahura Mazda is aided in his struggle against spiritual entities like Aeshma Daeva (the evil of wrath) are presented in some length. The physical manifestations of these spiritual entities and their interplay with earthly matters such as *apaosha*, drought, are also alluded to in this section.

Certain passages from the *Greater Bundahišn* have been included where the evil spirit, the 'world year' and its affiliated cosmology are discussed. Some of the materials presented in this section remind one of the creation stories in Judaism, Christianity and Islam. For example, there are references to how Ohrmazd or Ahura Mazda first created speech and then expanded the process of creation to include the material domain while viewing evil as an assault upon creation, the antagonism of the two spirits and the question of resurrection. All these teachings are in line with the central tenets of monotheistic religions.

In the section that follows, we have included a number of short excerpts from such works as *Vendidad*, *Hadhokht Nask*, *Maīnog-i Khirad*, *Zātspram*, *Dēnkart*, and *Šikand Gumānī Vazār*. A variety of themes are discussed here. In the *Vendidad* there is a discussion of eschatology and the fate of the soul in the hereafter and the Chinvat bridge that all the dead must cross before resurrection (similar to the Muslim *ṣirāṭ*). In the *Hadhokht Nask*, the precepts of good thoughts, good deeds, and good words as well as more on the question of the fate of the soul are discussed. The fate of the soul according to sources of the later Sasanian period is the subject of *Maīnog-i Khirad* and once again there are allusions to the crossing of the bridge as a test of the faithful. In the section on *Zātspram*, the mixing of the bounteous spirit and the destructive spirit, how light emanated from the good God and darkness from the evil god, and the interplay of these lights with the twelve creations are issues that are brought forth. The selection from *Dēnkart* deals with good and evil, their definitions, nature and other characteristics. It also offers a description of Ohrmazd and his omniscience, will and wisdom that comes very close to a monotheistic understanding of God. Ohrmazd is said to be the source of all that is good and his rule is perfect and joyful. Finally, there is the section from *Šikand Gumānī Vazār*. Of all the treatises included in this section, this part is the most philosophical in the strict sense of the word. It begins with a discussion concerning the impossibility of any existent thing being infinite, the nature of infinity, the relationship between epistemology, essence and quality, and the immutability of substance.

Next we have included a treatise of a dialogue between a learned Zoroastrian philosopher and the doctors of Islam (*faqīhs*) concerning major philosophical questions. Such questions include the possibility of resurrection, eternity and createdness of the world, the nature of time, sense perception, unity of the soul, intelligence and consciousness and of such spiritual beings as the *fravāhar*.

The last section of our chapter on Zoroastrian sacred writings comes from *Dēnkart*. This section deals primarily with moral issues and can be characterized as wisdom literature (*andarz* in Pahlavi). The Spirit of Wisdom appears to be offering moral advice to the people covering a wide range of topics among which one can name good deeds that are necessary for going to heaven, sin, the nature of righteousness, truthfulness, peace and avoidance of hell. Also among the themes discussed are what moral conduct is and how one should surrender oneself to religion, the maintenance of bodily and spiritual health, and the relationship between knowledge of religion and elimination of demons from the world.

Though cloaked in mythical language, the Zoroastrian writings included here represent a rich and diverse set of philosophical ideas and issues most of which later resurface in the writings of Muslim philosophers in Persia. These writings also firmly establish the presence of an active intellectual life in ancient Persia that stretches over one thousand years before the rise of Islam.

Mehdi Aminrazavi

1

The Original Creation
From *Bundahišn*

Reprinted from 'Bundahišn', tr. E. W. West, in F. Max Müller, ed., *The Sacred Books of the East: Pahlavi Texts*, (Delhi, 1977), vol. 5, pp. 3–20.

Chapter I

In the name of the creator Aûharmazd

1. The Zand-âkâs ('Zand-knowing or tradition-informed'),[1] which is first about Aûharmazd's original creation and the antagonism of the evil spirit,[2] *and* afterwards about the nature of the creatures from the original creation till the end, which is the future existence (*tanû-î pasînŏ*).

2. As *revealed* by the religion of the Mazdayasnians, so it is declared that Aûharmazd is supreme in omniscience and goodness, *and* unrivalled[3] in splendour,

1. The Pâzand and most of the modern Pahlavi manuscripts have, 'From the Zand-âkâs', but the word *min*, 'from', does not occur in the old manuscript K20, and is a modern addition to M6. From this opening sentence it would appear that the author of the work gave it the name Zand-âkâs.

2. The Avesta Angra-mainyu, the spirit who causes adversity or anxiety (see Darmesteter's *Ormazd et Ahriman*, pp. 92–95); the Pahlavi name is, most probably, merely a corrupt transliteration of the Avesta form, and may be read Ganrâk-maînôk, as the Avesta Spenta-mainyu, the spirit who causes prosperity, has become Spênâk-maînôk in Pahlavi. This latter spirit is represented by Aûharmazd himself in the Bundahišn. The Pahlavi word for 'spirit', which is read *madônad* by the Parsis, and has been pronounced *mînavad* by some scholars and *mînôt* by others, is probably a corruption of *maînôk*, as its Sasanian form was *minô*. If it were not for the extra medial letter in *ganrâk*, and for the obvious partial transliteration of *spênâk*, it would be preferable to read *ganâk*, 'smiting', and to derive it from a supposed verb *gandan*, 'to smite' (Av. *ghna*), as proposed by most Zendists. A Parsi would probably suggest *gandan*, 'to stink'.

3. Reading *aham-kaî*, 'without a fellow-sovereign, peerless, unrivalled, and independent'. This rare word occurs three times in §§ 2, 3, and some Pâzand writers suggest the meaning 'everlasting' (by means of the Persian gloss *hamîsah*), which is plausible enough, but *hâmakî* would be an extraordinary mode of writing the very common word *hamâî*, 'ever'.

the region of light is the place of Aûharmazd, which they call 'endless light', and the omniscience *and* goodness of the unrivalled Aûharmazd is what they call 'revelation'.[1]

3. Revelation is the explanation of both *spirits* together; one is he who is independent of unlimited time,[2] because Aûharmazd and the region, religion, and time of Aûharmazd were and are and ever will be; *while* Aharman[3] in darkness, with backward understanding and desire for destruction, was *in* the abyss, and it is *he* who *will* not be; and the place of that destruction, and also of that darkness, is what they call the 'endlessly dark'.

4. And between them was empty space, *that* is, what they call 'air', in which is now *their* meeting.

5. Both are limited and unlimited spirits, for the supreme is that which they call endless light and the abyss that which is endlessly dark, so that between them is a void, and one is not connected with the other; and, again, both spirits are limited as to their own selves.

6. And, secondly, on account of the omniscience of Aûharmazd, both things are in the creation of Aûharmazd, the finite and the infinite; for this they know is that which is in the covenant of both spirits.

7. And, again, the complete sovereignty of the creatures of Aûharmazd is in the future existence, and that also is unlimited for ever and everlasting; and the creatures of Aharman will perish at the time when[4] the future of existence occurs, and that also is eternity.

8. Aûharmazd, through omniscience, knew that Aharman exists, *and* whatever he schemes he infuses with malice and greediness till the end; *and* because He accomplishes the end by many means, He also produced spiritually the creatures which were necessary for those means, *and* they remained three thousand years in a spiritual *state*, so that they were unthinking[5] and unmoving, with intangible bodies.

---

1. The word *dînô* (properly *dênô*), Av. *daêna*, being traceable to a root *dî*, 'to see', must originally have meant 'a vision' (see Haug's *Essays on the Religion of the Parsis*, 2nd ed. p. 152, n. 2), whence the term has been transferred to 'religion' and all religious observances, rules, and writings; so it may be translated either by 'religion' or by 'revelation'.

2. This appears to be the meaning, but the construction of § 3 is altogether rather obscure, and suggestive of omissions in the text.

3. The usual name of the evil spirit; it is probably an older corruption of Angra-mainyu than Ganrâk-maîntôk, and a less technical term. Its Sasanian form was Aharmanî.

4. Substituting *amat*, 'when', for *mûn*, 'which', two *Huzvâris* forms which are frequently confounded by Pahlavi copyists because their Pâzand equivalents, *ka* and *ke*, are nearly alike.

5. Reading *aminîdâr* in accordance with M6, which has *amînîdâr* in Chap. XXXIV, 1, where the same phrase occurs. Windischmann and Justi read *amûîtâr*, 'uninjured, invulnerable', in both places. This sentence appears to refer to a preparatory creation of embryonic and immaterial existences, the prototypes, *fravashis*, spiritual counterparts, or guardian angels of the spiritual and material creatures afterwards produced.

9. The evil spirit, on account of backward knowledge, was not aware of the existence of Aûharmazd; and, afterwards, he arose from the abyss, and came in unto the light which he saw.

10. Desirous of destroying, and because of *his* malicious nature, he rushed in to destroy that light of Aûharmazd unassailed by fiends, and he saw its bravery and glory were greater than his own; *so* he fled back to the gloomy darkness, and formed many demons and fiends; *and* the creatures of the destroyer arose for violence.

11. Aûharmazd, by whom the creatures of the evil spirit were seen, creatures terrible, corrupt, and bad, also considered them not commendable (*bûrzis-nîk*).

12. Afterwards, the evil spirit saw the creatures of Aûharmazd; they ap-peared many creatures of delight (*vâyah*), enquiring creatures, and they seemed to him commendable, and he commended the creatures and creation of Aûharmazd.

13. Then Aûharmazd, with a knowledge[1] of which way the end of the matter *would be*, went to meet the evil spirit, and proposed peace to him, *and* spoke thus: 'Evil spirit! Bring assistance unto my creatures, and offer praise! So that, in reward for it, ye (you and your creatures) may become immortal and undecaying, hunger-less and thirstless.'

14. And the evil spirit shouted thus:[2] 'I *will* not depart, I *will* not provide assist-ance for thy creatures, I *will* not offer praise among thy creatures, and I am not of the same opinion with thee as to good things. I *will* destroy thy creatures for ever and everlasting; moreover, I *will* force all thy creatures into disaffection to thee and affection for myself.'

15. And the explanation thereof is this that the evil spirit reflected in this manner, that Aûharmazd was helpless as regarded him,[3] therefore He proffers peace; and he did not agree, but bore on even into conflict with Him.

16. And Aûharmazd spoke thus: 'you are not omniscient and almighty, O evil spirit! So that it is not possible for thee to destroy me, and it is not possible for thee to force my creatures so that they *will* not return to my possession.'

17. Then Aûharmazd, through omniscience, knew that: If I do not grant a period of contest, then it *will* be possible for him to act *so* that he *may* be able to cause the seduction of my creatures to himself. As even now there are many of the intermix-ture of mankind who practise wrong more than right.

18. And Aûharmazd spoke to the evil spirit thus: 'Appoint a period! So that the

1. The Huz. Khavîtûnast stands for the *Pâz. Dânist* with the meaning, here, of 'what is known, knowledge', as in Persian.

2. Literally, 'and it was shouted by him, the evil spirit, thus:' the usual idiom when the nomina-tive follows the verb.

3. The words *dên Val* stand for *dên valman*.

intermingling of the conflict may be for nine thousand years.' For he knew that by appointing this period the evil spirit *would* be undone.

19. Then the evil spirit, unobservant and through ignorance, was content with that agreement; just like two men quarrelling together, who propose a time thus: Let us appoint such-and-such a day for a fight.

20. Aûharmazd also knew this, through omniscience, that within these nine thousand years, *for* three thousand years everything proceeds *by* the will of Aûharmazd, three thousand years *there is* an intermingling of the wills of Aûharmazd and Aharman, and the last three thousand years the evil spirit is disabled, and they keep the adversary away[1] from the creatures.

21. Afterwards, Aûharmazd recited the Ahunavar thus: *Yathâ ahû vairyô* ('as a heavenly lord is to be chosen'), &c.[2] once, *and* uttered the twenty-one words;[3] He also exhibited to the evil spirit His own triumph in the end, and the impotence of the evil spirit, the annihilation of the demons, and the resurrection *and* undisturbed future existence of the creatures for ever and everlasting.

22. And the evil spirit, who perceived his own impotence and the annihilation of the demons, became confounded, and fell back to the gloomy darkness; even so as is declared in revelation, that, when one of its (the Ahunavar's) three *parts* was uttered, the evil spirit contracted *his* body through fear, and when two parts of it were uttered he fell upon *his* knees, and when all of it was uttered he became confounded and impotent as to the harm he caused the creatures of Aûharmazd, *and* he remained three thousand years in confusion.[4]

23. Aûharmazd created *his* creatures in the confusion of Aharman; first he produced Vohûman ('good thought'), by whom the progress of the creatures of Aûharmazd was advanced.

---

1. That is, 'the adversary is kept away'. In Pahlavi the third person plural is the indefinite person, as in English. These 9,000 years are in addition to the 3,000 mentioned in § 8, as appears more clearly in Chap. XXXIV, 1.

2. This is the most sacred formula of the Parsis, which they have to recite frequently, not only during the performance of their ceremonies, but also in connection with most of their ordinary duties and habits. It is neither a prayer, nor a creed, but a declaratory formula in meter, consisting of one stanza of three lines, containing twenty-one Avesta words, as follows:

Yathâ ahû vairyô, athâ ratus, ashâd kîd hakâ,
Vangheus dazdâ mananghô, skyaothnanãm angheus mazdâi,
Khshathremkâ ahurâi â, yim dregubyô dadad vâstârem.

And it may be translated in the following manner: 'As a heavenly lord is to be chosen, so is an earthly master (spiritual guide), for the sake of righteousness, *to be* a giver of the good thoughts of the actions of life towards Mazda; and the dominion is for the lord (Ahura) whom he (Mazda) has given as a protector for the poor' (see Haug's *Essays on the Religion of the Parsis*, 2nd ed., pp. 125, 141).

3. The word *mârîk* must mean 'word' here, but in some other places it seems to mean 'syllable' or 'accented syllable'.

4. This is the first third of the 9,000 years appointed in §§ 18, 20, and the second 3,000 years mentioned in Chap. XXXIV, 1.

24. The evil spirit first created[1] Mitôkht ('falsehood'), and then Akôman ('evil thought').

25. The first of Aûharmazd's creatures of the world *was* the sky, and his good thought (Vohûman), by good procedure,[2] produced the light of the world, along with which was the good religion of the Mazdayasnians; this *was* because the renovation (*frashakard*)[3] which happens to the creatures *was* known to him.

26. Afterwards *arose* Ardavahist, and then Shatvaîrô, and then Spendarmad, and then Horvadad, and then Amerôdad.[4]

27. From the dark world of Aharman *were* Akôman and Andar, and then Sôvar, and then Nâkahêd, and then Tâîrêv and Zâîrîk.[5]

28. Of Aûharmazd's creatures of the world, the first *was* the sky; the second, water; the third, earth; the fourth, plants; the fifth, animals; the sixth, mankind

---

1. It is usual to consider *dâdan* (Huz. *yehabûntan*), when traceable to Av. *dâ* = Sans. *dhâ*, as meaning 'to create', but it can hardly be proved that it means to create out of nothing, any more than any other of the Avesta verbs which it is sometimes convenient to translate by 'create'. Before basing any argument upon the use of this word it will, therefore, be safer to substitute the word 'produce' in all cases.

2. Or it may be translated, 'and from it Vohûman, by good procedure', &c. The position here ascribed to Vohûman, or the good thought of Aûharmazd, bears some resemblance to that of the Word in John i. 1–5, but with this essential difference, that Vohûman is merely a creature of Aûharmazd, not identified with him; for the latter idea would be considered, by a Parsi, as rather inconsistent with strict monotheism. The 'light of the world' now created must be distinguished from the 'endless light' already existing with Aûharmazd in § 2.

3. The word *frashakard*, 'what is made durable, perpetuation', is applied to the renovation of the universe which is to take place about the time of the resurrection, as a preparation for eternity.

4. These five, with Vohûman and Aûharmazd in his angelic capacity, constitute the seven Ameshaspends, 'undying causers of prosperity, immortal benefactors', or archangels, who have charge of the whole material creation. They are personifications of old Avesta phrases, such as Vohûmanô, 'good thought;' Asha-vahista, 'perfect rectitude;' Khshathra-vairya, 'desirable dominion;' Spenta-ârmaiti, 'bountiful devotion;' Haurvatâd, 'completeness or health;' and Ameretâd, 'immortality'.

5. These six demons are the opponents of the six archangels respectively (see Chap. XXX, 29); their names in the Avesta are, Akem-manô, 'evil thought;' Indra, Sauru, Naunghaithya, Tauru, Zairika (see *Vendidâd* X, 17, 18 Sp., and XIX, 43 W.), which have been compared with the Vedic god Indra, Sarva (a name of Siva), the Nâsatyas, and Sans. *tura*, 'diseased', and *garas*, 'decay', respectively. For further details regarding them, see Chap. XXVIII, 7–13.

Chapter II

On the formation of the luminaries.

1. Aûharmazd produced illumination between the sky and the earth, the constellation stars and those also not of the constellations,[1] then the moon, and afterwards the sun, as I *shall* relate.

2. First he produced the *celestial* sphere, and the constellation stars are assigned to it by him; especially these twelve whose names *are* Varak (the Lamb), Tôrâ (the Bull), Dô-patkar (the Two-figures or Gemini), Kalakang (the Crab), Sêr (the Lion), Khûsak (Virgo), Tarâzûk (the Balance), Gazdûm (the Scorpion), Nîmâsp (the Centaur or Sagittarius), Vahik[2] (Capricornus), Dûl (the Water pot), and Mâhîk (the Fish);

3. Which, from their original creation, *were divided* into the twenty-eight subdivisions of the astronomers,[3] of which the names are Padêvar, Pêsh-Parviz, Parviz, Paha, Avêsar, Besn, Rakhvad, Taraha, Avra, Nahn, Miyân, Avdem, Mâshâha, Spûr, Husru, Srob, Nur, Gêl, Garafsa, Varant, Gau, Goî, Muru, Bunda, Kahtsar, Vaht, Miyân, Kaht.[4]

4. And all his original creations, residing in the world, are committed to them;[5] so that when the destroyer arrives they overcome the adversary *and* their own persecution, and the creatures are saved from those adversities.

5. As a specimen of a warlike army, which is destined for battle, they have ordained every single constellation of those 6,480 thousand small stars as assistance; and among those constellations four chieftains, appointed on the four sides, are leaders.

---

1. The word *akhtar* is the usual term in Pahlavi for a constellation of the zodiac; but the term *apâkhtar*, 'away from the *akhtar*', means not only 'the north', or away from the zodiac, but also 'a planet', which is in the zodiac, but apart from the constellations. The meaning of *akhtar*, most suitable to the context here, appears to be the general term 'constellation'.

2. Written Nahâzîk here, both in K20 and M6, which may be compared with Pers. *nahâz*, 'the leading goat of a flock;' but the usual word for 'Capricornus' is Vahîk, as in Chap. V, 6. None of the other names of the signs of the zodiac are written here in Pâzand, but it may be noted that if the *ah* in Vahîk were written in Pâzand (that is, in Avesta characters), the word would become the same as Nahâzîk in Pahlavi.

3. Literally, 'fragments of the calculators', *khurdak-i hâmârîkân*. These subdivisions are the spaces traversed daily by the moon among the stars, generally called 'lunar mansions'.

4. All these names are written in Pâzand, which accounts for their eccentric orthography, in which both K20 and M6 agree very closely. The subdivision Parviz is evidently the Pers. *parvên*, which includes the Pleiades, and corresponds therefore to the Sanskrit Nakshatra Krittikâ. This correspondence leads to the identification of the first subdivision, Padêvar, with the Nakshatra Asvinî. The Pâzand names are so corrupt that no reliance can be placed upon them, and the first step towards recovering the true Pahlavi names would be to transliterate the Pâzand back into Pahlavi characters. The ninth subdivision is mentioned in Chap. VII, 1 by the name Avrak.

5. That is, to the zodiacal constellations, which are supposed to have special charge of the welfare of creation.

6. On the recommendation of those chieftains the many unnumbered stars are specially assigned to the various quarters and various places, as the united strength *and* appointed power of those constellations.

7. As it is said that Tîstar is the chieftain of the east, Satavês the chieftain of the west, Vanand the chieftain of the south, *and* Haptôk-ring the chieftain of the north.[1]

8. The great *one* which they call a Gâh (period of the day), which they say is the great *one* of the middle of the sky, till *just* before the destroyer came was the midday (or south) *one* of the five, that is, the Rapîtvîn.[2]

9. Aûharmazd performed the spiritual Yazisn ceremony with the archangels (*ameshôspendân*) in the Rapîtvîn Gâh, and in the Yazisn he supplied every means necessary for overcoming the adversary.[3]

---

1. Of these four constellations of stars, which are said to act as leaders, there is no doubt that Haptôk-ring, the chieftain of the north, is Ursa Major; and it is usually considered that Tîstar, the chieftain of the east, is Sirius; but the other two chieftains are not so well identified, and there may be some doubt as to the proper stations of the eastern and western chieftains. It is evident, however, that the most westerly stars, visible at any one time of the year, are those which set in the dusk of the evening; and east of these, all the stars are visible during the night as far as those which rise at daybreak, which are the most easterly stars visible at that time of the year. Tîstar or Sirius can, therefore, be considered the chieftain of the eastern stars only when it rises before daybreak, which it does at the latter end of summer; and Haptôk-ring or Ursa Major is due north at midnight (on the meridian below the pole) at about the same time of the year. These stars, therefore, fulfil the conditions necessary for being chieftains of the east and north at the end of summer, and we must look for stars capable of being chieftains of the south and west at the same season. Now, when Ursa Major is near the meridian below the pole, Fomalhaut is the most conspicuous star near the meridian in the far south, and is probably to be identified with Vanand the chieftain of the south. And when Sirius rises some time before daybreak, Antares (in Scorpio) sets some time after dusk in the evening, and may well be identified with Satavês the chieftain of the west. Assuming that there has been a precession of the equinoxes equivalent to two hours of time, since the idea of these chieftains (which may perhaps be traced to Avesta times) was first formed, it may be calculated that the time of year when these leading stars then best fulfilled that idea was about a month before the autumnal equinox, when Ursa Major would be due north three-quarters of an hour after midnight, and Fomalhaut due south three-quarters of an hour before midnight, Sirius would rise three hours before the sun, and Antares would set three hours after the sun. In the Avesta these leading stars are named Tistrya, Satavaêsa, Vanant, and Haptôi-ringa (see Tîstar Yt. 0, 8, 9, 12, 32, &c., Rashnu Yt. 26–28, Sîrôz. 13).

2. This translation, though very nearly literal, must be accepted with caution. If the word *mas* be not a name it can hardly mean anything but 'great;' and that it refers to a constellation appears from Chap. V, 1. The word *khômsâk* is an irregular form of the Huz. *Khômsyâ*, 'five', and may refer either to the five chieftains (including 'the great one') or to the five Gâhs or periods of the day, of which Rapîtvîn is the midday one (see Chap. XXV, 9). The object of the text seems to be to connect the Rapîtvîn Gâh with some great mid-sky and midday constellation or star, possibly Regulus, which, about 960 BC, must have been more in the daylight than any other important star during the seven months of summer, the only time that the Rapîtvîn Gâh can be celebrated (see Chap. XXV, 7–14). Justi has, 'They call that the great one of the place, which is great in the middle of the sky; they say that before the enemy came it was always midday, that is, Rapîtvîn.' Windischmann has nearly the same, as both follow the Pâzand MSS. in reading *hômîsak* (as a variant of *hamîsak*), 'always', instead of *khômsâk*.

3. Or 'adversity'.

10. He deliberated with the consciousness (*bôd*) *and* guardian spirits (*fravâhar*) of men,[1] and the omniscient wisdom, brought forward among men, spoke thus: 'Which seems to you the more advantageous, when[2] I shall present you to the world? *that* you shall contend in a bodily form with the fiend (*drûg*), and the fiend shall perish, and in the end I *shall* have you prepared again perfect and immortal, and in the end give you back to the world, *and* you *will* be wholly immortal, undecaying, and undisturbed; or *that* it be always necessary to provide you protection from the destroyer?'

11. Thereupon, the guardian spirits of men became of the same opinion with the omniscient wisdom about going to the world, on account of the evil *that* comes upon them, in the world, from the fiend (*drûg*) Aharman, and *their* becoming, at last, again unpersecuted by the adversary, perfect, and immortal, in the future existence, for ever and everlasting.

Chapter III

1. On the rush of the destroyer at the creatures it is said, in revelation, that the evil spirit, when he saw the impotence of himself and the confederate[3] (*hâm-dast*) demons, owing to the righteous man,[4] became confounded, *and* seemed in confusion three thousand years.

2. During that confusion the archfiends[5] of the demons severally shouted thus: 'Rise up, *thou* father of us! For we *will* cause a conflict in the world, the distress and injury from which *will* become those of Aûharmazd and the archangels.'

3. Severally they twice recounted their own evil deeds, and it pleased him not; and that wicked evil spirit, through fear of the righteous man, was not able to lift up *his* head until the wicked Gêh[6] came, at the completion of the three thousand years.

4. And she shouted to the evil spirit thus: 'Rise up, *thou* father of us! For I *will* cause that conflict in the world wherefrom the distress and injury of Aûharmazd and the archangels *will* arise.' And she twice recounted severally her own evil deeds, and it pleased him not; and that wicked evil spirit rose not from that confusion, through fear of the righteous man.

6. And, again, the wicked Gêh shouted thus: 'Rise up, *thou* father of us! for in that conflict I *will* shed thus much vexation[7] on the righteous man and the labouring ox

1. These were among the *fravashis* already created (see Chap. I, 8).

2. Reading *amat*, 'when', instead of *mûn*, 'which' (see note to Chap. I, 7).

3. The Pâzand MSS. have *garôist*, for the Huz. Hêmnunast, 'trusted'. Windischmann and Justi have 'all'.

4. Probably Gâyônard.

5. The word *kamârakân* is literally 'those with an evil pate', and is derived from Av. *kameredha*, 'the head of an evil being', also applied to 'the evil summit' of Mount Arezûra (*Vend*. XIX, 140, 142), which is supposed to be at the gate of hell (se Chap. XII, 8). That the chief demons or arch-fiends are meant, appears more clearly in Chap. XXVIII, 12, 44, where the word is *kamârîkân*.

6. The personification of the impurity of menstruation.

7. The word *vêsh* or *vîsh* may stand either for *bêsh*, 'distress, vexation', as here assumed, or for

that, through my deeds, life *will* not be wanted, and I will destroy their living souls (*nismô*);[1] I *will* vex the water, I *will* vex the plants, I *will* vex the fire of Aûharmazd, I *will* make the whole creation of Aûharmazd vexed.'

7. And she so recounted those evil deeds a second time, that the evil spirit was delighted and started up from that confusion; and he kissed Gêh upon the head, and the pollution which they call menstruation became apparent in Gêh.

8. He shouted to Gêh thus: 'What is thy wish? so that I may give *it* thee.' And Gêh shouted to the evil spirit thus: 'A man is the wish, so give *it* to me.'

9. The form of the evil spirit was a log-like lizard's (*vazak*) body, and he appeared a young man of fifteen years to Gêh, and that brought the thoughts of Gêh to him.[2]

10. Afterwards, the evil spirit, with the confederate demons, went towards the luminaries, and he saw the sky; and he led them up, fraught with malicious intentions.

11. He stood upon one-third[3] of the inside of the sky, and he sprang, like a snake, out of the sky down to the earth.

12. In the month Fravardîn and the day Aûharmazd[4] he rushed in at noon, and thereby the sky was as shattered and frightened by him, as a sheep by a wolf.

13. He came on to the water which was arranged[5] below the earth, and then the middle of this earth was pierced *and* entered by him.

14. Afterwards, he came to the vegetation, then to the ox, then to Gâyômard, and then he came to fire;[6] so, just like a fly, he rushed out upon the whole creation; and he made the world quite as injured and dark[7] at midday as though it were in dark night.

15. And noxious creatures were diffused by him over the earth, biting and venomous, such as the snake, scorpion, frog (*kalvâk*), and lizard (*vazak*), so that not so much as the point of a needle remained *free* from noxious creatures.

---

vish, 'poison', as translated by Windischmann and Justi in accordance with the Pâz. MSS.

1. That this is the Huzvâris of *rûbân*, 'soul', appears from Chap. XV, 3–5, where both words are used indifferently; but it is not given in the Huz.-Pâz. Glossary. It is evenly equivalent to Chald, *nismâ*, and ought probably to have the traditional pronunciation *nisman*, an abbreviation of *nismman*.

2. This seems to be the literal meaning of the sentence, and is confirmed by Chap. XXVIII, 1, but Windischmann and Justi understand that the evil spirit formed a youth for Gêh out of a toad's body. The incident in the text may be compared with Milton's idea of Satan and Sin in *Paradise Lost*, Book II, pp. 745–765.

3. Perhaps referring to the proportion of the sky which is overspread by the darkness of night. The whole sentence is rather obscure.

4. The vernal equinox (see Chap. XXV, 7).

5. Literally, 'and it was arranged'.

6. For the details of these visitations, see Chaps. VI–X.

7. Reading *khûst tôm*; but it may be *hangîdtûm*, 'most turbid, opaque'.

16. And blight[1] was diffused by him over the vegetation, and it withered away immediately.

17. And avarice, want, pain, hunger, disease, lust, and lethargy were diffused by him abroad upon the ox and Gâyômard.

18. Before *his* coming to the ox, Aûharmazd ground up the healing fruit,[2] which some call '*bînâk*', small in water openly before *its* eyes, so that *its* damage *and* discomfort from the calamity (*zanisn*) might be less; and when it became at the same time lean and ill, as *its* breath went forth and it passed away, the ox also spoke thus: 'The cattle are to be created, *and* their work, labour, and care are to be appointed.'

19. And before *his* coming to Gâyômard, Aûharmazd brought forth a sweat upon Gâyômard, so long as he might recite a prayer (*vâg*) of one stanza (*vikast*), moreover, Aûharmazd formed that sweat into the youthful body of a man of fifteen years, radiant *and* tall.

20. When Gâyômard issued from the west he saw the world dark as night, and the earth as though not a needle's point remained *free from* noxious creatures; the *celestial* sphere was in revolution, *and* the sun and moon remained in motion: *and* the world's struggle, owing to the clamour of the Mâzînîkân demons,[3] was with the constellations.

21. And the evil spirit thought that the creatures of Aûharmazd were all rendered useless except Gâyômard; and Astô-vîdâd[4] with a thousand demons, causers of death, were let forth by him on Gâyômard.

22. But his appointed time had not come, *and* he (Astô-vidâd) obtained no means of noosing (*âvizîdanô*) *him*; as it is said that, when the opposition of the evil spirit came, the period of the life and rule of Gâyômard was appointed for thirty years.

23. After the coming of the adversary he lived thirty years, and Gâyômard spoke thus: 'Although the destroyer *has* come, mankind *will* be my entire race; and this one thing is good, when they perform duty and good works.'

24. And, afterwards, he (the evil spirit) came to fire, and he mingled smoke and darkness with it.

25. The planets, with many demons, dashed against the *celestial* sphere, and they

1. The word *makhâ*, 'blow, stroke', is a *huzvâris* logogram not found in the glossaries; M6 has *dâr*, 'wood', but this may be a misreading, due to the original, from which M6 was copied, being difficult to read.

2. The word *mîvang* is an unusual form of *mîvak*, 'fruit'. It is probably to be traced to an Av. *mivangh*, which might mean 'fatness', as Windischmann suggests.

3. The *Mâzainya daêva* of the Avesta, and Mâzendarân demons, or idolaters, of Persian legends.

4. The demon of death, Astô-vîdhôtu in the Avesta (Vend. IV, 137, V, 25, 31), who is supposed 'to cast a halter around the necks of the dead to drag them to hell, but if their good works have exceeded their sins they throw off the noose and go to heaven' (Haug's *Essays*, 2nd ed. p. 321). This name is misread Asti-vihâd by Pâzand writers.

mixed the constellations; and the whole creation was as disfigured as though fire disfigured every place and smoke arose over it.

26. And ninety days *and* nights the heavenly angels were contending in the world with the confederate demons of the evil spirit, *and* hurled *them* confounded to hell; and the rampart of the sky was formed so that the adversary should not be able to mingle with it.

27. Hell is in the middle of the earth; there where the evil spirit pierced the earth[1] and rushed in upon it, as all the possessions of the world were changing into duality, *and* persecution, contention, and mingling of high and low became manifest.

1. See § 13.

2

Greater Bundahišn

Reprinted from 'Greater Bundahišn', in R. C. Zaehner, tr., *Zurvan: A Zoroastrian Dilemma* (Oxford, 1955), pp. 312–321.

(1) This, the Knowledge of the Commentary, (deals) first with the primal creation of Ohrmazd and the aggression of the Destructive Spirit; next with the nature of material creatures from the original creation up to the consummation as it is revealed in the Mazdayasnians religion; next with the things contained in the world together with an interpretation of their nature and properties.

(2) Thus is it revealed in the Good Religion. Ohrmazd was on high in omniscience and goodness: for infinite Time he was ever in the Light. That Light is the Space and place of Ohrmazd: some call it the Endless Light. Omniscience and goodness are the totality of Ohrmazd: some call them 'religion'. The interpretation of both is the same, namely the totality of Infinite Time, for Ohrmazd and the Space, Religion, and Time of Ohrmazd were and are and ever shall be.

(3) Ahriman, slow in knowledge, whose will is to smite, was deep down in the darkness: (he was) and is, yet will not be. The will to smite is his all, and darkness is his place: some call it the Endless Darkness.

(4) Between them was the Void: some call it Vāy in which the two Spirits mingle.

(5) Concerning the finite and infinite: the heights which are called the Endless Light (since they have no end) and the depths which are the Endless Darkness, these are infinite. On the border both are finite since between them is the Void, and there is no contact between the two. Again both Spirits in themselves are finite. Again concerning the omniscience of Ohrmazd—everything that is within the knowledge of Ohrmazd is finite; that is, he knows the Norm (pact) that exists between the two Spirits until the creation of Ohrmazd shall rule supreme at the Final Body for ever and ever: that is the infinite. At that time when the Final Body comes to pass, the creation of Ahriman will be destroyed: that again is the finite.

(6) Ohrmazd in his omniscience knew that the Destructive Spirit existed, that he would attack and, since his will is envy, would mingle with him; and from beginning to end (he knew) with what and how many instruments he would accomplish his purpose. In ideal form he fashioned forth such creation as was needful for his instrument. For three thousand years creation stayed in this ideal state, for it was without thought, without movement, without touch.

(7) The Destructive Spirit, ever slow to know, was unaware of the existence of Ohrmazd. Then he rose up from the depths and went to the border from whence the lights are seen. When he saw the light of Ohrmazd intangible, he rushed forward. Because his will is to smite and his substance is envy, he made haste to destroy it. Seeing valour and supremacy superior to his own, he fled back to the darkness and fashioned many demons, a creation destructive and meet for battle.

(8) When Ohrmazd beheld the creation of the Destructive Spirit, it seemed not good to him—a frightful, putrid, bad, and evil creation: and he revered it not. Then the Destructive Spirit beheld the creation of Ohrmazd and it seemed good to him—a creation most profound, victorious, and informed of all: and he revered the creation of Ohrmazd.

(9) Then Ohrmazd, knowing in what manner the end would be, offered peace to the Destructive Spirit, saying, 'O Destructive Spirit, bring aid to my creation and give it praise that in reward therefore thou mayest be deathless and unageing, uncorrupting and undecaying. And the reason is this that if thou dost not provoke a battle, thou shalt not thyself be powerless, and to both of us there shall be benefit abounding.'

(10) But the Destructive Spirit cried out, 'I will not bring aid to thy creation nor will I give it praise, but I shall destroy thee and thy creation for ever and ever: yea, I shall incline all thy creatures to hatred of thee and love of me.' And the interpretation thereof is this that he thought Ohrmazd was helpless against him and that therefore did he offer peace. He accepted not but uttered threats.

(11) And Ohrmazd said, 'Thou canst not, O Destructive Spirit, accomplish all; for thou canst not destroy me, nor canst thou bring it about that my creation should not return to my possession.'

(12) Then Ohrmazd, in his omniscience, knew that if he did not fix a time for battle against him, then Ahriman could do unto his creation even as he had threatened; and the struggle and the mixture would be everlasting; and Ahriman could settle in the mixed state of creation and take it to himself. Thus even now, in the mixed state, there are many men who work unrighteousness more than righteousness—that is they work chiefly the will of the Destructive Spirit.

(13) And Ohrmazd said to the Destructive Spirit, 'Fix a time so that by this pact we may extend the battle for nine thousand years'. For he knew that by fixing a time in this wise the Destructive Spirit would be made powerless. Then the Destructive Spirit, not seeing the end, agreed to that treaty, just as two men who fight a duel fix a term (saying), 'Let us on such a day do battle till night falls'.

(14) This too did Ohrmazd know in his omniscience, that within these nine thousand years three thousand would pass entirely according to the will of Ohrmazd, three thousand years in mixture would pass according to the will of both Ohrmazd and Ahriman, and that in the last battle the Destructive Spirit would be made powerless and that he himself would save creation from aggression.

(15) Then Ohrmazd chanted the *Ahunavar*, that is, he recited the twenty-one words of the *Yatā ahū vairyō*: and he showed to the Destructive Spirit his own final victory, the powerlessness of the Destructive Spirit, the destruction of the demons, the resurrection, the Final Body, and the freedom of creation from all aggression for ever and ever.

(16) When the Destructive Spirit beheld his own powerlessness and the destruction of the demons, he was laid low, swooned, and fell back into the darkness; even as it is said in the Religion, 'When one third thereof is recited, the Destructive Spirit shudders for fear; when two thirds are recited, he falls on his knees; when the prayer is finished, he is powerless'. Unable to do harm to the creatures of Ohrmazd for three thousand years the Destructive Spirit lay crushed.

(17) I shall now speak of the ideal creation, then of the material.

(18) Ohrmazd, before the act of creation, was not Lord: after the act of creation he became Lord, eager for increase, wise, free from adversity, manifest, ever ordering aright, bounteous, all-perceiving,

(19) [First he created the essence of the gods, fair (orderly) movement, that genius by which he made his own body better] for he had conceived of the act of creation: from this act of creation was his lordship.

(20) And by his clear vision Ohrmazd saw that the Destructive Spirit would never cease from aggression and that his aggression could only be made fruitless by the act of creation, and that creation could not move on except through Time and that when Time was fashioned, the creation of Ahriman too would begin to move.

(21) And that he might reduce the Aggressor to a state of powerlessness, having no alternative he fashioned forth Time. And the reason was this that the Destructive Spirit could not be made powerless unless he was brought to battle. And the interpretation of battle (*kārēčār*) is this, that action (*kār*) must be performed with resourcefulness (*čārōmandīh*).

(22) Then from Infinite Time he fashioned and made Time of the long Dominion: some call it finite Time. From Time of the long Dominion he brought forth permanence that the works of Ohrmazd might not pass away. From permanence discomfort was made manifest that comfort might not touch the demons. From discomfort the course of fate, the idea of changelessness, was made manifest, that those things which Ohrmazd created at the original creation might not change. From the idea of changelessness a perfect will (to create) material creation was made manifest, the concord of the righteous creation.

(23) In his unrighteous creation Ahriman was without knowledge, without method. And the reason and interpretation thereof is this, that when Ahriman joined battle with Ohrmazd, the majestic wisdom, renown, perfection, and permanence of Ohrmazd and the powerlessness, self-will, imperfection, and slowness in knowledge of the Destructive Spirit were made manifest when creation was created.

(24) For Time of the long Dominion was the first creature that he fashioned forth: for it was infinite before the contamination of the totality of Ohrmazd. From the infinite it was fashioned finite; for from the original creation when creation was created until the consummation when the Destructive Spirit is made powerless there is a term of twelve thousand years which is finite. Then it mingles with and returns to the Infinite so that the creation of Ohrmazd shall for ever be with Ohrmazd in purity.

(25) As it is said in the Religion, 'Time is mightier than both creations,—the creation of Ohrmazd and that of the Destructive Spirit. Time understands all action and order (the law). [Time is better informed.] Time understands more than those who understand. Time is better informed than the well-informed; for through Time must the decision be made. By Time are houses overturned—doom is through Time—and things graven shattered. From it no single mortal man escapes, not though he fly above, not though he dig a pit below and settle therein, not though he hide beneath a well of cold waters.'

(26) From his own essence which is material light Ohrmazd fashioned forth the form of his creatures—a form of fire—bright, white, round, and manifest afar. From the material (form) of that Spirit which dispels aggression in the two worlds—be it Power or be it Time—he fashioned forth the form of Vāy, the Good, for Vāy was needed: some call it Vāy of the long Dominion. With the aid of Vāy of the long Dominion he fashioned forth creation; for when he created creation, Vāy was the instrument he needed for the deed. (Then he created the essence of the gods, fair (orderly) movement, that genius by which he made his own body better.)

(27) From the material darkness which is his own essence the Destructive Spirit fashioned forth the body of his creation in the form of coal (?), black and ashen, worthy of the darkness, damned as the most sinful noxious beast. From material self-will he fashioned forth the form of Varan (heresy) whose religion is the worse (?); for Varan was needed. Next he created the essence of the demons, evil (disorderly) movement that genius from which destruction came to the creatures of Ohrmazd: for he created a creation through which he made his own body more evil that (in the end) he might be powerless.

(28) For from material darkness which is the Endless Darkness he created lying speech: and from lying speech the harmfulness of the Destructive Spirit was manifest. [For, he created that creation, through which he made his own body more evil that he might be powerless.] For from the Endless Darkness he fashioned forth

that form and he created his creation within that form: and through his own act of creation he will become powerless.

(29) From material light Ohrmazd created true speech: and from true speech the productiveness of the Creator was revealed. For, he fashioned forth the Endless Form from the Endless Light and he created all creation within the Endless Form. The Endless Form is exempt from the passage of Time. From the Endless Form the *Ahunavar* came forth, the genius of the *Yatā ahū vairyō* through which creation and the end of the world are revealed: this is the Religion. For Religion was created simultaneously with the act of creation.

(30) From the *Ahunavar* the Spirit of the Year came forth which is now in a mixed state, half light and half dark, three hundred and sixty-five days and nights, and is a division (dispensation) of Time of the long Dominion. By means of it both creations were set in motion and strove with each other; as it is said, 'The creation of Ohrmazd was endowed with lordship, authority, orderliness, blissful in the heights; the creation of the Destructive Spirit was endowed with contumacy, rebelliousness, sinfulness, straitened in the depths.'

(31) Ohrmazd became lord over decisions through the Amahraspands. When they had been created, he made three Judges, for they were needed for the material world. In the latter days at the Final Body they shall carry evil away from it. Spiritually he sustains the spiritual creation. The material creation he created in ideal form: then he created it in material form.

(32) First he created the Amahraspands, six originally, then the rest; and the seventh is Ohrmazd himself. Of the material world he created first six (beings) in ideal form; and he himself was the seventh. For Ohrmazd is both spiritual (and material). Material creation is first from the Amahraspands, second from Vāy of the long Dominion.

(33) First he fashioned forth Vahuman by whom movement was given to the creation of Ohrmazd. The Destructive Spirit first created Akōman of the lying word. Of material creatures Ohrmazd first fashioned the sky; and from the goodly movement of material light he fashioned forth Vahuman with whom the good Mazdayasnians Religion dwelt: that is to say Vahuman knew what would befall creation even up to its rehabilitation. Then he fashioned Artvahišt, then Šahrēvar, then Spandarmat, then Hurdāt, then Amurdāt: and the seventh was Ohrmazd himself. (34) Eighth true speech, ninth the blessed Srōš, tenth Mānsraspand, eleventh Nēryōsang, twelfth the exalted judge Ratwōk Berzait, thirteenth Rašn the just, fourteenth Mihr of wide pastures, fifteenth Aršišvang the good, sixteenth Pārand, seventeenth Sleep, eighteenth the Wind, nineteenth Order (the Law), twentieth Dispute, prosecution and defence, and the fruitfulness of reconciliation.

(35) Of material creation (he created) first the sky, second water, third the earth, fourth plants, fifth cattle, sixth man; the seventh was Ohrmazd himself. And he fashioned forth creation with the aid of Vāy of the long Dominion: for when he

fashioned forth Vāy of the long Dominion, it too was as an instrument and needful for the act of creation.

(36) The Destructive Spirit, bent on aggression, first of the demons with monstrous heads fashioned forth Akōman, then Indar, then Sāvul, then Nāehait, then Tarōmat, then Tarič and Zērič, then the other demons: the seventh was the Destructive Spirit himself. Never does he think or speak or do anything that is righteous; nor did he need the good that is in the creation of Ohrmazd;—and the creation of Ahriman did not need the good that is in the creation of Ohrmazd.

(37) Ohrmazd does not turn his mind to anything he cannot do. The Destructive Spirit does turn his mind to what he cannot do and threatens to do it.

(38) The creation of Ohrmazd was fostered spiritually in such wise that it remained without thought, without touch, without movement in a moist state like semen. After this moist state came mixture like (that of) semen and blood; after mixture came conception, like a fetus; after conception came diffusion, such as hands and feet; after diffusion came hollowing—eyes, ears and mouth; after hollowing came movement when it came forward to the light. Even now on earth do men in this wise grow together in their mother's womb, and are born and bred.

(39) Ohrmazd by the act of creation is both father and mother to creation: for in that he fostered creation in ideal form, he acted as a mother; and in that he created it materially, he acted as a father.

(40) Concerning the material creation.

(41) When the Destructive Spirit was laid low, unable to act (as I have written above) for three thousand years he lay abject and low. During the period of the powerlessness of the Destructive Spirit Ohrmazd fashioned creation in material form. From the Endless Light he fashioned fire in material form, from fire wind, from wind water, from water the all-solid earth: as it is said in the Religion: 'The first creation of all was a drop of water, for all things arose from water except the seed of man and cattle: for that seed has the seed of fire.'

(42) First he created the sky as a defence. Some call it 'the first'. Second he created water to smite down the Lie of thirst: third he created the all-solid earth: fourth he created plants to help the useful kine: fifth kine to help the Blessed Man: sixth he created the Blessed Man to smite the Destructive Spirit and his demons and make them powerless. Then he created fire, a flame; and its brilliance derived from the Endless Light, a goodly form even as fire desires. Then he fashioned the wind in the form of a stripling, fifteen years of age, which fosters and keeps the water, the plants, and the kine, the Blessed Man and all things that are.

(43) Now I shall describe their properties. First he created the sky, bright and manifest, its ends exceeding far apart, in the form of an egg, of shining metal that is the substance of steel, male. The top of it reached to the Endless Light; and all

creation was created within the sky—like a castle or fortress in which every weapon that is needed for the battle is stored, or like a house in which all things remain. The [bottom of the] vault of the sky's width is equal to its length, its length to its height, and its height to its depth: the proportions are the same and fit exceeding well (?). Like a husbandman the spirit of the sky is possessed of thought and speech and deeds, knows, produces much, discerns.

(44) And it received durability as a bulwark against the Destructive Spirit that he might not be suffered to return (to whence he came). Like a valiant warrior who dons his armour that fearless he may return from battle, so does the spirit of the sky keep (don) the sky. And to help the sky, he (Ohrmazd) gave it joy, for he fashioned joy for its sake: for even now in the mixed state creation is in joy.

(45) Second from the substance of the sky he fashioned water, as much as when a man puts his hands on the ground and walks on his hands and feet, and the water rises to his belly and flows to that height. And as helpmates he gave it wind, rain, mist, storm, and snow.

(46) Third from water he created the earth, round, with far-flung passage-ways, without hill or dale, its length equal to its breadth, and its breadth to its depth, poised in the middle of the sky: as it is said, 'The first third of this earth he fashioned as hard as granite(?); the second third of this earth he fashioned of sandstone(?); the third third of this earth he fashioned as soft as clay.'

(47) And he created minerals within the earth, and mountains which afterwards sprang forth and grew out of the earth. And to aid the earth he gave it iron, copper, sulphur, and borax and all the other hard substances of the earth except … (?) …, for that is of a different substance. And he made and fashioned the earth like a man when he tightly covers his body on all sides with all manner of raiment. Beneath this earth there is water everywhere.

(48) Fourth he created plants. First they grew in the middle of this earth to the height of a foot, without branches, bark or thorn, moist and sweet: and every manner of plant life was in their seed. And to aid the plants he gave them water and fire; for the stem of every plant has a drop of water at its tip and fire for (the breadth of) four fingers before (the tip). By the power of these they grew.

(49) Fifth he fashioned the lone-created Bull in Ērānvēž in the middle of the earth, on the banks of the river Vēh Daitē, for that is the middle of the earth. He was white and shining like the Moon and his height was about three cubits. And to aid him he gave him water and plants; for in the mixed state he derives strength and growth from these.

(50) Sixth he fashioned Gayōmart, shining like the Sun, and his height was about four cubits and his breadth equal to his height, on the banks of the river Daitē, for that is the middle of the earth—Gayōmart on the left side, the Bull on the right side; and their distance one from the other and their distance from the water of the Daitē was as much as their height. They had eyes and ears, tongue and

distinguishing mark. The distinguishing mark of Gayōmart is this that men have in this wise been born from his seed.

(51) And to aid him he gave him sleep, the repose of the Creator; for Ohrmazd fashioned forth sleep in the form of a man, tall and bright, and fifteen years of age. He fashioned Gayōmart and the Bull from the earth. And from the light and freshness of the sky he fashioned forth the seed of men and bulls; for these two seeds have their origin in fire, not in water: and he put them in the bodies of Gayōmart and the Bull that from them there might be progeny abundant for men and kin.

3

The Answers of Manūskihar From *Dādistān-i Dīnīk*

Reprinted from 'Dādistān-i Dīnīk', tr. E. M. West in F. Max Müller, ed., *The Sacred Books of the East: Pahlavi Texts* (Delhi, 1977), vol. 18, pp. 11–25.

The Religious Opinions of Manūskihar, Son of Yudān-yīm

1. First you ask thus: Why is a righteous man created better than the stars and moon *and* sun and fire of Aûharmazd, and is called in revelation greater and better than the spiritual creation, *and* also than that which is worldly?

2. The reply is this that the greatness and goodness of advance in wisdom and just judgment over the creatures arise from proficiency (*hûnar*).

3. Justice is the one good proficiency over the creatures, the means of wisdom are great, and praise bestowed is the most effectual performance of what is desirable (*kâmisn-karîh*).

4. For all three are mutually connected together; since the manifestation of justice is through wisdom, and its advantage is the performance of what is desirable for the creator; wisdom is the performance of what is desirable for the requirements of the creator, and its weapon (*zênô*) is justice; and the desire of the creator, which is progress, is in wisdom with justice.

5. All three are great among the creatures, and their lodgment in the superior beings and righteous men is spiritual, in the spirit which is the pure guardian angel,[1] *in* the understanding for encountering, averting, smiting, and prostrating (*khvâpâk*) the fiend, *in* the army of angels, and *in* the sovereignty of the far-seeing (*dûr-vênâkŏ*)[2]

1. The *fravâhar* or *fravashi*, which is the prototype or spiritual counterpart supposed to have been created in the beginning for each good creature and creation afterwards produced, whether material or immaterial, and whose duty is to represent the creature and watch over its interests in the spiritual world.

2. This word is badly written in K35, so that it has become *zôrînâk* in later MSS, which might

spirit, Aûharmazd; and, materially, in the worldly equipment and mutual connection of body *and* life.

6. And their appliances are the wisdom and worldly efficacy of treatises on the wise adoption of good thoughts, good words, *and* good deeds, *and* the relinquishment *and* discontinuance of evil thoughts, evil words, *and* evil deeds.

7. And their acquirer is the worldly ruler who is providing for Aûharmazd, and approving and stimulating the pure religion, a praiser of the good and pure creator, and a director of persistence in destruction of the field.

8. And in the promulgation (*rûbâkŏ-dahisnîh*) of the good and religious liturgy (*mânsar*), the coming of the good cause of the resurrection and the production of the renovation *of the universe*[1] are *his* cooperation and his own thanksgiving; and over the creatures of *this* prior world *he* is a guardian, defender, and manager.

9. And *such rulers* are great and pre-eminent; yet every man is not for that greatness, but it is mentioned as to superior beings *and* concerning righteous men, in whom it *has* arisen, and the best are the three who are the beginning, middle, *and* end of the creation.

10. One is the pure man, Gâyômard, who was its first rational praiser; he in whose keeping *was* the whole creation of the sacred beings, from *its* beginning and immaturity unto the final completion of the worldly creatures, over which *was* the exercise of goodness of his well-destined progeny, such as Hôshâng, Tâkhmôrup, Yim, and Frêdûn,[2] such as the apostles of the religion, like Zaratûst, Hûshêdar, and Hûshêdar-mâh,[3] and the producers of the renovation *of the universe*, like Sôshâns,[4] Rôshanô-kashm, and Khû-kashm.[5]

11. The approver[6] of the enterprises (*rûbâk-dahisnîhâ*) of cooperators, the purely-praising and just worshipper of the sacred beings through the strength of the spirit, the disabler of the worldly activity of the fiend as regards worldly bodies, and the one of pure religion—which is his charge (*spôr*),[7] the revelation of

perhaps mean 'strength-exerting'.

1. Which is expected to take place about the time of the resurrection (see Bd. XXX, 32).

2. The first four rulers of the world (omitting the usurper Dahâk) after Gâyômard (see Bd. XXXI, 1–3, 7). The five names of these primeval sovereigns are corruptions of the Avesta names, Gaya-maretan, Haoshyangha, Takhmô-urupa, Yima, and Thraêtaona. The third name is always written Tâkhmôrîdŏ in Dd.

3. Corruptions of Av. Zarathustra, Ukhshyad-ereta, and Ukhshad-nemangh. The last two are future apostles still expected by the Parsis to restore their religion to its original purity, in preparation for the resurrection (see Bd. XXXII, 2–10, Byt. III, 13, 43–48, 52, 53).

4. Av. Saoshyās. The last of the future apostles, in whose time the universe is expected to be renovated and the resurrection to take place (see Bd. XXX, 4–27, XXXII, 8, Byt. III, 62).

5. These two names, which mean 'bright-eyed' and 'sunny-eyed', are the Av. Raokas-kaêshman and Hvare-kaêshman of Fravardîn YT. 128 (see also Chap. XXXVI, 4).

6. This is Zaratûst (see § 12), the righteous apostle of the middle portion of the history of creation referred to in § 9.

7. Or 'which is wholly his'.

the place of the beneficent spirit and of the destruction of the depravity of the evil spirit,[1] the subjugation (*khvâpisnŏ*) of the fiend, the completion of the triumph of the creator, and the unlimited progress of the creatures—is the upholder of Mazda-worship.

12. And likewise through the goodness of Gâyômard, which is the begetting of Zaratûst, *he* is also just; likewise through the goodness of Sôshâns, by which he is the progeny of Zaratûst, *he* is also progressive in every good thought, good word, *and* good deed, *more* than the creatures which are produced with a hope of the religion, and equally thankful.

13. And one is the producer of bodies,[2] the renovator (*frashagar*) Sôshâns, who is the putter down, with complete subjugation from the world, of the glorification of fiends *and* demons, and of the contention with angels in apostasy and heterodoxy of various kinds and unatoned for; and the completer of the renovation through the full continuance of the glorification of the angels, and the perfect continuance of the pure religion.

14. And through that excellent, unblemished, brotherly work[3] *such a ruler* may be seen above the sun with swift horses, the primeval luminaries, and all removal of darkness, the advance of illumination which is the display (*tôgisnŏ*) of the days *and* nights of the world.[4] Regarding the same completion of the renovation *of the universe* it is said in the revelation of the Mazda-worshippers, that this great light is the vesture of the like righteous men.

Chapter III

1. The second is that which you ask thus: For what purpose is a righteous man created for the world, and in what manner is it necessary for him to exist in the world?

2. The reply is this, that the creator created the creatures for progress, which is his wish; and it is necessary for us to promote whatever is his wish, so that we may obtain whatever is our wish.

3. And, since that persistent creator is powerful, whatever is our wish, and so

1. These two spirits are supposed to be the authors of all the good and evil, respectively that exists in creation. They appear, originally, to have been both supposed to spring from Aûharmazd, who speaks of 'the more beneficent of my two spirits' in Yas. XIX, 21; but in later times, and throughout the Pahlavi literature, the beneficent spirit is identified with Aûharmazd, and the origin of the evil spirit is left in obscurity.

2. The renovated bodies of the future existence which are prepared for mankind at the resurrection (see Bd. XXX, 4, 7, 25–27).

3. Mentioned in §§ 7, 8.

4. M14 and J have '"*such rulers*" own praise is above the sun with swift horses, the primeval luminaries, and all good creatures; for that, too, which may be seen when the light of the sun is owing to the removal of darkness, and the removal is the advance of illumination of the world, is the display of days *and* nights.'

far as we remain very faithful, such is as *it were* deserving of his wish, which is for our obtainment of whatever is our wish.[1]

4. The miracle of these creatures was fully achieved (*âvôrîdŏ*) not unequally, and the gain (*gûâftâkŏ*) also from the achievement of the same miracle is manifest; that is, achieving, and knowing[2] that his achievement is with design (*kîm*) and his desire is goodness, when the designed achievement, which is his creature, and also the goodness, which is his wish, are certain, and likewise, owing to the perfect ability which is due to the creator, the wish is achieved, *it* is manifest.

5. And, afterwards, it is decided by wisdom that *he has* achieved it, and the creatures, as perfected for the complete progress which is his wish, lapse into evil; and since when evil exists good becomes the subjugation of evil—for when evil is not complete, and after it is expressly said that his creatures are created for his own will, the progress due to subjugations of evil is on account of the good completed—it is similarly testified, *in accordance* with the will aforesaid, that it[3] is achieved.

6. The creatures are for the performance of what is desirable for the creator, and the performance of what is desirable for the creator is necessary for two *purposes*, which are the practice of worship *and* contention.

7. As the worship is that of the persistent creator, who is a friend to his own creatures, *and* the contention is that with the fiend—the contender who is an enemy to the creation of the creator—that great worship is a pledge, most intimate to one's self, of the utmost contention also, and a pledge for the prosperity owing to the friend subjugating by a look which is a contender with the enemy, the great endeavour of the acquirers of reliance upon any mortals whatever.[4]

8. For when the persistent *one* accomplished that most perfect and wholly miraculous creation of the lord, and his unwavering look—which *was* upon the coming on of the wandering evil spirit, the erratic, unobservant spirit—*was* unmingled with the sight of an eye,[5] he made a spirit of observant temperament, which *was* the necessary soul, the virtuous lord of the body moving into the world.

9. And the animating life, the preserving guardian spirit, the acquiring intellect, the protecting understanding, the deciding wisdom, the demeanour which is itself a physician, the impelling strength, the eye for *what* is seen, the ear for *what* is heard, the nose for *what* is smelt, the mouth for recognizing flavour,

---

1. Reading *kâmakŏ* instead of the *dâmakŏ* of the MSS, which was, no doubt, originally *gâmakŏ*.

2. M14 has 'knowing perfectly'.

3. The subjugation of evil apparently.

4. Referring probably to the strong influence of a steady eye upon all living creatures.

5. This appears to be the meaning of *agûmêgisnŏ-î val vênâftâkŏ dîdag*; which phrase is followed by the conjunction 'and', so that the original text means that when the creator had done as in §§ 8, 9, he proceeded to act as in § 10. This conjunction, for the sake of clearness, is here transferred to the beginning of § 10.

the body for approaching the assembly (*pidrâm*) of the righteous, the heart for thinking, the tongue for speaking; the hand for working, the foot for walking, these which make life comfortable, these which are developments in creating, these which are to join the body, these which are to be considered perfected, are urged on by him continuously, and the means of industry of the original body are arranged advisedly.

10. *And* by proper regulation, and the recompense of good thoughts, good words, and good deeds, he announced and adorned conspicuous, patient, and virtuous conduct; *and* that procurer of the indispensable did not forget to keep men *in* his own true service and proper bounds, the supreme sovereignty of the creator.

11. And *man* became a pure glorifier and pure praiser of that all-good friend, through the progress which is his wish.

12. Because pure friendship is owing to sure meditation on every virtue, and from its existence no harm whatever arose; pure glorifying is owing to glorifying every goodness, and from its existence no vileness whatever arose; and pure praising is owing to all prosperity, and from its existence no distress whatever arose.

13. And pronouncing the benedictions he is steadfast *in* the same pure friendship, just glorifying, and expressive praising, *which* are performed even as though Vohûman were kept lodging in the thoughts, Srôsh in the words, and Ard in the actions.[1]

14. That, moreover, which is owing to the lodgment of Vohûman in the thoughts is virtuously rushing into true propitiation from the heart, and keeping selfishness away from the desires; the lodgment of Srôsh in the words is owing to him who is intelligent *being* a true speaker, *and* him who is unintelligent being a listener to *what is* true and *to* the high-priests; *and* the lodgment of Ard in the actions is declared to be owing to promoting that which is known *as* goodness, *and* abstaining *from* that which *one* does not know.

15. And these three benefits[2] which *have been* recited are sent down (*farôstakŏ*) in two ways that the ancients *have* mentioned, which are *that* deliberately taken and *that* they should deliberately leave,[3] whose means are wisdom and proper exertion.

16. And his (man's) high-priest is he whose instigation is to keep him truly *in accordance* with the revelation (*dînô*) of the sacred beings, and is the origin of his pure meditation which is truly through goodness like Vohûman's.

---

1. These three angels are personifications of the Avesta terms *vohû-manô*, 'good thought', *sraosha*, 'listening, obedience', and *areta*, 'righteous'. The coming of Vohûman ('the good spirit' of § 17) and of Srôsh is mentioned in the Gâthas (Yas. XLIII, 16, c d).

2. The lodgments of the three angels.

3. Meaning, probably, the deliberate adoption of good conduct and relinquishment of evil (compare Chap. VII, 7).

17. As the religious of the ancients *have* religiously said, that of him who keeps the goodness of Vohûman lodging in the thoughts the true way is then that of the good spirit.

18. The Mazda-worshipper understands the will of the creator in the true way, and grows and acquires by performing what is desirable for the creator, which obtains the benefit of the renovation.

19. A more concise reply is this, that a righteous man is the creature by whom is accepted that occupation which is provided for him, and is fully watchful in the world as to his not being deceived by the rapacious fiend.

20. And as a determiner, by wisdom, of the will of the creator—*one* who is himself a propitiator and understander, and a promoter of the understanding of goodness—and of whatever *pertains* to him (the creator), *he* is a giver of heed thereto; and it is necessary for him to be thus, so that such greatness *and* goodness may also be his more securely in the spiritual *existence*.

Chapter IV

1. The third question is that you ask thus: For what reason does this greatness[1] of a righteous man exist?

2. The reply is this that *it* is for the performance of what is desirable for the creator by the Mazda-worshipper; because he strives unhesitatingly that the way for the performance of what is desirable for the creator *may* be the propitiation[2] which is his desire, and that desired propitiation becomes perfect through sound wisdom.

3. The wisdom by which he understands about the desire of the heavenly angels is not appointed (*vakht*), but is the true, pure religion which is knowledge of[3] the spirits, the science of sciences, the teacher of the teaching of the angels, and the source of all knowledge.

4. And the progress, too, of the pure religion of the Mazda-worshippers is through the righteous man, as is shown of him in revelation thus: 'I created, O Zaratûst the Spîtamân! The righteous man who is very active,[4] and I will guard his hands from evil deeds; I *will* also have him conveyed unto those who are afterwards righteous and more actively wise.[5]

5. And *at* the same time the religion of me who created him is his desire, *and* it

---

1. Referring to Chap. II, 1, and not to Chap. III, 20; otherwise it might be supposed that the questions were contrived to suit the replies.

2. Or, perhaps, 'understanding'.

3. K35 has 'obedience to' by inserting a medial stroke in *dânisnŏ*, which converts it into *sinvisnŏ*, but is probably a mistake.

4. M14 and J here insert 'I will guard his mind from evil thoughts, *his* tongue from evil-speaking.'

5. In the future existence.

is the obtainment of a ruler which is to be changed by the well-organized renovation *of the universe.*[1]

6. As through wisdom is created the world of righteousness, through wisdom is subjugated every evil, and through wisdom is perfected every good; and the best wisdom is the pure religion whose progress is that achieved by the upholders of religion, the greatness of the best men of the righteous, in whose destiny *it is*, such as that which *was* shown about Gâyômard, Zaratûst, and Sôshâns.[2]

Chapter V

1. The fourth question is that which you ask thus: Of this destruction (*zadam*) and terror which ever happen to us from the retribution[3] of the period, and are a cause of the other evils and defects of the good religion, what kind of opinion exists? And is there a good opinion of us among the spirits, or not?

2. The reply is this, that it is said in the revelation of the Mazda-worshippers that the impediments (*râs-bandîh*), through which *there* is vexation in righteousness, are because its doctrine is this, that, regarding the difficulty, anxiety, and discomfort which occur through good works set going, it is not desirable to account *them* as much difficulty, trouble, and discomfort.

3. Whereas it is not desirable to account *them* as anxiety and difficulty, it is then declared by it[4] thereof, that, as its recompense, so much comfort *and* pleasure will come to the soul, as that no one is to think of that difficulty and discomfort which came upon him through so many such good works, because he is steadfast to maintain the good religion, and utters thanksgivings (*va stâyedŏ*).

4. And as regards the discomfort,[5] which the same good religion of ours *has* had, it comes on from the opponents of the religion.

5. Through the coming of religion we have full enjoyment (*barâ gûkârêm*), and owing to religion, unlike bondsmen (*abûrdŏgânvâr*), we do not become changeable among the angels; our spiritual life (*ahvôîh*) of praise then arrives in readiness, and owing to the angels *there* are joyous salutation, spiritual life, and glory for the soul.

---

1. M14 and J have '*and* it is the obtainment of a ruler who is a wise upholder of religion, from time to time, even unto the change of the last existences by the well-organized renovation *of the universe*.' But the additional words appear to have been suggested by the word 'ruler' being taken literally, whereas it seems to have been figuratively applied to the religion which is to rule the righteous till the future existence.

2. In Chap. II, 9–13.

3. Reading *pâdâsân*, but by a slight alteration M14 and J have *pâdakhshahân*, 'monarchs', which is equally suitable.

4. By revelation.

5. M14 and J have 'and he remains thereby certain that his good works are in the statement (*mâdîgânŏ*) of good works, *and* as regards all that terror, anxiety (*vayâdŏ*), and discomfort', &c.

Chapter VI

1. The fifth question is that you ask thus: Why does evil always happen more *to* the good than to the bad?

2. The reply is this, that not *at* every time and every place, *and* not *to* all the good, does evil happen more—for the spiritual welfare of the good is certainly more—but in the world it is very much more manifest.[1]

3. And the reasons for it are many; one which is conclusive is even this, that the modes and causes of *its* occurrence are more; for the occurrence of evil is more particularly appointed (*vakhtŏ*) by two modes, one by the demons, the appointers of evil, *and* one by the vile, the doers of evil; even to the vileness of creation and the vile they cause vexation.

4. Moreover, incalculable is the evil which happens to the vile from the demons, and that to the good from the demons and also from the vile, and the mode of its occurrence is in the same way without a demon.

5. This, too, is more particularly such as the ancients *have* said, that the labour and trouble of the good are much more in the world, and their reward *and* recompense are more certain in the spiritual *existence*; and the comfort and pleasure of the vile are more in the world, and their pain *and* punishment in the spiritual *existence* are more severe.

6. And this, too, is *the case*, that the good, through fear of the pain and punishment of hell, should forsake the comfort and ease in the world, and should not think, speak, *or* do anything improper whatever.

7. And through hope for the comfort and pleasure in heaven they should accept willingly, for the neck,[2] much trouble *and* fear in the practice of virtue in thought, word, *and* deed.

8. The vile, through provision with temporary enjoyment[3]—even that enjoyment of improprieties for which eventually there is hell—then enjoy themselves therein temporarily, and lustfully on account of selfishness; those various actions also, through which *there* would be a way to heaven, they do not trouble themselves with.

---

1. M14 and J have 'but the worldly evil and bondage are incalculably more manifest about the good, much more in the season (*zêmânîh*) of Srôsh.' The 'season of Srôsh' may perhaps mean the night-time or the three nights after death, when the protection of the angel Srôsh is most wanted; but Dasûr Peshotanji Behramji, the high-priest of the Parsis in Bombay, prefers reading *zîmânash* (with a double pronominal suffix), and has favoured me with the following free translation of the whole passage: 'At every time and every place much evil does not happen *to* all the good; for the good, after having been separated from this world, receive (as a reward for their suffering evil) much goodness in the next world, which goodness is (regarded as) of a very high degree in religious doctrines (*srôsh*).' Perhaps, after all, Srôsh is a miswriting of *saryâ*, 'bad, and evil'.

2. The word can be read *garêvan*, 'collar', or *gardûn*, 'neck', and is the usual Pâz. of the Huz. *kavarman* (Chald. צוורא), 'the neck', though 'neck' is often expressed by *gardûn*. The meaning is that the yoke of trouble and fear should be accepted.

3. M14 and J have 'through provision with the enjoyment of improprieties which is temporarily theirs.'

9. And in this way, in the world, the comfort and pleasure of the vile are more, and the anxiety, vexation, despondency, and distress of the good *have* become more; the reason is revealed by the stars.

4

Opinions of the Spirit of Wisdom From *Dīnā-i Maīnog-i Khirad*

Reprinted from 'Dīnā-i Maīnog-i Khirad', tr. E. W. West in F. Max Müller, ed., *The Sacred Books of the East: Pahlavi Texts* (Delhi, 1977), vol. 24, pp. 3–17.

Through the name and power and assistance of the creator Aûharmazd, the archangels *who are* good rulers and good performers, and all the angels of the spiritual and the angels of the worldly *existences*, by a happy dispensation (*dahisn*) and well-omened we write the Opinions of the Spirit of Wisdom through the will of the sacred beings.[1]

Chapter I

(1)[2] In the name and *for* the propitiation of the all-benefiting creator Aûharmazd, (2) of all the angels of the spiritual and worldly creations, (3) *and* of the learning of learnings, the Mazda-worshipping religion, (4) forth from which this, *which is* such a source of wisdom, is a selector.[3] (5) Through the glory and will of the creator

1. This heading is prefixed to the original Pahlavi text in K43, a facsimile of which was published by Andreas in 1882; as, however, the text which follows it in that codex, begins in the middle of Chap. I, p. 28, this heading must have been composed by some copyist, after the first folio of the text had been lost from some previous copy. It is, therefore, doubtful whether the name he gives to the work, 'Opinions (or decision) of the Spirit of Wisdom', be the original title, or not; but it is, at any rate, preferable to the modern appellation, 'the Spirit of Wisdom'. In Pâzand this title is *Mainyô-i Khard*.

2. The beginning of this chapter, enclosed in brackets, as far as § 28 (being lost from the Pahlavi text of K43, and no copy of it from TD2 being available) is here taken from the Pâzand version contained in L19. The division into sections, adopted throughout, is that of the alternating Pâz.-Sans. text of Nêryôsang.

3. That is, this work is a selection of wisdom from the religion. The Pâz. *vas* is a misreading of Pahl. *Agas*, 'from it', which is identical in form with Pahl. *Afas*, the correct equivalent of Pâz. *Vas*.

Aûharmazd, *who is* promoting the prosperity of the two existences[1]—(6) and of all the greatly powerful angels, (7) and *through* the completely calm repose of the sacred beings, the princely,[2] purpose-fulfilling sages, (8) presentations of various novelties for the appropriation of wisdom, (9) through largely acquiring reasoning thought,[3] are most wholesome for the body and soul *in* the two existences.

(10) As in the pure marvel of marvels, the unquestionable and well-betokened good religion of the Mazda-worshippers, by the words of the creator, Aûharmazd, and Zaratûst the Spîtamân,[4] it is in many places decided, (11) this he, who is the all-good creator, created these creatures through wisdom, (12) and his maintenance of the invisible revolutions[5] is through wisdom;

(13) And the imperishable and undisturbed *state*, in that which is immortality *for* ever and everlasting, he reserves for himself by means of the most deliberative[6] means of wisdom.

(14) For the same reason *it* is declared, (15) that *there* was a sage, who said, (16) that 'if this be known, that the religion of the sacred beings (*yazdân*) is truth, and *its* law is virtue, and *it* is desirous of welfare and compassionate as regards the creatures, (17) wherefore are *there* mostly many sects, many beliefs, and many original evolutions[7] of mankind? (18) And, especially, that which is a sect, law, and belief, causing harm to the property (*khêl*) of the sacred beings,[8] and is not good?

(19, 20)[9] And this, too, *one has* to consider, that, in order to become a chooser in this matter, trouble is to be undergone; (21) and it is necessary to become acquainted with this matter, (22) because, in the end, the body is mingled with the dust, and reliance is on the soul.

---

1. This world and the next.

2. The angels are here compared to the *vâspûharakân*, the highest class of Sasanian nobles, called *barbêtân*, 'sons of the house', in Huzvâris (see Nöldeke's Gesch. Pers. Sas. pp. 71, 501). As these nobles ranked next to the royal house, so do the archangels and angels rank next to Aûharmazd. The title *vâspûhar* is evidently connected with the ancient Pers. equivalent of Av. *vîsô puthra*, 'son of the village or town', which, as Darmesteter points out (*Études Iraniennes*, II, p. 140), is used in *Vend.* VII, 114 as the title of a person who has to pay the same medical fees as the *zantu-paiti*, 'tribe-ruler', mentioned in the earlier § 108, and who must, therefore, have been a man of equal rank.

3. Reading *vîrmat*, both here and in § 13, instead of the Pâz. *Nîrmad*, which is a misreading of the same letters.

4. Av. Zarathustra Spitama, the great apostle of the Mazda-worshippers, whose conversations with Ahura Mazda (Pahl Aûharmazd) constitute a considerable portion of the Avesta, or scripture of the Mazda-worshippers.

5. Of the spheres, or firmaments, which are supposed to carry along the heavenly bodies.

6. Reading *vîrmat-hômandtûm*.

7. Reading *bûn gast* (see Sg. IV, 73 n).

8. It may be questioned whether this allusion to a heterodox religion injuring the property of the orthodox faith is sufficient to identify the former with Muhammadanism.

9. These two sections are improperly separated by Nêryôsang.

(23) And every one is to undergo trouble for the soul, (24) and is to become acquainted with duty and good works; (25) because that good work which a man does unwittingly is little of a good work, (26) and that sin which a man commits unwittingly amounts to a sin in *its* origin.[1]

(27) And *it* is declared by the Avesta[2] (28) thus:[3] 'Nothing *was* taken by him by whom the soul *was* not taken (29) hitherto, and he takes nothing who does not take the soul (30) henceforward likewise;[4] (31) because the spiritual and worldly *existences* are such-like as[5] two strongholds, (32) one *it* is declared certain that they shall capture, and one it is not possible to capture.

(33) After *being* replete *with* those good actions *of*[6] which *it* is declared certain that it is not possible to capture, (34) and when he[7] surveyed the incitement for this, (35) he started forth (*fravaftŏ*), in search of wisdom, into the various countries and various districts of this world; (36) and of the many[8] religions and beliefs of those people who are superior in their wisdom he thought and enquired, and he investigated and came upon *their* origin.[9]

(37) And when he saw that they are so mutually afflicting (*hanbêshin*) and inimical among one another, (38) he then knew that these religions and beliefs and diverse customs, which are so mutually afflicting among one another in this world, are not worthy to be from the appointment of the sacred beings; (39) because the religion of the sacred beings is truth, and *its* law is virtue.

(40) And through this he became without doubt that, *as to* whatever[10] is not in this pure religion, *there* is then doubtfulness for them in everything, (41) and in every cause they see distraction.

(42) After that he became more diligent in the enquiry and practice of religion;

(43) and he enquired of the high-priests who have become wiser in[11] this religion

1. The original text was, no doubt, *vinâs pavan bûn val yehevûnêd*, which would be *gunâh pa bun ô bahôd* in Pâzand; but L19 has omitted the p in *pa*, and Nêr, has mistaken the preposition *val* for the pronoun *valman*, which blunders have misled the writers of later MSS. into a variety of inconsistent readings.

2. The sacred literature of the Parsis in its original language.

3. The extant Pahlavi text of K43 commences at this point.

4. By this division of §§ 28–30 Nêr, found himself compelled to add another Sanskrit clause in explanation, which would have been unnecessary if he had separated them as here pointed.

5. K43 omits 'as'.

6. L19 has 'after those good actions of a store'.

7. The sage mentioned in § 15.

8. L19 has 'every'.

9. L19 omits 'origin', having merely *vagôst*, 'investigated', instead of bun *gûstŏ*, 'investigated the origin'.

10. L19 has 'every one who', having read *kolâ mûn* instead of *kolâ maman*. The meaning, however, is that all details of foreign faiths that are not found in the Mazda-worshipping religion are doubtful.

11. K43 has 'of', by omitting pavan, 'in'.

and more acquainted *with* the religion, (44) thus: 'For the maintenance of the body *and* preservation of the soul what thing[1] is good and more perfect?'

(45) And they [spoke[2]], through the statement [from revelation, (46) thus: 'Of the[3] benefit which happens to men] wisdom is good; (47) because it is possible to manage the worldly *existence* through wisdom,[4] (48) and it is possible to provide also the spiritual *existence* for oneself through the power of wisdom.

(49) And this, too, is declared, that Aûharmazd has produced these creatures and creation, which are in the worldly *existence*, through innate wisdom;[5] (50) and the management of the worldly and spiritual *existences* 'is also through wisdom'.

(51) And when, in that manner, he saw the great advantage and preciousness of wisdom, he became more thankful unto Aûharmazd, the lord, and the archangels of[6] the spirit of wisdom; (52) and he took[7] the spirit of wisdom as a protection.

(53) For the spirit of wisdom *one* is to perform more homage and service than *for* the remaining archangels.

(54) And this, too, he knew, that it is possible to do for oneself every duty and good work and proper action through the power of wisdom; (55) and it is necessary to be diligent for the satisfaction of the spirit of wisdom.

(56) And, thenceforward, he became more diligent in performing[8] the ceremonial of the spirit of wisdom.

(57) After that the spirit of wisdom, on account of the thoughts and wishes of that sage, displayed *his* person unto him.

(58) And he spoke to him (59) thus: 'O friend *and* glorifier! Good from perfect righteousness! (60) Seek advancement from me, the spirit of wisdom, (61) that I may become thy guide to the satisfaction of the sacred beings and the good,[9] and *to* the maintenance of the body in the worldly *existence* and the preservation of the soul in the spiritual *one*.'

---

1. L19 has 'what one thing'.
2. K43 omits the words in brackets, by mistake.
3. Sans. Has 'this'.
4. L19 has 'through the power of wisdom'.
5. The *âsnô khiradŏ* (Av. *âsnô khratus*) is 'the durable or innate wisdom' supposed to be implanted in one's nature, as distinguished from the Av. *gaoshô-srûtô khratus*, 'the ear-heard or acquired wisdom', obtained by experience.
6. That is, 'produced by' this spirit, as mentioned in § 49 regarding the world, and here extended to the archangels. L19 omits the particle î, so as to convert this spirit into the wisdom of Aûharmazd and the archangels. It is very probable, however, that we ought to read 'and the spirit of wisdom'.
7. L19 has 'made;' these two verbs being written alike in Huzwâris.
8. L19 has 'to perform', by omitting 'in'.
9. Meaning, specially, the priests.

Chapter II

(1) The sage asked the spirit of wisdom thus: (2) 'How is it possible to seek the maintenance and prosperity of the body [without injury of the soul, and the preservation of the soul without injury of the body.[1]]'

(3) The spirit of wisdom answered thus: (4) 'Him who is less than thee consider as an equal, and an equal as a superior, (5) and a greater than him as a chieftain,[2] and a chieftain as a ruler.

(6) And among rulers *one* is to be acquiescent, obedient, and true-speaking; (7) *and* among accusers[3] be submissive, mild, and kindly regardful.

(8) Commit no slander; (9) so that infamy and wickedness *may* not happen unto thee.

(10) For it is said (11) that slander is more grievous than witchcraft; (12) and in hell the rush of every fiend[4] is to the front, *but* the rush of the fiend of slander, on account of the grievous sinfulness, is to the rear.

(13) 'Form no covetous desire; (14) so that the demon of greediness *may* not deceive thee, (15) and, the treasure of the world *may* not be tasteless to thee, and that of the spirit unperceived.

(16) 'Indulge in no wrathfulness; (17) for a man, when he indulges in wrath, becomes then forgetful of his duty and good works, of prayer and the service of the sacred beings, (18) and sin and crime of every kind occur unto his mind, and[5] until the subsiding of the wrath (19) he[6] is said *to be* just like Aharman.[7]

(20) 'Suffer no anxiety; (21) for he who is a sufferer of anxiety becomes regardless of enjoyment of the world and the spirit, (22) and contraction happens to his body and soul.

(23) 'Commit no lustfulness; (24) so that harm and regret *may* not reach thee from thine own actions.

(25) 'Bear no improper envy; (26) so that thy life *may* not become tasteless.

(27) 'Commit no sin on account of [disgrace];[8] (28) because happiness and adornment,[9] celebrity (*khanîdîh*) and dominion, skill and suitability are not through the will and action of men, but through the appointment, destiny, and will of the sacred beings.

---

1. The passage in brackets is omitted by K43, and is here supplied from L19.
2. In L19 the text is corrupt, but has nearly the same meaning.
3. L19 has 'associates', which seems equally appropriate; the two words are much alike in Pahlavi writing.
4. The word *drûg*, 'fiend', is usually supposed to mean a female demon, and is often understood so in the Avesta, perhaps because it is a feminine noun. It is usually an impersonation of some evil passion (see Chap. XLI, 11).
5. L19 omits 'and'.
6. L19 has 'wrath;' making § 19 a separate sentence.
7. The evil spirit, Av. *angra mainyu*.
8. K43 omits 'disgrace', by mistake.
9. L19 omits 'adornment'.

(29) 'Practise no sloth; (30) so that the duty and good work, which it is necessary for thee to do, *may* not remain undone.

(31) 'Choose a wife who is of character; (32) because that *one* is good who in the end is more respected.

(33) 'Commit no unseasonable chatter;[1] (34) so that grievous distress *may* not happen unto Horvadad and Amerodad, the archangels,[2] through three.

(35) 'Commit no running about uncovered;[3] (36) so that harm *may* not come upon thy bipeds and quadrupeds, and ruin upon *thy* children.

(37) 'Walk not with one boot;[4] (38) so that grievous distress *may* not happen to thy soul.

(39) 'Perform no discharge of urine (*pêsâr-vâr*) *standing* on foot;[5] (40) so that thou mayst not become a captive by a habit of the demons, (41) and the demons may not drag thee to hell on account of that sin.

(42) 'Thou shouldst be (*yehevûnes*) diligent and moderate, (43) and eat of thine own regular industry, (44) and provide the share of the sacred beings and the good; (45) and, thus, the practice of this, in thy occupation, is the greatest good work.

(46) 'Do not extort from the wealth of others; (47) so that thine own regular industry *may* not become unheeded. (48) for it is said that (49) 'He who eats anything, not from his own regular industry, but from another, is such-like as *one* who holds a human head in *his* hand, and eats human brains.'

(50) 'Thou shouldst be an abstainer from the wives of others; (51) because all these three would become disregarded by thee, alike wealth, alike body, and alike[6] soul.

---

1. A free translation of the name of the sin which is usually called *drâyân-gûyisnîh*, 'eagerness for chattering;' here, however, K43 omits the latter *y*, so that the name may be read *drâyân-gal-isnîh*, 'chatteringly devouring', and a similar phrase is used in A V. XXIII, 6. The sin consists in talking while eating, praying, or at any other time when a murmured prayer (*vâg*) has been taken inwardly and is not yet spoken out; the protective spell of the prayer being broken by such talking. If the prayer be not taken inwardly when it ought to be, the same sin is incurred (see Sls. V, 2, Dd. LXXIX, 8).

2. Instead of *amahraspend*, 'the archangel', L19 has Mârspend, the angel of the 'righteous liturgy;' but this is probably a misreading, due to the fact that, when the chattering interrupts prayer, the angel of the liturgy would be as much distressed as the archangels Horvadad and Amerodad, who protect water and vegetation (see Sls. XV, 25–29), would be when it interrupts eating and drinking. These archangels are personifications of Av. *haurvatâd*, 'completeness or health', and *ameretâd*, 'immortality'.

3. That is, moving about without being girded with *Kustî* or sacred thread-girdle, which must not be separated from the skin by more than one thin garment, the sacred shirt (see Sls. IV, 7, 8).

4. We should probably read 'without a boot', as *aê-mûkŏ* and *amûkŏ* are much alike in Pahlavi; otherwise we must suppose that walking with only a single covering for the feet, and without outer boots, is meant. At any rate, walking or standing on unconsecrated ground with bare feet is a serious sin for a Parsi, on account of the risk of pollution (see Sls. IV, 12, X, 12).

5. Whereby an unnecessary space of ground is polluted; hence the sin.

6. K43 has *hômanam*, 'I am', the Huzvâris of am, used by mistake for ham, 'alike', which is written exactly like am in Pahlavi.

(52) 'With enemies fight with equity. (53) with a friend proceed with the approval of friends.

(54) With a malicious[1] man carry on no conflict, (55) and do not molest him in any way whatever.

(56) With a greedy man thou shouldst not be a partner, (57) and do not trust him with the leadership.

(58) With a slanderous man do not go to the door of kings.

(59) With an ill-famed man form no connection.

(60) With an ignorant man thou shouldst not become a confederate and associate.

(61) With a foolish man make no dispute.

(62) With a drunken man do not walk on the road.

(63) From an ill-natured man take no loan.

(64) 'In thanksgiving unto the sacred beings, and worship, praise, ceremonies, invocation, and performing the learning of knowledge thou shouldst be energetic and life-expending.

(65) For it is said that: (66) 'In aid of the contingencies (*gahisnŏ*)[2] among men wisdom is good; (67) in seeking renown and preserving the soul liberality is good; (68) in the advancement of business and justice complete mindfulness is good; (69) and in the statements of those who confess (*khûstîvân*),[3] with a bearing on the custom of the law,[4] truth is good.

(70) In the progress of business energy is good, (71) for[5] every one to become confident therein steadfastness is good, (72) and for the coming of benefit thereto thankfulness is good.

(73) In keeping oneself untroubled (*anaîrang*)[6] the discreet speaking which is in the path of[7] truth is good; (74) and in keeping away the disturbance of the destroyer[8] from oneself employment is good.

(75) Before rulers and kings discreet speaking is good, and in[9] an assembly good recital; (76) among friends repose and rational friends[10] are good; (77) and with an associate to one's own deeds the giving of advantage (*sûkŏ*) is good.

(78) Among those greater than one (*agas masân*) mildness and humility are

1. K43 has *kîkvar*, instead of *kênvar*, but this is doubtless a miswriting.

2. L19 has *zahisn*, 'issue, proceedings'.

3. L19 has read *aûstîkân*, 'the steadfast', by mistake.

4. Reading *dâdŏ-khûk-barisŏîhâ*. L19 has 'conveying intercession (*gâdangô* = *dâdŏ-gôk*);' this small difference in reading may be a clerical error in K43. The Sans. Version omits the phrase altogether.

5. L19 omits *pavan*, 'for'.

6. Nêr. Has 'unblemished'.

7. L19 omits 'path of'; and it may possibly be superfluous.

8. Or it may be 'the destroyer and adversary', as in L19; the last word being defective in K43.

9. L19 omits *pavan*, 'in'.

10. L19 has 'friendship'.

good, (79) and among those less than one flattery[1] and civility are good.

(80) Among doers of deeds speaking of thanks and performance of deeds of generosity are good; (81) and among those of the same race the formation of friendship (*hûmânŏîh*)[2] is good.

(82) For bodily health moderate eating and keeping the body in action are good; (83) and among the skilled in thanksgiving performance is good.

(84) Among chieftains unanimity and seeking advantage are good; (85) among those in unison and servants good behaviour and an exhibition of awe are good; (86) and for having little trouble in oneself contentment is good.

(87) In chieftainship to understand thoroughly the good in *their* goodness and the vile in *their* vileness is good; *and* to make the vile unseen, through retribution,[3] is good.

(88) In every place and time to restrain oneself from sin and to be diligent in meritorious work are good; (89) and every day to consider *and* keep in remembrance Aûharmazd, as regards creativeness, and Aharman, as regards destructiveness, is good.

(90) *And* for dishonour not to come unto one a knowledge of oneself is good.'

(91) All these are proper and true and of the same description, (92) but occupation and guarding the tongue (*pâd-hûzvânîh*)[4] above everything.

(93) 'Abstain far from the service of idols[5] and demon-worship. (94) because *it* is declared that: (95) 'If Kaî-Khûsrôî[6] should not have extirpated the idol-temples (*aûgdês-kâr*) which *were* on the lake of Kêkast,[7] then in these three millenniums *of* Hûshêdar, Hûshêdar-mâh, and Sôshâns[8]—of whom one of them comes separately at the end of each millennium, who arranges again all[9] the affairs of the world, and utterly destroys the breakers of promises and servers of idols who are in the realm, the adversary[10] would have become so much more violent, that it would not have been possible to produce the resurrection and future existence.'

1. Or 'adaptation'.

2. L19 has *humatî*, 'good intention'.

3. L19 has 'to cause the reward of the good and the punishment of the vile.'

4. L19 has 'preserving pure language.'

5. More correctly 'temple-worship', as *aûzdês* means 'an erection'.

6. Av. Kavi Husravangh, the third of the Kayân kings, who reigned sixty years, and was the grandson of his predecessor, Kâî-Ûs, and son of Sîyâvakhsh (see Bd. XXXI, 25, XXXIV, 7).

7. The present Lake Urumiyah according to Bd. XXII, 2. This feat of Kaî-Khûsrôî is also mentioned in Bd. XVII, 7, and his exploits in the same neighbourhood are stated in Âbân Yt. 49, 50, Gôs Yt. 18, 21, 22, Ashi Yt. 38, 41, 42; but it is possible that the Avesta name, Kaêkasta, may have been transferred to Lake Urumiyah in later times.

8. The three future apostles who are supposed to be sons of Zaratûst, whose births have been deferred till later times (see Bd. XXXII, 8). Their Avesta names are Ukhshyad-ereta, Ukhshyad-nemangh, and Saoshyās.

9. L19 omits 'all'.

10. The evil spirit.

(96) 'In forming a store[1] of good works thou shouldst be diligent, (97) so that it *may* come to *thy*[2] assistance among the spirits.

(98) 'Thou shouldst not become presumptuous through any happiness of the world; (99) for the happiness of the world is such-like as a cloud that comes or a rainy day, which one does not ward off by any hill.

(100) 'Thou shouldst not be *too* much arranging the world; (101) for the world-arranging man becomes spirit-destroying.

(102) 'Thou shouldst not become presumptuous through much treasure and wealth; (103) for in the end it is necessary for thee to leave all.

(104) Thou shouldst not become presumptuous through predominance; (105) for in the end it is necessary for thee to become non-predominant.

(106) Thou shouldst not become presumptuous through respect and reverence; (107) for respectfulness does not assist in the spiritual *existence*.

(108) Thou shouldst not become presumptuous through great connections and race; (109) for in the end thy[3] trust is on thine own deeds.

(110) Thou shouldst not become presumptuous through life; (111) for death comes upon thee[4] *at* last, (112) the dog and the bird lacerate the corpse,[5] (113) and the perishable *part* (*segînakŏ*)[6] falls to the ground.[7]

1. L19 has 'in always doing;' having read *hamvâr*, 'always', instead of *ambâr*, 'a store'.

2. K43 omits 'thy'.

3. L19 omits 'thy'.

4. L19 omits 'thee'.

5. Referring to the mode of disposing of the dead adopted by the Parsis (see Sls. II, 6 n, Dd. XV, 5, XVII, 17, XVIII, 2–4).

6. L19 has *ast*, 'bone'.

7. Including the day of death. The fate of the soul after death, as detailed in §§ 114–194, is also described in Vend. XIX, 90–112, Hn. II, III, Aog. 8–19, AV. IV–XI, XVII.

5

Selected Readings

FROM THE GATHAS

2.2.2. **Verses from Yasna 30**[1]

From 'Yasna', in M. Boyce, ed. and tr., *Textual Sources for the Study of Zoroastrianism* (Manchester, 1984), pp. 35–36.

(1) Truly for seekers I shall speak of those things to be pondered, even by one who already knows, with praise and worship for the Lord of Good Purpose, the excellently Wise One, and for Truth … .

(2) Hear with your ears the best things. Reflect with clear purpose, each man for himself, on the two choices for decision, being alert indeed to declare yourselves for Him before the great requital.

(3) Truly there are two primal Spirits, twins renowned to be in conflict. In thought and word, in act they are two: the better and the bad. And those who act well have chosen rightly between these two, not so the evildoers.

(4) And when these two Spirits first came together they created life and not-life, and how at the end Worst Existence shall be for the wicked, but (the House of) Best Purpose for the just man.

---

1. Ahura Mazda has an Adversary, here called, in v. 5, 'Dregvant', the Deceitful or Wicked One, i.e. one who upholds 'drug', the lie or falsehood, opposed to '*asha*'. In v. 6 he is named the Deceiver. Wicked men also are called '*dregvant*', opposed to the just, '*ashavan*'. 'Worst Existence' is a term for hell, i.e. a place for retributive punishment (seemingly a new concept then in religious thought). The '(House of) Best Purpose' is a name for heaven, parallel to the traditional 'House of Song' (cf. 2.2.3.8 et pass.). 'Hardest stone', v. 5. is the substance of the sky, see 1.2.6. The Daevas, v. 6, are shown by the tradition to be Indra and other warlike divinities, cf. 2.3.1.55. Fury or Wrath, Aesthma, is a great demon; for the prophet, it is suggested, he hypostatized the battle-fury of war bands, cf. 1.2.7, 1.3.1. On the Ahuras see 1.2.3, 1.3.3. Devotion 'gave body and breath', v. 7, as guardian of earth. At the last day the world will be 'made frasha-', v. 9, i.e. transfigured, made free once more from evil, made wonderful.

(5) Of these two Spirits the Wicked One chose achieving the worst things. The Most Holy Spirit, who is clad in hardest stone, chose right, and (so do those) who shall satisfy Lord Mazda continually with rightful acts.

(6) The Daevas indeed did not choose rightly between these two, for the Deceiver approached them as they conferred. Because they chose worst purpose, they then rushed to Fury, with whom they have afflicted the world and mankind.

(7) With Power He came to this world, by Good Purpose and by Truth. Then enduring Devotion gave body and breathes … .

(8) Then when retribution comes for the sinners, then, Mazda, Power shall be present for Thee with Good Purpose, to declare himself for those, Lord, who shall deliver the Lie into the hands of Truth.

(9) And then may we be those who shall transfigure this world. O Mazda (and you other) Lords (Ahuras), be present to me with support and truth, so that thoughts may be concentrated where understanding falters.

(10) Then truly on the world of lie shall come the destruction of delight; but they who get themselves good name shall be partakers in the promised reward in the fair abode of good thought, of Mazda, and of Right.

(11) O men! When you learn the commands which Mazda has given, and both thriving and not-thriving, and what long torment (is) for the wicked and salvation for the just—then will it be as is wished with these things.

2.2.3 Verses from Yasna 45[1]

(1) Then shall I speak, now give ear and hearken, both you who seek from near and you from far … .

(2) Then shall I speak of the two primal Spirits of existence, of whom the Very Holy thus spoke to the Evil One: 'neither our thoughts nor teachings nor wills, neither our choices nor words nor acts, not our inner selves nor our souls agree.'

(3) Then shall I speak of the foremost (doctrine) of this existence, which Mazda the Lord, He with knowledge, declared to me. Those of you who do not act upon this *manthra*, even as I shall think and speak it, for them there shall be woe at the end of life.

(4) Then shall I speak of the best things of this existence. I know Mazda who created it in accord with truth to be the Father of active Good Purpose. And His daughter is Devotion of good action. The all-seeing Lord is not to be deceived.

(5) Then shall I speak of what the Most Holy One told me, the word to be listened to as best for men. Those who shall give for me hearkening and heed to Him, shall attain wholeness and immortality. Mazda is Lord through acts of the Good Spirit.

(6) I will speak of him who is the greatest of all, praising him, O Right, who is

1. In v. 2 the Adversary is called Angra Mainyu, the 'Hostile' or 'Evil Spirit'. This became his proper name, YAv. Angra Mainyu, Pahl: Ahriman.

bounteous to all that live. By the holy spirit let the Mazda Ahura hearken, in his adoration I have been instructed by good thought. By his wisdom let him teach me what is best,

(7) Even he whose two awards, whereof he ordains, men shall attain, who so are living or have been or shall be. In immortality the soul of the righteous be joyful, in perpetuity shall be the torment of liars. All this doth Mazda Ahura appoint by his Dominion.

(8) Him shall I seek to turn to us by praises of reverence, for truly I have now seen with my eyes (the House) of Good Purpose, and of good act and deed, having known through Truth Him who is Lord Mazda. Then let us lay up supplications to Him in the House of Song.

(9) Him shall I seek to requite for us with good purpose, Him who left to our will (the choice between) holy and unholy. May Lord Mazda by His power make us active for prospering our cattle and men, through the fair affinity of good purpose with truth.

(10) Him shall I seek to glorify for us with sacrifices of devotion, Him who is known in the soul as Lord Mazda; for He has promised by His truth and good purpose that there shall be wholeness and immortality within His Kingdom (*khshathra*), strength and perpetuity within His house.

PASSAGES FROM THE ZAND OF LOST AVESTAN TEXTS

Reprinted from 'Greater Bundahišn', in M. Boyce, ed. and tr., *Textual Sources for the Study of Zoroastrianism* (Manchester, 1984), pp. 45–53.

2.3.1 Chapter 1. About Ohrmazd, Ahriman and the Spirit Creation[1]

(1–5) It is thus revealed in the Good Religion that Ohrmazd was on high in omniscience and goodness. For boundless time He was ever in the light. That light is

1. The following selections are from the Greater Bundahišn, see 1.1.1.14. In them what appear to be glosses and extensions to the actual translation of the lost Avestan texts are omitted without indication. The final redaction of those texts must have taken place many generations after the composition of the Gathas, for they show scholastic developments of Zarathushtra's great vision. Thus in 2.3.1 what appears to have been Zarathushtra's own adaptation of the ancient Iranian creation myth (see 1.2.6) has been further developed through priestly speculation, notably about the 'world year' (see 1.8). The influence of the Zoroastrian calendar is also plain in 2.3.3.11 ff. (see 1.7 for it and for all the names of the divinities concerned). The myth of man's creation in 2.3.6 is probably older than Zarathushtra, while 2.3.7 sets out clearly what appear to have been his own wholly original concepts (often alluded to in the Gathas) of a Last Day and a Last Judgment, with resurrection of the body (see 1.2.5) postponed until the time when Ahura Mazda's kingdom (*khshathra*) will come on an earth made once more perfect, as He had created it. Middle Persian Druj (2.3.3.23–4) represents Avestan Drug, 'the Lie', cf. 2.2.2. Amahraspand (2.3.1.53–4 *et pass.)* is a dialect variant of Amashaspand, both representing Avestan Amesha Spenta.

the space and place of Ohrmazd. Some call it Endless Light. Ahriman was abased in slowness of knowledge and the lust to smite. The lust to smite was his sheath and darkness his place. Some call it Endless Darkness. And between them was emptiness. (6–10) They both were limited and limitless: for that which is on high, which is called Endless Light. And that which is abased, ... which is Endless Darkness—those were limitless. (But) at the border both were limited, in that between them was emptiness. There was no connexion between the two. Then both two Spirits were in themselves limited. On account of the omniscience of Ohrmazd, all things were within the knowledge of Ohrmazd, the limited and the limitless; for He knew the measure of what is within the two Spirits.

(11–12) Then the entire kingship of the creation of Ohrmazd, in the future body for ever and ever, that is limitless. The creation of Ahriman, at the time when the future body will be, shall be destroyed. That truly is limited.

(13–14) Ohrmazd by His omniscience knew that the Evil Spirit existed, what he plotted in his enviousness to do, how he would commingle, what the beginning, what the end; what and how many the tools with which He would make an end. And He created in the spirit state the creatures He would need as those tools. For 3,000 years creation remained in the spirit state.

(15–17) The Evil Spirit, on account of his slowness of knowledge, was not aware of the existence of Ohrmazd. Then he arose from the deep, and came to the boundary and beheld the light. When he saw the intangible light of Ohrmazd he rushed forward. Because of his lust to smite and his envious nature he attacked to destroy it. Then he saw valour and supremacy greater than his own. He crawled back to darkness and shaped many *devs*, the destructive creation. And he rose for battle.

(18–19) When Ohrmazd saw the creatures of the Evil Spirit, they appeared to Him frightful and putrid and evil; and He desired them not. When the Evil Spirit saw the creatures of Ohrmazd they appeared to him most profound and fully informed. And he desired the creatures and creation of Ohrmazd.

(20–23) Then Ohrmazd, in spite of His knowledge of creation and the end of the affair, approached the Evil Spirit and proffered peace and said: 'Evil Spirit! Aid my creatures, and give praise, so that in recompense for that you may be immortal ... .' The Evil Spirit snarled: 'I shall not aid your creatures and I shall not give praise, but I shall destroy you and your creatures for ever and ever. And I shall persuade all your creatures to hate you and to love me.'

(24–25) And Ohrmazd said: 'You are not all-powerful, Evil Spirit; so you cannot destroy me, and you cannot so influence my creatures that they will not return to being mine.' Then Ohrmazd in His omniscience knew: 'If I do not set a time for that battle of his, then he will be able eternally to make strife and a state of mixture for my creatures. And in the Mixture he will be able to lead my creatures astray and make them his own.'

(26–27) Then Ohrmazd said to the Evil Spirit: 'Set a time, so that according to this bond we may postpone battle for 9,000 years.' For, He knew that through this setting of a time He would destroy the Evil Spirit. Then the Evil Spirit, not being able to foresee the end, agreed to that pact.

(28–29) This too Ohrmazd knew in His omniscience, that within these 9,000 years, 3,000 years will go according to the will of Ohrmazd; 3,000 years, in the Mixture, will go according to the will of both Ohrmazd and Ahriman; and at the last battle it will be possible to make Ahriman powerless, and to ward off the assault from His creatures. Then Ohrmazd recited aloud the Ahunavar. And He showed to the Evil Spirit His own final victory, and the powerlessness of the Evil Spirit, and the destruction of the *dev*s, and also the resurrection and the future body, and the freedom of creation from the Assault for ever and ever.

(30–33) When the Evil Spirit saw his own powerlessness, together with the destruction of the *dev*s, he fell prostrate and unconscious. He fell back again into hell, even as He says in the scriptures that when He had spoken one third, the Evil Spirit crouched in fear; when He had spoken two thirds, the Evil Spirit sank upon his knees; when He had spoken it all, the Evil Spirit became powerless to do evil to the creatures of Ohrmazd. For 3,000 years he lay prostrate.

(34–35) Before creation Ohrmazd was not Lord. And after creation He was Lord, seeking benefit, wise, free from harm, making reckoning openly, holy, observing all things. And first He created the essence of the *yazata*s, namely goodness, that spirit whereby He made himself better, since His lordship was through creation.

(36–38) When He pondered upon creation, Ohrmazd saw by His clear vision that the Evil Spirit would never turn from the Assault; the Assault would not be made powerless except through creation; creation could not develop except through time; but if He created time, Ahriman's creation too would develop. And having no other course, in order to make the Assault powerless, He created time.

(39–42) Then, from Limitless Time He created Time of long dominion. Some call it Limited Time. All that which Ohrmazd created limited, was from the limitless. Thus from the creation, when He created creatures, until the end, when the Evil Spirit will be helpless, is a period of 12,000 years. That is limited. Afterwards the creatures of Ohrmazd will join the limitless, so that they will abide in purity with Ohrmazd for ever.

(44) Ohrmazd fashioned forth the form of His creatures from His own self, from the substance of light—in the form of fire, bright, white, round, visible afar.

(47–49) The Evil Spirit shaped his creation from the substance of darkness, that which was his own self, in the form of a toad, black, ashen, worthy of hell, sinful as is the most sinful noxious beast. And first he created the essence of the *dev*s, namely wickedness, for he created that creation whereby he made himself worse, since through it he will become powerless.

(49–50) From the substance of darkness, which is Endless Darkness, he created lying speech. From lying speech the wickedness of the Evil Spirit was manifest … . From the substance of light Ohrmazd created true speech; and from true speech the holiness of the Creator was manifest.

(53–54) And Ohrmazd parted Himself among the Amahraspands when He created them … . First He created the Amahraspands, originally six, and then the rest. Of the Amahraspands … He first created Vahman, through whom movement was given to the creation of Ohrmazd, for the good religion of the Mazda-worshippers was with him … . Then He fashioned Ardvahisht, then Shahrevar, then Spendarmad, then Hordad and Amurdad. The seventh was Himself, Ohrmazd.

(55) The Evil Spirit, aggressively inclined, shaped of the chief *dev*s first Akoman, then Indar, then Savol, then Nanhaith, then Taromad, then Turiz and Zairiz; then the rest of the *dev*s. The seventh was himself, the Evil Spirit.

2.3.2 Ch. Ia. About the Material Creation

(1–4) When the Evil Spirit was helpless in prostration, he lay prostrate for 3,000 years. During the helplessness of the Evil Spirit, Ohrmazd created the creation materially. First, He created the Sky as a defence; second, He created Water, to defeat the demon of thirst; third, He created the all-solid Earth; fourth, He created the Plant, to help the beneficent Animal; fifth, He created the beneficent Animal, to help the Just Man; sixth, He created the Just Man, to smite the Evil Spirit together with the *dev*s and to make them powerless. And then He created Fire and linked its brilliance to the Endless Light.

(5–6) And I shall describe their nature. First, He created Sky, bright, visible, high, its bounds afar, made of shining metal. And He joined its top to the Endless Light, and created all creation within the sky, like a castle or fort in which are stored all the weapons needed for a struggle. The Spirit of the Sky accepted it as a strong fortress against the Evil Spirit, so that he will not allow him to escape. Like a heroic warrior who has put on armour so that he may be fearlessly victorious in battle, so the Spirit of the Sky is clad in the sky. And to help the sky He created joy. Now indeed in the Mixture creation abides through joy.

(7–10) Second, He created Water. And to help Water He created wind and rain. Third, after Water He created Earth, round, very broad, without hill or dale …, set exactly in the middle of this sky. And He created in the Earth the substance of the mountains, which afterwards waxed and grew out of the earth. And to help Earth He created iron, copper, sulphur, borax, chalk, all the products of the hard earth. Beneath this Earth there is water everywhere.

(11) Fourth, He created the Plant. At first it grew in the middle of this earth, several feet high, without branch or bark or thorn, moist and sweet. And it had in

its essence the vital force of all plants. And to help the Plant He created water and fire; ... through their power it kept growing.

(12) Fifth, He fashioned the Uniquely-created Bull in Eranvej in the middle of the world, on the bank of the river Veh Daiti. It was white and bright like the moon, and it was three measured rods in height. And to help it He created water and plants, for in the Mixture its strength and growth are from these.

(13) Sixth, He created Gayomard, bright as the sun, and four measured rods in height, on the bank of the river Daiti, where is the middle of the world—Gayomard upon the left side, the Bull upon the right side. And to help him He created sleep, the giver of repose.

2.3.3 Chapter 3. The Material Creation, continued

(7–9) Seventh (He created) Fire, whose radiance is from the Endless Light, the place of Ohrmazd. And He distributed Fire within the whole creation. And He commanded Fire to serve mankind during the Assault, preparing food and overcoming cold.

(10) And He appointed and stationed the Amahraspands for working together during the battle of creation, so that when the Assault came each one laid hold of his own adversary in the struggle.

(11–13) And I shall speak further of their nature. The first of the invisible beings is Ohrmazd. And of the physical creations He verily took mankind for His own. And His fellow workers are the three 'Dai's' (Creators), of one place, one religion, one time. All are called Creator, being the spirit from which all creation proceeds. And He created man in five parts: body, breath, soul, form and *fravahar*. Thus body is the physical part; breath that which is connected with the wind; soul that which, together with the consciousness in the body, hears, seeks, speaks and knows; form is that which is in the station of the sun; and the *fravahar* that which is in the presence of Ohrmazd the Lord. For that reason He created him thus, so that when during the Assault men die, the body rejoins the earth, the breath the wind, the form the sun, and the soul the *fravahar*, so that the *devs* should not be able to destroy the soul.

(14) The second of the invisible beings is Vahman. And of the physical creations he took for his own all kinds of cattle. And for aid and fellow-working there were given him Mâh and Gosh and Ram. And he created cattle in five parts: body, breath, soul, form and spirit, so that during the Assault Gosh Urun may receive the seed of beneficent animals from the Moon (Mâh), and with the help of the good Ram may propagate them in the world; and when they die, the body rejoins the earth, the breath the wind, the soul Gosh Urun, the form the moon, and the spirit Vahman, so that the *devs* should not be able to destroy it.

(15) The third of the invisible beings is Ardvahisht. And of the physical creations he took fire for his own. And for aid and fellow-working there were given him Adar,

Srosh, and Vahram, for that reason that during the Assault Vahram should establish and set fire within the house, and give it a stronghold. When it goes out, through Vahram it rejoins Srosh, through Srosh Adar, through Adar Ardvahisht, so that the *dev*s should not be able to destroy it.

(16) The fourth of the invisible beings is Shahrevar. And of the physical creations he took for himself metal. And for aid and fellow-working there were given him Khvar, Mihr, Asman and Anagran, so that through this fellow-working during the Assault the *dev*s should not be able to overcome metal.

(17) The fifth of the invisible beings is Spendarmad. And of the physical creations she took for herself earth. And for aid and fellow-working there were given her Aban, Din, Ard and Amahraspands. Through this fellow-working it (the earth) is kept in good order.

(18) The sixth of the invisible beings is Hordad. And of the physical creations she took for herself water. And for aid and fellow-working there were given her Tir and Vad and the Fravahars—Tir is the same as Tîstar—so that through the help of the Fravahars she takes the water and entrusts it unseen to the Wind (Vad). The Wind guides and sends the water swiftly to the regions. By means of the clouds, with these fellow workers, she causes it to rain.

(19) The seventh of the invisible beings is Amurdad. And of the physical creations she took for herself plants. And for aid and fellow-working there were given her Rashn and Ashtad and Zam-yazad—the three Khwarrahs who are there at the Chinvat Bridge, who during the Assault judge the souls of men for their good and evil deeds.

(20–21) Innumerable other invisible beings of creation were arrayed to help them .... And He divided also the day into five periods (*gah*). And for each period He appointed a spirit: thus the spirit Havan keeps the period from daybreak as his own, the spirit Rapithwin noon, the spirit Uzerin the period till sunset, the spirit Aiwisruthrim the first part of the night, the spirit Ushahin the period till dawn. And He assigned them as to help (other divine beings); for He appointed Havan to help Mihr, Rapithwin Ardvahisht, Uzerin Burz Yazad [i.e. Ahura Berezant], Aiwisruthrim the *dev* of the just, ... and Ushahin Srosh. For, He knew that when the Assault came, the day would be divided into these five periods. Until the coming of the Assault it was always noon.

(23–24) During the noon-period Ohrmazd with the Amahraspands solemnized a spiritual *yasna*. During the celebration of the *yasna* He created all creations; and He consulted with the *dev* of men. He bestowed the wisdom of all knowledge upon (the *dev* of) men, and said: 'Which seems to you the more profitable, that I should fashion you for the material world, and that you should struggle, embodied, with the Druj, and destroy the Druj; and that at the end I should restore you, whole and immortal, and recreate you in the physical state, for ever immortal, unageing, free from enemies; or that you should be protected for ever from the Assault?' And the *dev* of men saw by the wisdom of all knowledge the evil which would come upon them in the world through the Druj and Ahriman; yet for the sake of freedom in the end from the enmity of the Adversary, and restoration, whole and immortal, in the future body for ever and ever, they agreed to go into the world.

2.3.4 Chapter 4. Concerning the Rushing of the Assault upon Creation

(10–11) Then the Evil Spirit rose up with the powerful *devs* to attack the lights. And he saw the Sky, which had appeared to them in the spirit state when it had not yet been created materially. Jealously he assailed it. Like a snake he rushed upon the Sky beneath the Earth and sought to cleave it. On the day Ohrmazd in the month Fravardin, at noon, he rushed in. And the Sky feared him as the sheep the wolf. Then he came to the Water, of which I said that it is set below the Earth. Then he bored into the middle of the Earth. He entered, and came to the Plant. Then he came to the Bull and Gayomard. Then he came to the Fire. Like a fly he rushed upon all creation. And he made the world at midday quite dark, as if it were black night. He made the sky dark below and above the earth.

(13 ... 28) And he brought a bitter taste to the Water. And he loosed noxious creatures upon the Earth. And he brought poison to the Plant, and straightway it withered. And he loosed pain and sickness upon the Bull and Gayomard. Before his coming to the Bull, Ohrmazd gave a narcotic to the Bull to eat, so that its suffering and distress would be less from his blow. Straightway it became weak and ill, and the pain left it, and it died. Before his coming to Gayomard, Ohrmazd brought sleep to Gayomard. And the Evil Spirit thought: 'I have made all the creation of Ohrmazd powerless except Gayomard.' And he loosed Astvihad upon Gayomard, with a thousand death-bringing *devs*. Then he came to the Fire and mingled with it smoke and darkness. And so he defiled the whole creation. Hell was in the middle of the earth where the Evil Spirit had bored through the earth and rushed in through it. So the things of the material world appeared in duality, turning, opposites, fights, up and down, and mixture.

2.3.5 Chapter 5. Concerning the Antagonism of the Two Spirits

(1–2) Thus Ahriman is against Ohrmazd, Akoman against Vahman, Indar against Ardvahisht, Savol against Shahrevar, Nanhaith ... against Spendarmad, Turiz against Hordad and Zairiz against Amurdad, Eshm against Srosh. Falsehood and deceit are against Truthfulness, the sorcerer's spell against the holy *manthra*, excess and deficiency against right measure. Bad thought, word and deed are against good thought, word and deed, ... aimless lust against innate wisdom, ... idleness against diligence, sloth against (needful) sleep, vengefulness against peace, pain against pleasure, stench against fragrance, darkness against light, poison against ambrosia, bitterness against sweetness, parsimony against generosity, avarice against discriminate giving, winter against summer, cold against heat ... defilement against cleanness, pollution against purification, discontent against contentment. And other devilish spirits are against other divine spirits ... .

(3) Likewise among the physical creations, hell is against the sky, drought against water, impurity and noxious creatures ... against the earth, insects against plants, hunger and thirst against beneficent animals, death and sickness and ... diverse ills against mankind, extinguishing and blowing out against fire ... . The lion and predatory wolf-species are against the dog and cattle, the toad against fishes, the owl and other noxious winged creatures against birds. Wicked apostates are against just men, the whore against women, and the demon of destruction against life-prolonging lineage.

2.3.6 Chapter 14. On the Nature of Mankind

(2–4) When sickness came upon Gayomard, he fell upon his left side. And death entered the body of Gayomard from the left side. (Thereafter), until Frashegird, death comes to all creatures.

(5–6) When in passing away Gayomard emitted seed, that seed was purified through the light of the sun. Two parts Neryosang guarded, and one part Spendarmad received, and it remained for forty years in the earth. And after forty years Mashya and Mashyanag grew up out of the earth in the form of a '*rivas*' plant, with a single stem and fifteen leaves, in such a way that their hands were resting on their shoulders, and one was joined to the other, and they were of the same height and shape.

(10–35) Thereafter both grew from plant bodies into human bodies and that glory which is the soul entered invisibly into them ... . From them were born six pairs of twins, male and female, all brothers and the sisters whom they married ... . One of those six pairs was a man named Siyamak and a woman named Vasag; and from them was born a pair of whom the man was named Fravag and the woman Fravagen. From them fifteen pairs of twins were born, of which every pair became a race; and from them was the full populating of the world.

2.3.7 Chapter 34. Concerning the Resurrection[1]

(4–5) Zardusht asked Ohrmazd: 'From where shall the body be reassembled which the wind has blown away, and the water carried off? And how shall the resurrection take place?' Ohrmazd answered: 'When I created the sky without pillars ... ; and when I created the earth which bears all physical life ... ; and when I set in motion

1. For 2.3.7.6ff., cf. the texts in 7.

the sun and moon and stars ... ; and when I created corn, that it might be scattered in the earth and grow again, giving back increase ... ; and when I created and protected the child in the mother's womb ... ; and when I created the cloud, which bears water for the world and rains it down where it chooses; and when I created the wind ... which blows as it pleases—then the creation of each one of these was more difficult for me than the raising of the dead. For ... consider, if I made that which was not, why cannot I make again that which was?'

(6–9) First, the bones of Gayomard will be raised up, and then those of Mashya and Mashyanag, and then those of other people. In fifty-seven years the Soshyant will raise up all the dead. And all mankind will arise, whether just or wicked.

(10–20) Then the assembly of Isadvastar will take place. In that assembly, everyone will behold his own good or bad deeds, and the just will stand out among the wicked like white sheep among black. Fire and the yazad Airyaman will melt the metal in the hills and mountains, and it will be upon the earth like a river. Then all men will be caused to pass through that molten metal .... And for those who are just it will seem as if they are walking through warm milk; and for the wicked it will seem as if they are walking in the flesh through molten metal. And thereafter men will come together with the greatest affection, father and son and brother and friend.

(23) The Soshyant with his helpers will perform the *yasna* for restoring the dead. For that *yasna* they will slay the Hadayans bull; from the fat of that bull and the white *haoma* they will prepare ambrosia and give it to all mankind; and all men will become immortal, for ever and ever.

(27) Then Vahman will seize Akoman, Ardvahisht Indar, Shahrevar Savol, Spendarmad ... Nanhaith, Hordad and Amurdad Turiz and Zairiz, Truthful Utterance Lying Utterance, and the just Srosh Eshm of the bloody club. Then there will remain the two Druj, Ahriman and the Demon of Greed. Ohrmazd will Himself come to the world as celebrating priest, and the just Srosh as serving priest; and He will hold the sacred girdle in His hands. And at that Gathic liturgy the Evil Spirit, helpless and with his power destroyed, will rush back to shadowy darkness through the way by which he had entered. And the molten metal will flow into hell; and the stench and filth in the earth, where hell was, will be burnt by that metal, and it will become clean. The gap through which the Evil Spirit had entered will be closed by that metal. The hell within the earth will be brought up again to the world's surface, and there will be Frashegird in the world.

THE FATE OF THE SOUL, FROM YOUNGER AVESTAN TEXTS

Reprinted from 'Vendidad', 'Hadhakht Nask', 'Dādistān-i Dīnīk', and 'Arda Virāz', in M. Boyce, ed. and tr., *Textual Sources for the Study for Zoroastrianism* (Manchester, 1984), pp. 80–86.

6.1.1 from Vendidad 19[1]

(26) Zarathushtra said to Ahura Mazda:

(27) 'O Creator! Where shall the rewards be, where shall the rewards be adjudged, where shall the rewards be concluded, where shall the rewards be reckoned up, which a man earns for his soul in the material world?'

(28) Then said Ahura Mazda: 'After a man is dead, after his time is over, after the wicked demons, evil of thought, rend him completely, at dawn of the third night, the Radiant One (the Dawn) grows bright and shines, and Mithra, having good weapons, shining like the sun, arises and ascends the mountains which possess the bliss of Asha.

(29) The demon named Vizaresha ('He who drags away'), O Spitama Zarathushtra, leads the bound soul of the wicked man, the worshipper of demons .... It (the soul) goes along the paths created by time for both the wicked and the just, to the Mazda-created Chinvat Bridge .... .

(30) There comes that beautiful one, strong, fair of form, accompanied by the two dogs .... She comes over high Hara, she takes the souls of the just over the Chinvat Bridge, to the rampart of the invisible *yazata*s.

(31) Vohu Manah rises from his golden throne. Vohu Manah exclaims: 'How have you come here, O just one, from the perilous world to the world without peril?'

(32) Contented, the souls of the just proceed to the golden thrones of Ahura Mazda and the Amesha Spentas, to the House of Song, the dwelling-place of Ahura Mazda, the dwelling-place of the Amesha Spentas, the dwelling-place of the just.'

6.1.2a From Hadhokht Nask, chapter 2[2]

(1–2) Zarathushtra asked Ahura Mazda: 'Ahura Mazda, Most Holy Spirit, Creator of the material world, just! When a just man dies, where dwells his soul that night?'

(3–6) Then said Ahura Mazda: 'It sits at the (corpse's) head, chanting Gatha Ushtavaiti, invoking for itself the wished-for things: "May Lord Mazda, ruling at will, grant wishes to him whosoever has wishes!" On this night the soul feels as much joy as all that it had felt in life.'

1. The 'beautiful one' of (30) is at the Daena of the just man, cf. 2.2.7 and 6.1.2a.22–3. In Vd. 13.9 there is a reference to two dogs which guard the Bridge, cf. 1.2.5.

2. See 1.1.11. The quotation in (3–6) is from Y. 43 = 2.2.9.1.

(7 ff.) 'On the second night, where dwells the soul?' 'It sits at the head … .

(12 ff.) 'On the third night where dwells the soul?' 'On this night also it sits at the head … .

(18–20) At the end of the third night, the dawn appearing, it is as if the soul of the just man were amid meadows and breathing in sweet scents. It is as if a wind blew on it from the most southerly quarter, from the most southerly quarters, fragrant, more fragrant than any other wind.

(21) Then it is as if the soul of the just man breathed that wind in its nostrils. 'From where blows this wind, which is the most fragrant wind that I have ever breathed in my nostrils?'

(22–23) As that wind blows on him, his own Daena appears in the form of a maiden, beautiful, queenly, white-armed, … in shape as beautiful as the most beautiful of creatures.

(24) Then the soul of the just man said to her, inquiring: 'What girl are you, the most beautiful in form of all girls that I have ever seen?

(25) Then his own Daena answered him: 'Truly, youth of good thoughts, good words, good acts, good inner self (*daena*), I am your very own Daena.'

(26) 'And who has loved you for that stature and goodness and beauty …, as you appear to me?'

(27) 'You have loved me, youth of good thoughts … .

(28–29) When you would see another who mocked, and worshipped devils, and practised oppression, and crushed plants, then you would seat yourself and chant the Gathas, and worship the good Waters and the Fire of Ahura Mazda, and show hospitality to the just man, whether he came from near or far.

(30) Then you would make me, who was beloved, more beloved, who was beautiful, more beautiful, who was desired, more desired.

(31–32) You would set me, who was sitting in a high place, in a higher place, by this your good thought, ….'

(33–34) First the soul of the just man advanced a step, he set it in 'Good Thought'. Second, he advanced a step; he set it in 'Good Word'. Third, he advanced a step; he set it in 'Good Act'. Fourth, he advanced a step; he set it in Endless Light.

(35–36) Then a just man, who had died before, said to him, inquiring: 'How, O just one, did you die? How did you depart from the dwellings with cattle …, from the material world to the spirit world, from the perilous world to the world without peril? How has long happiness come to you?'

(37) Then said Ahura Mazda: 'You shall not question him. He whom you question has come hither on a grim, fearful, calamitous road, this is, the separation of body and consciousness.

(38) Let there be brought to him as food some spring butter, that is the food after death for a man of good thought, good word, good act, good inner self; that

is the food after death for a woman of excellent thought, excellent word, excellent act, well instructed, ruled by a master, just.'"

6.1.2b From Hadhokht Nask, Chapter 3

(1) Zarathushtra asked Ahura Mazda: 'Ahura Mazda ... When a wicked man dies, where his soul dwells that night?'

(2) Then said Ahura Mazda: 'Truly, O just Zarathushtra, it scuttles about there near the (corpse's) head, chanting the Gatha Kam nemoi: "To what land to flee? Whither shall I go to flee?" On this night the soul feels as much distress as all that it had felt in life.'[1]

(3–16) 'On the second night ....'

(17) 'At the end of the third night, O just Zarathushtra, the dawn appearing, it is as if the soul of the wicked man were in a wilderness and breathing in stenches.

(18) It is as if a wind blew on it from the most northerly quarter, from the most northerly quarters, foul-smelling, more foul-smelling than any other wind.

(20) Then it is as if the soul of the wicked man breathed that wind in its nostrils. "From where blows this wind, the most foul-smelling wind that I have ever breathed in my nostrils?"

(21–33) First the soul of the wicked man advanced a step, he set it in "Bad Thought" ... . Fourth, the soul of the wicked man advanced a step; he set it in Endless Darkness.

(34) Then a wicked man, who had died before, said to him, inquiring: "How, O wicked one, did you die?

(35) How, O wicked one, did you depart from the dwellings with cattle ... How has long woe come to you?"

(37) Then snarled Angra Mainyu: "You shall not question him ... .

(38) Let there be brought to him as food poisonous and poisonous-smelling things, that is the food after death for a man of bad thought, bad word, bad act, bad inner self; that is the food after death for a harlot of exceeding bad thought, exceeding bad word, exceeding bad act, ill-instructed, not ruled by a master, wicked.'"

1. The quotation is from Y. 46 = 2.2.13.1. For (33–8) cf. Y. 49 = 2.2.10.11.

THE FATE OF THE SOUL, FROM PAHLAVI SOURCES

6.2.1 From the Maīnog-i Khirad, Chapter 2

Reprinted from 'Maīnog-i Khirad', in M. Boyce, ed. and tr., *Textual Sources for the Study for Zoroastrianism* (Manchester, 1984), pp. 80–86.

This, the book of the 'Spirit of Wisdom', is a compilation of the later Sasanian period, which contains much ancient material.

(110–113) Do not trust in life, for in the end death will overcome you, and dog and bird will rend your corpse, and your bones will lie on the ground.

(114) And for three days and nights your soul will sit at the body's head.

(115) And on the fourth day at dawn, accompanied by the just Srosh and the good Vay and mighty Vahram, and opposed by Astvihad and the worse Vay and the demon Vizarsh ... it will reach the high and terrible Chinvat Bridge, to which everyone comes, just or wicked.

(116) And there many adversaries wait, (117) (such as) Eshm with bloody club, malevolently, and Astvihad, who swallows all creatures and is never sated.

(118) And to mediate there are Mihr and Srosh and Rashn.

(119–120) In the weighing Rashn the just, who holds the balance for souls, never makes it dip to one side, neither for the just nor for the wicked, neither for a lord nor for the ruler of a land.

(121) He does not swerve by as much as a hair's breadth, and has no regard for persons ... .

(123) When then the soul of the just man crosses that bridge, the bridge becomes as if a mile wide, (124) and the just soul crosses accompanied by the just Srosh.

(125–126) And his own good acts will come to meet him in the form of a girl, more beautiful and fairer than any girl in the world ... .

(158) When a wicked person dies, then for three days and nights his soul scuttles about near the evil head of that wicked one.

(159) It weeps, saying: 'Whither shall I go and whom shall I now take as refuge?'

(160) And it sees with its eyes, during those three days and nights, all the sins and wickednesses which it has done in the world.

(161–162) On the fourth day the demon Vizarsh comes and binds the wicked man's soul in the harshest way and, in spite of opposition by just Srosh, leads it to the Chinvat Bridge.

(163) Then just Rashn will discover that wicked person's soul in its wickedness.

(164) Then the demon Vizarsh will seize that wicked person's soul and will beat and torment it scornfully and wrathfully.

(165) And the wicked person's soul will cry out with loud lamentation, and will weep and utter many pleas, entreatingly, and make many desperate struggles in vain.

(166) And since his struggles and entreaties are of no avail at all, and no good being nor yet devil comes to his aid, the demon Vizarsh drags him evilly to … hell.

(167) And then a girl approaches, not like other girls. (168–9) And the wicked man's soul says to that hideous girl: 'Who are you, than whom I have never seen a girl more hideous and hateful?'

(170–171) And answering him she says: 'I am no girl, but I am your own acts, O hateful one of bad thought, bad word, bad act, bad inner self.

(172–173) For when indeed while in the world you saw someone who worshipped the *yazad*s, you sat down and worshipped the *dev*s, and served the *dev*s and she-devils.

(174–175) And when indeed you saw someone providing shelter and hospitality for good people, and giving them gifts, whether they came from near or far, then you despised and humiliated good people, and did not give them gifts and indeed barred your door.

(176–177) And when you saw someone giving true judgment and not taking bribes, and bearing true witness, and holding pious discourse, then indeed you sat down and gave false judgment, and bore false witness, and held wrongful discourse.

(178) I am this your bad thought, bad word and bad act, which you have thought and said and done.'

ZĀTSPRAM

Reprinted from 'Zātspram', R. C. Zaehner, tr. in *Zurvan: A Zoroastrian Dilemma* (New York, 1972), pp. 341–343.

On the Mixing of the Bounteous Spirit and the Destructive Spirit

(1) Thus is it revealed in the Religion: the light was above and the darkness beneath; and between the two was the Void. (2) Ohrmazd in the light and Ahriman in the darkness. Ohrmazd knew of the existence of Ahriman and of his coming to do battle: Ahriman knew not of the existence and light of Ohrmazd.

(3) In the dismal darkness he wandered to the nether side: then, rushing, he came up and beheld a point of light, and because it was of a different substance from himself, he strove to attain it, and his desire for it waxed so mightily that (it was as great as his desire) for the darkness.

(4) When he came to the boundary, Ohrmazd, wishing to hold Ahriman back from his kingdom, advanced to join battle. By the pure word of the Law he laid him low and hurled him back into the darkness. As a protection against the Lie he fashioned in the heights the 'ideal' sky, water, earth, plants, cattle, man, and fire—all in ideal form. For three thousand years he held him back.

(5) Ahriman too was preparing weapons in the darkness.

At the end of three thousand years he returned to the boundary, and threatening said, 'I shall smite thee, I shall smite thy creatures. Art thou of a mind to create a creation, O thou who art the Bounteous Spirit? Verily I shall utterly destroy it.'

(6) Ohrmazd answered (and said), 'Thou canst not, O Lie, accomplish all.'

(7) Again Ahriman threatened (saying), 'I shall bring all corporeal existence to hate thee and to love me.'

(8) Ohrmazd, in his spiritual wisdom, saw that what Ahriman had threatened he could do unless the time of the conflict was limited.

(9) He begged Time to aid him, for he saw that through no intermediary belonging to the light would (Ahriman) desist. Time is a good helper and right orderer of both: there is need of it.

(10) (Ohrmazd) made it in three periods, each period three thousand years.

(11) Ahriman desisted.

(12) Ohrmazd saw that unless Ahriman was encompassed, he would return to his own principle of darkness whenever he so willed and would prepare more weapons, and the conflict would be without end. After fixing the time, he chanted the Ahunavar.

(13) And in the Ahunavar he showed him three things.

(14) First that every righteous thing is the will of Ohrmazd:

(15) And from this it is plain that since righteousness is the will of Ohrmazd, obviously there are things which are not according to the will of Ohrmazd—and these can only be whatever has its root in Vay who is of a different substance.

(16) Secondly this that he who does the will of Ohrmazd, reward and recompense are his; and he who does not the will of Ohrmazd, punishment and retribution are his.

(17) This shows the reward of the virtuous and the punishment of sinners, and thence, too, heaven and hell.

(18) Thirdly it shows that the sovereignty of Ohrmazd prospers him who keeps affliction from the poor.

(19) This shows that the wealthy are to help the needy: as the learned teach the ignorant, so should the rich generously lend a helping hand to the poor; for the creatures of Ohrmazd are in strife and battle one with another.

(20) For the final rehabilitation will be effected by these three things.

(21) First orthodoxy, that is the belief in two principles, in this wise and manner that Ohrmazd is all good and devoid of evil and his will is all-holy; and that Ahriman is all evil and devoid of good.

(22) Second, the hope of reward and recompense for the virtuous and the fear of punishment and retribution for sinners, striving after virtue and shunning vice.

(23) Third, that those creatures should help one another: for from mutual help comes solidarity; from solidarity victory over the enemy, and this is the final rehabilitation.

(24) By this word (Ahriman) was laid low and fell back into the darkness.

(25) (Then) Ohrmazd projected creation in bodily form on to the material plane, first the sky, second water, third earth, fourth plants, fifth cattle, sixth man: and fire permeated all six elements, and the period for which it was inserted into each element lasted, it is said, as much as the twinkling of an eye.

(26) For three thousand years creation was corporeal and motionless. Sun, Moon, and stars stood still in the heights and did not move.

(27) At the end of (this) period Ohrmazd considered, 'What profit have we from our creation if it neither moves nor walks nor flies?' And with the aid of the firmament and Zurvān he fashioned creation forth.

(28) Zurvān had power to set the creation of Ohrmazd in motion without giving motion to the creation of Ahriman, for the (two) principles were harmful to each other and mutually opposed.

(29) Pondering on the end he (Zurvān) delivered to Ahriman an implement (fashioned) from the very substance of darkness, mingled with the power of Zurvān, as it were a treaty, resembling coal (?), black and ashen.

(30) And as he handed it to him, he said, 'By means of these weapons Āz (concupiscence) will devour that which is thine and she herself shall starve, if at the end of nine thousand years thou hast not accomplished that which thou didst threaten, to finish off the treaty, to finish off Time.'

(31) Meanwhile Ahriman, together with his powers went to the station of the stars.

(32) The bottom of the sky was in the station of the stars: from there he dragged it into the Void which lies between the principles of light and darkness and is the field of battle where both move.

(33) And the darkness he had with him he brought into the sky; and he dragged the sky down into the darkness so that within the roof of the sky as much as one third only could reach above the region of the stars.

On the Final Rehabilitation

(1) It is revealed in the Religion that Zoroaster asked Ohrmazd (saying), 'Shall bodily creatures that have passed away on earth, receive their bodies back at the final rehabilitation or shall they be like unto shades?'

(2) Ohrmazd said, 'They shall receive their bodies back and shall rise again.'

(3) And Zoroaster asked (saying), 'He who hath passed away is torn apart by dog and bird and carried off by wolf and vulture: how shall (their parts) come together again?'

(4) Ohrmazd said, 'If thou who art Zoroaster hadst to make a wooden casket, would it be easier to make it if thou hadst no wood and yet hadst to cut and fit it, or if thou hadst a casket and its parts were sundered one from the other and thou hadst to fit it together again?'

(5) Zoroaster said, 'If I had a branch of wood, it would be easier than if I had no wood; and if I had a casket (and its parts were sundered one from the other), it would be easier … .'

(6) Ohrmazd said, 'When those creations were not, I had power to fashion them; and now when they have been and are scattered abroad, it is easier to fit them together again.

(7) For I have five store-keepers who received the bodily substance of those who have passed away. One is the earth which keeps the flesh and bone and sinews of men: one is the water which keeps the [flesh and] blood: one is the plants which preserve the hair of the head and the hair of the body: one is the light of the firmament (?) which receives the fire: and yet another is the wind which (gives back) the spirit of my own creatures at the time of the rehabilitation.

(8) I call upon the earth and ask of it the bone and flesh and sinews of Gayomart and the others.

(9) The earth saith, 'How shall I bring them, for I know not which is the (bone, flesh, and sinews) of the one (and which of the other)?'

(10) I call upon the water of the Arang which is the Tigris among rivers (saying), 'Bring forth the blood of those men who are dead.'

(11) (The water) saith, 'How shall I bring it, for I know not which the blood of the one is and which of the other?'

(12) I call upon the plants and ask of them the hair of the dead.

(13) The plants say, 'How shall we bring it, for we know not which the hair of the one is and which of the other?'

(14) I call upon the wind and ask him for the spirit of those men who are dead.

(15) The wind saith, 'How shall I bring it, for I know not which is the spirit of the one and which of the other?'

(16) When I who am Ohrmazd look down upon the earth, water, plants, light,

and wind, in my clear sight I know and distinguish the one from the other: for in my omniscience and clear thought I distinguish the one from the other even as when a man milks the milk of female beasts and it runs down upon this earth in the same channel, one stream into the other, he knows of which of his beasts it is. I recognize them even as when a man hath thirty horses and each horse has a caparison with a mark on it (to show) to which horse it belongs, and those thirty caparisons stand together, and the man (then) wishes to know; he takes off the caparisons and knows by the mark on the caparison which of his horses is which.

(17) I shall send forth Airyaman the Messenger among whose duties is the fulfilment of the end.

(18) He will bring the bone and blood and hair and light and spirit of Gayōmart and Mašyē and Mašyānē.

(19) And first shall I fit together again the bones of Gayōmart—and the bones of Mašyē and Mašyānē lie together near him, to the right and to the left—these shall I bring forth.

(20) And it is easier for me to fit together and create again the twelve creations that I created in the beginning: first when I created the sky without pillar or support which no material creature supports from any side; and second when I established the earth in the middle of the sky so that it was nearer to neither side, like the yolk of an egg in the middle of an egg; and third when I fashioned the Sun; fourth when I fashioned the Moon; (fifth when I fashioned the stars;) sixth when I created many hues, colours, and tastes in the plants; seventh when I created fire within the plants and it did not burn; eighth when I brought corn to the earth, and when it is full grown, it bears fruit and serves as food for man and kine; ninth when I formed the embryo within female creatures and covered it up so that it did not die and, as it grew, I revealed one by one the bone, blood, hair, phlegm, sinews, and nails; tenth when I made birds in bodily form to fly in the air; eleventh when I gave the water feet moving forward like unto a hare(?); twelfth (when I created the clouds) that carry the water up and rain it down.'

(21) The creating of creation, the progress of Religion, and the final rehabilitation are like unto the building of a house.

(22) For a house can only be completed by means of three things, that is the foundation, the walls, and the roof. Creation is the foundation, the progress of Religion the walls, and the rehabilitation the roof.

(23) As when a man desires to build a house, he chooses three men of whom one is most skilled in laying the foundation, one in raising the walls, and one in making the roof; and each is assigned to his proper work. Till the foundation is laid and the walls raised, it was not possible (to make the roof).

(24) He who bade the house (be built) knows clearly how many things are needed to complete it, and because he has no doubt concerning the skill of the maker of the roof, long does he confidently wait. When the walls are completed, it

is as easy for him whose business is the roof, to roof (the house) in as (it is) for the other two in the work that is assigned to them.

DĒNKARD

Reprinted from 'Dēnkart', in R. C. Zaehner, tr., *Zurvan: A Zoroastrian Dilemma* (New York, 1972), pp. 386–391.

From the Exegesis of the Good Religion

On goodness, the origin of goodness, the movement of goodness, the definition of goodness, the cause of goodness, the reason of goodness, what it is summed up in, and the categories of the offspring of goodness. On the movement of evil, the definition of evil, the reason of evil, what evil is summed up in, the categories of its abortions, the promotion of evil at the beginning, middle, and end.]

This that he whose ground is goodness and whose essence is goodness is the Bounteous Spirit. The origin of goodness is also in the Good Religion, that is to say whatever causes benefit when it supervenes and is put into practice. The movement of the goodness of the good Bounteous Spirit, that is his essence, is eightfold: it is Wisdom and the Light of Wisdom which are proper to his distinct nature, and Will, Power, Means, Effort, Space, and Time. It is revealed that of all those (powers), spiritual and material, which promote goodness in the world and are distinguished by the promotion of goodness, it is Wisdom that descends from the Light on to the earth and by which (men) see and think well; the Good Religion and Will by which goodness is desired; and Power, Means, Effort, Time, and Space which have the potentiality of goodness, and through which the world practises goodness. The definition of goodness is that which of itself develops, while hindrance of its development comes from outside itself; just as life in itself is desirable and worthy of praise, and that which is undesirable and unworthy of praise comes from outside itself, such as illness, disease, old age, sin, damnation. The cause of goodness in creatures is the essential goodness and generosity of the Father of Creation, the Lord and Creator, Ohrmazd. His intention, wish, and will for his creatures is that the benefit of his goodness shall come to them. Goodness is summed up in the Mean: its offspring is the Law. The categories of this offspring are wisdom, good character, modesty, love, generosity, rectitude, gratitude, and the other virtues inherent in the essence of the Amahraspands and the other spiritual gods. Thence is the life of man, sound prosperity, lordship, knowledge of the Religion, salvation by virtue together with the promotion of welfare among the good creatures of the world. The promotion of goodness consists, in the beginning, in the act of creation and the setting of it in motion; in the middle, in directing and continuing creation and the conquest of evil; at the end, in the complete conquest of the Aggressor, whence is the salvation of all creation, purity, eternal well-being, and bliss.

He whose ground is evil and whose essence is evil is the Destructive Spirit of evil knowledge. The origin of evil is also in the evil religion, that is to say whatever causes harm when it supervenes. The movement of the evil Destructive Spirit is in Lying Falsehood and the Darkness of Lying Falsehood which are proper to his distinct nature; and Will, Power, Effort, Means, Space, and Time. It is revealed that of the evil-doers in evil deeds, they hold that it is the Dark Falsehood by which they perceive and think evil, Will that by which evil is desired; Power, Striving, Means, Time, and Space that through which evil is practised in the world. The definition of evil is that which essentially does not develop, while its development is from outside: just as death in itself is undesirable and unworthy of praise, and that which is desirable and worthy of praise (to itself) comes from outside, such as illness, disease, old age, poverty, and torment, which are worse than death. The cause of evil in spiritual and material creatures is the origin of all evil, the Destructive Spirit, the Aggressor. The reason for its coming upon the goodness of creation is the Lie's desire of destruction, inherent in an aggressor, for the harm of the creatures of the Bounteous Spirit, and for their defilement by means of evil, the original cause of all injury. Evil is summed up in Excess and Deficiency: and the abortion of evil is Lawlessness. The categories of this abortion are concupiscence, anger, vengeance, envy, deception, guile, avarice, ingratitude, and the other vices that are inherent in the evil essence of the Demon and the Lie. Thence is tyranny over men, heresy, illness, poverty, evil knowledge, damnation in sin, together with all the other injury and confusion of worldly creatures. The promotion of evil consists, in the beginning, in the defilement of creatures; in the middle, in strife and confusion in the contaminated state; at the end, in the wise control of the good Bounteous Spirit and the defeat (of evil) by the power of goodness.

The religion of those sectaries who (favour) one principle is forced to declare that that principle is Bounteous and Destructive, good and evil, praiseworthy and blameworthy.

Matter is ruled by these six things, by Time, Space, Wisdom, Power, Means, and Effort. A wise man has explained that of these six three are spiritual and three material. Time, Space, and Wisdom are spiritual; Power, Means, and Effort are material.

On the Wisdom, Will, Action, and Time of Ohrmazd

This that Ohrmazd, by his omniscient Wisdom and the projection of his Will, fashioned a limit for Time through action, and for action through Time. Their course proceeds from the first term to the last. Action, at its fulfilment, returns to its original state of rest: Time, when its full term has elapsed, returns to its source which is the Infinite;—that is the rehabilitation, the defeat of the Lie, the Resurrection and the Final Body, eternal bliss delivering all creation. His Wisdom, Will, Action, and Time are immutable. From the first projection of his Will till the last they are effective and in motion: in particular the forward motion of the Mazdayasnian Religion together with creation proceeds within them till it reaches the rehabilitation, so that every destructive thing is rendered ineffective, especially that which causes the separation of the Mazdayasnian Religion and creation from the rehabilitation. The rule for man's will and action is the Mazdayasnian Religion; and the end of all that is Ohrmazd's is benefit, even though on earth some harm should accrue to it owing to its vilification by the Adversary. But the end of the rule of all that is destructive is harm, even though on earth the semblance of benefit should accrue to it owing to the wiles of the Adversary. Thus it appears that the Wisdom of Ohrmazd and the projection of his Will are an immutable benefit to the whole of creation.

The religion of those sectaries for whom the will of God is mutable and, every day, has a different character, and for whom the word of God threatens to fill Hell with men (makes) him whom they hold to be God resemble the Destructive Spirit, in that his will is unstable and injurious to his creatures and that his words threaten them with distress.

On that which, revolving, returns to its origin and that which is regularly continuous from beginning to end.

This, from the Exegesis of the Good Religion, concerns that which, revolving, returns to its beginning, Time; and that which continues from beginning to end, Wisdom. Of Time thus it is taught. From action *in potentia*, the original seed the Avestan name of which is *aršnōtačin* (semen-flowing) first (arose), through the Creator's creation, the performance of action with which coincided the entry of Time into action. From the performance of action (arose) the completion of action with which coincided the limit of finite Time. The limit of finite Time merges into Infinite Time the essence of which is eternity, and (which means) that at the Final Body what is contingent on it cannot pass away. Even as the religious authorities have said concerning Time: Time was originally infinite; then it became subject to limitation; at the end it returns to the Infinite. The law of Time is (to proceed) from original infinity through limitation involving action, motion, and passage, and finally to return back to ultimate infinity.

Of Wisdom thus it is taught. By the Creator's marvellous power—in infinite Time and through its power wisdom entered (the stage of) knowing (the immutability of Ohrmazd's essence is contingent on Infinite Time). Contingent on this is the rising up of the Aggressor, against the will (of God), to destroy the essence and properties (of Wisdom) by false speech. Contingent on this was the reapplication of (Wisdom's) essence and properties to the knowing of its own ground. So much knowing was necessary for the Creator to rise up for the creative act. The first result of this rising up was the Endless Light. From the Endless Light is the Spirit of Truth which derives from Wisdom (animated) by the energy of power (and which thus) comes to the knowledge of all. From the knowledge of all is power to do all he wills. Thence creation and the Aggressor's defeat thereby and the return of creation to its proper sphere of action and the eternal rule of Ohrmazd in perfect joy, viz. the origin of good things, the origin of good, the seed of good, the potentiality of all that is good. All good creatures are from him as a first result by creation or by emanation (lit. by connexion with him) as sheen is from shining, shining from brilliance, and brilliance from the light.

On that which was before, and that which was with, and that which was after creation.

This is that which was before creation was (Infinite Time): that which coincided with the very act of the Creator's creation was Finite Time: that which was after creation was action (continuing) till the rehabilitation.

On the limited nature of knowledge and the possible, the infinity and limitation of Time and the essence[1] of infinite and finite Time.

This that since knowledge is wholly limited to what is present and past[2] and the potential to the possible, it is clear that the possible (too) is limited. Thus the limitation of omniscience and omnipotence gives an indication of infinity.[3] Thus Time is the source of creation and the eternity of Ohrmazd. Its limitation was necessary, for creation takes place in a definite time. The essence of Infinite Time is eternal duration, undivided into past and future; that of finite time is transient duration, divided into future and past.

1. From the context the reading **khuwatāi* seems certain: *khuwat* in philosophical contexts seems to render Greek καθ αυτό.

2. Menasce reads *hast būt bavēt* and translates 'la science porte sur ce qui a été, est, sera, tout cela étant limité'. This can scarcely be right: for the point seems to be that we know only that which is past and present: the future (i.e. that which will come to pass or can come to pass) cannot be actually known since it is still only in potency (*tavān* = δύαμις). *Sahmānōmand* is best taken with *dānišn* as *sahmānōmandih i dānišn* in line 6 shows.

3. Menasce's 'nous offre une analogie pour la notion d'infinité qui s'applique au temps' does not seem to be a possible rendering, since *ahanārakīh* is separated from *zamān* by *ʾōh-ič* and cannot therefore be construed with it. *ʾŌh* means 'thus' and marks the beginning of a new clause.

ŠIKAND GUMĀNĪ VAZĀR

Reprinted from 'Šikand Gumānī 'Vazār', in R. C. Zaehner, tr., *Zurvan: A Zoroastrian Dilemma* (New York, 1972), pp. 394–396.

(53) Now I shall first discuss the impossibility of any existent thing being infinite except only the Void and Time, which I call infinite. All entities which are within locality and temporality are seen to be finite. Thus if they stipulate unity or duality (it will be found) that unity cannot exist except in an object that is completely self-contained: for the one is that which is not two, and two is that of which the origin is one and the separation of the one part from the second. Though this cannot be called two, for the one is not conceivable except as completely self-contained in its unity; and duality cannot exist except through the separation of the two ones. The one is that which is one in unity and confirmed in unity. Unity and duality are at the source of quantity and numerality. Quantity, numerality, totality, and separability, as I have said, can be nothing but finite. This is clear even to the moderately intelligent.

(66) Again the Infinite is that which cannot be comprehended by the intellect: and since it cannot be comprehended by any intellect, it follows that it cannot be comprehended by the intellect of God. Thus to the intellect God, his own essence and that of the Dark Principle, as wholes, are incomprehensible. Since his own essence is not comprehensible even to his own intellect, to call him all-good and all-seeing is false. How should one explain a complete totality?

(71) A totality, because it is encompassed on all sides, is called total. That which is encompassed on all sides, is necessarily finite. A God, who is aware that he is encompassed on all sides, must be considered finite. If he were infinite, he would be unaware of it. The first knowledge of an intelligent being is precisely to know his own essence, quality, and quantity. To assert that one, who is unaware of all his essence, quality, and quantity, should be cognizant of the quality and quantity of others is false. Thus the Infinite not being encompassed in any way cannot be comprehended by the intellect. It follows that it is not aware whether its whole essence is wise or ignorant, light or dark, alive or dead.

(79) Again (we must consider) whether the light and the living soul, which we receive on this earth, receive a part (lot) from that same Zurvānic substance or not. If it does receive such a part from the essence of Zurvān, then let them note that a thing from which a part can be divided must itself be composed of parts. What is composed of parts cannot but be joined together: and what is joined together is only distinguishable in so far as it is joined together by a joiner. And since the part is obviously made and finite, so also the source from which the part is derived must undoubtedly be made and finite, in accordance with the argument that has been put forward that every result and part bears witness of its source. So, since we find

the part to be made and limited, it cannot be that the source is other than made and composed of parts and finite.

(86) Further the Infinite is not susceptible of division: for the part is divided from the whole and totality implies limitation, as I have demonstrated above. For, I cannot conceive of the existence and quality of the source except by comparison and analogy with the result. Whatever is perceptible in the result must certainly, in like manner, apply to the source. Since it is to be perceived in the result that it is made and finite, it may without doubt be deduced that the source from which the result derives is also finite.

(94) Again the Infinite is that which is uncircumscribed in Space and boundless in essence; and there is no other place or abode that is devoid of it. Now if it is said that the two Principles are infinite and boundless in essence, then boundless too are the heavens and earths together with corporeal and growing things, souls, lights, gods, Amahraspands, and the numerous complex entities which are variously named because they differ from one another: they cannot be bounded. Then in what and where were all these things created? If the two Principles were always uncircumscribed in Space, how is that possible unless their infinite essence was made finite and the place of all things that are and were and shall be? If an all-infinite substance can become finite, it is certainly possible that it may also become non-existent. What they say about the immutability of substance is untrue.

(102) Now you must know that the Infinite is that without which nothing from the first is. Nothing can exist without it or separate from it. But in so far as it is infinite, it cannot be understood. So what, pray, is the point of obstinately discussing a thing which one does not know, of disputing and bandying words, and so deceiving the immature and those of immature intelligence? If one stupidly (?) asserts that its essence is infinite and that its intellect is infinite, and that with its infinite intellect it knows that it is infinite, that is false and doubly false. For one thing intellect can only be predicated of a thing which is within the scope of the intellect and comprehensible to the intellect. Nothing can be perfectly understood except that which is completely comprehensible to the intellect and within its scope. Knowledge of a thing is only attained by complete understanding of it; and the complete understanding of a thing is obtained by the complete comprehension of it in the intellect.

PERSIAN RIVĀYĀT; HORMAZYĀR: THE SECOND ʿULAMĀ-YI ISLAM

Reprinted from 'Hormazyār', in R. C. Zaehner, tr., *Zurvan: A Zoroastrian Dilemma* (New York, 1972), pp. 409–418.

(1) Six hundred years after Yezdigird (sc. III) according to the Religious Era the doctors of Islam asked certain questions of one who was learned in our religion. The conversation took place in this manner, and a book has been compiled on this matter, and this book is called '*The Doctors of Islām*', or '*The explanation of the nature of the world and the soul of man from the beginning of time till the end*.'

(2) They asked: 'What do you say concerning the raising (of the dead)? Do you believe it or not?'

(3) The High Priest of the Magians said: 'We believe in the raising (of the dead), and the resurrection will take place.'

(4) Then the Doctors of Islām said: 'Has the world (always) existed? And what is your opinion concerning God's creation of man, non-existence, death, and the resurrection in life?'

(5) The religious leader of that time answered: 'In this matter of which you ask concerning the raising (of the dead), first we must know what creation is and what it is to cause death and wherefore man is resurrected in life: and we must say whether the world has (always) existed or whether it has been created.

(6) 'First I will speak of the world and discuss whether it has (always) existed or whether it was created. If it should be said that it has (always) existed, this opinion is untenable: for ever anew do things wax in the world and then again wane [and wax], decrease and then again increase. Further all that is susceptible of coming to be and passing away and is the effect of a cause is not proper to God. Thus it is established that the world has not (always) existed and that it has been created. Moreover, a created thing necessarily implies a Creator.

(7) Now it must be known that in the Pahlavi religion to which the Zoroastrians adhere, the world is said to have been created. After saying that the world has been created we must further say who created it and when, how, and why he created it.

(8) 'In the religion of Zoroaster it is thus revealed. Except Time all other things are created.[1] Time is the creator; and Time has no limit, neither top nor bottom. It has always been and shall be for evermore. No sensible person will say whence Time has come. In spite of all the grandeur that surrounded it, there was no one to call it creator; for it had not brought forth creation.

1. So, reading *juz* as in Spiegel's text instead of *khudā* as in Hormuzyār. With the reading *khudā* no satisfactory sense is obtained. Blochet translates: 'Dieu a créé toutes les choses du Temps, et le Temps est le Créateur.' This is obviously inadequate.

(9) Then it created fire and water; and when it had brought them together, Ohrmazd came into existence, and simultaneously Time became Creator and Lord[1] with regard to the creation it had brought forth.

(10) Ohrmazd was bright, pure, sweet-smelling, and beneficent, and had power over all good things. Then, when he looked down, he saw Ahriman ninety-six thousand parasangs away, black, foul, stinking, and maleficent; and it appeared fearful to Ohrmazd, for he was a frightful enemy.

(11) And when Ohrmazd saw this enemy, he thought thus: 'I must utterly destroy this enemy', and he considered with what and how many instruments he could destroy him.

(12) Then did Ohrmazd begin (the work of creation). Whatever Ohrmazd did, he did with the aid of Time; for all the excellence that Ohrmazd needed, had (already) been created. And Ohrmazd made Time of the long Dominion manifest[2] which has the measure of twelve thousand years, and within it he attached the firmament, the artificer[3] (and heaven).[4]

(13) And each of the twelve Signs of the Zodiac which are bound to the firmament he appointed for a thousand years. During three thousand years the spiritual creation was made; and Aries, Taurus, and Gemini held sway each for a thousand years.

(14) Then Ahriman (with the aid of Time) turned towards the heights that he might do battle with Ohrmazd: he saw[5] an army marshalled and drawn up in ranks, and rushed back to hell. From the foulness, darkness, and stench that was within him, he raised an army. This was possible for him.[6] in this matter much has been said. The meaning of this is that when he (saw he) was empty-handed, he rushed back to hell.

(15) Because of the righteousness he saw in Ohrmazd for three thousand years he could not move, so that during these three thousand years material creation was made.[7] The control of the world passed to Cancer, Leo, and Virgo. In this matter much has been said.

(16) 'I will say a few words on this subject. In the creation of the material world first he manifested the sky, and the measure of it was twenty-four (thousand) by

1. Reading *khudāvand* with Spiegel and the MS. Bk. quoted by Dhabhar.

2. Ohrmazd must be the subject, for he is already existent whereas there has been no mention of Time of the long Dominion: yet Blochet, following Vullers, translates, 'Le Temps de la Langue Souveraineté créa Ormazd'.

3. Literally 'the painter' (*naqqāš*): Dhabhar unaccountably translates 'its chart'.

4. *va mīnū* : not in Spiegel. The word is obviously a transcription of Phl. *mēnōk* which in this context would mean 'in ideal or spiritual form'.

5. So following Spiegel's text, *dīd*: Hormazyār has *az dīv*.

6. *va mumkin būd*: the sense is not clear. Blochet has 'Il est possible que cela soit': similarly Dhabhar. Vullers, 'Wann dieses möglich gewesen'.

7. This episode corresponds to the first defeat of Ahriman described in text Z 1, § 7, and Z 4, § 4.

twenty-four thousand parasangs, and its top reached Garōdmān ... .[1] After forty-five days he caused the water to appear (from the sky):[2] after sixty days the earth appeared out of the water: after seventy-five days he manifested plants, large and small: after thirty days the Bull and Gayōmart appeared: and after eighty days Adam and Eve[3] made their appearance.

(17) When the three thousand years we have mentioned (had elapsed) and Man, the material world, and the other creatures we have mentioned had come into existence, the accursed Ahriman again bestirred himself: and (Time brought it about that Ahriman)[4] bored a hole in the sky, the mountains, and the earth, rushed into the material world and defiled everything in it with his wickedness and impurity.

(18) As he possessed no spiritual thing, he did battle for ninety days and nights in the material world; and the firmament was rent, and the spiritual beings came to the assistance of the material world.

(19) And they seized the seven most evil demons and brought them to the firmament[5] and bound them with unseen (spiritual, *mīnū*) bonds. And Ahriman

---

1. The text is corrupt: Hormuzyār has *tā bā-garōthmān bar šudeh*; Spiegel, *ta ba-garōthmān bi-rasad bar šudan bar rūy-i āsmān*. Neither makes sense, and Vullers wisely left a *lacuna* in his translation. Blochet translates 's'élevant jusqu'au Garôthmân et sur la sphère céleste'. Dhabhar has 'upwards to G. which was over the heavens'. This involves a slight emendation of the text.

2. All MSS. appear to read *ab* except Bk. which has *āsmān*. I would therefore read *az āsmān āb* corresponding to GrBd. 19. 5 (text Z 1, § 45), *'hač gōhr-i āmān 'āp brēhēnīt*.

3. That is, the first human couple, Mašyē and Mašyānē.

4. Spiegel's text: Hormuzyār omits.

5. From here on Spiegel's text is completely different. In translation it runs as follows:

'Of the seven demons they seized the four who were the worst, and they bound them with unseen bonds to the eighth heaven which they call the heaven of the fixed stars; and they appointed the star Vanand over those four demons so that they could do no harm. Of the other three demons they put Saturn who has a very evil influence in the seventh heaven; and in the Āyīn(?) heaven which is the sixth heaven they put Jupiter who has a very good influence. The second demon who is Mars and who has only a slightly evil influence, they put in the fifth heaven: and in the fourth heaven which is the centre of the heavens they placed the Sun and they presented him with sovereignty over the heavens [over against the heavens (?)]. They placed Saturn and Mars higher than the heaven of the Sun so that the poison and filth which they let fall upon the earth should be melted by the heat of the Sun and come to the earth in smaller quantities. In the third heaven they put Venus who has only a slightly good influence. The third demon which is Mercury, whose nature is mixed, they placed in the second heaven, and they bound him to the hand of the Sun so that (the Sun) should control the affairs of the heavens over him: but he does not escape from the Sun; for since his heaven is below that of the Sun, all the poison and filth which he lets fall comes to the earth. They call him 'mixed' because he is inclined to do evil, but since he is a prisoner in the hand of the Sun, he cannot do excessive harm as he would wish to do. His place is between two planets of good influence. Necessarily when he is with a good influence, he does good; and when he falls together with an evil influence, he does evil. For this reason they do not call him an evil influence, but mixed. In the first heaven they put the Moon. Below the heaven of the Moon there is another heaven which they call the heaven of Gōčihr, and the tail and the head of the serpent (For 'serpent' the text has the incomprehensible *WKYD*, but the meaning is assured

afflicted Gayōmart with a thousand torments till he passed away. And from him certain things came into existence. About this much has been said. From the Bull too certain things and animals came into existence. About this much has been said.

(20) Then they seized upon Ahriman and carried him off to hell by that very hole through which he had entered the world; and they bound him with unseen bonds. Two angels, even Ardībihišt, the Amahraspand, and Varhrām, the god, stood in guard over him.

(21) 'If it is objected that since all this suffering comes from him, they should have slain him when they captured him, then it must be known that when one kills a living creature and says, 'I have killed so and so', and that creature is (actually) killed, the fire that is in him goes to the Fire, and the water that is in him to the Water, and the earth that is in him to the Earth, and the air that is in him to the Air: and at the time of the raising (of the dead) he will be raised up; and what does it matter if in the meantime (the elements) were separated?

(22) Thus it is plain that none of these things which we have mentioned is annihilated, but that each of them is, as it were, separated from the four elements. Further, how could Ahriman with all his density[1] be slain unless they slew him gently and by degrees, and mingled evil with good, and darkness with light, and foulness with purity, so that mastery should remain, not vengeance and enmity?

(23) 'If it is objected that since (Time) possessed all this mastery, why did it create Ahriman, we (reply that as) we said in the beginning, Ohrmazd and Ahriman both came into existence from Time. Every sect holds a different opinion.

(24) One party says that it created Ahriman so that Ohrmazd should know that Time has power over (all) things: another says that there was no need to create him, and that Time[2] said to Ohrmazd, 'I have power to do this without bringing pain upon Ohrmazd and ourselves': another says, 'What pain or pleasure has Time from the evil of Ahriman or the goodness of Ohrmazd?' Another says that

---

by GrBd. 52.12: *gōčihr miyān <i> āsmān 'bē 'ēstāt mār humānāk, 'sar 'pat dōpatkar 'ut dumb 'pat nēmāsp.*—'Gōčihr was in the middle of the sky, like a serpent, with its head in Gemini and its tail in Centaurus.') are in that heaven. When the period of control of Aries, Taurus, and Gemini had passed and control passed to Cancer and it was its turn, they prepared the horoscope of the world; and they placed every constellation in the twelve Signs of the Zodiac in the house of its ascendant in the form in which they are (now) fixed so that it should be easier to understand. Then Ahriman afflicted Gayomart with a thousand torments until he passed away. From him certain things came into existence; and from the Bull, too, many kinds of things and animals came into existence. Then they seized upon Ahriman and carried him off to hell by that hole through which he had come into the world; and they bound him with unseen bonds, for the Amahraspand Ardībihišt and the god Vahram were appointed over him).'

1. For *siṭabrī* Blochet's 'vil et méprisable' is wrong.

2. Taking 'Time' as the subject with Vullers. Taking Ahriman as the subject Dhabhar produces regularly poor sense: 'He (Ahriman) said to Ormazd: I can do such (evil) things and therefore it is not necessary to attribute evil unto Ohrmazd or unto me.'

it created Ohrmazd and Ahriman so that it might mingle good and evil, and that things of different kinds and colours might come into existence: another says that Ahriman was an honoured[1] angel, and that because of some disobedience of which he had been guilty he became the target of malediction. In this matter much has been said.

(25) 'Now we will proceed to the end of our story. After the spiritual beings had bound Ahriman in hell and had bound the seven demons on to the firmament[2]—the names of the demons are as follows: Zēriēĵ, Tariĵ, Nānghaith, Tarmad, Xišm, Sēĵ, and Bēš—Ohrmazd surrounded every one of the seven with light and gave them Ohrmazdean names—Kēvān (Saturn), Ohrmazd (Jupiter), Bahrām (Mars), Šēd (the Sun), Nāhīd (Venus), Tīr (Mercury), and Māh (the Moon).

(26) When these deeds were duly performed, the firmament began to resolve, and the Sun, Moon, and stars began to rise and set; and hours, days, nights, years, and months appeared, and the 'givers'[3] appeared. In this matter much has been said.

(27) 'For three thousand years men existed and the demons too were plain to see, and there was war between men and demons. In Man there are some things that are Ohrmazd's and some that are Ahriman's. In his body there is fire, water, earth, and air, and further soul, intelligence, consciousness, and *fravahr*; further five senses, sight, hearing, taste, smell, and touch.

(28) Should anyone say that all these derive from the soul, it is not so; for there are many people who are dumb and lame. If anyone should object saying, 'If the soul does not possess these faculties and provisions, what then can it do?'—(we reply) that this is not a fair question (*lit.* this is not so): for we see that fire has no mouth, yet it consumes food; and it has no feet, yet when you put fuel before it, it goes in pursuit of fuel; and it has no eyes, yet it gives light to the eyes. This has been said that we should know that provided though we are with all these faculties and provisions, we are nothing without His favour despite all the pride and selfishness we show in our relations with one another. Since we have recorded those things which are Ohrmazd's, we will now record[4] those which are Ahriman's, that people may know. These are Concupiscence (Āz), Want, Envy, Vengeance, Lust, Falsehood, and Anger. These are the demons had in their bodies; and they were (mixed with) the four elements.[5]

1. So, reading *muqarrab*. Blochet read *mutazarrib* and translated 'qui se châtie lui-même.'

2. Hormuzyār adds *tavānand kard*, which yields no sense.

3. As Spiegel saw, the 'givers' must be the twelve Signs of the Zodiac (*Eranische Alterthumskunde*, ii, p. 182). *dahandagān* is in fact a literal translation of Av. *baya-*, Phl. *bay* 'bestower', then 'constellation': so ŠGV. 4. 8: *baya i nekī-bakhtāra*.

4. For the *yād kunand* of the text *yād kunīm* must be read.

5. The text reads: *dar dīvān kālbud dāshtand ṭabā'iʿ chahār gūneh būdī*. In his translation Dhabhar appears to have substituted *agar* for *dar*—'Had the demons been incarnate, their natures would have been of these four kinds.' I would prefer to emend the text to *divān dar kālbud dashtand bā ṭaba'iʿ chahār-gūneh būdand*, since *ṭabā'iʿ* must surely refer to the elements and not to the 'natures' of the demons.

(30) For the power of Ahriman comes to the demons of the firmament, and thus does he ever anew bring evil to the world through them, until the power of Ahriman wanes and the evil of Ahriman diminishes, till through the resurrection all his evil decreases and is annihilated.

(31) 'And the men of that time walked according to the paths of righteousness and smote the demons until Jamšīd became king. For six hundred and sixteen years and six months did he reign; and the demon of Wrath entered him and he claimed to be God. And the Arab Dahāk seized him and slew him and settled at the king's court.

(32) He reigned a thousand years and mixed men and demons together and worked much sorcery in the world until Farīdūn, son of Ātfi, came and bound him. Dahāk means ten sins.[1] Now he is commonly called Ẓaḥḥāk. After this, war broke out among men because some had mixed with the demons and some had fallen into error. Then Farīdūn strove to call men back to the path of righteousness. When Āfrāsyāb appeared from his family, disorder increased: and when Kay Xusrau appeared, he purged the world of evil men.

(33) Then Zartušt (Zoroaster) Isfantaman came as a prophet and brought the Avesta, Zand, and Pāzand. King Guštāsp was converted and spread it abroad in the world;[2] and one quarter of the world was converted to the religion of Zartušt and spread it abroad in the world; and for three hundred years it went every day better with the followers of the Religion until Alexander the Roman (Macedonian) came, and once again confusion increased.

(34) After this Ardašir, son of Pāpak, lessened the confusion and five hundred years passed by. After that the army of the Arabs rose up and brought the Persians beneath its yoke; and every day they became weaker (till) the time when Bahrām, the mighty, comes and takes to himself the throne of the kingdom of the Sasanians.

(35) 'Then Ōšēdar, the bright, will come and will bring one Nask of the Avesta and Zand in addition to that which Zartušt Isfantaman had brought and Bahrām, the mighty, will spread it abroad in the world; and of those three quarters who were not converted in the time of Zartušt, one quarter more will be converted and for four hundred years will spread it abroad.[3] Then once again will confusion appear. In this matter much has been said.

---

1. The *DH* ‘‘ of the text is meaningless. We must emend to *DH'I'* = *dahāy* : from the explanation *dah 'aib* it is to be assumed that the word was understood as *dah ay* <Av. *aya-* 'evil', Phl. *ay-* in *aydēn*, &c. According to Dhabhar the MS.Bk. enumerates the sins; these Blochet translates as follows: 'odieux, inique, petit, tyran, sans pudeur, mangeant beaucoup, parlant mal, menteur, téméraire, ayant mauvais coeur, sans intelligence.'

2. Text has *qabūl dar jahān kard*: read, with Dhabhar, *qabūl kard va dar jahān ravā kard.* Dhabhar reads *ravān* rather than *ravā*.

3. Reading *ravā kunand* for *ravā bāshand*. For Hormazyār's *sih bāreh ōshīdarmāh yakī ziyādat kunad* read with MSS. T30 and Bk. (Dhabhar p. 454) *sih yakī ziyādat qabūl kunad.*

(36) Then again Ōšēdar-māh will come and will make an end of confusion and will bring one more Nask of the Avesta in addition to that which Ōšēdar, the bright, had already brought, and will spread it abroad in the world. One half of those who are without religion will be converted to the Good Religion. Once again a period of welfare will pass away and a period of evil will set in and in its turn pass away.

(37) Then Sōšyans[1] will bring one Nask of the Avesta in addition to that which Ōšēdar-māh had already brought and all men will be converted to the Good Religion and confusion will vanish from the world. Fifty-seven years will pass and the resurrection will come to pass. In this matter much has been said, but I have been brief so as not to bore the reader.

(38) 'Now we have come to the end of our story. When it is said that a person dies or is killed, the air that is within him is united to the Air, and the earth within him to the Earth, the water within him to the Water, and the fire within him to the Fire. His soul, intelligence, and consciousness all become one and united with the *fravahr*, and the whole becomes one. If one has a preponderance of sin, one is punished: if one has a preponderance of virtue, one is taken up to heaven. Then the demons who were with these persons will all be worn down and slain.

(39) With regard to the punishment that they endure, the Amahraspand Ardībihišt acts as mediator and does not permit that they be punished beyond the measure of their sin. Whoso is worthy of heaven is borne to heaven; and whoso is worthy of Garōdmān is borne to Garōdmān; and whoso is worthy of Hamēstagān (the place of the mixed, i.e. purgatory) is borne to Hamēstagān.

(40) Then up to the resurrection the power of the demons is worn down and their wickedness is reduced to nothing because men endure punishment; and thus the demons that are within men are worn down.

(41) After this they raise up the bodies of the denizens of heaven and hell even from the primal substances: they collect (spirit) from spirit, fire from fire, water from water, earth from earth, and air from air, and the soul returns to earth.

(42) At the time of the resurrection the evil that is in the body of man no longer remains, and men will be free from death, old age, and want, so that they live for ever; and no evil will remain.

(43) 'Beasts, birds, and fish have no soul, but the fourfold spirit is reunited with them. They are exempt from the reckoning and judgement because they have no soul or *fravahr*. It is the soul that shows that man is possessed of reason, knowledge, righteousness, and height (!) and the ability to speak words with his tongue and to do deeds with his hands. Otherwise all living creatures partake of the four elements. But man has all this besides, and because he possesses a soul, he must undergo the reckoning and judgment while other creatures do not.

(44) 'With regard to what has been said about what creation is and what it is

1. The text reads *siyāvushānī*.

to cause death and why there is hope of resurrection in life, we must know that creation is due to his mercy and grace, and the cause of death is this, that (if) we were like the Amahraspands who do not die, Ahriman would have been unable to mingle with us, and his evil, darkness, foulness, and stench would have remained forever: (but now) since he has mingled with us and torments us, he has propagated himself and thinks that he can annihilate us, and he does not know that it is his own wickedness that he is destroying. That is how death is caused.

(45) The resurrection in life is a holy duty for Him since we have laboured much both in the material world and in the spiritual. So because of His mercy and kindness it is a holy duty for Him to bring us to life, although there is no question of anything being (really) dead. Rather He brings together what was scattered abroad and raises up the person and gives him his recompense from the good things that are His.

(46) 'With regard to the twenty-one Nasks of the Avesta of which they speak, Avesta is the tongue of Ohrmazd, and Zand is our tongue and Pāzand that tongue in which everyone knows what he is saying.

(47) The Avesta, Zand, and Pāzand of the twenty-one Nasks are as follows. The Zand and Pāzand of seven Nasks treat of those matters which we have discussed. The Zand and Pāzand of another seven Nasks treat of what is proper and what is improper, of what to do and what not to do, of what to say and what not to say, of what to take and what not to take, of what to eat and what not to eat, of what is pure and what is impure, of what to wear and what not to wear, such matters. If I recounted all, the book would (never) end: and so I have been brief. The Zand and Pāzand of the other seven Nasks treat of medicine and astrology. In this matter much has been said.

(48) 'They say that the Sun revolves round the earth; and everywhere the Sun goes, as for example here where we are, the sky and the stars follow (*lit.* are). It can go under the earth or to the side of the earth, so that we ourselves may be under the earth though we say that we are on the top of the earth. In the Avesta and Zand it is said that all men that have been or are or shall be, will go to heaven, and that their souls shall undergo punishment before the resurrection.

(49) 'More wonderful is this that we send our children to school and teach them good conduct and keep them far from evil. Yet when you consider, they still come to know evil before good. But good is good in the sight of God and before men; and evil is evil before the Creator and before men. And in man there is good and evil; and in the world there is good and evil; and in the firmament there is good and evil; and in the spiritual world there is heaven and hell.

(50) We were created by the Creator, and to Him is our return. Had it not been necessary, the Creator would not have created us. And with regard to the fact that evil should never have been created and yet exists, a veil is drawn over this, or else our intelligence cannot attain it. Yet since this is so, we must leave what is God's concern to God.

(51) 'What thou art told to do, thou shalt do; and what thou art told not to do, thou shalt not do; and what thou art told to think, thou shalt think; and what thou art told not to think, thou shalt not think; and what thou art told to say, say; and what thou art told not to say, thou shalt not say; and what thou art commanded to eat, eat; and what thou art commanded not to eat, thou shalt not eat; and what thou art told to wear, wear; and what thou art told not to wear, thou shalt not wear, and other such things as these. And our law is to busy ourselves with the service of God.'

(52) Greetings and blessings upon the pure and good and those who show the way. May the good prevail. Amen.

6

Exegesis of the Good Religion
Dēnkard VI

Reprinted from Ārturpāt-ı Ēmetān, *The Wisdom of the Sāsaniān Sages* (Dēnkard VI), tr. Sh. Shaked (Boulder, CO, 1979), pp. 7–212 (selected passages).

(6) They held this too: Character is not in wisdom, (but) wisdom is in character; and religion is in both wisdom and character. Spiritual things are known by disciplining character, the body is held by wisdom, the soul is saved by the union of both.

(7) They held this too: 'Shame' is that which does not let (one) commit a sin; 'disgrace' is that which does not let (one) perform a good deed.

(8) They held this too: The main thing in the way of the ancient sages is lack of sin.

(9) They held this too: A person who fulfils his duty is such with regard to that which he knows.

(10) They held this too: The deliberation which is in religion is wholly craftsmanship; but he who knows as much, performs it in action.

(11) They held this too: Ohrmazd the Lord created these creatures through character, he holds them with wisdom, and takes them back to himself by religion.

(12) They held this too: Ahriman did every thing for the harm of Ohrmazd. When it was done, it constituted harm to himself and benefit to Ohrmazd. Ohrmazd does every thing for his own benefit; when it is done, it constitutes benefit to himself and harm to Ahriman.

(13) They held this too: These three things are the greatest duties of men. To have one's eye on the world, not to reproach a sinner for an accidental sin committed, and to seek the reward of good deeds from the spirits. They said: to have one's eye on the world is this, one who looks at himself (saying): 'What have I desired? What am I doing?'

(14) They held this too: There are three things which are very difficult to do,

these are as follows: One, not to reproach a sinner for his sin; one, not to praise a deceitful man for the sake of authority and wealth; and one, to seek the reward of good deeds from the spirits, not from that which is material.

(15) They held this too: One ought not to reproach one who is worthy of forgiveness and not to praise one who is worthy of reproach.

(16) They held this too: Each man, whoever he may be, should hold the things of the spirit in memory at every moment and time—both the goodness of paradise and the evil of hell. At a moment when comfort, good things and joy have accrued to him, he should think this: 'It will indeed be good there in paradise, when even here it is so good; when from the great evil of Ahriman, with which there is no goodness intermixed over there, it is (still) so good here.' At a period when distress, grief, evil and pain have accrued to him, he should think this: 'It will indeed be bad there in hell when it is so bad even here; when from the great goodness of Ohrmazd, with which there is no evil intermixed over there, it is (still) so bad here.'

(17) They held this too: That man is happiest who at the time of bodily health and young age has grasped and done those things (only) concerning which on the ultimate day, when he departs from this world, such may be his desire: 'Would that I had done more.' He ought to beware most from those things concerning which on the ultimate day his desire may be this: 'Would that they had not been grasped and done by me.'

(18) They held this too: Righteousness should be held as a thing to perform. Sin should be held by that which repels pain.

(19) They held this too: Righteousness in substance is that thing which every person can perform, and which Ohrmazd the Lord desires from every person. Whoever does not perform that is under guilt.

(20) They said: That thing is this. Whoever is a friend of the gods never removes his thought from the friendship of the gods.

(21) They held this too: Heresy has destroyed (its own) source. When it first came to the world, it made people mostly believe in the soul, and because it had not come to power it grew. When it came to power those who mostly had abandoned faith were with the power and authority which belonged to it. After this, indeed, because people have abandoned faith, it does not grow.

(22) They held this too: One should take goodness from everyone; one should not take evil from any one.

(23) They held this too: There are five best things in religion. These are: truthfulness, generosity, being possessed of virtue, diligence and advocacy. This truthfulness is best: one who acts (in such a manner) to the creatures of Ohrmazd that the recipient of his action has so much more benefit when he acts like that to him.

This generosity is best: One who makes a present to a person from whom he has no hope of receiving anything in reward in this world, and he has not even this (hope), namely, that the recipient of his gift should hold him abundantly in gratitude and praise.

This possession of virtue is best: One who makes battle against the non-material demons, whatever they may be, and in particular does not let these five demons into his body: Greed, Envy, Lust, Wrath and Shame.

This diligence is best: One who does the work which he is engaged in doing in such a manner that at every moment he has certainty in himself with regard to the following: were he to die at that hour it would not be necessary to do anything whatsoever in a way different from that in which he is doing it.

That advocacy is best: One who speaks for a person who is inarticulate, who cannot speak his own misery and complaint; that person speaks out the voice of his own soul and of that of the poor and good person to the people of this world and these six Amahraspands.

(24) They held this too: Wisdom is manifest in work, character in rule, and a friend in hardship.

(25) They held this too: The wisdom which is best of all wisdoms is that, viz. one who can hold this body in such a way that no evil comes to it because of the soul, and who can hold the soul in such a manner that no evil comes to it because of the body. And when it is different and he cannot act thus, he ought to abandon the body and keep the soul.

(26) They held this too: Authority is the shield of wealth, wealth is the shield of the body, and the body is the shield of the soul. A person to whom a misfortune comes in connection with which there is the fear that wealth from among these four things may be removed let him abandon authority. When there is no hope with regard to authority, let him abandon wealth too with it. When there is no hope with regard to wealth, too, let him also abandon the body together with it. After this he should not reject the soul.

(27) They held this too: Righteousness and making religion dwell (in oneself) consist in this: holding well, having a good share, and being content.

(28) They held this too: Every person should make an offering of himself and deliver himself to the gods, and from then on be confident that nothing will ever reach him from whose coming there will be harm.

(29) They held this too: One should be a person who suppresses complaint, patient, diligent and confident in doing good works, and who seeks gratitude from the spirits.

(30) They held this too: One ought to hold the mind as lord and be obedient to it in the same way as one is to a lord and ruler. One ought not to do any work without the authority of mind.

(31) They held this too: The desire of Ohrmazd from men is this: 'Know me', for he knows: 'If they know me, every one will follow me.' The desire of Ahriman is this: 'Do not know me', for he knows: 'If they know me no one will follow me.'

(32) They held this too: Ohrmazd desires from men this, namely, 'Whatever you do, do it for your own selves, and do as much (of it) as you wish to do.' Ahriman desires from men this, namely, 'Do not do it for your own selves, (but) do as much (of it) as you wish to do.'

(33) They held this too: Every person has one thing which is dearer and more precious to him than other things. When he disciplines that thing, even though other things be neglected and not at his disposal, he is joyful. That thing is his religion.

(34) They held this too: Religion is that which one always does.

(35) They held this too: One who believes in advocacy for the sake of (his) soul (has) less evil than one who does not believe at all.

(36) They held this too: Religion is that, namely: one who causes comfort to every creature.

(37) They held this too: '*Bazag*' is that which concerns the law. '*Wināh*' is that which is (committed) through negligence and contempt. '*Māndag*' is that which is going to stay on.

(38) They held this too: The main thing in transgression is excess and deficiency. The main thing in a virtuous work is the (right) measure.

(39) They held this too: Religion is the (right) measure.

(40) They held this too: In every thing, being free from defect is the (right) measure. The following is manifest from this religion: the greatest (keeping of) the measure is the virtuous deed. This is the (right) measure: good thought, good speech, and good deed.

(41) They held this too: Whoever is righteous is righteous in religion.

(42) They held this too: Excess is this, viz. one who thinks, speaks and makes that which is not to be thought, spoken or made. Deficiency is this, viz. one who does not think, speak and act that which is to be thought, spoken and done. The (right) measure is this, viz. one who thinks, speaks and makes that which is to be thought, spoken and made.

(43) They held this too: These three things are most important in the religion: union, the right measure and separation.

This is union: one who is associated with the gods and the good ones in every righteousness in thought, speech and deed. That union never perishes.

This is separation: one who is detached in every iniquity and sin from Ahriman, the demons and the evil ones.

This is the right measure: one who is a protector of that union and separation. It will never perish.

(91) They held this too: These five things are very good, namely: generosity, truthfulness, manly virtue, eloquence, and sagacity.

Generosity is this: a man who surrenders himself to the gods solely for the sake of religion and love of the soul. Truthfulness is this: a man who only says that which is necessary, and who speaks with such circumspection as if the gods and the *Amahraspands* visibly stop in front of him.

Manly virtue is this: confession of faith. Confession of faith means to accommodate religion in one's body and to vanquish the demons from it.

Eloquence is this: a man who intercedes on behalf of that person for whom there would be no intercessor but for him; (it means) to intercede for the sake of one's own soul.

Sagacity is this: a man who begins a thing that he knows how to complete.

(92) They held this too: A man who is a trespasser with regard to one of these three relationships is wicked. One, the relationship of the world; one, the relationship of religion; and one, the relationship of the Renovation. The relationship of the world is this: being helpful and keeping one's door open; these things form relationships among people. The relationship of religion is this: a man who adopts a righteous authority in time, and does not deviate from the authority. The relationship of the Renovation is this: a man who takes a wife in time, who seeks children and who provides (for himself) a family.

(102) They held this too: Faith in the spirits is of many kinds. This too is faith in the spirits: People who believe that the spirits are capable of giving the goodness of this world to men, and who seek the goodness of this world from the spirits.

(103) They held this too: The most important thing in the body of men is substance, and after it (come) the other faculties. The faculties are necessary even for this function, to manifest the substance and bring it into action.

(104) They held this too: There is nothing which is more difficult to know than the substance of men, whether it is good or bad. For there are many people whose substance has been so much damaged and harmed that even in an extremely small matter much talent and education are necessary before it is possible to bring out whether they are good or bad. (But) it is easy to test and know the one who is of much [ability].

(105) They held this too: It is possible best to know the substance of men by this one thing: when education is brought upon a man, and he is made acquainted with righteous things and is given certainty, (to see) whether he does good deeds or sins. Having been tested, his substance is manifest.

(106) They held this too: When a man stands in the religion of the gods, the gods notice the pain endured by him in the world—even the fact that he came to pain by foot and that he lives lawfully on the work of his hands; and they carry and keep for him in the Reckoning of the Spirits the discomfort, hunger, thirst, worry and disease which affect him.

(113) They held this too: People have seven things which are best. These are: Good fame, righteousness, nobility, lordship, authority, health and satisfaction.

Good fame is this: a man who always keeps his door open to good people.

Righteousness is this: a man who performs good works for the sake of the soul.

Nobility is this: a man who gives presents to the good and the worthy.

Lordship is this: a man who restrains himself from doing sin.

Authority is this: a man who causes the preservation of the good and the uprooting of the wicked.

Health is this: a man who separates his body and soul from aliens and those of different substance, and who associates with those of the same substance as himself.

Satisfaction is this: a man who holds the spiritual gods in reverence for a good thing which has come and the gods bring him satisfaction which has not come to him and take away from him misfortunes which have come to him, and to whom good always comes from the mind.

(114) They held this too: This thing is best for men: love of men, desire for peace, truthfulness, support of one's kinsmen, reverence, humility, generosity, gratitude, consultation and keeping the measure.

The law of Ohrmazd is love of men; the law of Wahman is desire for peace; the law of Ašawahišt is truthfulness; the law of Šahrewar is support of one's kinsmen; the law of Spandārmad is reverence and humility; the law of Xurdād is generosity and gratitude; the law of Amurdad is consultation and keeping the measure.

(115) They held this too: people have several things which are very good, these are: religion, character, wisdom, virtue and fortune. When they are not accompanied by their instruments, they are of no account.

The instrument of religion is this: a man who has faith. Confession of faith is this: a man who takes a friend of good nature, pure and a good man, to be master over himself, says (to him): 'Tell me the faults which you know, so that I may correct them', listens eagerly and willingly to what he says, and obeys him.

The instrument of character is this: righteous habit, associating with good people, learning good from every person and not learning evil from any one.

The instrument of wisdom is this: maintaining good people and being respectful to them.

The instrument of virtue is this: doing one's duty and diligence.

The instrument of fortune is this: truth and keeping one's word.

(124) They held this too: Ohrmazd the Lord created the best character and religion. A man who has no character has no religion; a man who has no friendship of the good does not possess goodness. A man, who is a friend of the good for the sake of goodness, possesses goodness.

(125) They held this too: [He who] wishes to be endowed with fortune, let him worship the sun openly; he who wishes that the worship which he performs should reach the gods best, let him wash his hands clean and keep his body and clothes in cleanliness; he who wishes (to obtain) in the best way the thing which he desires

of the gods, let him worship the gods openly; he who desires that his world should come well in the assembly, let him recite the Avesta of Urination openly.

(126) They held this too thus: A man who shows reverence towards the gods in connection with a misfortune which has come or with one which has not come, the gods will save him from that which has come, and the one which has not come will not reach him in the first place.

(127) They held this too: In the life of man satisfaction is best, and in satisfaction bodily health is best.

Secondly, character is best, and in it the profession of the true religion is best.

Thirdly, wisdom is best, and in it patience and meekness are best.

Fourthly, wealth is best, and in it contentment and worthiness are best.

Fifthly, joy is best, and in it a woman who is a respectful housewife, loved by her husband, is best.

Sixthly, friendship is best, and in it obedience is best.

Seventhly, generosity through truth is best, and in it giving great benefit [is best].

Eighthly, apart from the salvation of one's own soul, it is best to strive for saving other people's souls.

Ninthly, to do good deeds in great accordance with the law, and much to avoid sin and inclination to sin is best.

Tenthly, good completion is best, and in it the salvation of the soul from hell is best.

(141) They held this too: It has been said in *Andarz* to men. Poverty is best, make provision of it. Stand firm in poverty, which is the best thing. A man who stands in poverty not out of constraint but solely because of the goodness and praise of poverty banishes Ahriman and the demons from the world. Every good deed which may be held in the world by that (man) would proceed like a river which is always navigable (?). And this too is thus: He can stand in poverty who has more joy in the scantest substance which is necessary for the body than in the bulkiest substance. One who acts thus can stand fortunate in poverty, and he who acts differently will be made to issue forth (?) from poverty.

(142) They held this too: Nobility is this: One who holds the powerful means of the material world, prosperous and satisfied, for beneficial work, and who knows (how) to consume and to give them. The powerful means are not harmful to that man or to (other) people. In whatever comes about he is an advocate for the poor and does good to them. He praises the poor and acts in such a manner that (his) wealth and riches are open to all men, and that they hold them as their own and are confident: 'If evil or misfortune come to us, he will seek a remedy to carry it away.'

(143) They held this too: Poverty is this: One whose self is prosperous and satisfied as regards the powerful wealth of the material world, whose mind turns away

from it (?), whose thought is content in it, who is not angry concerning it, and who is not contemptuous of a man who is wealthy and opulent, but acts in this manner (thinking): 'My poverty is together with the wealth and riches of that man. After all, we are the same, he and I.'

(147) They held this too: If the poor set right this one thing, the contempt of wealthy people of high standing, in a century not one of them will go to hell.

(148) They held this too: In this world there is no one whose authority and wealth are loved. One who is fortunate should (be loved) through righteousness, and a person who is unfortunate should (be loved) in any way.

(149) They held this too: One should not embellish the things of the material world in excess of the measure. For a man who embellishes the material world in excess of the measure becomes a destroyer of the spiritual world.

(150) They held this too: One ought to embellish the things of the material world to such an extent (only) as not to destroy the things of the spiritual world.

(151) They held this too: One ought to do the things of the material world in time, in such a way as if one knew: 'I shall live a thousand years, and what I do not do to-day I shall do tomorrow.' One ought to do the things of the spiritual world in thought and effort constantly in such a way as if one knew: 'I shall live one day, and what I do not do to-day I shall not be able to do later.'

(156) They held this too: Whoever desires authority and wealth and attains it, keeping them for the benefit and good of men, the gods make him a potentate in the world. Whoever stands in poverty and beneficence, being at peace in it, the gods establish him firmly in the world.

(161) They held this too: Many are those works of virtue which are so petty that (even) if a man performs very many of them he is unable to become righteous through them. And (there is) that word which is so great that (even) if a man performs (only) one he becomes righteous through it. We men should be very diligent so that the great works of virtue may become ours.

(162) They held this too: Every person has a mind. When the mind of that person is healthy and free from damage [even if the man says or does something bad (?)] that thing is yet available to him. When (the mind is) otherwise, even if the man says or does something very bad which is free from defilement, that thing is destroyed.

(163) They held this too: The mind of religion is Zoroaster, the mind of righteousness is the sacred word, the mind of Iranian dignity is the position of the ruler.

(164) They held this too: Every thing has a sea. The sea of knowledge is character, the sea of light is the sun, the sea of water is Vorukaš and the sea of the soul is mind.

(165) They held this too: One should strongly seek a friend in religion. For a friend who is always with one is a friend in religion. For a friend in religion is with one in both (worlds), here and there.

(166) They held this too: To every person religion is that for which he believes (he would) surrender his self. One ought to consider in his desire what that thing is for which he believes (he would) surrender his self, and religion is the several things for which the surrender of self is to be made. That person is steadfast in religion who surrenders himself when a thing comes for which he ought to surrender his self. However, as regards those several things for which the surrender of self ought to be made, one should not commit an unatonable sin. This is (that): one who surrenders his self, when the need arises, for the sake of religion, wife, children, righteous preceptors and other good people.

(167) They held this too: In this religion one word has much substance, it is even thus: Being free from doubt concerning the religion of the gods. Being free from doubt concerning the religion of the gods is this: those who, come what may (?), do not turn away from the things of the gods.

(170) They held this too: A man who, having come into harm and evil, yet desires a boon from the gods, (acts) with faith in the spirits. The reason for this is that although the action (of such people) is unrighteous out of ignorance, they believe the gods to be able to do good and evil.

(171) They held this too: The wise man knows well this: little and much, near and far, easy and difficult.

(172) They held this too: The road to paradise is the religion, which is the measure. When Ohrmazd paved this road, Ahriman at the same time laid two roads, one excess and one deficiency. He set them each to (the limit of) darkness; from that point on he can set no more.

(173) They held this too: Happy is the man who walks on the king's road, for even though he should walk with much gravity (?), he will come to the house on time. Unfortunate is that man who walks on a pathless road, for no matter how much he may exert himself he will still be farther from the house. The king's way is the religion and the house is paradise.

(174) They held this too: As regards the soul, to be able with measure is not to be able; as regards possessions, to dispose of them with measure is not to dispose.

(175) They held this too: The matter of disposing or not disposing varies according to people. For some people there is no power to dispose unless they are respectable (?) and possess a sufficient amount of gold, silver and other property. Some people have the power to dispose even when their desire does not go beyond one head of cattle.

(176) They held this too: There is power of disposition (only) over the whole of religion. There is power of disposition when people do not commit sins, and there is no power of disposition unless they perform good works.

(180) They held this too: That man is most fortunate who mixes this thing of the material world, which is transient, with that which is intransient, so that when he passes away from the material world he may become of the spiritual world.

(181) They held this too: In religion there are four sayings which are of much substance. These are: Not to reproach a sinner for a sin; not to praise a deceitful man for the sake of authority and wealth; to seek the reward of good deeds from the spirits; and to be a disciple. The most important is to be a disciple, for all those too become known through being a disciple.

(198) They held this too: When the spirit of lust and greed comes into the body of a man and displays to him the desire for material things, this stratagem is best, that the man should display to himself the transience of the body and of material things and that he should think: 'It is useful (?) when it is done. But what should I do if I have to abandon it soon? From now on I shall not do it, so that the disgrace which ensues from [that] should not reach me.' For with material things, it is much easier when they are not done than to abandon them.

(199) They held this too: A man of wisdom is one who keeps in mind everywhere the end of material things.

(210) They held this too: A man who stands in faith for the sake of the gods and the soul alone, and the thing by which he stands is not the religion and the way of the gods, the gods do even this act of favour to him, that they turn his head towards the religion and the path of the gods.

(213) They held this too: The soul of men never stands in one place, for it always only increases or diminishes. They said that 'increasing' and 'diminishing' is this: as long as a man has the desire of the soul, the soul increases. When he has the desire of the body, the soul diminishes.

(229) They held this too: The fruit of material things is a meal; the fruit of a meal is the preservation of the body; the fruit of the body is the [soul], the fruit of the soul is the future body, the fruit of the future body is intransient joy that always is and always will be.

(230) They held this too: The coming of the divine spirits from the spiritual into the material world is first at the fire of Warhrān and later in other places.

(231) They held this too: When heretics come to the religion and raise controversy over the existence or non-existence of the religion and the gods, no other person should go under his own leadership to the debate and speak anything except a priest whose duty it is and who is capable of speaking in such a way as to save himself and defeat the heretic. Other people can go only if they are sought and asked to do so. If anyone speaks (against this rule), mischief ensues and the man himself has to atone for it. When, however, a man is sought and asked (to speak), he ought to speak truthful things even to a ... (?). Anyone who does not is under guilt.

(236) They held this too: Never depart from the things of the gods in your thoughts. A man ought to be attached to them in such a manner that he should never think a sinful thing in his mind. For death comes to men at every hour, and fear only at that time when, upon the coming of death, the man thinks something sinful, even in such a manner that he becomes an enemy of the soul before he

becomes a doer of righteousness. For as long as the man thinks good deeds and righteousness the gods stay in his body and the demons are made powerless and depart, and when he thinks sinful things the demons rush into his body. If the man dies, and the demons at that hour are in his body, it is harder for the soul, and it is later more difficult for the gods to snatch that body from the hands of the demons than it would be for a man himself to make the demons powerless over his body in the material world.

(239) They held this too: The life of the soul is from righteous habit, the life of habit is from character, the life of character is from love of people. When a man is capable in all other good things, but his character is bad, there is no life to the soul of that man because of his action.

(240) They held this too: The life of wisdom is from patience, the life of religion is from truthfulness, the life of consciousness is from the worship of the gods in awe, the life of worship is from the ritual, the life of the ritual is from a (religious) authority, the life of authority is from association with religion through love.

(241) They held this too: A man who does not believe in spiritual things is much under guilt. For there is no salvation to a man who has not heard a thing in this world, unless a man has no doubt concerning spiritual things at least in so far, (namely:) 'All manners of things exist.'

(250) They held this too: A man who desires to be wise should first do this, namely: he should be reverent towards the gods, he should associate with the wise and he should always make his mind peaceful, as if he has eaten a sweet food, and he should always keep his body under guard so that the demons do not become victorious and ruling over his body.

(251) They held this too: A man who is reverent towards the gods is one who does not do a thing, either small or great, without consulting good people.

(252) They held this too: That friend is best: a man who takes his own soul as a friend, and who does not abandon it either in abundance or in destitution. That authority is best, a man who takes his own mind as authority, and who never departs from (its) authority. That shelter is best, a man who makes his character into a shelter and who never departs from (its) shelter.

(261) They held this too: The substance of religion is like a mirror; when a man looks at it he sees himself in it. This is in the following manner: a man who knows how to look sees all goodness and evil in it.

(262) They held this too: There are many kinds of masculinity and femininity. Masculinity and femininity are even this: innate wisdom and acquired wisdom. Acquired wisdom occupies the place of the masculine, and innate wisdom occupies the place of the feminine. As much as there is in the body of innate wisdom, there is; every thing that is known is known by innate wisdom. A man who has obtained no acquired wisdom knows nothing. When he has obtained it, whatever he knows is by character and innate wisdom. Innate wisdom without acquired wisdom is

like a female without a male, who does not conceive and does not bear fruit. A man who possesses [acquired] wisdom, but whose innate wisdom is not perfect, is like a female who is not receptive to a male; for a female who is not receptive to a male does not bear fruit in the same manner as one who does not have a male in the first place.

(273) They held this too: A man who does everything for the sake of the gods alone, in whatever manner he does it he is righteous by it.

(274) They held this too: People who do not adhere to the religion of the gods are of two kinds: One, a deceiver, and one, a deceived one. A deceiver is a man who knows by himself that what he is doing should not be done: he does it out of greed and bodily desire. A deceived one is a man who believes that what he is doing stands in righteousness, and he is doing it for the sake of the soul. Every deceiver is *druwand*; a deceived one may even be *ahlaw*.

(285) They held this too: People should be diligent so that they may join their bodily desire to the soul. For a man whose bodily desire is joined to the soul, religion is with his body; and a man the desire [of whose soul] is joined to the body, has demons joined to his soul.

(318) They held this too: One ought to live in the world without sin and in harmony. For the thing consists of these two (elements): one is the body and one is the soul.

(323) They held this too: It is necessary to direct a man's soul mostly to these three places: the houses of sages, the houses of good people, and the houses of fire. To the houses of sages, so that he may become wiser and that the religion may dwell more in his body; to the houses of good people, so that he may be aware of good and evil and that evil may be carried away from him; to the houses of fire, so that the spiritual demon may turn away from him.

(324) They held this too: The religion is bound to the sacred word and is in harmony with it in the same way as flesh is with skin and as a vein is with its enveloping hide.

(C53) This too is thus: From humility there comes about knowledge of the gods; from knowledge of the gods there comes about faith in the spiritual world; from faith in the spiritual world there comes about love of the soul; from love of the soul there comes about being of good disposition (?); from being of good disposition (?) there comes about the doing of good deeds; from doing good deeds the soul is justified.

(C54) This too is thus: From arrogance there comes about lack of knowledge of the gods; from lack of knowledge of the gods, lack of faith in the spiritual world; from lack of faith in the spiritual world, lack of possession of soul; from lack of possession of soul, lack of good disposition; from lack of good disposition there comes about the committing of sins and offences; because of committing sins and offences people come to be wicked.

(C75) This too is thus: From knowledge of the religion there comes about consideration of the sacred word; from consideration of the sacred word there comes about increase of (one's) calling in religion and worship of the gods; from increase of the calling in religion and of the worship of the gods, the elimination of the demons from the world; from the elimination of the demons from the world there comes about immortality, the Renovation and the Resurrection.

(C76) This too is thus: From lack of knowledge of the religion people turn to demon-worship and idolatry; because of demon-worship and idolatry the demons are in the world, [and because of the fact that the demons are in the world] there comes about death and calamity.

(C77) This too is thus: A man who surrenders himself to the gods and good people, this much goodness inhabits his body and he is guilty of fault and evil (only) by accident.

(C83b) The material world is governed by these six things: Time, instruction (?), knowledge, help, power and effort. The wise have decreed that of these six, three are of the spiritual and three are of the material world: time, instruction (?), and knowledge are of the spiritual world, and help, power and effort are of the material world.

(D1b) A man who performs the worship of the gods with certainty as to the gods and with (faith in) the reality of the thing, is a son of the gods and his place is in the highest heaven.

A man who performs the worship of the gods with (faith in) the existence of the gods but with doubt as to the thing, is a brother of the gods and his place is in Paradise.

A man who performs the worship of the gods with doubt as to the gods and with doubt as to the thing, is a slave of the gods and his place is in the Middle Region.

A man who performs the worship of the gods with the thought that the gods do not exist and that the thing does not exist, is an enemy of the gods and his place is in Hell.

(D7d) Ādurbād said this too: Come hither, so that you may make yourselves worthy, for happy is he who is worthy. The gods, besides, know the benefit; they know how it is most seemly for a good thing to be done to a person, in the material or in the spiritual world; they contemplate and assess, and assign the reward of the worthy to the place where it is best to assign it to, for both worlds belong to them, the material and the spiritual. For this reason there is always satisfaction to a worthy man.

(E1) It has been said: When a man has disciplined his character and surrenders himself to the gods in obedience, from that time on the gods guard and maintain him like a man who has a promising calf, who ties a cord around its horn and leads it to tilled fields, letting it forth in places where there is pasture and keeping it away from places where there is harm.

(E2) It has been said: Every person must look into himself at least three times every day (and enquire): 'Who is with me, a god or a demon?' If a god is with him he ought to make him to dwell more in himself, and if a demon is with him he ought to make him powerless over him.

(E13) It has been said: One is not a little and a thousand is not much. 'One' is spiritual things; 'a thousand' is material things.

(E14) It has been said: In taking care of material things a thousand rituals are nothing. In taking care of spiritual things one ritual is that (very) thing.

(E15) It has been said: A thousand men cannot cause one man to believe by words in such a way as one man can cause a thousand men by action.

(E16) It has been said: A man who is an excessive adorner of the material world becomes a destroyer of the spiritual world. For this reason it is necessary to take the material world in measure to such an extent (only) that the spiritual world should not be destroyed. When the wise men, i.e. the ancient learned men, considered and saw the transience of material things and the permanence of spiritual things, it seemed to them reasonable when material things are being taken care of, except that which it is not possible to take care of in measure, provided that the person does not cause harm and destruction to the spirit. One ought to relinquish material things which are in excess of the measure, so that one should not lose, because of the delusion of the material world, that which is better than material things.

(E22b) He said this too: A man who does not neglect this does not grasp that; and a man who does not see that does not neglect this. 'This' is the material world and 'that' is the spiritual world.

(E28) They said: An authority said: Just as repentance cleanses the soul of every sin, so does contentment mainly keep the fierce demon away from the soul.

(E30a) It has been said: One should be a person who suppresses complaint, a man of patience, diligent in doing good works, who seeks gratitude from the spirits, not from material beings.

When a thing comes about the remedy of which, for the love of the soul, is to be happy (?) in poverty, one should willingly step into poverty, because the comfort of the body and the security and freedom from Reckoning for the soul occur from it. That man can step into poverty who derives more joy from things of least substance necessary for the preservation of the body than from those of most substance. A man who is not like this cannot step into poverty. A man who steps into poverty not out of constraint but for the sake of the benefit which accrues from it, drives out of the world, for his own part, Ahriman and his misbegotten creatures. There cannot be in him at any moment anything which (leads to) the damnation of the soul and the ill-fame of the body.

(E31d) A man should be contrite and repentant of every sin and offence committed during his lifetime with the following thought: 'I shall not do this again.'

(E38c) It is possible to save the soul best by these several things: by gratitude, contentment and tenderness.

(E38d) It is necessary to have reverence for the gods, so that if a calamity has come, they will save (the man) from it, and if it has not come, less may come to him. The reason why the gods are eternal is that they benefit each other, and the reason why the demons will be destroyed is that they deceive each other. The Evil Spirit first deceived himself, and then his creatures, because from what he thought, did and is doing his own end and the destruction of his creatures will come about. Whatever a man is doing, if it does not increase the soul, or does not diminish it, all of it is a matter of inclination (?).

(E39) It has been said: A person sees that which he contemplates, and hears that which he listens to, and finds that which he seeks. A man who contemplates the spiritual world when the work of the material world is in his hands, his spirit is ineffective, with the exception of one (man) in one or two places.

(E45c) A man who has memorized the whole Avesta with Zand and does not know these five ritual formulae even with labour (?), should not be allowed to sit in the place of priests and to issue orders: 'upwardness' and 'downwardness' of an object; 'beforeness' and 'afterwardness' of a thing: 'greatness' and 'smallness' of a work: 'way' and 'passage' of a speech; 'escape' and 'inevitability' of poverty.

'Upwardness' is the consideration of the spiritual world; 'downwardness' is the consideration of the material world. 'Beforeness' is disciplining one's character; 'afterwardness' is inquiring with wisdom. 'Greatness' is storing up the religion; 'smallness' is doing good deeds. 'The way' is consultation; 'the passage' is listening. 'Escape' is striving and acting according to the measure; 'inevitability' is contentment and humility.

(E45d) A man who considers (the following) ten things not together but separately is not a follower of the ancient faith but a heretic: the spiritual world and the material world; the body and the soul; innate wisdom and acquired wisdom; action and fate; religion and the sacred word.

(E45g) The root of religion, in summary, is this: The root is Ohrmazd and all goodness is from him. A cognizant person is one who is always satisfied. That man is always satisfied who is always aware. That man is always aware whose thoughts, speech and actions are all from the gods.

(E45n) (The following question) was asked: 'Is goodness better or (mental) powers?' (The following) was said (in reply): 'Since (mental) powers are necessary for goodness, one ought to know that a man who has made goodness his own is a man who possesses great (mental) powers.

Part II

Early Persian Philosophy: Manichaeism

Introduction

Manichaeism is the name of the third-century Iranian religion founded by Mani (216–277 CE). Generally regarded to be a gnostic religion, Manichaeism incorporated many of the features of Christianity, Zoroastrianism and Hinduism as well as other indigenous Iranian religions. Within a century, it had spread both to the East towards India and to the West where it became one of the major religions of the Roman Empire. Traces of this religion can be found as far as Algiers.

Mani is believed to have been born near the ancient Persian city of Ctesiphon to an affluent family. His mother Maryam, was related to the Arsacid dynasty and his father was a prominent religious figure and a patriarch of the Ekesaite Mughtasilist cult, a mysterious gnostic sect with Christian tendencies, and a devotee of an obscure figure by the name Elkesai. At the age of four Mani was initiated into a baptismal group and when he was twelve he claimed to have received a revelation. The angel of revelation whom Mani called 'the twin' commanded him to leave this group and when he was twenty-four the angel of revelation appeared to him again commanding him to begin his public mission by preaching the revealed doctrine.

As is often the case, the new message was not received well by the traditional authorities even though Mani had incorporated many elements of the existing faith into his doctrine. The major point of contention may have been over Mani's interpretation of what true baptism means. Traditional authorities emphasized the ritual of baptism as having the power of cleansing but Mani put the emphasis on asceticism and argued that redemptive purity comes from the actual separation from matter, which he equated with darkness and evil.

Advocating that Truth is perennial, he argued that other prophets such as the Buddha, Zoroaster and Jesus had spoken the truth but their message was contaminated. Having declared himself the seal of prophets, Mani proclaimed that he had come to restore the truth that lies at the heart of all the divinely revealed religions. In this respect, Manichaeism was the final revelation intended for humanity.

Mani and his ardent followers devoted themselves to the task of propagating the new faith by travelling and advocating the teachings of the new religion. Mani himself is one of the few founders of a new faith who during his own lifetime composed the revealed sacred scripture. He composed seven works in the Aramaic language: *The Living Gospel, The Treasure of Life, The Pragmateia, The Book of Mysteries, The Book of Giants, The Letters* and *The Psalms and Prayers*. In addition to these works that are considered to be the canons of Manichaeism, Mani wrote Shāpūrgān, which according to some scholars is also a canonical work, perhaps as a replacement for *The Psalms and Prayers*. To this day, no complete text of any of these works has been found and what we do know comes from the many quotations found in such works as the *Acta Archelai*, the writings of Muslim authors Bīrūnī and Ibn Nadīm and of St. Augustine of Hippo.

Mani may have been inspired by Thomas the apostle who is said to have travelled to India to preach his faith, and he decided to go East. It was there that he converted Tūrān-Shāh, the Buddhist king of Tūrān and a large number of his courtiers to Manichaeism. Returning from Tūrān, Mani journeyed through Persia, Susiana and Mesene where he had some success in propagating his religion. Following the death of Ardashīr I, his son Shāpūr I who was known for his tolerance towards other religions provided Mani with an opportunity to promulgate his ideas freely. Mani met with Shāpūr I and was allowed to preach his religion throughout the empire resulting in the conversion of not only Shāpūr's own family but many important courtiers and the masses as well. Under the patronage of the emperor Mani decided to compose a synopsis of his teachings in Middle Persian titled *Shāpūrgān* which he dedicated to Shāpūr himself. Mani accompanied Shāpūr in numerous military campaigns and was at the battle of Edessa in 260 CE when the Roman emperor Valerian was captured by the Persians.

Mani's popularity and his success in converting people alarmed the traditional Zoroastrian high priests who decided to conspire against him. After Shāpūr's death, his successors, Hurmuz and Bahrām were persuaded by the high priest Kardar to persecute Manichaeans. Mani was arrested and brought to Gundīshāpūr where he was interrogated for a month by Kardar. It was there that Mani was put to death.

Manichaean Texts

Major discoveries have been made during the twentieth century with regard to Manichaean texts. These sources can be categorized into four divisions: Central Asian and Chinese, Greek, Latin and Coptic.[1] A detailed consideration of these sources goes beyond the scope of our work here but suffice it to say that these new discoveries have provided us with a wealth of information about Manichaeism.

1. For more information see *The Gnostic Bible*, Boston, 2003.

We have selected a number of passages from the *Kephalaia* (Greek for 'Central Principles') with a short commentary of Iain Gardner that places the writings in their proper context showing the salient features of Manichaeism.

The *Kephalaia* is a complex work that claims to be the verbatim teachings of Mani. It is, however, clear that it is a work that has evolved as terminologies and concepts changed from an earlier state. We are not concerned here with the accuracy of the materials and the extent to which they are actually Mani's; rather we have included selections from this text because it is considered part of the sacred literature of the Manichaean tradition and possesses at the same time philosophical significance. Some of the elements and motifs of later Persian philosophical thought can be found in these pages which discuss such topics as light and darkness, morality, asceticism, the duality of spirit and body, cosmology, creation and primordial essences. These are themes that have left their mark on the intellectual life of Iran throughout later centuries.

Blocks and brackets are incorporated by the translator and commentator to facilitate the reading of the text.

Mehdi Aminrazavi

7

Central Principles
The *Kephalaia*

Reprinted from Iain Gardner, *The Kephalaia of the Teacher: The Edited Coptic Manichaean Texts in Translation with Commentary* (Leiden, 1995), pp. 27–28, 31–33, 49–50, 86–87, 133–134, 200–202, 209–216, 266, 288–289.

Chapter 3 (23, 14–25, 6)

The Interpretation of Happiness, Wisdom and Power; what they signify,

Mani contrasts true happiness, wisdom and power to their perceived meaning in the world. In a schema that will be repeated throughout the Kephalaia, these principles are successively identified with the various levels of divinity (here five) as it descends into time and the universe.

Thus the archetypes are the great Gods in the eternal kingdom, untouched by the conflict with darkness; reflected then in the first evoked gods who have entered into time for the purpose of redemption, and who inhabit the two ships (the sun and moon), which can be regarded as the gateways to eternity for the purified light; then the divine elements and subsidiary gods who have descended into the mixed universe; and finally the human members of the church.

[Once again the enlightener speaks into his disciples, while / he sits in the assembly of the church: What are these three things that in the world are called 'happin[ss', 'wisdom]', and 'power'? People boa[s]t of th[em / …] the happiness of the world [… / …] in the world is has a [… / …] of the world shall pass by. /

[People boa]st of them. They praise [… / …] Now, [the] thing is revealed in a [… / …] as I have told you. /

[I will t]each you of another happiness [… / and another wi]sdom […] and together another power […] / So, now, listen that I may reveal to you [how] it is [with] these three: [ha/pines], wisdom and power. /

[The happin]ess of the glorious one is the Father, the God of / [truth, who] is established in the great land of [light]. (24) His glorious wis[d]om is his Great Spirit that [… / …] below, which flows through all his aeons, / and t[h]ey float therein. His great power is all the / gods, the rich ones and the angels who were summoned from him as they […] t/hey that are called aeons [… / … /

… / which is called] the sun [… the ship of] living fire, […the Third / Amba]ssador, the second greatne[ss … The] / glorious

[happiness] is the [Living] Spirit, [… / … the wisdom] is the Mother of Lif[e … / … and great power] is [all] the gods, [the rich o]nes and the angels who are within the ship. /

Again, [h]appiness, wisdom and power exist in the s[hip of liv/ing waters …] the happiness [… / …] the Mind of the Father. / Also, wisdom [is the Vir/gi]n of [Li]ght. And the power that is [i]n the ship is [all] the go[ds], the [ri]ch ones and the angels who are established i[n it].

Again, these three exist in the elements: happiness, wis/d[o]m and power. The happiness is [the Pillar of Glory], / the Perfect Man. Wisdom is the [five sons of the] / Living Spirit; and great powe[r is … the fi]ve songs of the First Man [… who are encl]/osed and compounded in the totality, that […] / while he supports the totality. /

Now, moreover, happiness, wis[dom and power ex/ist] in the holy church. Great, glorious, [happiness]s is the Apostle of Light [who has been s]/ent from the Father. Wisdom [is the leaders / and] the teachers who travel in the [holy] church, [proclaim-ing] / wisdom and truth. Great [power is … (25) …] all [the] elect, the virgins and the c[ontinent; / together with the] catechumens who are in the [holy] church. /

[…] five happinesses, the five wisdoms, [a]nd five powers [… / …] in the five chur[ches]. Blessed, [therefore], is every one who will know them, for he may [… / …] the kingdom forever.

Chapter 5 (28,1–30,11)

Concerning Four Hunters of / Light and Four of Darkness

The parallel reverse imagery evident in this kephalaion *is typical of Manichaean doctrine. In this instance the powers of light and darkness are compared to hunters trawling various seas from ships and with nets. The teaching is structured in terms of the cosmic history, presupposing a prior knowledge of the entire cycle from the descent of the First Man to the ascent of the Last Statue and the everlasting death of sinners. Thus, the redeeming work of the Third Ambassador, achieved by the revelation of his image in the heavens, is prior to that of Jesus, whose net is the wisdom cast from the church.*

Once again the apostle speaks to his discipl[es]; There are four hunters who were sent from [the li]/ght to fulfill the will of the greatness. /

The first hunter is the First Man who was sen[t] / from the greatness. He threw himself down to the five storehouses / [of] d[ar]kn[ess, h]e caught and seized the enmity [... ...] his net also [.. / ...] out over all the children of darkness [... / ...] His ship is his four sons who are swathed / over his body. The sea is the la[nd of darkness ... / ...] his net is [...] and his powers.

The second [hunter is the Th]/ird Ambassador. This one, for by his [lig]ht image, / which he revealed to the depths be[low], / he hunted after the entire light that is in al[l] things; [as it is establ/i]shed in them. His net is his light image, [...] the whole universe and took it prisoner, / to this likeness [... His] / ship is his light ship. [The sea] is the universe [...] / which were hunted after by his n[et ... / ...] his [glorious] image. /

The third hunter is Je[sus the Splendour, who came from the] great/[ness], who hunts after the light and lif[e; and he ...] it / to the heights. His net is his wisdom, [the] lig[ht wisdom] / with which he hunts the souls, catching them in the n[et]. His ship is his holy church [... The sea is / the] error of the universe, the law o[f sin ...] / the souls that are drowning in it [...] He catch[es] / them in his net. They are the souls [... / th]em by his light wisdom.

[The fourth] hunter is the great counsel that [...] / that lives in the circuit [...] (29) entire universe in it today. Yet, at the end, in the dissoluti/[on] of the universe, this very counsel of life / [will] gather itself in and sculpt its soul in the / Last [St]atue. Its net is its Living Spirit, becau[se] with its Spirit it can hunt after the light and the life that is in / all [t]hings; and build it upon its body. Its ship, in which it / [is est]ablished, is this light cloud whereby it itself trav/[els] in the five elements [... / the] great fire that will burn all the buildings of [... ...] in its net is the light and the [life. It can] / rescue and free it from all bonds and fetters. /

Blessed is ev[ery] o[n]e who will be perfect in his deeds, so that / at his end [he may escap]e the great fire that is prepared for the uni/verse at [the end of] its time!

O[nc]e again he [s]peaks: As I have revealed to you the four / living hunters of light who belong to the greatness, / [I will] also [t]each you about four other evil hunters who ca/me from the darkness.

The first hunter is the King / of they who belong to the darkness, who hunted after the living soul with his net at the beginning of the worlds. His net is his fi/re and his lust that he has put upon the living soul, / with which he has entangled it [...], through all his powers. /

[The] sec[ond] h[unter i]s the evil counsel that lives in / [...] that hunts after [the] light [...] and [...] / up from [...] the earths to heaven. It binds them with / its powers, which b[ring] them to the heavenly worlds above. / [i]ts net is [...] whereby they are drawn up / [fr]om the abyss [to the heig]hts.

The third hunter is lust [...] walks in every power of the flesh that wa/[lks ...] in the [...] the living souls [... / ... t]hem in its bodies, which [.... / ... / ...]

The fourth [hunter is the spirit] of darkness, the law of sin and (30) death, that rules in every sect. It hunts after the so[ul]/s of people and entangles them with this erroneo[us] teaching. / Then it drives them to eternal punishment. It[s] / net, whereby it hunts souls to death, is its erroneous teaching full of guile and villainy / and wicked turns. It imprisons foolish people wi[th] / its teaching, subduing them under its net and co[mpelling them to] eternal punishment.

Blessed is e[very] one [w]/ho will recognize these evil hunters through know[ledge, and it will s]ave and free them from their bond and fetter [for ever] and ever!

Chapter 11 (43, 22 –44, 18)

Concerning the Interpretation of] all [the] Fathers of / [Light], who are distinguished from one another.

Summary of the characteristics of principal divinities; perhaps for catechetical instruction.

[Onc]e again [the enlig]htener speaks: Happen you know, / [m]y beloved ones, that [the begin]ing of every good grace is the / [gr]eat Father of the [ligh]ts; since [a]ll [graces] are given by his hand. /

The beginning of each blessing and every prayer / is the Mother of [L]ife, the first Holy Spirit.

Also, [the] beginning [of] every good [co]unsel is the T[h/i]rd Am[bassad]or, the king of the glorious realm that lies in this / [wo]rld, [...] of the King of the lights.

The beginning of / [... and] each [hono]ur (?) is the Beloved of the Lights, who is honour/[ed.

The beginning of a]ll [the trappers] and hunters is the First [Man.

... of] all fighters is (44) [the] Living [Spirit], the Father of Life, who has distribu[ted about] / his five sons from place to place.

The beginning of all the archit[e]/cts and builders is the Great Builder, who is glo/rious.

Also, the first of all the porters of the gr[e]a[tness is the Pillar of Glory ... / ...]

The beginning of [all] the delivers [is Jesus the Splendour]; / or the one who delivers, as he frees whoever belongs [...] / from his words.

The beginning of every wisdom of / truth is the Virgin of Light, [...]

[The beginning of] all [the great]est honored ones [...] / is the Light Mind; who is the awakene[r of they] / who sleep, the gatherer in of the ones who are sc[att]ered. /

Blessed is he who shall lodge this treasure within hi[m, and] fasten [the knowledge] / of these fathers in his heart! For they a[re] the [root (?) of] all the lights, and such as belong to all life; as […] / of all souls besides them.

Blessed is he who wi[ll kn]/ow them, and continue in their belief, that he may inh/erit with them eternal life for ever.

Chapter 31 (84, 5 –85, 18)

Concerning the Summons, / in which Limb / of the Soul it descended to the First Man. /

This chapter discusses the relationship between the First Man, who was saved from the abyss by the Living Spirit; and his limbs or sons, the living soul that is scattered throughout the material universe. The summons is the call to salvation, and together with the answer or obedience it forms the counsel of life. This is the active will for redemption that drives the soul (see 178.1 – 5).

Mani shows that the First Man is the head upon which the soul depends for its life. Although hidden in this time and space, his presence is still with us in his image and love which is the virginal soul. The Man gathers in the soul, and builds it up, so that as his trunk it eschatologically ascends back to the land of light. This trunk is the Pillar of Glory which reunites with the First Man at its head. At the end of time it is the Last Statue.

Once again one of the teachers questioned the enlightener. He says to h[im]: In which limb of [the liv]i[ng] sou[l] did [the] summons descend / [to] the Man, who exists in the [a]eon? F[o]r it is written in / the [s]criptures about the Man that he spread himself through the […] / aeon as to a wooden house.

The [enli]ghtener speaks: / Indeed, the First Man dispersed himself and he […] limb o[f] the living soul as I have written f[or you …] / of the living soul; he has […] he did not know [… / …] but the blessed, glorious Man c[a]me [in] / secret; in his image; in his shape; in h[i]s lo/ve; in his holy virgin, she who is the v[ir]gin of light, the soul of the father. /

After the fashion of this fleshly body; as the root of / all the lim[bs] hang upon the head, so that should one of / the person's limbs be cut off, while the head exists he has hope for […] / but if his head should be cut off, the entir[e] body [w]ill d[ie] and he is lost.

This is also the case for the Firs[t] Ma[n]. / He is the head, while his sons attach to it the l[i]mbs [of] / his soul. Or, conversely, like the l[i]ving air, on [w]/hich all flesh entirely lives as it breathes an[d …] / therein. His head is placed on the body of the Pill[ar] of Gl]ory in the heights of the universe.

[This i]s also the case [for] / the father, the blessed Man; as he is like the he[ad that is upon the] / body and the air that upon the Pillar is set I[n …] / being made strong by his l[ight] virgin, [she] who is / his soul that he clothes […] (85) t[h]ose

[...]: the mind, thought, insight, counsel and / c[on]sideration that he produced and sent forth from / hi[m to] do his will. He sprang and travelled behind them. / [...] of his living soul, which is entwined among the revels; as they are like the limbs of its body, and / [...] universe.

And when they were sent, / at [that ti]m[e] he was found with the Virgin of [Lig/ht an]d [he] stood up, asking and entreating for a p[o]wer. / [... he] gave him peace and a ki[ss ...] he [gave] him goo[d] tidings / [... M]an. The Man him[s]elf gave [his / ...h]is limbs and gathered his soul i[n / ...] he built it in its place like this to[w]er / [...] shaped it and beautified it skillfully [... ...f]or[m ...] the voices that he se[n]t / [... he] might sink in and [q]uench [... / ...] so[u]l that was crushed by the enemy. They were gathered in. They came, / [s]et firm onc[e] more, in the image of their father.

Chapter 50 (125, 25 – 126, 29)

Concerning these Na[mes]: God, Rich One, / and Ange[l]; who they are. /

The many divine emanations in the Manichaean system exist at various levels, depending upon their function in the overall history, and on the directness of their evocation from the supreme Father. In this kephalaion Mani distinguishes the three categories of 'god', 'rich one' and 'angel'.

He then applies these to three distinct movements: the archetypes in the eternal land of light; the emanations who have entered into time and the cosmos; and those who belong to the households of the Great Spirit, the Beloved of the Lights, and the Ambassador. This last sequence is probably intended eschatologically, these being principal figures in the three series of emanations: descent, creation and redemption.

[Onc]e again the enlightener speaks: This one, a name is given to him in / the world. For people pronounce it with their mouths: 'go[d', 'ri]ch one', and 'angel'. Who are they? Who are the gods? Or / [who] are the rich ones? Or who are the angels? Who are these / [three] archetypes?

His disciples asked him. They say: T/[ell] us, our master, who they are! /

[The a]postle [speaks] to them: There are these three archetypes [in the land of light, and there is no measure to] them!

[So], the ones who are call[ed] (126) 'god', are the gods whom the Father has summoned / from himself. He has establ[ished them] after the likeness / of his greatness.

Conversely, these who are named / 'rich [...]', are the evocations of the right ri[ch] gods [of] the Father; because, when the Father had summoned (the first), / they themselves summoned evocations. They called them / 'rich'.

They too, the rich ones, have summoned their / evocations. They call them 'angel'.

These are the three / [archety]pes who occur in the land of light. There is no measure to apply to them!

Once again, listen! Other persons / who are named 'god' are the emanations who have / come f[r]om the Father; the evocations of the Father whom he summoned forth. / They came out to the contest and humiliated the enmity. /

Conversely, the 'rich ones' are [the ev]ocations of these first living words. They too, the rich ones, have come and performed and fulfilled the plea/sure of the greatness; [in the] worlds that are above and / below.

On the other hand, the ones who are named the 'ange/ls' are the evocations of the rich ones; who had come from the three / living words. They have been sent in an embassy and an apostolate to this building. They have come to the entire divinity, / which is established in silence and in hiddenness. [An]/d, also, they have come to all the souls who have been entangled in the en[emy]. / They have brought them hope and confidence.

On[ce again] / the enlightener speaks: Again, they are called 'go[d]', all the gods who belong to the household of the Great Spirit. /

Conversely, the ones who are called 'angel', are al[l] the rich ones who belong to the house[hold of the] glorious [Amb]/assador.

Chapter 79 (191, 9 – 192, 3)

Concerning the Fasting of the Saints.

Once more the enlightener speaks to his disciples. The fa/sting that the saints fast by is profit[able] / for [four] great works.

The first work: S[hall] / the holy man punish his body by fasting, [he sub]dues the entire ruling-power that exists in him. /

The second: The soul that come in [to] him in the adm[ini]/stration of his food, day by day; it shall be made holy, [cl]/eansed, purified, and w[ash]ed from the adulteration [of] / the darkness that is mixed in with it.

The third: Th[at] person shall make every deed a holy one; / the mystery of [the children] of light [i]n whom there is neither corruption / nor [...] the food, nor wound it. / [Rat]her, they are holy, [there is nothing] in them that defiles, as they li/[ve] in peace.

The fourth: They make a [... ...] the Cross, they restrain their hands from the hand / [... not] destroy the living soul. /

[The] fasting is profitable to the saints for these four great / [wo]rks should they persist; that is if they are constant in th/[em] daily, and cause the body to make all its [memb]ers to fast [with a] holy [fa]st. /

[...] faith: They who have not strength / [to fast d]aily should make their fast (192) [on] the lord's day. They too make a contribution [to the wor/ks] and the fasting of the saints by their faith and their / alms.

Chapter 80 (192, 3 – 193, 22)

The Chapter of the Commandments of Righteousness.

Summary of essential precepts held by the elect and the catechumens; arranged in two sets of two (by three).

The first righteousness of the elect has three parts: to refrain from all sexual activity; to take great care not to harm the light soul trapped everywhere in matter and especially vegetation (the Cross of Light), for instance by plucking fruit; and not to consume meat or alcohol (192.8 – 13). These correspond to the three seals of mouth, hands and breast discussed by Augustine (signacula oris, manuu, et sinus, mor. Manich. VII, 10; IX, 18); and also referred to in eastern Manichaean texts.

The second: to multiply wisdom, faith and grace.

The first righteousness of the catechumenate: fasting, prayer and almsgiving. The catechumens had to support the elect who could do no labour, farming or cooking.

The second: to give someone to the church; to share in their good works; to construct something. The catechumens were allowed to marry and procreate, but were expected to compensate in this way.

[Once more] the enlightener speaks to his disciples: Know [and] / understand that the first righteousness a per[son] / will do to make truly righteous is this: he can embra/[ce] continence and purity. And he can also acquire 'the rest [of the] hands', so that he will keep his hand still before the Cross of Li[gh/t]. The third is purity of the mouth, so that he will / keep his mouth pure of all flesh and blood; and not take any taste / at all of the 'wine' name, nor fermented drink. This is the fir/[st] righteousness. If a person will do it in his bo[dy], he is pronounced righteous by all mankind. /

Then, the second righteousness that he should do is this: / He can add to it [...] wisdom and faith so that / [...] from his wisdom he can give wisdom, to every person who will he/ar it from him. And also from his faith he can give faith, [to th]ese who belong to the faith. >From hi[s grace] he can give freely / of love, shower it upon them, that he might join them to him. / For, when that one acquires a great riches [...] / in righteousness. By this second godliness / he may cause others to be sent, resembling him in [righteous]ness.

Just as this righteous one should fulfill the se/cond and become a perfect elect; so too, / if the catechumen shall be a catechu/men of the faith, he is perfect in two stages.

The first work of the catechumenate that he does is fasting, prayer, and almsgiving. Now, the fa[stin]/g b[y] which he can fast is [thi]is: / he can fast on the [lord]'s day [and rest from the] / deeds of the world. [And] the pra[yer is this]: (193) he can pray to the sun and the moon, the great li[ght-givers. The alms]/giving also is this: he can place it [...] / in the holy one, and give it to them in righteous[ness ...] /

[The] second work of the catechumena[te that he] does is this: A person will give a child to the [ch]/urch for the (sake of) righteousness, or his relative [or member]

/ of the household; or he can rescue someone beset by troub[le; or] / buy a slave, and give him for righteousness. Accordingly, every [go]/od he might do, namely this one whom he gave as a fit [for righ]teousness; that catechumen [...] / will share in with them. Thirdly: / A person will build a dwelling or construct some pl[ace]; / so they can become for him a portion of alms in the holy ch[urch]. /

If the catechumen shall ful[fill] these three great works, these three great alm[s that he] / gives as a gift for the h[oly] church [...] / which these alms will achieve. Also, that cate[chu]men / himself, who gave them, he can [... / ...] as he shares in them. The catechumens who will give [...] have great lo[ve ther]ein, and a share of eve[ry] grace / and good in the holy church. They will find many / graces.

Chapter 83 (200, 9 – 204, 23)

Concerning the Man who is ug[l]y / in his Body, [but] beautiful / [in his Soul].

This chapter begins with a touching story about how Mani publicly embraces one of the elect, despite his deformity, in front of the assembled congregation who are laughing at his ugliness. It is the inner new man, formed by the Light Mind and religious practice, that is of lasting value.

This then leads Mani to develop an extended parable about pearls in their shells (the living soul in the physical body), pearl divers (the apostles), and traders (the sun and the moon). Mani like Jesus frequently used parables for effective teaching, and this motif of the pearl without price has an obvious heritage stemming from the Gospels through early Syriac Christian literature.

However, one distinctive feature of Mani's teaching was his desire to combine religious truths with total scientific knowledge, in order to establish a complete and integrated understanding of the world. Thus this parable begins with a lengthy discourse on the formation of pearls and their shells. While such features are of great historical interest for modern scholars, they did make Manichaeism a rather static religion, its teachings too easily undercut by advances in science.

[Once] again it happened one time, while the apost[l]e is [sitting among / a] great gathering, as some [... be]fore [the] teachers and elders [... / ...] by the leaders and first citi[zens]. Now, he / [is s]itting down in their midst. All of a su[dden] one / of the elect came in to his presence, but no[t ... / ... he] is an elect [... ...] his commandments. He is an ugly [man] in his / [bod]y, having [... / ...] in his midriff; but he is perfec[t in] his [h]oly righteousness[s]. / He is a man who is upright in his truthfulness[s. /

W]hen he came in, he spread himself on the ground and paid hom[age b]efore the apostle in love. The mass[es o/f] well-born men and free women cast their [ey/e]s about and saw that elect crying o/ut in his joy, exulting loudly and giving praise. When [they] / looked and saw him, ugly or body, havin[g], they

[a]ll mocked him and [sc/of]fed at him. They were speaking to one another a[bout him] / with laughter and scorn [... but the laugh]/ter did not trouble [that] ele[ct. (201) He was paying hom]age all the time, giving praise [... / ...] the glorious one stood u[p / from the ju]dgement seat; where he is s[itt]ing. He drew and gathered him [in / to him], and hugged him to his body, kiss[ing] that elect. He sat do[wn / ...]

And [when] he had sat upon his judgment seat [... / ...] with the entire congregation of well-born men a[nd] / free women sitting before him. He says to them: W[h]/y do you laugh at this man, in whom the [Lig]ht Mind and belief dwell? For what reason a[re you / g]aping at a person who is ugly of body [... / ...] in front of you because of the flesh [... / ...] outwardly; yet within great is [... / ...] is like a great [... ...] if he has no worth by his deeds, by [his / p]rayer and fasting and humility. He is like [a] / sharp [k]nife that might devour its [... / ...] its humiliations [...] that you see [... / ...] he destroys [...] and [... ...] while the [o]ld man [... / ...] you [...] he sculpts [... / ...] he is perfect in his limbs [... / ...] a young royal child, who is beautif[ul ... / ...] shape, as the beauty and loveliness is despoiled [... ...] the image that is fixed outwardly [... / ...] and is displayed and unveiled to you. / Its heart would not bear you to laugh at this old man [... / ...] because whoever will laugh at him possesses a g[reat / sin] be[f]ore God. For the [saviour] says: [He who sha]res something with these least of the faithful, who [... / ...] their angels see the face of the Father daily.

(202) [...] all heard these words [that the apost/le] uttered about this elect [... / ...] they gazed at him, he [... / ...] and he was in their presence like the [... ...] truth, when its worth is perfected [... / ...] upon him. When they were settled, they sat [... / w]hile his disciples stand.

They [paid homage, saying] / to him: Tell us, our master, [... / ...] how (pearls) came about and were formed in [the s]e[a ...]

The enlightener said to them: Pearls shall ar/[ise not] in every place in the sea, nor be formed / [in the s]ea as a whole. Rather, in various places that are in this s/[ea]. Pearls are formed in them [... / ...] that [sea, in which]h the [pearls] shall be formed [...] this [... / ...] what the sea shall [... / ...] its fire (blazes) above and comes [down ... / ...] and it makes foam like the drop of water that flows / [...] down in rainwater [... ...] is the water [... / ... d]own first [... / ...] foam and comes down [... / ...] the sweet waters [... / ...] the waters. This drop of water shall [... d]own to the sweet waters and [...] / and they absorbed them and were combined with the [... They did not / d]escend to the depths of the sea, but they [... / ...] it floated on the surface of the waters [... / ...] to it. The foam and the pearl-shell shall be formed [... ...] this wholesome drop [... / ...] it, and it becomes a pe[arl ...] / that makes a drop of rainwater [...] / waters [...] (203) it not being whole. It breaks and separates out into [m]any droplets, / and it has time to becomes a drop of sweet water [...] / and comes up in the sea of [...] rain / [a]nd sweet water; and it is accommodated in the shell, which at first is foam. They shall be joined with each other at [this] / time, and are shaped and become a great pea[rl], / a great and valued kind. When, however, a / drop of rainwater falls, and that drop / breaks into many droplets and various {particles of water}, they shall be formed into and be confined in [n]umerous pearls; / in the shell and the pearl-shell. One might [for]/m two pearls, another may form three, / others may form five; some mould more than t/hese, so[me] fewer.

Now, when you might [find a] whole drop, and the shell receives it, it shall become a great and valued [pe]/arl as its worth is perfected. [However], if / these two droplets will have time (to adhere) to one another / before any [water particle] escapes, and they mix with e[ach / o]ther, and the shell [...] before they break into [... ...] within [...] in a great kind [... / ...] the drop of rain, which [... / ...] another one, that [... / ...] the [w]aters form them in [... and] / in a great, valued commodity.

Behold, [I have] taught you how / sea-pearls shall be formed. I have told you that as a pe/[a]rl shall come into existence by means of rainwater that has [ti]/me to become foam, the pearl-shell shall come into existence by means of the foam, a/nd the foam itself comes into being by means of the transformation and the [...] of the sea.

Then immediately at the time when [... / ...] the pearl divers know it, they shall [...] and they / [... d]own to those places [and t]hey bring pearls up from the depths of the sea, and / each pearl diver finds according to the fortunate that is / [ordai]ned for him. The pearl divers shall [gi]ve them to the traders, and the t/[ra]ders give them to the kings and the nobles.

This is also what the holy church is like. / It shall be gathered in from the living soul, / gathered up and brought to the heights, raised from the s/ea and placed in the flesh of mankind; while the flesh / of mankind itself is like the shell and the pearl-shell.

[The] booty that shall be seized is like the dr[op of / r]ainwater, while the apostles are like the divers. / The traders are the light-givers of the heavens; the kings and no/b[le]s are the aeons of greatness.

[F]o[r a]ll the souls / that ascend in the flesh of [ma]nk[ind] and are freed shall be brought back to the great aeons of light. / A place of rest comes about for them, at that place in the ae/ons of greatness.

You to[o, my] / b[elo]ved ones, struggle in every way so that you will become good pea/rls and be accounted to heaven by the light diver. He will come to you and bring [you] back to [... the] great / chief merchant, and you will rest in the life for e/[ve]r. You have [... / ...] and the light.

Chapter 84 (204, 24 – 208, 10)

Concerning Wisdom; it is far superior when on the Tongue / than in the Heart of the Person. /

Mani uses the analogies of a child who is born, and of fire that blazes from wood, to explain why wisdom is superior when it is proclaimed to when it lies silent in the heart.

However, wisdom is not always listened to, nor well-received. In a second speech Mani extends the same two analogies, showing that strangers may reject a child, and the blind cannot see the fire.

Once again, on one occasion, one of the disciples sto/od up before the apostle. He questioned him, saying: / I entreat you, my master, that you might instruct me. Behold, when a person will be taught wise wisdom / in his heart, and he seals it in his doctrine, so sh[al]l you find / him rejoicing greatly about it. However, [sh]all his [… / …] to him, more th[an] when he may proc[laim …] (205) and utter it. He shall be enlightened by it, and [t]hat [wisdom] / shall shine forth the more in him. It is unveil[ed be]/fore him, and through it he assumes power and truth.

That disciple speaks further before the a[po]stle: I understand […] / that this word I have uttered is correct. I know that the w[i]s/dom I have been taught is spread through my heart and perfected in [m]y / soul. (However), it is not found like the splendour in me, so that I regard it / [ad]vanced, except when I shall proclaim it by my mouth and utter it to others. Indeed, when / I proclaim it, I am giving it to the ears [of] / others to hear. Would I do these same things, even if I had never heard it / in [my] days of being? Would I desire greatly and [m]y / [h]eart be drawn to the wisdom I now proclaim? [I entreat y]ou, my master, that you might instruct me as to [w/hy] this wisdom becomes more advanced when I / [p]roclaim it, than when it is sealed in my heart.

Then / the apostle [s]peaks to that disciple: Well / [do] you ask! And great is this lesson for which you have sought, [that is] whence comes my great joy, on account of this wis/dom that I utter? […] it is superior in my mouth when / [I] proclaim it than when it is set in m[y heart]. / [Y]ou yourself rejoice in it; and the other one who / [h]ears it from you, he shall rejoice in it, and be enlightened [by] it and receive thereby permanent strength. /

For like this matter, just so is a small b/[o]y who is conceived in the belly of his mother. He / [… he] turns in his mother's womb, filling her womb. / [The m]other knows and understands that this child she conceives is alive within her. She rejoices over him until / [the tim]e when she gives birth. And he comes from her alive with his / [limbs whole] and perfect in beauty, without defect, (206) [in] the living open air that is more sp/[ac]ious than the first air he was in. / [He] fills his eyes with the light and speaks with his livi[ng] voice / in the way of those who are born.

Now, the time w[h]en this woman conceives the child in her belly, / her joy at conceiving him in her womb is not so [ve]ry great as / when she gives birth and sees him; and is full of his / [be]auty and stature in the space of a single moment. / [T]he love and joy over him shall be a hundred [t]imes greater than it was, now that she has given birth and seen him.

For / the first time when she conceived him in her belly, / [h]is beauty and the sight of his eyes was hidden from his m[o/th]er; but when she gave birth to him she saw his beauty. His / s[t]ature and his loveliness came before the e[ye]s of his fathe[r a]nd his mother and all his relatives. They shall rejoic[e] / over him more and more when they look upon him / face to face and see his beauty and delightfulness. /

Just as in this simile, the wisdom that is present [in] / the heart of the person is like the living child who is co[nceived] in the belly of his mother. And when he / is taught and seals it in his heart, it becomes like / the child who shall be born, and they see his beauty. /

So, in this way, the wisdom that the person proclaims, speak[ing] / it from his heart, shall be advanced more and mor[e]. Its enhancement and glory shall double from the time when the bea/uty and splendour of the saying will be displayed before the eyes [of / t]hey who hear it, and it shall also advance for you [... / ...] your hearing, and you are astonished at what you proclai[m]. /

Once again, the wisdom is like this, while it is hidden in the heart of the person. [Bef]/ore he has uttered it, it is just like [the blaze] / of fire that is hidden in wood. An[d] that wood is [set aflame] / by the blaze of the fire, but the garment of fir[e that exists in] / the wood is not apparent. Indeed, you can see [...] (207) wood and they put them in a single house. It is impossible to [put] time when they are added to the fire, and the light [comes f]/orth from them. It is possible for that entire house [to be] lit by the light of a single piece of wood. /

This is also the case with the wisdom that is in the heart of the person. [It] / is like the fire that is hidden in the wood, as its light is / not [d]isplayed. For its part, the wisdom is like this: its li/ght is hidden and its glory is hidden in the heart; but when the person will proclaim it, its glory shall be displayed be/fore the eyes and the ears of a multitude.

Once / again, for a second time this disciple speaks to the apostle: / So, if the wisdom is like the paradigms / you have taught me, why are there some people who shall hear the word of wisdom and rejoice in it and give glory / to it; when others shall listen to it and neither rejoice / [i]n it nor receive glory amongst them? /

[Beh]old, the apostle speaks to him: I will persuade you and / satisfy you about this belief, so that I teach you with clarity of vision.

For in this respect the wisdom is / like this child about whom I have told you, the one who / [was] born from the woman. Now, when he will be born, / his father and mother and family circle shall / [r]ejoice over him. However, you find others grieving by reason of him, [s]ince they are strangers to him. These are not reckoned among his family. / [They do n]ot rejoice over him, because he is not of their race. /

This is also [the case] with the wisdom. When / it is proclaimed by the mouth of the teacher, these who / are [a]kin to it shall receive it to them and rejoice in it; but [those] who are strangers to it neither rejoice in it / [...] nor receive it to them. /

Just like the light of / [the fire, which I] proclaim[ed] to you, that shall come from the wood / [and be apparent o]utside before the eyes of every one. (208) So, [wh]oever looks shall see the light that has [come / fro]m the wood; but whoever is blind does not see the / [fir]e.

This is also the case with the wisdom, / when it will be proclaimed. The person, in whom is the [Mi]nd, of him is the wisdom. Whenever he may hear it, / he shall receive it in to him; but the one who has no Mind in him is a / stranger to it. He neither receives it in to him, nor shall he listen to [it]. /

When that disciple heard these things, he rejoiced gre/atly. He was persuaded in his heart about what had been proclaimed to him. He made obeisanc[e] and sat down.

Chapter 10 (260, 28 – 261, 13)

Concerning the Form of the Word, that [... ...] /

The process of forming a word is compared to the production of a coin.

Once again he speaks about the production of the word t[hat comes] / from the mouth and is heard by the [ears]. / He says [... (261) ...] and the throat draws it up and the tongue / spreads it out and the teeth cut it and the lips g[at]/her it! The word shall come forth through the power of th[ese five] / members and be heard outside.

Simila[rly] the coin: One shall pour it out and an[othe]/r beat it and another trim it as it is turned, and a[nother] / put the stamp on it and another wipe it in the sieve (?). [Behold], / these five craftsmen shall shape and beautify [their] / coin, and it comes amongst mankind. It becomes a posse[ssion] to be received and given.

This is also the case with the [wor]d, / as it is formed and embellished by five [member]s. / It comes forth and is heard by the ears [of] / others.

Chapter 120 (286, 24 – 288, 18)

Concerning the Two Essences.

In this chapter Mani makes forceful attack upon monotheism. The initial context is unclear, but possibly he is preaching directly to Christians. If there was nothing apart from God at the beginning, then where did all the evils in the world come from? He scornfully asks his listeners why they reject evil deeds, surely they should perform them if everything comes from God! Indeed, by not doing so they are committing the double crime against their God of rejecting his deeds, and then forgiving the sins of those who fall into them.

Alternatively, if evil did not come from God, the Manichaean position, his listeners have lied against God who will judge them. Mani asserts that Jesus, like all the true apostles, taught dualism. Here Mani develops the favourite proof-text about the good and evil trees, in his five-fold version (see 30.20 48.14 – 19 and Kephalaion 2). He ends by warning that at the last judgment his listeners will receive their condemnation.

Once again, when our father looked, he saw a [...] / person [...] before him. [He] says [... the] / two essences that are present at the beginning [...] the [lig]/ht and the darkness, that which is good and that which is evi[l, life and] death.

You, however, the creatures of the [... / i]s a single essence that exist[s ...] / every thing, [from] which everything came abou[t ... / ...[it, the evil and the [... (287) ...] God. Now, therefore, if the [... / ...] among you that only one essence exist[s ... / ...a]nd they say that there is nothing else [apart / from] God.

So, tell me that lying, fal[se] testimony, slander and accusation, sorceries [for] / sake of adultery, theft, the worshipping of id[ols], / robbery, the consuming fire, [...] that i[s / i]n the body of a person like a moth, the lustful[ness] / and fornication in which people revel, the [... ...] struggling with his breath as he shall not be quiet a si[ngl]e hour, / the insatiability of Mammon that the pers[on] shall [...] / as he shall not be satisfied for his lifetime, all these idola[tries], / the evil spirits that are like the night [... / ...] what they are or who cast them in the heart of peop[l]e so [that] they both would die by them, and be tortured / [on their] account.

If they came about from [the] G/[od o]f truth, then why do you annul [... / ...] them not. If they are his, you do them! [...] / will receive two woes: one, that you did not do them; the other [...] woe [...] received it, because you annul them and [... / ...] them. You forgive their sins upon the [... / ...]

For if God has hi[mself] created them, / the one who does them [h]as [no] sin therein! If they did not come / [about] from him, nor did he command them to be d[on]e, [y]ou are the one who will speak a lie against God, saying / [that] all [these e]vil things come about from him [... /... f]rom him, and you may bring two woes to that place. / [...] God (brings) a judgment against you, for while it / [...] through his beloved son in the [manner of] all [the apos]tles, he proclaimed l[ik]e ess/[ence ...] do these evil things, he set a [... / ...] saying that these evil things are / [...] which is the wicked (288) [...] for in this way [... / the] bitter trees that give not fruit [... / ...] the hard earth.

Once again he says: [... / ...] the father plants it, they will [... ... / be]loved [...] every fruit that is o/[n these] five tre[es ...] the and his belov[ed] son/ [and hi]s holy spirit and the entire kingdom of they that [... / ...] they say th[at] all the [wic]kednesses are his. They come about from / him. He is the one who established them because of this [… / …] to separate the good from the darkness. / You will [be c]on[de]mned by this in the presence of God with a great […] / an[d be]fore his beloved son and his h[oly] spirit at the last [da]y, at his advent.

You shall [come f]/rom your body and see these things that I have recou[nted to] / you; that they occur in truth before the Jud[ge] / of truth, the one who shall not favour anyone.

Part III

Early Islamic Philosophy: The Peripatetics

Introduction

What is known as Peripatetic or *mashshā'ī* philosophy in Islam is not simply Aristotelian philosophy in Arabic dress, despite the identification of the school with that of the Stagirite. Actually, from the beginning—that is, the third/ninth century when al-Kindī set the foundations for this school—the Muslim Peripatetics saw Aristotle through the eyes of his Alexandrian and Athenian commentators, al-Kindī being more related to the Athenian interpretation and Fārābī and Ibn Sīnā the Alexandrian, especially Themistius, Alexander Aphrodisias, and Simplicius. Now it must be remembered that these later commentators were mostly Neoplatonists, while one can also detect certain Stoic and even Hermetic elements in *mashshā'ī* thought. Furthermore, a recension of Plotinus's *Enneads* appeared in Arabic not under the name of the father of Neoplatonism but under that of Aristotle, the work becoming famous as the *Ūthūlūjiyā,* or 'Theology' of Aristotle.

Of even greater significance is the fact that the Islamic *mashshā'ī* philosophers were Muslim, lived individually as Muslims, and functioned in a society in which revelation loomed as the most dominant of realities on the horizon. Therefore, they not only sought to harmonize the Aristotle of the *Metaphysics* with the 'Aristotle' of the *Enneads*—that is, to achieve a synthesis of Aristotelianism and Neoplatonism—but also to integrate both of them into the Islamic worldview, thereby creating not simply Greek philosophy in Arabic but also Islamic philosophy. That is why Islamic philosophy has been quite correctly called by some prophetic philosophy. It is a philosophy that recognizes beyond reason and the senses, the channel of revelation—and by extension intellection—which at the highest level is its microcosmic counterpart, as a means of gaining access to knowledge of the most elevated level.

Mashshā'ī philosophers were consequently concerned, in addition to philosophical issues dealt with by the Greeks, with such questions as the relation between faith and reason, the created versus 'eternal' nature of the world, and survival of the soul after death—questions that were discussed extensively by the major figures of this school. They were also confronted with Islamic doctrines such as God's knowledge of particular existents and events in this world, the Qur'anic doctrine of the origination of the cosmos corresponding to the Biblical *fiat lux*, resurrection of the body, and other major beliefs that could not be explained by means of *mashshā'ī* philosophical tenets, although they usually accepted these doctrines individually as Muslims, as seen in the case of Ibn Sīnā. Nevertheless, the *mashshā'ī* were attacked over these and other issues by theologians and other schools of Islamic philosophy, especially in later centuries.

Although, in contrast to what one finds in most Western histories of Islamic philosophy, *mashshā'ī* philosophy was not the whole of Islamic philosophy, even during the early centuries of Islamic history, it was nevertheless the most important during the period from the third/ninth century to the fifth/eleventh century, culminating with Ibn Sīnā as far as Persia is concerned, although in Spain the school reached another peak with Ibn Rushd—who, however, followed a path that led more to medieval European thought than to later Islamic philosophy. But the works of the eastern Peripatetics, especially Fārābī and Ibn Sīnā, became a permanent heritage of all later philosophy in Persia. So many ideas, even of followers of later philosophical schools opposed to the *mashshā'ī* school, originated with this or that thought of Ibn Sīnā, as is clear in an even cursory reading of the works of Suhrawardī or Mullā Ṣadrā. Furthermore, the early *mashshā'ī* school, the thought of whose major figures follows, was revived in Persia in the seventh/thirteenth century, having been eclipsed for near two centuries as a result of attacks by theologians (*mutikallimūn)* such as Ghazzālī, Shahrastānī and Fakhr al-Dīn Rāzī. This revival carried out by Naṣīr al-Dīn Ṭūsī re-established the *mashshā'ī* philosophy of the early period, with which this section of Part 2 deals, as a permanent feature of the philosophical landscape of Persia for the next seven centuries.

From Mīr Dāmād and Mullā Rajab 'Alī Tabrīzī in the tenth/sixteenth and eleventh/seventeenth centuries to Mīrzā Abu'l-Ḥasan Jilwah in the thirteenth/nineteenth century, Ibn Sīnā continued to have followers who were usually called simply *mashshā'ī* but who should perhaps be called more specifically Ibn Sīnian. Even today the texts of this early period of *mashshā'ī* philosophy, especially *al-Shifā'* and *al-Ishārāt wa'l-tanbīhāt* of Ibn Sīnā, are taught in the traditional *madrasahs* of Persia, and no one is allowed to delve into the works of Suhrawardī and Mullā Ṣadrā without having mastered Ibn Sīnā. Therefore, in the same way that temporarily this early *mashshā'ī* school preceded the later schools of Islamic philosophy, intellectually it served as the first floor of the intellectual edifice of later Islamic thought as far as theoretical aspects of philosophy are concerned.

As for what these philosophers called practical philosophy, including ethics and politics, here again the early *mashshā'ī* texts are foundational for later schools of thought in Persia. This is especially true of Fārābī, whose political philosophy was the basis and fountainhead of all later Islamic political philosophy; its influence can even be seen in certain strands of Shiʿi political thought of the recent past and the contemporary period. Likewise, later philosophical ethics identified with Ṭūsī and others were developed mostly by proponents of *mashshāʾī* thought, most of whom were influenced in this domain, not only by Fārābī and Ibn Sīnā, but also and especially by Miskawayh. In the domains of both theoretical and practical philosophy (*al-ḥikmat al-naẓariyyah* and *al-ḥikmat al-ʿamaliyyah*), therefore, the works of the *mashshāʾī* masters under consideration here are seminal to an understanding of the thousand years of philosophical speculation that has followed upon their wake.

S. H. Nasr

8

Abu'l-'Abbās Muḥammad Īrānshahrī

While the history of Islamic philosophy usually begins with al-Kindī (third/ninth century), there are those who aver the philosophical significance of his Persian contemporary, Īrānshahrī. Abu'l-'Abbās Muḥammad ibn Muḥammad Īrānshahrī was from the city of Nayshāpūr. While no exact account of his life is available, Nāṣir-i Khusraw and Bīrūnī make references to his life and thought that help us to place him within the appropriate historical context.

Nāṣir-i Khusraw tells us that Īrānshahrī was the teacher of Muḥammad Zakariyyā' Rāzī, who was therefore influenced by his teacher. Rāzī's knowledge of such religions and sects as Dayṣāniyyah, Muḥammirah, and Mannāniyyah, as well as his book *al-Radd 'alā saysān al-mannānī*, are indications of the influence of his teacher Īrānshahrī. In addition, from the references made by Bīrūnī and others, it is apparent that Īrānshahrī had a thorough knowledge of Abrahamic religions, as well as Zoroastrianism and Manichaeism. His knowledge of Hinduism, however, was not as thorough and it appears that he familiarized himself with Hinduism through the writings of Muḥammad ibn Shaddād ibn 'Īsā Mūsā, known as Zarqān.

Bīrūnī tells us that Īrānshahrī did not belong to any religion and that he had invented his own religion, which he advocated avidly. While Īrānshahrī's alleged religion has not survived, it is believed that he composed a book in Persian, claiming that its contents had been revealed to him by an angel whose name was *Hastī* (Being). Furthermore, Īrānshahrī is said to have claimed that his book is the Persian Qur'ān and that just as Muḥammad was the prophet of Arabs, he was the prophet of Persians. These views are, however, conjectural and cannot be considered as being definitely true.

Īrānshahrī appears to have believed that there are four eternal substances: matter, space, time, and motion as understood by him. Contrary to al-Kindī, who advocated the same notion, Īrānshahrī seems to have offered a more Neoplatonic interpretation.

While it is difficult to state with precision the philosophical perspectives of Īrānshahrī, it is clear that he saw the fundamental governing principles of the world to be the unfolding of an ultimate Being, which is a profoundly Neoplatonic perspective. Īrānshahrī represents an important beginning, since he attempted a rapprochement between reason and revelation, an effort that has remained the salient feature of Islamic philosophical thought in Persia to this day.

This chapter includes the philosophical perspectives of Īrānshahrī, based on Nāṣir-i Khusraw's remarks, as presented in *Zād al-musāfirīn* (Provisions for Travellers). Since Bīrūnī's comments on Īrānshahrī are of historical significance only and do not shed light on the nature of Īrānshahrī's thought, they have not been included.

M. Aminrazavi

THE IDEAS OF ĪRĀNSHAHRĪ

From Nāṣir-i Khusraw, *Zād al-musāfirīn* (Provisions for Travellers)

Translated for this volume by M. Aminrazavi from Nāṣir-i Khusraw, *Zād al-musāfirīn* (Berlin, 1923), pp. 98–110.

Muḥammad Zakariyyā᾽ Rāzī restated the teachings of Īrānshahrī in a repugnant and heretical manner. The content of his [Rāzī's] master and predecessor was placed in a frightening and deniable context, so that those who have not studied the texts of the *ḥukamā* (philosophers) might suspect that these concepts have been extracted by himself [Rāzī].[1]

Ḥakīm Īrānshahrī, who has reiterated the philosophical concepts in a religious language in the *Kitāb-i jalīl, Kitāb-i athīr,* and others, has guided the people to the true religion and [has called for] the understanding of unity.[2] 'This much that we mentioned are the sayings of the group that considers space to have been eternal, such as Īrānshahrī.'[3]

Ḥakīm Īrānshahrī has said that time (*zamān*), aeon (*dahr*), and duration [*muddat*] are names whose meanings are derived from one substance. Time is a sign of divine knowledge, just as space is a sign of divine power, motion is a sign of divine action, and an existent being is a sign of God's ability. Each of these four are limitless and eternal.[4]

Īrānshahrī said that God, Most High, was always a creator (*Ṣāniʿ*), and there was not a time when He was not creating, such that His state of being noncreative would change to being creative. Since it is necessary that He always be creator, then of necessity that upon which His creation appears is eternal. His creation appears in matter, therefore matter is eternal. Matter is a sign for the apparent power of God, and since matter is not but in space and that [matter] is eternal, necessarily space is eternal.[5]

Those fine words and subtle meanings [of Īrānshahrī] are placed in a deplorable context so that his followers, from nonbelievers to contemplatives, think that the statements all came from his scientific views.[6]

Among the *ḥukamā᾽* [there are] those who said matter and space are eternal; they conceived of a substance for time and said that time is a substance, long and eternal. They rejected the opinion of those *ḥakīms* who conceived of time in terms of the movements of bodies. They said that if time were the number of movements

1. *Zād al-musāfirīn*, p. 98.
2. Ibid.
3. Ibid.
4. Ibid., p. 110.
5. Ibid., p. 102.
6. Ibid., p. 103.

of objects, then two objects in motion at one time would move in two different degrees. Ḥakīm Īrānshahrī has said that time, aeon, and duration are all names whose meanings are derived from the same substance.[1]

And time is a substance that flows and is restless, and the statement that Rāzī has attributed to Īrānshahrī says the same thing. He [Īrānshahrī] said that time is a transient substance.[2]

1. Ibid., p. 110.
2. Ibid.

9

Abū Naṣr Fārābī

Abū Naṣr Muḥammad ibn Tarkhān ibn Uzlugh Fārābī, who was known among later Islamic philosophers as the Second Teacher (*al-muʿallim al-thānī*) and the philosopher of Muslims (*faylasūf al-muslimīn*), is not only the founder of logic in Islamic philosophy but is also considered by many to be the real founder of Islamic philosophy itself. Little is known of his life and even his ethnic background has been disputed among traditional authorities. Ibn Nadīm in his *al-Fihrist,* which is the first work to mention Fārābī, considers him to be of Persian origin, as does Muḥammad Shahrazūrī in his *Tāʾrīkh al-ḥukamāʾ* and Ibn Abī Uṣaybiʿah in his *Ṭabaqāt al-aṭibbāʾ*. In contrast, Ibn Khallikān in his *Wafayāt al-aʿyān* considers him to be of Turkish descent. In any case, he was born in Fārāb in the Khurāsān of that day around 257/870 in a climate of Persianate culture. As an already mature scholar, he came to Baghdad, where he studied logic with the Christian scholar Yūḥannā ibn Haylān and with Ibn Bishr Mattā, who was a translator of Aristotle into Arabic. Fārābī was to become a teacher himself of the famous Christian theologian Yaḥyā ibn ʿAdī and the grammarian Ibn al-Sarrāj. Some time before 330/942, Fārābī left Baghdad for Syria, where he travelled to Aleppo and possibly also went to Egypt, but settled in Damascus, where he died in 339/950 and where he is buried.

Fārābī was a truly encyclopedic figure, at once master of many languages, logic, political philosophy, ethics, and metaphysics, as well as music. Some hundred works have been mentioned in diverse sources as having been composed by him. Many of these treatises are now lost, but a number of important ones have been discovered recently so that our view of his philosophy has been modified in recent years. His works include several commentaries upon the logical works of Aristotle, as well as his own writings on logic, which together form a major part of his intellectual output. They also include a number of foundational texts on political philosophy and ethics, chief among them *Mabādī ārāʾ ahl al-madīnat al-fāḍilah* (Principles of the Opinion of the People of the Virtuous City), perhaps his greatest work, and *al-Sīyāsat al-madaniyyah* (Politics of the City) and *Taḥṣīl al-saʿādah* (Attainment of Happiness). In the domain of political thought, his aim was to synthesize the theses of Plato, rather than Aristotle, with the teachings of Islam.

Fārābī also wrote a number of metaphysical works based on the wedding of Aristotelian and Neoplatonic doctrines in the bosom of Islam and dealt with questions of ontology, emanation, and the like, which set the background for the grand synthesis of Ibn Sīnā. Works in this category include his attempt to harmonize the teachings of Plato and Aristotle (by whom he also understood the author of the *Enneads* or Plotinus) in the work *al-Jamʿ bayn ra'yay al-ḥakīmayn Aflāṭūn al-ilāhī wa Arisṭū* (The Book of Reconciliation of the Opinions of the Two Sages, Divine Plato and Aristotle), as well as independent treatises on Plato and Aristotle and the *Aghrāḍ mā baʿd al-ṭabīʿah* (Purposes of the Metaphysics), which had such an influence on Ibn Sīnā. Fārābī's influential treatise *Fi'l-ʿaql* (On the Intellect) also belongs in this category.

Being concerned with logic as well as method in the various sciences, Fārābī turned his attention to the subject of classification in the sciences. He thus wrote *Fī iḥṣā' al-ʿulūm* (On the Enumeration of the Sciences), a treatise of great influence in both the East and West. It is mostly because of his effort to classify the sciences and discuss the boundaries and methods of each science that he was given by Muslims the title of Second Teacher—in the same way that Muslims called Aristotle the First Teacher as a result of his work in the context of Greek learning.

Fārābī was deeply interested in the relationship between language and thought, including logic. His *Kitāb al-ḥurūf* (The Book of Letters) is a masterly testament on this subject, devoted to the issue of language as a vehicle for meaning and intelligibility.

Finally, a word must be said about Fārābī as a musician. He is said to have created musical compositions. To this day there are melodies in Anatolian music and *rags* in classical North Indian music attributed to him, sung and performed by masters of these musical genres. Moreover, he was a master of music theory; his *Kitāb al-mūsīqā al-kabīr* (The Great Book on Music), known in the West as a book on Arabic music, is in reality a study of the theory of the Persian music of his day as well as presenting certain general philosophical principles about music, its cosmic qualities, and its influence on the soul.

Fārābī did not enjoy teaching too many students and so trained only a small number of scholars. But his influence was immense in all later Islamic philosophy and most particularly in later *mashshā'ī* philosophy, which culminated with Ibn Sīnā. Indeed, Ibn Sīnā paid the highest tribute to Fārābī by saying that he owed his understanding of Aristotle's *Metaphysics* to Fārābī's short but pertinent commentary on the work.

The selection of Fārābī's works that follows is a representative sample of his vast corpus of writings. The first is a section of *Kitāb al-burhān*, dealing with the paraphrase of Aristotle's famous treatise *Analytica Posteriora*, which marks the capstone of his logical system. The selections deal with certainty (*yaqīn*), assent (*taṣdīq*), conception (*taṣawwur*), and definition (*ḥadd*).

The second selection is from *Kitāb al-jamʿ bayn ra'yay al-ḥakīmayn Aflaṭūn al-ilāhī wa Arisṭū*. In this brief excerpt, Fārābī gives his readings of Plato and Aristotle on what is philosophy, methodology, knowledge of forms, and the soul, along with the differences he finds between the two philosophers.

The third selection is from *Mabādī āra' ahl-madīnat al-fāḍilah*, translated as 'The Perfect State'. This work deals with political philosophy and presents Fārābī's interpretation of Plato's *Republic*. But it begins with a treatment and elaboration of the First Cause, which has been presented here along with some discussion of the perfect ruler.

S. H. Nasr

A PARAPHRASE OF ARISTOTLE'S *ANALYTICA POSTERIORA*
From *Kitāb al-burhān*

Translated for this volume by Majid Fakhry from al-Fārābī, *Kitāb al-burhān*, ed., M. Fakhry (Beirut, 1987), pp. 19–50.

Chapter 1. Of the Specific Matters whereby each Type of Cognition is Acquired

Since we have already discussed[1] those matters by means of which we generally acquire the knowledge of every object we seek to know, as well as those which divert the reflecting mind from what it intends to know, and thereby cause it to err,[2] let us discuss now those specific matters by means of which each particular type of cognition is acquired.

Cognitions are of two types—conception and assent[3]—and each one of these is either more perfect or less perfect. We have already summarized in the preceding parts the manner in which we acquire each of those two types (of assent) in an absolute way. Now, since the matters through which we acquire perfect cognitions are different from those through which we attain those cognitions which are less perfect, and since the statements which summarize them absolutely are not sufficient in determining what is more perfect or less perfect, we have seen fit to supplement what has preceded with a summary of what pertains to perfect cognitions and to those which are less perfect. Of these two, we begin with an exposition of what pertains to perfect cognitions.

Of Perfect Assent

Perfect assent signifies certainty, whereas perfect conception signifies the conception of a thing in a manner which sums up its essence with respect to what belongs to it essentially; this consists in conceiving a thing by means of what its definition signifies.

Of these two, we begin by summarizing what belongs to perfect assent, as follows. Assent in general is the way in which man believes that the existence of an object of judgment outside the mind corresponds to what is believed in the mind, the true being the correspondence of what exists outside the mind with what is

1. That is, in the preceding paraphrases, which include the *Isagoge* (of Porphyry), the *Categories*, the *Interpretation*, *Analytica Priora* and *Sophistica* of Aristotle.

2. The reference is to *Sophistica*. al-Fārābī has accordingly departed from the traditional sequence of Aristotle's *Organon* by deferring the discussion of demonstration until the end of *Sophistica*.

3. Or judgment; in Arabic, *taṣdīq*. This classic division corresponds to Aristotle's definition and judgment or proposition, respectively.

believed in the mind. In fact, assent may indicate what is true or what is false in reality, and it consists of (a) that which is certain, (b) that which is nearly certain, and (c) the kind of assent designated as the soul's acquiescence in the object, which is the furthest kind of assent removed from certainty. As to false assent, it can never be an object of certainty, for certainty is possible only with respect to assenting to what is true.

Now, certainty consists in believing that the existence of what has been recognized as true can never be other than what we believe, and to believe, in addition, with respect to that belief that it cannot be otherwise, so that if it is taken as belief with respect to the first belief, then it cannot be otherwise, and so on *ad infinitum*. As to what is uncertain, it consists in believing that what has been assented to may, or at least that it is not impossible, that it could be otherwise than it is believed to be. The nearly certain consists either in our not being aware of its opposite or in being aware of it in such a way that the object of this awareness is so obscure that it cannot be articulated or its opposite easily refuted.[1]

The soul's acquiescence consists of assenting to that whose contrary is apprehended and could be articulated. This acquiescence can also differ according to the force of its opposite or its weakness. The assent which is nearly certain corresponds to dialectical assent; whereas the soul's simple acquiescence to a certain matter corresponds to rhetorical assent.[2]

The matters which constitute the objects of the nearly certain type of assent are (a) generally accepted premises and their like, (b) necessary inferences from syllogisms made up of generally accepted premises, or (c) necessary inferences from those inductions in which the inspected particulars have not been exhausted.[3] That in which the soul acquiesces is either received opinions or necessary inferences from a syllogism based on received opinions or, finally, necessary inferences from syllogisms based on possible (or contingent) premises. That could also result from other matters which we have enumerated in those parts in which we have discussed rhetorical discourses.

Assent to generally accepted or received opinions altogether depends in general on testimony. However, the generally accepted denotes what is attested to by everybody, the majority or the like;[4] whereas the received refers to what are attested to by one person, a group accredited by one person, or simply one group. N of those two types induces certainty, but confidence in the testimony of everybody or the majority is stronger and more common than that of one person or a smaller group.

1. I read *ya'sur*.

2. In *Analytica Priora* I, 25b, Aristotle distinguishes between demonstrative, rhetorical, and dialectical arguments on the basis of the degree of certainty proper to their premises and conclusions. Sophistical arguments are the result of fallacious reasoning. Formal and informal fallacies are discussed in the *Sophistica*.

3. That is, incomplete inductions.

4. This could refer to a relatively large group or two 'just witnesses', as in Islamic law.

However, it may happen that a certain matter forming part of what is attested to is really true, whereupon certainty is predicated of it by accident. That is why many people assume that testimony by itself can induce certainty but not accidentally; others feel that testimonies by themselves do not give rise to certainty and accordingly believe that those testimonies which are objects of certainty are a matter of divine command,[1] especially when attended by the soul's acquiescence.

Of Certainty and its Varieties

Let us now discuss certainty and that which is an object of certainty. We assert that certainty is either necessary or nonnecessary (contingent). Necessary certainty consists of believing, with regard to what cannot be otherwise in reality, that it cannot at any time be otherwise than it was originally believed. The nonnecessary refers to what was certain at one time only, whereas the necessary can never change and thereby become false. Instead, it always exists in the same manner it exists in the mind, whether only negatively or only affirmatively. The nonnecessary, on the other hand, can change and thereby become false without any corresponding change occurring in the mind. Necessary certainty in fact is possible only with respect to eternally existing entities,[2] such as the whole is greater than the part, for this matter can never change. However, the nonnecessary might bear on entities which are transient and changeable in actuality, such as the certainty that you are now standing up and that Zayd is in the house and such like.

The necessary is that the existence of whose opposite is impossible. That is why it is false and impossible, whereas the nonnecessary is that whose existence is not impossible. Thus the opposite of nonnecessary certainty is the false whose existence is possible, whereas the opposite of necessary certainty is the false whose existence is impossible. It follows that the false is of two types—either absurd or not absurd; necessary certainty and necessary existence are convertible. For what is an object of necessary certainty is necessarily existent and that which is necessarily existent is an object of perfect certainty, and this is identical with necessary certainty.

Let us leave aside now the consideration of nonnecessary certainty. Necessary certainty may result from deduction or without deduction.[3] That part thereof which results from deduction results either *per se* or *per accidens*. For instance, this man is walking and what walks is an animal; man is therefore an animal. Necessary certainty resulting from a deduction, but not *per accidens*, actually depends on two premises which are known likewise with certainty in a necessary way, either

1. The Arabic says *amr*, which clearly refers to divine revelation. In the Qur'ān, the term often refers to a verbal statement or command.

2. Cf. Aristotle, *Analytica Posteriora*, I, 75b 21.

3. The Arabic *qiyās* normally translates *syllogism*, but I have preferred the more general term *deduction* here.

without deduction from the beginning or by going back analytically to premises which have been known with certainty without deduction.[1]

Premises which are objects of this kind of certainty are either universal or particular. Of the two, let us consider universal premises only, since they are those mostly used in the sciences and since consideration of universals will encompass particulars.

Chapter 2. Of Demonstration and its Kinds

As for the universal premises by means of which necessary certainty is attained without deduction, they are of two kinds: one is that which occurs by nature, the other that which occurs by sense-experience. That which occurs by nature is that wherein certainty is achieved without our knowing wherefrom or how it has arisen, nor indeed our having sensed at any time that we had been ignorant thereof or desired to know it, or even have desired at any time to know it. Rather, we find that it is as though our souls were born with it from our very coming-to-be, or as though it was innate in us, never having been divested of it. These premises are called the primary premises native to man and are also called the primary principles.

We need not determine in this book how or wherefrom these premises came about because our ignorance of the manner of this coming about will not nullify the certainty, diminish it, or prevent us from forming therefrom a syllogism productive of the certainty consequent upon it in us. The manner in which these primary cognitions come about is one of the questions sought in the sciences and in philosophy.

It is clear that we achieve certainty regarding their coming about by means of such syllogisms that may be formed from such premises. If, however, the latter are not true or the knowledge wherefrom and how they have come to be known is not possible, they cannot be used in explaining anything at all. Now, if the manner of the latter[2] coming about cannot be known except through these syllogisms and these[3] cannot be used in explaining them, it follows that there can be no knowledge of anything at all. That is why he who stipulates the investigation of the manner in which such premises are known in the art of logic is in error.[4] Instead, we need only to know in this art how they are described or characterized and how their kinds are enumerated, as well as the manner in which they are used as parts of the syllogism and the way in which other cognitions lead to them.

Opinions have differed with respect to their coming about. However, we need

1. That is, intuitively. Aristotle calls these premises indemonstrable first principles of demonstration. *Analytica Posteriora*, *r*, 72b.

2. That is, the premises.

3. Ibid.

4. al-Fārābī may be referring here to the Stoics who dwelt at length on the origin of concepts, especially the so-called common notions.

not know when we use them how or wherefrom they came about, although it appears that with respect to most of these universal premises, their particular instances are sensible. That is why some[1] have said that they arise from sensation. However, it may appear herein that although these premises arise from sensation, sensation alone is not capable of giving rise to them fully. For, if we confine ourselves therein to the measure of what we have sensed, it being the case that we have only sensed a limited number of their (instances), it follows that the premises resulting from them would be particular rather than universal. We find, however, that they[2] were known to us as universals, so that we were able to judge of the subjects of these premises in a universal way, comprising both what we have sensed and what we have not sensed.

From the preceding statement it appears that the soul performs an activity, regarding sensible objects, in excess of what we actually sense in them. If, however, understanding these matters is hard in this context, we might leave it aside and confine ourselves to the measure which has already been expounded with respect to them. We are then able to ignore how they have been apprehended and whether the soul's apprehending them is a form of apprehension peculiar to it, even when we do not sense their particular instances. Our knowledge of them, in fact, arises once we have perceived their particular instances. Those which arise by experience are the universal premises of which we are certain in that manner of certainty consequent upon intending to perceive their particular instances, whether few or many. For experience consists in inspecting the particular instances of universal premises as to whether their predicates exist in each one of them, and then following them up in all or most of them until necessary certainty is attained by us. That kind of judgment applies to all the members of that species and is analogous to induction.

The difference between that judgment and induction is that induction does not give rise to necessary certainty through universal judgment, whereas experience gives rise to certainty through universal judgment. However, many people use those two terms[3] interchangeably; we ourselves do not care how these two notions are expressed and will also show that the soul is not satisfied in this matter with what can be inspected thereof, but resorts in the wake of that inspection to a general judgment which comprises both what is inspected and what is not inspected. But following that inspection, how it derives that general judgment is a question which, as we said above, should be deferred; for its knowledge will not contribute to the certainty consequent upon it nor the ignorance thereof increase or decrease the certainty of the premises, or bar us from using them. Let us call those premises the first principles of certainty.

1. The Stoics.
2. The premises.
3. Induction and experience.

Of Certain Knowledge (‘ilm*) and its Varieties*

Let us now discuss those cognitions which result from the primary premises of which that certainty has been attained. I say that the term scientific knowledge, as we stated earlier, is used in general in two senses: the first is assent, the second is conception. Assent may be either certain or not certain; certain assent is either necessary or not necessary. It is obvious that the term scientific knowledge is applied to necessary certainty more frequently than to what is not certain or to what is certain but not necessary. Let that be called certain scientific knowledge.

Now the certain sciences are three types. The *first* is the certainty of the existence of the thing only, and this is the knowledge of being; some people call it the knowledge *that* the thing is. The *second* is the certain knowledge of the cause of the existence of the thing only; some people call this knowledge the knowledge of *why* the thing is. The *third* is the certain knowledge of them both. The objects sought by means of certain principles are in fact such that their knowledge is sought in one of those three ways of inquiry, the purpose of the inquiry being one of those three ways of knowing.

It is clear that that of which the cause alone is sought must be such that the knowledge of its existence has already been gained by us. It is most fitting that, of the three, certain knowledge should be applied to that in which the certainty of existence and the cause together are attained.

It follows, then, that the syllogisms based on premises which are known in a necessary and certain manner fall into three kinds: the *first* conveys by itself the knowledge of the existence of the thing only; the *second* conveys by itself the knowledge of the cause only; and the *third* conveys of itself the two together. As to the syllogism which is formed with a view to gaining thereby the knowledge of the thing only, it is formed from that whose existence is already known, either in the manner in which first principles are known,[1] or through a syllogism which conveys the knowledge of existence only. Now the syllogism, which rests upon premises known with necessary certainty and conveys one of those three kinds, is called demonstration (*burhān*). Demonstration is, then, of three kinds: the *first* is the demonstration of existence, which is called the demonstration *that* the thing is; the *second* is the demonstration *why* the thing is; and the *third* is that which combines both, and that is demonstration in the absolute sense. Demonstration in an absolute sense, then, denotes that kind of certain syllogism which conveys, by itself and not accidentally, the existence and the cause of the thing in conjunction. Every demonstration is, then, the cause of the scientific knowledge acquired thereby, but not all demonstration conveys the knowledge of the cause of the thing's existence.[2]

---

1. That is, *intuitively*, as against the second which is known *deductively*.

2. Since some demonstrations, as mentioned earlier, simply seek to prove the existence of the thing only.

Of Absolute Demonstration

Let us discuss now demonstration absolutely—I mean that which conveys the knowledge of the existence and the cause of the thing together. Now the causes are four: (1) the matter of the thing and whatever is reckoned as part of matter or its concomitant; (2) the definition of the thing, the parts of its definition, and whatever is reckoned as part of the definition also; (3) the agent and whatever is reckoned as a concomitant thereof, and finally (4) the purpose and whatever is reckoned as a concomitant thereof.

Now each of these causes is either proximate or ultimate, is either *per se* or *per accidens,* is either more general or more specific, either in potentiality or in act. Such syllogisms as convey the knowledge of the cause, which is a cause *per accidens,* are not considered part of demonstration as such, unless they are called demonstrations *per accidens.* However, everything else which conveys to us all the kinds of causes is rightly called demonstration. However, that demonstration which conveys the knowledge of the cause, which is *per se*, is proximate, is more specific, and is in act deserves to be called a demonstration more than anything else. In fact, the objects sought in the first instance through demonstrations which convey the knowledge of the causes are actually of this type.

It is clear that each of these causes occupies, in relation to the parts of the syllogism, the position of the middle term. Thus, any syllogism of which the middle term is taken as one of the four kinds of causes is such that the knowledge which it conveys in the conclusion is identical with the knowledge of that cause only, whether it is ultimate, proximate, or anything else of the causes which we have already summarized.

Knowledge gained through demonstration is either universal or particular. Now since the consideration of what produces universals includes what produces particulars, it follows that we should first learn about those demonstrations which produce universal conclusions. For it is clear that those demonstrations which produce universal conclusions must have universal premises.

Let us now discuss the conditions of the parts of demonstrations in relation to each other and how they should be, as well as the conditions proper to the parts of the conclusions. Now since the conclusions which lead to necessary certainty must exist of necessity, it follows that the premises of the syllogism which produce them *per se* must be premises whose existence is necessary.

Necessary premises are either categorical or conditional, and the same is true of problems. Necessary categorical premises are those whose predicates are necessary to their subjects, whereas the necessary conditionals are those in which the concomitants of the premise are necessary. However, any conditional problem can be converted into a categorical one. Conditional problems are like our saying 'If two sides of a triangle are equal to the two sides of another triangle (each side being equal to its counterpart), and the two angles which are enclosed by the corresponding sides are equal, then those two triangles are equal', and so on with respect to similar problems. Or like our saying 'If a body moving in a circle is infinite, then the lines emanating from its centre will extend to infinity; and if the lines which emanate from its centre extend to infinity, then the distances intervening between those lines are infinite', and the like. Each of these conditional propositions may be converted into a categorical one indifferently, regardless of whether it is considered as categorical or hypothetical. Now whatever the existence thereof is sought, its existence will be sought either absolutely or in some particular way. Whatever the existence thereof is sought absolutely is that which is denoted by a single term, or that which stands for a single term; that, however, can be demonstrated only through a hypothetical syllogism. However, that whose existence is sought in some particular way can be demonstrated through a categorical and a hypothetical syllogism together. Anything which is posited and whose existence is sought absolutely, while we intended to demonstrate it through a categorical syllogism, will be replaced by a statement which defines it, and then we are able to demonstrate it. By the necessary here we mean the necessary essentially, since it is believed that not every necessary [predicate] is essential. That is why we should expound the essential predicates, whether we mean the essential concomitants, as in conditionals, or the essential predicates, as in the categoricals.

Of Essential Predicates

Essential predicates are of two kinds. The first is that which is such that the essence of its subjects or nature is to be predicated of those predicates, as for example 'Every man is an animal' and the like. The second kind is that whose essence and nature consist in existing in its subjects. These are called the essential accidents, such as motion and rest in relation to physical bodies. The nature of those subjects requires that their predicates be predicated thereof and are either definitions (as when we say man is a rational animal or the circle is a plane surface of a certain type) or parts of definitions.

Now the parts of definitions consist either of an approximate or an ultimate genus or the like, a proximate or ultimate differentia, or the like. An example of the proximate genus is the statement 'The circle is a plane surface'; an example of the ultimate is the statement 'The circle is a figure, or that it has a certain magnitude.' What is analogous to the genus is like the statement 'Man is made up of flesh and bone.' An example of the proximate differentia is the statement 'The circle is circumscribed by a single line'; that of the ultimate differentia is the statement 'The circle is circumscribed by a line.' An example of what is analogous to the differentia is the statement regarding the heart: 'It is the source of natural heat.'

Essential accidents are of two types. The first consists of those predicates whose subjects are used as parts of their definitions, not insofar as they are their genera but rather insofar as they are set up as differentiae, such as laughing in relation to man. The second kind consists of those essential predicates the genera of whose subjects are used in their definitions but not as genera thereof, such as the statement 'Every odd number multiplied by an even number gives an even sum.'

Now each of the two kinds of essential predicates, predicated of its subjects in a universal way, is either primary or not primary. A primary predicate is one which must be predicated of the genus of its subjects in a universal way, as when we say of the triangle that its angles are equal to two right angles. For, that would be predicated of the triangle in a primary way, insofar as it cannot be predicated in a universal way of the genus of the triangle. For, we cannot say correctly 'The angles of every plain figure, bounded by more than one straight line, are equal to two right angles.'

The nonprimary predicate is one predicated of its subject in a universal way, such as predicating the equality of right angles of the figure with two equal sides[1] or that of unequal sides.

Primary predicates are either proper to the subject or not proper to the subject. That which is proper to the subject is like (the statement) 'Every line which intersects with two straight lines, making the two angles collateral to each other equal to two right angles will make those two lines parallel.'[2] For their being parallel is predicated of these two lines, as well as the two lines with which a straight line intersects, rendering the external angle equal to the internal angle which faces it. Parallelism is then predicated of them in a primary way. If the primary predicate is of this kind, then you may know which one of the essential kinds is predicated of its subject in a primary way and which is not, and which is proper to its subject and which is not.

The proximate differentia may be proper to its subject, but the highest genus[3] and the differentia which constitutes the genus and what is above it is not primary. However, if the genus of the constitutive differentia is not a genus thereof or of its genus, then it can be regarded as a primary predicate; the same is true of the differentia which constitutes the differentia of the thing in question.[4] The essential accidents, however, are either primary predicates or are not. Now, of the essential predicate, what is always proper to the subject is the definition, for the definition is proper to its subject. The same appears to be true of the last differentiae.[5]

1. That is, an isosceles triangle.
2. In this figure, if $a + b = 180°$, then lines L & L^1 are parallel.

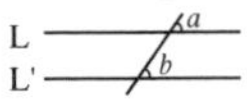

3. The Arabic says: 'the genus of the genus'.
4. That is, the differentia of the differentia.
5. That is, the most specific parts of the definition, as rational in the definition of man, who

Of essential accidents, that in which the genus of the subject itself is taken as part of its definition is proper to that subject such as laughing, but that in which the genus of its subject or the genus of the genus is taken in its definition, it is not necessary for it always and in every case to be proper to the subject, as for instance, 'Every even number multiplied by an even number is even', for even is an essential predicate of that which is multiplied by the even number being taken in its definition, and that is the genus of the subject or the genus of its genus, but is not proper to it. However, that the angles of a triangle are equal to two right angles requires that the genus of the triangle or the genus of its genus should be taken in its definition; for it is proper to the definition as such.

Essential concomitants are similar to essential predicates; for essential predicates as such can be taken as concomitants. For instance, if one is a man, then he is an animal, and if he is a man, then he is a rational and living being. Concomitants may also be taken as predicates. For instance, if a movable can move in an infinite body, then it will be able to cover an infinite distance in a finite time. For this concomitant can be taken as a predicate. For example, every movable in an infinite body may cover, as it moves, an infinite distance in a finite time. Now it is clear that the primary predicate, the genus of whose subject is taken in its definition, is more specific than that genus, or else that predicate cannot be considered primary with respect to what is beneath that genus. If so, then that genus as such may be taken in the definition of the opposite of that predicate and the definition of other things not opposite to it as well; so that that genus will be part of the definition of all the accidents in the definition of which that genus is taken. That, for instance, is the case of the odd and the even pertaining to number; for each of them pertains to part of what is subsumed under number in a universal and primary manner. However, their pertaining to number absolutely is particular,[1] since each one of them is more specific than number. These accidents are said to be essential to number in a certain sense, and to the species of number in another sense. Since number itself is taken in its definition, from the species of number, then its genus is also part of its definition. Now, essential accidents pertaining to a certain genus, in the same way as even and odd pertain to number, are either opposites, such as even and odd with respect to number, and straight and curved with respect to the line; or not opposites such as even and magnitude,[2] pertaining to number.

Opposite essential accidents are either essential to a certain genus primarily or not essential primarily. Primary opposites are those into which the genus of that genus cannot be divided, like even and odd, which are opposites; for the genus of number cannot be divided into them exhaustively. Thus we cannot say 'Every

is also a mammal, two-footed, etc.

1. Rather than universal. al-Fārābī appears to mean that odd and even, being more specific than number as such, cannot be identified with number in general.

2. The Arabic says *jism*, or body.

magnitude is either even or odd' since the line is a magnitude, but it is not, in so far as it is a line, either even or odd. Similarly, in the case of straight and curved which pertains to the line, we cannot say that every magnitude is either straight or curved. For if this was true, number, which is a magnitude, would be either curved or straight.

As for the opposite essential predicates which are not primary attributes of a certain genus, like equal and unequal with respect to number, number may be divided into either of them and the genus of number may also be divided into them in an exhaustive way. For, every magnitude is either equal or unequal, and the same may be said with respect to proportionate and unproportionate, the common and the uncommon. For it may be thought that every magnitude is common or uncommon, proportionate or unproportionate. Therefore, some opposite essential accidents are proper to a certain genus and some are common to it and to other genera. Now, common properties are of two kinds: some are like the way in which animal is common to man and horse, and some are like being or thing which are common to all genera. Some opposites, then, are primary and proper to that which is common in the sense in which animal is common to man and horse, even and odd are common to number, and equal and unequal to magnitude; whereas some are primary in the sense in which being and thing are common. For instance, every being exists either actually or potentially, and every thing may be said to be, either affirmatively or negatively. For these opposites are primary with respect to what is common in the sense in which being and thing are common.[1]

As to universal and primary premises, if their predicates are accidents proper to a certain genus and their subject's species of that genus, then they are the suitable premises proper to that genus. Likewise, whenever their subjects are species of that genus, and their predicates either that genus *per se* or other species of that genus, then they are also premises proper to that genus. If, however, the predicates of the premises are accidents of a certain genus which are not primary, and their subjects are species of that genus, then those premises are not proper to that genus. Of the premises of demonstration, then, some are proper to the genus and some are common.

These, then, are the modes of predicating the parts of the parts of the premises of demonstration one of the other. Now, since demonstrations which yield both the being and the causes are such that their middle terms are among the kinds of causes which have been mentioned,[2] and the modes of predicating the parts of demonstration are these, it follows necessarily that the causes which are taken as middle terms have the same character with respect to either of the two terms.[3]

1. Namely, in the highest degree of community, both being and thing are regarded as highest genera or 'transcendentals' in Aristotelian logic.

2. That is, the material, the formal, the efficient, and the final.

3. The reference is to the minor and major terms (or extremes), i.e. the subject and predicate, of the proposition.

It also follows necessarily that all the causes must be either definitions or parts of the definitions of both terms[1] or of only one of them, or have a share in their definitions in some way, either approximate or ultimate.

Of Demonstrations and Causes

As for the demonstrations which give the causes only, these consist of matters whose existence is already known to us, either by themselves, through the senses, or through those demonstrations called proofs.[2] It then remains for us, once their existence is known, to seek their causes.

Now the causes of things are known either through sense, through proofs, or through demonstrations. And it is thought that much of that whose essential causes are sought, that they do not necessarily belong to that in which they exist, such as baldness and hoariness in relation to man and the like. They exist, however, essentially in that in which they exist, it being clear that necessity therein consists in the relation of their causes to them only. If so, then it is not the case that whatever is essential for a thing is necessary thereto in the sense in which we have defined the necessary.

The kinds of primary causes are four which are divisible into the divisions that we have mentioned earlier. Each one of these is found in the answer to the question 'Why is the thing as it is?' For the question 'Why the thing is' may arise in connection with what we have already learned the existence thereof. Thus we say, 'Why does the man die?' when we have learned that he dies, to which the answer would be 'Either because he is made up of contraries or because he is a living rational, dying being, or because it is more fitting that he should die; or because that which preserves or produces him is changing and its relation to him (i.e., as the effect) is not the same.' The first answer pertains to his matter, the second to his form, the third to his final cause, and the fourth to his agent. However, what pertains to its matter, if given, will not necessarily entail the existence of that which exists in matter. The same is true of that which exists as an agent; but that which exists as a final cause, once it is posited, entails necessarily the existence of that through which the thing exists, and the same is true of the form. For these last two causes are concomitants of the existence of that which exists through them.

In some causes, even if posited, it will not appear at once how they are causes of that thing, nor how it exists through them or derives from them. For instance, why does the vine shed its leaves in winter? If we answer: 'Due to the fact that its leaves are broad', that cause would be an essential cause, but it is not clear from it how it is a cause of the vine's shedding its leaves in winter. That would happen

1. Ibid.
2. Singular *dalīl*, a less logically stringent proof or evidence than a demonstration.

when its proximate causes are not given. Accordingly there would still be room for asking about the cause in such matters. For instance, why is it that that whose leaves are broad sheds its leaves in winter? If it is said 'Because the humidity due to which the leaves which cause tree-leaves to stick together in winter causes that whose leaves are broader to scatter more quickly', such an answer would be more pertinent to knowing how the breadth of leaves is the cause of their being shed [in winter]. The same might be said about what Hipparchus[1] states with respect to the land of the Slavs not having any pipes,[2] due to the fact that it does not have any vines. Similarly, what Aratos says to the effect that the southern stars set more quickly than the northern, due to the fact that they are distant from the North Pole and that the moon is eclipsed due to its passing in the centre of the ecliptic. For such causes are remote, and therefore it does not appear therefrom how an existing thing comes to be through them.

Now, since the middle terms of demonstrations consist of such causes, it follows that they will almost constitute proofs. That is why we should seek, in the case of everything whose cause is given, its proximate cause and should not be content with its remote causes. For instance, we should not be content in explaining the eclipse of the moon with saying that it is parallel to the centre of the ecliptic circle without adding that, when it is parallel to the circle of the ecliptic and is facing the sun, the earth interposes between it and the sun and conceals thereby the light reaching it from the sun's rays.

The same thing may have many causes, according to the variety of causes that we have mentioned. Similarly, a number of things may have the same causes. The same cause may either be the same in genus, the same in species, or the same in proportion. An example of that whose causes are one in genus are the echo and the rainbow; for the genus of their cause is reflection,[3] the echo being caused by the reflection of sound and the rainbow by the reflection of light. As for two things the species of whose cause is the same, the rainbow and the object seen in a mirror may be given as instances, since both are seen due to the reflection of sight, although one of them is caused by the reflection of light from a cloud, whereas the second is from a polished iron surface.

Things whose causes are the same may be such that some of them may be causes of each other, and the remotest cause the cause of them all. However, some may not be causes of each other. An example of what may be causes of each other is our asking 'Why does the water of the Nile abound at the end of the month?' or 'Why does the air become more humid at the end of the month?' or 'Why does air at the end of the month become similar to that of winter?' The

1. Hipparchus was a second-century BC astronomer who was influenced by Aratos. Both were major sources of Ptolemy's astronomy.

2. Or flutes.

3. Or, rather, refraction.

cause in all these cases is the recession of the light of the moon. However, the cause of the abundance of the Nile is the excess of humidity in the air, the cause of this is the correspondence of the air's condition, then, to the air's condition in winter; the cause of the latter is loss of heat in the air, the cause of which being the lack of heat due to the moon's light, the cause of which being the recession of the moon's light emanating from its face which is opposite to the earth on its higher side, and finally the cause of this being the moon's proximity to the sun. Hence, the sun's proximity to the moon is the cause of all these conditions and some of these are causes of each other.

Very often, the proximate cause of the thing is given, and this leaves room for the question as to why that is so. For example, why are the angles of the isosceles triangle equal to two right angles? Its proximate cause may be to say that it is a triangle, but this would leave room for questioning till we say 'Because its angles are equal to the two right angles which lie on the two sides of one of its sides once its other side is drawn.'[1] Hence, every two angles on the opposite sides of a straight line intersecting with a straight line are equal to two right angles. Thereupon, there is no room left for asking why it is like that.

That is why we should not be content; with respect to whatever cause is being sought, with that which leaves room for asking why it is so. As for that whose being is not necessary, either absolutely or with respect to something else, it is of two kinds: one is the being which exists at most times or that which exists in most subjects, or that which combines the two conditions; the other is that which exists for the least part or in equal measure. This second kind is such that no science investigates its two conditions at all; whereas that which exists for the most part is the subject of investigation in many sciences.

Now the premises which are of this type will give rise to essential conclusions which are of this type also, the conclusions which are of this type being such that the syllogism which gives rise to them essentially will have premises of this type also. These premises are regarded as necessary principles in most of the sciences and are treated as such, and in these only essential premises are appropriate and are used in the sciences.

Chapter 3. Of Definitions and their Kinds

Let us now turn to conceptions. We have already summed up their kinds and shown which are more and which are less perfect, and listed the things from which the various kinds of conceptions actually derive. The least perfect of conceptions are

1. al-Fārābī's proof appears to be that $<b + <d = 180^{\circ}$, as in the figure.

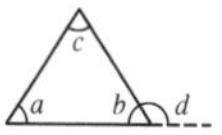

those which arise from single terms which designate a particular thing and their like; the most perfect are those conveyed by definitions.

Let us then discuss definitions and the things defined. These may be the ones which single terms denote, such as man, sun, and moon, or are denoted by a statement the form of its construction is not that of the construction of an affirmative statement.

Now definitions are formed out of a number of things similar to what demonstrations are formed from, the mode of forming definitions being different from the mode of forming demonstrations. (We have already summed up how demonstrations, and in general syllogisms and the parts of syllogisms, are constructed.) The mode of constructing the parts of definitions is not the mode in which some parts are a judgment and other parts are the object of judgment and whose combination may be used as part of an affirmative statement.

The smallest number of parts of which definitions may be formed is two; some parts of a definition may be predicated of the definiendum, some may not be predicated of the definiendum. For example, the definition of a circle is that it is a figure bounded by a single line at the centre of which is a point, all the straight lines emanating therefrom toward the circumference are equal. Now the statement that it is a figure may be predicated of the circle, for the circle is a figure; but the statement that it is a single line may not be predicated of the circle because it is not true to say that the circle is a single line, but rather that the circle is bounded by a single line. Thus the line would be part of the term predicated of the circle and it is, then, part of the differentia, the differentia being our saying 'Bounded by a single line.' Now whatever cannot be predicated of the definiendum is part of its part, not its whole part. For, its whole part may be predicated of the definiendum, and likewise, its whole parts may be predicated of each other, in either a universal or a particular way. That is why it is not excluded that predicating one of its parts to the other may be demonstrated; likewise, predicating each of its parts of the definiendum may also be demonstrated.

The parts of the definition may be prior to the definiendum or posterior thereto. That whose parts are prior to the definiendum is the one which explains the essence of the thing in an explicit way through those things which indicate the being of that thing essentially, rather than accidentally. The term definition applies more frequently to that thing whose parts are posterior to the definiendum. As to those things through which the being of the thing is given, some are intrinsic to the thing itself and some are extrinsic to that thing. That which explains the thing in an explicit way through those things which indicate its being and are intrinsic to that thing is more frequently referred to as the definition than that whose parts are extrinsic to that thing. Now as for the parts of definitions which are definitions absolutely, each one thereof is prior to the definiendum, although some are prior to the others. The priority of the parts of the definition to the definiendum is analogous to the priority of the parts of the demonstration to the conclusions.

The most prior parts of the definition in the order of discourse are the most posterior; and that of its parts which is posterior must be more prior and more prior in that order. By priority, then, we mean in fact the priority of the cause of the thing to the thing. Therefore, the most prior of the parts of the definition may be used to demonstrate the posterior, regarding either its existence in the definiendum or its existence absolutely; the same holds when the definition is made up of many parts in excess of two.

Of the complete parts of the definition, some are denoted by a compound expression, some by a single term, and some by a statement. As for what is denoted by a compound expression, its inherence in the definiendum may be demonstrated through the other parts. If to these other parts belongs that which can be predicated of each other, then the inherence of either of its two parts in the other may be proved through a categorical demonstration, while the other part thereof will serve as the middle term. If, however, its parts cannot be predicated of each other, then it is demonstrated through a conditional compound statement. As for what is denoted by a single term, it is similar to that which is denoted by a statement whose parts cannot be predicated of each other.

The complete parts of the definition which are each denoted by a statement are either such that some of them are more general than the *definiendum*, or some are such that each part thereof is equivalent to the *definiendum*. Now the complete parts of the definition denoted by a statement are such that those equivalent to the *definiendum* may each be taken separately as a definition of the *definiendum*. Then the posterior of these two parts will be called the conclusion of the demonstration, and the prior will be called the definition which is the principle of demonstration, whereas their combination will be called the definition which is a transferable demonstration. This is the most perfect of definitions, for there is no difference between this definition and demonstration except in the arrangement of the parts. If this is the case, then if a thing is demonstrated through an absolute demonstration, it will be possible to take the parts of the demonstration themselves as parts of definition; conversely, if a thing is defined, the parts of its definition can be taken as parts of demonstration. If it happens that we have a matter denoted by a single term, and we needed to prove its existence through a categorical demonstration, and so we took the statement explaining it and proved it through an absolute demonstration, and took the middle term therein as an intention denoted by a compound expression, then that which was originally an explanation of the expression will become a definition of that matter insofar as it is the *conclusion* of a demonstration. Thus the middle term will become a definition thereof, insofar as it is a *principle* of demonstration. For instance, if we wished to prove the existence of thunder and explained the connotation of the term thunder as a sound emanating from a cloud, then changed the order of this statement so that it would be capable of demonstration and said 'There is a sound in the cloud', making the middle term 'the rippling of the wind in the cloud' and constructed the proof as follows: 'There is in the cloud a rippling wind; therefore there is in it a sound; therefore there is a sound in the cloud.' This construction is the kind of proof proceeding continually and leading to a determinate conclusion. If, however, we wish to take these parts themselves in the definition of thunder, we would have to change the order of these parts as follows: 'Thunder is a sound emanating from a cloud due to the rippling movement of the wind in it.' Then that which has become prior in the proof would be posterior in the definition and that which is posterior in the former is now prior in the latter.

As for definitions whose parts are regarded as extrinsic to the *definiendum*, these extrinsic factors are of three kinds: (l) the purposes of the thing, (2) its agents, or (3) something in which the *definiendum* inheres. When, however, it is the case that a part denotes the purpose and another part denoting that in which the thing inheres combine in its definition, then that which denotes the purpose is the principle of demonstration with respect to that definition and the other part is the conclusion of the demonstration. For instance, in the definition of the soul, that it is the perfection of a natural, organic body from which apprehension[1] and the actions consequent on apprehension arise, we note that both these two parts (I mean our saying a natural, organic body and our saying apprehension and the actions consequent on apprehension arise) are two things extrinsic to the soul. However, a natural, organic body denotes that in which the soul inheres, whereas the other part denotes the purpose of the soul. That is why this part is used as a principle, of demonstration and the other as a conclusion of a demonstration. Similarly, if a part of the definition denoting the agent and a part denoting the purpose combine, then the part denoting the purpose is the principle of the demonstration and the other the conclusion of the demonstration. For instance, if we define the wall by saying it is a structure[2] which the builder constructed to hold up the ceiling, then the phrase 'to hold up the ceiling' is the principle of the demonstration and the other the conclusion of the demonstration.[3]

This discourse will summarize all the kinds of definitions, but since many people in both ancient and modern times have been accustomed to saying that they consist of genera and differentiae, it will be necessary to consider what they say on that subject and show in which kind that enters. Accordingly, we say that none of those people believe that the part which they call the genus defines the thing by reference to what is extrinsic to it essentially. But as regards the part which they call the differentia, it may be thought that a lot of it is defined by reference

1. *Idrāk*, which includes both sensuous perception and rational thought. The definition of the soul given above is Aristotle's, in *De anima*, II, 412 *b*.

2. The original has *jism*, i.e., body.

3. That is, the purpose or final cause is logically prior to the agent or efficient cause.

to that which is external to the thing defined, whereas a lot of it is not believed to be thus, such as the definition of man and the definition of triangle. As for that of which the differentiae are believed to denote something extrinsic to it, we give as an example our definition of the wall as a structure which holds up the ceiling. For holding up the ceiling is extrinsic to the essence of the wall. Similarly, the definition of God by some people as a being[1] who moves the world, and similar definitions of this kind.

That which is used as genus and differentia in definitions is of two kinds. The first is similar to what is said of the animal that it is a genus, and of rational that it is a differentia. The second is that which is denoted by fully analogous terms, such as one, being, perfection, potentiality, relation, and the like. The first kind is more fittingly called a genus, and it is genus in the absolute sense so that definitions which are made up of such genera and differentiae while their differentiae are not extrinsic to the definiendum, but are intrinsic to it, the parts of their definitions necessarily denote that through which the thing exists, as well as its identity.[2] However, the genus either designates that which functions as the conclusion of a demonstration or designates the whole compound,[3] but its designation of what functions as the *conclusion* of a demonstration is more fitting, more frequent, and stronger. The differentia, on the other hand, either designates the part thereof which functions as a *principle* of a demonstration or designates the whole compound,[4] but its designation of what functions as a principle of demonstration is more frequent. As for that whose differentia designates something extrinsic to the definition, that differentia is of two kinds. The first consists in being a definition of that which is equivalent to the form, so that the definition of the form is used instead of the name of the form in those cases in which the form happens not to have a name. For example, if we were to define a palm tree as the tree which yields fruit, then our saying a tree is the genus of the palm tree, and our saying yields fruit is a differentia, denoting something extrinsic to the palm tree and denoting a specific action thereof. Now, since specific actions arise from the specific form of the thing, it follows that the actions of the form are the ends of the form, and so it is defined by reference to them. And since it happens with reference to the form whereby the palm tree is a palm tree that it has no name, its definition is used as a substitute of its name.[5] And this is what we do in the case of whatever is such that its form is hard to conceive or is not possible at all. The second kind refers to whatever is such that its differentiae denote things extrinsic to it, as we have already stated. Thus, in those definitions which are made up of genera and differentiae which are of this type, the genus

1. The Arabic says 'thing', or *shay'*.
2. Arabic *huwiyyah.*
3. Of terms.
4. Ibid.
5. Namely, the palm tree is a fruit-yielding plant.

denotes in the definition what the genus denotes in the first kind, and so does the differentia. However, with respect to definitions which are made up of those remaining parts, that which is used as a substitute of the genus in the definition is either not a genus at all, but rather is an equivocal or analogous noun, or it is said to be a genus in a sense other than the sense in which animal is said to be the genus of man. For instance, one being and thing and their like are either not genera at all or are genera in a different sense. For these appear to enable us to visualize the thing generally in some way, without denoting a part which is constitutive of the thing essentially. If so, genus is of two kinds: one is what gives a general visualization of the thing in some way only and the other which gives a general visualization, but denotes nonetheless a part which is constitutive of the thing itself. This latter kind is more fittingly called genus than the former, but both should be called genera.[1]

A RECONCILIATION OF THE OPINIONS OF THE TWO SAGES, DIVINE PLATO AND ARISTOTLE

From *al-Kitāb al-jamʿ bayn raʾyay al-ḥakīmayn, Aflāṭūn al-ilāhī wa Arisṭū*

Translated for this volume by Shams Inati from al-Fārābī's *Kitāb al-jamʿ bayn raʾyay al-ḥakīmayn, Aflāṭūn al-ilāhī wa-Arisṭū*, ed. Albert Naṣrī Nādir (Beirut, 1960), pp. 80–101.

After seeing that the majority of the people of our times argue and dispute about the coming into being (*ḥudūth*) and eternity (*qidam*) of the world, and that they claim that the two prominent ancient sages, Plato and Aristotle, differ with regard to the proof for the existence of the First Creator, the existence of the secondary causes from Him, the issue of the soul and intellect, retribution for good and bad actions, and many civil, ethical, and logical matters, I wish in this essay to begin reconciling the opinions of these two sages and uncovering what is indicated by the meaning of their discourses. Thus agreement between their beliefs will be revealed, and doubt and suspicion in the hearts of those studying their books will be eliminated. I will point out the subjects of suspicion and the areas of doubt in the discourses of these two sages; for this matter is among the most important things whose demonstration is intended in this essay and the most useful object whose explication and clarification are sought.

1. In medieval logic, the first kind is referred to collectively as transcendentals, rather than genera, for the reason mentioned by al-Fārābī.

1. The Consensus that Plato and Aristotle are the Primary Source for Philosophy; the Meaning of the Difference of Opinion Regarding Them

The definition or quiddity of philosophy[1] is that it is knowledge of the existents inasmuch as they exist. These two sages created philosophy, introduced its first principles and fundamentals, and completed its ends and branches. On them one relies for its small and large matters, and to them one resorts concerning its simple and difficult issues. Whatever the two of them produced in every branch of knowledge is the only dependable foundation of that branch, owing to its being free from extrinsic and turbid elements. This truth was expressed by the tongues and witnessed by the minds of the majority of those with clear hearts and pure minds, if not by all of them.

If a statement or a belief is true only when it corresponds to the thing which is other than it, and if there is a difference between the opinions of these two sages regarding the majority of the branches of philosophy, then there must be one of three improper things: either the definition signifying the essence of philosophy is untrue, or the opinions and beliefs of all or of the majority about the philosophy of these two men are weak and emaciated, or the knowledge of those presupposing that there is a difference between the two regarding these fundamentals is incomplete.

2. The Meaning and Definition of Philosophy

Philosophy includes all the sciences. Both Plato and Aristotle made inquiries regarding it. The sound definition of philosophy corresponds to the art of (*ṣināʿt*) philosophy. This is clear from grasping the particular parts of this art. This is so because the subjects and matters of the sciences cannot but be either metaphysical, physical, logical, mathematical, or political. The art of philosophy is that which deduces and brings out these parts, in such a way that there is no existent in the world that is not penetrated and sought by philosophy and is made the source of knowledge in accordance with human capacity. The path of division favoured by the sage Plato expresses and clarifies what we have mentioned. One who employs division seeks to include everyone of the existents. Had Plato not trodden this path, the sage Aristotle would not have undertaken the challenge of treading it (p. 81).

1. Text: *ʾīḍāḥ al-falsafah ḥadduhā wa-māhiyyatuhā*, literally, since the definition and quiddity of philosophy. 'Since' has been dropped because it is confusing and unnecessary for conveying al-Fārābī's meaning. 'Definition and quiddity' has been replaced by 'definition or quiddity', to ensure that the reader understands that the definition and quiddity of a thing are the same, except that the former is a linguistic expression of the latter. The quiddity or essence of a thing is that thing's whatness, which consists of the genus and difference or differences of that thing. An example of this is the quiddity or essence of 'human being', which is 'rational animal'. The definition of a thing is simply a statement of that whatness.

3. Aristotle's Method of Treating These Sciences: The Use of Demonstration and Syllogism

When Aristotle found that Plato had captured, demonstrated, perfected, and clarified the method of division, he concerned himself with enduring hard work and exerting effort to establish the method of syllogism. He began explicating and refining this method, for the purpose of using syllogism and demonstration in every part necessitated by division. Thus he would be the adept, the perfecter, the aide, and the giver of advice. The truth of what I say will be evident to the person who is trained in the science of logic and is a master of the science of ethical conduct, and who then begins investigating physics and metaphysics and studies the books of these two sages. Such a person will find that the two of them had intended to record the sciences in accordance with the existents of the world and had made an effort to clarify the states of these existents as they are, without intending to invent, introduce extrinsic elements, create, embellish, or induce desire, but so that the two of them may fulfil their portion and share of duty, which is in accordance with their power and capacity. If that is the case, then the definition made of philosophy—that it is knowledge of the existents inasmuch as they exist—is a sound one that demonstrates the essence of the definiendum and signifies its quiddity.

4. Consensus Is Evidence, Especially If It Is That of the Intellectuals

The mind does not accept or acknowledge that the opinions of all or of the majority of people and their belief that these two sages are two recognized and eminent masters of this art[1] are weak and emaciated. This is because reality testifies to the contrary, for we know with certainty that no evidence is stronger, more beneficial, and more solid than the testimony of the various sciences of the same thing and than the agreement of many opinions regarding that thing, for the mind is evidence to all. There is need for the agreement of many different minds because a certain mind may imagine a thing posterior to that thing and contrary to what it is, owing to the similarity of the signs that signify the thing itself. There is no stronger evidence nor more solid certitude than that of the different minds when they are in agreement. Do not be deceived by the fact that there are many people with emaciated opinions, for a group that follows one opinion and adheres to a leader who guides them regarding the matter they agree on are of the rank of one mind (p. 82). But, as we already mentioned, the one mind may err with regard to the same thing, especially if this mind does not reflect frequently on the opinion to which it adheres and does not consider it with an examining and critical eye. Acceptance of a thing at face value or negligence in inquiry about it may veil, blind, and elude a mind. If different minds, however, are in agreement after their reflection, experience,

1. That is, the art of philosophy.

study, criticism, rebuke, and drawing parallel points, then nothing is sounder than what they believe in, testify to, and agree on. We do find that different speakers[1] agree on the prominence of these two sages, on setting them up as examples for doing philosophy, and on resorting to them in the consideration of matters. To the two of them is referred the attribution of profound philosophies, careful sciences, marvellous conclusions, and penetration into the exact notions that lead in every case to the pure truth.

If this is so, then the view of those who assume that the two sages have differences over fundamentals falls short of the truth. You must know that there is no erring view or faulty factor without a reason or something that calls for it. We shall show at this point some of the reasons that led to the assumption that there are differences between the two sages over fundamentals. We will follow that with reconciliation of the opinions of the two of them.

5. It is Impermissible to Draw a Universal Judgment from the Perception of Particulars

You must know that drawing universal judgments from the perception of particulars is among what is known with certainty to belong to the natures of things, such that these natures do not abandon it, and cannot be free from it or dispense with it in the sciences, opinions, and beliefs and in the reasons for rules and religious laws, as well as in civil associations and relationships. In physics, this is exemplified by our judgment that every stone sinks in water, but perhaps some stones float; that every plant burns in fire, but some plants do not burn in fire; that the universal body is finite, but perhaps it is infinite. In religious matters, this is exemplified by our judgment that whoever manifests good deeds on the whole is therefore just and of sound testimony in many things, though that person is not observed in all cases. In civil associations, this is exemplified by our judgment that calmness and tranquillity, whose (p. 83) limits in our souls are confined,[2] yet from those definitions there are only general conclusions[3] without their being observed under all of their conditions.

Since the condition of the universal judgment is as we have described it to be, namely, that it takes hold and captures the natures of things, how can the mind determine a link between Plato and Aristotle—in spite of imagining and grasping the universal differences between them—when the two of them emerged with apparent differences between them in terms of their lives, actions, and many statements. This is so, though the mind considers both statements and actions as

1. Text: *alsun* (tongues). It is taken for granted here that a tongue is a representation of the mind or that language is an expression of intention.

2. Text: *ḥadduhumā fī anfusinā maḥdūd.*

3. Text: *istidlālāt.*

consequent upon beliefs, especially when the beliefs are free from hypocrisy and embarrassment regardless of the length of time.

A Discussion of the Manners in which Plato and Aristotle Differ

First, Plato's Way of Life Differs from that of Aristotle

Among Plato's and Aristotle's dissimilar actions and different ways of life are Plato's abandonment of many worldly matters, his rejection of such matters, and his expressing in many of his statements caution of them and preference for avoiding them. In contrast is Aristotle's attachment to what Plato abandoned. Thus Aristotle acquired many properties, married, begot children, and became a minister for King Alexander. Of worldly matters, he possessed what cannot be concealed from those who concern themselves with the study of books of information about the ancients.

In appearance, this matter requires belief that the two doctrines of Plato and Aristotle differ with regard to the two worlds;[1] but in reality that is not the case. Plato is the one who wrote and refined politics and showed the just life, the civil, human relationships, demonstrating their virtues and manifesting the corruption that happens to the actions of those who abandon civil relationships and depart from cooperation in them. His essays regarding what we have mentioned are well known and have been studied by different nations from his time to ours. But when he found that the soul itself and its rectification are the first things with which a human being begins—such that when a human being ensures the equilibrium and rectification of the soul that human being moves on to rectify other souls—and found that he did not have in his soul the kind of strength that would enable him to preoccupy himself with those things that[2] concerned him about it, he devoted his time to his most important obligations. He was determined that when he finished with the first most important thing he would advance to the next lower thing, as he advocated doing in his discourses on politics and ethics (p. 84).

In his statements and essays on politics, Aristotle followed in the footsteps of Plato. However, especially when he returned to his soul itself, he felt that it is able, forbearing, of a generous character, and with perfection. With this, he was able to rectify his soul and to preoccupy himself with cooperation with, and enjoyment of, many civil matters. A person who reflects on these circumstances will know that there is no difference between the opinions and beliefs of the two sages. The apparent dissimilarity between these opinions and beliefs is caused by a deficiency in the natural powers of one of these sages and a supply of such power in the other, nothing else. This dissimilarity is in accordance with what belongs to two human individuals.[3] Thus the majority of people may know what is preferable, better, and

1. That is, the material and the spiritual.
2. Text: *mimmā* (from those things that).
3. That is, inasmuch as they are two individuals, not inasmuch as they are human.

worthier, yet do not have the capacity and power to do it, or perhaps they may have the capacity and power to do some of it but not the rest.

Second, Plato's and Aristotle's Methods of Writing Books Differ

Plato's and Aristotle's dissimilar doctrines regarding the writing of the sciences and the composition of books are also among the ways in which these two sages appear different philosophically. Thus in ancient times Plato used to forbid the writing of the sciences and their inclusion in books, rather than in the pure hearts and the responsible minds. When he feared absent-mindedness, forgetfulness, the disappearance of his inferences, and the difficulty of grasping them again, considering the abundance of his knowledge, wisdom, and penetration into wisdom, he then chose symbols and riddles with the intention to record his knowledge and wisdom. This he did in accordance with the method that renders his knowledge and wisdom accessible only to those worthy of them and those who must grasp such knowledge and wisdom through search, investigation, scrutiny, and effort.

Aristotle's doctrine, on the other hand, is one of clarity, exposition, organization, deliverance, disclosure, and declaration, as well as the completion of whatever is possible of that. The two methods are in appearance different. However, one who investigates Aristotle's ideas and studies his books with perseverance cannot but know his doctrine of the various manners of closure, veiling, and complication, in spite of the apparent intentional explication and clarity. Illustrations of this doctrine are found in his discourses, such as the elimination of the necessary premise from many physical, metaphysical, and ethical syllogisms which he mentioned. The place of such a premise was indicated by interpreters of such syllogisms. This doctrine is also illustrated by the elimination of many major ideas,[1] as well as the elimination of one of the two ideas under consideration, limiting oneself to one of the two. This is exemplified by (p. 85) his saying in his letter to Alexander on the politics of the particular cities: 'One who prefers the choice of justice in civil dealings[2] is worthy of being set apart from others by the city administrator with regard to punishment.' But the completion of this saying is this: 'One who prefers the choice of justice over wrongdoing is worthy of being set apart from others by the city administrator with regard to punishment and reward. This means that one who prefers justice is worthy of being rewarded, and one who prefers wrongdoing is worthy of being punished.[3]

1. Text: *al-mashā'ikh*.

2. Text: *al-ta'āwun*.

3. Owing to space limitations, only one more issue, that of knowledge, the tenth point in al-Fārābī's discussion of what he considers apparent rather than real differences between Plato and Aristotle, will be translated here. This point has been selected considering its importance and interest to the general reader.

Tenth, the Issue of Knowledge: The Issue of Forms in Plato and Aristotle's View regarding Such Forms

Also, among those apparent differences between Plato and Aristotle is that in his book *Posterior Analytics*, Aristotle had expressed the suspicion that one who seeks a certain knowledge must seek it in one of two ways. One seeks either what one does not know or what one knows. If one seeks what one does not know, then how can one be certain that knowing it is knowing that which one was seeking? If, on the other hand, one seeks what one knows, then one's seeking a second knowledge of it is superfluous and unnecessary. Aristotle then pursued his discourse, saying: 'One who seeks the knowledge of a certain thing seeks in something else only what has been attained in one's soul.' Thus, for example, equality and inequality are found in the soul. Therefore one who seeks to know whether a piece of wood is equal or unequal to another piece seeks only what the soul has attained of those forms. Thus, if one finds one of these two qualities, it is as if one recollects what is in one's soul. If one finds that piece of wood equal to another piece, then equality is in one's soul; if unequal, then inequality is in one's soul.

In his well-known book *Phaedo*, Plato pointed out that knowledge is recollection. In support of that, he provided evidence from what he related about Socrates' questions and answers on the subject of the equal and of equality. He asserts that equality is that which is in the soul, and as for the equal, it is that which is like the piece of wood or another thing that is equal to something else. A human being perceiving that piece of wood recollects the equality which is in the soul and, thus, knows that this equal thing is equal only in accordance with the equality which resembles that equality which is in the soul. Similarly, whatever is learned is only recollection of what is in the soul. God knows best.

The Soul and its Fate

Most people had adhered to beliefs that exceed the bounds of reasonable interpretation of the discourses of Plato and Aristotle concerning the eternity of the soul. Those who upheld the eternity of the soul after its separation from the body exaggerated in their interpretation of these discourses and distorted their ideas. They thought so well of these discourses that they placed them in the same class as demonstrations, not knowing that Plato related them about Socrates only as one would, who wishes to confirm a concealed matter through signs and indications. But a syllogism in signs is not a demonstration, as the sage Aristotle taught in *Prior Analytics* and in *Posterior Analytics*. As for those who reject the eternity of the soul, they too exaggerated in charging their opponents with falsehood. They claimed that Aristotle is opposed to Plato with respect to this belief. They were unmindful of Aristotle's statement at the beginning of the book *Posterior Analytics*, where he begins by saying: 'All teaching and all learning is only from knowledge that has prior existence.' A little later, he says: 'A human being may know something where his knowledge is prior and eternal and something the knowledge of which occurs simultaneously with its knowledge.' An example of this latter thing is all the things that fall under universal things.

How then[1] does the essence of this discourse of Aristotle depart in any way from what Plato had said? But a rectified mind, a sound opinion, and an inclination toward truth and justice are lacking in the majority of people. Thus a person who fully reflects on the occurrence of the primary premises and the condition for learning realizes that in this regard there is no difference, separation, or opposition between the opinions of the two sages. We have indicated only a small portion of this[2] sufficient to reveal this common meaning in the discourses of the two sages, so that doubt concerning that meaning would be removed.

Fārābī's Opinion Concerning Knowledge and the Soul

We say that it is clearly evident that an infant's soul has knowledge in potentiality and possesses the senses as instruments for apprehension. Sense apprehension is only of particulars, and from particulars, universals are attained. Thus universals are in reality sense experiences. However, some sense experiences occur by intention. It has become the custom of the multitudes to call the universals that occur by the intention 'experiential principles'. As for those universals which occur to a human being not by intention, the multitudes have no name for them because they do not concern themselves with them, but the scholars have a name for them. Thus the scholars call them 'primary knowledge', 'principles of demonstration', and similar names. In *Posterior Analytics*, Aristotle pointed out that one who loses a certain sense loses a certain knowledge, for knowledge occurs in the soul only by means of the senses. Since knowledge occurs in the soul at the very beginning of one's existence without intention, a human being does not remember this fact when this knowledge occurred bit by bit. That is why most people may imagine that this knowledge had been in the soul eternally and that it has access to[3] a path other than the senses.

Thus if knowledge occurs in the soul as a result of sense experience, the soul becomes rational, for reason is nothing other than sense experience. The more there is of this type of experience, the more the soul is rational. Furthermore, no matter how a human being seeks the knowledge of a certain thing, he desires to understand one of the states of that thing and makes an effort to attach that thing in that state to what has already been known. This is nothing other than seeking

1. Text: *layta shiʿrī*.
2. That is, of the fact that upon reflection one finds no real difference between Plato and Aristotle.
3. Text: *taʿlam*.

what is present of that thing in his soul. For example, when he desires to know whether a certain thing is alive or not alive, and when the meaning of 'alive' and that of 'not alive' have already been attained in his soul, he then seeks one of these two meanings either through his mind, or through his senses, or through both of them. If he encounters this meaning, he rests at it, feels at peace with it, and enjoys the removal in him of the harm of wonder and ignorance.

This is what Plato said: Knowledge is recollection, reflection is making the effort to know, and recollection is making the effort to remember. The seeker of knowledge is one who has desire and who makes an effort. Whatever he finds important, he seeks knowledge of it by way of indications, signs, and the meaning of what was earlier in his soul. Therefore, it is as if he remembers at that point, as one would who looks at a body, some of whose accidents resemble the accidents of another body which he had known but forgotten. Thus he remembers it[1] from what he knows about that which resembles it.[2] Reason has no act specifically concerned with it[3] without the senses and the apprehension of all things and of contraries, as well as the imagining of the states of things other than they are. The senses apprehend the united states of a being as united, the separate states of a being as separate, the ugly states of a being as ugly, and the beautiful states of a being as beautiful.[4] The same is true of the rest of such states. Reason, on the other hand, apprehends the states of every being that have been apprehended by the senses, as well as their contraries. Thus reason apprehends the united and the separate states of a being simultaneously and the separate and the united states of a being simultaneously. The same is true of the way reason apprehends the rest of the similar states.

One who reflects on what we have posited briefly concerning the matter about which the sage Aristotle exaggerated in describing at the end of the book *Posterior Analytics* and in the book *De Anima*, which has been commented upon by thinkers and whose subject was studied by them, knows that what the sage mentioned at the beginning of the book, *Posterior Analytics* and which we related in this discourse is close to what Plato stated in the book *Phaedo*. However, there is a difference between the two subjects in which the two sages mentioned this matter. Thus the sage Aristotle mentioned it when he wished to clarify the subject of knowledge and syllogism. Plato, on the other hand, mentioned it when he wished to clarify the subject of the soul. For this reason, the majority of those who reflect on the discourses of these two sages find a problem. What we have cited is sufficient for one who seeks the right path.

---

1. That is, the former body.
2. That is, the latter body.
3. That is, with the former body.
4. In other words, the senses grasp only the specific states that are presented to them.

THE PERFECT STATE

From *Mabādi' ārā' ahl al-madīnat al-fāḍilah*

Reprinted from Abū Naṣr al-Fārābī, *On the Perfect State* (Mabādi' ārā' ahl al-madīnat al-fāḍilah), ed. and tr. R. Walzer (Oxford, 1985), pp. 58–89, 229–259.

Metaphysics: The First Cause is One and Mind

1. The First Existent is the First Cause of the existence of all the other existents. It is free of every kind of deficiency, whereas there must be in everything else some kind of deficiency, either one or more than one; but the First is free of all their deficiencies. Thus its existence is the most excellent and precedes every other existence. No existence can be more excellent than, or prior to its existence. Thus it has the highest kind of excellent existence and the most elevated rank of perfect existence. Therefore its existence and substance cannot be adulterated by non-existence at all. It can in no way have existence potentially, and there is no possibility whatsoever that it should not exist. Therefore it is without beginning, and everlasting in its substance and essence, without being in need of any other thing, which would provide its permanence in order to be eternal; its substance suffices for its permanence and its everlasting existence. No existence at all can be like its existence; nor is there any existence of the same rank of its existence which the First would have and which it does not have already. It is the existent for whose existence there can be no cause through which, or out of which, or for the sake of which, it has come to exist. For it is neither matter nor is it at all sustained by a matter or a substratum; its existence is free of all matter and substratum. Nor does it have form, because form can exist only in matter. If it had form, its essence would be composed of matter and form, and if it were like that, it would be sustained by the two parts of which it would be composed and its existence would have a cause. Likewise its existence has no purpose and no aim, so that it would exist merely to fulfil that aim and that purpose; otherwise that would have been a cause of its existence, so that it would not be the First Cause. Likewise it has not derived its existence from something else prior to it, and even less so from inferior to it.

2. The First Existent is different in its substance from everything else, and it is impossible for anything else to have the existence it has. For between the First and whatever were to have the same existence as the First, there could be no difference and no distinction at all. Thus there would not be two things but one essence only, because, if there were a difference between the two, that in which they differed would not be the same as that which they shared, and thus that point of difference between the two would be a part of this species that exists: what is perfect in beauty is that apart from which no beauty of its species exists; equally

what is perfect in substance is that apart from which no substance of its species exists. Equally, in the case of every perfect body nothing else can be in the same species, as in the case of the sun, the moon and each one of the other planets. If, then, the First has perfect existence, it is impossible that any other existent should have the same existence. Therefore the First alone has this existence and it is unique in this respect.

3. Further, the First cannot have a contrary. This will become clear when the meaning of 'contrary' is understood. For, a thing and its contrary are different, and it is impossible that the contrary of a thing should ever be identical with that particular thing. Not everything, however, that differs from another thing is its contrary, nor is everything that cannot be that particular thing its contrary, but only that which is, in addition, opposing it, so that each of the two will annihilate and destroy the other when they happen to meet: it is of the nature of such contraries that the absence of B entails the existence of A in all places where B exists (now) and that the existence of B being established where A is established now entails the absence of A from that place. This generally applies to everything which can possibly have a contrary. For if a thing is the contrary of the other in its actions only and not in its other modes, this description will apply only to their actions; if they are contrary to each other in their qualities, this will apply only to their qualities; and if they are contrary to each other in their substances, this description will apply (only) to their substances. Now, if the First were to have a contrary, this would be its relation to its contrary. It would follow, then, that each of them would tend to destroy the other, and that the First could be destroyed by its contrary and in its very substance. But what can be destroyed cannot derive its own subsistence and permanence from its own substance, but also its own substance is not sufficient to bring it into existence. Nor is its own substance sufficient for producing its existence; this would rather be caused by something else. But what may possibly not exist cannot be eternal. And anything whose substance is not sufficient for its permanence or its existence will owe its existence or its permanence to another, different cause, so it will not be the First. Again, the First would in this way owe its existence to the absence of its contrary, and then the absence of its contrary would be the cause of its existence. The First Existent would then not be the First Cause in the absolute meaning of the term.

Again, it would follow that they both should have some common 'where' to receive them, either a substratum or a genus, or something else different from both of them, so that by their meeting in it, it would be possible for each of them to destroy the other. That 'where' would be permanent, and the two would occupy it in turn. And that 'where' would then be prior in existence to each of them.

Now should someone posit as 'contrary' something which does not answer this description, the thing posited would not be a contrary. Rather would it differ from the First in another way. We do not deny, indeed, that the First may have other things different from it, but not a contrary nor something which has the same existence which it has. Thus no existent can be of the same rank of existence as the First, because two contraries are (always) in one and the same rank of existence. Thus the First is unique in its existence, and there is no other existent to share its species. Hence it is one and, in addition, utterly unique by virtue of its rank. And it is one in this respect as well.

4. Again, the First is not divisible in thought into things which would constitute its substance. For, it is impossible that each part of the explanation of the meaning of the First should denote one of the parts by which the First's substance is constituted. If this were the case, the parts which constitute its substance would be causes of its existence, in the same way as the meanings denoted by the parts of the definition of a thing are causes of the existence of the thing defined and in the same way as matter and form are causes of the existence of the thing composed of them. But this is impossible in the case of the First, since it is the First and since its existence has no cause whatsoever.

If it is thus not divisible into these parts, it is still less possible to divide it into quantitative parts or into any other kinds of parts. This necessarily entails also that it has no magnitude and is absolutely incorporeal. Hence it is also one in this respect, because one of the meanings denoted by 'one' is 'the indivisible'. For whatever is indivisible in some respect is one in that respect in which it is indivisible. If it is indivisible in its action, it is one in that respect; if it is indivisible in its quality, it is one according to its quality. But what is indivisible in its substance is one with regard to its substance.

5. If then the First is indivisible with regard to its substance, the existence it has, by which it is distinguished from all other existents, cannot be any other than that by which it exists in itself. Therefore its distinction from all the others is due to a oneness which is its essence. For one of the meanings of oneness is the particular existence by which each existent is distinguished from all others; on the strength of this meaning of oneness each existent is called 'one' inasmuch as it has its own particular existence. This meaning of the term 'one' goes necessarily with 'existence'. Thus the First is one in this respect as well, and deserves more than any other one the name and the meaning (of 'the one').

6. Because the First is not in matter and has itself no matter in any way whatsoever, it is in its substance actual intellect; for what prevents the form from being intellect and from actually thinking (intelligizing) is the matter in which a thing exists. And when a thing exists without being in need of matter, that very thing will in its substance be actual intellect; and that is the status of the First. It is, then, actual intellect. The First is also intelligible through its substance; for, again, what prevents a thing from being actually intelligible and being intelligible through its substance in matter. It is intelligible by virtue of its being intellect; for the

One whose identity (*ipseitas*) is intellect is intelligible by the One whose identity is intellect. In order to be intelligible the First is in no need of another essence outside itself which would think it but it itself thinks its own essence. As a result of its thinking its own essence, it becomes actually thinking and intellect, and, as a result of its essence thinking (intelligizing) it, it becomes actually intelligized. In the same way, in order to be actual intellect and to be actually thinking, it is in no need of an essence which it would think and which it would acquire from the outside, but is intellect and thinking by thinking its own essence. For the essence which is thought is the essence which thinks, and so it is intellect by virtue of its being intelligized. Thus it is intellect and intelligized and thinking all that being one essence and one indivisible substance—whereas man, for instance, is intelligible, but what is intelligible in his case is not actually intelligized but potentially intelligible; he becomes subsequently actually intelligized after the intellect has thought him. What is intelligible in the case of man is thus not always the subject which thinks, nor is, in his case, the intellect always the same as the intelligible object, nor is our intellect intelligible because it is intellect. We think, but not because our substance is intellect; we think with an intellect which is not what constitutes our substance; but the First is different; the intellect, the thinker and the intelligible (and intelligized) have in its case one meaning and are one essence and one indivisible substance.

7. That the First is 'knowing' is to be understood in the same way. For it is, in order to know, in no need of an essence other than its own, through the knowledge of which it would acquire excellence, nor is it, in order to be knowable, in need of another essence which would know it, but its substance suffices for it to be knowing and to be known. Its knowledge of its essence is nothing else than its substance. Thus the fact that it knows and that it is knowable and that it is knowledge refers to one essence and one substance.

8. The same applies to its being 'wise'. For wisdom consists in thinking the most excellent thing through the most excellent knowledge. By the fact that it intelligizes its essence and through the knowledge of it, it knows the most excellent thing. The most excellent knowledge is the permanent knowledge, which cannot cease to exist, of what is permanent and cannot cease to exist. That is its knowledge of its essence.

9. The same applies to its being 'real' and 'true'. For real and true go with existence, and 'reality' and 'truth' go with existence. For, the reality and truth of a thing is its particular existence and the most perfect state of the existence which is its lot. Further, real and true are said of the intelligible through which the intellect happens to meet an existent, so as to grasp it. It is then said of that existent that it is real and true, inasmuch as it is intelligible, and that it exists with regard to its essence and by not being related to what intelligizes (thinks) it. But now, in the case of the First, it can be said that it is real and true in both these senses at once,

in that its existence is the most perfect and in that it is the intelligible by means of which he who thinks it comes into contact with the existent as it exists. In order to be real and true it is by the fact of its being intelligible in need of no other external essence which would think (intelligize) it. It also deserves more than anything else to be called real and true in both these senses at once. And its reality and truth are nothing else but its being real and true.

10. The same applies to its being 'living' and 'life': these two terms denote not two essences but one. In the case of the First, the meaning of 'living' is that it intelligizes the most excellent intelligible through the most excellent intellect, or that it knows the most excellent knowable through the most excellent knowledge. Likewise it is in our case, when we apprehend the lowest apprehensible through the lowest kind of apprehension, that we are called 'living' in the first instance. For we are called 'living' only when we apprehend the sensibles, that is the lowest knowables, through sensing, which is the lowest kind of apprehension, and making use of the lowest apprehending faculties, that is the sense perceptions. But the First, which is the most excellent intellect, thinks and knows the most excellent intelligible through the most excellent knowledge. It deserves in a higher degree to be called 'living': for it thinks inasmuch as it is intellect. That it is thinking and that it is intellect and that it is knowing and that it is knowledge has, in its case, one and the same meaning. And that it is 'living' and that it is 'life' has in the same way one and the same meaning.

Again the word 'living' may be predicated metaphorically of non-animals as well, so that it can be predicated of any existent which has come to its ultimate perfection and of everything which has reached that state of existence and perfection in which it produces that whose nature it is to proceed from it. In the same way, since the First has the most perfect existence, it deserves also in the highest degree that the word 'living' be predicated of it in this metaphorical sense as well.

11. When any thing whose existence is utterly perfect is thought (intelligized) and known, the result of that process of thinking of the thing which goes on in our minds and conforms to its existence will be in accordance with its existence outside our minds. If its existence is deficient, what we think of it in our minds will be deficient. Thus, in the case of motion, time, infinity, privation and other existents like them the result of our thinking each of them in our minds will be deficient, since they are themselves deficient existents. In the case of number, triangle, square and their like, the result of our thinking them in our minds will be more perfect, because they are themselves more perfect. Hence, since the First has the highest perfection of existence, it follows that what we think of it in our minds ought to have utmost perfection as well. We find, however, that this is not the case. One ought to realize that for the First it is not difficult to apprehend itself, since the First itself is of the utmost perfection. But it is difficult and hard for us to apprehend (perceive) it and to represent it to ourselves because of the weakness of our intellectual faculties,

mixed as they are with matter and non-being: we are too weak to think it as it really is. For, its overwhelming perfection dazzles us, and that is why we are not strong enough to represent it to ourselves perfectly (completely). Likewise, light is the first and most perfect and most luminous visible, the other visibles become visible through it, and it is the cause of the colours becoming visible. Hence our visual apprehension of any colour which is more perfect and powerful (strong) should have been more perfect. But we see that just the opposite happens. The more perfect and the more powerful a visible is, the weaker is our visual apprehension of it, and not because of its being hidden or deficient—it has, on the contrary, in itself the utmost brightness and luminosity—but because the perfection of its splendour dazzles our sight so that our eyes are bewildered. Thus are our minds in relation to the First Cause, the First Intellect and the First Living. Our thinking it is deficient, not because of any deficiency in the First, and our apprehension of it is difficult for us, not because of its substance being difficult to apprehend, but because our minds are too weak to represent it to ourselves. That is why the intelligibles within our minds are deficient. Our representation of them is of two kinds: one kind of intelligible is in itself impossible for man to represent to himself or to think of by way of perfect representation, because of the weak nature of their existence and the defects of their essences and substances. The other kind of intelligible could in itself be represented completely and as perfectly as they are, but since our minds are weak and far from the substances of these objects, it is impossible for us to represent them to ourselves completely and with all the perfection of their existence. Each of these two things is at opposite extremes, one being of the utmost perfection, the other of the utmost deficiency. Since we are mixed up with matter and since matter is the cause of our substances being remote from the First Substance, the nearer our substances draw to it, the more exact and the truer will necessarily be our apprehension of it. Because the nearer we draw to separating ourselves from matter, the more complete will be our apprehension of the First Substance. We come nearer to it only by becoming actual [or 'actually'] intellect. When we are completely separated from matter, our mental apprehension of the First will be at its most perfect.

12. The same applies to its greatness, its majesty and its glory. For majesty, greatness and glory exist in a thing in proportion to its perfection, either with regard to its substance or to one of its (special) properties. Whenever this is said of us, it is mostly said on account of the perfection of some 'accidental' things (goods) which we possess, such as riches or knowledge or some bodily quality. But since the perfection of the First surpasses every perfection, its greatness, majesty and glory surpass all those (others) which are endowed with greatness, and glory; in this case, surpassing greatness and glory are in its substance and not in anything else apart from its substance and its essence. For it is its essence which is possessed of majesty and glory, and it does not make any difference whether anybody else exalts it or does not, praises its greatness or does not, glorifies it or does not.

13. Beauty and brilliance and splendour mean in the case of every existent that it is in its most excellent state of existence and that it has attained its ultimate perfection. But since the First is in the most excellent state of existence, its beauty surpasses the beauty of every other beautiful existent, and the same applies to its splendour and its brilliance. Further, it has all these in its substance and essence by itself and by thinking (intelligizing) its essence. But we have beauty and splendour and brilliance as a result of accidental qualities (of our souls), and of what our bodies have in them and because of exterior things, but they are not in our substance. The Beautiful and the beauty in the First are nothing but one essence, and the same applies to the other things predicated of it.

14. Pleasure and delight and enjoyment result and increase only when the most accurate apprehension concerns itself with the most beautiful, the most brilliant and the most splendid objects. Now, since the First is absolutely the most beautiful, the most brilliant and the most splendid, and since its apprehension of its own essence is most accurate in the extreme and its knowledge of its own substance most excellent in the absolute meaning of the term, the pleasure which the First enjoys is a pleasure whose character we do not understand and whose intensity we fail to apprehend, except by analogy and by relating it to the amount of pleasure which we feel, when we have most accurately and most completely apprehended what is most perfect and most splendid on our level, either through sensing it or representing it to ourselves or through becoming aware of it intellectually. For we experience in this state an amount (degree) of pleasure which we assume to surpass every other pleasure in intensity and are filled with a feeling of utmost self-enjoyment as a result of the knowledge which we have attained. But whereas this state in us lasts but a short time and disappears speedily, the First's knowledge and the First's apprehension of what is most excellent and most beautiful and most splendid in its essence is, as compared with our knowledge and our apprehension of what is most beautiful and most splendid on our level, like its pleasure and its delight and its enjoyment of itself as compared with the limited amount of pleasure and delight and self-enjoyment which is attained by us. And since our apprehension and its apprehension have nothing in common nor do the object of our knowledge and the object of its knowledge nor the most beautiful on our level and the most beautiful in its essence—and if they had anything in common, it would be insignificant—then the pleasure which we feel and our delight and our enjoyment of ourselves and the corresponding state of the First have nothing in common. If they had anything in common it would be very insignificant—for how can that which is only a small part and that whose extension is unlimited in time have anything in common, and how can that which is very deficient have anything in common with that which is of utmost perfection?

15. Since the more something enjoys its own essence and the greater pleasure and happiness it feels about it the more it likes and loves its essence and the greater is

the pride it takes in it, it is evident that the relation which exists between the First is necessary love and liking of its essence and its pride in it and our love of ourselves, which arises from our enjoyment of the excellence of our essence, is the same as the relation between the excellence and the perfection of its essence and our excellence and perfection of which we are proud. In its case, subject and object of affection, subject and object of pride, subject and object of love are identical, and that is just the opposite of what exists in our case. What is loved in us is excellence and beauty, but what loves in us is not excellence and beauty, but is another faculty, which is however not what is loved in us. What loves in us, then, is not identical with what is loved in us. But in the First's case, subject and object of love and affection are identical. It does not make any difference whether anybody likes it or not, loves it or not: it is the first object of love and the first object of affection.

Politics: Perfect Association and Perfect Ruler; Faulty Association

1. In order to preserve himself and to attain his highest perfections every human being is by his very nature in need of many things which he cannot provide all by himself; he is indeed in need of people who each supply him with some particular need of his. Everybody finds himself in the same relation to everybody in this respect. Therefore man cannot attain the perfection, for the sake of which his inborn nature has been given to him, unless many (societies of) people who co-operate come together who each supply everybody else with some particular need of his, so that as a result of the contribution of the whole community all the things are brought together which everybody needs in order to preserve himself and to attain perfection. Therefore human individuals have come to exist in great numbers, and have settled in the inhabitable (inhabited?) region of the earth, so that human societies have come to exist in it, some of which are perfect, others imperfect.

2. There are three kinds of perfect society, great, medium and small. The great one is the union of all the societies in the inhabitable world; the medium one the union of one nation in one part of the inhabitable world; the small one the union of the people of a city in the territory of any nation whatsoever. Imperfect are the union of people in a village, the union of people in a quarter, then the union in a street, eventually the union in a house, the house being the smallest union of all. Quarter and village exist both for the sake of the city, but the relation of the village to the city is one of service whereas the quarter is related to the city as a part of it; the street is a part of the quarter, the house a part of the street. The city is a part of the territory of a nation, the nation a part of all the people of the inhabitable world.

3. The most excellent good and the utmost perfection is, in the first instance, attained in a city, not in a society which is less complete than it. But since good in its real sense is such as to be attainable through choice and will and evils are

also due to will and choice only, a city may be established to enable its people to co-operate in attaining some aims that are evil. Hence felicity is not attainable in every city. The city, then, in which people aim through association at co-operating for the things by which felicity in its real and true sense can be attained, is the excellent city, and the society in which there is a co-operation to acquire felicity is the excellent society; and the nation in which all of its cities co-operate for those things through which felicity is attained is the excellent nation. In the same way, the excellent universal state will arise only when all the nations in it co-operate for the purpose of reaching felicity.

4. The excellent city resembles the perfect and healthy body, all of whose limbs co-operate to make the life of the animal perfect and to preserve it in this state. Now the limbs and organs of the body are different and their natural endowments and faculties are unequal in excellence, there being among them one ruling organ, namely the heart, and organs which are close in rank to that ruling organ, each having been given by nature a faculty by which it performs its proper function in conformity with the natural aim of that ruling organ. Other organs have by nature[1] faculties by which they perform their functions according to the aims of those organs which have no intermediary between themselves and the ruling organ; they are in the second rank. Other organs, in turn, perform their functions according to the aim of those which are in the second rank, and so on until eventually organs are reached which only serve and do not rule at all. The same holds good in the case of the city. Its parts are different by nature, and their natural dispositions are unequal in excellence: there is in it a man who is the ruler, and there are others whose ranks are close to the ruler, each of them with a disposition and a habit through which he performs an action in conformity with the intention of that ruler; these are the holders of the first ranks. Below them are people who perform their actions in accordance with the aims of those people; they are in the second rank. Below them in turn are people who perform their actions according to the aims of the people mentioned in the second instance, and the parts of the city continue to be arranged in this way, until eventually parts are reached which perform their actions according to the aims of others, while there do not exist any people who perform their actions according to their aims; these, then, are the people who serve without being served in turn, and who are hence in the lowest rank and at the bottom of the scale. But the limbs and organs of the body are natural, and the dispositions which they have are natural faculties, whereas, although the parts of the city are natural, their dispositions and habits, by which they perform their actions in the city, are not natural but voluntary—notwithstanding that the parts of the city are by nature provided with endowments unequal in excellence which enable them to do one thing and not another. But they are not parts of the city by their inborn nature alone but rather by the voluntary habits which they acquire such as the arts and

1. Or better, with *P*: 'to make its (i.e., the body's) life perfect and to preserve it.'

their likes; to the natural faculties which exist in the organs and limbs of the body correspond the voluntary habits and dispositions in the parts of the city.

5. The ruling organ in the body is by nature the most perfect and most complete of the organs in itself and in its specific qualification, and it also has the best of everything of which another organ has a share as well; beneath it, in turn, are other organs which rule over organs inferior to them, their rule being lower in rank than the rule of the first and indeed subordinate to the rule of the first; they rule and are ruled. In the same way, the ruler of the city is the most perfect part of the city in his specific qualification and has the best of everything which anybody else shares with him; beneath him are people who are ruled by him and rule others.

The heart comes to be first and becomes then the cause of the existence of the other organs and limbs of the body, and the cause of the existence of their faculties in them and of their arrangement in the ranks proper to them, and when one of its organs is out of order, it is the heart which provides the means to remove that disorder. In the same way the ruler of this city must come to be in the first instance, and will subsequently be the cause of the rise of the city and its parts and the cause of the presence of the voluntary habits of its parts and of their arrangement in the ranks proper to them; and when one part is out of order he provides it with the means to remove its disorder.

The parts of the body close to the ruling organ perform of the natural functions, in agreement—by nature—with the aim of the ruler, the most noble ones; the organs beneath them perform those functions which are less noble, and eventually the organs are reached which perform the meanest functions. In the same way the parts of the city which are close in authority to the ruler of the city perform the most noble voluntary actions, and those below them less noble actions, until eventually the parts are reached which perform the most ignoble actions. The inferiority of such actions is sometimes due to the inferiority of their matter, although they may be extremely useful—like the action of the bladder and the action of the lower intestine in the body; sometimes it is due to their being of little use; at other times it is due to their being very easy to perform. This applies equally to the city and equally to every whole which is composed by nature of well ordered coherent parts: they have a ruler whose relation to the other parts is like the one just described.

6. This applies also to all existents. For the relation of the First Cause to the other existents is like the relation of the king of the excellent city to its other parts. For the ranks of the immaterial existents are close to the First. Beneath them are the heavenly bodies, and beneath the heavenly bodies the material bodies. All these existents act in conformity with the First Cause, follow it, take it as their guide and imitate it; but each existent does that according to its capacity, choosing its aim precisely on the strength of its established rank in the universe: that is to say the last follows the aim of that which is slightly above it in rank, equally the second existent, in turn, follows what is above itself in rank, and in the same way the third

existent has an aim which is above it. Eventually existents are reached which are linked with the First Cause without any intermediary whatsoever. In accordance with this order of rank all the existents permanently follow the aim of the First Cause. Those which are from the very outset provided with all the essentials of their existence are made to imitate the First (Cause) and its aim from their very outset, and hence enjoy eternal bliss and hold the highest ranks; but those which are not provided from the outset with all the essentials of their existence, are provided with a faculty by which they move towards the expected attainment of those essentials and will then be able to follow the aim of the First (Cause). The excellent city ought to be arranged in the same way: all its parts ought to imitate in their actions the aim of their first ruler according to their rank.

7. The ruler of the excellent city cannot just be any man, because rulership requires two conditions: (a) he should be predisposed for it by his inborn nature, (b) he should have acquired the attitude and habit of will for rulership which will develop in a man whose inborn nature is predisposed for it. Nor is every art suitable for rulership, most of the arts, indeed, are rather suited for service within the city, just as most men are by their very nature born to serve. Some of the arts rule certain (other) arts while serving others at the same time, whereas there are other arts which, not ruling anything at all, only serve. Therefore the art of ruling the excellent city cannot just be any chance art, nor due to any chance habit whatever. For just as the first ruler in a genus cannot be ruled by anything in that genus—for instance the ruler of the limbs cannot be ruled by any other limb, and this holds good for any ruler of any composite whole—so the art of the ruler in the excellent city of necessity cannot be a serving art at all and cannot be ruled by any other art, but his art must be an art towards the aim of which all the other arts tend, and for which they strive in all the actions of the excellent city.

8. That man is a person over whom nobody has any sovereignty whatsoever. He is a man who has reached his perfection and has become actually intellect and actually being thought (intelligized), his representative faculty having by nature reached its utmost perfection in the way stated by us; this faculty of his is predisposed by nature to receive, either in waking life or in sleep, from the Active Intellect the particulars, either as they are or by imitating them, and also the intelligibles, by imitating them. His Passive Intellect will have reached its perfection by [having apprehended] all the intelligibles, so that none of them is kept back from it, and it will have become actually intellect and actually being thought. Indeed any man whose Passive Intellect has thus been perfected by [having apprehended] all the intelligibles and has become actually intellect and actually being thought, so that the intelligible in him has become identical with that which thinks in him, acquires an actual intellect which is superior to the Passive Intellect and more perfect and more separate from matter (immaterial?) than the Passive Intellect. It is called the

'Acquired Intellect' and comes to occupy a middle position between the Passive Intellect and the Active Intellect, nothing else being between it and the Active Intellect. The Passive Intellect is thus like matter and substratum for the Acquired Intellect, and the Acquired Intellect like matter and substratum for the Active Intellect, and the rational faculty, which is a natural disposition, is a matter underlying the Passive Intellect which is actually intellect.

9. The first stage, then, through which man becomes man, is the coming to be of the receptive natural disposition which is ready to become actually intellect; this disposition is common to all men. Between this disposition and the Active Intellect are two stages, the Passive Intellect which has become actually intellect, and [the rise of] the Acquired Intellect. There are thus two stages between the first stage of being a man and the Active Intellect. When the perfect Passive Intellect and the natural disposition become one thing in the way the compound of matter and form is one—and when the form of the humanity of this man is taken as identical with the Passive Intellect which has become actually intellect, there will be between this man and the Active Intellect only one stage. And when the natural disposition is made the matter of the Passive Intellect which has become actually intellect, and the Passive Intellect the matter of the Acquired Intellect, and the Acquired Intellect the matter of the Active Intellect, and when all this is taken as one and the same thing, then this man is the man on whom the Active Intellect has descended.

10. When this occurs in both parts of his rational faculty, namely the theoretical and the practical rational faculties, and also in his representative faculty, then it is this man who receives Divine Revelation, and God Almighty grants him Revelation through the mediation of the Active Intellect, so that the emanation from God Almighty to the Active Intellect is passed on to his Passive Intellect through the mediation of the Acquired Intellect, and then to the faculty of representation. Thus he is, through the emanation from the Active Intellect to his Passive Intellect, a wise man and a philosopher and an accomplished thinker who employs an intellect of divine quality[1] and through the emanation from the Active Intellect to his faculty of representation a visionary prophet who warns of things to come and tells of particular things which exist at present.

11. This man holds the most perfect rank of humanity and has reached the highest degree of felicity. His soul is united as it were[2] with the Active Intellect, in the way stated by us. He is the man who knows every action by which felicity can be reached. This is the first condition for being a ruler. Moreover, he should be a good orator and able to rouse [other people's] imagination by well chosen words. He

1. Reading of *Y*. Reading of *PC*: 'who employs an intellect in which the Divine resides (indwells).'

2. The French translation follows the erroneous reading of *B* : 'son âme est parfaite et unie à l'intellect agent.'

should be able to lead people well along the right path to felicity and to the actions by which felicity is reached. He should, in addition, be of tough physique, in order to shoulder the tasks of war.

This is the sovereign over whom no other human being has any sovereignty whatsoever; he is the Imam; he is the first sovereign of the excellent city, he is the sovereign of the excellent nation, and the sovereign of the universal state (the *oikumen ē*).

12. But this state can only be reached by a man in whom twelve natural qualities are found together, with which he is endowed by birth. (1) One of them is that he should have limbs and organs which are free from deficiency and strong, and that they will make him fit for the actions which depend on them; when he intends to perform an action with one of them, he accomplishes it with ease. (2) He should by nature be good at understanding and perceiving everything said to him, and grasp it in his mind according to what the speaker intends and what the thing itself demands. (3) He should be good at retaining what he comes to know and see and hear and apprehend in general, and forget almost nothing. (4) He should be well provided with ready intelligence and very bright; when he sees the slightest indication of a thing, he should grasp it in the way indicated. (5) He should have a fine diction, his tongue enabling him to explain to perfection all that is in the recess of his mind. (6) He should be fond of learning and acquiring knowledge, be devoted to it and grasp things easily, without finding the effort painful, nor feeling discomfort about the toil which it entails. (7) He should by nature be fond of truth and truthful men and hate falsehood and liars. (8) He should by nature not crave for food and drink and sexual intercourse, and have a natural aversion to gambling and hatred of the pleasures which these pursuits provide. (9) He should be proud of spirit [*megalopsychos*] and fond of honour, his soul being by his nature above everything ugly and base, and rising naturally to the most lofty things. (10) Dirham and dīnār and the other worldly pursuits should be of little amount in his view. (11) He should by nature be fond of justice and of just people, and hate oppression and injustice and those who practise them, giving himself and others their due, and urging people to act justly and showing pity to those who are oppressed by injustice; he should lend his support to what he considers to be beautiful and noble and just; he should not be reluctant to give in nor should he be stubborn and obstinate if he is asked to do justice; but he should be reluctant to give in if he is asked to do injustice and evil altogether.[1] (12) He should be strong in setting his mind firmly upon the thing which, in his view, ought to be done, and daringly and bravely carry it out without fear and weak-mindedness.

13. Now it is difficult to find all these qualities united in one man, and, therefore, men endowed with this nature will be found one at a time only, such men being altogether very rare. Therefore if there exists such a man in the excellent city

1. Cf. al-Fārābī [10] p. 84 n.1.

who, after reaching maturity, fulfils the six aforementioned conditions—or five of them if one excludes the gift of visionary prophecy through the faculty[1]—he will be the sovereign. Now when it happens that, at a given time, no such man is to be found but there was previously an unbroken succession of sovereigns of this kind, the laws and the customs which were introduced will be adopted and eventually firmly established.

The next sovereign, who is the successor of the first sovereigns,[2] will be someone in whom those [twelve] qualities are found together from the time of his birth and his early youth and who will, after reaching his maturity, be distinguished by the following six qualities: (1) He will be a philosopher. (2) He will know and remember the laws and customs (and rules of conduct) with which the first sovereigns had governed the city, conforming in all his actions to all their actions. (3) He will excel in deducing a new law by analogy where no law of his predecessors has been recorded, following for his deductions the principles laid down by the first Imams. (4) He will be good at deliberating and be powerful in his deductions to meet new situations for which the first sovereigns could not have laid down any law; when doing this he will have in mind the good of the city. (5) He will be good at guiding the people by his speech to fulfil the laws of the first sovereigns as well as those laws which he will have deduced in conformity with their principles after their time. (6) He should be of tough physique in order to shoulder the tasks of war, mastering the serving as well as the ruling military art.

14. When one single man who fulfils all these conditions cannot be found but there are two, one of whom is a philosopher and the other who fulfils the remaining conditions, the two of them will be the sovereigns of this city.

But when all these six qualities exist separately in different men, philosophy in one man and the second quality in another man and so on, and when these men are all in agreement, they should all together be the excellent sovereigns.

But when it happens, at a given time, that philosophy has no share in the government, though every other condition may be present in it, the excellent city will remain without a king, the ruler actually in charge of this city will not be a king, and the city will be on the verge of destruction; and if it happens that no philosopher can be found who will be attached to the actual ruler of the city, then, after a certain interval, this city will undoubtedly perish.

15. In opposition to the excellent city are the 'ignorant' city, the wicked city, the city which has deliberately changed its character and the city which has missed the right path through faulty judgment. In opposition to it are also the individuals who make up the common people in the various cities.

16. The 'ignorant' city is the city whose inhabitants do not know true felicity, the thought of it never having occurred to them. Even if they were rightly guided

1. Literally: 'the gift of foreseeing and warning of things to come.'

2. Reading the plural instead of the singular of all the MSS.

to it they would either not understand it or not believe in it. The only good things they recognize are some of those which are superficially thought of as good among the things which are considered to be the aims in life such as bodily health, wealth, enjoyment of pleasures, freedom to follow one's desires, and being held in honour and esteem. According to the citizens of the ignorant city each of these is a kind of felicity, and the greatest and perfect felicity is the sum total of all of them. Things contrary to these goods are misery such as deficiency of the body, poverty, no enjoyment of pleasures, no freedom to follow one's desires, and not being held in honour.

17. The ignorant city is divided into a number of cities. One of them is the city of necessity, that is the city whose people strive for no more food, drink, clothes, housing and sexual intercourse than is necessary for sustaining their bodies, and they co-operate to attain this. Another is the city of meanness; the aim of its people is to co-operate in the acquisition of wealth and riches, not in order to enjoy something else which can be got through wealth, but because they regard wealth as the sole aim in life. Another is the city of depravity and baseness; the aim of its people is the enjoyment of the pleasure connected with food and drink and sexual intercourse, and in general of the pleasures of the senses and of the imagination, and to give preference to entertainment and idle play in every form and in every way. Another is the city of honour; the aim of its people is to co-operate to attain honour and distinction and fame among the nations, to be extolled and treated with respect by word and deed, and to attain (gain, achieve) glory and splendour either in the eyes of other people or amongst themselves, each according to the extent of his love of such distinction or according to the amount of it which he is able to reach. Another is the city of power; the aim of its people is to prevail over others and to prevent others from prevailing over them, their only purpose in life being the enjoyment which they get from power. Another is the 'democratic' city: the aim of its people is to be free, each of them doing what he wishes without restraining his passions in the least.

18. There are as many kings of ignorant cities as there are cities of this kind, each of them governing the city over which he has authority so that he can indulge in his passion and design.

We have herewith enumerated the designs which may be set up as aims for ignorant cities.

19. The wicked city is a city whose views are those of the excellent city; it knows felicity, God Almighty, the existents of the second order, the Active Intellect and everything which as such is to be known and believed in by the people of the excellent city; but the actions of its people are the actions of the people of the ignorant cities.

The city which has deliberately changed is a city whose views and actions were previously the views and actions of the people of the excellent city, but they have been changed and different views have taken their place, and its actions have turned into different actions.

The city which misses the right path (the 'erring' city) is the city which aims at felicity after this life, and holds about God Almighty, the existents of the second order and the Active Intellect pernicious and useless beliefs, even if they are taken as symbols and representations of true felicity. Its first ruler was a man who falsely pretended to be receiving 'revelation'; he produced this wrong impression through falsifications, cheating and deceptions.

20. The kings of these cities are contrary to the kings of the excellent cities: their ways of governing are contrary to the excellent ways of governing. The same applies to all the other people who live in these cities.

10

Abu'l-Ḥasan 'Āmirī

Without doubt the most important figure in *mashshā'ī* philosophy between Fārābī and Ibn Sīnā is Abu'l-Ḥasan Muḥammad 'Āmirī, a native of Khurāsān who spent most of his life in that land, where he died in 381/992. He did, however, make two journeys to Baghdad, until then the centre for study of Islamic philosophy; he also lived in Rayy between 350/961 and 365/976. In Baghdad, 'Āmirī debated with the philosophers and scholars of the city—such men as al-Ṣīrāfī, who became hostile toward him and whom he criticized later in his life. He was also quoted but criticized by Ibn Sīnā, who did not hold 'Āmirī's philosophical acumen in great esteem.

Although Ibn Sīnā's criticism eclipses the writings of 'Āmirī to an extent, some of his works and ideas survived and played a role in later Islamic philosophy. 'Āmirī wrote several well-known treatises, such as *al-Amad 'ala'l-abad* (Time Within Eternity) dealing with the soul and its destiny; *al-Sa'ādah wa'l- is'ād* (On Seeking and Causing Happiness) on ethics; and a work unique in the annals of Islamic Peripatetic philosophy, *al-'Ilām bi-manāqib al-Islām* (An Exposition of the Virtues of Islam). This latter work is a philosophical defence of the religion of Islam and also contains important sections on other religions, including Judaism, Christianity, Zoroastrianism, and Sabaeanism.

Of particular interest among 'Āmirī's philosophical theses is the unity of the intellect and the intelligible (*ittiḥād al-'āqil wa'l-ma'qūl*), rejected by Ibn Sīnā but espoused by Afḍal al-Dīn Kāshānī and especially Mullā Ṣadrā, who quotes 'Āmirī in his *al-Asfār al-arba'ah* (The Four Journeys).

'Āmirī calls for a rational approach to the question of knowledge, arguing that the final cause of knowledge is virtuous action. It is 'Āmirī's view that Islamic doctrine is receptive to rational discourse and goes on to maintain the superiority of religious sciences over secular ones. It is for this reason that he vehemently attacks the Ismailis and other adherents to esoteric Islam who, according to him, do not emphasize the significance of the *Sharī'ah*.

Relying on a lost Neoplatonic commentary of Plato's *Phaedo* and the Aristotelian classification of psychology, ʿĀmirī offers arguments for the immortality of the soul. He is also important in the history of philosophy, since he offers a summary of the thought of such figures as Empedocles, Pythagoras, Socrates, Plato, and Aristotle. Also, ʿĀmirī sought to develop a political philosophy based more on the integration of pre-Islamic Persian ideas, as contained in the *tāj-nāmah* literature of the Sasanid period and Islam and less on Greek sources, as we find in Fārābī and other Islamic political philosophers.

Free will and determinism, superiority of prophetic intellect over reason, optics, and theology are among other issues upon which ʿĀmirī comments. His works are an attempt to reconcile his brand of Neoplatonism, reason, and discursive philosophy with faith and revelation. Although his works were overshadowed by Ibn Sīnā's, ʿĀmirī remains a significant figure in the history of Islamic thought.

This chapter presents two selections. The first is a translation of a segment of ʿĀmirī's *al-Iʿlām bi-manāqib al-Islām* (An Exposition of the Merits of Islam). Following a prolegomenon on 'What Must Be Known First', the author treats such issues as the nature of knowledge and the nobility of the religious sciences. The second selection, a portion of ʿĀmirī's *al-Amad ʿala'l-abad,* translated by Everret Rowson as *A Muslim Philosopher on the Soul and Its Fate*, deals with questions of an eschatological nature. Of particular interest here are ʿĀmirī's numerous references to the Greek philosophers, in particular Socrates, Plato, and many of the pre-Socratics.

S. H. Nasr

KNOWLEDGE AND THE RELIGIOUS SCIENCES

From *al-Iʿlām bi manāqib al-Islām* (An Exposition on the Merits of Islam)

Translated for this volume by E. K. Rowson from ʿĀmirī's *al-Iʿlām bi-manāqib al-Islām*, ed. A. A. Ghorab (Cairo, 1967), pp. 77–122.

Prolegomenon: What Must be Known First

If the act[1] which is specific to the human substance is that one know the truth and act in accordance with the truth, then surely the most perfect person will be the one who possesses the fullest knowledge of the truth and is most capable of acting in accordance with the truth, and the most contemptible person will be the one who possesses the least knowledge of the truth and is the least capable of acting in accordance with the truth. And surely nothing could be more useful for him who wishes to spare himself distress than the realization that when he commits evil deeds he will be unable to stop the mouths of people from mentioning them; if he seeks to silence them, then, he should not do so by abusing the one who reproaches him for such deeds, but rather by reforming his morals.

This being acknowledged, we say:

A party of the philosophers,[2] and a group of the Bāṭinīya,[3] have claimed that the one who distinguishes himself in mastering the various kinds of knowledge is no longer obligated to adhere to any of the ritual duties, other than providing guidance for mankind, and that the intelligent person among us is obligated to seek knowledge, not as a means to performing virtuous acts, but only in order to avoid the misery of ignorance; for ignorance is in itself ugly and painful,[4] while its opposite is in itself beautiful and pleasurable. There can be no doubt, they continue, that one who engages in a given craft will undergo the trouble of pursuing[5] it only to the point that he attains proficiency in it; once his skill has become manifest and his expertise solid, he need take no further trouble in it other than guiding (others) and imposing it (on them). Clearly then, they claim, it would be a dreadful thing to put the one who is advanced in wisdom on a level equal to that of the masses of the ignorant in being obliged to weary himself in fulfilling the divinely ordained

1. Reading *fiʿl* for the text's *ʿaql*, 'intellect'.
2. Perhaps to be identified with al-Fārābī, whose Aristotelian intellectualism and social elitism somewhat parallels the stance described here.
3. The 'esotericists'—that is, the Ismaili Shiʿa—also criticized by al-ʿĀmirī by this name in other works. The opinions outlined here do not point clearly to any specific known subgroup of tenth-century Ismailis.
4. Reading *mu'limah* for the text's *muẓlimah*, 'dark'.
5. Reading *takalluf* for the text's *taklīf*, 'imposing'.

duties; if it were possible to imagine such a thing, there would be no reason for the ignorant to follow the leadership of the learned. This is the essence of the sophistical argument advanced by this group.

We reply that anyone who adopts for himself such a belief is guilty of a grave error. For knowledge is the basis of action, and action is the completion of knowledge; and the excellence of knowledge of various sorts is desirable only for the sake of virtuous actions. If God's intention for human nature had been simply the acquisition of knowledge, without the rectification of action, then the practical faculty would be either a superfluous addition or an accidental appendage; and if this were so, the lack of it would entail no deleterious effects on the prosperity of societies or the governance of human beings. But no! To imagine such a thing leads to delegating virtuous actions in their entirety to the ignorant and foolish; and if this were the case, then human nature could dispense entirely with the various sorts of true knowledge in performing virtuous actions.

We have treated this subject in full detail in our book 'The Perfecting of the Virtues of Man'.[1]

This being established, we must turn our attention to the subject of good actions. In a first analysis, these can be divided into three types:

1. The rectification of that whose proper state is dependent on some sort of human assistance.
2. The preservation of that whose continued existence is in need of some sort of human power.
3. The use of that whose benefits are enjoyed[2] by means of some sort of human management.

Each of these three divisions is then connected with three sorts of attainment related to human authority.[3]

Now whoever fall short of the psychological attainments—that is, those which bring about the rectification, preservation, and (beneficial) use (of the soul)—must necessarily fall short of the household attainments—that is, those which bring about the rectification, preservation, and (beneficial) use (of the household). But the reverse is not the case. Correspondingly, whoever falls short of the household attainments—that is, those which bring about the rectification, preservation, and (beneficial) use (of the household)—must necessarily fall short of the political attainments. But the reverse is not the case.

---

1. This work is lost.

2. Reading *mā fāʾidat manāfiʿihi* for the text's *fāʾidat manāfiʿihi* and the editor's proposed *ʿāʾidat manāfiʿihi*.

3. As is clear from the following paragraph, these three attainments involve exercising authority over oneself, one's household, and one's polity, a schema which reproduces the traditional Greek distinction between ethics, economics (household management), and politics. Something may have fallen out of the text here.

We must therefore turn our attention in this analysis to establishing the nature of the attainments which are connected with each of these three categories. We say:

Rectification of the soul is connected with three concerns:

a. Concern with suppressing the concupiscent faculty.
b. Concern with training the irascible faculty.
c. Concern with giving the intellective faculty authority over the (other) two faculties—that is, the concupiscent and irascible.

(These can in fact be reduced to) a single concern,[1] namely, being trained to submit to the intellect everything by which concupiscence and irascibility are moved, in order that it may be the intellect which manages (the soul's) attainment of its goal in a perfect way.

As for household rectification, it is connected with four binary relations:

a. The relation of a man to his wife.
b. The relation of a father to his children.
c. The relation of a possessor to his possessions.
d. The relation of a monarch to his subjects.

Household preservation is in turn a matter of maintaining these four relations to one's individual self in a way which accords with the demands of manly virtue for a person of one's rank and status.

As for the rectification and (beneficial) use of political authority, the Sages[2] have had a great deal to say in their works about this, and their books on its divisions are well known. The central point of all these divisions is that one must strive to preserve different groups of people and their occupations in their proper ranks, according to their mutual relations, observing the dictates of sound religion and unbiased judgment.

If this is acknowledged, and if the True Religion[3] is found to be superior in rank to other religions in its insistence on reaching these attainments and in its guidance toward adherence to what is required by these concerns—as will be demonstrated in what follows—then one is justified in recognizing the exalted excellence and superior rank of this religion.

Having now summarized what is connected to virtuous actions, out of a desire to make the clear elucidation of this matter a prolegomenon to what we intend to treat in the body of this book, we must now proceed directly to the latter and turn our attention to the points we intend to make in the following chapters. We will

1. The text may be defective at this point.

2. *al-Ḥukamāʾ*, referring to the Greek philosophers, and perhaps pre-Islamic Persian authors as well.

3. *al-Millat al-ḥanīfiyyah* the religious community associated with the original Abrahamic religion, neither Jewish nor Christian—that is, Islam. See *EI2*, s.v. *ḥanīf*.

begin by discussing the nature and nobility of knowledge, and the benefits of its various types.

Chapter I. The Nature of Knowledge and the Benefits of Its Various Types

Faith is true, certain belief, and its locus in the soul is the intellective faculty. Infidelity is uncertain, false belief, and its locus in the soul is the imaginative faculty. The imaginative faculty is capable of true belief, but the intellective faculty is incapable of false belief. Now a person is obligated to submit all the various beliefs that occur to his imaginative faculty to his intellective faculty, in order than he may thereby be secure from the afflictions of falsehood. Sometimes, however, he dislikes doing this, out of a desire to avoid being thought imperfect and reproached for falsehood. But just as the most well-grounded action is that which is undertaken only after careful consideration and the most well-grounded speech is that which is uttered only after deliberation, so also the most well-grounded knowledge is that to which belief is accorded only after careful revision.

This being acknowledged, we must turn to our primary subject, and say:

Knowledge is comprehension of a thing as it is, without error or oversight. It is divided into religious and secular.[1] The masters of the religious sciences are the chosen prophets, and the masters of the secular sciences are the recognized sages. Every prophet is a sage, but not every sage is a prophet.

The religious sciences consist of three disciplines:

1. One of them deals with matters of sense perception; this is the discipline of the traditionists (*muḥaddithūn*).
2. The second deals with matters of intellect; this is the discipline of the theologians (*mutakallimūn*).
3. The third deals with matters of both sense and intellect; this is the discipline of the jurisprudents (*fuqahā'*).

Finally, the discipline of language functions as an adjunct instrument for these three disciplines.

The secular sciences also break down into three disciplines:

1. One of them deals with matters of sense perception; this is the discipline of the physicists.
2. The second deals with matters of intellect; this is the discipline of the metaphysicians.
3. The third deals with matters of both sense and intellect; this is the discipline of the mathematicians.

---

1. *Millī* and *ḥikmī*—that is, connected with a religious community (*millah*) or with 'secular' wisdom (*ḥikmah*).

Finally, the discipline of logic functions as an adjunct instrument for these three disciplines.

In addition, the masses sometimes apply the term 'science' indiscriminately to any trade or profession, and those concerned with empirical observation sometimes apply it to things having to do with empirical testing, such as various sorts of augury from birds[1] and from the scapulae of beasts,[2] and the art of making deductions from traces on the ground.[3]

There are also some sciences which are considered blameworthy by the sages and which are not to be learned by the masses; that is because the sages are convinced that the harm in practising them outweighs the benefit. Examples of these are magic, *wahm*,[4] conjurations, and alchemy.[5]

This being established, we must advance a bit in our elucidation, and say:

One of God's greatest gifts to His servants is that He created them such that in themselves they love knowledge. Furthermore, since human nature is essentially such that a single person is incapable of mastering all the divisions of knowledge, a hidden connection and essential relation has been made between different persons' natures and the various sorts of things known. That is, each individual will find his interest attracted to a given division, either by his own choice, or by the choice of the one who has the authority to determine this for him; his intimacy with the chosen field will become close and his passion for it intense, and he will single it out for wholehearted love and prefer it to anything else, even if it is objectively less valuable. Thus it has been said, 'A man is an enemy to that of which he is ignorant.'[6]

This being known, and there being no doubt that understanding the benefit which we acquire from each branch of knowledge is of great help in choosing among them, we must turn our attention to this question. So we say:

The secular sciences have been attacked by a group of the Ḥashwiyyah,[7] who claim that they are opposed to the religious sciences and that whoever inclines to them and undertakes to study them has lost both this world and the next. They say that these sciences consist of nothing but frightful terms and fancy names which have been fixed

1. *Zajr* and *'iyāfah*, technically, divination from the flight of a bird at which a stone has been thrown, and zoomancy generally. See *EI2*, s.v. *'iyāfa*.

2. *'Ilm al-katif*; see *EI2*, s.v. *katif*.

3. *Qiyāfah*, also originally comprising physiognomancy; see *EI2*, s.v. *ḳiyāfa*.

4. A form of magic associated with India, whose exact nature is unclear; see E. K. Rowson, *A Muslim Philosopher on the Soul and Its Fate: al-'Āmirī's* Kitāb al-amad 'ala'l-abad (New Haven, CT, 1988), p. 287.

5. al-'Āmirī follows al-Kindī in rejecting alchemy, in contrast to some philosophers, notably Miskawayh.

6. A famous saying usually attributed to 'Alī b. Abī Ṭālib, and quoted by al-'Āmirī frequently in his works.

7. 'Idle babblers', a term of opprobrium applied by rationalist scholars, especially the Mu'tazilites, to conservative traditionists who vaunted the authority of received texts over the conclusions of human reason.

up with concocted meanings, so that the foolish and ignorant will be taken in by them and the naive and superficial be seduced by them.[1] But this is not so. In fact, they consist, root and branch, of beliefs which are in conformity with the unbiased intellect and supported by sound proofs, just like the religious sciences. Clearly there can be no opposition or conflict between what is ascertained by proof and necessitated by the intellect and what is required by true religion. Moreover, he who has achieved mastery of the secular sciences may consider himself fortunate in three ways:

1. He knows what it means to achieve perfection in human virtue, by attaining command over the realities of things and the capability of controlling them.
2. He perceives wherein the wisdom lies in the Creator's creation of various things, and can establish their causes and effects and the wondrous order and elegant structure which connects them.
3. He is trained to require proof rather than accepting transmitted claims, and is free from the disgrace of following blind tradition[2] in adhering to untenable positions.

Having shown this, and described the secular sciences altogether as divided into three disciplines—those of the mathematicians, the physicists, and the metaphysicians, with the discipline of logic serving as an instrument—we must now briefly explain the benefit and value of each of these four disciplines, before turning our attention in turn to the various religious sciences. So we say:

The discipline of the mathematicians has five branches: arithmetic, geometry, astronomy, harmony,[3] and mechanics.

Training and proficiency in arithmetic bring a man to gates through which his thought plunges into intellectual pleasure; for anyone who contemplates the properties of numbers, in themselves and in their mutual relations, will never be satiated in his enjoyment of them, and will be convinced that the greatness and importance of this subject is such that one's wonder at it will never cease. Add to this that arithmetic is by its very nature unencumbered by disagreement or the occurrence of doubt, and is called on to serve a practical function in everyday transactions. God has said, 'He does take an account of them (all) and has numbered them (all) exactly',[4] and 'He takes account of everything one by one.'[5]

---

1. This argument is advanced, for instance, by a certain al-Jarīrī (a follower of the legal school of Muḥammad b. Jarīr al-Ṭabarī) in an attack on al-ʿĀmirī, the Brethren of Purity, and others, recorded by al-Tawḥīdī in his *Kitāb al-imtāʿ wa'l-mu'ānasah*; see Joel L. Kraemer, *Humanism in the Renaissance of Islam* (Leiden, 1993), pp. 168–174.

2. *Taqlīd*, in legal parlance the opposite of *ijtihād*, 'independent reasoning', and the crux of the conflict between traditionists and rationalists.

3. Or 'composition' (*ta'līf*), here replacing the more usual term, 'music' (*mūsīqī*), and referring to the study of mathematical ratios, both as applied to audible tones and more generally.

4. Qur'ān 19:94

5. Qur'ān 72:28.

Geometry ranks next to arithmetic in greatness and importance. It is easier to grasp because it is amenable to illustration perceptible by the senses; and it is broader in its application, since without it, it would be impossible for those engaged in computation to extract surd roots, or for those engaged in surveying to determine the shapes of plots of land, or for minds in general to determine the length and breadth of the seas or the area and height of mountains. Not only this—may God be your support—but there are also the benefits it provides trained architects, carpenters, artists,[1] and goldsmiths, as well as its contribution to the design of astronomical instruments such as celestial globes,[2] astrolabes, armillary spheres, and sun-clocks.[3]

No one can deny the nobility of astronomy, since it is concerned with investigation of the structure of the celestial world, both quantitatively and qualitatively, and the motions of each of its bodies, and with determining the causes of eclipses and the various phenomena associated with the planets,[4] such as retrograde and direct motion, and moving and stopping, as well as the apparition and occultation, and orientality and occidentality, of the fixed stars. Unquestionably, when an intelligent person acquires a comprehensive knowledge of what the heavens contain, he gains access to a major source of happiness. This is why God blamed certain persons who were quite content to be bereft of this excellence, saying, 'Have they not pondered upon [themselves? God] created [not] the heavens and the earth, [and that which is between them,] save with truth';[5] and He praised other persons who rejoiced in this sort of excellence, saying, 'Those who remember God, standing, sitting, and reclining, and consider the creation of the heavens and the earth, (saying,) 'Our Lord! You have not created (all) this in vain. Glory be to You! Preserve us from the doom of Fire.'[6]

The nobility of (the science of) harmony cannot be denied, for on it depends the establishment of proofs regarding what is harmonious and what is not, among powers and quantities in both the celestial world and the terrestrial world—indeed, in both the spiritual world and the corporeal world. Were it not for the power of this discipline, the astronomers would not have been able to establish the truth of what they have claimed about the applications[7] of the planets and the mixing of their rays,[8] and the prosodists would not have been able to offer rational explanations of

1. *Naqqāshun*, referring ambiguously to stone-carvers, painters, or engravers.

2. *Kurā*; see *EI2*, s. v. *kura*.

3. *Rukhāmāt*; see al-Khwārazmī, in G. Van Vloten, ed., *Mafātīḥ al-ʿulūm* (Leiden, 1895), p. 126.

4. Literally, 'the receding and running', (*al-khunnas al-jawārī*), quoting Qur'ān 81:15–16.

5. Qur'ān 30:8.

6. Qur'ān 3:191.

7. *Ittiṣālāt*, that is, their coming into aspect with one other; see Abū Maʿshar al-Balkhī, *al-Mudkhal al-kabīr ilā ʿilm aḥkām al-nujūm*, facsimile edition (Frankfurt, 1985), pp. 389–403.

8. Reading *ashiʿʿatihā* for the text's impossible *ashyiʿatihā*. The theory of 'rays' also concerns the astrological aspects of the planets; see Abū Maʿshar, *al-Mudkhal al-kabīr*, pp. 408–410.

the poetic meters and systematize their fifteen sorts into the five circles.[1] And the Apostle of God has said, 'Adorn the Qur'ān with your voices'.[2]

Mechanics is a composite branch of science, partly mathematical and partly physical. It is useful in extracting water hidden in the bowels of the earth and bringing it up to the surface, by means of either water-wheels or fountains;[3] in producing the power to transport heavy objects with the expenditure of relatively little manpower; in helping to construct arches over deep valleys and erect wonderful bridges over deep rivers; and in many others things which we cannot go into here.

These, in sum, are the benefits of the discipline of the mathematicians. Clearly, there is no opposition or conflict between it and the religious sciences.

The discipline of the physicists is concerned with corporeal things perceived by the senses. Now all the substances of the world can unquestionably by divided into two sorts:

1. Those which are created by God's unlimited divine power, such as the celestial spheres, the planets, and the four elements.
2. Those which are generated from these by means of divine subjugation.[4] These are in turn divisible into three sorts:
   a. That which is produced in the atmosphere: snow, rain, thunder, lightning, thunderbolts, meteors, and the like.
   b. That which is produced in the inert earth: gold, silver, iron, copper, mercury, lead, and the like.
   c. That which is produced between the other two. This is in turn divisible into plants and animals.

Various noble disciplines have been generated secondarily from this science, including medicine, cooking, dyeing, plating, and the like.

Such, in sum, is the benefit of the discipline of the physicists. Clearly, between it and the religious sciences there is neither opposition nor conflict.

The discipline of the metaphysicians is too exalted for any of its aims to be conceived of except by the faculty of the unencumbered intellect. This faculty is called the 'heart' (*lubb*), the 'heart' of anything being its very core.

---

1. On al-Khalīl b. Aḥmad's prosodical circles, see *EI2*, s. v. *'arūḍ*.

2. For this *ḥadīth*, see A. J. Wensinck et al., *Concordance et indices de la tradition musulmane* (Leiden, 1936–), vol. 2, p. 376, and, in the context of the controversy over music in Islam and especially in Quranic recitation, K. Nelson, *The Art of Reciting the Qur'ān* (Austin, TX, 1985), pp. 32–100.

3. *Dawālib* and *fawwārāt*. On these devices, see Ibn al-Razzāz al-Jazarī, *The Book of Knowledge of Ingenious Mechanical* Devices, tr. and annotated Donald R. Hill (Islamabad, 1989), pp. 158–169, 272–273, 275.

4. *Taskhīr*, a term appearing frequently in the Qur'ān to refer to God's control of natural process; see, for example, Qur'ān 14:32–33.

This is a discipline devoted exclusively to investigating the first principles of the occurrence of things generated in the world, and to establishing the True Unique First, which is, in Its glory, the ultimate end of all endeavour, by way of (establishing) that which can be freed from all doubt. The achievement of such blessedness as this is undoubtedly what leads to eternal happiness. But it will be extremely difficult to reach such a height unless we first utilize other sorts of knowledge as a means to attaining it—as we have explained in our book entitled 'Care and Study'.[1]

This is why the Ancients were unwilling to call anyone a sage unless he had attained this knowledge. And it would be absurd to maintain that between a discipline which bears such fruits as these and the religious sciences there should be any opposition or conflict.

With regard to logic, however, a party of theologians[2] have been influenced by the contempt for it displayed by the Ḥashwiyyah, and advanced two arguments in support of their position:

First, they say: We, who are known for our proficiency in the discipline of theology, have looked into the books on logic, and have found nothing in them except abstruse words and strange terms. But if those who composed these books had been so fortunate as to discover something which accords with the truth, one would certainly find them eager to present it in all clarity, and there would surely exist one book which we could consult and which would spare us the trouble of finding someone to elucidate for us what it is all about.

This—may God be your support!—is an invalid argument. For the fact that the theologians are incapable of understanding the contents of books on logic is not evidence that the latter are incorrect. Indeed, anyone who confesses that he is incapable of understanding all the concepts contained in the discipline of logic testifies thereby to the absolute invalidity of any verdict he renders on them, whether he maintains that they accord with the truth or that they disagree with it, and to his necessary obligation to turn to the one he has blamed or praised for an explanation of their content, before rendering a verdict as to their correctness.

Their second argument is as follows: The masters of this discipline have agreed that the great benefit of acquiring it is the attainment of proficiency in understanding the rules for correctly arguing from the known to the unknown, and that its position in relation to the theoretical sciences as a whole is comparable to that of the discipline of prosody in relation to the various types of poetry. But it is quite

1. This work is lost.

2. The locus classicus for polemics against logic is the debate between the Muʿtazilite grammarian Abū Saʿīd al-Ṣīrāfī and the Christian philosopher Abū Bishr Mattā over the respective merits of grammar and logic, recorded by al-Tawḥīdī in his *Kitāb al-imtāʿ wa'l-mu'ānasah*, ed. A. Amin and A. al-Zayn (Beirut, 1953), vol. 2, pp. 104–128. Al-Ṣīrāfī does not advance the arguments presented here, but does offer a parody of the awkward and opaque style of the philosopher al-Kindī. For an overview of the problem, see A. Elamrani-Jamal, *Logique aristotélicienne et grammaire arabe* (Paris, 1983).

clear to us that when one of us is able, by means of his instinctive taste, to compose fine poetry, the science of prosody is quite irrelevant to him. Correspondingly, he who is able, by means of his understanding, to use syllogisms properly must then have no use for the discipline of logic. Now any intelligent person who can boast of proficiency in the discipline of theology has only been guided to this proficiency by his own understanding; logic, then, could only do him harm.

Nor does this argument have any force. For suppose an intelligent man among us does happen to apply his syllogisms correctly, but then his opponent contests their correctness with him and maintains against him the correctness of a syllogism which fails to conform to his rules. He will then be unable to confirm the correctness of that which has been contested unless he can turn to this sure balance whose accuracy can be depended on. This is like the situation of someone with whom the correctness of a line of verse has been contested, with the claim that it is metrically incorrect: he can only confirm which claim is correct, his or his opponent's, by force of the discipline of prosody.

Having refuted these two arguments, we must now explain the primary benefit of this discipline. So we say:

It is an intellectual instrument whereby the rational soul is able to distinguish completely between truth and falsehood in theoretical matters, and between good and bad in practical matters. Its position with regard to the souls which make use of it is comparable to that of an equalizing gauge by which one weighs various items of knowledge. By means of it, one is able to scrutinize questions and answers, objections, contradictory assertions, and refutations, and indeed to resolve ambiguities, expose sophisms, and perform other operations which contribute to determining the validity of claims. And another benefit gained by it is the pure intellectual pleasure which comes from making use of it, and the sense of security about what one knows, by which the soul can claim for itself to be one of those who have acquired wisdom, not in order to win the praise of one's fellows, but for the gratification of having achieved the truth on its own and for the repose of certainty.

Now we have also found that a party of ascetics[1] disparage literary accomplishments[2] and claim that there are only two sorts of men who yearn to attain them: those who wish to be praised for the chasteness and eloquence of their speech, and those who show off this eloquence to nobles and aristocrats in an effort to derive material gain and status from their brilliance. In either case they have been beguiled from holding fast to God's service or directing their efforts to the pursuit of the truth.

1. Beyond noting the general Sufi disdain for worldliness, it is difficult to identify the 'party' of ascetics (*nussāk*) intended here.

2. *Ādāb*. It is unclear whether al-ʿĀmirī has been led to defend literary activity here because of the relation between logic and speech (*manṭiq* refers to both), or because he has conflated literary activity with 'the science of language', defined above as the instrument of the religious sciences but not discussed with the religious sciences proper in the following chapter.

This party is also guilty of a grave error. For this is a discipline which contributes to effective communication, which itself functions as a rein and bridle to sensitive souls, since the man blessed with an eloquent tongue is able thereby to draw them from one position to another. Moreover, words have a relation to meanings analogous to that of bodies to souls; for just as the praiseworthy actions of noble souls are manifested only in those particular bodies which have an excellent temperament, so also true meanings can only be adequately expressed in attractive words. The Apostle of God has said, 'In some eloquent expression there is magic';[1] indeed, God has said, 'He created Man, and taught him eloquence.'[2]

The point of having a broad knowledge of language, then, is not simply to attain a good facility at chaste speech; the point is rather to achieve natural and effective speech, in forms such as poetry, oratory, epistolography, and proverbs. Each of these four genres has its own effective means which are useful for sharpening the intellect, such as those of pithy aphorisms and striking similes; and it is for this reason that such forms of speech have been immortalized in books, to the point that their longevity has resulted in their being called 'living speech'. Furthermore, he who contemplates their fruits as demonstrated in assemblies called to reconcile differences, the power of their influence in putting an end to hostility and aversion and inclining the hearts of kings and nobles, and the way they serve to adorn testimonia from transmitted accounts of such men's noble deeds and fair words, will be in no doubt that whoever disparages them is recklessly belittling something of great value. For the memorization and recital of them motivates lofty ambitions to seek the heights, and induces those who delight in listening to them to acquire some portion of them for themselves with which to adorn their own speech.

Having now sufficiently described the benefits to be gained from the secular and metaphysical sciences, and bearing in mind that our original intention in writing was directed toward the religious sciences, which are what is really pertinent to our topic in this book, and that we were obliged to speak at such length about the secular sciences only in order that we might then show how the benefits of the religious sciences are superior to them, we must now turn our attention to the latter.

It is God Who gives help and success.

Chapter 2. Clarification of the Nobility of the Religious Sciences

To gain knowledge is to civilize the heart.

Keeping company with scholars and sages clears one's vision.

The manifestation of one's position as a scholar is dissociation from the various sorts of ignorant men.

---

1. A particularly celebrated *ḥadīth*; see Wensinck, *Concordance*, II, p. 435.
2. Qur'ān 55:4.

The most useful thing in sharpening the intellect is submission to learning.

If these truths are acknowledged, we must embark upon our intended topic in this chapter, and say:

The sciences in themselves are multiple, and in their multiplicity some are nobler than others. Prosody and grammar, for instance, although both noble sciences, cannot match the nobility of jurisprudence, which enables one to manifest his servitude to God, nor the nobility of theology, which is the defence of religion with the tongue.

But this inequality in nobility is not peculiar to the sciences; indeed it is common to all things. For who can doubt that the Dais and the Throne[1] are nobler than the substances of the lower world, or that the sun and the moon are nobler than lanterns and meteors, or that the falcon is nobler and more comely than the worm, or that grapes and dates are nobler than apricots and medlar? God has said, 'We have honoured the children of Adam; we have carried them on land and sea, have made provision of good things for them, and have preferred them above many of those whom We created with a marked preferment.'[2] He has also spoken of the inequality to be found among people, saying, 'He it is who has placed you as viceroys of the earth and has exalted some of you in rank above others.'[3] And He has spoken of the inequality among the prophets, saying, 'Of those messengers, We have preferred some above others.'[4] And so also some places and times enjoy preferment over others, except that in this case it is a matter of convention and is subject to alteration.

The relative inequality in these things does not, however, prevent them from all being of benefit, such that if one were to imagine them removed from the world there would appear some breach in its order. Still, that whose purpose is nobler, or whose power is more pervasive, is worthier of being judged superior. The purpose of hearing and vision, for example, is nobler than the purpose of fingernails and hair, and the power of the brain and the heart is more pervasive throughout the body than the power of the stomach or the foreskin.

Every single type of knowledge, then, no matter how relatively insignificant, is in itself noble and exalted. Lowliness and imperfection are to be found only in ignorance and stupidity. God has said, 'God will exalt those who believe among you, and those who have knowledge, to high ranks.'[5] And the noble Imām ('Alī) said, 'The value of every man is what he does well.'[6]

This being established, we must turn our attention to a discussion of the

1. God's *ʿarsh* and *kursī* are both mentioned in the Qur'ān, the former frequently and the latter at 2:255.

2. Qur'ān 17:70.

3. Qur'ān 6:165.

4. Qur'ān 2:253.

5. Qur'ān 58:11.

6. al-ʿĀmirī quotes this famous statement repeatedly in his works.

excellence of the religious sciences. We will begin by stating the position of those who disparage them and belittle their worth, and resolving the sophisms and confusions in their claims. So we say:

Some of the sophisticates,[1] whose dissolute and profligate ways have led them to find the ritual obligations onerous and to reject the duties imposed by the divine command, have claimed that there is not a single religion which rests on any knowledge that the intellect would require one to acknowledge or take seriously. They are all in reality simply legal paradigms and conventional postures, each religious community adopting its share of these and making use of them in establishing its own way of life and defending itself from whatever might undermine it. If they had any reality, they would have no need of explicit revelation, but would depend entirely on the intellect; and if that were the case, people would not be divided into various sects and divergent parties.

These people further claim that any mortification of the self not required by the intellect is vain effort which does no one any good. Therefore, the best course for anyone who consults his own intellect and follows its dictates is to adhere to what he finds all the different sects agreeing on as desirable—justice, truthfulness, faithfulness, trustworthiness, helping the weak, and succouring the troubled—and to make this his way of life, rejecting all the other things about which communities wrangle and individuals contend.

This is the gist of what this group advances as a claim and argument. Only one of two sorts of men will be inclined to accept it: a man whose strength is not up to giving inquiry its due, and falls back in his beliefs on confusion and doubt; or a man who abandons himself to the pleasures he lusts after today, without worrying his head about how things will turn out in the sequel. Now you will not find some specific realm whose denizens are men of these two types; indeed, people in every realm find them detestable, war against them, and judge them to be the most despicable of men in their adopted position and the vilest of men in their actions. For people agree that there is nothing more outlandish to the intellect than maintaining the existence of a true Creator who neither commands nor forbids, neither tests nor obligates, neither promises nor threatens, and neither invites nor deters, but Who abandons those of his servants who possess intelligence to a vain existence, so that one lingers for a few years in this world, with all its worries and cares, toil and trouble, and then vanishes into eternal oblivion. But we should take a closer look at the arguments advanced by these sophisticates and test their reliability. So we say:

First of all, their statement that the religious sciences 'are all simply legal paradigms and conventional postures' is a false premise. For the primary foundations of all religions can be divided into four things: beliefs, services to the divinity, rules of

1. *Mutaẓarrifah*. On the self-styled 'beautiful people', see M. F. Ghāzī, 'Un groupe social: 'Les Raffinés' (*Ẓurafā'*)', *Studia Islamica*, 11 (1959), pp. 39–71.

human interaction, and deterrents.[1] Furthermore, these are essentially intellectual entities, and they cannot be done without so long as the lower world continues to be populated by human beings. By this I mean that the unbiased intellect will not permit intelligent persons to leave off serving their Master, or interacting in a good way with their fellows, or deterring evil persons from wicked behaviour. And whatever the intellect does not permit one to leave off and neglect, it requires one to affirm and adhere to. On the other hand, our partial intellects are incapable of knowing the modality and quantity of these requirements, and this weakness puts us in need of the creator and commander, particularly as the specific forms and degrees of what is beneficial will vary in accordance with the varying characteristics of successive epochs.

Second, their statement that 'the best course for anyone who consults his own intellect is to adhere to what he finds all the different sects agreeing to' is a specious premise. For despite their disagreements about the specific injunctions of religious laws, people do agree that anyone who rejects all forms of divine service, abandons all rules of human interaction, and is impervious to the various sorts of deterrence, is good for nothing in either his religious or secular life, and is doomed in both this world and the next. But if this is what people believe, and the basic assumption on which they act, then anyone who turns away from religious laws because of his excessive desire to follow what the intellect requires will in fact be following something that all communities agree in opposing. And besides, the intellect will not require that one simply abandon everything that intelligent people have had disagreements about; rather, it will require that one direct himself toward that position among them which is most correct.

Having explained our reply to the position advocated by these sophisticates, we must now return to our principal concern. Before taking it up, however, we must first deal with a preliminary matter which will serve as an introduction to the main point we wish to elucidate. So we say:

In their relation to the intellect, things may be divided into three types:

1. What is required by the intellect.
2. What is considered possible by the intellect.
3. What is rejected by the intellect.

Whatever is required by the intellect must be accepted and embraced; whatever is rejected by the intellect is to be disavowed and cast off; and for whatever is considered possible by the intellect judgment is to be suspended until something is found among the intelligibles which entails either a positive or a negative verdict on it. For example, for a son to protect his father from peril is required by the intellect, and for him to force him into peril is rejected by the intellect, while for him to stand

1. *Iʿtiqādāt, ʿibādāt, muʿāmalāt, zawājir.* Al-ʿĀmirī here follows the structure of Islamic law treatises, *zawājir* serving in place of *ḥudūd*, 'fixed punishments', or, approximately, penal law.

in his presence out of respect is considered possible by the intellect. But then if his father commands him to stand in his presence, or to withdraw from his presence, this becomes required and incumbent upon him. Thus what is possible according to the intellect is resolved in favour of one of the two alternatives, not in itself, but through its being commanded.

Thus it appears that all God's servants follow one of two paths in serving their Master:

1. The intellectual path, which is a response to noble character, and earns praise; or
2. The traditional path, which is a response to duties which have been commanded, and merits a reward.

Moreover, it appears that, were it not for the traditional path, there would be no apparent difference between the profligate and the obedient; and that the intellectual path is taken, not to manifest obedience, but to gain commendation and praise. And furthermore, it appears that the reason why the intellect, in the case of what is possible, must await the arrival of a command is that it is incapable on its own of apprehending all the realities, but is in need with regard to many of them of external input.

Finally, it appears that it is incumbent on every person to undertake to teach those who are beneath him, and learn from those who are above him, in a chain which must culminate in a unique individual to whom all the others can turn to discover whatever their own natures are incapable of learning—a person whose position assures the dissemination of knowledge, and whose superiority guarantees the maximum benefit for all. But surely this person will be able to fulfil his function of making up for the deficiency in a perfect way only if his position is accompanied by certain indications which confirm to the people his exalted status in the eyes of the Creator and Commander—blessed be His name!—so as to strengthen their trust in the veracity of his tongue in what he transmits to them from their Master.

It is true that this preliminary point will be acceptable as a premise only to those who already acknowledge the Creator—be He glorified!—and are convinced that they are His servants, enjoying His blessings, and that it is incumbent on them to be assiduous in obeying Him, diligent in offering their gratitude for His favour, and zealous in manifesting their humble servitude to Him.

Now we have finally reached the point where we can fulfil our promise to describe the virtues of the religious sciences. So we say:

These are the noblest, loftiest, and most exalted of all the sciences, in three respects:

1. The fruit of all the sciences is the attainment of good things. But a servant can hope for nothing better than to attain a position of intimate favour with his

master, and this is a blessing he can obtain only by means of devout service and single-minded attention to seeking his good pleasure. And there can be no doubt that a person will be rightly guided toward fulfilling the claims incumbent on him from the Creator and Commander—glory to His name!—only if he has knowledge of His true religion, regardless of any knowledge he may have of other sciences. It is thus religion alone among the sciences that provides the servant with an eternal good, and with perpetual bliss. This is a fruit which cannot be surpassed.

2. No religion has ever been instituted for the sake of a particular benefit or a partial advantage; rather, all religions have always aimed at the general welfare. There has always been a more pressing need for that which benefits all creatures generally than for that whose advantage is restricted to a single individual. This is why Muʿāwiya was criticized for loading the idols into ships to be sent off to India, even if this meant a windfall for the treasury, to the point that people said, 'We do not know whether Muʿāwiya is a man who has been deluded into seeing his bad actions as good, or a man who has despaired of the other world and determined to maximize his enjoyment in this one.'[1] Thus, while the other sciences are in themselves precious things, they only count as such in relation to individuals among God's creatures; so if one of the intelligent people turns away from acquiring them, he does not thereby incur blame. In comparison with the science of religion, they are all petty and trivial.
3. Religious science can serve as a foundation on which to build the other sciences. For it is derived directly from that niche of light[2] which is the ultimate source for the original establishment of every theoretical discipline, namely divine inspiration, which is safe from doubt and immune to any error or oversight. But not one of the other sciences is such as to be capable of serving as a foundation for the science of religion or determining any part of it.

We may conclude that religious science must necessarily in itself occupy the same position as the roots and first principles of the theoretical disciplines, in its veracity and power. By this I mean that the physicians, while attributing the origin of their discipline to their master known as Asclepius, claim that he was one of those who were taken up spiritually into the heavens and observed the conditions obtaining there; and the astronomers, while attributing the origin of their discipline to their master known as Hermes, claim that he also was one of those who were taken up spiritually into the heavens and observed the bodies there;[3] and so also the sages of India, while maintaining their own insight into

1. See al-Balādhurī, *Futūḥ al-buldān* (Beirut, 1983), p. 237, and al-Bīrūnī, *Taḥqīq mā l'il-Hind* (Beirut, 1983), p. 87. The idols are said to have come from a raid on Sicily.

2. *Mishkāh*, derived from Qur'ān 24:35 and commonly identified with prophecy.

3. Hermes' celestial ascent is a commonplace in Arabic, and derives from the *Hermetica*. Al-ʿĀmirī also refers elsewhere in his works to the quasi-prophetic origins of astronomy and

various types of knowledge, do not hesitate to attribute it to prophetic revelation or divine inspiration.

Insofar as he appreciates these three points, the intelligent man will recognize the distinctive superiority of the religious sciences and will be eager to enjoy the possession of as much of them as he possibly can.

It is God Who gives help and success.

Chapter 3. Virtues of the Religious Sciences

Only he who feels bereft of people's esteem will take the route of attacking those who possess knowledge and attempt to kill off any desire for it, out of resentment at the position he sees these people holding in the eyes of God's servants.

When a scholar wishes to be looked on with respect he should complement his knowledge with moderation and abstemiousness; to the extent that he does so, he will become a beacon of guidance through the darkness of uncertainty. And in associating with his fellows he should avoid acting as if what he knows defines who he is, rather showing himself affable and refraining from any condescension; for when someone's knowledge leads him to self-admiration he is beguiled into arrogance and vanity, and exposes himself to hostility and hatred.

The best piece of advice for men of merit is that they not boast of that which makes them more meritorious than the masses. No one can be completely safe from people, for fault-finders have ever been the plague of the worthy, and the child of Adam is quicker to pounce on his brother's fault than a lion on his prey.

There is no one baser in rank than he who hunts out the bad to extract it from the folds of the good.

This being acknowledged, we must turn to our intended topic, prefacing it with the following introduction:

The basis on which some things in themselves are found worthy of preferment over others of the same category is sometimes one of quantity and sometimes one of quality. With regard to quantity, this can take the form of greater number or larger magnitude, for these can dazzle the eyes and ears before one undertakes to ascertain a thing's real nature. This is why any mention of the 'consensus of the community'[1] or the 'mainstream'[2] has such an effect on the souls of one's audience; for people are naturally disposed to be impressed by things of imposing appearance, such as lofty

---

medicine, an argument which also appears in al-Ghazzālī and Ibn Ḥazm; see E. K. Rowson, *A Muslim Philosopher*, pp. 12, 241.

1. *Ijmāʿ al-ummah*, a central concept in Sunni law; see *EI2*, s.v. *idjmāʿ*.

2. *al-Sawād al-aʿẓam*, recommended as a referent in a well-known prophetic Tradition ("*alaykum bi'l-sawād al-aʿẓam*'; see Wensinck, *Concordance*, vol. 2, p. 19), and adopted as the name of a creed composed by the Ḥanafī *qāḍī* al-Ḥakīm al-Samarqandī and promulgated as orthodoxy by the Samanid rulers of Transoxania; see W. Madelung, *Religious Trends in Early Islamic Iran* (Albany, NY, 1988), p. 30.

mountains, magnificent buildings, tall trees, and huge animals. God has said, 'And when you see them their bodies please you, and when they speak you give ear to their speech—as though they were blocks of wood propped up.'[1] And He has said, 'And He gave you growth of stature; so remember God's bounties.'[2] With regard to quality, we may point to the parity between a single male and a number of females, such as a stallion and his mares, a male camel with his females, a rooster with his hens, or a man with women.

Having confidence in this judgment, and having mentioned that the religious sciences are all divisible into four disciplines, namely, those of jurisprudence, tradition, theology, and philology, we must now come to see how they stand in merit with regard to their quantity and quality. Regarding quantity, the relevant point is that any science which has a larger number of subdivisions and a greater wealth of branches has a greater right to being accorded merit; and regarding quantity, it is that any science which is of greater utility and superior benefit is worthier of being considered distinguished. Now there can be no doubt that the science of tradition has been made to function as matter for the religious sciences, and thus has the merit of priority; that the science of theology has been made their final objective, and thus has the merit of perfection; that the science of jurisprudence has been made to be the intermediary between these two, and thus has the merit of balance; and that the science of language functions as an instrument for all of these, and thus has the merit of easing and facilitation.

At this point our exposition leads us back to our intended topic, and we say:

A group of the theologians[3] has agreed in disparaging the science of tradition, calling its exponents '*ḥashw*' and 'rabble'. They even go so far as to exclude them from the ranks of the scholars, arguing that knowledge of traditional reports is comparable to knowledge of what is perceived by the eye, and that just as one cannot call someone a 'scholar' because of the knowledge he has from vision, so one cannot call someone a 'scholar' because of the knowledge he has from hearing reports. Only that can be called 'scholarship', they claim, the learning of which is connected to activity by the cognitive soul and the probing of reflection and deliberation.

We reply that anyone who adopts this stance regarding the science of reports shows himself to be guilty of great ignorance. For the science of tradition is not simply a matter of aural perception. Rather, it is equivalent to writing, which encompasses meanings, despite the fact that it is the forms of the letters which are perceived by sight. Furthermore, this science subsumes a variety of methods, and ramifies into different disciplines. Indeed, there is not a single branch of the sciences in which one does not find transmitted reports, either from the revealed

1. Qur'ān 63:4.
2. Qur'ān 7:69.
3. The Mu'tazilites.

books, or from the prophets and religious leaders, or from the ancient sages, or from the pious forebears. Thus it serves as matter for all of them.

It is because of the need of the innate intellect for heard reports that God reinforced His appeal to the intellect with one to hearing, saying, 'Can you then make the deaf to hear even though they do not exercise intelligence?'[1] and 'Have they hearts wherewith to exercise intelligence and ears wherewith to hear?'[2] The very structure of the religion is founded on the Book of God and the Sunna of His Apostle, and just as the human race has been presented with irrefutable arguments in what has reached them in God's Book, so also is this true of the (Prophetic) heritage—and especially so as it has been said 'Whoever obeys the Apostle obeys God.'[3] We see how the caliphs rejoice in the mantle and staff of the Apostle,[4] and we see how the Children of Israel found joy in the Ark of the Covenant, containing 'a remnant of that which the house of Moses and the house of Aaron left behind.'[5] But if these things merit such consideration, despite their lowly status, what are we to make of that which is the very essence of the Prophet's heritage?

Unquestionably it is the traditionists who undertake to become acquainted with historical information which yields knowledge of what is beneficial and harmful, and it is they who are knowledgeable about men of bygone times—their genealogies, locations, and life spans, and who consorted with them and took knowledge from them. Indeed, it is they who confirm which religious traditions are valid and invalid, strong and weak; who impose on themselves the rigours of travelling near and far, working at home and abroad to glean the reports of the Apostle of God from trustworthy sources; and who strive to become discerning critics of the prophetic heritage, and acute evaluators of prophetic reports, in order to know which of them have chains of transmission which fail to reach back to the Prophet and which do so reach, which of them mention the link between the Prophet and the next generation and which do not, which of them give all the links and which lack one or more, which chains belong with their reports and which have been grafted on, and which are well known and which forged,[6] and to ground their discipline so effectively that were someone to wish to manufacture a false tradition, or change a chain of transmission, or tamper with a text, or treat these traditions in

1. Qur'ān 10:42.

2. Qur'ān 22:46.

3. Qur'ān 4:80.

4. See D. Sourdel, 'Questions de cérémonial 'Abbāside', *Revue d'Etudes Islamique*, 38 (1960), p. 135.

5. Qur'ān 2:248.

6. The technical terms are, respectively, *mawqūf* and *marfū'*, *musnad* and *mursal*, *muttaṣil* and *munqaṭi'*, *nasīb* and *mulṣaq*, and *mashhūr* and *mudallas*. See, for the first six and last two, Ibn al-Ṣalāḥ (d. 642/1244), *Muqaddima Ibn al-Ṣalāḥ fī 'ulūm al-ḥadīth* (Beirut, 1988), pp. 22, 22, 21, 25, 21, 26, 134, 34, respectively; there is, however, considerable variation in the definitions given these terms. I have not found attestation for the technical use of *nasīb* and *mulṣaq*, whose meaning remains uncertain.

the same cavalier way as occurs with literary accounts such as those of conquests, biographies, entertaining tales, and battles, he would encounter the most violent rejection from them all.

This being the nature of their efforts, and the focus of their endeavours, we must grant them the fullest acknowledgment of the care they have taken, as well as our deepest gratitude, greatest admiration, and highest praise. So much for this question.

But then some among the bearers of the prophetic heritage[1] have ventured to malign the theologians, and have shown zeal in blaming the discipline of theology, charging its practitioners with heresy and error, and advancing against them the argument that they are properly known as 'masters of disputation'[2] and that disputation is something that God has made the object of blame, saying 'And if they dispute with you, say: God knows best what you are doing.'[3] God also said, 'They dispute with you over the truth after it has been made manifest',[4] and even mentioned disputation in conjunction with indecency and iniquity.[5] This is why the Companions of the Apostle were not found to be engaging in it or inclining to it; it is clear that they would have had no reason for avoiding it unless they knew that it was something forbidden them.

We reply that anyone who adopts this stance regarding the science of theology shows himself to be guilty of great ignorance, for the following reasons:

1. God says, 'Call to the way of God with wisdom and exhortation, and dispute with them by means of that which is better.'[6] But a blameworthy thing cannot be the occasion for that which is better.

2. When 'Umar b. al-Khaṭṭāb disputed with the Jews with regard to Gabriel, advancing arguments which silenced them, and returned to the Apostle of God to inform him of what had occurred, he immediately received confirmation of what he had argued against them in God's saying, 'Whoever is an enemy of God, His angels, His apostles, Gabriel, and Michael, (God is an enemy of the unbelievers)';[7] and 'Umar thereby became firmer in his belief.[8] There are also the replies of the

---

1. Ḥamalat al-āthār, that is, the traditionists, many of whom were opposed to *kalām* in all its forms.

2. *Aṣḥāb al-jadal.*

3. Qur'ān 22:68.

4. Qur'ān 8:6.

5. A reference to Qur'ān 2:197: 'And whoever is minded to perform the pilgrimage in (the appropriate months) (should remember that there is to be) no indecency, no iniquity, and no disputation during the pilgrimage.'

6. Qur'ān 16:125.

7. Qur'ān 2:98.

8. According to al-Bayḍāwī's commentary on this verse (*Commentarius in Coranum*, ed. H. O. Fleischer (Leipzig, 1846–48), vol. 1, pp. 74–75), 'Umar disputed the Jews' claim that Gabriel, whom they considered their enemy, was also an enemy to the angel Michael, although the two angels stood on God's two sides; he retorted that whoever was an enemy of either of them was

glorious Imām ʿAlī b. Abī Ṭālib to skeptical questions, which are so well known and so powerful that no intelligent person could, in view of them, ascribe avoidance of the discipline of theology to the Companions.[1]

3. Religion is divided into things which count as roots—that is, what the believer is obliged to subscribe to, including the Unity of God and the affirmation of the Apostles and the Hereafter—and things which count as branches—that is, the laws and ordinances which the Muslim is obligated to observe. But clearly, the root is prior to the branch, since the branch is invalidated if the root is; and this is why error in the roots of religion is considered unbelief. But it is those who engage in the discipline of theology who are concerned with consolidating the foundations of the religion.

4. This is a discipline which can be utilized with the non-Muslim scripturalist (*dhimmī*) as well as the member of the Muslim community (*millī*), and employed with the profligate as well as the observant. With it a man enters the ranks of the elite, who judge what they will accept and what they will reject on the basis of insight, and escapes from the class of the masses, who consign the reins in their affairs to those who will lead them without argument. And God says, 'Say: This is my way; I call on God with insight, I and whoever follows me.'[2]

Since, then, those who pursue this discipline are found to be defending the sacred precincts of religion, freeing it from clinging aspersions, and protecting its roots from disfiguring wounds, it must be acknowledged that their achievements are no less worthy of gratitude and admiration than the achievements of those who defend it with steadfastness, might, weapons and armour. So much for this question.

Finally, a branch of the Imāmiyyah[3] and a group of the Ḥanbalites[4] have found fault with the discipline of jurisprudence, and charged its practitioners with heresy, saying that with regard to religious ordinances (*aḥkām*) it is proper to follow the Book and the Sunna, to the exclusion of personal judgment (*ra'y*)[5] and analogy (*qiyās*), and particularly so in questions of what is permitted and what is forbidden. For God says, 'And speak not falsely in that which your tongues describe, saying "this is permitted and that is forbidden."'[6] He has also said, 'He who does not judge

---

an enemy of God, and then returned to Muḥammad to discover that the present verse had been revealed.

1. The *Nahj al-balāghah* (Beirut, n.d.), II, p. 99, records 'Alī's reply to the question whether he had seen his Lord; perhaps it is statements of this nature which are referred to here.

2. Qur'ān 12:108.

3. That is, the Twelver Shiʿa. On their consistent hostility to personal judgment (*ra'y*) and analogy (*qiyās*), see R. Brunschvig, 'Les *uṣūl al-fiqh* imamites à leur stade ancien (Xe et XIe siècles)', in T. Fahd, ed., *Le Shīʿisme imamite* (Paris, 1970), pp. 201–213.

4. For Ḥanbalite polemics against *ra'y* and *qiyās*, see H. Laoust, *La Profession de foi d'Ibn Baṭṭuṭa* (Damascus, 1958), p. 6 and n.1.

5. This term is particularly associated with the legal theory of the Ḥanafī school, patronized by the Samanids of Transoxania, under whom al-ʿĀmirī probably wrote this work.

6. Qur'ān 16:116.

(*yaḥkum*) by what God has revealed—those are unbelievers',[1] and 'Believe in God and His Apostle, the illiterate prophet, who believes in God and His words, and follow him, so you may be rightly guided.'[2]

We reply that anyone who adopts this stance regarding the science of jurisprudence (*fiqh*) shows himself to be guilty of great ignorance, for the following reasons:

1. God says, 'Of every troop of them, a party only should go forth, that they (who are left behind) may gain understanding (*yatafaqqahu*) in religion, and that they may warn their folk when they return to them, so that they may beware.'[3] And the Apostle of God said, 'Many a one bears understanding (*fiqh*) to one more understanding (*afqah*) than he.'[4] Furthermore, when the Apostle of God sent Mu'ādh ibn Jabal to Yemen and asked him 'On what basis will you render judgment, after the Book of God and the Sunna of the Apostle?' He was pleased with him when he answered, 'I will endeavour to exercise my own judgment.'[5]
2. After the death of the Apostle of God, the Companions all belonged to one of two groups: one group ventured to use analogies, while the other group preferred to abstain from doing so, but without directing any criticism against the first group. But if such a procedure were forbidden by religion, some party of them would undoubtedly have objected to the first group's engaging in it. Therefore, the fact that they were silent about it is evidence for their not believing that it is forbidden; and in fact its use has become a form of judgment validated by consensus.[6]
3. Transmitted records of the prophetic heritage, no matter how numerous, are nevertheless limited, such that no further increase in them is to be expected. But novel events befalling humanity are potentially infinite. If, then, independent reasoning is to be forbidden to the jurisconsults, there will be no alternative to having recourse to one of two other strategies: either one must affirm the existence of an infallible Imam, as the Twelvers claim, or one must declare permitted whatever the intellect considers best (*istaḥsana*), as claimed by al-Naẓẓām.[7] But

1. Qur'ān 5:44.
2. Qur'ān 7:158.
3. Qur'ān 9:122.
4. See Wensinck, *Concordance*, vol. 5, p. 191.
5. *Ajtahidu ra'yī* . For a discussion of the jurisprudents' reliance on this celebrated tradition, see Wael B. Hallaq, *A History of Islamic Legal Theories: An Introduction to Sunnī Uṣūl al-Fiqh* (Cambridge, 1997), pp. 86, 106.
6. *Ḥukman ijmā'iyyan.* For a discussion of the use of the argument from the Companions' 'tacit consensus' (*ijmā' sukūtī*) to defend the employment of analogy in jurisprudence, see Bernard G. Weiss, *The Search for God's Law: Islamic Jurisprudence in the Writings of Sayf al-Dīn al-Āmidī* (Salt Lake City, UT, 1992), pp. 645–648, and for 'tacit consensus' itself, ibid., pp. 226–228.
7. On al-Naẓẓām (d. *c.* 225/840), see Josef van Ess, art. Abū Isḥāq Naẓẓām in *Encyclopaedia Iranica*, ed. E. Yarshater (London, 1982–), and on his jurisprudential views in particular, see idem, 'Ein Unbekanntes Fragment des Naẓẓām', *Der Orient in der Forschung: Festschrift Otto Spies*

the infallible Imam's location cannot be determined, and it will be impossible to have recourse to him on the occasion of the occurrence of novel events; and resolving to follow what the intellect considers best is considered by the Ḥanbalites and the Imāmiyyah to be an even greater heresy (than the use of independent reasoning).[1] Therefore, there really is no alternative to referring the branch (*farʿ*) back to the root (*aṣl*), in adherence to the Sunna of the excellent Companions.

4. An indication of the power of this discipline is that it is found to share with the ruler in the governance of mankind. By this I mean that, were rulers to turn away from all the traditionists and all the theologians, without relying on the assistance of a single person from either group, they would be abandoning what is a basic stay in the maintenance of their rule; and similarly, were they to persist in turning away from all the jurisprudents, they would be undermining their rule. For the jurisprudents' situation in deriving rules for human intercourse, in order to render verdicts, settle disputes, draw up documents, and apply legal stipulations, parallels that of the physicians who prepare medications for deadly diseases before their advent, so that those who seek to be cured of the latter may have recourse to their healing effects. And just as God has set up the root forms (*uṣūl*) of nourishment for mankind and then led them to discover the various sorts of distinction among them so that they might extract through their independent reasoning their particular benefits, so also has He legislated general root principles (*uṣūl*) in their religion and then granted them sound intellects so that they might utilize them in referring the branches back to these root principles.[2]

As for investigating God's ordinances in order to make independent claims about what is permitted and what forbidden, and forging lies against God, and rendering judgments in conflict with what God has revealed—this is something of which not a single one of the masters of this discipline can be suspected. Take Abū Ḥanīfa, who is one of those whom the Ḥanbalites and the Imāmiyyah slanderously accuse of having disseminated the method of exercising personal judgment (*ra'y*)[3] through the Community. When asked about analogy, 'Shall we forgo it when there exists a report from the Apostle?' he said 'Yes'; when asked 'Shall we forgo it when there

---

(Wiesbaden, 1967), pp. 170–201.

1. A good representative of the traditionalist Imāmīya described by al-ʿĀmirī is his contemporary Ibn Bābawayh (d. 381/991). In the next generation, al-Shaykh al-Mufīd resolved the legal problems posed by the occultation of the Imām by appealing to use of reason (*ʿaql)*, while avoiding the more specific terms *qiyās*, *ijtihād*, and *istiḥsān*; see M. J. McDermott, *The Theology of al-Shaykh al-Mufīd (d. 413/1022)* (Beirut, 1978), pp. 289–298.

2. In legal terminology, the 'branches' (*furūʿ*) are the judgments of positive law, decided on the basis of the 'roots' (*uṣūl*), which in Sunni theory consist of Qur'ān, *Sunnah*, *ijmāʿ*, and *qiyās*.

3. The Ḥanafīs were generally known at this time as 'the people of personal judgment' (*ahl al-ra'y*).

exists a statement from a Companion?' he said 'Yes'; when asked 'Shall we forgo it when there exists a statement from one of the leaders among the Followers?' he said, 'The Followers were men and we are men.'[1] He thus made a distinction between the Companions and the Followers, on the basis of his knowledge that the Companions had been blessed with being witnesses to the circumstances of the revelation, and indeed with being witnesses to the circumstances of the Apostle, with regard to both his words and his acts. Now we have no doubt that one who witnessed them could appreciate their true significance in a way those who were not there could not, while the situation of the Followers is comparable to that of pious men (of later times) in their not having witnessed the evidence provided by these circumstances.

And since this discipline stands in a place of particular honour such as we have described, then we should find its masters entitled to gratitude and admiration, rather than levelling censure and calumny at them. So much for this question.

Since the particular merit to which each of the religious sciences is entitled has now become clear to us, we must turn our attention to an exposition of the particular requirements of each of these three disciplines. So we say:

To ensure the proper conduct of the discipline of tradition, he who pursues it should, in addition to his memorization of accounts and his knowledge of the classes of transmitters, manifest sincere rectitude and evident self-restraint, and be untouched by any suspicion of lying and free of any tendency toward laxity. For his discipline constitutes matter for the intellect in bringing out knowledge, and things are just as liable to corruption from the one who supplies their matter as they are from the one who supplies their form. His eagerness to seek rare accounts should not lead him to listen to traditions from untrustworthy sources, nor should his love of faithfully following (*taqlīd*) the leaders among the traditionists lead him to harbour hatred for the disciplines of jurisprudence and theology; for his discipline is one of conservation, while (in them) it confronts a discipline of thought.

To ensure the proper conduct of the discipline of theology, he who pursues it should, in addition to his knowledge of the various types of analogies, models for independent reasoning, and the composition of premises for the derivation of conclusions, manifest acumen in his beliefs and a solid command of the teachings of his school, and be chary of following his shaykhs out of mere good opinion, aloof from resorting to deceit when pressed in argument, and wary of becoming combative or overweening with his opponent out of arrogance. For if he does not

1. More commonly cited is another statement attributed to Abū Ḥanīfa, to much the same effect: '(In) what comes to us from the Companions we follow them, but (in) what comes to us from the Followers we (consider ourselves authorized to) contest them (*zāḥamnāhum*).' For a discussion, see al-Sarakhsī (d. 483/1090), *Uṣūl al-Sarakhsī*, ed. Abu'l-Wafā' al-Afghānī (Beirut, 1973), vol. 1, p. 313, and vol. 2, p. 114.

discipline himself in this fashion he runs the danger of inciting faction, which will lead to his ruin in both this world and the next.

To ensure the proper conduct of the discipline of jurisprudence, he who pursues it should, in addition to his command of the force of the various kinds of report—that is, the multiply-verified report, the isolated report, the generalized report, and the articulated report[1]—and his command of the force of the various kinds of consensus—that is, general consensus, specific consensus, text-based consensus, and intent-based consensus[2]—be extremely wary of employing legal devices[3] in the various sorts of legal findings (*fatāwā*) he issues, and not over eager to find legal concessions[4] in dealing with novel events that occur; indeed, he should be readier to avoid and stand aloof from them than to rush in and embrace them. For he renders judgments on the lives, property, and sexual honour of the Muslims, and these are an immense trust for which he has taken responsibility and a difficult burden which he has undertaken faithfully to bear.

Finally, it is incumbent on the masters of all three of these disciplines that not one of them be induced by his pride in himself and his profession to belittle the others, and that he not be induced by vanity about his expertise in his own discipline to plunge into areas which are not his own. Rather, he should make a point of consigning the work of each discipline to those who are masters of it, granting in full to those who are knowledgeable and pre-eminent in it all the respect and honour that they merit. Nor should he contest what is required by the unbiased intellect out of love of following previous decisions (*taqlīd*), especially those of someone whose infallibility is unattested; for truth is not known by the man, but rather by itself, and only then is it known who has attained it and who has missed it. He should also follow the advice of the glorious Imam ʿAlī b. Abī Ṭālib when he says 'Knowledge is bountiful, so take the best of everything';[5] this is the point of God's statement, 'Therefore give good tidings to my servants who hear advice and follow the best thereof; such are those whom God guides, and such are men of understanding.'[6]

1.. The technical terms are *al-khabar al-mutawātir, khabar al-āḥād, al-khabar al-mujmal,* and *al-khabar al-mufaṣṣal*. For the first two, see Hallāq, *History*, pp. 60–68; for the last two, see al-Tahānawī, *Kashshāf iṣtilāḥāt al-funūn* (Beirut, n.d.), p. 250.

2. The terms are *al-ijmāʿ al-ʿāmmī, al-ijmāʿ al-khāṣṣī, al-ijmāʿ al-naqlī,* and *al-ijmāʿ al-gharaḍī*. None of these seem to have become established in the technical vocabulary of later works of legal theory. The first two presumably refer to the distinction between the consensus of the Muslim community at large and that of the legal scholars (on which see Weiss, *Search*, pp. 188–190, 212–214); the last two, less certainly, would seem to indicate the difference between a legal consensus grounded on a precise textual indicator (Qurʾān or Sunna) and one not so grounded (on which see Weiss, *Search*, pp. 230–237).

3. *Ḥiyal*, particularly favoured by the Ḥanafī school; see *EI2*, s. v. *ḥiyal*.

4. *Rukhaṣ*; see M. J. Kister, 'On 'Concessions' and Conduct: A Study in Early *ḥadīth*', in G. H. A. Juynboll, ed., *Studies on the First Century of Islamic Society* (Carbondale, IL, 1982), pp. 89–107.

5. A celebrated statement, repeated often by al-ʿĀmirī in his works.

6. Qurʾān 39:17.

ON THE SOUL AND ITS FATE
From *al-Amad ʿala'l-abad*

Reprinted from E. K. Rowson, *A Muslim Philosopher on the Soul and Its Fate: al-ʿĀmirī's* Kitāb al-amad ʿala'l-abad (New Haven, CT, 1988), pp. 59–87.

Chapter I

1. God has said in the unambiguous part (*muḥkam*) of His Book, 'Therefore give good tidings to My servants who hear advice and follow the best thereof' (Qur'ān 39:17–18). And according to Tradition, the Prophet said, 'Knowledge is abundant, so take the best of everything.' And it is told that the exalted Imam ʿAlī said, 'The value of every man is that which he (knows) best', and 'A man is an enemy to that of which he is ignorant.'

2. We have found that the various classes of people can be divided into four groups on the basis of the fields of cognition: (1) those who admit reality to sensual perceptibles, but not to intellectual concepts; (2) those who admit reality to intellectual concepts, but not to sensual perceptibles; (3) those who deny altogether the reality of things both sensual and intellectual; and (4) those who affirm the reality of both kinds together.

3. It is doubtless true that sensual entities (*maʿānī*) cannot be perceived by pure intellects; for if they were, the sensual powers would be superfluous and unneeded. Nor can intellectual entities be perceived by the sensual powers; for if they were, pure intellects would be superfluous and unneeded. And if both kinds were ruled out, then all senses and all intellects would be useless and futile. So it is clear that of these four groups the one which conforms to the truth is that which acknowledges the reality of both kinds together, that is, sensual and intellectual.

4. But those who deny all realities, sensual and intellectual, are the furthest from the correct group, and are characterized by obstinacy and sophistry. It would appear that the reason for their being afflicted with this ignorance and defect is the multitude of disagreements among the dialecticians (*jadaliyyūn*) in their dealings with theoretical matters (*maʿānī*), and among the traditionists in their transmissions of reported matters. What I mean is this: these people encountered many situations where two factions maintained propositions with mutually opposed meanings. But they did not have the capacity to examine and text these propositions, and to distinguish between the correct ones and the erroneous ones. So they (simply) adjudged them all to be mutually contradictory and branded them as mutually exclusive. Thus their initial acceptance of the statements of the negative parties came to lead them in the end to considering all of those involved to be liars.

5. Now just as the perfected, superior people who can differentiate between veracity and mendacity when transmissions disagree, and can distinguish between true and false in much-disputed matters, are very few, in the same way, those who ignorantly shed all beliefs and repudiate all realities are also only a few people. And it is quite reasonable for them to be so; for they stand at the two extremes, and doubtless opposite extremes in any species will be small in number. For instance, people who are extremely large or small, beautiful or ugly, strong or weak are found only sporadically; and the same is true of other species, such as horses, oxen, and donkeys. But the numerical majority falls in the middle between the two sides.

6. This being acknowledged, we say: The person afflicted with ignorance who stupidly repudiates the sciences may think of himself as being brilliant in understanding and intelligence. And with his deceptions, pretensions, and affectations he may manage to fool anyone whom he finds to have only rudimentary knowledge and average intelligence. This is what a merchant does when he tries to sell off fraudulent goods to someone who does not understand very much about them. And in doing that, he may deck himself out falsely with philosophy and claim fraudulently to be a follower of one of the famous philosophers, in order to conceal more effectively the ignorance with which he contents himself, and to instill a deeper belief in his fabricated philosophy; for he is certain that most books of philosophy, though they have achieved immortal fame and renown, remain full of symbols and obscure, so that careful attention is needed to be sure of their meanings. So he claims to be an expert on them, and devotes himself to building up their prestige, in order to provide himself with weapons with which to derogate from religious learning and to speak ill of the leaders of the Muslims.

7. The people of (our) religion are not safe from the evils attendant on this situation. But it seems to me that we can provide an effective treatment in the following way. We will summarize the opinions of the philosophers, especially those who are noted for metaphysical wisdom. We will give an account of what their leaders claim about the Unity of God, and we will indicate their opinions on the Hereafter.

8. It is true that the defenders of Islam have done their utmost to fill people's hearts with aversion for the philosophers' teachings, and to frighten their souls away from occupying themselves with their doctrines. Despite this, however, the philosophers have enjoyed widespread fame among the various peoples, together with continuing esteem from the caliphs. This has led those who are weak in understanding to acknowledge the truth of (doctrines) attributed to the philosophers which are at variance with the religious tenets. And it may be that prohibition has acted as an incentive, and blame as a temptation.

9. We will begin by giving an account of the eras of the different nations, for this will be very useful in determining the circumstances and ranks of these philosophers.

Chapter III

1. The first one to whom wisdom was attributed was Luqmān the Sage, as God says: 'And verily we gave Luqmān wisdom' (Qur'ān 31:12). He lived at the time of the prophet David; they were both residents of the land of Syria.

2. It is said that Empedocles the Greek used to keep company with Luqmān and learn from his wisdom. But when he returned to the land of Greece, he spoke on his own authority about the nature of the world, saying things which, if understood literally, offend against (the belief in) the Hereafter. The Greeks attributed wisdom to him because of his former association with Luqmān; indeed, he was the first Greek to be called a Sage. A group of the Bāṭinīs claim to be followers of his wisdom and speak of him with high esteem. They claim that he wrote in symbols whose hidden meanings are rarely comprehended.

3. Another Greek who was described as wise was Pythagoras. In Egypt he kept company with the companions of Solomon son of David, after they moved there from the land of Syria. Having (already) learned geometry from the Egyptians, he then learned the physical and divine/metaphysical (*ilāhiyyah*) sciences from the companions of Solomon. These three sciences—that is, geometry, physics, and the science of religion (*ʿilm al-dīn*)—he transferred to the land of Greece. Furthermore, by his own intelligence he discovered the science of melodies and submitted them to ratios and numbers. He claimed that he had acquired these sciences from the niche of prophecy.

4. After him, another Greek who was described as wise was Socrates. He derived (his) wisdom from Pythagoras, but limited himself to the divine sciences, to the exclusion of the other kinds. He turned away from worldly pleasures and publicly declared his disagreement with the Greeks on religion, confronting the leaders of the polytheists with rational arguments and logical demonstrations. So they stirred up the mob against him and compelled their king to kill him. The king consigned him to prison in order to appear praiseworthy to them; and he gave him poison to drink, in order to guard against their wickedness. The story of Socrates is well known, by a strong, continuous tradition of reports.

5. Then, after him, another one described as wise was Plato. He was of noble lineage and pre-eminent among them. He agreed with Socrates in deriving (his) wisdom, and with Pythagoras. However, he did not limit himself to the divine sciences, but combined with them the physical and mathematical sciences. The books he undertook to write are famous, although they are full of symbols and obscure. At the end of his life, when a number of his pupils had become proficient with him, he entrusted the instruction and the school to his most capable associates and withdrew from the people, in order to devote himself exclusively to the worship of his Lord.

6. In his time the plague spread through the land of Greece. The people made entreaty to God about it, and asked one of the Israelite prophets the reason for it.

God revealed to him that when they doubled a cube-shaped altar of theirs, the plague would be lifted from them. So they built another altar like it, and added it to the first. But the plague intensified. They returned to the prophet and asked him the reason. And God revealed to him that they had not doubled the altar, but had only put next to it another like it. This was not a doubling of the cube.

7. So they turned to Plato for help. He said, 'You have been driving people away from wisdom and frightening them off from geometry. Therefore, God has afflicted you with the plague as a punishment. For God holds the sciences of wisdom in esteem.' Then he told his associates, 'When you are able to discover two lengths intermediate between two (other) lengths in a continuous geometrical proportion, you will have arrived at the duplication of the altar; for there is no other way for you except to discover that.' So they worked on it, and succeeded in completing the operation of doubling the altar. And the plague lifted from them. Thus, they ceased to disparage geometry and the other theoretical sciences.

8. Another of the Greeks after Plato who was described as wise was Aristotle. He was the teacher of Alexander, who is known as Dhu'l-Qarnayn. Aristotle studied with Plato for nearly twenty years in order to derive wisdom (from him). In his youth he was called 'Spiritual' because of his extraordinary intelligence; and Plato used to call him 'Intellect'. It was he who composed the books on logic and made them an instrument of the sciences. For this he was dubbed the 'Master of Logic'. And it was he who organized the subjects of physics and metaphysics, and composed a separate book on each subject, being careful to proceed systematically in it. In his days the kingdom was put in good order by Dhu'l-Qarnayn, and polytheism was suppressed in the land of Greece.

9. These five were described as Sages. But none of the Greeks who came after them were called Sages. Rather, to every one of them was ascribed an art or a way of life—for example, Hippocrates the Physician, Homer the Poet, Archimedes the Geometer, Diogenes the Cynic, and Democritus the Physicist.

10. Now Galen, in his time, having composed many works, aspired to be described as wise—that is, to be called 'the Sage' instead of 'the Physician'. But people made fun of him and said, 'Go back to your ointments and laxatives, and to treating sores and fevers. For, the source of wisdom is too subtle to be found by anyone who has doubts about its informational content (*ma'ālim*). For he who testifies against himself that he is in doubt whether the world is without temporal beginning or created in time, and whether the Hereafter is real or not, and whether the soul is a substance or an accident, occupies too humble a rank to be called a Sage'.

11. The extraordinary thing about the people of our own time is that, when they see that a man has read Euclid's book and mastered the principles of logic, they describe him as a Sage, even if he completely lacks (knowledge of) the divine sciences. Thus they ascribe wisdom to Muḥammad b. Zakarīyā' al-Rāzī because of his

proficiency in medicine—this in spite of his various ravings about the five eternal principles and about the corrupt spirits.

12. Now our shaykh, Abū Zayd Aḥmad b. Sahl al-Balkhī, was at home in the various kinds of knowledge, and his procedure in questions of religion was sound. Nevertheless, when one of his admirers ascribed wisdom to him, he would recoil from him and say, 'Alas for a time in which an imperfect one like me has ascribed to him the honour of wisdom!—as if they have never heard the world of God, "He gives wisdom to whom He will; and he to whom wisdom is given has been given much good. But no one remembers except men of understanding"'. (Qur'ān 2:272). And this was (also) the case with *his* master, Ya'qūb b. Isḥāq al-Kindī.

13. Knowing this, you must know further that one of the famous stories about Plato is that he used to say to his associates, 'Even if you should know everything, still do not consider yourselves as knowing anything, so long as you do not know God.' And one of the famous stories about Aristotle is that he used to say, 'Before today I used to drink and be thirsty; but now that I have learned of God, my thirst has been quenched without drinking.'

14. And the followers of these five Greeks who were called Sages without qualification regarded with disdain and contempt all those who did not acknowledge the Creator and were not certain of the eternal Reward after their deaths, and they treated them in the same scornful way as the monotheist treats the heretic (*mulḥid*). However, their belief about the form of the Hereafter differed from the True Religion (*al-millat al-ḥanīfīyah*) in one point: namely, they did not acknowledge the resurrection of the body, but affirmed the eternal Reward only for human spirits. This is why Islam has adjudged all of them to be misled and in error. But as for the affirmation of the Creator and the Unity of His essence, and the denial of rivals and adversaries to Him—this they have granted willingly and brought forth proofs of.

15. But our reason for wanting to describe their situation in this way is the following: They undertook to master arts which are useful in producing prosperity in the land, and are beneficial in promoting the well-being of men—arts such as medicine, geometry, astronomy, music, and others. They have written well-known books on them, which have been translated into various languages, and which right-minded people in the various nations have approved of. And these wise men have attained high rank in these places.

16. But then we have found the filthy heretics (*zanādiqah*) hunting down people of weak intelligence, one here and one there, by exploiting these wise men and their renown, and leading these people gradually into the profligacy (*khalā'ah*) with which they are themselves defiled. They even make them imagine that if the Religion of God possessed true reality, these wise men with their perfect intellects and their abundant intelligence would surely have adopted it and adhered to it.

17. And furthermore, we have also found that the dialecticians accuse these wise men of denying God's attributes (*ta'ṭīl*), and of heresy (*ilḥād*); and they make the

masses imagine that the Religion of Truth has powerful adversaries, and that 'were it not for our exclusive devotion to the struggle against them and our zeal to refute their falsehoods, heresy would pervade the pale of Islam.' Now, upon my life! the dialecticians have made an effort worthy of thanks in aiding the truth and supporting the religion. But their ascription of the denial of God's attributes to these wise men has perhaps contributed to making heresy attractive and encouraged people to be impressed by freethinking—and that is something which supports the party of the materialists (*dahrīyah*) against weak creatures.

Chapter IV

1. The teaching of Empedocles on the attributes of the Creator is this: Although Knowledge, Beneficence, Will, and Power are attributed to Him, He does not have distinguishable qualities (*maʿānī*) peculiar to (each of) these different names. For as we say that every existent in the world is known by Him, under His Power, willed by Him, and an emanation of His Beneficence, without (thereby) affirming manifold qualities in the existent, in the same way we attribute Knowledge, Beneficence, Will, and Power to Him Who gives the existents their being (*mūjiduhā*), although He is a unique One.

2. Furthermore, the Creator's existence (*wujūd*) is not like that of any of the existents in the world. For things existing in the world do so with contingent existence, that is, depending on creation (*ṣanʿah*), while He is essentially of necessary existence (*dhātuhū wājib al-wujūd*), not depending on creation. In the same way, His Unity is not like the unity of any of the existents in the world. For in the world unities are subject to multiplicity, either of parts, or of qualities, or of (only numerically distinct) exact equivalents, but His essence is exalted above this.

3. So, although one may properly attribute to Him Knowledge, Beneficence, Power, and Will, His most particular attribute is that He is Truth (*Ḥaqq*) in essence, and is Wise (*Ḥakīm*) in essence. The meaning of 'Truth' is that His existence is such that it is impossible to apply 'non-existence' to Him in any way. The meaning of 'Wise' is that He brings everything into existence having as much perfection as befits its purpose.

4. But then, having acknowledged the truth of this excellent statement, Empedocles got mixed up about the Hereafter. For it is well known that in his teaching he used to speak of Love (*maḥabbah*) and Mastery (*ghalabah*). These refer to two qualities possessed by the substance of the soul, namely, nature and intellect. The soul may have a disposition which is in accord with nature, in which case it will perform its acts in accordance with Love; and a disposition which is in accord with intellect, in which case it will perform its acts in accordance with Mastery. And each of these two dispositions has a temporal period equal to that of the other. One of

the two dispositions is pleasurable, the other is painful. But there are absolutely no proofs for these claims which Empedocles made up.

5. Pythagoras agreed with Empedocles in what he believed about the attributes of the Creator, except on one point. This is that, according to Pythagoras, our describing Him as [Truth is dependent on our describing Him as] Wise; for Wisdom is prior to Truth, and with Wisdom the Truth becomes Truth.

6. Furthermore, he also disagreed with Empedocles about the Hereafter. For it is well known that in his teaching Pythagoras used to say the following: The world in its entirety is divided into twelve parts. Four of them are the lower bodies, that is, earth, water, air, and fire; and eight of them are the upper bodies, that is, the seven heavens and the Throne (*kursī*) which surrounds them. And above this world is a luminous world whose beauty and splendour are beyond the grasp of intellects, and which pure souls long for. These divisions are arranged in layers, one above the next; and each division is, as it were, the sediment (*thufl*) of the one above it.

7. Now any man who has succeeded in putting his soul right by freeing himself from vanity, pride, [hypocrisy,] envy, and other corporeal desires, has become worthy of reaching the highest of these divisions and beholding (*iṭṭalaʿa ʿalā*) all the divine Wisdom pervading the substances of the world. When he has that good fortune, he has attained true happiness and true glory, and the pleasurable things then come to him gently, as musical melodies come to the sense of hearing, and he need not burden himself with seeking them at all.

8. Socrates agreed with Pythagoras about this, except on two points. One of them is that, according to Socrates, our describing the Creator as Wise is dependent on our describing Him as Truth; for Truth is prior to Wisdom, and whenever knowledge attains its utmost perfection, it is described as Wisdom.

9. The other point is this: Socrates said that at the Second Raising (*al-nash'at al-thāniyah*) the heaven will become starless. For, the reason for the stars' being fixed in it is the rapid motion of the spheres which carry them along. But everything in motion comes to some rest; and whenever the spheres cease their revolution, their stars will fall off and come to surround the earth, being all contiguous with one another, like a flaming circle. Every soul which has been defiled and wicked will remain on this earth surrounded by flame. But for the pure souls the heaven will become like the earth, and their heaven will be a luminous heaven, nobler than this one. And there, there will be pure beauty and pure pleasure.

10. Socrates also went beyond Pythagoras in saying that any man who is ennobled with the acquisition of pure wisdom thereby becomes a possessor of absolute goodness. And the highest rank of (God's) servant (man) in goodness is that he finds his True Lord sufficient for him, without needing an intermediary between him and his Lord. But he who needs an intermediary between him and his Lord in acquiring wisdom is inferior in the ranks of service. And the more intermediaries one has between himself and his Lord, the lower is his standing in service.

11. Now the body requires the effect of nature in its concerns; nature requires governance by the soul in performing its acts; the soul requires the direction of the intellect in its choosing; and there is no revealer (*fātiḥ*) above the intellect except divine guidance. Therefore, we ought to grant that he who has recourse to pure intellect in all that he does has the bliss of finding—sufficiency in his Lord; but he who pursues the desires of the body, allows himself to be led by the biddings of nature, and goes along with the cravings of the soul, is far from his Lord and inferior in rank, since he does not hold fast to what the intellect enjoins. So there is no goodness in him who clings to the many first things, not ascending with his intellect to the First Truth.

12. As for Plato, he varied in his teaching. In his book the *Statesman*—that is, 'the governance of cities'—he said that the world is eternal (*abadī*), not generated (*ghayr mukawwan*), abiding forever (*dā'im al-baqā'*). Proclus the Materialist commented on this statement and composed his book on the eternity (*azaliyya*) of the world—the book which John the Grammarian refuted. But then, in his book known as *Timaeus*, Plato said that the world was generated, the Creator (*Bārī'*) having created (*abdaʿa*) it, from non-order to order; and that all the substances of the world are composed of matter and form, and every compound is subject to decomposition.

13. Now if his pupil Aristotle had not explained what he meant by making these two different statements, he would have been judged confused. But Aristotle made it clear that the word 'generated' falls among the homonymous nouns. Plato's intention in saying that 'the world is eternal, not generated' is that no time preceded it, and it was not created in time (*yuḥdath*) from anything. But his intention in saying that 'it was generated, the Creator having turned (*ṣarafa*) it from non-order to order' is that its existence is dependent on the creative act (*ṣanʿah*) which brings the matter into order with the form. Now, neither of these (matter and form) has existence in itself without union with the other. Therefore, the Creator (*Mubdiʿ*) of the two brought both into existence by means of an ordering act of unifying. So, by His creative (*ibdāʿī*) act, he turned the world from non-order to order, that is, from non-existence to existence.

14. Indeed, Plato has explained this clearly in the book of the *Laws*, where he says that the world had a causative beginning, but not a temporal beginning—that is, it has an Agent Who produced (*ikhtaraʿa*) it atemporally. And if someone should inquire of the reason for His producing it, we reply that He Wills by Himself to emanate His Beneficence, and has the Power to bring into existence (*ījād*) what He Wills.

15. In the same way, Plato said in his book named after *Phaedo* that the substance of the soul is not generated, and that it does not die. But then he said in the book *Timaeus* that it is generated and that it is mortal and does not endure. Aristotle undertook to clarify his intention in the two differing statements, saying, 'He meant by his first statement that the soul, in its creation in time (*ḥudūth*), did not

progress from potentiality to activity, but was created in time (*uḥditha*) all at once; and death will not befall it in the Abode of Reward. And by his second statement he meant that the soul is subject to the qualitative change (*istiḥālah*) from ignorance to knowledge and from vice to virtue; and it would not be able by itself to endure eternally, were it not that God preserves it forever.' Indeed, Plato has stated this plainly in the book *Timaeus*, where he says that the Creator of the universe revealed to the spiritual substances that 'You are not such that you do not die, but I preserve you with My divine power (*quwwa*).'

16. And in the same way, Aristotle made clear what is really correct in what Pythagoras and Socrates differed on—whether Wisdom is prior to Truth, or Truth prior to Wisdom. Aristotle said: Truth is more general than Wisdom, but it may be manifest or it may be hidden. Wisdom is more specific than Truth, but it can only be manifest. Therefore, Truth is extended throughout the world, and includes the Wisdom emanated in the world. And Wisdom is emanated in the world, and makes manifest the Truth extended throughout the world. But neither of the two is separate from the creation (*ṣunʿ*) of God which gives the world existence, and from His power (*quwwa*) which holds the world fast. Therefore, both statements are acceptable, each in a way.

17. This, then, is a summary of our conception of the teaching of these four, and of what we have gleaned from the major figures connected with philosophy. But the books which they have composed on these subjects are not comprehensible without a revealer (*fātiḥ*) to explain them, for they are filled with symbols and enigmas. The authors did this intentionally, for three reasons. One was an abhorrence lest someone should plunge into a search for the secrets of wisdom who was not worthy of them; they could thus become a tool for him in acquiring some sort of evil. The second was that he who loves wisdom should not slacken his efforts in applying himself to acquire it, even though it cost him labour to attain it; and so that the lazy man would find these books difficult, due to their obscurity, and simply disdain them. And the third was to hone (the learner's) nature (*tabʿ*) by requiring much toilsome reflection, so that the learner would not incline to pleasant rest and relaxation of the soul, but rather devote his efforts to understanding that which (his) nature turns away from.

18. As for the teaching of Aristotle, we have given a summary of it in our book called *Care and Study*, and have made clear his approach to (the questions of) the Unity of God and the Hereafter.

11

Abū Sulaymān Sijistānī

Abū Sulaymān Muḥammad ibn Ṭāhir Sijistānī (390/999) appeared during the most intense period of the translation movement, in the third/ninth and fourth/tenth centuries. What we know of him is through his major work, *Ṣiwān al-ḥikmah*, and his student Abū Ḥayyān al-Tawḥīdī's writings. Sijistānī, in pursuit of a more cogent scholarly ambiance, went to Baghdad and joined the school of Yaḥyā ibn 'Adī, a learned Christian scholar from whom Sijistānī learned the ancient sciences, as well as Arabic literature and poetry. Baghdad at the time had reached a fascinating degree of acculturation in which different religious groups such as Muslims, Jews, Christians, Sabaeians, and Mazdaeans, unified by their common interest in ancient sciences, worked together. Sijistānī, who had mastered Aristotle and Neoplatonism, also pursued some of the occult sciences of late antiquity.

Sijistānī and his intellectual circle were deeply concerned with the integration of ancient philosophy into the Islamic religious perspective. Al-Tawḥīdī tells us that Sijistānī belongs to the Baghdad school of philosophy, and was opposed to the type of harmonization to which the Bretheren of Purity adhered. Sijistānī is often included among a group of thinkers who have been referred to by some scholars as Islamic humanists. While Sijistānī emphasized the use of reason, he did not deny the significance of religion. Religious faith as a phenomenon remains an integral part of people's lives, whereas the use of reason, Sijistānī maintained, is appropriate for the intellectual elite.

Sijistānī attempted to bring about a rapprochement between grammarians and logicians. He argued that grammar and logic are essentially two distinct aspects of the same phenomenon. Logic, he maintained, is inclusive of the internal aspect of expression, whereas grammar governs their external dimension. Sijistānī argued that logic is universal and therefore inclusive of all languages.

Sijistānī's teleological view of the world bears resemblance to Hegel's, arguing for a gradual progression of history toward perfection. Despite his interest in rational discourse, Sijistānī did not condemn faith as a possibility of knowledge beyond sensory perceptions, and he maintained that Greek discursive philosophy and Islamic sciences can be harmonized with intellectual intuition and religious faith.

In this chapter there are translations of three treatises that can be attributed to Sijistānī with confidence. These treatises, which always exist together in various editions, have been translated by Joel Kramer in his book *The Renaissance of Islam*. The first two are thematically related, and the third is addressed to the king ʿAḍud al-Dawlah and therefore must have been written after 367/977, when the title ʿAḍud al-Dawlah was bestowed upon him.

In the first treatise, *The Supernal Bodies Possess Rational Souls*, Sijistānī discusses the nature of the heavens and their difference from the four elements, and the soul which also acts as their principle of motion and constitutes their relationship to the First Mover. Sijistānī's argument that motion is an inherent characteristic of nature is similar to that of such philosophers as Alexander of Aphrodisias, John Philoponus, and Mullā Ṣadrā, as seen in his principle of the 'trans-substantiality of motion' (*al-ḥarakah al-jawhariyyah*).

The second treatise, *On the First Mover*, discusses the nature of the First Mover as presented by Aristotle in two of his treatises, *Physics*, Book VIII and *Metaphysics*, Book Lambda. Sijistānī concludes that the First Mover in *Physics* is the mover of the outermost spheres, different from the First Mover in the *Metaphysics*, who is the Ultimate Principle transcending all forms.

The third treatise, *On the Specific Perfection of the Human Species*, examines the relationship between the Ultimate Principle and an individual who establishes peace and harmony in the world and rules justly. From a discussion concerning those who are recipients of divine emanation, Sijistānī goes on to examine the source of that emanation and presents the opinion of those who believe in the unifying power of the Ultimate Principle.

M. Aminrazavi

PHILOSOPHICAL TREATISES
Muṣannafāt

Reprinted from 'Muṣannafāt', in J. L. Kraemer, tr., *Philosophy in the Renaissance of Islam: Abū Sulaymān al-Sijistānī and His Circle* (Leiden, 1986), pp. 279–304.

5. The Supernal Bodies Possess Rational Souls (Treatise No. 1)

5.1.1 Every natural body has an essential motion toward something specific to it alone.[1] I mean by saying 'natural' what has a cause in itself moving it toward what is specific to it. This cause is what is called 'nature', and it is defined as 'the principle of motion and rest in what it resides primarily and essentially, not accidentally.'[2] The natural bodies so qualified are the heavenly bodies and the four elements, which are fire, air, water, and earth, and what is composed of these, I mean of the elements.[3]

1. Cf. S. Pines, 'A Refutation of Galen by Alexander of Aphrodisias', *Isis*, 52 (1961), p. 43, n. 87, on the beginning of Alexander's argument in a treatise that has been preserved in Arabic, *Fī mabādī' al-kull* (*On the Principles of the Universe*), in *Arisṭū 'ind al-'Arab*, ed. Badawī, pp. 253–277. Pines' translation deserves quotation for its stylistic and substantive resemblance to our text: 'Every natural body is naturally moved *per se*. For that which has in itself a principle or a cause of motion is moved *per se*; every natural body has in itself a principle of motion, I mean thereby nature … .' Alexander's treatise will be further cited as a source of a number of Sijistānī's arguments. He is mentioned specifically in connection with the subject of the present treatise (below, 6.3.2, p. 290). *Fī mabādī' al-kull* resembles Alexander's *Quaestiones naturales*, I, I and ii, 3, ed. I. Bruns, *Scripta Minora* (Berlin, 1892); cf. S. van den Bergh, *Averrveos' Tahāfut al-Tahāfut* (London, 1954), vol. 2, p. 254; and Pines, 'Une version arabe de trois propositions de la *Stoicheiōsis theologikē* de Proclus', *Oriens*, 8 (1955), p. 199. The initial arguments in the present treatise correspond, *grosso modo*, to the discussion in *De caelo*, 1, 2 and 3, beginning with 1, 2, 268b14: 'All natural bodies and magnitudes we hold to be, as such, capable of locomotion; for nature, we say, is their principle of movement.'

2. *Mabda al-ḥarakat wa al-sukūn fī shay' al-ladhī huwa fīhi awwalan wa bi'l-dhāti lā bi'l-ṭarīq al-'araḍ*; *Physica* 192b21. For the same definition, see above, 2.1.4 (6), p. 173; and below, 8.4, p. 307. The Arabic translation of the definition before us differs but slightly from that of Isḥāq b. Ḥunayn in his translation of the *Physica*, where *tou kineisthai kai ēremein* is rendered *li-an yataḥarraka wa-yaskuna*; ed. Badawī, vol. 1, 79.7–9. The difference between the two renditions corresponds to that between the translation of Wicksteed and Cornfold ('of motion and rest') and the translation of Gaye ('of being moved and of being at rest').

3. It is noteworthy that Sijistānī mentions the heavenly bodies among the natural bodies after having cited the definition of nature from *Physica* 192b21, where it is stated that nature is a principle of both motion and rest. The heavens do not partake of rest, however. How, then, can they be considered natural bodies? Aristotle did include the heavens in some enumerations of natural bodies; see A. Mansion, 'La notion de Nature dans la Physique aristotélicienne', *Annales de l'Institut Supérieur de Philosophie*, 1 (Louvain and Paris, 1912), p. 477, and *idem*, *Introduction à la Physique aristotélicienne* (2nd rev. ed., Louvain and Paris, 1946), p. 98, note 11, citing *De caelo* 298a30, *Metaph*. 1028b8–13, and 1042a7–11 (add *De caelo* 268b27). But where nature is described as a principle of both motion and rest, as in *Physics* 192b21 (and 192b14), the heavenly bodies are not included among the natural bodies (see 192b8–10). This prompted Alexander of Aphrodisias to observe that the omission was by design; i.e. that when Aristotle defines nature as a principle

Each one of these four elements has an essential motion when it is outside its place toward its coordinate—the place where its totality is—resting there upon reaching it.[1] It has, then, a specific nature, which is the principle of its motion and rest. Since the supernal bodies are natural bodies having essential motion, they have a nature that is the principle of their motion.[2] And inasmuch as the nature of each one of

---

of motion and rest he thinks of other physical bodies apart from the heavens, as their motion is perpetual and they do not contain a principle of rest; see Alexander *apud* Simplicius, *In Physica*, 264.18–20; and *Quaestiones naturales*, II, xxv. It may be noted that Alexander describes the divine body (*al-jism al-ilāhī* [*to theion sōma*]) as a natural body in *Fī mabādī' al-kull*, p. 254.3 (and see p. 255.18), but this follows a reference to nature as a principle of motion, not of both motion and rest. Aristotle speaks of nature as simply a principle of motion in *Physica* 200b12; and *Metaph.*, V, 4.

Simplicius (*loc. cit.*) attempted to solve the *aporia* by arguing that the heavens *do* partake of stationariness (*stasis*) (see *Physica* 192b14), though not rest (*ēremia*), as the centre and poles are immovable (cf. Alexander, *Quaestiones naturales*, II, xxv [p. 76.19]). Philoponus attempted to solve the difficulty by explaining that the heavens are always in a state of perfection, and can thereby be said to be at rest (*In Physica*, 198.9–199.20). On the *aporia* and its proposed solutions, see also Mansion, *Introduction*, p. 98, note 11; Sambursky, *The Physical World of Late Antiquity*, pp. 123–124.

Discussion of this question was carried on in the Baghdad school of Aristotelian studies. In the Arabic translation of the *Physica*, I, 87, Yaḥyā b. 'Adī is quoted as having commented that the heavens do not move; for their motion is not the actualization of a potentiality, which is what motion must be according to Aristotle (see *Physica*, 201a10). Miskawayh treated the problem in his brief *Risālah fi' l-ṭabī'ah*, Ms. Rāghib Pāshā 1463, fol. 60a, citing the view of Simplicius, though not in his name. It may be added that al-Rāzī, in his *Maqālah fī mā ba'd al-ṭabī'ah*, *Opera Philosophica*, ed. P. Kraus, p. 117.11–19, undertook to criticize what he calls the solution of Philoponus, which appears to be instead the proposal of Simplicius as cited anonymously by Philoponus. Finally, we have a statement of Sijistānī himself on the question whether the world is at rest or in motion. Asked whether the world, i.e. the first heaven, is at rest or in motion, he replied: 'If it were in motion in the ordinary way, it would totter and shake, bow over and collapse. It rather moves in a rotary motion, and therefore cannot be considered to be at rest, and it is at rest in receiving the emanation, and therefore cannot be considered to be in motion. Aspiration [toward the First Mover] is a kind of motion but it is intellective, and persistence in aspiration is a kind of rest but it is intellective' (*Muqābasāt* 33, p. 156).

1. 'Its totality' refers to the whole of the element in its natural place; cf. *RIS*, II, 2 (II, 48.10): *kawn ajzā'ihī fī jawfi kulliyyātihi*. In Aristotle's view, a fragment of earth, for instance, does not tend to move toward the mass of earth, i.e. the totality of the element, but toward the centre—its natural place—where the mass of earth is located and toward which it moves only *per accidens*; see *De caelo* 310b5–7, and note 2 *ad loc.* in the Oxford translation. Sijistānī thus expressed the situation precisely in speaking of the proper place, in which the totality of the element is, as being the goal of motion. The view that the goal of motion is not the natural place of the element but its collective mass was held by Thābit b. Qurrah; see Pines, *Beitrage*, p. 42, note 2 (p. 43).

It is also possible that *kulliyyātuhu* should be emended to read *kamāluhu*, 'its perfection;' cf. Alexander, *Fī mabādī' al-kull*, p. 254.8–9, translated by Pines, 'A Refutation of Galen', p. 44: 'For in this way the destination of every body is the natural place which is peculiar to it. And when it is established in that place it achieves the perfection that is peculiar to it' (cf. *Quaestiones naturales*, II, iii [p. 48.11]). We also have it on Simplicius' authority that Alexander regarded the natural places of bodies as their actualities or perfections (Pines, p. 37). Cf. *De caelo* 311a5.

2. Cf. *De caelo*, I, 2. The principle of motion which a body contains in itself is, according to

the elements differs from that of the others, insofar as its motion differs from that of the others, it neither moves toward what the others move nor rests where the others rest, it follows that the nature of the supernal bodies also differs from the natures of the elements. And since these are four, this is a fifth.[1]

5.1.2 Fire is absolutely light, and earth is absolutely heavy; for the former moves away from the centre and the latter moves toward the centre.[2] Air is light relative to water and heavy relative to fire, and water is heavy relative to air and light relative to earth.[3] The supernal bodies, however, are neither light nor heavy; since they move neither away from the centre nor toward the centre but rather about the centre.[4] The motion of these bodies, which is locomotion,[5] is of two kinds: rectilinear and circular. Circular [motion] is nobler than rectilinear [motion] inasmuch as it is capable of continuance and permanence, whereas rectilinear [motion] is limited and finite.[6] It is apparent that the eternal and permanent is more excellent than the transitory and limited. The nature that is the principle [of circular motion] is therefore nobler than the nature that is the principle of rectilinear [motion], and the body which moves by the former is more excellent than the body which moves by the latter. The nature of the heavenly bodies is consequently nobler than

---

Physica 255b32, not a principle of moving something, or of *causing* motion, but of *undergoing* it. Aristotle made this qualification as a consequence of his principle *omne quod movetur necesse est ab aliquo moveri* (*Physica* 241b24ff.), and so as to distinguish the motion of inanimate bodies from the motion of animate bodies (*Physica* 255a5–10); see Mansion, *Introduction*, pp. 236f. Sijistānī, however, regards a body's principle of motion, or nature, as an intrinsic, active movement. Alexander held the view that natural bodies contain intrinsic, active principles of motion, analogous to the souls of animate bodies (Pines, 'A Refutation of Galen', p. 41). This position is not without support in Aristotle, as Pines shows. Furthermore, the views of Philoponus on natural inclination and impetus were current within Islamic philosophy; Pines, p. 48; and *idem*, 'Un précursuer bagdadien de la théorie de l'impetus', *Isis*, 44 (1953), pp. 246–251.

1. For the fifth nature in Arabic sources, see Pines, *Beiträge*, p. 43, note 1. The argument here approximates the text of *De caelo* 269a32ff. Sijistānī follows Aristotle in considering the natural motion of the four elements in terms of their parts and outside their natural places, and that of the fifth element in its totality and its natural place. But between the time of Aristotle and Sijistānī this double viewpoint had been criticized by Xenarchus and Philoponus; Simplicius, in *De caelo*, ed. I. L. Heiberg (Berlin, 1894), p. 33. Their objection was that fire and air in their totality and natural place do move rotarily, and that this motion, being eternal, cannot be forced and must be natural. It consequently cannot be argued that rotary motion is natural to only one body, viz. the heavens. See E. Evrard, 'Les convictions religieuses de Jean Philopon et la date de son Commentaire aux Météorologiques', *Bulletin de l'Académie Royale de Belgique*, 5, 34 (1953), p. 318, and Sambursky, *The Physical World of Late Antiquity*, p. 130.

2. *De caelo* 269b23 and 311a19.

3. *De caelo* 269b28 and 311a23.

4. *De caelo* 269b30.

5. Ed. Badawī: *al-ḥarakat al-thaqīlah*, 'heavy motion'. A number of Mss. read *al-ḥarakat al-'aqliyya*, 'intellective motion'. Neither reading makes sense here. Read: *al-ḥarakat al-naqliyyah*, with Ms. Teheran Parliament 634 (and Yazd 605?—the reading is unclear).

6. *De caelo* 269a18ff.; *Physica*, VIII, 8 and 9; *Metaph.* 1052a28.

the natures of the four elements.[1] Their substrate is likewise nobler than all other substrates, since no other forms belong to nobler substrates.[2] And their form is their nature.[3] The supernal bodies are thus the most excellent bodies in their substrates, natures, and motions. And since their motion is single, continuous, uniform, and homogeneous, no other motion may impel them.[4] Now if no other motion may impel them, the substance of their substrate does not admit transition from one state to another, as this occurs by means of some [other] motion.[5]

5.1.3 Since an animate body is more excellent than an inanimate body,[6] and we find animate and inanimate beings among compounds of the elements; and as it has been demonstrated above that the supernal bodies are superior to the elements, they are, consequently, animate. For if this were not so, then a part of what is inferior in excellence to [the supernal bodies] would be superior to them, and this is absurd.[7] Since they are animate, their nature is soul, which is the principle of their

1. *De caelo* 269b16.

2. It is presumably not perchance that Sijistānī uses the term 'substrate' instead of 'matter'. Cf. al-Fārābī, *al-Siyāsat al-madaniyyah*, p. 41.5: '[the heavens'] substrates are not matters.' According to Aristotle the heavens have matter of a special kind (*Metaph.* 1044b7, 1050b22, 1069b28). That form and matter, or substrate, are correlative is a guiding principle of Aristotle's system; see e.g. *Physica* 194b9.

3. Cf. *Physica* 193a9–b21; and *Metaph.*, V, 4, definition 5. Sijistānī regards the form, nature, and soul of a heavenly body as identical.

4. Cf. *De caelo* 270a10: 'For neither naturally nor unnaturally can [heaven] move with any other motion but its own;' Alexander, *Fī mabādī' al-kull*, p. 256.4–8: 'Since the divine body is simple, and its motion is single and simple, it has no other natural motion apart from the soul;' and al-Kindī, *al-Ibānah 'an sujūd al-jirm al-aqṣā*, in *Rasā'il*, I, 252.8: 'The ulterior body's motion is vital motion and is not acquired from another body.'

5. Cf. *De caelo* 270a10–35.

6. *Gen. an.* 731b29.

7. This manner of reasoning is labelled 'thinking in axiological antitheses' by Dijksterhuis, *The Mechanization of the World Picture*, p. 75. Axiological modes of thought underlie one of the most pervasive convictions of Greek cosmology—the belief that there is soul, or mind, in the universe. The argument runs, as formulated by Dijksterhuis (pp. 77f.): 'In fact, the living is more powerful than the lifeless, the animate nobler than the inanimate, and consequently ... it is incredible that the Cosmos should be dead.' As an argument for the vitality, animateness, or reasonableness of the cosmos, this mode of deduction was favoured by the ancient Stoics; see e.g. von Arnim, *Stoicorum veterum Fragmenta*, I, 32f. (Zeno, no. 111) and II, 191, 193 (Chrysippus, nos. 633, 641). The Stoic argument is traceable to Socrates; see Xenophon, *Memorabilia*, I, 4, 8 (ed. and tr. E. C. Marchant (Cambridge, MA, 1953), pp. 57–59), and Plato, *Philebus* 28e–30d (Festugière, *La révélation d'Hermès Trismégiste*, vol. 2, pp. 80–82).

The source of Sijistānī appears to have been Alexander of Aphrodisias, whose argument that the divine body must be animate because it is the superior body is set forth in *Mabādī' al-kull*, p. 254.13–17, and in *Quaestiones naturales*, I, I (pp. 3.11–13) (parallel in *Metaphysica*, ed. M. Hayduck (Berlin, 1891), 686.12–16). Alexander's argument for the animateness of the divine body was cited by Averroes, who rejected it as too simple and unsophisticated for his own purposes (*Die Epitome der Metaphysik des Averroes*, tr. S. van den Bergh (Leiden 1924), p. 109). Averroes' argument presupposes first the existence of an unmoved mover, which moves by virtue of being desired, and then posits the necessity of a soul as the seat of desire (*Tafsīr mā ba'd al-ṭabī'ah*, ed. Bouyges,

motion;[1] for the nature of every animate being, insofar as it is such, is its soul,[2] and a living being is a body endowed with a soul.[3]

5.2.1 What remains to be explained is: (1) Which soul is it? (2) Are they all endowed with souls, I mean, are the spheres and the stars all endowed with souls, or only the stars and not the spheres, or only the spheres and not the stars? (3) In what manner do their souls move them in a corporeal circular motion? The manner most reflecting the substance of their soul is by intellect and cognitive discrimination. (4) Toward what thing do they strive in their motion? (5) How many motions have they?

5.2.2 I say: We have found that every natural thing aspires toward something which moves it that is most fitting for it to assimilate itself to, its motion abating

---

VII, 1593; cf. Theophrastus, *Metaphysics*, ed. and tr. W. D. Ross and F. H. Fobes (Oxford 1929), II, 8, 5a, 28). Averroes knew Alexander's *Fī mabādī' al-kull* (*Epitome*, p. 113; *Tahāfut al-tahāfut*, p. 497.7/301). It is also possible that he found the passage in Alexander's Commentary on the *Metaphysics*; see J. Freudenthal, *Die durch Averroes erhaltenen Fragmente Alexanders zur Metaphysik des Aristoteles, Abhandlungen der Königlichen Akademie der Wissenschaften zu Berlin*, phil.-hist. Klasse, I (1884), p. 112, note 3.

The argument under consideration also appears in al-Kindī, *al-Ibānah 'an sujūd al-jirm al-aqṣā, Rasā'il*, I, pp. 254.13–255.7, where it is stated that the heavens are not only superior, they are the cause of reason in us, and therefore cannot be devoid of the same.

1. Aristotle described the motion of the heavens as natural in *De caelo*, II, 2; however, in *De caelo* 285a30 he appears to have contradicted this by saying that the heaven is animate (*empsuchos*) and possesses a principle of motion. This created a problem for commentators; see H. A. Wolfson, 'The Problem of the Souls of the Spheres from the Byzantine Commentaries on Aristotle through the Arabs and St. Thomas to Kepler', *The Dumbarton Oaks Papers*, 16 (1962), pp. 67–93; in *Studies*, I, pp. 22–59. The recourse adopted by Alexander was to consider the nature of the heavenly bodies as identical with their soul and as constituting an internal source of motion; see *Fī mabādī' al-kull*, p. 256.6; Simplicius, *In De caelo*, p. 380.29ff., and *In Physica*, p. 1219.3–5; Pines, 'A Refutation of Galen', p. 47; and Wolfson, pp. 69, 73. Alexander compared the soul and nature of the heavenly body—one and the same in his view—to the heaviness and lightness of the elements, e.g. earth and fire, which are their natures or powers. Simplicius objected on several grounds. He rejected Alexander's view that the soul is entelechy, i.e., an inseparable form, of a body and he criticized Alexander's understanding of nature as a principle of a body's motion rather than of its being moved. Simplicius' own view (see also *In De caelo*, pp. 78–80) was that the animateness of heaven does not preclude its having natural motion. Its natural motion would not be perpetual were it not for the presence of soul. Soul and nature are thus distinct but complementary. For Simplicius' views, see P. Duhem, *Le Système du monde* (Paris 1913–59), vol. 4, p. 426, and Wolfson, p. 75. Philoponus took the position, more as critic than commentator, that the heavens are not animate but are moved naturally like terrestrial bodies, *De opificio mundi*, pp. 231ff., cited by Pines, p. 50, note 137.

It is clear that Sijistānī follows the view of Alexander. Averroes also followed Alexander in considering the soul and nature of a sphere to be one and the same (*Epitome*, p. xxx and p. 241, note 2 *ad* p. 108). al-Ghazzālī appears to have followed Philoponus; see Averroes, *Tahāfut*, Discussion XIV, 476.12ff/290 and p. 479.9ff/292; Wolfson, *Crescas Critique of Aristotle*, pp. 535–538; whereas Avicenna's view resembles that of Simplicius; *al-Najāh* (Cairo, 1938), pp. 258–259; *al-Shifā', al-ilāhiyyāt*, ed. I. Madkour et al. (Cairo, 1960), vol. 2, p. 382.

2. *De anima* 415b25; *De part. an.* 641a28; *Metaph.* 1049b8–9.

3. *De anima* 434b12; *To zōon soma empsuchon esti*; and see H. Bonitz, *Index Aristoelicus* (Berlin, 1870; 3rd ed., Graz, 1955), p. 744b43–45.

upon reaching it. Water, for example, moves toward the place that accords with continuance of its form, namely, what lies between air, according with it in its moistness, and earth, according with it in its coldness. And likewise the rest of the elements and also animals. They aspire with respect to their body toward the thing that accords with their continuance, and with respect to their soul they aspire toward what the environment provides for their quest. Since, therefore, [animals] follow a natural course and necessary order in their movements, we intend to consider the faculty by which the animate being solely seeks its object, refraining from discussing anything else.

5.2.3 We say: A living being seeks either to avenge itself and assail another so as to wrest what it possesses by means of the spirited faculty, or it seeks desires and pleasures by means of the vital and voluntary faculty, or it seeks the virtues by means of the rational faculty.[1] Spirit and appetite are associated in the lower animal with its bodily needs: spirit to obtain what is outside itself for the welfare of its condition or to preserve it from its enemies, and appetite to obtain what compensates for the disintegration of its body and the voidance of its waste. The supernal bodies are exempt from all these things because of the remoteness of their substance from change, transition, deficiency, and need for what is outside them, as we have explained above. Since the matter is as we say, their soul is that by which the virtues are desired.[2]

5.2.4 Since the virtues are also of different kinds—some belonging to animals in accordance with the faculties we have mentioned; for example, courage,

1. The enumeration of the faculties of the soul follows the famous tripartition of the *Republic*, Book IV. For its role in Islamic philosophy, see Walzer, 'Some Aspects of Miskawayh's *Tahdhīb al-Akhlāq*' *Greek into Arabic*, pp. 221–222, and *idem*. 'Akhlāq', *EI*, vol. 1, pp. 327–328. The Platonic trichotomy of the soul is present in the Arabic translation of Galen's *Peri ēthōn* (*Fi'l-akhlāq*), a long quotation from which is contained in the *Ṣiwān al-ḥikmah*, pp. 274–275, in which the relation of the rational part of the soul to the spirited part is compared to the relation of a hunter to his dog or of a rider to his mount. See also *Ṣiwān al-ḥikmah*, p. 283, in al-Kindī's entry. The tripartition of the soul plays a prominent role in Yaḥyā b. ʿAdī's *Tahdhīb al-akhlāq*, in *Rasā'il al-bulaghā'*, ed. M. Kurd ʿAlī (3rd ed., Cairo, 1946), pp. 483–522. This trichotomy penetrated even into the Peripatetic stream, as can be determined from the fact that it is ascribed by al-Yaʿqūbī to Aristotle; M. Klamroth, 'Ueber die Auszüge aus griechischen Schriftstellern bei al-Jaʿqūbī', *ZDMG*, 41 (1887), p. 421.

2. The remoteness of appetite and spirit from the heavenly bodies is affirmed by Alexander; *Fī mabādī' al-kull*, p. 254.10–20. He asserts (p. 255.3–5) that the divine things (viz. the heavens) do not need appetite and spirit, which provide preservation; their desire (*shahwah*) is by rational wish (*ikhtiyār*), and the true, supreme rational wish is love of the good (cf. *Metaph*. 1072a27, and note of Ross *ad loc*., in *Aristotle's Metaphysics*, II, p. 376).

The freedom of the heavens from appetite and spirit was stressed by al-Kindī, *al-Ibānah ʿan sujūd al-jirm al-aqṣā*, p. 255.15ff. In the same work (p. 256.2–4), denying that the soul of the outer heavenly body possesses either the spirited or appetitive faculty, he affirmed that it is endowed with the rational faculty of the Platonic trichotomy. Al-Fārābī also denied that the motion of the spheres is due to appetite or spirit; they are said to be actuated by a desire to assimilate to the separate intelligences (*ʿUyūn al-masā'il*, ed. Dieterici, p. 62.10/trans., 102). See also Avicenna, *al-Najāh*, pp. 262–263.

temperance, and justice, which is the equipoise of the three faculties—the virtue that the supernal bodies seek must be the most exalted in rank, the most sublime in station: assimilation to the most excellent existent, the ultimate in nobility and perfection. [This is] like the striving of man, the most excellent of living beings in the world of generation and corruption.[1] He strives toward this notion either according to its true essence or according to what he imagines it to be.[2] He strives toward the good according to his estimation, erring concerning it because of the diversity of his ways, the alternation of his movements, and the abundance of his matter.

5.2.5 And these, I mean the supernal bodies, since their substance is remote from diversity and from being compounded of incompatible things, and they are of homogeneous parts in their configurations and motions, and the closest of all bodies to their Creator—and what is close to a thing is what is capable of assimilating to it, as in the levels of all other existents—they aspire toward Him and proceed to attain the perfection[3] fitting them in permanent continuance of circular motion. They strive for whatever of this is possible by virtue of their body, and by virtue of their soul [they strive] for conceiving and for discrimination among essences. The soul, which is their form, moves them by will toward assimilation with the First Cause and First Mover, and the First Cause moves them as the beloved and good moves its pursuer.[4]

5.2.6 As for their all being endowed with souls, it has become evident from what we have said above that all coincide in species, since the nature of all of them, which is the principle of their motions, tends to one kind of substrate, inasmuch as [the substrate] is the same in every one of them in its remoteness from change, alteration, and in motion, because they all move in utmost circularity. They all strive for assimilation to the First Cause and First Mover in permanent continuance and conceiving. And these intellective motions are more suitable to the animate body than to the inanimate.

---

1. Of the four cardinal virtues, which correspond to the three parts of the soul, the heavens possess wisdom (*sophia*), which merges here with the wisdom (*phronēsis*) of *Theatetus* 176b—i.e., the endeavour to assimilate to the divine.

That man is the most excellent being in the world thanks to his possession of reason is a common theme in Islamic philosophy; see e.g. al-Rāzī, *Kitāb al-ṭibb al-rūḥānī*, in *Opera Philosophica*, p. 18.

Assimilation to God is one of the definitions of philosophy known to the Arabs from the Neoplatonic introductions to the Aristotelian corpus; see e.g. al-Fārābī, *Fī mā yanbaghī an yuqaddama qabla taʿallum al-falsafah*, ed. Dieterici, p. 53.16/trans. p. 89; Rosenthal, 'On the Knowledge of Plato's Philosophy in the Islamic World', p. 409, note 1; Kraus, *Jābir ibn Ḥayyān*, II, p. 99, note 2; and Altmann and Stern, *Isaac Israeli*, pp. 197–200. The parent of the Arabic reference to this notion is Ammonius, *In Isagoge*, prooemium, ed. A. Busse (Berlin, 1891), p. 3.8. See, in general, H. Merki, *Homoiōsis Theōi* (Freiberg, 1952).

2. Cf. *De anima* 433a28; *Metaph.* 1072a28.

3. Ed. Badawī: *li-faḍli'l-kamāl*. See note 1 *ad loc.* (p. 370). the *li-* does not appear in most Mss., however, which give something like *y-t-ṣ-l al-kamāl*. Read, perhaps, *taḥṣīl al-kamāl*.

4. *Metaph.*, XII, 7, 1072b4.

5.2.7 As for the number of their motions, this can be explained on the basis of knowledge of the number of their movers above the spheres. To know this, one needs to refer to the science of astronomy. These can be determined in accordance with correct observations.[1]

Abū Sulaymān says: This is what occurs to me to say on this subject according to my ability, and I hope it will be helpful, God willing.

6. On the First Mover (Treatise No. 2)

6.1.1 The most suitable investigation concerning the first mover combines discussion of physical inquiry with metaphysical inquiry. I do not mean by 'the first mover' some particular mover, nor by 'what moves by it' some particular mobile, as the one did who surmised that when Aristotle demonstrated in the eighth treatise of the *Physica* that there is some first mover and some thing that moves by it primarily, and that the mover is in the circumference; he meant by 'the first mover' the being that is the First Cause, and by 'the first mobile' the sphere of the universe, and that this mover is in its circumference.[2]

6.1.2 My view is that [Aristotle] discussed in that book the universal principles and the general canons of physical entities as such, and that he did not concern himself with their essences.[3] This was so that the investigator of entities, in following a physical procedure, would comply with these canons, inasmuch as the truth concerning it is attained through them. The philosopher's discourse, however, in which he made statements relating to entities, leads the imagination to what was surmised. And this is how most of what he stated in the *Metaphysica* ought to be regarded; for the objective of inquiry is to pave the way and to provide understanding of the correct procedure toward the subjects of investigation proper to the two philosophies, I mean natural philosophy and divine philosophy, so that the investigator of the real essences of existents may employ them.[4]

---

1. Cf. *Metaph.* 1073b5.

2. Sijistānī's own view of the discussion concerning the first mover in *Physica* VIII is that in placing the first mover in the circumference of the outer sphere (*Physica* 267b9), Aristotle had in mind the notion of first mover in general rather than a particular first mover. The view he objects to is that espoused by Alexander of Aphrodisias (see Simplicius, *In De caelo*, p. 116; and *In Physica*, pp. 1260f., 1354f.), later associated with the names of Averroes and Zarabella (Ross, *Aristotle's Metaphysics*, I, p. cxxxvi).

3. Cf. *Physica* 184a14; Philoponus, *In Physica*, pp. 2.15–3.10; 219.16; Simplicius, *In Physica*, p. 2.8–11; *In De caelo*, p. 2.18; al-Fārābī, *Falsafat Arisṭūṭālīs*, ed. M. Mahdi (Beirut, 1961), p. 92.2–9; trans. Mahdi, in *al-Fārābī's Philosophy of Plato and Aristotle*, pp. 98f.; Mattā b. Yūnus, cited in the Commentary on the Arabic translation of the *Physica* (ed. Badawī, I, p. 166) (cf. Mattā with the view of Philoponus).

4. That is, the *Metaphysica* is concerned also with the universal principles and general canons of physical entities.

6.1.3 In my view, Aristotle was distinguished by this kind of philosophic inquiry from the ancients who preceded him; for they tended to confuse inquiry concerning essences with inquiry concerning statements aimed at knowing their conditions and the syllogisms and rules indicating their validity.[1] [Aristotle], however, reserved inquiry concerning syllogisms, rules and general canons of the intelligible, the object of opinion, what is naturally constituted, and what has a material substrate, for logic, which comprises demonstrative, dialectic and other arguments, for which verification and assent are required.[2] He then produced natural philosophy,[3] reserving inquiry concerning the rules and general canons regarding entities insofar as they are natural for the *Physica*. He then produced the divine science, reserving inquiry concerning the paths leading to it for what he asserted in the books of the *Metaphysica*. Inquiry in the *Metaphysica* does not concern the essences of the divine entities; it concerns rather the manner of investigating the essences insofar as they are divine.[4]

6.2.1 And now I shall return to what we intended to discuss, having mentioned something that is not the specific matter of investigation in this place. We say: Every first mover, insofar as it is such, has a first mobile. And the first mobile, insofar as it is such, has the motion most deserving of priority, namely locomotion,[5] and of it the noblest motion of its kind, namely, circular motion.

6.2.2 Everything that moves does so either essentially or accidentally.[6] What moves essentially is prior to what moves accidentally.[7] And the first mobile, which moves by a first mover, is prior to and nobler than everything that moves essentially. What moves essentially is first; hence, the first mobile of a first mover is the first that moves essentially.[8]

6.2.3 What moves essentially contains its principle of motion.[9] Every body that contains its principle of motion is a natural body, and that notion from which the principle of its motion derives is natural.[10] The motion of every mobile and

1. That is they confused *ousia* and *logos*; cf. Ibn al-Ṭayyib, Introduction, fol. 13a.

2. Logic, which is propaedeutic to philosophy, treats the standards, rules, and canons of all objects of knowledge. In listing the objects of knowledge, Sijistānī tends to confuse their *ratio cognoscendi* with their *ratio essendi*.

3. Ed. Badawī and Mss.: *bi'l-falsafat al-ilāhiyyah*. Read *bi'l-falasafat al-ṭabī'iyyah*. The radical emendation is required by the context. The procedure of chronological arrangement ('Then he brought forth … ') is found also in al-Fārābī's *Philosophy of Aristotle*.

4. Cf. above, ch. III, part 3, note 167 (p. 210).

5. *Physica* 260a26ff.

6. *Physica* 254b7ff.; 224a21ff.; 226a19ff.; and cf. *De anima* 406aff.

7. *Physica* 198a7; *Metaph.* 1065b2. This appears to follow from the sense of priority in *Categoriae* 14b10ff., and *Metaph.* 1019a1ff. (fourth sense).

8. Cf. *De caelo* 292b28.

9. To move essentially *per se* (*kath' hauto*) means to move independently of everything else; to move essentially *a se* (*huph' hautou*) means to have an internal cause of motion; hence, only that which moves both *per se* and *a se* has the cause of its motion in itself (Wolfson, *Crescas' Critique of Aristotle*, p. 532).

10. Cf. *Physica* 192b14; 254b14–17.

mover exists in the mobile rather than in the mover.[1] The rotary mobile, which contains its principle of motion, and owing to which motion exists, is the circumference rather than the centre.[2] The first mover, then, is in the circumference of every rotary mobile rather than the centre.[3] And the first mover is a natural form for the first rotary mobile and is moved accidentally.[4] However, the mover

---

1. *Physica* 202a13–b22; 224b25.
2. Cf. *Physica* 267b6–9.
3. *Physica* 267b9.
4. Sijistānī regards the first mover in the circumference of the outer, or first, sphere as its natural form or soul. He does not distinguish between the soul of the sphere and its intelligence. The more usual view in Islamic philosophy (Fārābī, Avicenna, Averroes) is that the intelligences, or unmoved movers, of Book *Lambda*, chapter eight, move as separate final causes, and that the souls move as inherent efficient causes.

In holding the view that the sphere-movers do not transcend their respective spheres but reside in them as the soul of an animal inheres in its body, Sijistānī apparently followed Alexander of Aphrodisias (Simplicius, *In Physica*, pp. 1261.30–1262.13; W. Jaeger, *Aristotle*, tr. R. Robinson (2nd ed., Oxford, 1955), p. 361).

As the sphere-movers are said to be natural forms or souls of their respective spheres, they are moved *per accidens* like the souls of living beings (cf. *Physica* 259b8). This conflicts, however, with Aristotle's view (*Physica* 259b28–31) that the sphere-movers are not moved accidentally like the souls of animals, their accidental motion being due to the attraction of their respective spheres into the revolution of the outer sphere; Jaeger, p. 361; H. A. Wolfson, 'The Plurality of Immovable Movers in Aristotle and Averroes', *Harvard Studies in Classical Philology*, 63 (1958), p. 237; *idem*, 'The Problem of the Souls of the Spheres', pp. 67f. Alexander rejected Aristotle's argument on the ground that even the accidental motion he admits implies that the sphere-movers are immanent in the spheres as the soul is in the body. The view that the sphere-movers are moved accidentally on the analogy of the soul in the body was also held, it appears, by Themistius (*In Metaphysica, librum Lambda paraphrasis*, ed. S. Landauer (Berlin, 1903), Heb., p. 23.9–11/Lat., p. 26.8–9; Arabic translation, ed. Badawī, *Arisṭū ʿind al-ʿArab*, p. 19.3–4).

Sijistānī parted company with Alexander in a crucial respect. Alexander distinguished between the first mover of the first aplanetary sphere and the movers of the subsequent planetary spheres (Simplicius, *loc. cit.*). In his view, the first mover of the first sphere is a separate substance, independent of the motion of the sphere; it causes motion as a final cause (Simplicius, *In Physica*, p. 1354.12ff.). The first mover, unmoved both essentially and accidentally, is identical, in Alexander's view, with the God of Book *Lambda*. Sijistānī, in contrast, considered the first mover of the first sphere as the first of the series of sphere-movers and on a par with them insofar as all are immanent in the spheres and moved accidentally.

Simplicius was not convinced that Alexander had successfully accounted for the absolute immovability of the first mover in view of its spatial relation to, and direct operation upon, the sphere (*In Physica*, p. 1355.15ff.). Alexander's discussion concerning the absolute immovability of the first mover (in *Mabādī' al-kull*, pp. 258f.) gives the impression that he was responding to arguments of those who maintained that the first mover cannot be demonstrated to be absolutely immovable (e.g. p. 258.2: 'If someone should say … ').

Among those who held this opposing view was Galen. We know from quotations from Galen's non-extant works, *On the First Mover* (cf. the title of the present treatise) and *On Demonstration* (in Jābir b. Ḥayyān, *Kitāb al-baḥth*, in *Textes choisis*, ed. P. Kraus (Paris and Cairo, 1935), p. 518. ff.), that Galen argued against the idea that the first mover is immovable, maintaining that the first mover, in causing motion, must itself be moved. Galen's *On the First Mover* is also cited by Maimonides, in *Medical Aphorisms*, 25th discourse (J. Schacht and M. Meyerhof, 'Maimonides

that does not move accidentally is nobler than the mover that does. Since this is so, there exists some mover that does not move in any respect.[1] For whatever is

---

against Galen, On Philosophy and Cosmology', *BFA*, 5 (1937), p. 80.1/67). Galen's treatise bore the title *Eis to prōton kinoun akinēton auto*) (see Galen, *On his own Writings, Scripta Minora*, ed. I. von Mueller (Leipzig 1891), vol. 2, p. 123.4 [and praefatio, p. lxxxix]), and is cited by Ḥunayn b. Isḥāq in his list of Galen's writings, under the title *Fī anna al-muḥarrik al-awwal la yataḥarrak* (G. Bergsträsser, 'Ḥunain ibn Isḥāq, Uber die syrischen und arabischen Galen-Übersetzungen', *AKM*, 12 (1925), p. 51.5/41 [no. 125]). See also I. von Mueller, 'Über Galens Werk vom wissenschaftlichen Beweis', *Abhandlungen der philosophisch-philologischen Klasse der Königlich-Bayerischen Akademie der Wissenschaften*, 20 (1897), p. 471, n. 97; I. Ilberg, 'Über die Schriftstellerei des Klaudios Galenos', *Rheinisches Museum*, 51 (1896), p. 604; H. Zeller, *Dei Philosophie der Griechen* (4th ed., Leipzig 1909), vol. 3, p. 859, n. 5; and Kraus, *Jābir ibn Ḥayyān*, vol. 2, pp. 327f., where the above references are cited.

Sijistānī agreed with those who asserted that the first mover of the first heaven is moved accidentally, but he did not view this as fatal for the Aristotelian system. He posited the existence of a first unmoved mover beyond the first sphere (see below), unmoved both essentially and accidentally, as the first unmoved mover must be (see *Physics* 258b15 and 259b24). It is possible that a similar position was adopted by al-Sarakhsī, who wrote a treatise against Galen's *On the First Mover*; see F. Rosenthal, *Aḥmad b. al-Ṭayyib al-Sarakhsī*, p. 57, II A (21): *Kitāb fi'l-radd 'alā Jālīnūs fi'l-maḥall al-awwal* (amend *al-maḥall* to read *al-muḥarrik*). A treatise bearing the title *Kitāb al-tawassuṭ bayn Arisṭūṭālīs wa Jālīnūs fi'l-muḥarrik al-awwal*, written by Abū Sahl 'Īsā b. Yaḥyā al-Masīḥī, an associate of Bīrūnī, contained an attempt to mediate between the views of Aristotle and Galen (see Bīrūnī, *Risālah*, p. 45; Kraus, *Jābir ibn Ḥayyān*, II, p. 328, note 5; and cf. S. H. Naṣr, *An Introduction to Islamic Cosmological Doctrine* (Cambridge, MA, 1964), p. 109). This may also have been the intention of a treatise by al-Fārābī, mentioned by Ibn abī Uṣaybi'ah, *'Uyūn al-anbā'*, II, 139.22, which bore the title *Kitāb al-tawassuṭ bayn Arisṭūṭālīs wa Jālīnūs*.

1. The view that there exists a first mover unmoved in every respect, i.e., the God of Book *Lambda*, which is not the first mover at the circumference (the subject of *Physica*, VIII), was apparently held by Themistius, according to Mūsā b. Yūsuf al-Lāwī, who stated that al-Fārābī, Avicenna, and other Muslim philosophers, in claiming that God, or the First Cause, is not the first mover, since God must have absolute perfection, were following the viewpoint of Themistius; see M. Steinschneider, *al-Fārābī (Alpharabius), des arabischen Philosophen Leben and Schriften, Mémoires de l'Académie Impériale des Sciences de St. Pétérsbourg*, Sér. 7, 13, 4 (1869), p. 151; *idem*, *Die hebraeischen Übersetzungen des Mittelalters und die Juden als Dolmetscher* (Berlin, 1893; repr., Graz, 1956), p. 410; H. A. Wolfson, 'Notes on Proofs of the Existence of God in Jewish Philosophy', *HUCA*, 1 (1924), p. 588; in *Studies*, vol. 1, pp. 574–575; *idem*, 'Averroes Lost Treatise on the Prime Mover', *HUCA* (1950–51), pp. 683–684; in *Studies*, vol. 1, pp. 402–403; G. Vajda, 'Un champion de l'avicennisme: le problème de l'identité de Dieu et du prémier moteur d'après un opuscule judéo-arabe inédit du xiie siècle', *Revue Thomiste*, 48 (1948), pp. 480–508; *idem*. 'La conciliation de la philosophie et de la loi religieuse' de Joseph b. Abraham ibn Waqār', *Sefarad*, 9 (1949), pp. 311–350; (1950), pp. 25–27, 281–323, esp. p. 43.

Fārābī distinguishes between the first mover and God in his *Risālah fi'l-'aql*, ed. Bouyges, p. 35.4–6. 'Therefore, the mover of the first heaven cannot be the first principle of all existence; no it must of necessity have a principle [itself], and that principle is certainly of more perfect existence than it;' and see Averroes, *Tafsīr mā ba'd al-ṭabī'ah*, VII, 1648–51; and Wolfson, 'Averroes' Lost Treatise', p. 704.

The question whether the first mover is identical with the first cause, or God, became a cause célèbre as result of the divergence between Avicenna and Averroes on the issue; Avicenna, as noted above, following the view of Thermistius; Averroes, the view of Alexander. Maimonides, who stood, it appears, on the side of Avicenna (see *Guide of the Perplexed*, II, 1 and 4; and Wolfson,

accidental comes after what is essential, and a part of it is present in whatever it is posited.[1]

6.3.1 Now that it has been explained that the first mover is of two kinds: a first mover that is moved accidentally, which is a natural form for the moving body that is a first rotary mobile, and a First Mover that is not moved in any respect, it is necessary to inquire in what way each motivates what is moved by it. For this clarifies what each of the movers is, and that the one that the philosopher indicated as being in the circumference is not the First Mover which is the ultimate principle, and that the former exists together with what is caused by the latter, which is its cause in some way.

6.3.2 It has been demonstrated that the sphere is animate in the previous discussion in the treatise I composed, *The Supernal Bodies Are Animate and their Soul is the Rational Soul*, and in what Alexander [of Aphrodisias] and others demonstrated, which we need not repeat in this place. The soul of every natural, animate body motivates it by desire toward the most suitable thing for it to assimilate itself. That thing motivates it through desire toward its essence. The aim of an animate being is outside its essence, and its movement is combined with a kind of passivity and change to abandon its essence and to become something else. The Primal Principle[2] moves the things caused by it by bestowing its essence upon

---

Crescas' Critique of Aristotle, pp. 106, 110, and 606; but cf. Shem Tob b. Falaquera, *Moreh ha-Moreh* (Pressburg, 1837), p. 14, and Pines, in the Introduction to his translation of the *Guide*, (pp. cxiii–cxv), like Sijistānī, argued for the existence of a first principle beyond the first mover of the first sphere on the ground that the latter is moved accidentally (see Wolfson, 'Notes on Proofs of the Existence of God', p. 592). Fārābī and Avicenna, according to Averroes, were actuated to seek a transcendent First Mover by their emanationist principle that only a single effect could proceed from a simple cause. As the mover of the first heaven is the source of its soul and is simultaneously the mover of the next sphere, it is consequently not simple (Averroes, *Tafsīr mā ba'd al-ṭabī'ah*, VII, pp. 1649.1–7, 1652.5ff.; Wolfson, 'Averroes' Lost Treatise', p. 704).

The view expounded by Sijistānī has been championed in modern times by J. Paulus. Paulus argues that the first mover of book VIII of the *Physica* causes motion as the efficient, immanent cause of its sphere, on the analogy of a soul, whereas the First Mover of Book *Lambda* causes motion solely as a final cause ('La Théorie du Premier Moteur chez Aristote', *Revue de Philosophie*, 4 (1933), pp. 259–294, 394–424; cf. also W. K. C. Guthrie, 'The Development of Aristotle's Theology-I', *The Classical Quarterly*, 27 (1933), p. 163). Paulus has not been deemed convincing; see e.g. P. Merlan, 'Aristotle's Unmoved Movers', *Traditio*, 4 (1946), p. 2, n. 8.

For some of the philosophical consequences of the controversy between the Avicennists and the Averroists, see Wolfson, 'Notes on Proofs of the Existence of God', p. 590; van den Bergh, *Epitome*, pp. iii, 152, 253, 313; E. Gilson, *Jean Duns Scot* (Paris, 1952), p. 77; and Pines, pp. cxiv–cxv.

1. The translation is uncertain. The text evidently means that the mover which is not moved in any respect, unlike the mover which is moved accidentally, is neither inherent in, nor a part of, something else (cf. *Physica* 211a20ff.).

2. *Al-mabda' al-awwal*; cf. the rendition of *hē archē kai to prōton tōn ontōn* (*Metaph.* 1073a23) by *mabda' al-mawjūdāt wa-awwaluhā* in the Arabic translation of Book *Lambda*, edited by Badawī, *Arisṭū 'ind al-'Arab*, p. 7.15. Cf. also the Arabic translation of Book *Lambda*, p. 6.10, *ad Metaph.* 1072b11 and 13, and the *Lemma* of Averroes, *Tafsīr mā ba'd al-ṭabī'ah*, VII, 1642.14. The expression *al-mabda' al-awwal* occurs occasionally in the Arabic translation of Book *Lambda* in

them and by translating them to their noblest level. For, it is the pure bounty and the unadulterated good, perpetually overflowing upon all existents, everything obtaining from its good and bounty according to its merit and capacity.[1]

6.3.3 The First Mover, then, which is the Primal Principle, moves the sphere by arousing desire,[2] and the first mover, which is a natural form in the circumference, moves by desiring. It has consequently been demonstrated that the philosopher's intention in saying that the first mover is in the circumference is that it is a natural form of the circumference, and it is its soul, caused by the First Mover that is First Cause.[3]

6.4.1 We have stated at the beginning of our discourse that discussion concerning the first mover combines physical inquiry with metaphysical inquiry. Let us, then, state how this is so. Inquiry concerning the conjunction of effects with causes has two aspects: the first, insofar as it ascends through their connections to their cause; the second, insofar as the power of the cause pervades its effects. Inquiry in the first mode belongs to the physicist; in the second, to the science of metaphysics. There exists also a third mode that is not according to relation, namely, inquiry concerning the essence stripped of affinities and relationships. Its discussion belongs to divine philosophy.

6.4.2 We have discussed the first mover that is a natural form of the first mobile. Let us now consider the status of the First Mover that is a separate form.[4] I say: We

---

indirect reference, and it is used frequently in the Arabic translation of Themistius' Commentary on Book *Lambda*, ed. Badawī, *Arisṭū 'ind al-'Arab*, pp. 12.7, 19.17, 21.10, etc.

1. Blending Aristotelian with Neoplatonic themes, Sijistānī associates the idea of the first unmoved mover of the Lyceum, which moves as an object of desire and love, with the absolute, or pure, effluent good of the Arbor Porphyreana. The phrase 'the pure bounty and unadulterated good' (*al-jūd al-maḥḍ wa'l-khayr al-khāliṣ*) is reminiscent of the Arabic title of the *Liber de causis* (*Kitāb al-īḍāḥ fi'l-khayr al-maḥḍ*) and of similar expressions in that work and in the *Theology of Aristotle.*

The association of the First Mover of Book *Lambda* with the effluent good of Neoplatonism was facilitated by the use of the expression *to on kalon* in *Metaph.* 1072a28. In addition, the parable of the general and the army, used by Aristotle in Book *Lambda*, chapter ten, to express how the good (*to agathon*) and the highest good (*to ariston*) are present in the universe was naturally associated with the Neoplatonic idea of emanation; see e.g. Avicenna, *Sharḥ kitāb ūthūlūjiyā*, ed. Badawī, *Arisṭū 'ind al-'Arab*, p. 33.3ff. (and cf. *Ārā' ahl al-madīnat al-fāḍilah*, ed. F. Dieterici (Leiden, 1895), pp. 55ff.).

2. Ed. Badawī and some Mss.: *sābiq*, 'prior'. Read with Ms. Teheran University 393: *Shā'iq*.

3. The first immovable mover is not specifically designated as a first cause by Aristotle in Book *Lambda*. However, in the Arabic translation of this book (ed. Badawī, p. 5.17–18), the expression *al-'illat al-ūlā* renders *archē* of *Metaph.* 1072a30 (cited by Pines, 'A Tenth Century Philosophical Correspondence', p. 117, n. 62; and see *idem*, 'Un texte inconnu d'Aristote en version arabe', *Archives d'histoire doctrinale et littéraire du Moyen Âge*, 31 (1956), p. 18, note 3, citing the Arabic translation, p. 8.17–18, *ad Metaph.* 1074a31–33). Cf. also, in the same translation, p. 5.1–2 *ad Metaph.* 1072a14 (*al-'illa al-ūlā* = *to prōton*).

4. The expression 'separate form' (*eidos kechōrismenon*), as applied to the First Mover, is employed by the commentators on Aristotle; see e.g. Alexander, *Quaestiones naturales*, I, xxv (p. 39.18). Themistius, in his Commentary on Book *Lambda*, p. 25.18/29.5, *ad Metaph.* 1074a35, calls the First Mover 'the First Form and the First Mover' (which appears in the Arabic translation, ed.

designate it 'form' according to its relation to what is outside it; for if its essence is viewed abstractly, in this sense it is said to be 'the nature of the universe'.[1] Our saying 'form' entails that of which it is a form. And likewise our saying 'nature'. For *ṭabīʿah* ('nature') is the *faʿīla* form of *ṭabʿ*, and it is *faʿīl* in the sense of *mafʿūl*; so the meaning of *ṭabīʿah* is *maṭbūʿah*.[2] For this reason, the term 'the first nature' indicates the form.[3]

6.4.3 In physical inquiry we indicate by the term 'form' the entity that occurs in matter; in metaphysical inquiry, the entity that informs matter, bestowing its forms upon it;[4] and in divine inquiry, the being which the levels of the powers reach, and beneath which terminate the attributes that accord with the different passive states of the things caused. And the forms may be correlated according to their receptivity of the overflow.[5]

6.4.4 One definition of 'nature' is that it is 'the principle of motion and rest in the thing in which it resides primarily and essentially, not accidentally'.[6] This is according to physical inquiry. Its definition as 'a power that pervades bodies, bestowing forms of each of them' is according to metaphysical inquiry.[7]

6.4.5 We may find that in discussing the movers of the spheres and their number, the philosopher (scil. Aristotle) indicated that, despite their diversity and multiplicity, they revert to one unmoving being, which is the mover of the universe. This is an explicit statement of the view we are maintaining, that the First Mover which

---

Badawī, p. 19.11, as simply 'the First Mover'); and in the same work, p. 30.16–17/31.19–20, God is called 'the form of all things.' Cf. also Themistius *In Physica paraphrasis*, p. 33.9–11.

1. *Ṭabīʿat al-kull*. Themistius, in his Commentary on Book *Lambda*, calls God 'Nature' (ed. Badawī, p. 15.14, 16; ed. Landauer, p. 17.12, 15/19.20, 24) and the expression *ṭabīʿat al-kull* appears in the Arabic translation of Themistius' Commentary, ed. Badawī, p. 16.13 (Landauer, 19.15/21.33–34), rendering *hē phusis* in *Metaph*. 1072b13, where this expression, however, has the meaning of 'the nature and system of the whole' (see Alexander of Aphrodisias, *In Metaphysica*, p. 716.8) rather than *natura naturans* (cf. *Metaph*. 1075a11: *tou holou phusis*).

2. See above, ch. III 2.1.4(9), pp. 173, 177.

3. *Al-ṭabīʿat al-ūlā*. The expression 'First Nature' is used at least thrice by Themistius in his Commentary on Book *Lambda*, ed. Landauer, pp. 25.24/29.13, 33.25/38.2, 35.8/39.26. The first instance is not paralleled in the Arabic translation—a not unusual occurrence—and the last two come after the Arabic text breaks off. In the second citation, the First Nature (Heb. trans.—*ha-ṭevaʿ ha-rishon*) is contrasted with the last nature, i.e. sensible nature (*natura naturata*), and in the third citation the identity of the First Nature with the First Mover is made explicit (cf. also the use of the expression 'First Form' for God by Themistius in his Commentary on the *Physica*, p. 33.9–10).

4. Presumably the hypostasis intellect, although the most proximate purveyor of forms to the realm of physical bodies is nature.

5. The term *epitēdeiotēs*, which expresses the idea of fitness, is rendered here by the word *qubūl*. See also the Arabic translation of Alexander, *Quaestiones naturales*, II, xv (p. 60.1), in *Arisṭū ʿind al-ʿArab*, ed. Badawī, p. 284.12.

6. See above, ch. III 2.1.4(6), pp. 173, 175; and 5.1.1, p. 278.

7. The definition of nature according to philosophical inquiry in *Muqābasāt* 79, above, ch. III 2.1.4(7), pp. 173, 176, has *ḥayāt*, 'life', instead of *quwwah*, 'power'.

is the First Cause is not the first mover in the circumference, since in this sense it is a form of the first mobile. It becomes form, and it and what is informed are one in substrate and differ [only] relatively. And if the First Mover is assumed to arouse desire, and the first mover by which the first mobile [is moved] desires and assimilates itself to it, they differ in definition. And the First Mover which arouses desire is not in the circumference. This extent of discussion is sufficient for the purpose of demonstrating what we wished.

7. On the Specific Perfection of the Human Species (Treatise No. 3)

7.1.1 Praise to God,[1] who cleaves the dawn[2] of tenebrous nothingness with the light of bounty, who furnishes evidences of divinity and proofs of unity, confutes the doubts of denial and rejection, and marks the signs of the worlds of creation and wonders of innovation as witnesses for the perception of rational intellects and pure senses; who gave everything, articulate and dumb, its natural disposition, and bestowed intellect upon the worthy among the family of kneeling and prostration [the angels]. He appointed them as archangels, cherubs, those arrayed in ranks and giving praise, recorders for individuals of the human species, not for all of them, but for those of subtle insight.[3] He stands at the utmost extremity, arranging things in their ranks, from where body begins to the end of an extended line and computable quantity. What occupies a place[4] does not exceed it, and contraries are not in discord. If one exceeds its bounds, it returns to its own level, so that every effect depends upon its cause, and everything having a goal repairs to it. The inferior is linked with the superior; the powers arrive in intergraded succession at their supreme horizon; and all is combined by divine wisdom in an order that preserves for existents their specific and general perfections.

---

1. The introductory section (7.1.1) is placed by Kügel-Türker at the end of the treatise. A somewhat different version is given at the beginning. Ms. Tehran University Mishkāt 253 lacks the introduction altogether. It is not certain that it was written by Sijistānī.

2. Cf. Qur'ān 6:96. Mss. read: *fāliq ṣubḥ*; Badawī: *khāliq ṣubḥ*.

3. The angels mentioned here are: archangels (*muqarrabīn*), lit. 'those who are brought near' (Qur'ān 4:172/170 etc.); see e.g. al-Qazwīnī, *Cosmography*, ed. F. Wüstenfeld (Göttingen, 1849), vol. 1, p. 55; cherubs (*karrūbīn*), Heb. *kerubim*, often identified with the *muqarrabūn*; see Lane, *Arabic-English Lexicon*, 1,7, p. 2603, s. v.; and al-Bayḍāwī, *Tafsīr al-Qur'ān*, ed. H. O. Fleischer (Leipzig 1846–48), vol. 1, p. 243 (cited in *EI*, vol. 3, p. 190, s. v. 'Malā'ika'); those arrayed in ranks and giving praise (*al-ṣāffīn wa'l-musabbiḥīn*); cf. Qur'ān 24: 41; recorders (*safara*) (Qur'ān 80:15); see J. Horovitz, 'Jewish Proper Names and Derivatives in the Qur'ān', *HUCA*, 2 (1925), p. 209; A. Sprenger, ed., *Dictionary of the Technical Terms of the Sufis* (Calcutta, 1845), vol. 2, p. 1854; and Corbin, *Avicenna and the Visionary Recital*, p. 357, note 1.

On esoteric angelology in Islamic philosophy, see e.g. al-Ghazzālī, *Tahāfut al-falāsifa*, pp. 482.11–483.1/293; al-Shahrastānī, *al-Milal wa'l-niḥal*, p. 202.2: Walzer, 'New Studies on al-Kindī', p. 203, note 1; Corbin, Part I, ch. ii.

4. *Mutamakkin*; see Pines, *Beiträge*, p. 46, note 2, for this term, and above, chapter III, part 2, note 92 (p. 185).

7.1.2 A human being is distinguished among [the existents] by a most perfect form and superior aspect. [God] balanced his temperament (*mizāj*) and constitution (*ikhtilāṭ*), and caused to emanate upon him His bounty and the illumination of His substantiality, by which [a human being's] soul is enlightened and his body sustained. His power flows in the diverse existents below him, so that he controls them by coercion with the limbs of his body and by comprehension with the cognitions of his soul, which comprise their notions and the causes that are from them, to them, in them, and upon them. The substance and essence of each of them become clear, and by dint of his knowledge and intellect he scrutinizes its hidden reality.

7.2.1 The aim of this treatise is to elucidate the specific perfection of the human species and to describe the individual in whom this perfection has consummately appeared in this time, for the edification of our lord the king, may God preserve his dynasty and majesty and sustain his dominion. It is therefore necessary to allude to the notion I have asserted to be the power emitted from the ultimate principle, flowing over powers and souls until it brings all the virtues within it which tend to appear in this world to a pure soul, pristine nature, and intellect undefiled by the taint of views and opinions deviating from the truth. He then undertakes the regimen of the world, governing its inhabitants with just laws (*sunan*). He rescues them from the hands of despots, who have abolished the effects of lawful opinions, eliminated the regulations of political authorities, permitted the vilest subjects to vie with men of consequence, and ignited in the souls of the vicious the fire of fanatical partisanship, arousing the lesser over the greater and the base over the prominent. He ranks and classifies them. Each man knows his station and halts at the boundary set before him, obedient to whomever is above him and not inclining to contend with whomever is superior to him in power and authority. Matters thus move toward the ends which divine wisdom and the rational law (*al-sharīʿa al-ʿaqliyya*) have determined for them. Mankind is secure, the country prospers, and authorities proceed together, guided by one authority and one head.

7.2.2 Human authorities exist by virtue of the power that dominates the powers produced by soul, which activates everything in this world, manifesting its actions in the various kinds of animals, giving each of their species its specific perfection according to each of its faculties, to the extent allotted to it—excessive, moderate, or deficient. These [faculties] are agreement, inclination, desire, sensation, imagination, estimation, conception, cogitation, opinion, determination, resoluteness, conjecture, acumen, understanding, retention, memory, enlightenment, supposition, knowledge, and intellect.

7.2.3 [These faculties] have been allotted [to animals] equitably. To some of them a part of sensation is given, namely touch, with which the faculty of desire, inclination, and agreement is connected.[1] The existence of animals cannot be

1. Cf. *De anima* 414b2ff.

realized without all these.[1] A share of imagination is not assigned to them, for imagination belongs only to animals having all senses. Moreover, it is associated in particular with the sense of sight, and whatever lacks this sense is thus deprived of imagination.[2] This class of animals is exemplified by snails, worms, and many insects.[3] Some [animals] are given all the senses along with imagination, such as horses, oxen, donkeys, and so forth. Some [are given] along with these the faculty of estimation and a glimpse of the faculties of conception and cogitation, such as the animal called 'ape' (*nasnās*) and 'weasel' (*'irās*).[4] One of them, namely man, [is given], along with these, the faculties of conception, cogitation, retention, and memory, together with the rest of the faculties with which he is endowed, namely, conjecture, understanding, acumen, resoluteness, determination, opinion, supposition, knowledge, and intellect.

7.2.4 Some of them, namely the heavenly bodies, [are given] knowledge and intellect. These faculties are embodied in them in a spiritual way, so that in perceiving sensibles the correspondence of things outside themselves is not required, for they are not compounded of what the rest of the sensibles are compounded, namely fire, air, water, and earth.[5] The sentient perceives its sensum by the matter they have in common, receiving the qualities of these [sensible] bodies by way of opposites, I mean the hot by the cold and the fluid by the solid, and in general according to the fitness of the substrate that admits the various contraries. But these [heavenly bodies] are not compounded of [qualities]. I say that these (i.e. knowledge and intellect) are embodied in them because they belong to them by way of action and influence in this world of generation and corruption, not by way of passivity and receptivity that exist in fluctuating substance that alternates from

1. That animals must have sensation, at least touch, in order to survive is often stated by Aristotle; see e.g. *De anima* 434b14; *Hist. an.* 489a17; *De part. an.* 647a22.

2. For the connection between sight and imagination, see *De anima* 429a3.

3. Cf. *De anima* 428a11.

4. For the distinction between estimation (*tawahhum*), imagination (*takhayyul*), and intellect (*'aql*), see Goichon, *Lexique*, p. 787; and see the discussion in H. A. Wolfson, 'The Internal Senses in Latin, Arabic, and Hebrew Philosophic Texts', in *Studies*, vol. 1, pp. 268ff. The word *'irsa*, not *'irās*, as here, means 'weasel' (also *ibn 'irs*).

5. The scale of the faculties of the soul reaches its pinnacle in man, who possesses intellect as well as the lower powers; cf. *De anima* 415a8. The heavenly bodies, which are superior to man, are intelligent (*De anima* 414b17), but they are not endowed with, or in need of, the lower faculties of sensation and imagination. Their superiority does not reside in their possession of additional faculties but rather in their capacity to dispense with the lower; see D. J. Allan, *The Philosophy of Aristotle* (rev. ed., London 1963), p. 27; Walzer, 'New Studies on al-Kindī', pp. 202f. Fārābī denied that the heavens have sensitive and imaginative faculties (*al-Siyāsa al-madaniyya*, p. 34). The question was one of the issues upon which Avicenna and Averroes differed (*Tahāfut al-tahāfut*, p. 495/I, 301). According to Waltzer, the view which Aristotle propounded in his *On Philosophy*, that the heavens possess the two highest senses—seeing and hearing—was espoused by Kindī and Avicenna, whereas the stricter Aristotelians, like Averroes, denied this (as does Sijistānī). The question, Walzer observes, has bearing upon the question of divine providence.

one state to another.[1] Every agent acts upon its patient according to the paradigm of the form that is in its essence and to what this substrate is apt to admit. The heavenly bodies thus perform their activities according to the universal forms of each species of existents in the world of generation and corruption, and as they are in their sensate existence, which comprises parts, faculties, qualities, quantities, and different accidents. [The forms], however, are in [the heavenly bodies] in a spiritual, unitary mode *per se.*[2] Then by their partial corporeal motions they emit the forms into this world to the matter that receives them, so that it does, and the particular individuals come about which imitate the paradigm of their universals.[3] And they become perfect by reason of the agent and the universal form and deficient by reason of their substrate, owing to the fluctuation of its substance and the diversity—greater, lesser, and equipoised—of its parts and motions the many changes and transitions inherent in it, and its nearness to the bodies which move them by means of their motions.

7.3.1 Let us now depict the quality of the state to which the qualifications of [Primal] Being are applied and the intimations that past nations have made, with their different views and opinions concerning it.

7.3.2 Some of them claimed that this Being is conjoined with the essences of entities which they claimed it unites with. They then disagreed concerning these entities which they claimed it unites with. That is, the ancient adherents of the laws professed that they are the heavenly bodies, and they claimed that [this Being] appears in them, performing its activities through them. And they named [the heavens] 'secondary deities'.[4]

---

1. Cf. *De gen. et. corr.* II, 10.

2. On the manner in which the forms are in the heavens, cf. *Liber de causis*, ed. O. Bardenhewer (Freiburg im Breisgau, 1882; repr., Frankfurt, n.d.), p. 79/ed. Badawī, *Neoplatonici apud Arabes*, p. 12; Proclus, *Elements of Theology*, p. 155; *Theology of Aristotle*, X, 126ff. (tr. Lewis, pp. 459f.).

3. Alexander of Aphrodisias discusses the notion of the conveyance of forms to this world and their preservation within it in *Fi'l-tadbīrāt al-falakiyyah*, Ms. Jārullāh 1279, fols. 51a, 52a. *In fi'l-'ināyah*, Ms. Jārullāh 1279, fol. 49b, Alexander states that the divine bodies are the medium through which the power of nature is transmitted to the world. On this treatise, see P. Thillet, 'Un traité inconnu d'Alexandre d'Aphrodise sur la Providence dans une version arabe inédite', in *L'Homme et son destin d'après les penseurs du moyen âge* (Louvain-Paris, 1960) (Actes du Premier Congrès International de Philosophie Médiévale), pp. 313–324. The Greek original, *Peri pronoias*, is not extant. In *Fi'l-istiṭā'ah*, Ms. Jārullāh 1279, fol. 50a, the heavenly body is actually identified with nature (= *Peri tou eph' hēmin, Scripta Minora*, II, 1, 172.18–19), which maintains forms in things, as is stated in *Fi'l-tadbīrāt al-falakiyyah*, fol. 52b ('the heavenly power which we call nature') and 53a.

4. For 'secondary deities', see *Timaeus* 41e and 42e; Plotinus, *Enneads*, III, 5, 6, 22 (*tous horatous theous deuterous*); Bīrūnī, *India*, trans. Sachau, I, p. 35; Averroes, *Tafsīr mā ba'd al-ṭabī'ah*, VII, 1494.5.

Sijistānī apparently alludes to the religion of the Ḥarrānian Sābians. They were adherents of a religious law, believed to have been revealed by pagan prophets, and were regarded as ancient—Ibn Ḥazm, for instance, says that they represent the oldest religion of mankind; *al-Fiṣal fi'l-milal* (Cairo 1317–21/1899–1903), vol. 1, p. 35.

7.3.3 Some of them professed that the entities with which [this Being] unites are human substances. Some among them held that of all these substances that with which it unites is one, namely, the substance of the humanity (*nāsūt*) of the Messiah (*scil.* Jesus). These are the Christians, with their divergent opinions concerning this. The Jacobites claim that from the two substances, I mean the substance of humanity (*nāsūt*) and the substance of divinity (*lāhūt*), one substance and one hypostasis (*uqnūm*) emerge.[1] The Nestorians hold that the union is only through good pleasure,[2] and the two substances remain two and two hypostases. The Melkites hold that two substances and one hypostasis emerge through the union.[3]

7.3.4 And among those who profess union there are some who claim that [this Being] unites with more than one person. These are the Shiʿi extremists (*ghulāt*), those who profess incarnation (*ḥulūl*), and a group of Sufis who profess the essence of union (*ʿayn al-jamʿ*).[4]

7.3.5 And some of them hold that the entire world is composed of this and another substance, its opposite. These are the proponents of two roots—light and darkness.[5]

7.3.5 Most of the rational theologians (*mutakallimūn*) among the adherents of the laws have intimated this being by qualifications in accordance with the relation of the things caused by [this Being] to it, and by the effects of this Being evident to them in [the things caused]. And they considered among [these qualifications] the principles and roots of what is beneath [this Being], naming them 'essential attributes', which are life, power, knowledge, and the like, by which it should not be

---

Sijistānī intimates that the stars were not the ultimate divinities of the Sābians, but rather divine intermediaries (cf. also Shahrastānī, *al-Milal wa'l-niḥal*, p. 203.16–17). On the astral piety of the Sābians, see Corbin, 'Rituel sabéen et exégèse ismaélienne du rituel', *EJ*, 19 (1950), p. 189f.

1. For the terms *nāsūt* (= *anthrōpōtēs*) and *lāhūt* (= theotēs) in the context of discussions of the Trinity, see H. A. Wolfson, 'Saadia on the Trinity and Incarnation', *Studies and Essays in Honour of Abraham A. Newman* (Philadelphia, PA, 1962), p. 562; in *Studies*, vol. 2, p. 393f.; and for the probable derivation of the terms, see Kraus, *Jābir ibn Ḥayyān*, vol. 1, p. lii, n. 11. *Uqnūm* is from Syriac *qʿnōmā*. See also above, p. 215, n. 188.

2. *Mashī'ah* probably reflects Greek *eudokia*, 'good pleasure'. For the Nestorian use of this term, see H. A. Wolfson, *The Philosophy of the Church Fathers* (Cambridge, MA, 1956), vol. 1, p. 451.

3. According to Wolfson, 'Saadia on the Trinity and Incarnation', pp. 564–565, the normal order of the Christian sects in Muslim works is Melkites, Nestorians, Jacobites. He suggests that Saʿadya Gaon, in discussing them in a sequence like that before us—Jacobites, Nestorians, Melkites—reflected the order by which he became acquainted with them. But note that whereas Ibn Ḥazm, for instance, in discussing the history and geographical distribution of the Christian sects, treats them in their order of importance (*Fiṣal*, vol. 1, pp. 48–49), when discussing their respective views on the Trinity and Incarnation, he treats them (*Fiṣal*, vol. 1, p. 53) in the sequence followed by Saʿadya Gaon and Sijistānī.

4. L. Massignon and G. C. Anawati, 'Ḥulūl', *EI*, vol. 3, pp. 570–571. On *ʿayn al-jamʿ*, see Massignon, *La Passion de Ḥallāj*, vol. 4, Index, pp. 279–280. The expression is variously translated by Massignon, viz. 'l'union substantielle', 'essence de l'union', 'l'essentielle union'.

5. See R. Strothmann, 'Thanawiyya', *SEI*, p. 592.

qualified, nor [should it be qualified] by the opposite or as having potentiality[1] for the opposite. Among them are those who distinguish between essential and action attributes, such that it may be qualified by action attributes and by the opposite, and with potentiality for the opposite, whereas this is not possible in the case of essential attributes.

7.3.7 All these sects only comprehended some effect of this Being. Thus they judged it according to the effects evident to them, and each sect intimated by that with which it was most familiar, to the extent of its power of deduction and its access to acquaintance with it. The Christians described the Being by the attribute of the effect evident to them from the signs of perfection in the person of the Messiah. The adherents of light and darkness described the effect by an essential attribute. The most excellent philosophers, however, hold that the Being which creates existents surpasses the comprehension of any of its creations, and that none of the attributes confined by existence to this world may adhere to it. For what transcends the universe, comprehending it, may not be comprehended by it, nor may a power of any part of the universe reach it.[2]

7.4.1 Attributes are signs by which the human intellect signifies spiritually by inner speech the essences of existents which it apprehends that are outside it by means of the effects coming from them and to them, actively and passively. The soul then produces them, expressing them physically in external speech according to different national languages. This belongs to intellect by way of what is specific to its very substance.

7.4.2 Intellect is the cause of the order of existents and their harmonious combination, giving each of them its determined existence. Each of them seeks the help of intellect for its specific perfection. For nothing comes about coincidentally, from which perfect existence emerges and whose production is aimed at by wisdom, rather each thing is determinately related to another.

7.4.3 Intellect has two other functions: the first, insofar as it is primary, simple, activated, and caused by the First Cause and First Agent, praised and exalted, gives each existent—intellect, soul, and what is beneath them—the existence common to all of them. Intellect allots this existence to the essences of existents by giving them the forms specific to each one of them, ordering [existence] according to what [each existent] derives from it in its specific existence in preserving order. And [intellect] makes it appear to soul in possessors of bodies endowed with life, and the power called 'nature' is constituted in them. It pervades them and bestows shape and form upon them according to the specific forms of each, animate and inanimate.

---

1. For *qudrah ʿalā* in the sense of 'potentiality', see al-Ashʿarī, *Maqālāt al-islāmiyyin*, pp. 508.12ff.

2. Cf. the language in *Epistola de scientia divina*, par. 200, *ad Enneads*, V, 5, 9.34–38 (tr. Lewis, p. 353); and Simplicius, *In Physica*, p. 1335.13–15.

7.4.4 The second function is what [intellect] performs by means of soul, by conferring life upon everything ready to receive it. This activity belongs to soul *per se* and to [intellect] by its intermediacy. For soul is the form that occurs in the animate being, and intellect bestows it. [Intellect], therefore, is what merits being called 'complete', 'universal', 'perfect', and 'perfecting others'. Or [intellect] has completeness by virtue of the First Agent, insofar as it made it cause of the existence of every existent by ordering existents in harmonious relations. [The First Agent] did not make anything else a cause for its existence. Completeness also belongs to it insofar as conferring of existence in the manner described begins from it, while ascending and conceiving the First Form and all the powers ends with it, it being the intermediary between the Primal Principle and all other existents. This ordering [function] belongs to it specifically, truly, and by nature, and to all other things by convention. Furthermore, [intellect] contains the things through which an entity is what it is. Belonging to it is the form of triunity on account of which the Christians came to profess the three hypostases.[1] The philosophers used to extol triunity and venerate God through it. The philosopher Aristotle mentioned this in his book *De caelo et mundo*, as did the commentators on this book.[2] The intention herein, in my opinion, is to allude to intellect, by which the three existents are ordered, which are: the divine existence sustaining all existents, the orderly existence specific to [intellect], and the natural existence that is allotted to sensible existents, particular and general, by soul, which emits nature into them. The notion of universality also belongs to [intellect], since it contains all the notions of things outside it in universal forms. [Intellect] is perfection insofar as it is the aim at which the powers terminate in conceiving, whether spiritual conceiving according to the faculties of the soul, which are discrimination, discernment, and apprehension of what is in the essence of intellect, or corporeally conceiving according to the faculties of bodies, which acquire their existence from [intellect] insofar as it contains proportions that order the parts determined for them, whereas it need not assume the form of anything outside itself, for it is the form of forms and the power of powers.

7.4.5 Intellect's consciousness of the First Agent, its Creator and the Creator of the universe, is not by way of comprehending and apprehending it, for this is not its want, as we have described it above. Rather because of its need for what sustains its continuance and existence, so that it persists in producing order, [intellect] is conscious that [the First Agent] is a being from which it has its continuance and existence. [Intellect] therefore submits to [this Being], needing it to extend its life,

1. Sijistānī alludes to the equations: *ʿaql = ab, ʿāqil = ibn, maʿqūl = rūḥ*; see, for example, Yaḥyā b. ʿAdī, in *Petits traités apologétiques*, pp. 20–ff. and 24ff.; Abū ʿAlī ʿĪsā b. Zurʿah, in *Vingt traités philosophiques et apologétiques*, ed. P. Sbath (Cairo, 1929), pp. 9ff. and 68ff. And see below, 8.7, p. 309.

2. *De caelo* 268a10; Simplicius, *In De caelo*, p. 8.18ff.

which is the first power emitted from [this Being] to it.[1] The meaning of life herein is desire for the superior thing, to endure through it. And this submission is divine sanctification.

7.4.6 It has become evident that intellect perfects others from what we have described—that every existent, animate and inanimate, derives its existence and its form, by which it is what it is, from this form according to the fitting proportions, spiritual and corporeal, corresponding to souls and bodies.

7.5.1 Since the matter is as described, man among all that exists in the world of generation and corruption is the one in whom are united all the powers distributed among all that is in [the world], apportioned to every class, i.e. the powers of the heavenly bodies and the terrestrial bodies, both animate and inanimate. He is thus the multiple one, comprising separate units, just as the First Agent, praised and exalted, is the pure One, non-multiple in every way, from whom are emitted all the units and powers that flow into this world until they all reach the human form. The particular individual obtains them to the extent of his fitness for their reception—the extent of equipoise, excess, and deficiency of his temperament—and according to the motions of the heavenly bodies and their diverse influences by their synod, separation, and revolutions; their great, medium, and small conjunctions; and their transition through the zodiacal signs from one trigon to another. That which is manifested through them varies in strength and weakness, loftiness, and extent. Prodigious events and the appearance of the perfect individuals (*al-ashkhāṣ al-kāmilah*), who receive in full the powers of the First Principle, and who undertake to guide and rule the world, only occur by reason of these revolutions and the transition of these conjunctions from one trigon to another.[2]

---

1. Cf. *Liber de causis*, ed. Bardenhewer, 92.7/ed. Badawī, 19.5–6 = Proclus, *Elements of Theology*, 92.9–10 (and see the editor's note, pp. 252–254).

2. Sijistānī uses the expressions *al-shakhṣ al-kāmil* and *al-shakhṣ al-ilāhī* instead of the more common *al-insān al-kāmil*, familiar from Sufi literature. The perfect individual is regarded as the epitome of the human species. 'Just as the genus ascends to a perfect species, so the species ascends to a perfect individual' (*Imtāʿ*, vol. 3, p. 113).

The idea of the perfect man (*anthrōpos teleios*), which became prominent in Sufism, goes back to Iranian and Hellenistic (Gnostic) sources; e.g. A. Christensen, *Les Types du premier homme et du premier roi dans l'histoire légendaire des Iraniens* (Leiden-Uppsala, 1917–34); Molé, *Le Problème zoroastrien et la tradition mazdéene*, pp. 469ff.; H. H. Schaeder, 'Die islamische Lehre vom Vollkommenen Menschen', *ZDMG*, 4 (1925), pp. 192–268; A. E. Affifi, *The Mystical Philosophy of Muḥiyy al-Dīn ibn al-ʿĀrabī* (Cambridge, 1921), pp. 77ff.; F. Meier, 'Der Geistmensch bei dem persischen Dichter ʿAṭṭār', *EJ*, 13 (1945), pp. 283–353; and L. Massignon, 'L'homme parfait en Islam et son originalité eschatologique', *EJ*, 15 (1947), pp. 287–313 (*Opera Minora*, vol. 1, pp. 107–125). See also ʿA. Badawī, *al-Insān al-kāmil fi'l-Islam* (2nd ed., Kuwait, 1976). Quoting the present treatise on the basis of a manuscript in the possession of P. Kraus (p. 112), Massignon writes: ' … et Abū Sulaymān Sijistānī enseignera que la béatitude suprême est l'accès, possible dès cette vie, à la 'Nature Parfait' (*ṭibāʿ tāmm*), l'investissant de la Souveraineté divine.' The expression *ṭibāʿ tāmm* does not appear in the editions (or Mss.).

The classic works on the perfect man are ʿAbd al-Karīm b. Ibrāhīm al-Jīlānī (Jīlī), *al-Insān al-kāmil fī maʿrifat al-awākhir wa'l-awā'il* (Cairo, n. d.) (for al-Jīlānī, the perfect man is the Prophet

7.5.2 When the time comes to pass when the divine individual (*al-shakhṣ al-ilāhī*) is supposed to appear, by agreement of the spherical configurations, he appears in the vocation in which he is most fit for governance. [The spheres] influence by manifesting the virtues emitted from the Primal Principle, by which this individual is distinguished for governing nations, managing kingdoms, and establishing laws.[1] [These laws] preserve benefits for mankind by means of the various policies required at that time to bring advantages to people then, to parry injuries from them, and to acquaint them with the laws that unite a prosperous livelihood with a noble destiny.

7.6.1 The trigons in which the conjunctions take place differ in the influences and states arising from them in greatness, loftiness, and nobility. The igneous [trigon] indicates outstanding and prodigious things owing to its power of influence, like igneousness which transcends all the elements by position, acceding into their confines by influence and impression. From [the igneous trigon] arises the appetitive faculty directed toward all human cravings and political ambition. When the cycle [of the igneous trigon] arrives, the individual of perfect virtues must appear, manifesting his power, ordering things in their ranks by forbidding and permitting, and referring them to their principles—their sound foundations, chief props, and firm pillars.

Muḥammad); and ʿAzīz al-Dīn Nasafī, *Kitāb al-insān al-kāmil* (*Le Livre de l'homme parfait*): *Recueil de traités de soufisme en persan*, ed. M. Molé (Tehran and Paris, 1962). The ideal perfect man, in the eyes of the *Falāsifah*, was either a sage or a ruler; ideally, a combination of both. The human perfection (*al-kamāl al-insānī*) that the *Falāsifah* envisioned was thus reserved for the happy few.

The idea of the perfect or divine individual in our text has in common with the mystical notion of *al-insān al-kāmil*: (1) The belief in the periodic appearance of such a person at crucial points in history. (2) A soteriological conception of his appearance, his function as preserver and maintainer of the world. The perfect, divine individual is not the divine humanized but the human divinized, thus corresponding to the incarnate logos of Christianity (Massignon, 'L'homme parfait en Islam', pp. 110–111). The relationship of Sijistānī's soteriology to Shiʿi Imamology remains to be determined. It is not unlikely that Shiʿi conceptions of the Imām influenced Sijistānī's portrayal of ʿAḍud al-Dawlah. Cf. M. Arkoun, *Contribution à l'étude de l'humanisme arabe au IVᵉ/Xᵉ siècle; Miskawayh (320/325–421), philosophe et historien* (Paris, 1970), p. 98, on Miskawayh's conception of the Imam as a perfect sage, who installs a tolerant religion and integrates religion and philosophy—a nation that Arkoun relates to Miskawayh's Shiʿism. (3) The doctrine that the perfect individual is a microcosm, either insofar as his intellect encompasses all, or insofar as his existence comprises all things, i.e. the entire scale of being. This idea is stressed, for example, by al-Jīlānī. The notion of the perfect man who is the all or an epitome of the all, insofar as he comprises the entire universe, is traced by G. Quispel to Jewish conceptions concerning Adam (*Yalqut Shimʿoni*, Genesis, par. 34); see 'The Jung Codex and Its Significance', in F. L. Cross, ed., *The Jung Codex* (London, 1955), p. 77. For the primordial man in Gnosis, see especially E. S. Drower, *The Secret Adam: A Study of Nasorean Gnosis* (Oxford, 1960). See also R. Arnaldez, *'al-insān al-kāmil'*, *EI*, vol. 3, pp. 1239–1241, for general orientation.

1. For the idea of virtues (*faḍāʾil*) sent into this world through the medium of the heavens, see Alexander of Aphrodisias, *Fi'l-tadbīrāt al-falakiyyah*, fol. 52a; and for the notion that the powers of the planets are emitted from the Primal Principle, see fol. 51f.

7.6.2 Aries is the zodiacal sign of all signs of this trigon in which all the powers are united that preserve the order of existents in the way divine nature has ordered them. In its *medium caelum* is Capricorn, the domicile of supernal Saturn, which none of the planets transcends. It is the indicator of prominence, elevation, steadfastness, permanence, and continuance, and it is the first recipient of the divine powers that emanate upon existents. Its relation to that world is therefore one of compatibility, and to this world, one of incompatibility. It is, as it were, an incompatible contrary to the rapid changing moon, which indicates alternating, changing, natural powers.

7.6.3 Its ninth and its third, namely Sagittarius and Gemini, are the indicators of intentional movements toward views, opinions, and preferences in sciences and religions, and of locomotion. [They are] the domiciles of Jupiter and Mercury, which indicate these notions by nature. Jupiter, the lord of the ninth of Aries, is the planet indicating intellect. And it is in the conventional disposition of the planetary powers on the level of the root and the active principle of the sciences. And Mercury, the lord of the third domicile of Aries, is like the spreading branch that reveals what it receives from Jupiter, corresponding to it in the domicile of knowledge, which is the activity of intellect. Its seventh is Libra, the domicile of Venus, the indicator of the manifestation of what it receives from Mars, the lord of the sign of Aries, by an association that engenders existents corporeally by coupling and marriage and another [association that engenders] spiritually by conveying the notions that the soul produces through their declaration and expression. Its fourth is Cancer, the domicile of the moon and the exaltation of Jupiter, the indicator of consequences, which the moon indicates by nature owing to its situation in the last rank with respect to the other planets. Its fifth is the sign of Leo, the domicile of rejoicings and pleasures. Its lord is the sun, the lord of the exaltation of Aries, which indicates inclination for and enjoyment of political affairs. Then the rest of the astral bodies are ordered according to the natural order in conformity with what is required by the optimally proportionate and homogeneous arrangement.

7.6.4 The indicators must combine when the individual whose appearance is anticipated happens to come into existence, so that this sign [Leo] be his ascendant, and so that his authority and rule dominate all kingdoms when the conjunction comes about, such that the matter in [the political] order corresponds to the natural process and the flow of the perfect powers into the world unto him. The indicators conspire at his coming into being: the heavenly bodies in influencing and the matter that is prepared to receive the influence in the suitable place and the proper time. The powers and the notions necessary for his existence arrive so that no deficiency pervades the qualities of perfection that evoke obedience to him, submission to his jurisdiction and laws, and compliance with his command and prohibition, as has happened at this time with the appearance of the lord of lords, chief of chiefs, and king of kings, our master, the victorious king, benefactor of favours, Arm of the Dynasty ('Aḍud al-Dawlah) and Crown of the Faith (Tāj al-Millah), may God perpetuate his grandeur. He came to the world as succour[1] for its people, favouring them with the things that fecundate the specific perfections of every manner of its circumstances and every class of its people by management that brings them to their most excellent goal—security from harm—and governance conducive to their prosperity in their livelihood and undertakings, knowing the consequences of their affairs and assigning them to the procedures which the governance of subjects requires, so that the most negligible item of what is known to be incumbent upon them does not escape them, and arrogance is not excessive, such that they wrong each other, and so that the one deserving of honour is not shunted aside.

7.7.1 Let God give him good fortune, so that he reach every perfection through these qualities. He, may God perpetuate his sovereignty, perfect in himself and perfecting others, is most deserving in all creation of praise and prayer for the endurance of his rule, especially by the people of learning and culture; for he has invigorated them, enhanced their enterprise, and has given free rein to their tongues to promulgate what each of their sects professes, without dissimulation (*taqiyya*), so that it may reveal what it claims and proclaim what it believes. And it may discriminate the true from the false, secure that one will not assail another with the tongue of religious fanaticism.

7.7.2 Therefore praise to God who has favoured us with what He has withheld from other past nations, which desired some of the felicity with which we are favoured by living during his auspicious days. [God] is the one responsible for perpetuating them in His superior ways, for He is generous, beneficent, the doer of what He wills.[2] And He is for us as protector and helper. Prayer and peace upon Muḥammad and his family, the pure.

1. *Ghiyāthan*. Read perhaps: *aghyāthan* ('as abundant rain'). For the metaphor, as applied to the ruler, see Pseudo-Aristotle, *Sirr al-asrār*, p. 81.1–2. The word *lawāqih*, which appears in the next phrase, may then be translated 'fecundating winds'.

2. Sūrah 11: 107/109; 85:16.

12

Ibn Sīnā

The most famous and influential of Persian philosophers and scientists, Abū ʿAlī al-Ḥusayn ibn ʿAbdallāh ibn Sīnā (Avicenna), known by the later Islamic philosophers as al-Shaykh al-Ra'īs and Ḥujjat al-Ḥaqq, and in circles involved with his philosophy as simply Shaykh, was born in 370/980 in Afshānah, a village outside of Bukhārā. His father, originally from Balkh, had moved to Afshānah; when Ibn Sīnā was five years old, they moved once again, this time to Bukhārā itself, where Ibn Sīnā grew up.

The Ibn Sīnā household was a centre of intellectual activity visited by numerous scholars of the city. Extremely precocious, Ibn Sīnā showed remarkable attraction to the sciences from a very early age. By the time he was ten, he had memorized much of the Qur'ān and had mastered the Arabic language in addition to his mother tongue, which was Persian. According to his autobiography, completed by his lifetime student and companion Abū ʿUbayd Juzjānī, by the time Ibn Sīnā was eighteen years old, he was already master of the Islamic sciences, both transmitted and intellectual, and was an accomplished physician and philosopher. In 387/997, the Samanid ruler of Bukhārā gave him access to the royal library, which enabled him to further his mastery of the various sciences, especially philosophy and medicine. In 391/1001, at the age of twenty-one, he composed the first books of which we have any knowledge.

A year later, however, Ibn Sīnā's whole life was set in turmoil as the result of his father's death and Maḥmūd of Ghaznah's conquest of Bukhārā. Refusing to join his court and deeply saddened by the destruction of the order of his native home, Ibn Sīnā set out for Jurjāniyyah. He began a life of wandering from one Persian court to another, usually acting as court physician to the various Buyid rulers of the central regions of Persia. He journeyed from Jurjān (Gurgān) to Rayy and then to Hamadān, where he remained several years as court physician and *wazīr*. But he sought to reach the court of ʿAlā' al-Dawlah in Iṣfahān and refused further service at the Hamadān court. This decision resulted in his falling out of grace and being imprisoned for four months. Escaping in the garb of a dervish, he made it safely to Iṣfahān, which had become a great centre of learning under ʿAlāʾ al-Dawlah. Here he spent some fifteen years in respect, honour, and peace and wrote many of his major works, even beginning the construction of an observatory that was never completed. Yet, even this period of peace was to be disrupted by the attack upon the city by Maḥmūd of Ghaznah's son, Masʿūd. Ibn Sīnā then left Iṣfahān and returned to Hamadān, where he died of colic in 428/1037 and where his tomb, a celebrated monument, is to be found to this day. Some claim that he was buried in Iṣfahān but this is most likely not true. His school (*madrasah*) can be seen in the old quarter of the city, but his tomb is, according to the most authentic early historical sources, in Hamadān.

Ibn Sīnā led an extraordinary life, which has turned him into a legend—indeed, almost a mythological figure. Endowed with unlimited physical and intellectual energy, an exceptional memory, an acute sense of observation, a truly remarkable power of intellectual analysis and synthesis, a love of the sacred and the beautiful, and a power of concentration rarely seen in the annals of intellectual history, he was able to produce a vast body of works amid the outward turmoil and vicissitudes of his time. He wrote over two hundred works during a fairly short life, some of which, such as the *Shifāʾ*, are of monumental proportion. His writings are astounding from both the qualitative and the quantitative points of view. Many are devoted to medicine, including the *al-Qānūn fiʾl-ṭibb* (Canon of Medicine), the most famous single work in the history of medicine in both the Islamic world and the West—a work that gained Ibn Sīnā, or the Latin Avicenna, the title of Prince of Physicians in medieval Europe. But his scientific works also include treatises on mathematics (especially music) as well as language.

As for the philosophical works with which we are concerned here, they can be divided into two categories: those dealing with *mashshāʾī*, or Peripatetic philosophy, and those treating what Ibn Sīnā himself called *al-ḥikmat al-mashriqiyyah* (oriental wisdom), which can be read in Arabic orthography as either oriental or illuminative—a philosophy that he considered as having been written for the elite (*khawāṣṣ*). The first category includes his encyclopedic masterpiece, the *Kitāb al-shifāʾ* (The Book of Healing), which deals in four sections with logic, natural philosophy, mathematics, and metaphysics; it is the most voluminous work of its kind ever written by a single person. The section on logic is the most extensive in the annals of Islamic thought, while the natural philosophy and the metaphysics sections mark the peak of Peripatetic philosophy in Islam. The first category also includes shorter works such as the *al-Najāh* (Deliverance), *al-Mabdaʾ waʾl- maʿād* (The Origin and the End), and the *Dānish-nāmah-yi ʿalāʾī* (Treatise on Knowledge Dedicated to ʿAlāʾ al-Dawlah), the first work on Peripatetic philosophy ever written in the Persian language.

To the second category belongs his last great masterpiece, *al-Ishārāt waʾl-tanbīhāt* (Remarks and Admonitions)—at least its last chapters—and also the trilogy of visionary recitals *Ḥayy ibn Yaqẓān* (The Living Son of the Awake), *Risālat al-ṭayr* (Treatise of the Bird), and *Salāmān wa Absāl* (Salāmān and Absāl). We must also include his short mystical treatises in this latter category. As for his Qur'anic commentaries, which are the first by a Peripatetic philosopher, they occupy a category of their own. The *ḥikmat al-mashriqiyyah* of Ibn Sīnā was never known or taken seriously in the West; in Persia, however, it formed a bridge to the later School of Illumination (*ishrāq*) of Suhrawardī. What Ibn Sīnā writes in his *Manṭiq al-mashriqiyyīn* (Logic of the Orientals), which belongs to the second category, as setting out to expound a philosophy (that is at once oriental and illuminative) for the intellectual elite was seen by the later *ishrāqī* tradition as pointing to the *ḥikmat al-ishrāq* that was to be expounded by Suhrawardī less than two centuries after Ibn Sīnā.

Of special significance for the later history of Islamic philosophy in Persia is the fact that Ibn Sīnā wrote philosophical and scientific works in Persian, especially the *Dānish-nāmah-yi 'alā'ī*. Although his choice of words was sometimes contrived and the text is difficult to fathom in many ways, he set the background for the appearance of Persian as a major philosophical language—and in fact the second language of Islamic philosophy after Arabic. The lucid and rich Persian philosophical works of Nāṣir-i Khusraw, Suhrawardī, Naṣīr al-Dīn Ṭūsī, Quṭb al-Dīn Shīrāzī, and many others show evidence of the pioneering efforts of Ibn Sīnā.

The works of Ibn Sīnā mark a combination of early Islamic Peripatetic philosophy, Neoplatonism, Aristotelianism and general Islamic teachings, creating a synthesis that has cast its influence upon all later Islamic philosophy. The fundamental ontological distinctions between Necessary Being (*wājib al-wujūd*) and contingent existent (*mumkin al-wujūd*), the definition and distinction between existence and quiddity, and other basic concepts either developed or refined by Ibn Sīnā mark the foundation of ontology and what in the West is called medieval philosophy. Many have in fact called him the first 'philosopher of being'; it was always in the continuation of or reaction to his ontology that later Islamic, and even many Jewish and Christian, philosophers developed their ideas. This is seen especially in Persia, as the ontological discussions of such major later figures as Suhrawardī, Khwājah Naṣīr al-Dīn Ṭūsī, and Mullā Ṣadrā make clear. Ibn Sīnā also opened the door and pointed toward a path that was later to be followed by Suhrawardī.

The philosophical significance of Ibn Sīnā's synthesis is also to be seen in cosmology and psychology, including the master's critique of the Aristotelian theory of motion and the relationship between the psyche and the physical body. Ibn Sīnā's medical philosophy is in fact of great significance not only for the history of medicine but also for the current search for holistic understanding of medicine and the human psychosomatic reality. It would not be an exaggeration to say that Ibn Sīnā is the greatest cultural hero of Persia in the domains of philosophy and the sciences. In any case, little in those domains has remained untouched by his influence during the succeeding centuries of Persian history and his philosophical influence is alive in his native land today.

The first selection in this chapter deals with Ibn Sīnā's major Persian work, *Dānish-nāmah-yi 'alā'ī*. The focal point of this section, entitled *Ilāhiyyāt* (Metaphysics and Theology), is the Necessary Being. It is here that a wide range of issues, from God's knowledge of universals to the will of the Necessary Being, is treated.

The second selection is part three of *al-Ishārāt wa'l-tanbīhāt* concerning 'creation *ex-nihilo* and immediate creation'. The ninth treatise of *al-Shifā'* and book seven of *al-Ishārāt wa'l-tanbīhāt* are presented next. These sections treat such notions as providence, evil, and divine predestination; how evil has entered the created order is the central theme of this section.

The fifth selection is dedicated to the concept and nature of time, a translation of section two, parts eleven and twelve of the *Physics* of *al-Shifā'*.

The sixth selection turns to mystical aspects by offering a translation of *Maqāmāt al-'ārifīn* (On the Stations of the Knowers). This philosophical-mystical narrative is a translation of part four of the ninth class of *al-Ishārāt wa'l-tanbīhāt*.

The seventh selection is from the philosophical-mystical narrative of Ibn Sīnā, *Ḥayy ibn Yaqẓān*. Among different translations of this treatise, we have chosen Henry Corbin's because, despite his free style of translation, he stays faithful to the most profound meaning of the text and because of Corbin's contributions as a contemporary authority of Islamic philosophy.

In the final selection, we provide a translation of Ibn Sīnā's introduction to his *Manṭiq al-mashriqiyyīn* (Logic of the Orientals) that is part of a greater work in which Ibn Sīnā had expounded his 'oriental philosophy'.

S. H. Nasr

METAPHYSICS

From *Dānish-nāmah-yi ʿalāʾī* (Treatise on Knowledge, Dedicated to Prince ʿAlāʾ al-Dawlah)

Translated for this volume by Thomas Gaskil from *Dānish-nāmah-yi ʿalāʾī: Ilāhiyyāt*, ed. M. Muʿīn (Tehran, 1952), pp. 82–111, 122–146.

Ilāhiyyāt

28. Necessary Existence is Eternal and all these Things are Transitory

The being of bodies, accidents, and, in brief, the categories (*maqūlāt*) of this sensible world is clear. For all of these, quiddity (*māhiyyat*) is other than existence (*anniyyat*), which applies to all ten categories, and we have said [see *Ilāhiyyāt* §11 and §18] that these are all contingent beings (*mumkin al-wujūd*). Accidents subsist in bodies, and bodies are receptive to change, and bodies are composed of matter and form, and the two [together] are body. Matter does not subsist by an act of its own self (*bi-nafs-i khwīsh*). Form, likewise, does not do so. We have also said [see *Ilāhiyyāt* §20] that everything which exists in such a manner is a contingent being, and we have said that a contingent being is existent because of a cause. Its being is not from itself (*bi-khud*) and its being is from another thing, and this [contingent thing] is a transitory thing. [Moreover,] we have said that causes ultimately return to Necessary Existence, and Necessary Existence is unity (*yakī būd*).

Thus, it is evident that there is a First (*awwal*) to the world which does not reside in the world, and the being of the world is from It, and Its existence is necessary, and Its existence is from Itself (*bi-khud*). Moreover, it is, in its true reality (*ḥaqīqat*), Absolute Being. All things are in existence from It in the way that the light of the sun is from itself, and the light which comes from anything [else] is an accident from [the sun]. This analogy would be just if the sun were the source (*nafs*) of its light and subsisted in itself. However, it is not so, for the light of the sun is a created thing, and the being of Necessary Existence is not a created thing, for, moreover, It subsists through Itself.

29. What Must Be Understood of the Meaning of Intelligence (ʿālimī) *of Necessary Existence*

It will be evident later [*Ilāhiyyāt* §32, *infra*] that the cause by which the object of [knowledge] becomes known is that the form[1] and the true reality (*ḥaqīqat*) of it

1. For sake of consistency, *ṣūrat* will be consistently rendered as 'form'. However, it should not be interpreted as Platonic, since Ibn Sīnā was more than direct in his scathing criticisms of the

are separated from matter. In the very same way, the cause of the existence of a thing's knowledge is that its being is not in matter. Whenever the being, [when] disjoined[1] from matter, is form, knowledge of that being is in the [other] being [which is] disjoined from matter.[2] For example, whenever the form of humanity is disjoined from the matter of humanity, then there is knowledge of it [the form of humanity] in the soul (*nafs*). Since the form of the soul is itself disjoined from the matter in which it is [embodied], thus the soul itself is knowing itself through the soul itself,[3] because it is that which is separated from matter, as we will make clear in its proper place [*Ilāhiyyāt* §31, *infra*]. [This] knowledge proceeds from that which is not separated from it and also from that which arrives to it. Because it[4] is disjoined [from matter], it is known from itself, from that which is not separated from it, and it is not separated from itself (*khud az khud judā nīst*). Hence, its knowing proceeds from itself and is known to itself.

Necessary Existence is disjoined from matter by an absolute disjunction. Its essence (*dhāt*) is not veiled to [or, disjoined from] Itself, and is not separated [from Itself]. Hence, Its knowledge proceeds from Itself and is known to Itself, and, moreover, It is knowledge (*'ilm ast*). The disjoined [from matter], because it is disjoined, is such that its essence is knowledge of everything with which it is united (*bi-harchi paywandad*). Because it is a disjoined [thing, from matter], and because it is not separated from itself, its knowing proceeds from itself and it is known [to itself]. In true reality, what is known is knowledge, because that which is known to

---

Platonic doctrine of the Forms. *ṣūrat* has connotations of 'figure' and of Aristotelian *morphē*.

1. There is no adequate English equivalent for *mujarrad* ('disjoined'), which can be used for, among many meanings: bare, naked; without a veil; incorporeal, immaterial. It does not indicate *abstraction* from matter (which would be an act whose reality is solely within the mind), nor does it indicate *separateness* from matter (since, for example, the soul is *mujarrad* from the body even when the soul is embodied). The closest English equivalent may be 'disjoined', in the sense that there is a *logical* disjunction between matter and that which is *mujarrad*. Hence, 'disjoined' will be used for *mujarrad* consistently, even if it sometimes produces less than felicitous English. 'Separate' will be used consistently for *judā*.

2. This sentence is typical of Ibn Sīnā's compressed writing style, but its import is rather simple: knowledge is disjoined from matter, and knowledge exists only in a soul which is also disjoined from matter.

3. '*... pas nafs khud bi-khud binafs-i khud 'ālim ast, ...*.' The knowledge at hand is 'self'-referential. The human soul, although embodied and possessed of some material faculties, knows the real, intelligible forms through the immaterial faculty of intellect (see *Ilāhiyyāt* §37 and *Ṭabī'iyyāt* §43, *infra*). In the present case, the human soul is knowing the form of the human soul, not merely an individual material embodiment of a particular person, and, hence: it has knowledge *within* itself; that knowledge is knowledge *of* itself; and it has this knowledge *by means of* itself (i.e., its own intellectual faculty). Although such a self-referential example requires tortuous language, this example is a *necessary* prelude to the discussion of the bliss of Necessary Existence in Its 'self'-knowledge and of our ultimate bliss in imitating and receiving that knowledge (see *Ilāhiyyāt* §37, *infra*).

4. The ambiguous reference can be either to this knowledge or to the soul. Either would be consistent with the import of this passage.

you is, in true reality, the form which is within you, not that thing of which it is the form. The thing [as it is] known is another being and is not the true reality (*ḥaqīqat*) itself [as it exists outside of knowledge]. The sensible is the effect which resides in sense, not that external thing, and that effect is the sensation [see *Ṭabīʿiyyāt* §47]. Hence, in true reality, the known is identical with knowledge. When the known is the knowledge of the soul (*ʿilm al-nafs*), then in that case knower and known and knowledge are one thing.

Thus, Necessary Existence is a knower by its very essence (*dhāt*). Its essence gives being to all things which exist, in the order in which they exist. Hence, Its essence, which gives being to all things, is known to It. Consequently, all things are known to It from Its essence, not because things are a cause of the knowledge in It which It has of them, but, on the contrary, Its knowledge is the cause of the being of all things. [This is] like the knowledge which a carpenter has of the form of the house which he has conceived within himself. The form of the house, which is in the knowledge of the carpenter, is the cause of the form of the external house. It is not the form of the [external] house which is the cause of the carpenter's knowledge.

However, the form of the heavens is the cause of the form of our knowledge, because the heavens exist. The agreement (or order; *qiyās*) of all things by the knowledge of the First is similar to the agreement of things which we realize by our external reflection of them by our knowledge, since their external form is of that form which is within our knowledge.

30. How it is that Necessary Existence Knows Many Things Without Multiplicity in Its Essence

It is necessary to know: first, that the knowledge (*ʿilm*) of Necessary Existence is not like our knowledge nor is it analogous (*qiyās*) to our knowledge; and, second, that in us there are two kinds of knowledge. The first [kind of knowledge] requires multiplicity, and the second does not. That which requires multiplicity is called 'psychological' knowledge (*ʿilm-i nafsānī*), and that which does not require [it] is called 'intellectual' knowledge (*ʿilm-i ʿaqlī*). A precise explanation of these two as they truly are will be given later [e.g., *Ṭabīʿiyyāt* §49, *infra*], but here we present the sum of it by an example of an intelligent (*ʿāqil*) person, who is in a debate with someone or [who is] in a discussion.

That other person asks many questions, all of which call for an answer. A single 'thought' (*khātir*) comes to be in the soul [of the intelligent person], so that by that one thought alone he possesses the knowledge to answer all of [the questions], without that form, in his soul, of the answers in which they would be seen as separate from one another. Thus, that which proceeds by thought and speech, form by form, from the single thought in the soul is completely orderly, and the soul examines the forms one after another. Knowledge (*dānish*) comes to be knowledge to him by that act, and language produces the explanation from that form. Both of these two [the single thought and its discursive explication] are, in actuality, knowledge, since that person to whom the thought came previously is certain that he knows entirely [how to respond] to every question from the other person. That second manner also is knowledge in act.

That previous [single thought] is knowledge because it is the beginning and cause of making clear the intelligible forms. This knowledge is active (*fiʿlī*). That other [the discursive explication] is knowledge because it is a receptacle for multiple intelligible forms. This knowledge is passive. Here, many forms appear in the knower, and this makes multiplicity necessary because there (*ānjā*) there is a relation among many forms, which are from one thing, thus requiring multiplicity. Hence, it is made manifest how it can be that there is a knowledge of many things without multiplicity [in the knowledge]. The state (*ḥāl*) of the knowledge of all things by Necessary Existence is like the state of that one thought (*khātir*) knowing many things, but it is more sublime and more singular and more disjoined, for there is in him [the person] a receptacle for that thought, and Necessary Existence is disjoined [from a receptacle].

31. How the Contingent Can Be Known by a Knower

Of a thing which is contingent, for which it is possible (*mumkin*) that it exists and possible that it does not exist, it is not possible to know if it exists or does not exist. However, one can know that it is contingent, for contingency is necessary for the contingent, and existence and nonexistence are not necessary for a contingent [thing]. Since contingency is necessary, it is possible that it becomes known, and, because existence and nonexistence are not necessary, it is possible that it does not become known, for if it is known that it exists and that it is possible that it does not exist, [then] when it does not exist the knowledge is false, and falsity is not knowledge but is opinion (*gumān*). But it does not exist in the manner that it cannot be that it does not exist, and afterwards it is possible that it exists and it is possible that it does not exist.[1]

However, for everything which is contingent in itself (*binafs-i khwīsh*), it is necessary that its existence or nonexistence is due to a cause. Hence, when one knows it from its cause, one knows it under the aspect of necessity. Thus, there

1. In his many works on logic, Ibn Sīnā argued strenuously that 'knowledge' properly applies only to the universal (*kullī*), not to the particular (of which we can have only opinion). Hence, we can have only opinion of the existence of contingents and possibles, although we can have knowledge that contingents and possibles are contingent and possible. If (as is not truly the case) we could have knowledge of the complete causes of contingents and possibles, only then could we have knowledge (rather than mere opinion) of their existence. The import of this paragraph's final sentence (which has proved challenging to all translators, including the present one) seems to be that something which necessarily cannot exist is not a contingent, but an impossibility, and hence cannot later become possible.

can be knowledge of the contingent under the aspect in which it is necessary. For example, if someone says, 'a particular individual will find a treasure tomorrow', [that someone] does not have the power to know if [that individual] will find [the treasure] or will not find it, for this is contingent in itself. However, when one knows that a cause has inscribed in the heart of that particular individual [the cause] to set out [on a trip], and that a cause set him on a specific path, and that a cause makes him place his foot in a specific place, and it is known to be that the weight of his trampling is stronger than the cover [of the treasure], then in this case there is certitude that he will find the treasure. Thus, when this contingent is examined under its necessary aspect, it becomes known, and it is known that there has never been a thing which is not necessary.

Hence, there is a cause for everything, but the causes of things are not known to us completely (*bi-tamāmī*). Therefore, their necessity is not known to us. If we know some causes, it is opinion which prevails, and it is not certitude, because we know that all of the causes which we know do not make necessary the existence of [the contingent], for it is possible that there is another [intervening] cause or it is possible that an obstacle exists. If this [other cause or an obstacle] might exist or might not exist, this [i.e., the insufficiency of the known causes to provide certainty] is known to us with certainty.

Everything which exists returns to Necessary Existence, for it is necessary that they come from It. Therefore, all things are necessary in their relation to It, because they come to be necessary by Necessary Existence. Thus, all things are known by It.

32. How Necessary Existence Can Know Changeable Things without Change Becoming in Its Knowledge

It cannot be that the knowledge (*ʿilm*) of Necessary Existence happens within time, so that it could say that now it is so and tomorrow it is not so, and [so that] its judgment is according to how It exists today and It will be tomorrow, and then afterwards how It is tomorrow [and] It is not [any longer] today. [This is] because everything which is a knower of a thing has in it an attribute (*ṣifātī*) in [the knower] itself (*binafs-i khwīsh*), other than its relation to the [known] thing and other than that thing's coming-to-be, and other than that thing's existence. [That attribute] is not in the following manner: when a thing has disappeared, it is not in a relation between [the attribute] and that thing, in such a way that, if the thing is destroyed, it is lost to [the attribute]; and [if] now it has not disappeared, no change can be produced and its essence (*dhāt*) remains the same, but there is not a union with and relation to an existent thing.[1]

1. This argument, notwithstanding its abstruse formulation, is consistent with Ibn Sīnā's dual claims, in his works on logic, that: (1) there is a causal relationship between the object which is

On the contrary, knowledge (*'ilm*) is such that, when a thing is a knower, it is when the essence [of the knower] is known by that which is existent, and when that thing is not [a knower], it is when the essence is not known. It is not only that the essence would not be known [then], but also that a knower—which is the meaning and description of that essence—also would not exist. For knowing that thing is to add another thing to [the knower], rather than that thing not being in it. There must be a property in the essence (*dhāt*) of that which is a knower. For each distinct known [thing] there is a distinct state (*ḥāl*), or its one distinct state is united with each of the known [things], so that if one known [thing] does not exist, that distinct state does not exist.

Thus, if Necessary Existence is a knower in the present time, either: Its knowing is united with the present moment or with the possibility that something does not exist at a certain moment and with the [possibility that it] will exist at a certain time, when that time arrives; or It always knows that such a thing does not exist and will exist (and this is an error, not knowledge); or It does not know in this way but knows in some other manner. Therefore, It is not such a knower. [If it does know in this way], It would have turned from its first knowledge. Hence, It would be changeable, as we have demonstrated. Thus, it cannot be that the knowledge of Necessary Existence is related to the changeables in this manner.

But in what way can it [Necessary Existence's knowledge] be? It can be in such a manner that it is universal (*kullī*), not particular. What kind of universal is it? It is in the following manner, for example. An astronomer knows that a certain star is at rest here, later it goes there, and after so many hours will be in conjunction with a certain star, and at some time later, for example, will be in eclipse, and for some hours will remain in eclipse, and later will reappear. [He knows] how [all this] is without knowledge (*dānish*) of the present moment, for that [temporal] knowledge does not remain the same in him, and another knowledge will [come to] be, from the time that he knows (which is how it is now) to another time, and [such temporal knowledge] can be changeable. If that [knowledge] is in the manner of universal knowledge, it is always one knowledge, [that]: after a certain place [the star] is at [another] place, and after that movement will be that [other] movement. Before that movement and during that movement and after that movement, the knowledge (*'ilm*) is one and is not subject to change, so that whether [the movement is] in the future or in the present or in the past, [the knowledge] is entirely perfect, that a certain star after its conjunction with [another] star for some hours would be in conjunction with [yet another] star. This [knowledge] is true (*rāst*) if [the

known and our knowledge; but (2) what is known is not the thing itself, but our knowledge of it. (In medieval European terminology, what is known is our intention.) This must be the case, if Ibn Sīnā's psychology is correct, because our knowledge is not of the 'given' of perception, but rather of the 'given' of perception after it is thoroughly processed by several internal faculties. Hence, as Ibn Sīnā discussed in the next paragraph, the act of knowing is an act of knowing that which is within the knower.

conjunction] is in the past and it is true if [the conjunction] is in the future and it is true if the conjunction is in the present.

But, if one says that the star is in conjunction with a certain star right now, tomorrow it will be in conjunction with another star, [so] it cannot be that he says that very thing [tomorrow] and that it is true. [It is] exactly so in knowledge (*dānish*) so that it is known that, if right now it is in conjunction and tomorrow it will be in conjunction with another, [and] if tomorrow the very same knowledge [as today] is known [it will be] false.

Thus, the difference is clear between knowledge of things which is changeable and particular [and] completely temporal, and the completely universal. Necessary Existence knows all things completely universally, so that everything, small and great, does not escape from Its knowledge (*'ilm*), as has become clear from our discussion.

33. The Meaning of the Will of Necessary Existence

Every act which is from an agent is either by nature or by will or by accident, as has been explained herein [*Ilāhiyyāt* §15]. Every act which is by knowledge is neither by nature nor by accident, and such an act is not free of will. Whenever such an agent comes to know that act and the agent of that act, that act arises from it by knowledge. Every act which is from will has as its root either knowledge or opinion (*gumān*) or imagination. An example of that which proceeds from knowledge is an act of a geometer or a physician on the basis of a science which is known to them. An example of that which proceeds from opinion is to abstain from things which are dangerous. An example of that which proceeds from imagination is not to desire a thing which is like a defiled thing, or the heart's desire for a thing which is like something which appears beautiful, which resembles that which is sought after by the heart.

Action by Necessary Existence cannot happen from opinion or imagination, since opinion and imagination are accidental and are receptive to change, and Necessary Existence is unchangeable and necessary in every aspect, as was demonstrated earlier. Thus, it must be that the will of Necessary Existence is from knowledge. Is it not proper to provide an explanation of that will, to describe its manner and to offer examples?

In the way in which we desire a thing, there must first be a belief, knowledge, opinion, or imagination that this thing is efficacious. By 'efficacious' we mean that the thing is pleasant or advantageous for us. Then, after this belief, an inclination [or intention; *gharaḍ*] arises. The inclination then becomes strong, after which the bodily organs operate to bring about motion, and that outcome (which is desired) is brought about. For this reason, action follows from our desire.

We have made evident, however, that Necessary Existence is the completeness of Being or is greater than completeness. Hence, there cannot be a desire for action.

Likewise, it cannot be that it is possible in any way that a thing is efficacious to It, that an inclination should arise in It toward a thing.

Moreover, Its will proceeds from knowledge in the following manner. It knows that the being of some thing is in itself good and is pleasant, and the being of such a thing should be in a manner which is good and virtuous, and the existence of such a thing is better than its nonexistence. Then, It needs no other thing [i.e., no intervening desire, inclination or instrument], because that which is known by It is brought into existence. Thus, in knowing a thing to be, It brings into being all things and brings into being the best possible world which this world has the ability to be, [and this] is the requisite cause for all things such as are to come to exist. Similarly, knowledge by means of the faculty of knowledge is a cause within us, without intermediaries, of the movements of the faculty of desire, such as when we know that the best way is that the faculty of desire is put in motion by an absolute (*muṭlaq*) knowledge without conjecture (*gumān*) or without interference from the imagination (*wahm*), [so that] the faculty of desire is put in motion by that knowledge (without an intermediary from another faculty of desire). In just this way, the state of the creation of the being of all things proceeds from the knowledge of Necessary Existence.

While for us this faculty of inclination necessarily seeks that which is pleasant for our sense organs, it does not act thus [for Necessary Existence]. Thus, the Divine Will is no other thing but knowledge of the truth (*ḥaqq*) (that is, [knowledge] of how the order of the being of the world of things ought to be), and knowledge that the things are good [not only] for It but that the existence of each thing is good in itself, so that the meaning of the goodness is, for each thing, to exist such as it is. The Providence (*ʿināyat*) of [Necessary Existence] is that It knows, for instance, what kind of body is [proper] for humans or what is the best order for the heavens or what is the best world, without anything other [than knowledge] in It—no design or reason or inclination or desire—none of which would be worthy of It.

In summary, our consideration of what is beneath It and Its care of this aspect [of what is] as has been described, is not worthy of Its completeness and independence, as has been discussed earlier [*Ilāhiyyāt* §29–32, *supra*].

However, suppose someone said: 'We, too, act without desire, although with inclination. For example, we do good sometimes without any advantage for ourselves. If Necessary Existence looks upon those below It and attends to those inferior beings for their virtue rather than for Its own, it is not different.' To such a person, we respond: 'We never act, in this form (*ṣūrat*), without desire, because, although we desire to benefit someone else, we desire our [own] purposes, either to gain a good name or to gain a valuable reward or something which is even better.' This [last] is necessary if we are to choose the good and if we are to be the agents of necessity, so that, by doing what is necessary, praise and excellence and virtue are ours. If we do not do so, then that renown and virtue and praise are not ours. To seek after a universal state of benefit for all is our desire. We have made evident that it is desire which moves the agent and is effective in making him an agent. It is improper that Necessary Existence be the originator of action. Thus we have arrived at knowledge of the nature of the will of Necessary Existence, and knowledge that it has no attribute (*ṣifat*) other than knowledge (*'ilm*), and it has become known that Its knowledge is eternal, and it has become known that our will is [not[1]] in this manner.

34. The State of the Ability and Power of Necessary Existence

It is well known and widely accepted among people that one is powerful who acts when he wishes and does not act when he does not wish, not one who [simultaneously] wishes to act and wishes not to act. There are many things which they say that the Creator eternally neither wishes nor does which It has the power to do, such as to do an act of injustice. Thus, the conditional is not a categorical syllogism but rather is a hypothetical syllogism, that: if It wishes, it will act, and if it does not wish, It does not act. For a conditional to be true, it does not have to be the case that both parts of it are true, since it may be that both are false, such as when it is said, 'if a man flies, then he moves the air'. This [conditional] is true, although both the antecedent and the consequent are false. The antecedent could be false and the consequent true, as in when it is said, 'if man is a bird, then he is an animal'.[2] Thus, we say that [the conditional] 'if It does not wish, it does not act', does not necessarily entail the truth of [the antecedent] 'It does not wish', so that [the consequent] 'It does not act' is true.[3] It may be that it is true that It wishes and It acts, so that if It does not will (and it is suitable that It does not will), then It does not act, and if It wills (and it is suitable that It wills), then It does act. One or the other is true in a conditional.

If someone says that, 'if It does not wish' states a future case, and to be such is to be in time, and it is not suitable that Necessary Existence have a new will, and especially for it to have changed its principle', [then] we respond to this fantasy in two ways. First, this problem is such that the antecedent of the conditional is not true and cannot be true, and we have dismissed this earlier [*Ilāhiyyāt* §23, and §33 (*supra*)]. Second, we use the expressions 'if' and 'It does not wish' and 'It does not

1. All the manuscript traditions indicate that the will of Necessary Existence is like our will. It seems likely that this is an oversight by Ibn Sīnā or by the copyist of the archetype, since the will of Necessary Existence is, manifestly, quite different from our will.

2. A modern, Western, inaccurate dichotomy between birds and animals (the accurate dichotomy would be between birds and *mammals*) should be scrupulously avoided here. The Persian *parandah* could be rendered 'bird' *or* 'flying animal'.

3. Ibn Sīnā's sentence is quite compressed. His point, however, is one which is logically quite basic: a conditional does not necessarily entail the truth of the antecedent and, hence, does not necessarily entail the truth of the consequent.

will' figuratively here. It should be stated here that: whatsoever It wishes to be, is; and whatsoever It wishes not to be in what proceeds from It, is not; and that thing which It wishes, if it is not suitable that it is not wished to be, is; and that thing which It does not wish, if it is suitable that it is willed [not to be], is not. This is the meaning of that thing which is called 'powerful'. That is not powerful which sometimes acts or does not act, and sometimes wishes or does not wish.

From this it is evident that Its ability is identical with Its knowledge of the order of things. In essence (*dhāt*), Its knowledge and ability are not different.

35. Explanation of the Wisdom of Necessary Existence

Wisdom (*ḥikmat*), we believe, applies to two things: first, to complete knowledge (*dānish-i tamām*), and complete knowledge in conception (*taṣawwur*) is in recognizing a thing by its quiddity (*māhiyyat*) and by its definition, and in judgment (*taṣdīq*), is in certain (*yaqīnī*) judgment of the complete causes of things in the manner in which they are causes; and, second, to perfect (*muḥkam*) action. Perfection in action consists in whatsoever is the divine decree (*farīḍat*) for it to be, and it is whatsoever observes the divine decree to it, inasmuch as [its embodiment] in its matter it may allow, and it is whatsoever is ornament and addition to it, even if not decreed, to be.

Necessary Existence knows all things that are, and knows them in their complete causes, because It does not know things by means of other things, but It knows them from Itself, since all things are from It, and the cause of all things is from It. Hence, in this sense, It is wise, and Its wisdom is the same as Its knowledge (*'ilm*). Necessary Existence is that from which is the being of all things, and which has given the divine decree of being to all things, and to that which is outside of the divine decree. We shall write a book on this matter, if time permits. This idea is expressed in several passages in the Qur'ān: 'Our Lord is He Who gave unto everything its nature, then guided it aright' [Qur'ān 20:50],[1] and also, 'Who measureth, then guideth' [Qur'ān 87:3], and also, 'Who created me, and He doth guide me' [Qur'ān 26:78]. The wise have called the creation of the divine decree the first perfection, and the creation of abundance the second perfection. Hence, Necessary Existence is Absolute Wisdom.

36. The Generosity of Necessary Existence

Benefit and gain come from one thing to another in two ways: first, by commerce and, second, by generosity.

Commerce takes place when one thing is given and another is taken, and what is taken is not always concrete, since it can be a good name or joy or a prayer—in

1. All translations of the Qur'ān are by Muḥammad Marmaduke Pickthall.

sum, anything for which we have a desire. Whatever is in that way equivalent compensation is, in reality, commerce, although the vulgar people call commerce and recognize as commerce [exchange of] goods for goods, and reputation and gratitude are not given as equivalent compensation. However, a prudent person knows that whatever is his desire is a gain.

However, generosity is that which is not aimed at equivalent compensation or recompense, and is not an exchange of actions. It is that which proceeds from a will for a good thing without a desire for it. The act of Necessary Existence is thus. Hence, Its acts are Absolute Generosity.

37. The Most Delightful Happiness and the Greatest Bliss and Felicity Are in Union (paywand) *with Necessary Existence, although Most People Imagine that Other Things Are More Pleasant*

First, we must know what pleasure and pain are. We say that: whatever is not perceptible is neither pleasure nor pain. Hence, it must first be perceptible. Our perceptions are of two kinds: first is that belonging to the external senses, and, second, that which is imaginative (*wahmī*) or intelligible (*ʿaqlī*), which is internal to us. Each of these is of three kinds: first, perception of things which are agreeable and proper to the perceptive faculty; second, that which is not agreeable, not proper, and is destructive; and third, an intermediate which is neither the first nor the second. Hence, pleasure is in perception which is proper, and pain is in perception which is not proper. However, in perception in which there is neither the former nor the latter, there is neither pleasure nor pain. What is proper to each faculty is that which corresponds to its action, without harm: to anger, victory; and to appetite, flavour; and to a fancy, hope; and each of the senses of touch, smell, and sight has, analogously, that which is agreeable to it.

The prudent consider the pleasures of the internal faculties to be superior, while the small-souled and vile people and the ignoble regard superficial pleasures as superior. If one asks, 'Do you wish sweet, tasty, edible things or high station, grandeur and victory over an enemy?', to someone ignominious, of base desires, and at the level of children and of cattle, he will wish the sweets, and if one asks someone who is of noble and precious soul, he will always ignore the sweets and will not prefer them to another thing. He is of base inclination whose inner faculties within him are dead, and he does not have knowledge of the acts of his inner faculties, like children whose inner faculties are not yet completely actual.

For each faculty, pleasure is in perception of that thing which is appropriate to that faculty and for which it exists, and that thing which is agreeable to it. However, in this matter, the differences are of three species:

First, differences among faculties, so that the nobler and more powerful the faculty, the nobler and more powerful is its act.

Second, differences in the amount of apprehension and perception received, so that for each faculty in which perception is greater, the pleasure and pain is greater, and if two faculties are of the same kind, yet one is more acute, then the perception of the latter of pleasure or pain is greater.

Third, differences among faculties according to what is received by them, so that if the pleasure or lack of pleasure is more powerful, the faculty perceives more powerful pleasure or more powerful pain.

That thing is more pleasant which produces and possesses less deficiency and less inclination toward evil. That thing is more painful which produces and possesses more deficiency and inclination toward evil because there is vileness in the thing. Hence, how can there be a comparison made between the form which is perceived by the senses to be sweet, or between other ideas which resemble sweetness in sense perception because they are in perception vile things, and the form which is from Necessary Existence in intellect (*ʿaql*), which is the most excellent form and which actualizes our faculty of intellect?

However, if we consider the faculty, rather than its object, then the faculty of sensation is vile and weak, as will become evident [later in this section], for it shares in a vile existence and it arises from a corporeal organ. Whenever there is a powerful perception of pleasure in it, [the faculty] is diminished. For example, illumination is pleasant to sight, and darkness is unpleasant [to it], and yet a powerful light blinds it. In summary, strong sensations destroy the faculties of sensation, and powerful intelligibles improve the intellect and make it more powerful. The intellectual (*ʿaqlī*) faculties subsist in themselves and are not susceptible to change, as will be demonstrated. Their being is near[1] the being of Necessary Existence, as shall also be demonstrated [*Ṭabīʿiyyāt* §43 and 48–50, *infra*]. Hence, the faculty of sensation is not related to the intellectual faculty.

Furthermore, intellectual perception and sense perception are different in several aspects. First, intellect perceives a thing as it is in itself (*bi-khudish*), and sense perception perceives nothing whatsoever as it is in itself. Whenever the eye sees whiteness, it sees length, width and shape, and it sees motion and rest. Thus, the eye does not have the power to see whiteness as whiteness itself, and [it] sees more or less of the thing. It may be that it sees the thing as less than it is. Intellect perceives the thing without a veil (or disjoined; *mujarrad*) as it is, or it does not perceive it in any manner at all. Sense perception perceives vile and changeable accidents, and intellect perceives unchanging substances and attributes (*ṣifathāʾī*) and that thing from which goodness and order (*niẓām*) and happiness all arise. Hence, of what kind is the state (*ḥāl*) of happiness in which intellect is found when it receives the First Truth (*ḥaqq-i awwal*), that from which all beauty and order and splendour proceed, and how can such happiness be compared to the pleasures of the senses?

1. Ibn Sīnā may have intended a dual meaning here, since *nazdīk* can mean, figuratively, 'resembling' and, literally, 'near', both of which are appropriate. See *Ṭabīʿiyyāt* §43, *infra*.

However, it sometimes happens that one among the faculties receives a pleasure and it is inattentive to the pleasure, either: (1) because it is otherwise occupied and inattentive, as when someone wholly occupied [with something else] hears glorious melodies and beautiful verses and is unaware of their pleasantness; or (2) because an illness weakens its nature, so that it, because of the thing which makes it ill, desires that thing which can cure the illness. Thus, when some other thing besides that [which cures the illness] is given, although it is pleasant, it will not be perceived as pleasant, as when someone who finds eating clay pleasant finds a sour and bitter thing pleasant but finds a sweet thing unpleasant. Or, (3) because of habit and familiarity, as when an unpleasant food has become familiar to someone or when it becomes agreeable to him. Thus, this food appears more pleasant to him than does that which is, in reality (*ḥaqīqat*), pleasant. Or, (4) because the faculty in itself is diminished and has not the power to sustain a pleasant thing, as when the eye does not find a strong light pleasant, and the enfeebled ear finds the stronger and more pleasant [sounds] to be unpleasant.

Hence, for similar causes, we may also be inattentive to perceiving the pleasures of the intelligibles (*maʿqūlāt*), for example, when we are distracted from them and the faculty of intellect is weakened from the first action and completely, when we are embodied and are accustomed to and familiar with sensible things. It is often the case that pleasant things are unpleasant for these causes, and it is often the case that one has awareness neither of pleasure nor of unpleasantness, such as someone whose body has become numb, who does not know pleasure or unpleasantness when it is received, and when the numbness dissipates, one is able to perceive painful things which have happened, such as a burn or a wound. And it is often the case that a faculty has in it a thing either bad or pleasant, and it does not perceive it because of a disease.[1] For example, in the disease which the physicians call bulimia, the entire body is starving and [yet] hunger becomes diminished, but the stomach is unaware, because of this sickness, that it is ill from weakness or from moisture. When the cause of the illness is removed, misery arises from the lack of food.

The state (*ḥāl*) of our soul (*nafs*) in this world is just the same, for it is in a state of hunger.[2] In one in whom there is not the perfect intelligible, there is misery [see *Ṭabīʿiyyāt* §43, *infra*]. One possesses perfection who possesses happiness or to whose very self it is bound. However, when one is embodied, one is distracted from [true] happiness and pain, and when one is separated [from the body], one perceives them.

1. 'Because of a disease' (*az sababī ʿāriḍ rā*) could also be rendered, 'for an accidental [in the Aristotelian sense of 'accident'] cause' or, 'for an adventitious cause'. However, the discussion of bulimia that follows seems to indicate that the medical meaning is preferable here.

2. Literally, 'is defective (diminished, injured, or wanting; *bi-nuqṣān ast*).'

The Completion of the Discussion under This Heading

Thus, Necessary Existence is the most magnificent knower of the most magnificent in knowledge, which is Itself, the most complete, eternal knowledge, having the greatest splendour and grandeur and station (*manzilat*). Hence, the state (*ḥāl*) of highest happiness is the state It is in Itself, for It has no need of anything external to give It perfection and grandeur. Those beings which, in the first creation, were found complete, and which are pure intellect (*ʿaql-i maḥḍ*), and which are not like us, having no need of external things, and are not attached to lower things, are occupied with their own perfection, which is intelligible to them, and in that which they contemplate of the perfection and splendour of Necessary Existence, which illuminates them in the mirror of their substance. Their ultimate happiness and delight is the happiness in which they are in contemplation of Necessary Existence, in addition to the happiness which they have in the perception of their own perfection. They are occupied with the highest happiness and delight, because, eternally, they do not turn from the highest to the lower aspect [of what is]. Their whole selves (*khudī-yi khwīsh*) are consecrated to the contemplation of grandeur, that is, the regal presence, and to receiving the greatest happiness.

There is no sadness for them, for the cause of our sadness is another diversion, either an instrument (*ālat*)[1] of pain or an evil instrument. In summary, there must be matter which is receptive to change, and moreover sadness does not occur without a cause,[2] and whatever is subject to a cause which it receives is mutable. Fortunate is the man who seeks that state for his own life (*jān*), when it becomes separated from the body, in which he finds happiness. If he seeks to acquire the opposite state, he has, rather than happiness, pain, although he has, at present, no idea of the form of that pain, as when one has not experienced the pain of a burn from a fire, but knows of it by hearsay. How well has spoken the leader of the wise, and the guide and teacher of the philosophers, Aristotle, on this matter, i.e., that happiness which Necessary Existence has in Itself, and all things issue from It. He said:

If the First of all things perpetually has from Itself the same amount of happiness which we receive from It, at any given time when we contemplate It and meditate upon Its grandeur and present to ourselves a truth (*ḥaqqī*) which speaks of It, there is a great magnificence within It. This amount which our understanding conceives and which our state (*ḥāl*) necessitates is not at all comparable to that which It has in Itself, which is more magnificent and wonderful. Still more, the First Being is

1. This is the term which Ibn Sīnā customary uses for bodily organs, and it is likely that he so intends it here, given the discussion of embodiment which follows.

2. There are four highly divergent manuscript variants of this clause. The text may well be corrupt here. Hence, details of this clause should not be given excessive weight, but the overall import is reasonably consistent.

happiness, complete in Its own self (*binafs-i khwīsh*). Perhaps such a state should not be called happiness, but there is no word among known words which better conveys this meaning.

Ṭabīʿiyyāt (Physics)

42. The State (ḥāl) *of the Immortality of the Soul* (nafs) *and Which Faculties are Immortal*

It is evident that the soul (*nafs*), if it comes into being with the body, cannot exist because of a cause which is external to the body or which is prior to the body, since, if the souls exist prior to the bodies, they are either many or one.

If there is one, and if this one soul becomes many, then it is divisible into parts. We say that: this substance (*gawhar*) is not divisible into parts.

If there are many, then they become a single kind. They are distinguished, one separate from the other, by material accidents. Thus, they are material. Hence, the soul does not exist prior to the body, for its existence prior to the body is empty. Consequently, when it becomes existent (*mawjūd*) from the causes of [its] existence, so does its organ [the body].

When it becomes existent (*mawjūd*) and it is a substance, it subsists because the principle of its existence subsists. When its organ is destroyed, and it does not exist by or in the organ, it is not destroyed. Several faculties which reside in bodily organs—sense, imagination, desire, anger, and all others which reside in bodily organs—are separated, and are destroyed with the destruction of their organs.

43. The Agent Intellect (ʿaql-i faʿʿāl)

Insofar as the intelligibles are powerful in the soul (*nafs*), and come to it by act, it must be that there is an intelligent (*ʿaqlī*) thing which it endows them with from the power of act (*bi-fʿil*). It is indubitable that it is one of the intellects of which we have spoken in the *Ilāhiyyāt* [in §37, *supra*] and that [it is that] particular one which is the nearest [to this world]. That is called the Agent Intellect, which acts upon our intellects so that they come from potentiality (*quwwat*) to actuality.

However, when our sensations (*maḥsūsāt*) and our imaginings (*khayālāt*) do not exist, our intellect does not actualize, and when the sensations and imaginings come into being, there is a mixture of the forms with foreign accidents, and they are hidden like things in darkness. Thus, the splendour (or light; *tābish*) of the Agent Intellect falls upon the imaginings, in the way that the light of the sun falls on the forms [of things] which are in darkness. Hence, from those imaginings disjoined forms come to the intellect, just as because of light the visible forms are present in the mirror or the eye. As they are disjoined, they are universal (*kullī*), as whenever you make the superfluous separate from [the sensation of] humanity, a universal meaning remains, and the individualities disappear.[1] Hence, this intellect makes an essence (*dhātī*) and accidents separate from one another; makes clear subjects and predicates; and makes clear each predicate which is united with a subject without the mediator in the intellect; and [makes clear] all of those [predicates for which] the mediator must be separated by thought.

When the human soul recognizes the intelligibles disjoined from matter, and the need to perceive through sense is gone, when the soul becomes separated from the body, [the soul's] unity with the splendour above becomes complete, for its body is finally sent from it, however much an aid it was to it at first, just as, [for example, in the case of] a horseman who mounts a horse, in order to reach a place, and to reside there. If he cannot separate himself from the horse, and his heart is with the horse, and he remains upon it, then finally the horse is an obstacle to his goal, just as at first it had carried him. In this way, the cause of the perfection of the soul is the Agent Intellect, which is eternal and its splendour is constant, and the soul is its receptacle [for the intelligibles] by itself not by an organ [of the body], and the soul is eternal. Hence, the union of the soul with the Agent Intellect and [the soul's] perfection are perpetual, and [the soul] suffers neither obstacle nor falsehoods nor destruction.

It has become evident that the pleasure of each faculty is in the perception of that thing for which it is, by its nature (*ṭabʿ*), a receptacle.

And it has become evident that nothing is more pleasant than an intelligible idea (*maʿānī*).

It has become manifest previously that the sensible does not hold such pleasure as the intelligible—moreover, that it is not even comparable to it.

And it is evident that the cause is how it is that we perceive a pleasant thing and do not know a pleasant [thing]. It has become clear how this happens and does not happen.[2]

From that, it follows that: when the human soul becomes separated [from the body], and it arrives at its goal, as we have said, its delight and its felicity are incomparable; and when it desires the acquired perfection—and when the perfection is not acquired to a degree which is perfect, it holds to it in this manner [cf. *Ilāhiyyāt* §37, *supra*]—and there is sorrow. If it does not have this desire, it has an imaginary state in conformity with its belief in which it is bound, and its act which it has done. And one says, it chooses that thing by imagination, and from imagination it is not set free, so that for it the aspect of sense of the lower [realm] does not exist, and it must be the organ of imagination, for example: the heavenly bodies.

It has become known that: the body is an obstacle to the soul obstructing [the soul's] own proper act; and that each time that [the soul] turns toward this

1. Cf. the related discussion in *Ilāhiyyāt* §29, *supra*.
2. Each of these conclusions reiterates a discussion from *Ilāhiyyāt* §37, *supra*.

world, it is interrupted from intellectual thought. Moreover, each faculty puts up obstacles to the other faculties: lust to anger, and anger to lust; sight to hearing, and hearing to sight; external sense to internal sense, and internal sense to external sense.

And it must be known that: the body does not obstruct [the soul] because the soul is in it, because the soul is not in [the body], but [the body] obstructs [the soul] because the soul has the desire to turn toward it, and when this desire becomes a habit so that the soul binds itself to the form and the habit and the command of the body, [then] as long as the body exists, it obstructs [the soul] from attaining felicity. Moreover, it throws the soul into negligence and holds it in preoccupation, and [the soul has] no thought of defilement and the damage of its effects, so that it forgets its own proper felicity. When this [the body] departs and its effects remain, then the soul knows sorrow because of the proximity of the effects, as we have given an example in another place [*Ilāhiyyāt* §37, *supra*]. But these states are foreign [to the soul], and when the actions cease to exist, the effects of the habit disappear.

Hence, this sorrow which arises from action is not everlasting, and that which is from deficiency is everlasting, and the Law of God (*sharīʿat-i Ḥaqq*) says exactly this. In this way, the birth of the body makes necessary the birth of the soul (or life; *jān*): it is not possible that the soul (*jān*) goes from one body to another, for otherwise there are two souls for one body.

45. *The Cause of Dreams and Their Truth*

Moreover, dreams arise when the faculty of imagination (*mutakhayyilah*) rests alone, and is made free from preoccupation with the senses, and the soul (*nafs*) turns its face from the senses, and is free from preoccupation with the senses. It is the nature of the imagination to tell stories, and it is seldom quiet.[1] Hence:

Sometimes the disposition of the body makes the stories. For example, when there is yellow bile, it presents yellow colours, and when there is black bile, black colours. When heat is dominant, it presents fire, and when cold is dominant, it presents ice.

Sometimes past thoughts (*andīshahāʾī*) make the stories.

When the soul is weak, it [imagination] puts [stories] into it, just as sense [usually] puts [sensibles] into it.

If the soul is strong, or finds a respite from the imagination, it is free from labours, and it becomes adorned within it with the splendour of the spiritual be-

1. Ibn Sīnā has omitted a subordinate conclusion in his argument here. The nature of imagination is to tell stories; it does not have the material of sensation from which to make those stories; therefore [the omitted subordinate conclusion], the imagination must find some other source for the raw material of its tales.

ings. If the splendour of these is not in him, the cause for [the fact that] the soul is not receptible [to them] is that it is preoccupied with the inferior. When their splendour is in the soul, particularly that form the states (*ḥālhā*) of which are the most important in their being and [are most] agreeable to the soul, they shine in the soul, so that their reality (*maʿānī*) is the states which they are in their essences and [also] which they are [as] perceptions, as has been explained earlier [*Ilāhiyyāt* § 35–37].

Thus, those forms, if they are particular, are bound in the formative faculty, and their meanings remain in memory.

If the imagination does not interfere, and that form is represented well, [then] it is in sleep as it is [in reality], and an explanation and interpretation of the dream is not necessary.

Hence, if the imagination distinguishes among [the forms], the soul receives the form feebly. If [the soul] receives [the form] powerfully, the imagination is quiet, just as when it receives powerfully from sense. When a faculty makes a strong action, the soul turns [to it], [and] another faculty makes a weak action.[1]

When the imagination is in a quiet state, the dream is seen just as it really (*rāst*) is. Hence, if the union of the soul with the upper realm is weak, the imagination acts quickly, and it changes that vision from that condition (*ḥāl*) [which it really is] into another thing with an altogether other meaning in its place. Similarly, if you contemplate a thing as it is in itself (*bi-khud*), then the imagination is unable to interfere. Hence, if you hold weakly [to a reflection], the imagination acts quickly and you are carried far from the path of reflection, and the form of [that] reflection is stilled, and the imagination is in control, and you forget the nature of reflection (*andīshah*). You take a step [to discover] how you remember and you ask, 'How have I thought, when I have such a reflection in me involuntarily?' Afterwards, by machination of thought, you recover the prior reflection. Hence, for every dream such as this, an interpretation is needed.

The essence (*maʿānī*) of that interpretation is this. You ask, 'How have I seen the thing, from the invisible world, when the imagination has made it into another thing?' For example, 'How do I see when the imagination makes a tree?' Hence, dream interpretation is more by conjecture and by one's experiences, and each nature is another habit, and each time and each state is another representation to the imagination.

1. See the discussion of the mutual interference of the faculties of the soul in *Ṭabīʿiyyāt* §43, *supra*. If the intellect is powerful, then it interferes with the imagination, and *vice versa*.

46. *The Cause of the Union of the Human Soul* (jān) *with the Invisible World*

The union between the human soul (*jān*) and the spiritual world and the dwellings of the angelic substance is [because]: it [the soul] is so powerful that sense [is not hindered by] that which is from its own action. For example, a man may have, in a single state (*ḥāl*), great powers of understanding, listening, speaking, and writing. Thus, his soul (*nafs*) has the power to see in wakefulness the same which it perceives in sleep.

Or, because the faculty of the imagination (*takhayyul*), which is his instrument in this act, in attaining both the world below and the world above, aids the soul in union [with the world] above.

Or, [the soul is] negligent of sensory states, by the domination of black bile, and dryness in him, so that the heart is preoccupied more by [its] reflections [than] by the sensible world. That is like one who is talkative who is far from the sensible world. His soul [*rūḥ*] makes a weak current in the external in that manner and produces strong internal action from sharpness and dryness, which are the opposites of moistness and heaviness.

Or, by reason of sleep, in which sense is relinquished.

47. *The Cause of Forms which Are Seen and Are Felt in the Senses but which Do Not Exist*

The faculty of the soul which discovers the concealed does this in two ways: first, all those which are; and, second, the weaker and under the command of imagination (*khayāl*). [In the second case, the imagination] desires that it may possess a glance at that thing, and it interprets [the thing] by means of other things, and in that way, it [the thing] is not preserved [in the soul], as when anyone speaks words. When the faculty of imagination is powerful, it dominates the *sensus communis*,[1] and it places that imaginary form in him so that it is perceived. The *sensus communis* is a mirror, in this manner: if the external sense seizes a form in perception, then it is received.

In reality, the sensible is that form which is there [in the *sensus communis*] in perception, not the external form [cf. *Ilāhiyyāt* §32, *supra*].

If one calls both 'sensible', it ['sensible'] has two meanings. If that form is internal and it is strong, then it remains within him. When it remains within him, then it is sensible. So, the sensible is this form from whence an image came. There are two things which, during times of wakefulness, prevent the maintenance of this fo rm in the *sensus communis*: first, the dominance of external sense and the preoccupation

1. The *ḥiss-i mushtarak* is the faculty of the soul which gathers together and holds in unity the products of the other faculties (see *Ṭabīʿiyyāt* §34). Since it is the sense which is common to the other senses, it is sometimes translated as 'common sense'. 'Common sense' is nearly synonymous with 'prudence' in daily usage, though, and so the medieval Latin translation, *sensus communis* will be used herein.

the *sensus communis* comes to have with external sense; and, second, the weakness of the imagination, so that reason is frustrated by it, and the forms presented by the power of [the imagination] are possessed of falsehood.

If it [reason] is strong, external sense does not preoccupy it, and if the imagination is very strong, it seizes it [reason] by itself.

If intellect (*'aql*) is weak, or if it has ceased to act because of an illness, there is not anything [in it] from that which it [presented] to the imagination. Hence, the imagination manufactures the entire form of things. Thus, it is made to reside in the *sensus communis*. Because of this, whenever reason is not [active] in it [the soul], many impossible forms appear. If one is in a state such that fear comes to dominate reason, then reason becomes silent, and imagination has a free hand [to produce] a fearful apparition, or another faculty operates, so that there is perceived everything feared or everything which is desired.

48. Origin of Miracles and Their Coming to Be Done

It has been demonstrated, in the previous science [*Ilāhiyyāt*, e.g., §39 and §56], that: the matter of this world is obedient to the soul (*nafs*) and the intellect, and the forms which reside in the soul are the cause of the existence of those forms in this world. It is necessary that the matter of this world be obedient to the care of the human soul, for it is from that substance.[1] However, the human soul is weak, but, although it is weak, it resembles the soul of the world in several respects. For example, when an abominable form happens in it, the constitution of the body turns cold, and if it perceives a superior form, the temperament of the body warms. If it contemplates a libidinous form, in a short time a heat becomes present in the genitalia, and produces a swelling, and the sexual organ becomes such that it is desirous. This cold and heat are not from any other heat and cold, for they follow upon the form which is in the soul.

The human soul is not within the body, but the union with it is come to be manifest, for [the body] is the distinctive instrument for it [the soul], and existence with [the body] falls to [the soul]. It may observe it and have love toward it, as is its nature. In this case, [the soul] is most important (*alif*), because [the soul] is near to it, by nature and by principle. Thus, the human soul is able to make an effect from this which is prior, in this quantity of matter, with which it is united, and its ability is within [these] limits. Because of the power of this soul, it is not like the power of the soul of the world, [for] this effect [on the body] also continues to be weak.

1. The reference appears to be to the soul of the sublunary realm. In Ibn Sīnā's emanation scheme, which was in some difficulty when he wrote the *Dānish-nāmah*, each of the concentric spheres of the cosmos has a body, a soul, and an intellect. Our world is within the innermost sphere (the orbital sphere of the moon) and is governed by the soul and the intellect of the lunar sphere. Since our substance is of the same kind as that of the soul of the lunar sphere, and earthly matter obeys the soul of the lunar sphere, earthly matter should also obey our souls.

It happens that some few souls can produce an effect in the body (*jism*) of another person by apprehension (*wahm*) and by the evil eye. However, this is to say that it is not prohibited by reason that some few people happen to have a powerful soul which has great power to act upon material bodies in this world, by apprehension (*wahm*) and by its own will, so that this material world is submitted to a great change by its cause, particularly by heat and cold and movement. From this it brings about all miracles.

49. The State of Powerful Souls

It is known that one arrives at the unknown by means of the middle term [of syllogisms], and the middle term: either is apparent from the sharpness of the intellect, which intuition (*ḥads*) thinks within the soul, and that is from the freedom (*rastagī*) of the soul related to receptivity to the form (*faṭan*) [of the middle term] from the Agent Intellect; or, it is received from instruction.

Intuition is of two kinds: one with sluggishness and delay, and the other with swiftness.

It is not obligatory (*farīḍah*) that intuition perceives one proposition after another. Every proposition is discovered by intuition if it is grasped in true reality (*ḥaqīqat*). When, first, it is learned from someone, it is always unknown before it is learned from that other, but there has been someone who has discovered it by himself.

If someone makes a strenuous effort to know, by knowing the things of this world, things are, for the most part, known to him soundly, or are known by the power of conjecture, because he has been using deductive reasoning.

Now, among men, there is someone who may be a teacher of most things to them, and he does not have the power to make every intuition, and, moreover, it is also [the case] that he, too, does not have the power to understand but from a teacher.

It may be that there is one who knows most things by intuition so that there is little need of a teacher, and such a person is rare. When he wishes, without a teacher and in a moment, he knows the sciences by means of intuition, from beginning to end, from the goodness of his union with the active intellect. Then he does not need to reflect upon every thing, and in this manner he understands that it [knowledge] is finding a place in his heart. Moreover, this [knowledge] is the truth (*ḥaqq*) itself, and this one must be he who is the principal teacher of mankind. It ought not to surprise [us] that:

That which we see is not in the manner of this station (*manzilat*). Things learned by reflection and toil are, however, [learned] by the power of intuition free from toil—intuition which is in agreement with most things which are found in books. Hence, the toil of reading numerous books is not necessary. Such a person, by the age of eighteen or nineteen, has understood the sciences of wisdom (*'ulūm-i ḥikmat*)—logic, *ṭabī'iyyāt*, *ilāhiyyāt*, geometry, arithmetic, astronomy, music, and the science of medicine and many other abstruse sciences—such as no person other than himself has done. Thus, after many years pass and there is not an addition of many things to the first state, one knows that one has passed the years needed to learn every one of these sciences.[1]

50. The State of the Sanctified Soul Which Is That of the Prophets

Moreover, the sanctified soul is the rational soul of the magnificent prophets who know the intelligibles by means of thinking and of union with the knowledge (*'ilm*) of the angels, without teacher and without book. By imagination (*bā takhayyul*) in a state of vigilance and in a state of knowledge (*'ilm*), the concealed arrives within them and they receive revelation. Revelation is a union between angels and the life (*jān*) of man which endows knowledge from the states [of the angels]. Knowledge makes a mark in matter, so that it causes miracles and causes another form. This is a different degree of man, and is conjoined to an angelic rank, and in this manner one is the *khalīfah* of God on the Earth. His existence is received in intellect (*'aql*) and is necessary to the endurance of the species of man, and this is made clear in another place. This is a sufficient discussion of 'natural science'. Peace be with you.

---

1. It is clear that this passage is autobiographical, since it merely summarizes an extremely similar passage in Ibn Sīnā's *Autobiography*. See William E. Gohlman, ed. and tr., *The Life of Ibn Sīnā: A Critical Edition and Annotated Translation* (Albany, NY, 1974), pp. 36–39.

CREATION EX-NIHILO AND IMMEDIATE CREATION

From *al-Ishārāt wa'l-tanbīhāt* (Remarks and Admonitions)

Translated for this volume by Shams Inati from Ibn Sīnā, *al-Ishārāt wa'l-tanbīhāt,* Part Three (published with Part Four) fifth class, ed. S. Dunyā (Cairo, 1958), pp. 484–544.

Chapter 1. Delusion and Admonition

It appears to the imagination of the commoners that the dependency of a thing, which they call 'effect', on another thing, which they call 'agent', is in respect of the sense according to which the commoners call the effect 'an effect' and the agent 'an agent'. In this respect, the latter brings into existence, fashions, and causes while the former is brought into existence, is caused, and is fashioned. All this amounts to saying that after nonexistence a thing acquires existence from another thing.

They may also say that if a thing is brought into existence, the need for the agent disappears so that if the agent is missing, it is permissible that the effect remains in existence. This matter is exemplified in their observation of the missing of the builder, while the building still subsists. Many of them do not hesitate to say that if nonexistence were permissible for the Creator, the exalted, His nonexistence would not harm the existence of the world. For the world, according to them, needs the Creator, the exalted, only to bring it into existence, that is, to bring it out of nonexistence into existence. By doing so, He is an agent. But if the world is caused and acquires existence after nonexistence, then after that, how could it come into existence after nonexistence in a manner in which it would need an agent.

Again, they say that if the world needs the Creator, the exalted, inasmuch as it exists, then every existent needs another thing to bring it into existence. The same would be true of the Creator, and so on to infinity. We will clarify the manner concerning the modality of this and what must be believed regarding it.

Chapter 2. Delusion

We must analyse the meaning of the expressions 'fashions', 'causes', and 'brings into existence' into the simple elements of their comprehensions, eliminating from them those elements whose inclusion in what is under consideration is accidental.

We say that if a thing is nonexistent and then, if after nonexistence, it exists owing to a certain thing, we call it 'an effect'. We do not care at this point whether either of the two things has the other as its predicate—whether equal to it, more general than it, or more specific than it—so that one would, for example, need to add, saying: 'After not existing, it exists owing to that thing—by the movement of that thing with immediacy or through an instrument, by a voluntary design, or not (by nature, by generation, or by something else), or by what corresponds to these.' At present we do not pay attention to these things, since indeed they are additional to a thing's being an effect. That which corresponds to the effect, and due to whose causation the effect exists, is something we call 'agent'. What proves this equality between the agent and the effect is that if one says, 'I acted through an instrument', 'through a movement', 'through a design', or 'by nature', one does not thereby mention something that contradicts the act as an act or that includes a repetition in the comprehension of the act.

Regarding contradiction, if the comprehension of an act, for example, prevents the act from occurring by nature and one says, 'I acted by nature', it is as if one says, 'I acted and I did not act'. As for repetition, if the comprehension of an act, for example, includes choice and one says, 'I acted by choice', it is as if one says, 'an animal human being'.

If this is the meaning of an act, or if some of this is the meaning of an act, it will not harm us in our purpose; for in the comprehension of an act there is existence and nonexistence. The fact that that existence is after nonexistence is as if this fact is an attribute predicated of this existence.

Nonexistence, on the other hand, is not dependent on the agent of the existence of the effect. As for the fact that this existence is described as being after nonexistence, that is not due to the action of any agent or to the making of any maker, for this existence is of something like that for which it is permissible not to exist. Therefore, it remains that the dependency of this existence, inasmuch as it is this existence, is either the dependency of the existence of that whose existence is necessary or the dependency of the existence of that whose existence must be preceded by nonexistence.

Chapter 3. Completion and Remark

Let us, therefore, consider now for which of these two matters the existence that depends on other things depends.[1] Thus we say that the comprehension of its being not necessary in existence by itself but through another does not prevent it from being one of two divisions. The first is that whose existence is always necessary through another. The second is that whose existence is sometimes necessary through another. 'That whose existence is necessary through another' is predicable of these two divisions, while 'that whose existence is necessary through itself' is negated of both of them in view of its comprehension—unless something external prevents this from happening (p. 495). The existence that is preceded by

1. In other words, is it the case that the existence that depends on something else depends on it because that existence is possible in itself and necessary through another, or because it is something that comes into existence after nonexistence?

nonexistence has only one manner of existing through another. In comprehension, it is more specific than the comprehension of the former.

'Dependency on something else' is predicable of both comprehensions. If there are two ideas of which one is more general than the other, and if a third idea is predicated of the comprehensions of both, then that third idea belongs primarily to the more general by itself and secondarily to the more specific later on. This is because that idea does not attach to the more specific except if it had already attached to the more general. The reverse is not true. So that, if it were permissible that the existence of that which is preceded by nonexistence not be necessary through another, and if it were possible for it according to its definition, this would not be a dependency.

Therefore, it is clear that this dependency is due to the other manner.[1] Because this attribute is a permanent predicate of caused beings, not only in the state of their beginning to exist, it is, therefore, permanent. Similarly, if it belongs to its being preceded by nonexistence, then this existence is not only dependent at the time that it is, after not having existed, only so that after that, it can dispense with the agent.

Chapter 4. Admonition

That which begins to exist after not having been has a priority in which it does not exist, not like the priority that 'one' has over 'two' in which that which is before and that which is after can be together in actual existence. Rather, it is a priority of a before that does not persist with an after. In a priority of this kind, there is also a renewal of a posteriority after the discontinuity of a before.

This priority is neither the same as nonexistence, for nonexistence may be after; nor is it the agent itself, for the agent may be before, simultaneous with, and after. Therefore, this priority is something else in which interruption and renewal persist in a continuity. You had already learned that such a continuity, which corresponds to movements in measures, cannot be composed except of divisible parts.

Chapter 5. Remark

Because renewal is impossible except with the change of a state, and the change of a state is impossible except for that which has a capacity for the change of a state—I mean the subject—this continuity is then dependent on a movement and a movable—I mean on a change and a changeable thing. But that for which it is possible to continue and not be interrupted is circular position.

This continuity is susceptible to measurement, for a before may be further and a before may be closer. It is, therefore, a quantity that measures change. This is the

1. That is, of being necessary through another.

time which is the quantity of movement, not under the aspect of distance, but under the aspect of priority and posteriority that do not exist.

Chapter 6. Remark

Whatever begins to exist must have had possible existence before existing. Thus the possibility of its existence is realized. This possibility is not the capacity of that which has power over existing; otherwise, if it were said about the impossible that one has no power over it because it is not possible in itself, it would have been said that one has no power over it because one has no power over it, or that it is not possible in itself because it is not possible in itself. It is clear, therefore, that this possibility is other than the fact that that which has power over existing has power over existing.

Nothing intelligible in itself has its existence outside a subject. Rather, it is relative and, thus, in need of a subject. Hence that which begins to exist is preceded by a power to exist and by a subject.

Chapter 7. Admonition

A thing may be posterior to another in many ways, such as the posteriority of time and that of space. Now we do not need to consider in the group of posterior things anything except that which is required by existence, even though it is not impossible that it be in time simultaneous with that which is prior to it in existence. This happens when the existence of a thing is from another, and the existence of that other is not from it. The former does not merit existence except after the latter has already realized actual existence. The former does not mediate in existence between the latter and another thing; rather, existence comes to the latter not from the former. Existence does not reach the former except after having already reached the latter. This is exemplified by your saying: 'I moved my hand, thus the key moved' or 'following that, the key moved.' You do not say: 'The key moved, thus my hand moved' or 'following that, my hand moved.' This is in spite of the fact that both things moved simultaneously in time. This posteriority is with respect to the essence.

You also know that the state of a thing, that belongs to that thing according to that thing's essence and not according to anything else, is essentially prior to the state of that thing that is derived from something other than that thing itself. Whatever exists due to something other than itself merits nonexistence if isolated, or existence does not belong to it if isolated. Rather, existence belongs to it only owing to something else. Therefore, it has no existence before it has existence. This is the essential beginning of existence.

Chapter 8. Admonition

The existence of the effect depends on the cause, inasmuch as the cause is in a state by virtue of which it is a cause, such as the state of nature, volition, or some further thing that must be one of the external things that take part in the completion of the cause as an actual cause. Such things are exemplified by (1) the instrument, as in the carpenter's need for the hammer; (2) the matter, as in the carpenter's need for wood; (3) the assistant, as in the sawyer's need for another sawyer; (4) the time, as in a human being's need for the summer; (5) the motive, as in the eater's need for hunger; or (6) the removal of an obstacle, as in the washer's need for the removal of heavy rain.

The nonexistence of the effect depends on the nonexistence of the cause in a state by virtue of which it is an actual cause, whether the cause itself exists not in that state or whether it does not exist at all. If there is no external impediment, and if the agent itself exists, yet without being a cause by essence, the existence of the effect will depend on the existence of the above-mentioned state. Thus if such a state exists, whether as a nature, as a decisive volition, or as something else, the existence of the effect is made necessary. If, on the other hand, such a state does not exist, the nonexistence of the effect is made necessary. If the existence or nonexistence of such a state is assumed to be forever, that which corresponds to it will also be forever. If it is assumed to be for some time, that which corresponds to it will also be for some time. If it is permissible that a thing has a uniform state eternally,[1] and it has an effect, it is not far-fetched[2] that this effect will necessarily follow from it eternally. Therefore, if this is not called 'an effect' because it is not preceded by nonexistence, there is no problem of naming since its meaning has become clear.

Chapter 9. Admonition

Immediate creation (*al-ibdāʿ*) is a thing's giving existence to another that depends on nothing other than it—without the mediation of matter, instrument, or time. That which is preceded by temporal nonexistence, on the other hand, cannot dispense with an intermediary. Immediate creation is a nobler rank than material production (*al-takwīn*) and temporal production (*al-iḥdāth*).

Chapter 10. Admonition and Remark

It is evident to the first intellect that the tipping of balance of one of the two extremities of the possibility of anything[3] that had not existed and then existed became preferred over the other extremity owing to a certain thing or a cause, even though

1. Text: *fī kull-i shay'* (in everything), that is, in every case.
2. Text: *lam yabʿud*; but a stronger claim must be made here. It is not only not far-fetched but also necessary.
3. That is, the possibility of existence and the possibility of nonexistence.

it may be possible for the human mind not to pay attention to this evidence and to resort to other kinds of proof. This tipping of balance and appropriation owing to that thing occurs either after being already necessitated by the cause, or without yet being necessitated, but made by the cause in the realm of possibility, since in no way is this tipping of balance prevented from being produced by a cause. Thus we return to the original state of seeking the cause of the tipping of balance once again, and to this, there will be no succession. Therefore, the truth is that the tipping of balance is necessitated by the cause.

Chapter 11. Admonition

The comprehension of a certain cause inasmuch as (a) necessarily follows from it is other than the comprehension of a certain cause inasmuch as (b) necessarily follows from it. If that which is one necessarily produces two things, this is in virtue of two aspects different in comprehension and in reality. These two aspects are either among the constituents of that which is one, its necessary concomitants, or its individuating elements.[1] If these two aspects are assumed to be among the necessary concomitants of that which is one, once again the search goes back to the original case. Thus, you are led to two different aspects among the constituents of the cause, owing either to its quiddity, or to its existence, or to its individuating elements. Therefore, every being that necessarily produces two things simultaneously of which neither is mediated by the other has a divisible reality.

Chapter 12. Delusions and Admonition

A group of people said that this sensible thing exists by its essence and is necessary by itself. But if you recall what was mentioned to you concerning the condition for that which is necessary in existence, you will not find this sensible thing necessary and will recite the saying of God, the exalted: 'I do not love those things that disappear.'[2]

For that which is at the bottom of the realm of possibility is a certain kind of disappearing.

Others said: 'Rather, this sensible existent is caused.' Then they differed among themselves. Some of them claimed that its principal element and matter are not caused, but its makeup (*ṣunʿatah*) is caused. Thus this group posits two necessary beings in existence. You are well aware, however, of the impossibility of that.

Others of them attributed the necessity of existence to two contraries or to a number of things, and considered everything else as derived from that. This group is of the same judgment as those before them.

---

1. *Bi'l-tafrīq*, literally, by separation.
2. Qur'ān, 6:76.

Others agreed that that whose existence is necessary is one; then they differed among themselves. A group of them said that it continued without the existence of anything resulting from it. Then it began to desire the existence of something from it. Were it not for this, the renewed states of various types would have had an infinite past, but they exist in actuality. This is because every one of them exists, therefore, all of them exist. Thus, a totality limited in existence belongs to an infinity of succeeding things.

They say, but that is impossible. If there is a totality that limits its parts together, it falls under the same judgment. How could one of these states be described as not existing except after that which is infinite, such that it becomes dependent on the passage of that which is infinite and, thus, that which is infinite becomes interrupted at it? Following that, every time this state is renewed, the number of those states is increased. But how could the number of that which is infinite be increased?

Of this group, there are those who said that the world exists since it is better by existing. Others of them said that the existence of the world is impossible except at the time it exists. Still others of them said that the existence of the world does not depend on a time or on any other thing, but on the agent. However, they do not inquire about the reason for acting or not acting. Thus this group is the same as that group. Opposite to these, there is a group that asserts the unity of the First. They say that all the primary attributes and states of that whose existence is necessary through itself also have necessary existence, and that in pure nonexistence, no state can be distinguished in which it is more appropriate for the First not to bring into existence anything, or for things not to be primarily produced by the First, or an opposite state.

Furthermore, it is not permissible that a renewed volition arises except due to a motive, nor that it arises carelessly. Similarly, it is not permissible that a nature or that something else arises without the renewal of a state of the agent. How would a volition arise due to a renewed state, when the state of that which is renewed is the same as that which prepares the renewal for it—the latter being renewed? If there is no renewal, the state of that for which there is no renewal will be one and the same state that continues in the same manner—whether you consider the renewal as belonging to something present or to something that has already been removed. This is exemplified by the beauty of the action whenever present, or at a determined time, or in some other manner that has already been enumerated, or by the ugliness that had belonged to the action or had been removed, or an obstacle or something else that was but was removed.

They say that if the motive which hinders that whose existence is necessary from flowing into goodness and excellence is that the effect is preceded by nonexistence, then this motive is weak. Its weakness has already been revealed to the just minded since it subsists in every state, and is not more deserving of the affirmation of priority in one state than in another.

Regarding the effect as having possible existence in itself and necessary existence through another, this does not contradict its having permanent existence through another, as you have already been told.

As for that which is infinite being an existing totality due to the fact that every one has existence at a certain time, this is a false opinion, for if a judgment is true of every one, it is not necessarily true of the realized totality; otherwise, it would be proper to say that it is possible for an infinite totality to enter into existence because it is possible for every part of it to enter into existence. Thus possibility would be predicated of the totality as it is predicated of every one of the totality.

They say that the infinite states they have mentioned do not cease to be nonexistent, do not come into existence except one thing after another, and the nonexistent infinite may involve more or less without this causing a breach in the states that are infinite in nonexistence.

Regarding the dependency of one of these states on having prior to it that which is infinite, or the need of some of these states for having that which is infinite interrupted at reaching it, this is a false view; for the meaning of our statement: 'Such and such depends on such and such' is that the two things together are described as nonexistent, and the existence of the second cannot be except after the existence of the first nonexistent.

The same is true of need. Furthermore, it is never true to say at any one time that the latter depends on the existence of that which is infinite or has need for that which is infinite to reach it. Rather, if you suppose any time, you will find between it and a later one finite things.

Thus, at all times, such is its attribute, especially as the totality is present to you, and every part of it is one.

If by this dependency you mean that this thing does not exist except after the existence of things—every one of which being at a different time—then it is not possible to count the number of such things. This is absurd, for this is the same thing under dispute, namely, whether or not it is possible. How then could it be a premise in the refutation of it? Is it by changing the expression in a way that does not change the meaning?

Therefore, the consideration of what we have pointed out requires that the Artisan, the Necessary in existence does not have different relations to the diverse times and things that derive their existence primarily from it, and to the essential consequence of this consideration except as necessarily resulting from a diversity followed by change.

These are the doctrines. Choose among them in accordance with your intellect and not your passion after having posited that the Necessary in existence is one.

ON THEODICY AND PROVIDENCE (I)
From *al-Shifā'* (The Healing)

Translated for this volume by Shams Inati from Ibn Sīnā, *al-Shifā', al-Ilāhiyyāt*, II (hereafter *Ilāhiyyāt*, II), ed. G. C. Anawati and S. Zāyid (Cairo, 1960), pp. 414–422.

Metaphysics: Ninth Treatise
On Providence: Showing the Manner[1] of the Entry of Evil in Divine Predetermination

Having reached this point, it is appropriate for us to assert the view[2] concerning Providence.

No doubt, it had become clear to you from what was shown by us that it is impossible for the exalted causes to do what they do for our own sake or to be in general (p. 415) concerned about anything, motivated by a motive and subject to the occurrence of any preference. [In spite of this], there is no way for you to deny the amazing marks of the formation of the world, the parts of the heavens, and the parts of the animals and plants which do not come about accidentally, but require a certain governance.

Thus it must be known that Providence (*al-'ināyah*) is (1) the knowledge the First has in Himself [of the manner of arranging] existence (*al-wujūd*) according to the good (*al-khayr*),[3] (2) the fact that He is in Himself a cause of goodness and perfection (*al-kamāl*)[4] in as much as that is possible, and (3) the fact that He is satisfied with the order [of the good) in the way previously mentioned, He thus thinks the best possible order of the good, and hence what He thinks emanates from Him as the best order and good which He thinks—an emanation that most completely leads to [that] order in as much as that is possible. This, therefore, is the meaning of Providence.

---

1. *Manner: The Arabic text has it as *wa-kayfiyyāt* (and the manner).
2. Text: *al-qawl* literally, the saying.
3. The good is the desirable; the better, the more desirable (Ibn Sīnā, *al-Shifā', al-Manṭiq*, ed. A. F. al-Ahwānī (Cairo, 1965), p. 158. The true good is that which is desired for its own sake (ibid., p. 136). Pleasure is the good; this is to say that the more pleasurable, the better (ibid., p. 138). Good and evil are contraries (ibid., p. 223). The good is relative (Ibn Sīnā, *al-Ishārāt wa'l-tanbīhāt*, vol. 4, bk. 8, ch. 3).
4. 'The perfection of a thing is the good in relation to that thing, and which that thing has the capacity to attain.' (ibid.).

You must know that evil (*al-sharr*)[1] is said to be of [various] types: Thus, (1) 'evil' is said of what is deficiency (*al-naqṣ*), such as ignorance (*al-jahl*), weakness (*al-ḍa'f*) and deformity (*al-tashwīh*) in the natural constitution;[2] and (2) 'evil' is said of what is like pain (*al-alam*)[3] or grief (*al-ghamm*)[4] which is a certain realization (*idrāk*) that has a cause, and not only the loss of a cause.[5]

The cause that negates the good, that stands in the way of the good, and that requires its destruction may be: (A) something distant [from], and unapprehended by the harmed thing, such as the clouds when they cast their shade, preventing thereby the sun's rising on what needs to perfect itself by the sun. If this needy

1. Evil is relative (*al-Shifā', al-Manṭiq*, pp. 136–137). A being is evil not by virtue of the potentiality for evil in it, but by virtue of the actuality for evil in it. (ibid., p. 187).

2. *Ilāhiyyāt* II reads *fayuqāl sharr limithl al-naqṣ al-ladhī huwa'l-jahl wa'l-ḍa'f wa'l-tashwīh fi'l-khilqa*: evil is said of what is like deficiency, which is ignorance, weakness and deformity in the natural constitution. But I prefer the phrasing of this sentence as translated above and which appears in *al-Najāh*, p. 284. The reason for this is that this first type of evil is not *like* deficiency—it is deficiency; and 'such as' is a more appropriate term than 'which is' since there are other types of deficiency which to Ibn Sīnā are evil.

3. Pain is defined by Ibn Sīnā as: 'a being's realization and reception of what is defective and evil from the perspective of that being' (*al-Ishārāt wa'l-tanbīhāt*, vol. 4, bk. 8, ch. 3). This is to say that even if the cause of pain, i.e. the defective and evil, is present, but without the being's ability to realize its presence, there would be no pain. For example, there is no pain in the following two cases: (1) In the case of being close to death, since the power of realizing the defective and evil is weakened; (2) in the case of being sedated, for this power is hampered (ibid., ch. 7).

4. 'Grief is not the same as anger and cannot be predicated of it. Rather, it is prior to and necessitates the presence of anger' (*al-Shifā'*, pp. 184, 200). 'Anger is a consequence of pain [or] grief. Anger belongs to the sensitive faculty, and grief belongs to the appetitive and the rational faculties' (ibid., p. 185).

5. As is the case with the first type of evil, i.e., deficiency. Since only being or that which exists can have a cause, and since deficiency does not exist, for it is nothing in being, it follows that deficiency cannot have a cause. Evils such as pain and grief, on the other hand, do exist, and because of that they can and must have a cause.

It must be mentioned that one can also read this sentence as 'and (2) "evil" is said of what is like pain and grief which is a *certain realization of what has a* cause ... '. But since the emphasis here is on the contrast between the idea that the first type of evil has no cause, and the idea that the second type does, and since the second type of evil is something like pain and grief and not what is realized by them, the above translation seems more appropriate.

Let me finally point out a difficulty with the term *'idrāk* (realization). This term has several meanings, two of which are: (1) awareness or apprehension and (2) attainment of a certain reality or an actualization. Thus, the statements including *'idrāk* are not always free from ambiguity. Where what is intended by this term is clear, I have substituted for it a term that does not suffer from the same difficulty, and which makes the meaning more accessible to the reader. Where it is, for example, used in the sense of 'awareness' or 'apprehension', 'apprehension' has been used; where it is used in the sense of 'attainment of a certain reality' or 'an actualization', the meaning is conveyed in various terms depending upon the context—but in all cases *'idrāk* or any of its variants are parenthesized next to the translation. Where, on the other hand, it is not fully clear in what sense *'idrāk* is intended, 'realization' is kept, in order that the reader be made aware of the ambiguity. Since 'realization' is also used in the sense of *ḥuṣūl* (coming into being), the Arabic term expressed by 'realization' is consistently parenthesized next to it.

thing were capable of apprehension, it would apprehend that it is not benefiting; and in as much as it apprehends that, it does not apprehend that the clouds have stood in the way [of its benefiting], [although] it sees [the clouds].[1] [However], it is not because it sees [the clouds] that it is injured (*muta'adhdhīan*), harmed (*mutaḍarraran*) or made deficient by [them], but because it is something else.[2] Or (B) it may be continuous [with], and apprehended by, the one who suffers (*mudrik*) from the lack of health, such as someone who suffers from the loss of connection [with a power in] an organ due to the scorching heat. In as much as one apprehends the loss of the connection with a power in that organ itself, one also apprehends the injurious heat. Thus there result two apprehensions: an apprehension in the manner previously [mentioned] of our apprehending the nonexistent things, and an apprehension in the manner previously [mentioned] of our apprehending existing things.[3]

The apprehended existing thing is not evil (p. 416) in itself, but [only] in relation to the [harmed] thing. As for the lack of perfection and health [of the harmed thing] it is not evil only[4] in relation to [the harmed thing]—so that it would have a presence by virtue of which it is not an evil—rather its very presence is nothing but an evil in it, and in the manner of being evil.[5] Thus, blindness cannot be except in the eye; and inasmuch as it is in the eye, it cannot but be evil, with no aspect to it by virtue of which it would be other than evil. As for heat, for example, if it becomes evil in relation to the one who suffers from it, [also] it has another aspect by virtue of which it is not evil.

Thus, essential evil (*al-sharr bi'l-dhāt*) is privation (*al-ʿadam*),[6] but not just any

1. *Bal min ḥaythu huwa mubṣir* (but inasmuch as it is seeing). This is a curious phrase by which, I think, is meant that while a being who is capable of awareness, such as a man, can be aware of the fact that he sees a far away thing such as the clouds that have intervened between him and the sun, he is not, in as much as he is aware of that, also aware that such clouds act as a cause of evil by depriving him of the sunlight which he needs.

But the question is, why could not such a being also be aware that such clouds are doing so? It seems that all that is required in order for him to be aware of that is the knowledge that he needs the sunlight and that if the clouds stand between him and the sun, then they must harm him by preventing the sunlight from reaching him, a knowledge which is not only not impossible, but seems to be quite common. Ibn Sīnā's claim may be true only in the case of a being who is capable of awareness but incapable of such knowledge, but certainly not of every being who is capable of awareness. It is possible, for example, that a bird may see the clouds and be aware of his seeing them, without at the same time being aware that such clouds harm him.

2. That is, a being whose perfection may be impeded by an external cause such as the clouds when they intervene between it and the sun's shining on it.

3. *Al-umūr al-wujūdiyyah* literally, existential matters.

4. The sentence in *Ilāhiyyāt* II reads 'it is not evil in relation to [the harmed thing] only'. But it is the relation and not the harmed thing that Ibn Sīnā wants to qualify, as is clear from the remaining part of the sentence. Such a lack of perfection is an evil in relation to everything, and not only in relation to the harmed thing.

5. That is, of being a lack of what is normal or natural to a thing.

6. 'Privation is neither the absolute existence of being nor the absolute nonexistence of being.

[kind] of privation—rather it is privation that necessitates [removing from] the nature (*ṭibāʿ*)[1] of a thing the perfections that are fixed for the species and nature (*ṭabīʿatih*) [of that thing]. Accidental evil (*al-sharr bi'l-ʿaraḍ*), on the other hand is the nonexistent, the destroyer[2] or that which withholds perfection from what deserves it.

There is no good about absolute privation, except about the utterance of it. [For this reason], [absolute privation] is not a realized (*ḥāṣil*) evil.[3] Were it to have a certain realization (*ḥusūl*), there would be general evil.[4] Thus the existence of anything is perfection at its highest and has nothing in potentiality; hence, evil does not follow [that existence]. For evil follows only that which has in its nature what is potential; and [potentiality] is due to matter.

Evil follows matter due to a primary thing that happens to it [from] itself[5] or to

---

Rather, it is the lack of the existence of potential being' (*al-Najāh*, p. 164; J. Saliba, *Dictionnaire philosophique*, vol. 2, p. 64). Complete deficiency is absolute privation (ibid.).

1. Plural of *ṭabʿ* which is whatever belongs to the species, be that active or passive. *Ṭabʿ* is a more general term than *ṭabīʿah* (A. Goichon, *Lexique de langue philosophique d'Ibn Sīnā* (Paris, 1939), p. 199, also translated in English as 'nature' but refers specifically to the primary source of motion and rest of a being (ibid., p. 201). 'Whatever belongs to a thing by *al-ṭabʿ* is preferable to what does not belong to a thing in the same manner' (*al-Shifāʾ*, *al-Manṭiq*, p. 155). 'It is a specific property of a human being, in contrast to a horse, to have two legs. Unless it can be said that this is natural (*ṭabʿ*) [for a human being] this cannot be realized [in a human being]. But not every human being has two legs in existence. However, if it can be said that a human being is such by nature (*ṭabʿ*), i.e., in human form, and if at the time of his birth, it happens that the proper matter is present, free from any defects, and not hampered by any external causes, then he has [in existence] this specific property, i.e., two legs' (ibid., p. 222).

2. Some manuscripts of *Ilāhiyyāt* II have it as *al-maʿdūm* (the nonexistent) only, while *al-Najāh*, p. 248, and at least one manuscript of *Ilāhiyyāt II*, have it as *al-muʿdim* (the destroyer).

3. In order for anything to be realized or to exist it must be a being and hence to some extent be good, for being and the good, according to Ibn Sīnā, are in reality one and the same.

4. This statement seems to contradict the one just stated in the last note, namely that which asserts that if anything were to exist at all, it must to some extent be good. This statement, on the other hand, declares that there is at least one thing in the world, i.e., absolute privation, which if it were to exist, there would be nothing good about it; instead, there would prevail general evil.

But lest it be thought that Ibn Sīnā is contradicting himself, it must be said that he is not unaware of the contradiction between these two statements. The point he wants to make is that these two statements are both true of absolute privation, but because they are contradictory, absolute privation cannot be a real thing. In other words, his claim is that because in order for absolute privation to exist it must totally negate the good (i.e., go contrary to the natural and the real), and because at the same time in order for it to exist it must to some extent be good, absolute privation cannot exist; the notion of its existence is self-contradictory.

5. Literally, in itself. The reason for my translation is the fact that what, I think, Ibn Sīnā is trying to do here is to offer an enumeration and a discussion of the sources of evil which, according to him, happen to be two: matter and agents external to matter. In speaking of evil as due to the former type of source, it is more appropriate, therefore, to say that evil is due to what occurs *from* matter. To describe it as due to what occurs *in* matter, on the other hand does not say anything about its source, for it could be due to what occurs in matter, and still have as its source some external source or sources. Ibn Sīnā, I believe, preferred to use 'in' instead of something like 'from' in order not to give the impression to the reader that matter as a source of evil functions as an agent. But 'in' by itself leaves unsaid the very important point that he means to make, namely, that matter is the source of

an unforeseen [external] thing that happens to it later on. As for the thing [from] itself [this happens] when some external causes of evil occur to a certain matter at the beginning of its existence, such that they take hold of it in such a way that it impedes the special preparedness [of that matter for] the perfection which was stricken by a counter-balancing evil. An example of this is the matter from which a human being or a horse is formed. If unforeseen causes occur to it which make it worse in composition and more resistant in substance, it becomes unreceptive of designing, shaping and reforming. [If this happens], its natural constitution becomes then deformed, and what is required of the perfection of [its] composition and constitution is [then] not found—not because the agent deprived [the matter of the proper form] but because the receptive element did not accept [it].

As for the unforeseen thing that happens to [matter] from without, it is one of two things: either (A) something that stands in the way of, obstructs and makes distant the perfective, or (B) something that opposes [comes] in contact [with], and destroys the perfected (p. 417). An example of the first is the occurrence and accumulation of many clouds, and the shading of high mountains, [all of which] prevent the sun's influence from reaching the fruits which need to perfect themselves [by the sunlight].[1] And an example of the second is the cold's closing in upon plants that are approaching their perfection at the proper time so that [their] special preparedness [the perfection] and what follows it are corrupted.

All causes[2] of evil are only found in the sublunary world. And the whole of the sublunary world is small in relation to the rest of existence, as you have learned.

Furthermore, evil only strikes individuals, and at certain times. The species, [on the other hand], are preserved. Except for one kind of evil [the accidental one] real evil does not extend to a majority of individuals.[3]

You must [also] know that evil in the sense of privation is evil either (A) with respect to a necessary thing, or (B) [with respect to] a beneficial thing close to being

---

evil. As long as it is understood that matter is a source of evil, not in as much as it acts, but only in as much as it does not accept its proper form, then there is no harm in using '*from*'.

1. I am substituting *ikmāl*' (to perfect) for *kamāl*' (perfection).

2. I am substituting *asbāb* (causes) for *sabab* (cause). First, because *jamī*ʿ (all) cannot be said of any one thing—in this case any one cause; second, because we know that even if *jamī*ʿ can be used with *sabab*, the statement would still not express Ibn Sīnā's view, according to which there are many causes of evil in the sublunary world. The earthquake that kills thousands of people, the fire that burns a man's arm, the cold that corrupts plants, etc. are all different causes of evil.

3. There is a problem with this sentence as it stands in *Ilāhiyyāt II* where it reads, *wa laysa al-sharr al-ḥaqīqī yaʿumm akthar al-ashkhāṣ, illā nawʿan min al-sharr* (real evil does not extend to the majority of individuals, except for one kind of evil). 'One kind' is in the accusative, which means it is to be understood as the object of 'extend'. But real evil, the subject of the sentence, cannot be said to extend to evil no matter what kind the latter is. Thus, 'one kind' cannot be the object of 'extend'. The sentence as found in *Ilāhiyyāt* II is acceptable, but only if *naw*ʿ (one kind) is read in the nominative; for if it is so read, it would state that real evil does not affect the majority of individuals, but that there is a kind of evil, (i.e., the accidental one) that does so, and such a statement is in accordance with Ibn Sīnā's view.

necessary, or (C) it is evil not with respect to that, but with respect to something which is possible in a minority of individuals.

Were [what is possible in a minority of individuals] to exist, it would be among the additional perfections that [come] after the secondary perfections, and it would not be required by the nature [of the individual] in [which] the possible is found[1]. This division is other than the one with which we are concerned—it is the one we have excluded. [In addition to] this, [the privation of such an additional good] is not evil with respect to the species but with respect to a consideration additional to what is necessary for the species. An example of [such privation] is ignorance of philosophy, geometry, and the like. That is not an evil with respect to our being human beings, but with respect to the prevailing of the perfection that is most befitting.[2] You shall know that in reality it is evil only if [its contrary, i.e., knowledge of philosophy, geometry, or the like for example], is required by a particular human being, or his particular soul. An individual requires it not because he is a human being or a soul but only because the goodness of that which is missing has been confirmed to him, [such that] he desires it, and becomes fully prepared for it, as we shall explain to you later.

Prior to [the confirmation of the goodness of that which is missing, that goodness] is not among [those things] toward which a thing is moved to preserve the nature of the species, [as in the case of] being moved toward the secondary perfections which come after the primary perfection[s]. If [this goodness] did not exist, there would be privation of a thing not required[3] by the nature [of a being].

---

1. *Wa la muqtaḍan lahū min ṭibāʿ al-mumkin huwa fīhi*, literally, it is not required by the nature of the possible in it. But knowledge of geometry which, for example, is such an additional good *is* required by the nature of the possibility for such knowledge; yet it is not required by the nature of the individuals that have such possibility. The nature of such individuals is the same as the nature of any other human being which does not include in its definition knowledge of geometry. This is the reason for my translation. I believe that the literal form of the sentence leaves out some terms needed to help understand Ibn Sīnā's point; without these terms, the statement would not be in accordance with Ibn Sīnā's view. For it would be stating that something like knowledge of geometry is not required by the possibility found in some individuals for such knowledge. But it is precisely the possibility for such knowledge that does require such knowledge or good. The natures of the individuals themselves, (i.e., their being human beings) on the other hand, do not require that kind of knowledge.

2. The text reads: *kamāl al-iṣlāh* (the perfection of reform). But this sentence in *al-Najāh* (p. 288) seems to make more sense. It reads: *kamāl al-aṣlaḥ* (the perfection that is most befitting).

3. *Fī amr mā yuqtaḍā* (of a thing not required) could also be understood as 'of something required'. This is so because *ma* can be used in various senses. Among these senses are 'not' and 'some'. If *mā* is intended here in the sense of 'not', then the translation given above is satisfactory. If, on the other hand, it is intended in the sense of 'some', then the statement is about primary perfection and not the additional type of goodness with which we are now involved; for according to Ibn Sīnā, it is the primary perfection and not the additional one that is essential to and hence required by the nature of a thing. If we were to read *mā* here as 'some' instead of 'not' the sentence, then must be translated as: 'If [this primary perfection] did not exist, there would be a privation of something required by the nature [of a being].' Both interpretations of this sentence fit in well

Thus evil in particular existing things, is slight (p. 418). Yet, in spite of that, the presence of evil in things is a necessity consequent upon the need for the good. Were [the][1] elements not to oppose one another and be acted upon by the dominant [element among them], these noble kinds would not have arisen from them. If among these [elements] fire, [for example], were not such that, if the clashes occurring in the course of the whole led by necessity to the meeting of a noble man's garment, [that garment] necessarily burns, then fire would not be [something] from which general benefit could be derived.

Hence, it is required by necessity that the good possible in these things be a good only after [it is possible for] such an evil to occur from and with [such a good].

Thus, the emanation of the good does not require the exclusion of the dominant good [in order to avoid] a rare evil. For excluding [that good] is more evil than that [rare] evil. This is so because the privation of that whose existence in the nature of matter is possible is a greater evil than one privation [alone] since it consists of two privations.[2] It is because of this that the rational [person] prefers being burned

---

with Ibn Sīnā's scheme. But I tend to think that *mā* is here intended in the sense of 'not', and not in the sense of 'some', for the reason that the discussion at this point centres around the additional type of goodness rather than primary perfection.

1. Text: *hādhihī* (these).

2. *Idhā kāna 'adamān* (if it was two privations). On this phrase I have three comments to make:

(1) Ibn Sīnā makes the statement that the dominant good must not be excluded from the world, for if it were, that would create more evil than the evil already existing in the world as a result of this good. Then he goes on to give the reason for this: 'the privation of that whose existence in the nature of matter is possible is a greater evil than one privation [alone], *if* it consists of two privations.' (For an explanation of the nature of these two privations, see ch. 5, p. 3.) But in order for this to count as a reason at all, one of two things must be done: either *idhā* (if) must be replaced by *idh* (since); or an additional statement such as 'and the exclusion of the dominant good consists of two privations' must be supplied. Otherwise, even if we accept the claim that what consists of two privations is a greater evil than what consists of one privation only, there would be no reason for us to accept the claim that the exclusion of the dominant good is a greater evil than the rare evil resulting from that good. For after all nothing has been said about the fact that the exclusion of such a dominant good consists of two privations. Since an emendation must therefore be made, I prefer to read *idh* for *idhā*. The reason is this: since *idhā* is quite similar in form to *idh*—the only difference between them is an *a* at the end of *idhā*—mistaking one for the other is not too difficult; and since supplying a whole statement is a large emendation which can be taken care of by a smaller and simpler one, *idh* is therefore the more suitable emendation.

(2) 'Two privations', which is the predicate of *kāna* (was), must be in the accusative and not in the nominative, as it is in the text. This comment concerns the Arabic text and has no bearing on the English translation, especially since *kāna* is rendered in this translation as 'consists of'.

(3) Finally, it must be mentioned that three manuscripts have *'adaman* (privation) instead of *'adamān* (two privations) (p. 418). But I think that editors of the edition in hand are correct in choosing *'adamān* which, it must be mentioned, is also the term used in *al-Najāh*: for it makes no sense to say that the exclusion of something 'is a greater evil than one privation [alone] since it consists of privation [i.e., one privation]'.

by fire on condition he escapes from it alive, to death without pain.[1] Thus, if such a good were left out [of existence], that would be an evil over and above this evil which [comes about due to this good].

It lies within the requirement of the Intellect that knows the arrangement necessary in the order of the good to think the merit of such a mode of things as existing—allowing necessary evil that occurs with it. It is necessary, therefore, that the existence of [such a mode of things] emanate.

If someone says, 'It was possible for the First Governor to bring into existence absolute good, free from evil', we say that this was not possible in a mode of existence such as this, even though it was possible in absolute existence, since that mode of absolute existence free [from evil] is other than this one. [The mode of absolute existence] is a part of what emanated from the First Governor and came to exist in intellectual, psychical, and celestial things. [As for] this mode [of existence], it remained in possibility; and refraining from bringing it into existence was not due to the evil that may be mixed with it. If the principle [of this evil] had not [come] to exist in the first place, and had been left out [of existence]—lest this evil come about—that would have been an evil greater than that [resulting from] the presence of [the principle of this evil].[2] Thus, the presence of [such a principle] is the better of the two evils.

Also, it was not necessary not to bring into existence the good causes which [come] before the causes which lead accidentally to evil. For the existence of those [good causes] renders consequential [on it] the existence of these [causes that lead accidentally to evil; such that if the causes leading to evil did not exist, the good causes must also not exist.[3] But if [that happened], there would have been in [the world] the greatest fault in the universal order of the good.

But if we do not pay attention to that [fact], and limit our attention (p. 419) to what the possible inexistence divides into by way of types of existence that differ in their states, then [we see that] the existence which is free from evil had already been realized (*ḥaṣala*), and what remained [to be realized] was a mode of existence which is only in this way [i.e., not free from evil] and whose nonexistence is a greater evil than its existence. Because of that, its existence must necessarily emanate in as much as the most befitting existence emanates from Him, in the manner that has already been stated.

To begin with, we say that evil is spoken of in [many] ways: thus, (1) 'evil' is said

---

1. The idea is that while the former involves one privation, the latter involves two privations. The latter, hence, is a greater evil than the former even though it involves no pain.

2. 'The principle of this evil' seems to refer to this mode of existence without which there would not be the evil there is in the world, but without which there would be a greater evil than the one that is now present in the world.

3. The existence of the good causes serves as a sufficient condition for the existence of those causes that lead accidentally to evil. That is why, if the existence of the latter is denied, the existence of the former must also be denied.

of blameworthy acts; (2) 'evil' is said of the principles of character [behind those acts]; (3) 'evil' is said of pains, griefs, and the like; and (4) 'evil' is said of each thing's falling short of its perfection, and its loss of what belongs to it.

Even though the essences of pains and griefs are positive and not privative, it is as if privation and deficiency follow from them. Also, evil in acts exists only in relation to the one who loses perfection by the reaching of [evil] to that person's [evil] such as wronging (*al-ẓulm*),[1] or in relation to the perfection one loses which is required by religious policy, [evil] such as adultery. Similarly, principles of character are only evil by virtue of the proceeding of these [evils] from them—[such principles of character] are compared to the soul which is deprived of perfections that belong to it.

You find nothing among the acts that are called evil that is not a perfection in relation to its cause which enacts it. Rather it is only evil in relation to the cause [which is] receptive of it, or in relation to another agent prevented [by that act] from acting in that matter to which [this agent] has more right than that act. Thus, wronging proceeds, for example, from a power that seeks domination (*al-ghalabah*), i.e., the spirited power whose perfection is domination. For this reason, it was created to be spirited. This is to say that it was created to be directed toward domination, seeking it and rejoicing in it. Therefore, [domination] in relation to it is a good for it, [but] if it weakens from [exercising domination], in relation to it, [domination then] becomes an evil for it. [This power] is evil only with respect to the one suffering wronging or with respect to the rational soul whose perfection is to override it and control it. If [the rational soul] is unable to do this, (p. 420) this then would be an evil for it. The same is true of the cause enacting pains and burning, such as fire; if it burns, for example, burning is its perfection yet, [burning] is evil in relation to the one who has been deprived of health by it—due to the loss of what one has lost.

As for the evil whose principle[2] is the deficiency and shortcoming that occur in the natural constitution [of things, i.e., the evil] which is not enacted by an agent, but [comes about] because the agent does not enact [something][3] [this kind of evil] is in fact not good in relation to anything.

Regarding evils which attach to things that are goods, those are due to two causes: (1) matter[4] [in] that it is receptive of form and privation; and (2) the agent[5] [in] that material things necessarily come into being through it—it being

1. Ibn Sīnā defines wronging as 'intentional harming' (*al-Shifāʾ, al-Manṭiq*, p. 110).

2. *Al-ladhī sababuhū* (whose cause). Since the deficiency cannot be the cause of anything for only a being, according to Ibn Sīnā, can be a cause, the deficiency, on the other hand, is a nonbeing, and since the type of evil spoken of here is also a deficiency which, according to Ibn Sīnā, means it cannot have a cause—'cause' must here be read 'principle'.

3. If an agent were to enact something; there would have been an aspect of that thing by virtue of which it is good, i.e., good with respect to that agent. But since the kind of evil under consideration is not the result of an action of any agent, rather the result of an absence of such an action, it is evil in all respects.

4. Literally, a cause from the side of matter.

5. Literally, a cause from the side of the agent.

impossible for matter to have the type of existence[1] which enjoys the richness of matter and performs the action of matter except if [such matter][2] were receptive of form and privation—it being impossible for it not to be receptive of contraries. It is impossible for the active powers to have acts that are contrary to other acts whose existence has been realized (*ḥaṣala*) without having [such powers) perform such [acts]. For it is impossible to create the purpose intended from fire, [if fire] does not burn, [since] the whole is completed only by having in it that which is burned and that which is warmed, and by having that which burns and that which warms. It follows necessarily that the beneficial purpose of the existence of these, [types of things] have consequences that are defects and which accidentally occur from burning and from being burned. An example of this is the fire's burning of a hermit's organ. However, what [happens] in general, and what is also permanent is the realization (*ḥusūl*) of the good intended in nature. [What happens) in general is that the majority of individuals of a species are in safety from being burned; and what is permanent is due [to the fact that] many species are not preserved permanently except through the existence of [something] like fire in as much as it burns. And including what proceeds from fire, there is little harm that proceeds from it. This is also the case with all those causes that resemble [fire].

Thus, it would not have been good to leave out [of existence] the predominant and the permanent benefits [in order to avoid] evil accidentals[3] which are less than [good].

The goods that exist due to these things have been willed, therefore, by a primary will in the manner where it is proper to say: God, exalted, wills things; evil was also [so to speak] willed (p. 421) in an accidental manner—Since [He] knows it is necessary He minds it not. Thus, the good is required essentially; the evil is required accidentally; and each is predestined.

It is also the case that matter has been known to be incapable of [certain] things, and that in [certain ways] perfections fall short of [reaching] it; but the perfections

---

1. Texts: *wujūd al-wujūd* (the existence of existence) which does not make any sense. That is why it should perhaps be read as G. F. Hourani suggests, *wujūh al-wujūd*, which could be rendered 'the types of existence'.

2. *Ilā an yakūn* (except if [such an existence]) is changed here to 'except if [such matter]'. The reason for this change is that the statement as it is does not seem to fit in well with what Ibn Sīnā intends here. Existence to him is something that cannot be receptive of form and privation. Existence is an act, and as such it is complete; therefore, it is always at its highest perfection and can never be less or more than it is. In fact, to Ibn Sīnā the existence of a thing either is or is not. If it is, it is complete; if it is not, it is completely absent. Thus, the existence of matter, for example, stands in no need of anything to perfect it; it has neither a privation nor an ability to receive any form. What is receptive of form and privation, on the other hand, is matter and not its existence. *An yakūn qābilan li'l-ṣūrat wa'l-'adam* (were receptive of form and privation) indicates reference to a masculine noun which in this sentence must be 'existence'. It must be read *an takūn qābilatan li'l-ṣūrat wa'l-'adam* which would indicate reference to a feminine noun, 'matter' in this case.

3. Text: *li-aghrāḍ sharriyyah* (evil objectives). I have substituted *a'rāḍ* (accidentals) for *aghrāḍ*.

that it enjoys are by far more numerous than those that fall short of [reaching] it. If this is so, it is not of divine wisdom, therefore, that the superior, permanent, and predominant goods be left out [of existence in order to avoid] evils in individual matters which are nonpermanent.

Rather, we say that things in imagination are, if imagined as existing, either: (a) things which cannot but be absolutely evil,[1] (b) things whose existence is good—it being impossible for them to be evil and deficient, (c) things in which goodness predominates, if their existence comes about—anything other than this is impossible for their nature, (d) things in which evilness predominates, or (e) things in which the two states [goodness and evilness] are equal.

As for that in which there is no 'evilness', it exists in the nature [of things]. Regarding that which is completely evil, or that [in which evil] predominates, or also that [in which evil] equals [the good, these] do not exist. However, that in whose existence the good predominates it is more suitable that it exists—if what is predominant in it is its being good.

If it were [asked]: 'Why is evilness primarily not prevented from [being present in the last type of things just mentioned] so that it would be all good?', [one would] then say: [These things] would not be themselves if it can be said [of them] that their existence is the existence which cannot be such that evil would not occur from them. Thus, if they were made such that evil would not occur from them, their existence would not be the existence that belongs to them; instead, it would be the existence of other things that exist which are other than they and which are realized—I mean, what has been created such that evil does not necessarily follow from it primarily. An example of this [is the following]:

If the existence of fire consists in its burning something, and the existence of that which burns something is [such] that if it touches the poor man's garment, it burns it; and

[if] the existence of the poor man's garment [is such] that it is receptive of burning; and

[if] the existence of each one of them [is such] that it is subject to the occurrence of diverse[2] motions; and

[if] the existence of the diverse motions in things (p. 422) that are thus described[3]

1. Text: *Inna'l-umūr fi'l-wahm immā umūr idhā tuwuhhimat mawjūdah, yumtana' an takūn illā sharran 'alā'l-iṭlāq* (Things in imagination are either: (a) things which if imagined as existing, cannot but be absolutely evil) ... But the first type of things discussed here is, as we will soon see, distinguished from the other four only in that it is absolutely evil. If one claims that imagining this first category as existing is essential to the discussion, since it does not really exist, the answer is that so do (d) and (e). Hence, imagining things as existing has either to cover at least (d) and (e) or not be mentioned at all.

2. Text: *Ḥarakat shay'* (the motions of a thing); *al-Najāh*, however reads: *Ḥarakat shatta* (diverse motions) which better suits this argument.

3. As being subject to the occurrence of diverse motions.

is an existence of what is subject to the occurrence of coming together; and

[if] the existence of coming together of the agent and the patient is by nature an existence which necessitates action and reaction;

then if what [comes] second[1] is not, then what [comes] first[2] is not;

therefore, the active and the receptive, the celestial and the terrestrial, the physical and the psychical powers have only been arranged in the whole in such a manner that they would lead to the universal order—with the impossibility of their being what they are without leading to evils.

Thus, the states of the world in relation to each other necessitate in some soul the occurrence of a form of bad opinion, unbelief, or another evil in soul or body such that if this were not so, the universal order would not be sustained.

[God], therefore minds not and pays no attention to the corrupt concomitants which occur by necessity. And it has been said [by Him]: 'I created these for fire, and I care not; and I created these for paradise, and I care not.' It has been [further] said [by Him]: 'Everything is made to move with ease in the direction for which it has been created.'

If someone said, 'Evil is not a rare or a minor thing, but is predominant', [we answer that]: This is not so; on the contrary, evil is numerous but not predominant. And there is a difference between the numerous and the predominant—there are many things such as diseases that are numerous, but not predominant. [It must be repeated that such things] are numerous, but not predominant.

If you reflect on this type of evil we are now discussing,[3] you would find it less than the good which is its contrary, and which is present in its matter, [let alone] in relation to the other eternal goods which are over and above [this good]. Indeed, evils that are deficiencies of secondary perfections are predominant, however those are not the evils that our discourse is about. Examples of such evils are ignorance of geometry and the missing of radiant beauty and the like. [These evils] do not harm the primary perfections or the perfections that come after the primary ones and which manifest their benefit. These evils are not due to the action of an agent, but to the inaction of the agent either because[4] the recipient is not ready [to receive the form imparted by the agent], or does not move toward [such] reception. These evils are the privation of goods that fall under the type of superabundance and excess.

1. That is, that which is a reaction or a consequence, such as being burned.
2. That is action such as burning something.
3. That is essential evil.
4. Text: *li-ajl* (for the sake of).

ON THEODICY AND PROVIDENCE (II)
From *al-Ishārāt wa'l-tanbīhāt* (Remarks and Admonitions)

Translated for this volume by Shams Inati from Ibn Sīnā, *al-Ishārāt wa'l-tanbīhāt*, ed. S. Dunyā (Cairo, 1957–1960), vol. 3, pp. 729–746.

Chapter 22

Providence is the First [Being's] knowledge of the whole, and of the necessary [character] which the whole must have, so that [it] would have the best order, and [of the fact] that [it] is necessarily derived from Him and from His knowledge of it. Thus the existent corresponds to the known [which is] in the best order—without a motivating intention or quest from the First [Being], the Truth.

Thus, the First [Being's] knowledge of the manner of the befitting arrangement of the existence of the whole is the source of the emanation of the good in the whole.

Chapter 23. Remarks

Things that are possible in existence include: (1) things whose existence can primarily be altogether free from evil, disorder (*al-khalal*), and corruption (*al-fasād*); (2) things which cannot give their advantages except if they are such that a certain evil proceeds from them at the jamming of motions and the clashing of movable things; and in [this] division [of the things, that are possible in existence, there is also]; (3) things that are evil, either absolutely or for the most part.

If the Pure Good is the principle of the emanation of the good and befitting existence, [then] the existence of the first division must necessarily emanate, an example of which is the existence of the intellectual substances and the like. Also, the second division must necessarily emanate—for in the non-existence of much good, and in the nonproduction of it as a precaution against [the presence of] slight evil, is a great evil. [This fact] is exemplified in the creation of fire. For fire would not give its advantages and would not complete its help in perfecting existence, unless it is such that it harms and hurts whatever animal bodies happen to collide with it. The same is true of animal bodies: they cannot have their advantages, unless they are such that it is possible (a) for their states in their motions and rests, as is the case with the states of fire also, to lead to the coming together of clashes that harm; (b) for their states and the states of the things in the world to lead to the occurrence of error from them in the knotting of harm for the second life, and for the truth; or (c) to an excess of an acting predominant agitation such as desire, or anger that harms the affairs of the second life.

The above-mentioned powers [fire, for example], do not enjoy their richness unless they were such that accidental error and predominant agitation occur from[1] them on the occasion of clashes; this is so in individuals less in number than the safe ones, and [this is so] at times fewer than the times of safety .

Because this is known in the first providence, it is as if it is intended incidentally. Thus, evil enters destiny incidentally, as if it is, for example, pleasing [to God] incidentally.

Chapter 24. Delusion and Admonition

You may say that the majority of people are dominated by ignorance, or obedience to desire and anger; why then is this type [of evil] among them [described] as rare?

Listen then: the states of the body which in disposition are three: (1) the state of the one who excels in beauty and health; (2) the state of the one who does not [excel] in these two [qualities]; and (3) the state [of the one who suffers from] ugliness, illness, or chronic illness. The first and second [types] receive an abundant or a moderate portion [respectively] of worldly and physical happiness, or they are [simply] saved. So also are the states of the soul in its dispositions three: (1) the state of the one who has attained the full virtue of mind and character; [this kind of person] will have the highest degree of happiness in the future life; (2) the state of the one who has not attained that [level], especially in [those virtues concerning] the intelligibles; yet the ignorance [of such a person] is not an impediment to the second life, even though he does not have a large store of knowledge of great use for the second life; nevertheless, he is among those who are in safety and who receive a portion of the goods of the future life; and (3) another who, like the ill or the chronically ill, is subject to harm in the second life. Each one of the two extremes is rare. The middle is prevalent and predominant—and if the virtuous extreme is added to it, [the number] of the people saved becomes abundantly predominant.

Chapter 25. Admonition

Do not think that happiness in the future life is of one kind. And do not think that happiness is not received at all, except by perfecting [oneself] with knowledge, even though that makes its kind nobler. And do not think that the various sins affect the certainty of salvation; but that which creates eternal destruction is only a kind

1. 'From' replaces in this sentence *lahā* (to them). Anyone who is familiar with the material preceding this statement and the material in *al-Shifā'*, *al-Ilāhiyyāt*, vol. 2, bk. 9, ch. 6, understands that in this sentence Ibn Sīnā is repeating his view that something like fire cannot be itself unless it is such that accidental evil proceeds from it under certain circumstances (i.e., when it is put in contact with a combustible element). The substitution of 'from' for 'to them' is therefore necessary to render Ibn Sīnā's meaning.

of ignorance. And that which exposes [people] to limited suffering is only a kind of vice and a certain degree of it. [But] that [happens] to a minority of individual human beings.

Do not listen to the one who considers salvation limited to a certain number of people and denied to the ignorant and sinful to eternity—God's mercy is abundant. And about that, you will hear further explanation.

Chapter 26. Delusion and Admonitions

Or perhaps you will say: Was it not possible that the second division [of things possible in existence] might have been free from attachment to evil? The answer is: If it had been free from [attachment to evil], it would have been something other than this division. But[1] the first division had already been freed from [evil]. This division[2] in its basic construction is only among those things to which the great good cannot attach, unless it is such that evil attaches to it by necessity at the occurrence of clashes. Thus, if it were free from this [evil], it would have been made other than itself—so, as if fire were made other than fire and water other than water. Leaving out the existence of this division, as previously described,[3] does not befit the Good as we have shown.

Chapter 27. Delusion and Admonition

You will perhaps also say: If there is destiny, then why is there punishment? Reflect on the answer:

Punishment of the soul for its sin is, as you shall know, similar to the disease of the body for its gluttony. Thus, it is one of the necessary consequences to which past conditions have led which together with their consequences were inescapable. As for [the punishment] which falls in another class[4] and which has[5] its principle from without,[6] [this] is another story. Furthermore, if a punisher from without is accepted, that is also good, for it is necessary that fear be present among the causes that are confirmed, and are thus useful in general. Belief [in such punishment] ensures fear.

Thus, [even] if it happens that due to destiny one person transgresses the required fear and consideration, and so does wrong and commits a crime; [still], belief [in an external punisher] was made to exist for the sake of the general good,[7] even though it is not suitable for that person and not required by the Choicemaker and the Merciful.

1. Text: *Wa* (and).
2. That is the second division, in other words, the sublunary sphere.
3. As being mixed with evil.
4. Text: *jihat* literally, side.
5. Text: *min* (from).
6. In contrast to the class of punishment just discussed whose principle is from within.
7. Texts: *al-gharaḍ al-ʿāmm* (general purpose).

If there had been nothing other than the person afflicted by destiny, there would not[1] be in the particular corruption of him a considerable, general, and universal utility. For the sake of the universal, attention should not be paid from the point of view of the particular. Similarly, for the sake of the whole, attention should not be paid from the point of view of the part. Thus, an organ that hurts is severed in order that the body as a whole be saved.

As for the discussion about injustice and justice [that comes to us], and discussion about acts said to be unjust and acts contrary to them, and [about) the necessity of abandoning [the unjust ones] and adopting [those contrary ones]—on the assumption that [these] are primary premises, they are not of universal necessity, but most of [them] are among the widely accepted premises agreed on for the sake of interest. Perhaps there is among [these premises] what can be demonstrated as sound with respect to some agents.

If the truths are determined, attention must then be paid to the obligations without their contraries;[2] and you have learned the types of premises in their place.

ON TIME

From *al-Shifā'* (The Healing)

Translated by Yegane Shayegan from *Kitāb al-shifā'*, *Ṭabī'iyyāt* (Physics). With a commentary by Khwānsārī, lithographed, (Tehran, 1886), pp. 140–149.

On the Verification and Proof of What It Is To Be Time

72.2–8. We say that it is evident and clear that two moving bodies can start their movements and terminate them together, yet one of them covers a shorter distance and the other a greater distance, either due to the difference in 'slowness' and 'fastness' or owing to the number of rests which intervene—as some people think. It is [also] permissible that two [moving bodics] start and cover two equal distances but one of them reaches the end of the distance while the other has not yet reached it; and that, owing to the difference just mentioned. In every case, from the starting point of each movement up to its terminal point (A) it is possible to traverse this same distance with that motion which is uniform in its 'fastness' or 'slowness' or which is uniform in its combination with rests. (B) It is also possible to traverse a greater point of this distance with a 'faster' [movement] or with a 'fewer' rests mixed with it. (C) It is possible to cover a shorter distance with a 'slower' [movement] or with more rests mixed with it. And it is not permissible that it differs at all.

1. I am reading *lam* (would not) for *wa-lam* (and would not).
2. I have substituted *aḍdādihā* (their contraries) for *amthālihā* (their like).

72.8–12. It is thus already established that between the starting point and terminal point [of a movement] there is a limited possibility in relation to movement and speed. If we assume half of that distance with the same 'fastness' and 'slowness', there will be between the starting point of that distance and its end at the half-way point (D) another possibility in which it is possible to traverse only the half with this 'fastness' and 'slowness'; (E) similarly between this terminal point which is assumed at present and between the first terminal point. Thus the possibility of [covering the distance from the starting point] to the half-way point and that of [covering the distance] from the half-way point [to the terminal point] are equal and each one of them is half the possibility that was assumed first. Thus the possibility which was first assumed will be divisible.

72.12–15. You do not have now to take this moving thing as something really moving along spatial magnitude but rather as a part that one assumes moving by virtue of positing, resembling the moving thing along spatial magnitude—for it will be separated as one contact touching another [forming] a continuity of things touching one another, and one parallel to another [forming] a continuity of parallels—and if what it traverses is called 'distance'—however it may be—any judgment concerning our discussion will not differ due to that. We thus say it has been confirmed that this possibility is divisible and anything divisible is either a measure or possesses a measure.

72.15–19. This possibility is not devoid of measure [and two possibilities may follow], either its measure is that of the distance or that of something else. If it were the measure of the distance, then equal parts in this distance would be equal in this possibility, while it is not so. It is therefore the measure of something else; either it has to be the measure of the moving thing or not; but it is not the measure of the moving thing, [for] otherwise the greater moving thing would have been greater in this measure, while it is not so. Therefore it is neither the measure of the distance nor that of the moving thing.

72.19–22. It is known that motion is not the same as this measure itself either, nor is 'fastness' and 'slowness'. It is so, since motions as motions are [sometimes] the same and are the same in 'fastness' and 'slowness', [but] differ with regard to this measure. Sometimes motion may differ in 'fastness' and be the same in this measure.

Thus the existence of a measure of the possibility of occurrence of movements between the prior and the posterior in a way that requires finite distances has been proven.

72.22–28. It is neither the measure of a moving thing nor that of distances nor [even] that of motion as such. This measure cannot be self-subsistent. How can it be self-subsistent while it diminishes with that which is measured by it and any diminishing thing is destructible? Therefore it is in a subject or possesses a subject. Thus this measure depends upon a subject. And it is not permissible that its first subject be the matter of a moving body, according to what we have [already] explained [above]. For if its measure was matter without any intermediary, owing to it, matter would have become 'larger' or 'smaller'. Therefore it is in the subject through another disposition, and this cannot be a permanent disposition such as whiteness and blackness, otherwise the measure of this disposition would take place in matter as a fixed permanent measure. Hence, the only alternative is that it should be the measure of a successive disposition which is movement from one place to another or from one position to another between which there is a distance along which runs the motion which is that of position. This is what we call time.

72.28–73.2. You know that to be divided into a prior and a posterior is inherent in movement, but the prior exists in [motion] only along that which is the prior of spatial magnitude and the posterior exists in it only along that which is the posterior of spatial magnitude. But it follows from this that the prior in motion does not co-exist with the posterior in it as the prior and the posterior co-exist together in spatial magnitude. It is not permissible for that which corresponds to prior in movement along spatial magnitude that it becomes posterior; nor that which corresponds to posterior in movement along spatial magnitude that it becomes prior, as it is permissible in spatial magnitude.

73.2–6. The prior and the posterior in movement become properties which inhere in motion in so far as what they are of motion not in so far as what they are of spatial magnitude. The two are numbered by motion. Therefore motion by means of its parts numbers the prior and the posterior. Motion has a number inasmuch as having the prior and the posterior in spatial magnitude; it has a measure too as corresponding to the measure of spatial magnitude; and time is this number or measure. Time is the number of movement when it is divided into a prior or a posterior not in respect of time but in respect of spatial magnitude, otherwise the explanation will be a definition by way of vicious circularity. What one of the logicians who has not comprehended this, has assumed, namely, that a vicious circularity is contained in this explanation, his assumption is a fallacy.

73.6–17. This time is also a measure in its own right for it is that which *qua* itself possesses priority and posteriority, and the prior and the posterior do not co-exist in time as they do in other modes of priority and posteriority. This is that which in its own right, has some part of it 'before' and some part of it 'after', and it is owing to this that other things have some of their parts prior and some, posterior. This is so because the things in which the before-and-after exists in the sense that the before has vanished and the after does not exist with the before, are such not in their own right but owing to their existence with some part of this measure. Thus of that which corresponds to the part which comes before, it is said that it is 'before' and of what corresponds to the part which is after, it is said that it is 'after'. It is obvious that these are the things which undergo change, because that in which no change occurs, nothing vanishes in it and nothing appears [in it] either. This thing does not have a before and an after in respect of something else because if that were so, its past would have become past only in respect of its existing in the before of something else. This thing, or another thing toward which finally the gradual process would terminate, will then be that which in its own right possesses the before-and-after, that is, in its own right receives the relation by which it is before and after. It is known that this thing is that in which the possibility of changes occurs, according to the way which was mentioned [above], in a primary way, and it occurs in other things because of it; thus this thing is that measure which measures the mentioned possibility *qua* itself, and it is what we are concerned with, nothing else. We have granted the name time only to the meaning of that which, as such, is the measure of the mentioned possibility, and this latter occurs in it in a primary way.

73.17–26. It is evident from this that this mentioned measure is the same thing that, in its own right, receives the relations of before and after, or rather it is divisible in itself into before and after. I do not mean by this that time has a before not by means of a relation, rather I mean that this relation is a concomitant of time in its own right and is a concomitant of other things because of time. For, when about something other than time—such as motion and man and so on—it is said that it is before, it means that it exists with a thing which is in such a state that, that state, when it is compared to the state of the other, implies that the thing will have a before in its own right, that is, it will have this concomitant in its own right. Thus the priority of that which is prior is that it exists with the non-existence of some other thing which does not exist while [itself] it exists; It is prior to the other, when the latter's nonexistence is considered; and simultaneous with it when its existence alone is considered; and in the state of being simultaneous with it, it is not prior to it. Its essence is determinate in the two states. But the state of what is prior is not the state of what is simultaneous. For necessarily the priority it had is in some respect lost when it is simultaneous. Thus 'priority' or 'before-ness' is a concept of that essence, not in its own right, nor does it remain permanent with the permanence of that essence. It is absolutely and essentially impossible for this concept to remain the same in the latter state and it is impossible for [priority] to become simultaneous; and it is obvious that this [earlier state of] existence [as before] does not remain permanent with it, when the other comes to exist.

73.26–74.6. As for the thing to which this concept and this matter belong, it is not impossible for it to remain. For at times it exists while being prior; at others, while being simultaneous; and [still] at others, as after, while remaining one and the same. As for the very thing which is before and after, in its own right, even though it has a before in relation to an after, it is not permissible that it remains the same so as to be after, after having been before. For as soon as the concept by which the thing is after appears, that by which it is before ceases to be, while the thing possessing the after persists despite the cessation of the before. The relation of this thing [the before] cannot be merely to nonexistence or to existence; for the relation of the existence of the thing to its nonexistence is sometimes that of posteriority and sometimes that of priority, and similarly with respect to existence. Rather it is the relation to a nonexistence which is joined to something else which, when it is joined to it, will be prior and, when it is joined to something other than it, will be posterior, and the nonexistence in both states is nonexistence and similarly with respect to existence. Its counterpart [after], similarly, is joined to that to which it is related, because *vice versa* the related [thing] is also related to it, and the same principle applied [to the relatives]. This thing is time or it is a relation to time. If it is time, then our argument holds. If it is a relation to time, its priority is on account of time and it will be attributable to the fact that the primary subject of this priority and posteriority is time, for the before-and-after coincides in time in its own right, or rather that in which the before-and-after coincides, in its own right, is that which we designate as time, since we already explained that [time], in its own right, is the measure of the possibility to which we have pointed.

74.6–10. Now as it is [rightly] confirmed that time is not self-subsistent—how could it be self-subsistent as it has no determinate essence and is generated and destroyed and the existence of anything analogous to this is dependent upon matter—hence time is material and, despite being material, it exists in matter through the intermediary of motion. For if there were no motion and no change, there would be no time. For, how could there be time if there is no before and after? And how can before and after exist if nothing is generated step by step? For before and after are not simultaneous; rather the thing which is before is annihilated inasmuch as before because the thing which is after is generated inasmuch as after.

74.10–19. If there is no difference and change in that something is annihilated or something is generated, there will be nothing which is after since there has been no before, and nothing which is before since there is no after. Therefore time does not come to be except with the existence of renewal of states [of being]; this renewal must persist, otherwise there will not be time either, because if something occurs 'at once' and then there is nothing at all until something else occurs 'at once', two possibilities exist: either between those two there is possibility of renewal of things or there is not. If there is between them possibility of renewal of things, then there is between them a before and an after. The before-and-after is only realized through the renewal of things, while our assumption was that there is no renewal of things. This is an [utter] contradiction. If between the two, there is no such possibility, then the two are stuck together. In that case two [further] possibilities exist: either this sticking together goes on or it does not. If it goes on then that which we have assumed to be impossible has been produced, and its impossibility will be clarified later. If it is interrupted our argument returns to the beginning. Hence it is of the utmost necessity that, if there is time, there should be renewal of states either by way of sticking together or continuity; for if there is no motion there will be no time. And since as we have stated time is a measure and is continuous, and corresponding to the continuity of motions and spatial magnitudes, it has necessarily a separation in thought which is called the 'now'.

Concerning the Explanation of the 'Now'

74.19–22. We maintain that one knows the 'now' through knowing time, for since time is continuous it necessarily has a division in the mind; this is what is called the 'now'. This 'now' is not actually existent at all, in relation to time itself, otherwise the continuity of time is disrupted; rather its existence is merely in respect of the fact that the mind perceives it as that which divides in a rectilinear stretch; that which divides does not exist in actuality in the rectilinear stretch inasmuch as that which divides, otherwise—as we shall explain later—there will be those which divide *ad infinitum*; rather it can only be in actuality if time were to be disrupted in a certain [real] way; however, it is impossible that the continuity of time be disrupted.

74.23–29. This is so because if one considers a division for time, two possibilities will exist: either this division will be at the beginning of time or at its end. If it is at the beginning of time, it will necessarily follow from this that this time has no 'before'. But if it has no 'before', it ought not to be nonexistent, then come into existence. For if it is nonexistent, then comes into existence, its existence will be after its nonexistence and its nonexistence before its existence; it will necessarily have a 'before' and this 'before-ness' will be a notion other than the nonexistence described in the way we have stated in another place. The thing about which this kind of before-ness is said will have taken place, but not this time. Hence this time has before it a time which is continuous with it, the former is 'before' and the latter is 'after', and this division holds the two together, while it was assumed that it was that which divides. This is a contradiction.

74.29–75.7. Similarly if one assumes a division as being at the end of time, two possibilities will arise: either after it the existence of something is possible or it is not. If it is not possible that something exists after it, not even that which exists necessarily, so that it will be impossible that anything exists with the nonexistence of the end at which it terminates, then existence of something as necessary and absolute possibility are both removed; however, necessary existence and absolute possibility cannot be removed. If it is possible that after it [something exists] then it has an 'after' and [itself] it is 'before'; thus the 'now' unites and does not divide. Consequently time has no 'now' existing in actuality in relation to itself, rather [it exists] potentially; I mean, its potentiality is close to being actual, that is, time is always prepared that the 'now' constantly coincides in it, either in respect of someone's assumption or in respect of motions reaching a common boundary which is indivisible such as the starting point of the sunrise or sunset and so on. This in reality is not the occurrence of a division in the essence of time itself, but rather in its relation to movements, just as relative divisions occur in other measures, e.g., as one part of a body is separated from another either by being parallel or by contact or by being assumed by someone, without any division actually occurring in the body itself; rather actual division occurs in it in relation to some other thing.

75.7–12. If this 'now' is determined due to this relation, its nonexistence is not anywhere but in the whole of the time after it.

Someone's assertion that it ceases to be either in a 'now' which succeeds it or a 'now' which does not succeed it, [is possible] after he has admitted that it can begin to cease to be in a 'now'. However, the beginning of its ceasing to be is the limit of time in the whole of which it becomes nonexistent. For by ceasing to be is understood nothing other than that the thing is not existent after having existed and its existence in this case is that it is the limit of time in which it is nonexistent. It is as you would say that it is existent in the limit of time in which it is nonexistent and its ceasing to be has no beginning of ceasing to be which is a primary 'now' in which it ceases to be, rather between its existence and its nonexistence there is a division which is its existence and nothing else. You know that the moving thing, the resting thing, that which comes to be and that which ceases to be, do not have a primary 'now' in which they are either in movement or at rest, or come to be or cease to be, since time is potentially divisible *ad infinitum*.

75.12–21. The one who believes that it is possible to say about this that the 'now' either 'ceases to be gradually', so that it is stretches in a duration towards nonexistence; or else that it 'ceases to be at once', so that its nonexistence occurs in a 'now'—this is an argument whose invalidity ought to be made evident. We thus say that the nonexistent or the existent 'at once', in the sense that it is determined in one single 'now', is not a concomitant of the opposite of that which ceases to be 'gradually' or comes to be 'gradually', rather it is more particular than this opposite. This opposite is that which does not proceed gradually toward existence, nonexistence, alteration, and so on. This holds true of that which happens to it 'at once'; it holds true of the thing which in the whole of a certain time is not existent and at the extreme limit of it which is not time, is existent, or the thing which in the whole of a certain time is existent and at the limit of it which is not time, is not existent. For these last two do not come to be or cease to be gradually; and so is the first also, i.e., that whose existence or nonexistence is in a 'now'. But this latter mode is different from the first, because in the first [the 'now'] which is the extremity of time in its own right, has been assumed to be identical to the whole of time; and in the latter, the 'now' has been assumed to be different from time—all this without positing a 'now' that takes place after another different 'now', otherwise between the 'nows' contiguity would occur and this 'now' would be the limit of time in its own right.

75.21–76.1. Our argument is not concerned with whether this latter mode of existence holds true or not. We are not arguing about it inasmuch as we assent to its existence, but rather inasmuch as it is predicated of [the thing] as a certain negation. This negation is [the following]: 'it does not come to be and cease to be gradually.' In this it has a participant. That participant is more particular than this negation, and the more particular is not implied in the more universal. Whenever something is conceived as a subject or a predicate, it is not necessary that it be such that we assent or not assent to its existence. This has already been known in the art of logic. If our statement 'it does not come to be or cease to be gradually' is more general than our statement 'it comes to be at once' or 'it ceases to be at once' in the sense that the former state is in a first 'now', then someone's argument that this is either gradual or at once is not true as would be a disjunctive proposition which encompasses two sides of the contradictory or that encompasses the contradictory and the concomitant of its contradictory. Moreover, the opposite of 'that which comes to be at once' is 'that which does not come to be at once', that is, it does not come to be in a first 'now', and does not necessarily imply that 'it comes to be and ceases to be gradually', rather the mode mentioned above may hold true of it, unless one means by 'the existent at once' that which there is no 'now' in which it does not exist and there is no 'now' in which it is still in process, and similarly with regard to 'the not-existent at once'. If this is what is meant, then this will be the concomitant of the opposite and the proposition will be true, but it is not necessary that the beginning of its existence and its nonexistence be 'at once'.

76.1–6. There is here another thing which, even though it is not appropriate [to discuss] in this place, we have [nevertheless] to mention so that it will help verify what we have said. This is that it is best that we seek to know whether in the 'now' which is a common [boundary] between two times in one of which the thing is in a certain state and in the other it is in another state, the thing may be devoid of both states or be in one of the states to the exclusion of the other. Now, if two are contradictory states such as 'touching' and 'not-touching', 'existing' and 'not-existing' and so on, it is impossible that the thing be devoid of both of them in the assumed 'now'. It necessarily has to be in one of the two [states]. But in which of the two is it?

76.6–18. We say that something must necessarily adhere to the existing thing to render it nonexistent. Two possibilities exist: either this thing that has adhered is one that can adhere to a 'now', and this is the thing whose state is the same no matter which 'now' you may take in the time of its existence and it does not need to be in a 'now' whose [stretch] to another 'now' corresponds to duration; consequently, the thing in the common dividing boundary is qualified by whatever is of this characteristic such as touching, squaring, and other permanent dispositions whose existence is identical in every 'now' of the time of their existence. Or else the thing is different from this qualification and it exists in time not in the 'now'; it will then come to exist in the second of the two times only. The 'now' which divides the two is not necessarily predicated of it; and there will be in it [the 'now'] the opposite characteristic such as distinction and lack of contact and movement. Among these there is that whose states can be identical in the 'nows' of its time to the exclusion of the 'nows' which occur at the beginning, and that whose states cannot be identical at all. An example of that which it is permissible [that its states be identical] is 'the not touching' which is 'the different' for it does not occur unless in virtue of motion and difference of state; but they persist the same for some time as 'not touching', indeed as 'different'. If their states differ in some other respect, that is not in respect of being 'different' and 'not touching'. An example of that in which this is not permissible is motion, for its state is not the same in any 'now', rather in every 'now' it is renewed with a new proximity and distance both of which are [dependent on] the states of motion. If the unmoved thing moves and if the touching thing does not touch, it will be because of the 'now' which divides between its two times. For there is neither a beginning of distinction nor movement in [the 'now'], thus there is in it contact and privation of motion. Although this [topic] falls beyond the scope of our purpose, it is, [nevertheless], beneficial for it and for the other questions.

That about which we have argued is the 'now' which is encompassed by the past and the future. It is as if time were generated and after its being determined, it was defined by means of this 'now'.

76.18–77.8. Sometimes one may represent another 'now' in the mind with another qualification. For just as a 'now' [which is] the limit of the moving thing—let that be a certain point—by means of whose movement and flux one assumes a certain distance, or rather a certain line, as if it, I mean, that limit, is translated, then on that line a point is assumed which is not the [actual] generator of that line, rather that which is occurring to the one who represents it in the mind. Similarly, it seems that there is something analogous concerning time as well as movement—in the sense of *terminus motus*—and something like a point that is inserted in a line which it does not [actually] generate, but is rather represented in the mind after the generation of the line. This is due to the fact that one represents in the mind a translated thing and a limit in spatial magnitude and a time. The translated thing then generates a continuous translation to which corresponds a continuous time, it is as if the translated thing, or rather its state which is its concomitant due to its motion, is an indivisible limit which, owing to its flux, generates something continuous; in spatial magnitude a point corresponds to it and in time, a 'now'. For there is neither the line along spatial magnitude *with* this, for it has left it behind, nor motion, in the sense of *terminus motus*, for it is terminated, nor time, for it is past; it has with it from each one of these only a limit whose division is indivisible. Thus in time, the 'now' is always with it; in the traversing, the thing which we have explained that it is, in reality, motion, as long as the thing moves; and in spatial magnitude, the limit, whether it is a point or something else. Every one of these is an end, the translated thing is also an end in its own right, inasmuch as it is translated as though it is something that is extended from the starting point in the distance up to where it reaches; for it is, inasmuch as it is a translated thing, a thing extended from the starting point to the terminal point, while it itself, which is the existing continuous 'now', is a limit and an end in its own right inasmuch as being translated to this limit.

Hence it is appropriate for us to inquire whether, just as the translated thing itself is one, and in virtue of its flux it generates that which is its limit and its end and generates distance also, similarly with regard to time there is something which is the 'now' which flows and is itself indivisible *qua* being the same, and persists identical to itself because of that, but *qua* being a 'now' it does not persist, because it is a 'now' only when it is considered as that which limits time, just as the former is a translated thing when it limits that which it limits, but in itself it is a point or some other thing. And just as it coincides in the translated thing that *qua* translated thing it cannot exist twice but passes away with the passing away of its translation, thus also the 'now' *qua* 'now' does not exist twice; however, that which for some reason becomes a 'now' may exist at many times, just as the translated thing inasmuch as it is something in which translation is coincidental, may exist many times. Thus if such a thing is existent, it will be true to say that the 'now', by its flux, generates time. This is not the 'now' which is assumed between two times and which holds the two together, just as the point which by means of its motion is assumed as generating a distance, is not the point of the distance *in* which it is assumed to be. Thus if such a thing exists, it is the existence of a thing which is joined to the notion which we have established earlier [by determining] that it is motion without considering a prior, a posterior, or a correspondence. And just as by its having a 'where' when it persists flowing along a distance, it generates motion, similarly by its having that notion which we have called the 'now' when it persists in the prior and posterior of motion, it generates time. Thus the relation of this thing to the prior and posterior is [due to] its being a 'now' while in itself it is a thing which generates time and numbers time by what is generated.

77.8–27. When we consider a 'now' as one of the limits in two [motions], then the prior and posteriors will be generated as numbered, as the point numbers the line in that every point is a common boundary between two lines by means of two relations. The real numbered is that which first gives unity to the thing, and by way of repetition it gives multiplicity and number to it. The 'now' which has this characteristic, numbers time. For as long as there is no 'now', time will not be numbered. The prior and posterior numbers time according to the second manner, namely, by its being a part of it and its being a part is determined by the existence of the 'now', and because the prior and the posterior are parts of time and each part of it can be divisible like the parts of a line.

The 'now' is better suited for a unity, a unity is better suited for numbering, thus the 'now' numbers in the same way as the point numbers and it is not divisible. Motion numbers time in virtue of the prior and posterior that it engenders by means of distance. The measure of motion is the number of the prior and posterior, thus motion numbers time in that it engenders the number of time which is the prior and posterior. Time numbers motion in virtue of being the number of motion itself. An example for this is that people, because of their existence, are themselves the causes of the existence of their number which is, for instance, ten; thus due to their existence their 'ten-ness' exists, and the 'ten-ness' makes people, not existing or things, but numbered, that is, possessors of a number. The soul when it counts people, that which is counted is not the nature of men, but the 'ten-ness' realized due to—for example, separation of the human nature [into individual men]. Thus the human soul numbers the number ten. Similarly motion numbers time in accordance with the idea which was mentioned [above]. But if motion had not existed with the limits of the prior-and-posterior that it generates along spatial magnitude, time would not have possessed a number. However, time measures motion and motion measures time.

77.19–27. Time measures motion in two ways: on the one hand, it makes it possessor of measure; on the other, it signifies the quantity of its measure. Motion measures time inasmuch as it signifies its measure by means of the prior and posterior existing in it. There is a difference between the two [modes of measuring]. As for signifying the measure, it is at times like the fact that the measuring device signifies the measuring, and at others, like the fact that the measuring signifies the measuring device. Similarly, at times distance signifies the measure of motion; at others, motion signifies the measure of distance. For at times one says 'a journey of two parasangs'; and at others, 'a distance of bow shot'. But that which gives the measure to the other is one of the two, and this is that which is a measure in its own right. Because time is continuous in its substance, it is appropriate to say 'long' and 'short', and because it is a number in relation to the prior and posterior—in accordance with what we have explained [above]—it is appropriate to say 'few' or 'many'. Similarly in the case of motion, for 'continuity' and 'discontinuity' are coincidental in it, and it is spoken of as that which has the properties of 'the continuous' and those of 'the discontinuous', but these are coincidental in it due to what is other than itself; those which pertain to it specifically are 'fast' and 'slow'.

We have already indicated the mode of existence of the 'now' in actuality—if it has an existence in actuality—and its mode of existence in potentiality.

ON THE STATIONS OF THE KNOWERS

From *al-Ishārāt wa'l-tanbīhāt* (Remarks and Admonitions)

Reprinted from Shams Inati, *A Study of Ibn Sīnā's Mysticism* (Albany, NY, 1996). The translation is based on *al-Ishārāt wa'l-tanbīhāt, Part Four,* Ninth Class, ed. S. Dunyā (Cairo, 1958), pp. 790–852.

Chapter 1. Admonition Concerning the Stations of the Knowers

In their present lives, the knowers (*al-ʿārifīn*)[1] have stations and ranks that are reserved for them to the exclusion of others. It is as if, while being clothed by their bodies, they have shed their bodies, become free from them, and attained the world of saintliness. To them belong things concealed in them[2] and things manifested by them.[3] The latter are protested against by those who deny them and are considered as great by those who know them. We will relate these things to you.

If your hearing is stricken by one of the things that strikes your hearing and if, among the things you hear, the story of Salāmān and Absāl is related to you, then you must know that Salāmān is given as an example of yourself, and Absāl is given as an example of your rank in knowledge—if you are among those who know. Solve the riddle if you can.

Chapter 2. Admonition Concerning the Differences Among the Ascetic, the Worshipper, and the Knower

The name 'ascetic' is reserved for one who shuns the delights and goods of this world. The name 'worshipper' is reserved for one who persists in exercising worship by prostration, fasting, and what resembles them. The name 'knower' is reserved for one who disposes his thought toward the sanctity of divine power, seeking the perpetual illumination of the light of the Truth into his innermost thought.[4] Some of the above-mentioned definitions may be combined with each other.

---

1. *Al-ʿārifīn* are those who know by direct experience, as opposed to *al-ʿālimīn* who know by natural or rational means.
2. That is, the divine things that they see.
3. That is, the extraordinary things that they do.
4. Text: *fī sirrihī.*

Chapter 3. Admonition Concerning the Difference Between the Asceticism and Worship of the Knower and Those of the Nonknower

Asceticism for one who is not a knower is a kind of business deal, as if one buys the delights of the second life with the delights of the present one. But for the knower it is a kind of abstinence from that which distracts one's innermost thought from the Truth and an elevation over everything other than the Truth.

Worship for one who is not a knower is a kind of business deal, as if one acts in the present life for a salary that one will receive in the second life as a retribution and a reward. But for the knower, it is a kind of exercise of one's faculties (*himamihi*), including the estimative and imaginative powers of one's soul, to orient them by habit from the side of error to the side of the Truth. Thus, they become receptive to the private innermost thought of the soul, so that, when this thought seeks the revelation of the Truth, these powers will not be in conflict with it. Hence, the innermost thought arrives at the bright illumination. This arrival becomes a well-established habit. Whenever the innermost thought wishes, it views the light of the Truth without being rivalled by these faculties, instead, being warmly accompanied by them. Thus, the innermost thought will be totally involved in attaining sanctity.

Chapter 4. Remark Concerning the Social Need for a Religious Law and for a Prophet

Since a human being is not such that on his own he achieves independence in his personal affairs except by sharing with another being of his type through the exchange and commutative contract that are made between them—each of them setting his companion free from some occupation which, if the companion himself were to undertake, many things would accumulate for that individual (if this were possible to manage, it would be among the difficult things)—that is why it is necessary to have among people transactions and justice preserved by a law imposed by a legislator. This legislator is distinguished by meriting obedience due to his special possession of signs that indicate that they are from the Lord. It is also necessary that the performer of good deeds and the performer of bad deeds be retributed by their Lord, the Powerful and the Knower. Thus, knowledge concerning the retributer and the legislator is necessary. In addition to knowledge, it is necessary to have a cause of retaining knowledge. Therefore, worship, which reminds one of the Object of worship, is imposed on people to be repeated by them[1] in order that they preserve the remembrance by repetition until the call for justice that sustains the life of the species becomes known. Those who practise this worship have abundant reward in the second life, in addition to the great benefit they have in the present life.

1. Text: *wa-kurrirat ʿalayhim.*

Furthermore, for those who practise it and are knowers, a benefit reserved for them is added, inasmuch as they turn their faces toward Him.

Thus, reflect on the wisdom, mercy, and grace of God; you will notice an aspect whose marvels dazzle you. After that, establish the law and be upright.[1]

Chapter 5. Remark Concerning the Proper Objective of the Knower

The knower seeks the First Truth not for anything other than Itself and prefers nothing to the knowledge and worship of It alone (other than, of course, Itself).[2] This is because the First Truth merits worship, and because worship is a noble relation to It, and not because of desire or fear. If desire or fear were present, the desired object or the feared object would be the motive and the object of the search. The Truth then would not be the end, but a means to something other than It—this something being the end and the object of the search, to the exclusion of the Truth.

Chapter 6. Remark Concerning the Difference Between One Who Seeks the Truth as an Intermediary and One Who Seeks It for Its Own Sake

He who finds it permissible to place the Truth in an intermediary position receives mercy, but only in some manner; for he is not given the pleasure of having joy in the Truth so that he can seek this pleasure. His knowledge of pleasure is only of that which is by nature incomplete. Hence, he longs for this incomplete pleasure, disregarding that which is beyond it. Those who resemble him are in relation to the knowers just as young boys are in relation to those who are well experienced.

---

1. This view, whose seeds are found in Plato and al-Fārābī, asserts the following: (1) A human being requires other human beings for the fulfilment of his needs. (2) This requires social cooperation. (3) Social cooperation requires justice. (4) Justice requires the presence of law. (5) The presence of law requires a legislator to enact the law. (6) The legislator must have special qualities that distinguish him from others and that command their obedience to him. (7) Among these qualities, one finds the manifestations of signs, such as extraordinary behaviour which indicates that the law enacted is divine—this legislator is a prophet. (8) The law must impose on people hope and fear through retribution by God, Who knows everything and who has power over everything so that they would do the good and refrain from doing the bad. (9) The fear and hope from retribution require that people know God, the Retributer, and the legislator, the human being who conveys knowledge of retribution to them. (10) In order to establish this knowledge in their soul, people must practise worship, which consists of repetitive remembrance of God. (11) The worshippers will reap benefits both in this life and in the second life. The knowers among them have, in addition to this, a vision of the Truth that gives them blissful eternity.

2. See the passage that will follow in ch. 20 of the present class: '*Man āthar al-ʿirfān li'l-ʿirfān fa-qad qāla bi'l-thānī*' (he who prefers knowledge for the sake of knowledge professes belief in knowledge). The knower differs from those nonknowers who also seek knowledge of the Truth and practise asceticism and worship of God in that the former does so only for the sake of the Truth, while the latter do so for the sake of gaining reward.

Since young boys neglect the goods that are guarded by those who are mature, and since the experience of the former is limited to the goods of playing, the former become astonished at serious people when the latter turn away from the goods of playing, detest them, and resort to other things.

Similarly, he whose vision is curbed by deficiency from encountering the joy of grasping the Truth sticks his two palms to the pleasure that surrounds him, that is, the false type of pleasure. Thus, in the present life, he abandons this false type of pleasure unwillingly, and does not abandon it except for seeking double its amount in the second life. He worships God, the exalted, and obeys Him only so that God would grant him in the second life satiation of this pleasure such that he would proceed to delicious food, good water, and beautiful sex.

If one turns away from the Truth, one's vision cannot be raised—whether in the present or in the other life—except to the pleasures of one's belly and memory. But he who, by way of preference, seeks insight through the guidance of sanctity, has known the real pleasure and turned his face toward it, seeking mercy upon him who is led away from the right conduct to its opposite, even though what the latter seeks by his effort will be generously given to him in accordance with what he had been promised.

Chapter 7. Remark Concerning the First Preparatory Stage, Willingness, in the Knower's Movement Toward the Truth

The first step in the knowers' movement is that which they themselves call 'willingness' (*al-irādah*).[1] This is the desire that overcomes the seeker of insight—either by demonstrative certainty or by tranquillity of the soul due to the confirmation of faith—to establish a strong relation to the world of sanctity. Thus, his march proceeds to sanctity in order to attain the spirit of conjunction. Therefore, as long as he remains on this level, he is an adept (*murīd*).

Chapter 8. Remark Concerning the Second Preparatory Stage, Spiritual Exercise

Furthermore, the knower needs spiritual exercise. This kind of exercise is directed toward three goals. The first is to remove from the path of choice whatever is other than the Truth. The second is to render the commanding soul[2] obedient to the tranquil soul[3] so that the power of imagination and that of estimation will be attracted

1. *Al-irādah* is ordinarily translated as *will*. But since the will is usually considered to be a faculty, and since what is being referred to is a step in a movement—that is, an act in a process not a faculty, I have preferred to translate *al-irādah* as *willingness*.

2. That is, the animal soul.

3. That is, the rational soul.

to the ideas proper to the saintly affairs, abandoning those ideas that are proper to base things. The third is to render the innermost thought sensitive to attention.

The first is assisted by real asceticism. The second is assisted by a number of things: worship accompanied by thought, tunes employed by the powers of the soul for rendering the words put to the tune acceptable to the mind, and, finally, didactic words themselves that come from an intelligent speaker in an eloquent phrase, in a soft tune, and that involve some guidance. As for the third goal, it is assisted by sensitive thought and pure love, which is commanded by the qualities of the beloved and not by the rule of the appetite.

Chapter 9. Remark Concerning the First Step in Conjunction, Moment

Furthermore, if the will and spiritual exercise bring the knower to a certain limit, he will encounter pleasurable stolen looks at the light of the Truth, as if these looks are lightning that shines over the knower and then turns away from him. These stolen looks are what they call 'moments' (*awqāt*). Every moment is surrounded by two ecstasies: an ecstasy for the Truth and an ecstasy over the passing away of the Truth. After that, these overwhelming moments multiply if the knower persists in the spiritual exercise.

Chapter 10. Remark Concerning the Second Step, Seeing the Truth in Everything Once Conjunction with the Truth Becomes a Fixed Habit

He is then absorbed in those overwhelming moments until they overcome him even while not exercising. Thus, whenever he catches a glimpse of a thing, he returns from that thing to the side of sanctity, remembering something of the latter. He is then overcome by a fainting spell. Thus, he almost sees the Truth in everything.

Chapter 11. Remark Concerning the Third Step, Reaction to the Experience of Conjunction Before and After Familiarity with the Truth

Perhaps on his way to this limit, his veils are lifted up for him, and he ceases to be calm. Thus, the knower's companion pays attention to the knower's being provoked out of his stability. If his spiritual exercise is prolonged, he will not be provoked by the lifting up of any veil and will be guided to conceal his experience.

Chapter 12. Remark Concerning the Fourth Step, Effects on the Soul of Familiarity with the Truth

After that, spiritual exercise carries him to a point at which his moment is converted into tranquillity. Thus, that which is stolen becomes familiar, and the lightning becomes a clear flame. He acquires a stable knowledge of the Truth, as if this knowledge were a continuous accompaniment in which he delights in the rapture of the Truth. If he turns away from this knowledge, he will do so with loss and regret.

Chapter 13. Remark Concerning the Fifth Step, Manifestations Contrary to Inner Experience Due to Further Delving into Knowledge

Perhaps up to this point, he manifests what he undergoes. But if he delves into this knowledge, there will be less manifestation of this experience. Thus, he will be present while being absent, and stationary while marching on.

Chapter 14. Remark Concerning the Sixth Step, Accessibility of the Truth at a Wish

Perhaps up to this point, this knowledge is facilitated for him only at times. But then he moves gradually until he attains it whenever he wishes.

Chapter 15. Remark Concerning the Seventh Step, Conjunction with the Truth Without Even a Wish

Then he advances beyond this rank so that his situation does not depend on a wish. Rather, whenever he notices one thing, he also notices another,[1] even if his noticing is not for the purpose of consideration. Thus, it is available to him to move away from the world of falsehood to the world of Truth, remaining in the latter, while the ignorant move around him.

Chapter 16. Remark Concerning the Eighth Step, Becoming a Replica of the Truth While Remaining Aware of Oneself

If he crosses from spiritual exercise to attainment of the Truth, his innermost thought will become a polished mirror with which he faces the side of the Truth. The lofty pleasures are then poured on him, and he is pleased with himself due to the traces of the Truth that these pleasures involve. To him belongs a glance at the Truth and a glance at himself—for he is still reluctant.

Chapter 17. Remark Concerning the Ninth Step, Awareness of Nothing but the Truth: Real Conjunction

Following this, he abandons himself. Thus, he notices the side of sanctity only. If he notices his self he does so inasmuch as it notices the Truth, and not inasmuch

1. That is, the First Truth.

as it is ornamented with the pleasure of having the Truth. At this point, the arrival is real.

Chapter 18. Admonition Concerning the Deficiency of the Levels Below That of Real Conjunction

Paying attention to whatever the Truth transcends is preoccupation. Relying on whatever obeys the animal soul is weakness. Rejoicing in the ornament of pleasure, inasmuch as it is pleasure—even if it is in the Truth—is perplexity. And advancing in totality toward the Truth is salvation.

Chapter 19. Remark Concerning the Two Main Levels of Knowledge: The Negative and the Positive

Knowledge begins by the truly adept's separation, detachment (p. 839), abandonment, and rejection—concentrating on a togetherness that is the togetherness of the attributes of the Truth, reaching the One, and then stopping.

Chapter 20. Remark Concerning the Object of Knowledge and the Necessity for Experiencing It

He who prefers knowledge for the sake of knowledge professes belief in knowledge. He who finds knowledge, yet as if he does not find it but finds its object, plunges into the clamour of the arrival. Here there are steps not fewer in number than those that have preceded. We have preferred brevity concerning them, for conversation does not capture them (p. 842), a phrase does not explicate them, and discourse does not reveal anything about them. No power responsive to language other than the imagination receives even a semblance of them.[1] He who desires to know these steps must move gradually until he becomes one of the people of witnessing and not of speaking, one of those who arrive at the Truth Itself and not those who hear the trace.

Chapter 21. Admonition Concerning the Knower's Equal Treatment of Everything

The knower is bright-faced, friendly, and smiling. Due to his modesty, he honours the young as he honours the old. He is as pleased with the unclear-headed as he

1. The imagination does this not because of language but because it neighbours the rational soul, which can have direct experience of these highest levels. See the Tenth Class, where it is stated that, if a knower has vision of the realm of the Truth, his imagination will experience the appearance of objects that have a remote resemblance to the divine objects.

is with the alert. How could he not be bright-faced when he enjoys the Truth and everything other than the Truth, for he sees the Truth even in everything other than the Truth! Furthermore, how could he not treat all as equal when, to him, all are equal! They are objects of mercy, preoccupied with falsehoods.

Chapter 22. Admonition Concerning the Knower's States Before and After the Arrival

To the knower belong states in which he cannot bear the sound of a murmur, let alone the remainder of the attractive preoccupations. Such states are at the moments at which he turns his innermost thought to the Truth, if a veil—whether from himself or from the movement of his innermost thought—appears before the arrival. However, at the time of the arrival, he is either preoccupied with the Truth, to the exclusion of everything else, or he is open to the two sides[1] due to the broad range of his power. Similarly, when moving in the cloak of dignity, he is the most bright-faced of the creatures of God by virtue of his rapture.

Chapter 23. Admonition Concerning the Knower's Magnanimity

The knower is neither concerned with scrutinizing the states of others, nor with gathering information about others, nor is he inclined to anger at observing bad deeds, as he is filled with mercy. This is because he discerns God's secret regarding destiny. If he requests good deeds, he does so with kindness characterized by advice and not with violence characterized by pointing out disgrace. If he magnifies the value of good deeds, it could be because he wishes to protect such deeds from those who do not adopt them.

Chapter 24. Admonition Concerning Some Further Character Qualities of the Knower

The knower is courageous. How could he be otherwise, when he is in isolation from the fear of death? He is generous. How could he be otherwise, when he is in isolation from the love of falsehood? He is forgiving of others. How could he be otherwise, when his soul is more magnanimous than to be injured with evil by another? Finally, he is forgetful of grudges. How could he be otherwise, when his memory is preoccupied with the Truth?

---

1. The two sides being the Truth and everything else other than the Truth.

Chapter 25. Admonition Concerning the Difference in the Knowers' Attitudes

The knowers may differ in their endeavours according to their different thoughts that are based on their different motivating considerations. The knower may consider a rough life as equal to a luxurious life; or he may prefer the former to the latter. Similarly, he may consider a bad odour as equal to a good odour; or he may prefer the former to the latter. This is so when his soul is concerned about belittling whatever is other than the Truth. Again, he may be inclined toward ornament, love for the best in every genus, and hatred for the incomplete and the bad. This is so when he considers his habit of finding evidence for the Truth in the accompanying external states. Thus, he seeks beauty in everything, because it is a good quality given by the grace of the First Providence and is closer to being of the type toward which the knower's inclination is turned. All these attitudes may differ from one knower to another and may differ in the same knower from one time to another.

Chapter 26. Admonition Concerning the Knower's Exemption from Religious Duties While in the State of Conjunction

The knower may be inattentive to the thing by virtue of which he reaches the Truth. Thus, he becomes ignorant of everything around him. Therefore, he is in the same class as those on whom religious duties are not imposed. How could this be otherwise, when religious duties are imposed only on one who understands the imposition of religious duties at the time one understands it, and on one who becomes a sinner for not abiding by the religious duties,[1] even though he does not understand the imposition of religious duties at the time of imposition, but has the capacity for doing so.[2]

Chapter 27. Remark Concerning Conjunction as Possible Only for a Small Number of People with a Certain Type of Nature

The Truth Itself is loftier than to be a drinking place for every comer, or a thing to be viewed except by one after another. That is why what is included in this part of the work is an object of ridicule for the ignorant, and an idea for the scholar. Thus, one who listens to it and is then revolted by it must accuse his soul of not being appropriate for it. Every being is directed with facility toward that for which it was created.

1. Text: *ijtaraḥa bi-khaṭī'atihi.*
2. Such as one under anaesthesia.

LIVING SON OF THE AWAKE
From *Risālah Ḥayy ibn Yaqẓān*

Reprinted from H. Corbin, *Avicenna and the Visionary Recital*, tr. from the French by W. R. Trask (Princeton, NJ, 1990), pp. 137–150.

1. Your persistence, my brothers, in demanding that I set forth the *Recital of Ḥayy ibn Yaqẓān* for you has finally triumphed over my stubborn determination not to do so; it has untied the bond of my firm resolve to defer and delay. Thus I have found myself ready to come to your aid. May we look to God for help and support!

2. Once when I had taken up residence in my city, I chanced to go out with my companions to one of the pleasure places that lie about the same city. Now, as we were coming and going, making a circle, suddenly in the distance appeared a Sage. He was beautiful; his person shone with a divine glory. Certainly he had tasted of years; long duration had passed over him. Yet there was seen in him only the freshness proper to young men; no weakness bowed his bearing, no fault injured the grace of his stature. In short, no sign of old age was to be found in him, save the imposing gravity of old Sages.

3. When I had seen this Sage, I felt a desire to converse with him. From my inmost depths arose a need to become intimate with him and to have familiar access to him. So, with my companions, I went in his direction. When we had approached, he took the initiative; he wished us peace and honoured us with his salutation. Then, smiling, he addressed us in words that were sweet to our hearts.

4. Many words were exchanged between us, until at last the conversation led us to such a point that I questioned him about everything to do with his person, and sought to learn from him what his mode of life and profession were, and even his name and lineage and country. Then he said to me: 'My name is *Vivens*; my lineage, *filius Vigilantis*; as to my country, it is the Celestial Jerusalem [lit., the 'Most Holy Dwelling', *al-Bayt al-Muqaddas*]. My profession is to be forever journeying, to travel about the universe so that I may know all its conditions. My face is turned toward my father, and my father is *Vigilans*. From him I have learned all science, he has given me the keys to every kind of knowledge. He has shown me the roads to follow to the extreme confines of the universe, so that since my journey embraces the whole circle of it, it is as if all the horizons of all climes were brought together before me.'

5. Our conversation continued without interruption. I questioned him concerning the difficult sciences. I learned from him how to solve their obscurities, until finally, from transition to transition, we came to the science of physiognomy. I observed in him such penetration and sagacity in that science that I was filled with admiration; for it was he who took the initiative when we came to physiognomy and the various facts that have to do with it. He said to me: 'The science of physiognomy

is among the sciences the profit from which is paid cash down and whose benefit is immediate, for it reveals to thee what every man conceals of his own nature, so that thou canst proportion thine attitude of freedom or reserve toward each man, and make it befit the situation.

6. 'In thee, physiognomy reveals at once the most excellent of creatural types and a mixture of clay and of inanimate natures that receive every impression. It shows thee to be such that, to whichever side thou art drawn, to that side thou goest. When thou art held upon the right road and art called to it, thou becomest upright and pure. But if a deceiver seduce thee into the road of error, thou dost submit to be led astray. These companions who are about thee and never leave thee are evil companions. It is to be feared that they will seduce thee and that thou wilt remain captive in their bonds, unless the divine safekeeping reach thee and preserve thee from their malice.

7. 'That companion who walks ever before thee, exhorting thee, is a liar, a frivolous babbler, who beautifies what is false, forges fictions; he brings thee information without thy bidding and without thy having questioned him; he mingles false and true therein, he sullies truth with error, even though, in spite of all, he is thy secret eye and thy illuminator. It is through his channel that news reaches thee of what is foreign to thy neighbourhood, absent from the place where thou art. It is laid upon thee to separate the good money from among all the counterfeit coins, to glean what is true among the lies, to free what is right from the matrix of errors, since thou canst not wholly do without him. It may happen that sometimes divine aid will lead thee by the hand and rescue thee from the straying that leads nowhere, and that sometimes thou wilt remain in perplexity and stupor; and sometimes it may happen that false testimony will seduce thee.

'As for the companion on thy right, he is greatly violent; when he is roused by anger, no advice can restrain him; to treat him courteously nowise lessens his excitement. He is like a fire catching on dead wood, like a torrent dashing down from a height, like a drunken camel, like a lioness whose cub has been killed.

'Lastly, that companion on thy left is a sloven, a glutton, a lecher; nothing can fill his belly but the earth; nothing satisfies his appetite but mud and clay. He licks, tastes, devours, and covets. He is like a pig that has been starved and then turned loose among refuse. And it is to these evil companions, O wretch, that thou hast been bound. There is no way for thee to get loose from them save by an expatriation that will take thee to a country whose soil may not be trodden by such as they. But because the hour of that expatriation is not yet come, and thou canst not yet reach that country, because thou canst not break with them and there is no refuge for thee where they cannot come at thee, so act that thou shalt have the upper hand of them and that thine authority shall be greater than theirs. Let them not seize thine own rein, suffer them not to put the halter upon thee, but overcome them by acting toward them in the fashion of an experienced master; lead them by forcing them to remain in the right path, for each time that thou showest thy strength, it is thou who subduest them, no longer they who subdue thee; it is thou who mountest them, no longer they who make thee their mount.

8. 'As for stratagems and effectual means to which thou canst have recourse in respect to these companions, there is one that consists in subduing the slack and gluttonous companion by the help of the one who is violent and malicious, and in forcing the former to retreat. Conversely, another way will be gradually to moderate the passion of the intolerable angry one by the seduction of the gentle and caressing companion, until he is completely pacified. As for the third companion, the fine talker skilled in fictions, beware of trusting him, of relying on his words, unless it befall that he bring thee some weighty testimony from God. In that case, yes, rely upon his words, receive what he tells thee. Beware, that is, of systematically suspecting all his words, turning a deaf ear to the news he brings thee, even though he mingle true with false therein, for, in it all, there cannot but be something to be received and investigated, something whose truth it is worth-while to realize.'

When he had thus described these companions to me, I found myself very ready to receive what he had taught me and to recognize that his words were true. Submitting my companions to trial and setting myself to observe them, [I found that] experience confirmed what I had been told of them. And now I am as much occupied with curing them as with submitting to them. Sometimes it is I who have the upper hand of them, sometimes they are stronger than I am. God grant that I may live on terms of good neighbourhood with these companions until the time comes when I shall at last part from them!

9. Then I asked the Sage to guide me on the road of the journey, to show me how to set out on a journey such as he himself was making. I addressed him in the fashion of a man who burned to do so, who had the greatest desire for it. He answered me: 'Thou, and all those whose condition is like thine—you cannot set out on the journey that I am making. It is forbidden you; the road is closed to you all, unless thy fortunate destiny should aid thee, for thy part, to separate from these companions. But now the hour for that separation is not yet come: there is a time set for it, which thou canst not anticipate. For the present, then, thou must rest content with a journey interrupted by halts and inactivity; now thou wilt be on the road, now thou wilt frequent these companions. Each time that thou goest alone, pursuing thy journey with perfect ardour, I walk with thee, and thou art separated from them. Each time that thou sighest after them, thou turnest back toward them, and thou art separated from me; so shall it be until the moment comes when thou shalt break with them wholly.'

10. Finally, the conversation led me to question him concerning each of the climes to which he had travelled, all those that were included in his knowledge and of which he was fully informed. He said to me: 'The circumscriptions of the earth are threefold: one is intermediate between the Orient and the Occident. It is the best known; much information concerning it has reached thee and has been rightly understood. Notices even of the marvellous things contained in that clime

have reached thee. But there are two other strange circumscriptions: one beyond the Occident, the other beyond the Orient. For each of them, there is a barrier preventing access from this world to that other circumscription, for no one can reach there or force a passage save the Elect among the mass of men, those who have gained a strength that does not originally belong to man by right of nature.

11. 'What aids in gaining this strength is to immerse oneself in the spring of water that flows near the permanent Spring of Life. When the pilgrim has been guided on the road to that spring, and then purifies himself in it and drinks of that sweet-tasting water, a new strength arises in his limbs, making him able to cross vast deserts. The deserts seem to roll up before him. He does not sink in the waters of the ocean; he climbs Mount Qāf without difficulty, and its guards cannot fling him down into the abysses of hell.'

12. We asked him to explain that spring to us more fully. He said: 'thou hast heard of the darkness that forever reigns about the pole. Each year the rising sun shines upon it at a fixed time. He who confronts that darkness and does not hesitate to plunge into it for fear of difficulties will come to a vast space, boundless and filled with light. The first thing he sees is a living spring whose waters spread like a river over the *barzakh*. Whoever bathes in that spring becomes so light that he can walk on water, and can climb the highest peaks without weariness, until finally he comes to one of the two circumscriptions by which this world is intersected.'

13. Then I begged him: 'Teach me what the circumscription of the Occident is, for the Occident is nearer to our cities.' He said to me: 'At the uttermost edge of the Occident there is a vast sea, which in the Book of God is called the *Hot* (and Muddy), *Sea*. It is in those parts that the sun sets. The streams that fall into the sea come from an uninhabited country whose vastness none can circumscribe. No inhabitant peoples it, save for strangers who arrive there unexpectedly, coming from other regions. Perpetual Darkness reigns in that country. Those who emigrate there obtain a flash of light each time that the sun sinks to its setting. Its soil is a desert of salt. Each time that people settle there and begin to cultivate it, it refuses; it expels them, and others come in their stead. Would any grow a crop there? It is scattered. Is a building raised there? It crumbles. Among those people there is perpetual quarrelling or, rather, mortal battle. Any group that is strongest seizes the homes and goods of the others and forces them to emigrate. They try to settle; but in their turn they reap only loss and harm. Such is their behaviour. They never cease from it.

14. All kinds of animals and plants appear in that country; but when they settle there, feed on its grass, and drink its water; suddenly they are covered by outsides strange to their Form. A human being will be seen there, for example, covered by the hide of a quadruped, while thick vegetation grows on him. And so it is with other species. And that clime is a place of devastation, a desert of salt, filled with troubles, wars, quarrels, tumults; there joy and beauty are but borrowed from a distant place.

15. Between that clime and yours there are others. However, beyond this clime of

yours, beginning at the region in which the Pillars of the Heavens are set, there is a clime that is like yours in several ways. In the first place, it is a desert plain; it too is peopled only by strangers come from distant places. Another similarity is that that clime borrows its light from a foreign source, though it is nearer to the Window of Light than the climes we have described hitherto. In addition, that clime serves as foundation for the heavens, just as the preceding clime serves as the seat for this earth, its permanent base. On the other hand, the inhabitants who people that other clime are sedentaries there in perpetuity. Among the strangers who have come there and settled, there is no war; they do not seize each others' homes and goods by force. Each group has its fixed domain, into which no other comes to inflict violence upon it.

16. In relation to you, the nearest inhabited country of that clime is a region whose people are very small in stature and swift in their movements. Their cities are nine in number.

After that region comes a kingdom whose inhabitants are even smaller in stature than the former, while their gait is slower. They passionately love the arts of the writer, the sciences of the stars, theurgy, magic; they have a taste for subtle occupations and deep works. Their cities number ten.

After that region comes a kingdom whose inhabitants are extremely beautiful and charming; they love gaiety and festivities; they are free from care; they have a refined taste for musical instruments, and know many kinds of them. A woman reigns over them as sovereign. A natural disposition inclines them to the good and the beautiful; when they hear of evil and ugliness, they are seized with disgust. Their cities number nine.

Next comes a kingdom whose inhabitants are very tall in stature and extremely fair of face. The characteristic of their nature is that they are highly beneficial for whatever is at a distance, whereas their immediate neighbourhood is calamitous. Their cities number five.

Next comes a kingdom in which are settled people who bring destruction to the earth; they love to wound, kill, mutilate, and make examples, for their diversion and amusement. Over them reigns a red personage always inclined to hurt, to kill, to strike. Sometimes, as the narrators of their chronicles report, he is seduced by the fair-faced queen whom we just mentioned and who inspires him with passionate love. Their cities number eight.

After their country comes a vast kingdom whose inhabitants are endowed to the utmost with temperance, justice, wisdom, and piety, and bestow all necessary good on all parts of the universe. They maintain a compassionate friendship toward those who are near to them as toward those who are far from them; they extend their goodness to him who recognizes it as to him who knows it not. They are of extraordinary beauty and brightness. Their cities number eight.

After that, comes a country inhabited by a people whose thoughts are abstruse and inclined to evil. However, if they tend to goodness, they go to its utmost extreme. If they attack a troop, they do not lightly fling themselves upon it, but proceed in the fashion of a seducer full of wiles; they do not hurry over what they do, and do not refuse to wait for long periods. Their cities number eight.

Next comes an immense kingdom, with great scattered countries. Its inhabitants are numerous. They are solitaries; they do not live in cities. Their abode is a desert plain where nothing grows. It is divided into twelve regions, which contain twenty-eight stations. No group goes up to occupy the station of another except when the group preceding it has withdrawn from its dwelling; then it hastens to replace it. All the migrants expatriated in the kingdoms that we have described hitherto travel about this kingdom and perform their evolutions there.

Marching with it is a kingdom of which no one has descried or reached the boundaries down to this day. It contains neither city nor town. No one who is visible to the eyes of the body can find refuge there. Its inhabitants are the spiritual Angels. No human being can reach it nor dwell there. From it the divine Imperative and Destiny descend upon all those who occupy the degrees below. Beyond it there is no earth that is inhabited. In short, these two climes, to which the heavens and the earth are respectively joined, are on the left side of the universe, that which is the Occident.

17. Now when thou proceedest toward the Orient, there first appears to thee a clime in which there is no inhabitant neither human beings nor plants nor minerals. It is a vast desert, a flooding sea, imprisoned winds, a raging fire. Having crossed it, thou wilt come to a clime where thou wilt find immovable mountains, streams of living water, blowing winds, clouds that drop heavy rain. There thou wilt find native gold, silver, precious or base minerals of all kinds, but thou wilt find nothing that grows. Crossing it leads thee to a clime filled with the things already mentioned, but in which thou wilt also find all kinds of vegetation, plants and fruit trees and other trees, giving fruits with stones or seeds, but thou wilt find there no animal that whines or peeps. Leaving this clime in its turn, thou wilt enter another where thou wilt find all that was mentioned before, but also living creatures of every species not endowed with the logos, those that swim, those that crawl, those that walk, those that fly beating their wings and gliding, those that engender, and those that hatch, but no human beings are there. Thou wilt escape from it into this world that is yours, and thou knowest already through sight and hearing what it contains.

18. Then, cutting straight across toward the Orient, thou wilt come upon the *sun rising* between the two troops [lit., the two 'horns'] of the Demon. For the Demon has two troops: one that flies, another that plods. The troop that plods contains two tribes: a tribe that has the ferocity of beasts of prey, while the other has the bestiality of quadrupeds. Between the two there is perpetual war, and both dwell in the *left* side of the Orient. As for the demons who fly, their quarters are in the *right* side of the Orient. They are not all of the same constitution. Far from it, for one would say that each individual among them has his particular constitution, different from every other, so that some of them are constituted of two natures, others of three,

others of four, as a flying man would be or a viper with a boar's head. Some of them too are but a half, others but a fragment of a nature, like an individual who should be only one half of a human being, or the palm of a hand, or a single foot, or any other corresponding part of an animal. One would almost think that the composite figures that painters represent come from this clime!

The authority that governs the affairs of this clime has laid out five great roads there for the courier. It has made these roads so many fortified bulwarks for its kingdom, and has stationed men-at-arms upon them. If inhabitants of this world present themselves, the men-at-arms take them prisoners. They inspect all the baggage that the prisoners bring with them, then they deliver them to a Guardian who is in authority over the five men-at-arms and who stands watching at the threshold of that clime. The information that the captives bring and that is to be sent on is put into a letter on which a seal is placed, without the Guardian's knowing what the letter contains. Now, the duty that lies upon the Guardian is to send the letter on to a certain Treasurer, who will present it to the King. It is this same Treasurer who takes charge of the prisoners; as for their effects, he delivers them to another Treasurer for safekeeping. And each time that they take prisoners some troop from your world, whether of human beings, or of animals, or of other creatures, those creatures proliferate, whether by a happy mixture in which their forms are preserved or by engendering only abortions.

19. Sometimes a group from one of these two troops of demons sets out for your clime; there they surprise human beings, they insinuate themselves into their inmost hearts with their breath. As for the plodding tribe that resembles beasts of prey, it lies in wait for the moment when someone will do a man the slightest wrong. Then it stirs him up, shows him the worst actions in a fair light, such as killing, mutilating, ruining, inflicting suffering. It nourishes hatred in the secrecy of his heart; it urges him to oppress and destroy. As for the second of the two plodding tribes, it never leaves off talking secretly to a man, beautifying sins, unworthy acts, and scoundrelly behaviour; it inspires him to desire them, gives him a taste for them; riding the mount of obstinacy, it persists until it has succeeded in swaying him. As for the flying troop, it leads a man to declare that everything he does not see with his bodily eyes is false; it persuades him that it is excellent to adore what is only the work of nature or made by men; it suggests to his heart that after this earthly life there is no birth into another world, nor consequences for the good and the evil, and finally that there is no being who reigns eternally in the celestial kingdom.

20. Severing themselves from these two demoniac troops, there are, however, some groups who haunt the frontiers of a certain clime lying next after that inhabited by the *terrestrial angels*. Letting themselves be guided by these angels, they find the straight road; thus they depart from the aberrancy of the demons and choose the road of the *spiritual Angels*. When these *daimons* mingle with men it is neither to corrupt nor to misguide them; on the contrary, they beneficently help them to

become pure. These are the 'fairies' or 'genii' [*parī*], those who in Arabic are called *jinn* and *ḥinn*.

21. He who succeeds in leaving his clime enters the climes of the Angels, among which the one that marches with the earth is a clime in which the terrestrial angels dwell. These angels form two groups. One occupies the right side: they are the angels who know and order. Opposite them, a group occupies the left side: they are the angels who obey and act. Sometimes these two groups of angels descend to the climes of men and genii, sometimes they mount to heaven. It is said that among their number are the two angels to whom the human being is entrusted, those who are called 'Guardians and Noble Scribes'—one to the right, the other to the left. He who is to the right belongs to the angels who order; to him it falls to dictate. He who is to the left belongs to the angels who act; to him it falls to write.

22. He who is taught a certain road leading out of this clime and who is helped to accomplish this exodus, such a one will find an egress to what is beyond the celestial spheres. Then, in a fugitive glimpse, he descries the posterity of the Primordial Creation, over whom rules as king the One, the Obeyed.

There, the first delimitation is inhabited by intimates of that sublime King; they ever assiduously pursue the work that brings them near to their King. They are a most pure people, who respond to no solicitation of gluttony, lust, violence, jealousy, or sloth. The mission laid upon them is to attend to the preservation of the ramparts of that empire, and it is there that they abide. Hence they live in cities; they occupy lofty castles and magnificent buildings, whose material was kneaded with such care that the result is a compound that in no wise resembles the clay of your clime. Those buildings are more solid than diamond and jacinth, than all things that require the longest time to wear away. Long life has been bestowed upon that people; they are exempt from the due date of death; death cannot touch them until after a long, a very long term. Their rule of life consists in maintaining the ramparts in obedience to the order given them.

Above them is a people that has more intimate dealings with the King and that is unceasingly bound to His service. They are not humiliated by having to fill this office; their state is preserved against all attack, nor do they change their occupation. They were chosen to be intimates, and they have received the power of contemplating the highest palace and stationing themselves all about it. It has been granted them to contemplate the face of the King in unbroken continuity. They have received as adornment the sweetness of a subtle grace in their nature, goodness and penetrating wisdom in their thoughts, the privilege of being the final term to which all knowledge refers. They have been endowed with a shining aspect, a beauty that sets the beholder trembling with admiration, a stature that has attained its perfection. For each of them, a limit has been set that belongs to him alone, a fixed rank, a divinely ordained degree, to which no other contests his right and in which he has no associate, for all the others either are above him or each respectively finds sweetness in his lower rank. Among them there is one, whose rank is nearer to the King, and he is their 'father', and they are his children and grandchildren. It is through him that the King's word and order emanate to them. And among other marvels pertaining to their condition is this: never does the course of time expose their nature to the marks and witherings of age and decrepitude. Far from it, he among them who is their 'father', though the oldest in duration, is thereby all the more abounding in vigour, and his face has all the more of the beauty of youth. They all live in the desert; they have no need of dwelling places or shelter.

23. Among them all, the King is the most withdrawn into that solitude. Whoever connects Him with an origin errs. Whoever claims to pay Him praise that is proportionate to Him is an idle babbler. For the King escapes the power of the clever to bestow qualifications, just as here too all comparisons fail of their end. Let none, then, be so bold as to compare Him to anything whatsoever. He has no members that divide Him: He is all a face by His beauty, all a hand by His generosity. And His beauty obliterates the vestiges of all other beauty. His generosity debases the worth of all other generosity. When one of those who surround His immensity, undertakes to meditate on Him, his eye blinks with stupor and he comes away dazzled. Indeed, his eyes are almost ravished from him, even before he has turned them upon Him. It would seem that His beauty is the veil of His beauty, that His Manifestation is the cause of His Occultation that His Epiphany is the cause of His Hiddenness. Even so, it is by veiling itself a little that the sun can be the better contemplated; when, on the contrary, the heliophany sheds all the violence of its brightness, the sun is denied to the eyes, and that is why its light is the veil of its light. In truth, the King manifests His beauty on the horizon of those who are His; toward them He is not niggardly of His vision; those who are deprived of contemplating Him are so because of the wretched state of their faculties. He is mild and merciful. His generosity overflows. His goodness is immense. His gifts overwhelm; vast is His court, universal His favour. Whoever perceives a trace of His beauty fixes his contemplation upon it forever; never again, even for the twinkling of an eye, does he let himself be distracted from it.

24, 'Sometimes certain solitaries among men emigrate toward Him. So much sweetness does He give them to experience that they bow under the weight of His graces. He makes them conscious of the wretchedness of the advantages of your terrestrial clime. And when they return from His palace, they return laden with mystical gifts.'

25. Then the sage Ḥayy Ibn Yaqẓān said to me: 'Were it not that in conversing with thee I approach that King by the very fact that I incite thy awakening, I should have to perform duties toward Him that would take me from thee. Now, if thou wilt, follow me, come with me toward Him. Peace.'

THE INTRODUCTION

From *Manṭiq al-mashriqiyyīn* (The Logic of the Orientals)

Translated for this volume by S. H. Nasr from Ibn Sīnā, *Manṭiq al-mashriqiyyīn* (Cairo, 1910) pp. 2–4.

In the Manṭiq al-m(a)shriqiyyīn,[1] *which most likely is the section on logic, of* al-Ḥikmat al-m(a)shriqiyyah, *now mostly lost, Ibn Sīnā 'disowns' his own earlier Peripatetic works as being for the common crowd and announces that in his 'oriental philosophy'*[2] *he is going to expose his real views. This is a complete translation of the passage in which Ibn Sīnā presents his own view of his 'science of the elite'.*

We have been inspired to bring together writings upon the subject matter which has been the source of difference among people disposed to argumentation and not to study it with the eyes of fanaticism, desire, habit, or attachment. We have no fear if we find differences with what the people instructed in Greek books have become familiar with through their own negligence and shortness of understanding.[3] And we have no fear if we reveal to the philosophers something other than what we have written for the common people—the common people who have become enamoured of the Peripatetic philosophers[4] and who think that God has not guided anyone but them or that no one has reached Divine Mercy except them.

Although we admit the wisdom of the most learned predecessor of these philosophers [that is Aristotle], and we know that in discovering what his teachers and companions did not know, in distinguishing between various sciences, in arranging the sciences in a better manner than before, in discovering the truth of many subjects ... he was superior to those who came before him, the men who came after him should have brought to order whatever confusion had existed in his thought, mended whatever cracks they found in his structure, and expanded his principles. But those who came after him could not transcend what they had inherited from him.[5] Bigotry over whatever he had not found out became a shield, so that they remained bound to the past and found no opportunity to make use of their own intellects. If such an

1. Unable to convey this double meaning in the Latin transliteration, I have chosen to write the word as *m(a)shriqiyyah*, keeping the (a) in parentheses.

2. In English, and French also, the double meaning of the word 'Orient' points to the same symbolism.

3. Ibn Sīnā is indirectly criticizing those earlier philosophers who tried to emulate Greek philosophy in a literal fashion and without any independent thinking.

4. The whole enterprise undertaken by Ibn Sīnā in this work and his 'oriental philosophy' in general is based on the distinction of a philosophy meant for anyone and accessible for everyone or the common people (*al-'awāmm*) and the philosophy meant for the intellectual elite (*al-khawāṣṣ*). The latter are those to whom the present work is addressed.

5. Again, Ibn Sīnā is not so critical of Aristotle as of his later followers who accepted his thought blindly and without independent understanding.

opportunity did arise, they did not find it admissible to use it in increasing, correcting, and examining the works of their predecessors.

When we have turned our attention to their works, however, from the beginning the comprehension of these works became easy for us. And often we gained knowledge from non-Greek sources.[1] When we began on this project, it was the beginning of our youth, and God shortened the time necessary for us to learn the works of our predecessors. Then we compared everything word for word with the science which the Greeks called logic, and it is not improbable that the Orientals had another name for it.[2] Whatever was contrary by this means of comparison we rejected. We sought the reason for everything until the Truth became separate from error.

Since those who were the people of learning were strongly in favour of the Greek Peripatetics, we did not find it appropriate to separate ourselves and speak differently from everyone else. So we took their side, and with those philosophers who were more fanatical than any of the Greek sects, we too became fanatical. Whatever they sought but had not found and their wisdom had not penetrated, we completed. We overlooked their faults and provided a leader and tutor for them while we were aware of their errors. If we revealed some opposition it was only in matters in which no patience was possible. But in most cases we neglected and overlooked their faults . . . . We were forced to associate with people devoid of understanding who considered the depth of thought as innovation (*bidʿah*) and the opposition to common opinion as sin . . . .

Under these conditions, we longed to write a book containing the important aspects of real knowledge. Only the person who has thought much, has mediated deeply, and is not devoid of the excellence of intellectual intuition can make deductions from it . . . .

We have composed this book only for ourselves, that is, those who are like ourselves. As for commoners who have to do with philosophy, we have provided in the *Kitāb al-shifā*[3] more than they need. Soon in the supplements we shall present whatever is suitable for them beyond that which they have seen up to this time. And in all conditions we seek the assistance of the Unique God.[4]

1. This is very significant for an understanding of what the 'oriental philosophy' meant for later Persian philosophers. For these Persian-Greek sources could only mean ancient Persian philosophy. This is stated clearly three centuries later by Suhrawardī.

2. It is of interest to note that in Arabic and Persian the word for logic (*manṭiq*) and speech or the word (*nuṭq*) is more preserved than between these concepts in contemporary European language. It is difficult, however, to ascertain what term Ibn Sīnā was alluding to in his statement.

3. The *Shifā'* is the great synthesis of Peripatetic philosophy in Islam. It perpetuated Ibn Sīnā's Peripatetic thought for centuries, despite his criticism of this philosophy in the present text.

4. In the *Dānish-nāmah-yi ʿalāʾī*, for the first time, Ibn Sīnā begins with metaphysics (*ilāhiyyāt*) and from there proceeds to natural philosophy (*ṭabīʿiyyāt*) in contrast to Aristotle and many Muslim authors like Abu'l-Barakāt al-Baghdādī (in his *Kitāb al-muʿtabar*) and Fakhr al-Dīn Rāzī (in his *Mabāḥith al-mashriqiyyah*), who begin from natural philosophy and then proceed to metaphysics. Later Safavid and Qājār authors, including Ṣadr al-Dīn Shīrāzī, Mullā Muḥsin Fayḍ and Hājjī Mullā Hādī Sabziwārī, have followed the precedent of the *Dānish-nāmah-yi ʿalāʾī*.

13

Abū ʿAlī Aḥmad ibn Muḥammad Miskawayh

Muḥammad ibn Yaʿqūb Muskūyah, known in Arabic as Ibn Miskawayh, also entitled Abū ʿAlī al-Khāzin and sometimes known simply as Miskawayh, was born around 320/932 in Rayy, into a family that had converted to Islam from Zoroastrianism at least a generation earlier. (Some have said it was his father who converted, while others say it was his grandfather.) He spent most of his life in Iṣfahān, where he was under the patronage of the Buyid rulers of Persia and their *wazīrs*, for whom he served as librarian. He also travelled to Baghdad, where he rose to a position of influence. Miskawayh died in 421/1030, after having gained great fame as both a historian and a philosopher.

It is known that Miskawayh was a Shiʿa, but his attachment to a particular school of Shiʿism is not clear. He was also an accomplished linguist, having mastered several languages including Pahlawī, from which he translated some texts into Arabic. He also had avid interests in other fields of knowledge ranging from medicine and psychology to history and ethics. Of some eighteen works he is known to have written, the most notable from a philosophical point of view are *al-Fawz al-akbar* (The Greater Victory), which deals with metaphysics, psychology, and prophecy; *Tahdhīb al-akhlāq* (The Refinement of Character), his most important work on ethics and *Jāwīdān-khirad* (Perennial Philosophy), dealing with aphorisms concerning ethics and wisdom from different times and cultures. Then there is his major historical work *Tajārib al-umam* (The Experience of Nations), that deals with the history of the world from the Flood of Noah to 369/979.

Miskawayh sought to synthesize various currents of thought. He drew not only from Islam and earlier Islamic schools of thought, especially that of Abū Sulaymān Sijistānī, but also diverse Greek sources, including Plato, Aristotle, Galen, Themistius, Porphyry and other Neoplatonists, and the Stoics, as well as pre-Islamic Persian sources. This meeting of diverse currents is especially evident in his *Jāwīdān-khirad*, the first work in Islamic thought to bear the title of *Philosophia Perennis*, which was to be made famous in the West by Leibnitz in the seventeenth century.

Miskawayh's most important philosophical contribution was in the field of ethics, in which he produced several works. He was a notable ethicist and sought to live according to the ethical principles he preached. He is in many ways the father of Islamic philosophical ethics, which sought to integrate Islamic principles (especially Sufism) and Greek philosophical ethics. This is fully reflected in his *Tahdhīb al-akhlāq*, which reflects both Islamic and more particularly Sufi ethics and Porphyry's commentary upon Aristotle's *Nichomachean Ethics*. This work was to have extensive influence in later Persian history. The *Akhlāq-i nāṣirī* (Nāṣīrean Ethics) and *Akhlāq-i muḥtashamī* (Muḥtashamī Ethics) of Naṣīr al-Dīn Ṭūsī, the *Akhlāq-i jalālī* (Jalālī Ethics) of Jalāl al-Dīn Dawānī, and many later works of this genre, written both in Persia and India mostly in the Persian language, show the influence of Miskawayh's work. By combining ethics with psychology and virtue understood in its religious sense, Miskawayh created a distinctly Islamic philosophical discourse on ethics that wielded great influence over the ages and affected and interacted in numerous ways with other types of ethical discourse, especially Sufi ethics, as we find in the works of Ghazzālī and Mullā Muḥsin Fayḍ Kāshānī.

The two selections in this chapter have been chosen to emphasize Miskawayh's conception of philosophy as possessing a perennial and universal character and also present his ethical ideas.

The first is a first-time translation of his *Jāwīdān-khirad* or *al-Ḥikmat al-khālidah* (Perennial Philosophy), in which Miskawayh first considers a number of virtues, then quotes from various figures from both the Zoroastrian era and also Islamic Persia and offers, in addition, his advice regarding the proper manner and way of acting. Later in this selection there is a reply from Būzarjumihr, the wise Sasanid minister, to the letter of the Persian emperor Khusraw. This letter can be roughly classified as a treatise on political philosophy, in that Miskawayh offers his views regarding the art of governing. In the third part of this selection, Miskawayh paraphrases aphorisms from the emperor Anūshīrwān. This part is rather similar to the previous one, but the style is different. A hypothetical person asks the emperor Anūshīrwān questions concerning key virtues and the emperor responds to them. It concludes with a brief discussion of the emperor Bahrām's words of wisdom. These texts, drawn to a large extent from pre-Islamic Persian sources, are the historical precedents for the *Mirror of Princes* literature that became popular later in Persian history.

The second selection is a translation of the sixth discourse of Miskawayh's *Tahdhīb al-akhlāq*. The selection begins with a discussion concerning the health of the soul and covers a number of issues pertaining to the soul, such as its nature, faculties, and relationship to the body, as well as its survival after death.

The discussions on the soul take place, however, to expose—in Miskawayh's own words—'the diseases which affect the soul, indicate their treatment, and point out their remedies.'

S. H. Nasr

PERENNIAL PHILOSOPHY (WISDOM)

From *al-Ḥikmat al-khālidah or Jāwīdān-khirad* (Perennial Philosophy)

Translated for this volume by Alma Giese from Miskawayh's *al-Ḥikmat al-khālidah: Jāwīdān khirad*, ed. ʿA. Badawī (Tehran, 1979), pp. 5–28, 41–62.

In the Name of God, the Merciful, the Compassionate
and Through Him Comes Help

Aḥmad ibn Muḥammad ibn Yaʿqūb Miskawayh said—after giving the praise and laudation of which He is worthy, to God, and blessings on Muḥammad the Prophet and his noble outstanding family:

In my youth, I had read a book by Abū ʿUthmān al-Jāḥiẓ that was known as *Istiṭālat al-fahm*. In it he mentions a book known as *Jāwīdān khirad*, and he quotes a few sayings [contained] in it. He then glorifies it greatly, going beyond the usual glorification of anything comparable. I desired to obtain it in the countries in which I roamed around, until I found it in Persia with the Zoroastrian High Priest (*Mūbadh mūbadhān*).

When I looked into it I found that it had many similarities and parallels with the wise sayings of the Persians, the Indians, the Arabs, and the Byzantines. However, this book was more ancient and further back in time than those; for it was the testament of Hūshang [*Aushahnaj*] to his son and the kings [to come] after him, and this king came a little after the deluge. No biography of whoever was before him can be found nor any beneficial wisdom. So I thought it good to copy this testament as it was, and then to attach to it everything that I had collected from the testaments and words of proper conduct (*ādāb*) of the four communities—I mean the Persians, the Indians, the Arabs, and the Byzantines—for the young men to educate themselves with them, for the learned to remember what had come before them of wisdoms and knowledges (*ḥikam wa'l-ʿulūm*) I sought through this rectification of myself and of whoever may be rectified by it after me. My highest goal in this is the reward and recompense from God—mighty and great is He—and He is the patron of the good things and the one who rewards the good deeds, and there is no power except with God.

Hūshang said:[1]

In God is the beginning, and with Him everything ends, through Him comes success and He is rightly praised.

He who knows the beginning is thankful, and he who knows the end is faithful.

He who recognizes God-given success (*tawfīq*) is humble, and he who recognizes [God's] favour turns back [to God] with abandonment and assent.

1. The chapter headings have been added by the editor of the text.

Furthermore: The best that man can obtain in this world is wisdom, the best that he can attain in the Hereafter is forgiveness and the best that he can attain in himself is stern admonition; the best that man can ask for is well-being and the best that he can utter is the profession of the unity of God (*tawḥīd*).

The beginning of certainty (*yaqīn*) is knowledge (*maʿrifah*) of God.

The empowerment of knowledge (*ʿilm*) is the act (*ʿamal*), the empowerment of the act is normative tradition (*sunnah*) and following the tradition means staying with the golden mean.

Religion with its [different] branches is like a castle with its columns: when one of them breaks down the others follow after it.

Pious deeds consist of four branches: knowledge, action, soundness of heart, and abstinence. Knowledge is [knowledge] in the normative tradition; action is [action] with the aim of the normative tradition; soundness of heart [lies] in mortification of the body; abstention [lies] in endurance.

All of the matters of man [lie] in four properties: knowledge, forbearance, virtuousness, equitableness. Knowledge of the good is for acquisition, [knowledge] of the bad is for avoidance; forbearance in religion is for reconciliation, and [forbearance] in this world is for noble-mindedness; virtuousness in passion is for self-possession, and [virtuousness] in neediness is for preservation [of honour]; equitableness is for contentment, and anger is for justice.

Knowledge consists of four aspects: that you know the true origin without which nothing could exist, and its branches which are absolutely necessary, the aim at it, without which nothing comes to pass, and its opposite besides which nothing can corrupt it.

Knowledge and action are connected like spirit and body: the one is useless without the other.

The truth can be known in two ways: an obvious one that is known by itself, and an obscure one that is known by an inference from evidence. Likewise, the false.

There are four things, by which one gains the strength for action: health, affluence, determination, and God-given success.

The paths of salvation are three: the path of right guidance, perfection of God-fearingness, and good nutrition.

Knowledge is spirit, action is body; knowledge is a root, and action is a branch; knowledge is a parent, and action is an offspring. Action exists due to [the existence of] knowledge, but knowledge is not existent due to [the existence of] action.

Wealth lies in contentment, soundness lies in detachment, freedom lies in rejection of passion, and love lies in letting go of greed and desire.

You should know that enjoyment over long days comes about for the price of a few days' patience.

The great wealth consists of three things: a knowing soul from which you can seek help for your religion, a steadfast body from which you can seek help in obedience to your Lord and with which you can provide yourself for your return [to God] and for the day of your poverty, and contentment with that which God has provided: through renunciation of that which is with people.

Expel greed from your heart, and you will loosen the fetter from your foot and give rest to your body.

The oppressor will be a repentant, even if some people praise him; and the oppressed will be unblemished, even if some people blame him.

He who is content is rich, even if he is hungry and naked, and he who is greedy is poor, even if he is the king of the world.

Courage (*shajāʿah*) is a breast widened by fearlessness of deadly affairs.

Patience (*ṣabr*) is bearing of painful things and sudden calamities.

Generosity (*sakhāʾ*) is magnanimity of the soul for him who deserves things to be lavished upon him, and the lavishing of considerable wished-for gifts in their [appropriate] places.

Clemency (*ḥilm*) is forgoing revenge despite the possibility of using power.

Determination (*ḥazm*) is exploitation of opportunity.

This world is a house of work, the Hereafter is a house of reward.

The rein of well-being is in the hand of affliction, the head of soundness is under the wing of destruction, and the door of security is hidden under fear. So be not in one of these three states without expecting their opposites, and make not yourself a target for the destructive arrows [of time]. For truly, time is man's enemy, so be on guard against your enemy with the utmost preparedness, and when you keep thinking about yourself and your enemy, you have no need for warning.

Remember! There is soon-to-come death at the hand of someone else than you, and there is fast driving on the part of night and day. And when the allotted time comes to an end your preparation will not avail you, so anticipate that before being denied [through death] and honour death, as you will enter the company of those who went before you.

When soundness is your companion, feel abhorrence from destruction [at the same time], and when you enjoy well-being, be sad because of affliction [at the same time]: For to it (i.e., affliction) will be the return, and when hope makes you serene, make your soul anxious by the nearness of the determined end. For this is the [only true] appointment.

Ruse is better than severity, thoughtfulness is better than hurry, impetuosity in war is better than restraint, and the thought there [in the war] about the [final] outcome is a matter of anguish.

O you warrior, use stratagems and you will gain booty, and do not think about the outcome, lest you should be defeated!

Thoughtfulness in that which you do not fear will escape is better than hurry toward attaining [your] hope.

The weakest ruse is more useful than the harshest severity, the least amount of thoughtfulness is more advantageous than the largest degree of hurry; cunning is the harbinger of an inescapable fate; and when the king is obstinate with his own opinion, the straight paths are obscured for him.

It is forbidden to someone who listens to a speaker to declare him a liar except in three cases which are not right: the patience of the ignorant in suffering a misfortune, the intelligent one who hates the one who has done good to him, and the mother-in-law who loves her daughter-in-law.

There are three things, the wrongness of which cannot be put right by any ruse: enmity between relatives, envy between equals, lowliness in kings.

And there are three things, the rightness of which cannot be put wrong by any kind of cunning: religious observances in the scholars, contentment in those endowed with reason, and generosity in those that are of importance.

There are three things, of which one cannot have enough: well-being, life, and property.

When the malady is from heaven, the remedy is futile, and when the lord decrees, the caution of those who are ruled over is futile.

What a good cure is death! What a bad disease is hope [and wealth]!

There are three things that are the joy of the world, and three things that are its sorrow: As for the joys, they are contentment with [one's] share, acting with obedience in good times, and rejection of concern for tomorrow's livelihood. As for the sorrows [they are]: excessive greed, obtrusive beggary, and to desire that which brings grief.

The world is four things: housing,[1] women, wine, and song.

Four are the troubles of affliction: a great number of dependants, a small amount of property, an evil neighbour, and a disloyal wife.

The calamities of the world [lie] in four things: old age with loneliness, illness away from home, a great amount of debts with paucity, and a wide distance on the journey.

The good woman is a pillar of religion, flourishing of the house, and support in obedience.

Not perfect is he who goes to war without first consummating the marriage with a woman he has married, or he who builds a house that he does not complete, or who scatters seeds that he does not harvest.

There are three things that the intelligent one should not forget: the transitoryness of the house (i.e., this world), the vicissitudes of its states, the harmful damages against which there is no security.

There are three things that you cannot gain by three [other] things: richness through wishes, youth through dye, and health through medication.

Four are the properties which, when you attain them, no worldly lack will be detrimental to you: abstention from food, good character, sincere speech, and keeping of the trust.

1. One could also read *thanā'*, 'praise' instead of *binā'*, 'housing'.

Six things put the world in balance: wholesome food, a merciful master, dutiful offspring, an agreeable wife, clear and firm speech, and perfect intellect.

Your polishing the sword when it has none of its original substance left (i.e., the whole sword has turned into rust) is a mistake, your sowing of the grain before its time into the manured earth is ignorance, and your exposing an old recalcitrant camel to training is a toil.

Innate nature is a true guide and beautiful speech is a compassionate leader.

Smarting toil is the substitute talent for one who has no inborn talent.

An incurable disease is frivolity that snowballs.

A bad woman is a festering wound.

Anger is a heavy pregnancy.

There are three things which are good in three [different] situations: consolation with hunger, sincerity with exasperation, and forgiveness with power.

The intelligent man does not hope for anything for which he will be chided, he does not ask for that which he fears will be refused to him, and he does not vouch for that over which he cannot be confident to have power.

There are three things in the company of which one is not abroad: good behaviour, suppression of grievance, and avoidance of suspicions.

Eight ways of behaviour are among the characteristics of the ignorant: anger without sense, undeserving donations, tiring out the body in futile [things], a man rarely knowing his friend from his enemy, entrusting a secret to undeserving people, confidence in someone whom he has not put to the test, good opinion of someone who has no intelligence and no loyalty, and a lot of talk without any benefit.

A king who becomes unjust has left the high-mindedness of kingship and nobility and has moved to the lowliness of greed and deficiency and the imitation of subjects and slaves.

When loyalty leaves, affliction settles in.
When safeguarding dies, revenge comes to life.
When deceptions appear, blessings go into hiding.

Jesting is the ruin of seriousness, lying is the enemy of sincerity, oppression is the corruptor of justice: so when a king uses jesting, respect for him disappears, when he takes up with lying he is no longer taken seriously, and when oppression appears, his reign is ruined.

Resoluteness is exploitation of opportunity while it is in one's power, and avoiding slackness in things which you fear will pass you by.

Leadership is not complete save by good administration, and whoever seeks it endures its pains.

By undergoing toils rulership is cherished, by making a profit dangers are praised, by virtuous behaviour deeds thrive.

When discerning judgment is with somebody who is not obeyed, and a weapon with somebody who does not use it, when riches are with somebody who does not spend them—then all is lost.

It is the king's duty to make use of three ways of behaviour: deferment of punishment while anger is dominating, expediting rewards for someone who has done good deeds, and equanimity in whatever happens. For in the deferment of punishment he has the possibility for forgiveness, in the expediting of reward for the good deeds he gains hastening in obedience from subjects and army, and in equanimity ample room for discerning judgment and elucidation of that which is right.

Someone who is resolute in an opinion which is dubious to him is in the position of someone who lets a pearl get lost, then collects the dirt around the place where it fell, and then sifts it until he finds it. So also the resolute man collects the [different] kinds of opinions on dubious matters, then he refines them and discards some of them until he has distilled from it the true opinion.

[There is] no lowliness with resoluteness; no nobility with weakness: resoluteness is the mount of success, weakness causes deprivation.

There are four ways of behaviour [indicating] lowliness in kings and nobles: arrogance, the company of young men and women, consultation with them [i.e., women], and not doing the things he needs to do in what he carries out with his own hand and attends to personally.

The king will not become a [real] king unless he eats from his [own] plantation, is clothed from his [own] manufacture, marries from his old [clans], and takes mounts from his [own] stock.

Correct performance of these matters lies in proper management, proper management lies in consultation, consultation is with the viziers who give sincere advice and are worthy of their rank.

Conquer him who is beneath you with graciousness, him who is your equal with equity, and him who is above you with respect—then you hold on to the firm reins of right conduct.

Necessary for the intelligent man (*ʿāqil*) is: glorification and gratitude with respect to God—great and exalted is He, obedience and good advice with respect to the ruler, striving for the good and avoidance of the bad things with respect to your own self, loyalty in friendship and giving help with respect to the companions, and abstaining from doing harm and good companionship with respect to people in general.

Man is not perfect save for four things: old in nobility, young in soul, giving when there is property, telling the truth even if it can bring you harm.

Whom riches do not make vain, who does not become lowly in poverty, whom calamities do not frighten, who does not feel safe from misfortunes, and who does not forget the outcome—he is the perfect one.

Perfection lies in three things: understanding in religion, patience in the ups and downs [of life], and good estimation in your livelihood.

A man's fear of God can be concluded from three things: [absolute] trust in that which he has not [yet] obtained, perfect contentment with that which he has obtained, and perfect reassignment with that which has passed him by.

The summit of belief is in four ways of behaviour: patient endurance of the judgment, contentment with the divine decree, making your trust in God pure and absolute, and surrender to the Lord.

There is no substitute for religion, no replacement for time, and no successor for the soul.

Who is a mount for night and day will be moved along, even if he himself does not move along.

Who combines generosity and modesty has made a good loincloth and cloak.

He who does not care about complaints has thereby admitted to meanness.

Whoever reclaims his gift has consolidated his meanness.

[There are] four things of which a little is a lot: pain, poverty, disgrace, and enmity.

Who does not know his own worth knows even less the worth of someone else.

He who spurns doing work himself is forced to [seek] somebody else's work.

Who looks down on his parents has been barred from the well-guided path.

Who does not humble himself in his own eyes is not lifted up in somebody else's [eyes].

Think with every blessing about its end, with every trial about its removal, for that makes bliss more lasting, safer from vanity, and nearer to joy.

If justice is not victorious over oppression, all sorts of trials and evils will not cease to happen.

Nothing is more conducive for the reversal of a blessing and the quick meting out of punishment than persistence in injustice.

Expectation cuts off from everything good, abandoning ambitious desire prevents all fear, patient endurance leads to success, and the soul invites to all evil.

In rectifying the means of living the worshipper is made to thrive, by true trust [in God] subsistence is deserved, by sincere devotion recompense is deserved, by soundness of the breast love is laid down in the heart, by abstaining from the forbidden things the Lord's contentment is gained; through wisdom the cover is lifted from knowledge; with contentment life becomes good; through understanding the summit of things is reached; when affliction comes down the virtues of man become apparent; with a long absence consolation of brothers appears; in perplexity the intellects of men are disclosed; through travels characters are tested; with constraint appears generosity, in anger the sincerity of a man becomes known; by preferring others over oneself slaves are made kings; through sound behaviour knowledge is inspired; through abstention from sins one is free from defects; through asceticism wisdom comes to be; through God-given success deeds are strong; when there are extremes resolutions become apparent; through him who has sincerity one becomes strong enough for [all] matters; with get together there is an increase in friendships; with giving up worldly pursuits brotherliness is strengthened.

Loyalty brings forth continuing relations; accepting guidance from a scholar results in riding the mount of knowledge; an honest intention brings forth the choice of righteous companions; brushing against danger results in riding the sea; a powerful soul brings forth the necessity of contentment; the rule of certainty results in endurance in your religion;[1] entering into the secret of sincerity brings forth the meeting with that which the common people do not know; love of soundness results in the ending of passions; fear of the Return brings forth abstention from evils; striving for curiosity results in the fall into afflictions; and who does not feel a pain toward himself because of a misdeed does not feel within him a place where a good deed could settle.

Separation from a fool equals union with a sage.

The envious cannot rule.

Who fights the truth is defeated.

Most entitled to [receive] favours is he who returns his own favour most often.

That which helps most for the purification of the intellect is learning, and that which proves more cogently the intellect of a man is skilled planning.

He who asks for advice has protected himself from falling, and he who proceeds independently crashes down into error.

He who clothes himself in bashfulness, his garment covers his defects from [the eyes of] people.

The best of conduct is that a man does not praise himself for his good conduct, that he does not demonstrate power over somebody who has no power over him, and that he does not become slack in knowledge when he strives for it.

[There are] three types of people who do not feel lonely when away from home and one does not fail to see noble deeds from them: the hero, wherever he turns, for people have a need for his heroism and his courage; the scholar, for people have a need for his knowledge and his understanding; and he who has a sweet tongue, clear and lucid, for speech works for him through sweetness of his tongue and smoothness of his language. And when you cannot obtain self-composure and a bold heart, may knowledge and the reading of books not elude you, for that is a refinement and a knowledge that have been laid down for you by those who have gone before you, through which you will increase in intelligence.

Make gentle forbearance an instrument with which you withstand the foolish.

1. I prefer to leave out *man yaṭmaʿu*, 'who strives' in accordance with the variant given in the apparatus.

Abū ʿUthmān al-Jāḥiẓ said: Ḥasan ibn Sahl, the brother of Dhu'l-Riyāsatayn Faḍl ibn Sahl said:

This is a translation of that which was available to us of the pages which we took from the book *Jāwīdān-khirad*. However, we dropped a lot of it, the parts were disconnected from each other, because Dhūbān did not allow himself to turn the pages over to us in sequence, [appropriate] arrangement and compilation; and so we left out the rest of it, for we did not have any wish for it. For him who does not learn a lesson by a little, much is of no use. And in that which we have presented [there is] richness and sufficiency, and information for him who wants to benefit from it. Praise be to God alone!

Abū ʿUthmān al-Jāḥiẓ relates the story of this book in his book, entitled *Istiṭālat al-fahm*, and he said: al-Wāqidī reported to me and said: al-Faḍl ibn Sahl said to me:

When blessings for Ma'mūn were invoked in the districts of Khurāsān for his caliphate, presents from the kings were brought to us. And the king of Kābulistān sent an old man who was called Dhūbān and wrote mentioning that he was sending the most brilliant, refined, noble, and magnificent present on earth. Ma'mūn marvelled at this, and he said: 'Ask the shaykh: What are the presents that he has with him?' So I asked him and he said: 'I have nothing more with me than my knowledge.' Then he said: 'What is your knowledge?' and he replied: 'Devising, deciding and guiding.' al-Ma'mūn ordered to lodge him, to honour him and to keep his matter a secret. And when he decided on turning toward ʿIraq to fight against his brother Muḥammad, he called for Dhūbān and said: 'What do you think about the turning toward ʿIraq to fight against Muḥammad?' He said: 'A decision clear and a kingship near, won by a smart emir.'

Al-Jāḥiẓ then relates from Dhūbān through an uninterrupted chain of authorities that he used to speak in the rhymed prose of the soothsayers and that he hit the mark in everything that Ma'mūn asked him. When now the message of the conquest of Iraq was received by him, he called for Dhūbān, honoured him and ordered to give him one hundred thousand dirham. But he would not accept them, and he said: 'O king! My king,[1] has not sent me to you to reduce you [in your means]. So do not take my refusal of your benefaction in anger, for I do not refuse it because I find its amount too little. I will, however, accept from you something that is equivalent to this fortune and that [even] exceeds it. This is a book to be found in ʿIraq, in which there are the noble deeds of outstanding character and the knowledge of all regions from the books of the ruler of Persia. It can be found in the treasure crates underneath the vaulted hall in Madā'in (i.e., Seleucia-Ctesiphon).'

When Ma'mūn arrived in Baghdad and the seat of his kingdom became established in it, Dhūbān claimed from him what he desired. He then demanded of him

1. For better understanding I adopt the variant *malikī*, 'my king' mentioned in the apparatus, instead of *al-mālik*, 'the king' in the main text.

that he write down the details and mention the place [where it was to be found]. Dhūbān then wrote it down and defined the place, and he said: 'When you come to buildings and you reach the yard then pull it up, and you will find the desired object. But do not pay attention to anything else, or the result of offending it will stick with you.' Ma'mūn now dispatched in this matter a man endowed with sound judgment. He found there a small crate of black glass and upon it a lock of black glass. He took it up and restored the hole to its [former] state.

He said: 'Ḥasan ibn Sahl has related to me: I was with Ma'mūn when this crate was brought in.' He began to marvel at it. Then he called for Dhūbān and said: 'This is your object of desire?' He answered: 'Yes!' He (Ma'mūn) then said: 'Take it and leave! You shall not think that desire for that which may be found in it will cause us to ask from you to open it in front of us.' But he (Dhūbān) said: 'Certainly not, oh king! You are not one of those whose desire destroys the protection of his promise.' He then opened the lock, put his hand in, and pulled out a piece of brocade. He spread it out and from it fell leaves of paper. He counted them and lo!—they were a hundred leaves! Then, he shook out the crate, but there was nothing but the leaves in it. He returned the leaves to the piece [of brocade], took them up, and rose. Then he said: 'O king! This crate is appropriate for the hidden treasures of your treasury!' So he ordered it to be taken away.

Ḥasan ibn Sahl said: Then I said: 'Does the Commander of the Faithful approve of me asking him what is in the book?' He answered: 'O Ḥasan! Do I flee from rebuke and then return to it?'

After he had left I went to him in his home and asked him about it. He said: 'This is the book *Jāwīdān-khirad* which Kanjūr the *wazīr* of the ruler of Īrānshahr selected from the old word of wisdom.' I said: 'Give me one leaf of it so that I can look at it!' He then gave it to me. I let my eyes linger on it and my mind attend to it, but what was in it became ever farther removed from me. I then called for Khiṣr ibn ʿAlī, and that was in the early parts of the day. And it was not half over, when he had finished reading it for himself. Then he started to interpret it while I wrote it down. I then returned the leaf and took another one from him, while Khiṣr was [still] with me. He began to read and I wrote [it down] until I had taken from him about thirty leaves and then, I went away for that day. Then one day, I came to him and said: 'O Dhūbān! Is there in the world anything better than this knowledge?' He answered: Where it not for the fact that knowledge is grudged (i.e., you do not want to give it to the unworthy)—and this is the way of the world and the Hereafter—I would have deigned to hand it over to you in its complete form. However, there is no access to more than that which I took. The leaves which I took, were not compiled, because they contained things that could not possibly be brought out.

Ḥasan ibn Sahl has related to me: One day, Ma'mūn said to me: 'Which Arabic book is the most noble and the most excellent?' I started enumerating books on military expeditions of the Prophet (*maghāzī*) and history until I mentioned Quranic exegesis (*tafsīr*). He said: 'Nothing resembles the word of God Most High.' Then, he said: 'Which is the most noble Persian book?' I mentioned many of them, and then said: the book *Jāwīdān-khirad*, oh Commander of the Faithful!

He then ordered the catalogue of his books and started turning it about. But he did not see a trace nor mention of this book. He said: 'How could mention of this book be omitted from this catalogue?' I said: 'O Commander of the Faithful! This is the book of Dhūbān, and I have written down some of it.' He said: 'Bring it to me at once!' I sent away to fetch it, and a messenger brought it while he had just stood up for prayer. When he saw him approaching and that the book was with me he turned away from the *Qiblah*, took the book, and read in it. And every time, when he had finished a chapter he said: 'There is no god but [the one] God!' When this had lasted a while, I said: 'O Commander of the Faithful! The [time for] prayer will pass, but this [book] will not pass.' He said: 'You are right. However, I fear that I will be distracted in my prayer, because my heart is occupied with it.' Then he prayed and went back to his reading. He then said: 'Where is the end of it?' I replied: 'Dhūbān did not present it to me.' He said: 'Were it not that the covenant is a rope one end of which is in the hand of God and the other in my hand, I would take it from him! For this, by God, is wisdom, not what we do, namely turn our tongues in the openings of the corners of our mouths.'

Aḥmad ibn Muḥammad Miskawayh said:

This is the end of the book of Hūshang and its story with Dhūbān. I have heard of Ma'mūn's strong liking for it and people's reluctance to part with what it contains and from what we have added to it you will learn the genius of the wise, the fruits of their thoughts and their conformity in spite of their being separated [from each other] in their [different] lands—things that will clearly mean an increase in beauty over it.

I begin with words with which I introduce to you the hidden treasures of the wise, their secrets and their intentions, so that you may direct yourself to it with your genius and travel on its path until it leads you to your goal, and that you may not digress from it so that you do not go astray and get into the wilderness that has no end. For when the path is straight, one easily reaches the utmost goal by it. But if it is not straight, then whenever the attention for it increases, it grows in distance from its goal.

I ask God—in whose hands there are the keys of the good things—for protection and success. He is sufficient for us and how well He can be trusted!

Rules of Conduct of the Persians

Among these are the admonitions of Adharbādh. He spoke, admonishing his son:

O my son! Adopt a middle course in hospitality, and you will be taken in as a guest. Hold on to contentment, and you will be relaxed of mind; be filled with good will, and you will be composed; work hard in the quest, and you will find; avoid sins, and you will be safe; adhere to the golden mean, and you will be trusted; become an ally of proper conduct, and you will be knowledgeable; persevere in gratefulness, and you will be deserving; adhere to modesty, and you will have many brethren; and to your spouse be sincere, dutiful and pure.

Do not leave aside—for the sake of gaining property—that which is better than property. Do not abstain—because of the shares of the transitory world—from striving for the attainment of the shares of the everlasting Hereafter. Let knowledge be the most favoured and most noble thing for you. Pay thorough attention to the learned; pay good obedience to those who are in power. Associate closely with sincere friends in such a way that you will not be in need of a judge. Accustom yourself to being humble toward people; that will not humiliate you, but elevate you and increase your stature. Do not apply certainty to matters that are open to doubt. May thinking of your Return and fear of your punishment be on your mind. Do not place confidence in intercessors. Do not place confidence in women and do not reveal to them a secret. Do not worry about that which may not happen. Do not think of words and deeds that are past history for you, and use contentment and acceptance for that which has happened. Do not be obsessed with beginning the talking in gatherings before everybody else. Do not let a powerful man be indebted to you, for then you will be overcome by trouble while attempting to retrieve this [debt] from him. Do not quarrel with equals with regard to the seat [at table] nor the ranks [at court]. Do not acquaint the envious with your wealth. Do not wager with anybody. Do not, by any means, rely on anything in the world of generation and corruption (*ʿālam al-kawn wa'l-fasād*). Do not eat with the shameless glutton. Do not associate with a drunken man who has a bad character. Do not quarrel with a clever and eloquent man. Do not walk in the company of the sinner. Use the virtuous man as a doorkeeper, the sharp-witted free man as a messenger, the noble free man as a friend so that he will not be disloyal to you and will not disappoint you. Do not use deceit and fraud in any of your matters. Steer clear of arrogance and resignation, for the well-bred man of knowledge does not get drunk from prosperity and misfortune does not depress him. When you see something disagreeable and strange, you should not be seized by doubt of your lord and not regret the good and pious [things] that you have sent ahead [to the Hereafter]. Do not be sad about the riches that have escaped you, for fortune is like a bird that moves from top to top:[1] when it approaches it is quick in approaching, and when it retreats it is fast in its change of locality. Do not be friendly with the conceited ungrateful who finds fault with people; for through him you will be at the side of unjust damage. Furthermore, do not lack in intercessors at your door whom to reject would weigh heavily on you and who would be difficult to contradict in what they ask from you. Avoid taking an oath in the state of sincerity, and as to the lie, you should avoid it [i.e., the oath] in principle. Do not dispute with your brothers, even if you are eloquent and good in argument. Even if you are very skilful in [the art of] swimming, you should not rush to the stream in the *wādī*. Even if you are well versed in magic spells, you should not hasten to reach for snakes. When you begin with a good deed, do not have any doubt about its reward, and when you start with an evil deed, then you should watch out for punishment for it. Look after your fortune with an eye on profit, intense inspection, and thoroughgoing accounting so that the current proverb may not applicable to you: 'When fortune is present, the intellect is distant, and when the intellect is present, fortune is distant.' Persevere in the endeavour to store good deeds, so that grief and repentance may not overtake you at a time when you are in need of them. May not the insolent devil deceive you with his delusions and his distortions and so take possession of you; for he is like the people who set up a trap, obscure its traces, make its grains clearly visible, and hold it to be a ruse against the birds and a means for catching them. Likewise, the devil presents in a favourable light the [different] kinds of dangers and downfalls for people, trying to gain access to controlling their rein, seeking reasons to bring them into trouble and to expose them to damnation. Avoid a high rate of slaughtering of freely grazing livestock and observe in that the golden mean. For the consequence of it is severe in the Hereafter, and consider the evil outcome of it also in this world, because in every place, in which there is less killing and shedding of blood, there is a greater amount of people, in it the evil does not show excessively and their welfare is more common, the rule of harmful things and diseases is weaker and corruption of the devils and sorcerers is lesser and more feeble.

Measure things according to the evaluation of the intellect (*'aql*) and in accordance with the spirit (*rūḥ*), not in accordance with passion, the belly, and the genitals in the stage of the cattle.

The diligent man (*mujtahid*) hastens to finish a work that needs to be done here and now, before time is too short for him; and he will at every moment trust and perceive that his intention, when it suddenly occurs to him will not need any preparation and none of his means and conditions need to be corrected.

Belittle this world with the Return, concentrate your insight and thinking on your return, and be confident and [absolutely] certain that our Lord is victorious,

1. I prefer to read the variant *nashaz*, 'elevated place, high ground' mentioned in the apparatus, instead of *nashr*, 'unfolding, spreading etc' in the main text.

sovereign, and just and that the devil is ignorant and does not have full power, and that he has no knowledge of the presence of the appointed time when it comes near and the completion of time when it approaches—and this is the eye of certainty (*ʿayn al-yaqīn*).

What I Have Chosen of the Wise Sayings of Kisrā Qubādh

The answers of Kisrā Qubādh, to the Byzantine king to the questions he had asked him and the answers of somebody else to certain questions.

Somebody asked him: Is there somebody who does not have a defect? He said: No, because he who has no defect should not die.

And he was asked: What is it that makes men happiest when they achieve it? He said: [He is happiest] who strives for a truth and attains it, and whose wish is then in agreement with this.

He was asked: Who among people is considered happy? He said: Who possesses an intellect leading to success.

He was asked: Which man is among your people most praiseworthy as judged by the intellect? He said: He who clearly sees the short duration of this world, because he refrains from sins due to his insight into this, while this does not restrain him from obtaining [some] of the pleasures of this world with moderation.

He was asked: Does one in addition to faith (*īmān*) require the intellect (*ʿaql*)? He said: Yes, because with the intellect one distinguishes between the true and the false; and faith is belief in that which should be believed.

Someone said: How does one distinguish between the two of them? He said: Who is intelligent does not look into those matters of which he is not convinced, and does not refrain from research into that in which there is doubt.

Someone said: What is most useful for the intelligent? And what is most damaging for him? He said: The most useful thing for him is consultation with the learned, and consultation and circumspection; and the most damaging thing for him is laziness, following one's passions and hurrying things.

He was asked: What is it with the scholars that they are the most joyful and the least sad of all mankind? He said: They have joy because of the good which they have sent ahead for their Hereafter, and they have little sadness because of their patient endurance and contentment with whatever overcomes them.

Someone said to him: Which is the best adornment for mankind? He said: As for the learned it is adhering to an approved way of life, as for the heroes, it is victory and pardon after the victory.

He was asked: Do riches change the learned? He said: He is not a learned person whom riches change.

He was asked: Is it the learned who earn most praise among the forefathers or is it the heroes? He said: Nay, the learned, for we benefit today from their knowledge like those benefited from them who were with them in their time.

He was asked: How does one know the learned man? He said: By the perfection of his way of acting.

He was asked: Whom among the kings do you [Persians] see as most excellent in kingship? He said: Those who rule with goodness and during whose reigns the public well is all-pervasively established.

Someone said: What does the king have to do so that his righteousness embraces [all] the people of his kingdom? He said: That he will appoint [as deputies] the best people of his realm.

Someone said: What should kings be guided by in their behaviour towards their subjects? He said: [By] four characteristics which are the foundations of their authority: protection for them, acting according to the customs among them, beneficence toward common people, rectifying their affairs, and averting tyranny from them.

Someone said: What is the fruit of heroism? And what the fruit of knowledge? He said, the fruit of heroism is safety from the enemy, and the fruit of knowledge is safety from sins.

He was asked about the difference between joy, on the one hand, and pleasure and jest, on the other. He said: Joy remains, whereas pleasure will exist only as long as you are in it. Someone said: What is the meaning of this? He said: Because joy remains, and it is that the good of which one hopes for in the Hereafter. All the rest is considered pleasure, because it is transient.

He was asked: What is it that one has to do concerning God, the soul, the ruler, one's relatives and one's friends? He said: As to God Most High, it is praise and thanks; as to the soul, it is being diligent in knowing and doing and avoiding sins; as to the ruler, it is obedience and sincere advice; as to one's relatives, it is love and kinship; and as to one's friends, it is gentleness and support.

He was asked: Why did the kings of yore see a bad omen in the mention of death in their presence, while you now frequently mention death? He said: Because then they considered the continuity and management of their kingdom, and we now consider the separation from our kingdom and the arrangement of whatever comes after that.

Why do you not estimate the effect of intense joy and safety, when they come to you? He said: Because we know that we will be separated from them and they from us.

He was asked: Why do you boast of a great amount of riches? He said: Because we increase with it in our benefits and good deeds for people and in our power against the enemies.

He was asked: Which rule do you consider to be the most excellent? He said: [The rule of] him whom the innocent trusts and from whom the suspicious cannot be safe.

Someone said: We have heard you say: Someone who does not know for certain that it is not possible for him to be killed outside of his appointed time, need not consider himself as belonging to the people of battle. Why have you said this? He said: We have said this because when the horsemen are accomplished, we can educate them to have little fear of death. But who is not certain that his death is predetermined, his soul does not side with him.

Someone said to him: We have heard you say: It is unfitting that anybody be in doubt of four realities. What are they? He said: One is God—mighty and great is He, the second is doing good deeds, the third is [the fact] that no kingdom is in good order except through the Religious Law, and the fourth is the king's judgment.

Someone said: What is the meaning of your words: 'Envy people for avoiding sins, not for riches', while we see many of those who avoid sins being at a disadvantage and in severe trial, and we see those who are rich in good composure and a good life? He said: From riches those who have them gain a little joy and long-lasting sadness; and from the avoiding of sins those who do it gain a little hardship and long-lasting safety.

Someone said: We heard you say: 'One should exert oneself in that which lessens sadness at the time of death, not in that which increases the pain of death. What is it that increases the pain of death in severity? And what is it that lessens it? He said: That which increases the pain of death in severity is the occupation with pleasure and the things futile, a great number of enemies and children lacking good conduct. As to that which lessens the pain of death, it is pious deeds, true friends, and children with good conduct.

He was asked: Why does man surrender his soul to death, although there is nothing dearer to him than it? He said: Nobody does this except for four specific [reasons]: either for greed, or for fear of disgrace, for religion, or for want.

The messenger of the king of Byzantine asked Kisrā that he advise his master on whatever would be of use to him. Kisrā said: Instruct him to uphold thankfulness (*shukr*), that he strives for beneficence (*iḥsān*) toward him in whom he perceives good quality. Instruct him never to cease being alert and courageous. Instruct him not to trust in anything worldly, for there is no fulfilment and no soundness in it; not to assist anyone in committing a sin; not to be proud because of one good thing that happened to him, not to be depressed because of harm when it falls upon him. And instruct him not to be unhappy about whatever is bound to happen to him, that he not wish for anything he ought not to wish for. Also instruct him that he take to a way of life (*sīrah*) in which he does not [need to] have recourse to judges. And instruct him not to blame his brothers for anything he does not blame himself for.

Copy of a Letter from Būzarjumihr to Kisrā about the Latter's Questions to Him

You should know that there is for people—the kings among them as well as the subjects—nothing through which they can gain more favours and blessings nor greater adornment and beauty than [this]: the fear of God Almighty, His glorification together with their own belittlement, acknowledgment of His power and their own humbleness, the certainty of their annihilation and return to Him, that their lives go by until the end of the appointed time in search for the truth and whatever is necessary for them to know and whatever principles of the sciences (*ʿulūm*) and the cognitive skills (*maʿārif*) are necessary for them, and carrying out what they impose upon them. Through this is accomplished for them God-given success, following the path of their salvation, and attainment of whatever they love of this world and the Hereafter. This is the searched-for bliss and the cherished happiness. He whose intention is good and whose heart is pure, whose striving is permanent, gains knowledge of that which was his ancestor's duty toward God whose majesty is most high, he perseveres in God-fearing piety and follows God's custom (*sunnah*) in his justice and his wisdom.

Kingship is right for him whose rule is suitable for his subjects, and to whom what sets them aright is preferable to the attainment of his personal whims and who strives to benefit both the elect and the common people. The best kings are those who are most grateful to God Most High, who best judge in truth, who are most benevolent to their subjects and who have the best insight into what is right for the country and what makes it flourish. This can only be brought to completion through intelligent circumspection (*ʿaql*). The king whose rule is most beneficial for his subjects is the one who acts according to the well-known established customs among them and who appoints the best people his governors, who spares their blood and bars the enemy from his land. The most blessed of them is he who rules people during the time in which he is appointed for them with general fairness and charity. The highest bliss is reached by those whose knowledge is vast and who succeed in putting it into action. The most deserving [thing] for him (i.e., the king) to delight in is the good that is gained through him, and the provisions he makes through it (i.e., the good) for his subjects by which he merits gratitude from them and reward and recompense from God, so that the innocent will trust in him and the troublemakers will fear him. For the trust of the innocent makes him grow in exerting himself, and sincere behaviour and the fear of the troublemaker makes [people's] dread and awe for him increase. Through exertion and sincere behaviour[1] there comes health, vitality, and integrity and with fear and awe there comes uprightness and obedience. The best character traits of the kings are dignity in anger and a large amount of self-control and equanimity. But the ugliest of their character traits are irascibility, inability, lack of insight, crudeness, being overcome

1. I read *wa-* instead of *bi-*.

by avarice, cruelty, and lack of concern for the affairs of the common people.

Those in power should know that they cannot bring the common people not to mention the rulers' deficiencies and they should not exert themselves for the sake of preventing the people from seeing what is in them. Their earnest goal should be not to have any deficiency and not to open a door for people to gossip about them.

The ignorant among the people should not rule over them, for ignorance leads to error, and error leads to affliction and strife, and in strife there is destruction and ruin.

It is imperative for kings that they take for the weak from the powerful, for the poor from the rich according to both their shares in what is theirs by right and [both] their portion in justice; further, that they have a strong concern for the weak and the poor, that they are very benevolent to them, and that they thoroughly scrutinize the affairs of those two, because the powerful and the rich are protected from most kinds of oppression and injustice. As to the poor and the weak their protection will be through the power of their ruler and their strength[1] will be through their support by him (i.e., the ruler).

You should know that the rule of the kings of the world extends over the bodies which they rule and over their visible affairs as they become apparent. As to their intentions and the hidden aspects of their affairs, there is no way for them to get to it, because it is hidden and concealed from them. So the kings should not admonish the subjects for anything but that which appears of them to them. They should abstain from making assumptions, for assumptions lead to suspicion, and suspicion leads to tribulations.

Most useful to the ruler is the company of the learned and the quest to increase one's knowledge. For one of the virtues of knowledge is that he who possesses it, whenever he increases it, he wishes to make it grow further. This is the kind of greed that is praiseworthy.

People are being blamed for a strong desire in the pursuit of this world and wealth, but they are praised for a strong desire in the pursuit of knowledge and the companionship of the learned. So increase in splendour[2] and delight due to the knowledge that you possess and grow ever more greedy of it and persistent in it. Moreover, you should not look down on anybody who brings to you his knowledge and reject to accept it because of contempt of him, for knowledge is useful for you from wherever it comes to you. You should know that for everything there is a source, and the source of knowledge is the clear exposition. Neither progression of years nor age should keep you away from knowledge, for you are capable of pursuing it for as long as your life is destined for you, as knowledge is longer than the days of your life. So read and study many books, so that you may grow in insight and benefit by this. There is nothing more enjoyable or more joyful for those who

1. Instead of *qurratuhumā* I read *quwwatuhumā*, as mentioned in the apparatus.

2. Instead of *ḍannan* I read *ḍiyāʾan*.

have knowledge than doing good deeds, spreading them out extensively, to do a lot of it and to grow in it. These are the people with the least sadness through their perfect equanimity toward things that passed them by, and the most submissive people to that which has befallen them from God—great and mighty is He. Who has knowledge has no leisure for anything else but the pursuit of knowledge and the good. The moment he has leisure he would be capable of the good, but then would not do it. This would be a stupidity in his estimation and an error in his determination and evaluation. The leisure of a thinker would consist only in giving himself a rest, when his mind has become blunt and he has become unable to think about extracting the hidden treasures of wisdom. Then, he would revive his heart, so that his creative activity returns, his determination becomes forceful again and his thought pure.

The worst time is a time when the learned man hides his knowledge for fear of the ignorant and out of concern that he might be reproved for it. You should know that most worthy of being honoured and being drawn near to you, O King, is he who admonishes you and puts to rights your conduct. So, honour the learned, reward them, listen to their aphorisms of appropriate conduct (*adab*), keep in mind their admonishments, and beware of those who imitate the learned and yet do not belong to them, for these are the majority. So remove them and beware of their talk and of the phony leadership they exert themselves in. Do not follow your passion, do not compromise the truth, do not avail yourself of leisure, do not feel at home with indifference, do not be shy in acquiring knowledge and learning, do not let yourself be deceived by a worldly good that you have attained, do not repent of a kindness that you have committed, do not become bored by the study of books, for their study[1] is a perusal of the minds of all people, and knowledge of the virtues of those who had wisdom in the past, the prophets, and all nations (*umam*) and all the people of the various religious communities (*ahl al-milal*). However, most of that which they described and recorded consists of branches whose roots and causes they did not make clear, and the reason for which they did not unveil. These are praiseworthy things, except that they are numerous and the memory cannot retain and learning cannot encompass knowledge of all of them. But the wise have busied themselves with the roots of these branches and shown their causes and reasons and have subsumed the particulars under their universals. Whoever masters these roots extracts the treasures of truth from every object of investigation, and uncovers the secrets of wisdom from all that is concealed. He who acts like this has a long life even if his days are short.

1. Instead of *fa-inna ṭūl dirāsatihā innamā huwa* I read *fa-inna dirāsatihā innamā hiya* in the apparatus.

Words of Wisdom Related From Anūshīrwān

Whatever you have wasted on your lust and whatever you have won from it, be sure that you have not won it, rather it has won you and through it part of you has perished. The prudent man is, thus, he who has forgone passion that he become like someone who forgoes a meal[1] in order to attain [many] meals,[2] or like someone who eschews a visible abomination in order that invisible abominations remain closed to him. Otherwise,[3] nothing will intervene between him and it (i.e., his lust) and his living in it will become longer and his need with regard[4] to it will become stronger.

He also said: When desire conquers the mind it turns its good qualities into bad ones. So, it turns clemency into hatred, knowledge into hypocrisy, generosity into waste, moderation into avarice, and forgiveness into cowardice. When desire reaches this degree in the person concerned it leaves him such that he does not consider health to be anything but the health of his body, nor knowledge anything but what he can use for his own aggrandizement, nor does he see security in anything but suppressing people, nor good fortune in anything but the acquisition of riches, nor trust in anything but the availability of treasuries. All this is contrary to [true] aspiration, leading further away from the [true] goal, bringing nearer to destruction.

And he said: Drunkenness exists in twelve stages, and a man's drinking ends in drunkenness only with the help of all of them or some of them. They are: the drunkenness of youth, the drunkenness of pride, the drunkenness of beauty, the drunkenness of lust, the drunkenness of wine, the drunkenness of desire and the drunkenness of power. You should know, that gorging on food is drunkenness, much sleep is drunkenness, being overcome by ignorance is drunkenness, being possessed by sorrow is drunkenness, and bad habit is drunkenness.

He also said: Whoever is lacking in intelligence, ruling will not make him grow in power; who is lacking in contentment, riches will not make him grow in wealth; one who is lacking in faith, the transmission of religious knowledge (*riwāya*) will not make him increase in the religious understanding (*fiqh*). Man is, indeed, mind in a form: He whom the mind has missed and to whom [only] the form adheres is not a complete human being, he is like a statue in which there is no spirit of life.

---

1. Arab. *akla*. One could also read *ukla*, 'morsel'.

2. The many morsels must be on another plane, i.e., forgoing worldly pleasure will result in many spiritual pleasures. Since in the subsequent simile (*ka-mujtanib* …) the consequence (*li-takhfā* …) is the avoidance of something worse (at least it looks that way), one might, for the sake of strict parallelism, consider a slight textual emendation here, by reading *li-allā yaṣila* … . for *li-yaṣila* … . Thus: 'in order not to end up with (many) meals', because one gets 'hooked'.

3. At this point, to make any sense at all, I have inserted *wa-illā*.

4. Unfortunately, the text has *minhā*, while *ḥājah* requires *ilayhā*; for this reason I have not translated it 'his need for it'.

He was asked: What is the greatest fortune? He said: Purity of the soul and mastering of desire.

He was asked: Which [kind of] awesomeness is most beneficial for the ruler in his rule and of greatest benefit for his subjects? He said: the awesomeness of justice and impartiality, and putting a stop to misfortunes [caused] by evil and fickle people.

Someone said: What is more useful for the kings, good luck [as brought on by the stars] or intelligence? He said: Good luck is connected with intelligence, inasmuch as its effects become clear through signs.

He was asked: Which men are most worthy of kingship? He said: Those who have the most love for the maintenance of people's well-being and who are most knowledgeable in policy-making (*tadbīr*). Someone said: And then who else? He said: Those who are the strongest in mastering their desire and who best suppress it.

Someone said: How does the ruler know if his Lord is content with him? He said: God is not content with a ruler who does not give up his pleasure and his desire and does not refrain from his passion while [at the same time] looking after the well-being of his subjects, spreading justice among them and lifting oppression away from them.

He was asked: What is the joy in which the king rejoices? He said: The joy for the king as well as others is that which is accompanied by hope for his good Return. Anything else is strongly rejected by men of insight.

Someone said: Is there some kind of joy in which one finds pleasure when it is detached from this hope? He said: I do not know anything which has pleasure while being detached from this hope except for the pleasure of being healed from grudges that is felt by those who are so healed.

Someone said to him: What is contentment and what is humility? He said: As to contentment, it is being satisfied with the allotted share and the soul's forgoing what should not be aspired to. As to humility, it means to endure wrongs from everybody and to be gentle to those who are beneath you.

Someone said: What is the fruit of contentment, and what is the fruit of humility? He said: The fruit of contentment is peace, and the fruit of humility is love.

He was asked: What is conceitedness, and what is eye service? He said: Conceitedness is when a man thinks of himself as something that he is not, so that he sees his opinion as the right one and the opinion of somebody else as the wrong one. Eye service is that he keeps up a pretence for the eyes of the people and makes a show of righteousness while he is devoid of it. Someone said: Which one of the two is more damaging for him? He said: As to his soul, it is pride, and as to his companions, it is eyeservice, for they have confidence in him as to their concerns, because of what he shows them of himself; so one cannot be safe from his deception.

Someone said: What is greed and what avarice, and which one of the two is more damaging? He said: Greed is man's desiring what is not his due, and avarice is his withholding from people their proper rights. Greed is the more damaging of the two, because greed is the root of evil and the source of injustice. And from greed comes avarice, because nothing in the world satisfies such a man's appetite.

Someone said to him: What is the seed of all virtues? He said: Intelligence and knowledge. It was asked: And is there something beyond intelligence and knowledge? He said: God-given success embellishes them and god-forsakenness disgraces them.

Someone said: What is praiseworthy patience? He said: Perseverance in everything noble and restraining the desire from everything ignoble. It was asked: And then what? He said: That neither happiness nor distress change you so that you do not get transformed from praiseworthy to blameworthy. It was asked: And then what? He said: Power over passion at the intemperance of ambitious desire, and suppression of anger in a state of boiling rage. It was asked: And what then? He said: Bearing of every adversity from which one can gain a virtue. Patience has four homesteads: perseverance, abstention, endurance, and daring. Perseverance in noble pursuits; abstention from forbidden things and sins; endurance of [unwanted] concomitants in acts which virtue dictates and manliness brings to the fore; daring in the face of momentous affairs in which lies salvation and success.

He also said: Steadfastness issues from thankfulness, and thankfulness issues from a virtuous constitution. There are two kinds: Steadfastness in obedience to God Most High and in abstaining from disobedience toward God Most High. Steadfastness in obedience to God is the performance of the religious duties, and [steadfastness in] abstaining from disobedience toward God is refraining from the forbidden things.

He was asked about policy-making, and he said: In it is the medicine of the world. He was asked: And what is the medicine of the world? He said: Knowledge of the malady and the remedy in the body politic (*kull*). Someone said: And is there another goal in policy-making beyond this one? He said: Yes! and he was asked: And what is it? He said: Your attaining in both, knowledge and action, that which makes you strong enough to bring out the virtues and the advantages of things so that you can reach the utmost degree of both of them. But that does not easily happen except through his sovereignty and his willing.

Someone said: What is the sign of bliss? He said: If someone is content with the divine decree in things liked or disliked, and is satisfied with what he gets from the world, if his heart adheres to remembrance of Him, and if he removes desires for evil things from his heart—this is the sign of bliss!

Someone said: What is genuine nobility? He said: Fulfilment of obligations.

Someone said: And what is genuine meanness? He said: False accusation like the wolf who intends to eat the lamb born this year and says to it: You have abused me last year!

Someone said: Which is the beneficial [kind of] right conduct? He said: That you take [what happens to] others as a warning, but [let not anything happen to you that] others would take as a warning.

Someone said: What is the fulfilment of the intellect? He said: That you fling away from you the onslaught of worries with the resolution of perseverance.

Someone said: Why is it that you devote yourselves intensely to studying books, so that people almost attribute all your resolve back to this and assign to it your leadership? He said: That is so, because we do not want knowledge for self-aggrandizement, but we want it for its benefit.

Someone said: How is it that you bear upon yourselves the burden of compassion to such a degree that it spoils for you what you are just doing? He said: That is so because we know that there is no worldly joy in which one can be safe from damage and change.

Someone said: How is it that you reject that kind of praise which does not get rejected with other kings? He said: Because of the multitude whom we have seen from among the praised who are more deserving of blame than of praise.

Someone said: Which are the things that are most bitter? He said: Need for people, when it is sought from the wrong people.

Someone said: What thing is most disappointing? He said: Consultation with the ignorant.

Someone said: Which negligencies by which you are inflicted are hardest on you? He said: That we have the possibility to do something good and then postpone it, for it may be that this is the [right] time and it never returns.

Someone said: In which situations are you most afraid of your enemies? The situation in which we are is of the utmost confidence in ourselves and the least confidence in our Lord as well as the least reliance on our kingship and our glory.

Someone said to him: We heard you say: The mindful man ceases to pursue that which makes death difficult for him when it descends upon him and goes after that which will make [death] easy for him on the day of its descent. We would like to explore this. He said: What makes death difficult when it descends are the passions and desires in which men are easily led,[1] and he cannot make any use of them at the time of his need for benefits. What makes death and its pain easy on him are the good works which he has sent before him and whose benefit is returning to him on the day on which only the good works take a man's hand [to lead him] to his joy.

Someone said: We have heard you say: There are three things which we never saw perfected in anyone. Which are they? He said: [Absolute] certitude, intelligence, and knowledge.

Someone said: We have heard you say: There are four things which a mindful man should not forget under any circumstance. We would like to know what they are. He said: Yes! I shall tell you about them, so do not forget them. [They are:] the transitoriness of the world, taking it as a warning, heeding the changing flow of its

1. Lit.: 'in which the leading rope becomes smooth for man.'

[different] states, and the misfortunes against which there is no safeguarding.

Someone said: We have heard you say: He who endeavours to steer clear from four things, for him it is only natural that no hateful thing shall come to him, so that he would commit a crime against himself. We would like to know these things. He said: [They are:] haste, conceitedness, obstinacy, remissness. The fruit of haste is repentance; the fruit of conceitedness is hatred; the fruit of obstinacy is confusion and destruction; and the fruit of remissness is poverty and loss.

He was asked: Is man capable of acting piously at all times? He said: Yes! For no piety is superior to being sincere in thankfulness to God—Great is His praise!—and purifying the intention of corruption.

Someone said: Is man capable to encompass all people with his goodness and his kindness? He said: With the mass of his property, no. But if he wants goodness for them in his intention and his heart, then he has already encompassed them with his goodness.

He was asked: How can man live in immunity [from punishment]? He said: By fearing sins, and not becoming saddened by that which is decreed and is bound to happen to him.

He was asked: What is the correct view with regard to one's way of life? He said: For him who wants a life of joy, it is contentment. For him who wants a life of good reputation, it is striving for good order and encompassing all people with kindness. For him who wants the comfort of this world and its superfluities, he has to accustom himself to sin, grief, and fatigue.

Someone said: Which is the most helpful endeavour for gaining the praiseworthy good reputation? Which is most helpful for putting life in good order? And which is most helpful for being safe [from punishment]? He said: The most helpful for a praiseworthy good reputation is equity issuing from the soul, then the avoidance of injustice. The most helpful for safety [from punishment] is abstaining from sins. And the most helpful for the improvement of life is striving for the truth and rejection of evil and greed.

Someone said: Who among men is mindful? And who of them is smart? And who of them is shrewd? He said: The mindful man is he who has insight into that which is necessary for him in the matter of his return [to God], he who realizes his insight with his determination. The smart one is he who knows what is necessary and what is indispensable in the matter of his world. The shrewd one is he who is perspicacious in the subtle manoeuvres in all kinds of flatteries that he needs in the relationships between himself and all other people.

Someone said: Is there a time for pleasure? He said: If there is, then [it would be] at the time when man is not distracted by it from the improvement of his Return, and from that which is beneficial for his life.

Someone said: Which [kind of] calm makes most happy? He said: That which is there after a decision of important matters.

Someone said: Which person has the most perfect joy? He said: As to this world, it is he who has no need for anyone else in what he means [to do], and whoever does not own his slave without property right. As to the Hereafter, it is he who is most abounding in good deeds.

Someone said: Which are the most peaceful people? He said: Those who do not hurry anyone towards ruin and who are not hurried by anyone to their own ruin.

He was asked: Which is the most beneficial knowledge for the ruler? He said: That he knows that he is not able to close the mouths of people on his defects and bad deeds, so that, this being so, he does not aim at silencing them by threats and harsh treatment nor aim at pleasing them and moving them away from mentioning his bad deeds and his defects except by removing from his soul, mind and character those defects.

He was asked: What is the fruit of intelligence? He said: Its honoured and noble fruits are many. However, I shall enumerate for you those that are present in my mind. One of them is that man preserves his earthly portion [i.e., his wealth, etc.] by fixing his intention on recompensing all his benefactors and that he does as much as he can in this respect. Another one is that he does not relinquish his caution and wariness of sins; one is that he does not rely on any worldly condition and does not strive for it when he is not prepared for it. Also, that he does not acquire any of the evils; and that he does not abstain from kindness for those who detest him. Another one of them is that he does not take as a model the foolish, not even when an enormous worldly benefit is involved, and as to the benefits of the Hereafter, there is no part in it for the fools. Also one of them is that he only performs a deed after circumspection, tact, and weighing the options. And one of them is that good luck does not lead him into vanity and misfortune does not lead him into resignation. Also, that between him and his enemy he pursues a way of acting in which he does not need to fear the judgment of a judge and in [the relationship] between him and his friend there should be a way of acting in which there is no need for blame. One of them is that he does not consider anyone too insignificant for being humble toward him and that he does not consider the poor to be less perfect than the rich, except if the rich man is knowledgeable and the poor man is ignorant. Also one of them is that he does not honour immoral people, when they happen to be rich relatives or intimate companions. And one of them is that he is not the one to begin with wrongdoing and does not pay back with it, and when he stands up for someone, then in so aiding him, he does not go beyond the limit of justice and right. Another one of them is that, side by side with the intellect, desire with him is trifling. Also, one of them is that he does not consider the weak man lowly and that he does not scorn the endeavour for right conduct. Another one is that a past sin that is all over and from whose consequence he is safe does not encourage him to do a similar thing again. And one of them is that in none of his [different] circumstances does he suppress clemency and dignity, and that he does not enjoy the praise of someone who praises him for something which he knows he is lacking. Also, one of them is that he does not hate someone who finds fault with him for something that he knows to be part of himself. And one of them is that he does not undertake anything of which he fears that it may be followed by repentance. Another one of them is to bear the hardship of righteousness, and to restrain the soul from all pleasure that has to do with a sin.

He was asked: What is it that is obligatory for kings toward their subjects? And what is obligatory for the subjects toward [their] kings? He said: It is the duty of kings toward the subjects to treat them equitably and to do them justice, to set their mind at rest and safeguard their borders. And it is the duty of subjects toward kings to give good advice and be thankful.

He was asked: What is joy? And what is pleasure? He said: Joy is that with which [comes] hope of the Hereafter, and any other joy is distraction and pastime, and this will vanish.

He was asked: Is there distraction without sin? He said: No!

He was asked: What is haughtiness and what is aloofness? He said: Aloofness is under certain circumstances praised, because whoever is aloof scorns the lowly thing and any attention given to it. Haughtiness is not praised, because whoever has it elevates himself above his [actual] position, to such a degree that he sometimes is too arrogant to return the greeting to someone below him.

Someone said: What is eye service and what is hypocrisy? He said: Eye service is that he is an evil man and he makes a show of the good and the beautiful. Hypocrisy is that he shows of himself the opposite of what he is. Someone said: Which of them is worse? He said: With regard to himself, hypocrisy is, but with regard to action, eye service is.

He was asked: What is it that wards off the flaming rage? He said: Remembering the wrath of the Lord—mighty and great is He—at the disobedience of His servants and at their pursuit of vile deeds, and then His clemency regarding him.

Someone said: What are the four ways of behaviour about which, as you said, there should be no doubts? He said: Obedience to God Most High, preference of the Hereafter to this world, obedience to the king in whatever is in accordance with the right, just claim, and that man does not doubt the reward for the doer of good deeds and entrusts the dealing with the evildoer to his Maker.

Someone said: We have heard you say that the ruin of kings here and in the Hereafter lies in one attitude with which no good deed will rise up. We would like to know this attitude unmistakably. He said: Belittling the people of knowledge and virtue.

Someone said: We have heard you say: He who loathes dishonour should avoid five attitudes. What are they? He said: Yes! They are greed, avarice, contempt of people, following desire and procrastinating a promise.

Someone said: What is dishonour for you? And is there a dishonour that is more serious than that which you have described? He said: Yes! The mortal sins! Someone said: What are the mortal sins (*kabā'ir*)? He said: Withholding what is due,[1] and worse than that is that he makes a promise and then breaks it, and the grave offences (*mūbiqāt*)—they are that you turn your eye to what you do not possess and to which you have no right. The highest of all mortal sins is contempt of the divine statutes.

Someone said: Which is the most pleasant and comfortable life? He said: A life in ease and sufficiency neither in poverty nor in wealth.

Someone said: How is it possible for man to live in security? He said: In the morning he is obedient to God, and in the evening he exerts himself in his obedience to Him and desires to worship Him.

He was asked: How is it possible for man to remember God Most High in all his [different] states and not be forgetful? He said: That is [possible] when, in all his states, he is cautious and fearful concerning sin.

He also used to say: Avarice is better than delaying the fulfilment of a promise, because resignation cuts off hope and longing, while the delay spoils the gift, even if its benefit is great.

He was asked: What is necessary for the one who lives in this world? He said: comfort without consequence, joy without sin, composure without slackness and neglect.

And he said: The pious' death is peace for them, and the evil doers' death is peace for the world.

He was asked about a man who is afflicted by a rupture of the relations with his brothers. What is the reason for this? He said: This comes from his lack of loyalty, from his failure to offer them what they offer him, and it may be from his difficulty in coping with the humble status of his brothers.

He was asked about [the relationship between] sins and thankfulness. He said: He whose thankfulness to God Most High is sincere is freed from sins.

Someone said: Which is the biggest sin for man? He said: That he is not aware of his own fault.

Someone said: Which is the thing that is most worthy of not being forgotten? He said: For those who are intelligent, it is their perpetration of sins, and for those who are ignorant, it is blood-vengeances.

Someone said: Which are the things that are the best help for the envious to let go of envy? He said: That he know that this is a pain which he inflicts on himself, and that he has no authority to move a grace of God from its place, and that he can only impair himself with his envy.

Someone said: Is it then possible for the envious to cause damage to the object of his envy? He said: How could he be able to do that if he can only come to it through

1. I prefer to make an emendation and read *wājib* instead of *wājid*.

something evil that comes to himself? [Even] if the good life of the object of his envy comes to an end, it will not come to him.

Someone said: Which is the finest thing by which the kings are distinguished? He said: Abstinence. It was asked: From what? He said: From the forbidden things. It was asked: Then who? He said: Who abstains from that which belongs to the subjects. It was said: Then what? He said: That he is not known for greed to such a degree that it is attributed to him, nor for submissiveness to such an extent that the splendour of dignified comportment falls away from him.

Someone said: What epitomizes praise, what determination and what blame for the kings? He said: As for praiseworthy things, they are [epitomized] in one single characteristic and that is: when they intend something good they carry it out. As to determination, it also consists of one single characteristic, and that is to gain the upper hand in the things [they do]. And as to blameworthy things, they are [also] combined in one single characteristic: when they are angry, they attack.

Someone said: What is the one comprehensive characteristic for the warding off of the speech of the envious and of the enemies from the kings? He said: That he adheres to sessions with the learned and meritorious people, taking over the merits of their [good] deeds.

Someone said: What is the particular behaviour that results in everything worthless and all the evil deeds that come with it? He said: Sitting with fickle people, and with those who are immoral and ignorant.

Someone said: What is the utmost degree of the human intellect? He said: Belittlement of the world and its value while he views something of the precious things of the Hereafter, and rejection of the deceptions in it [created] by pleasures, from the consequences of which he is not safe.

Someone said: Is there something for kings that they have to consider for themselves that is not for the subjects? He said: Yes, thinking about the rapidity of the passing of their power, the shortness of their lives and the excess of their craving for sinful things.

Someone said: Is enjoyment and pleasure uglier for the kings or for the subjects? He said: Nay, for the kings, since they know the brevity of enjoyment from those who have gone before, and the frequency of its being spoiled and [the multitude of] happenings that befall their worldly goods.

Someone said: Which virtues of man are an adornment for him? He said: Clemency while there is anger, forgiveness together with power, generosity without asking for recompense, and striving for the everlasting abode, not the one that perishes.

Someone said: Of which people should one beware most? He said: The tyrannical ruler, the powerful enemy, and the deceiving friend.

Someone said: Which faults are most difficult to remedy? He said: Haughtiness and obstinacy.

Someone said: Which are the most important things to be avoided? He said: Those that most participate in desire.

It was said: Which thing is rarest? He said: The sincere friend.

When Anūshīrwān had completed the book *Questions* he said at the end of it: I have held the intellect in high esteem in my youth, I loved knowledge and I searched for every kind of instruction. I regarded the intellect as the biggest and greatest of all things, a sound nature the best of things, clemency the most beautiful of qualities, beneficence the most excellent of deeds, moderation the best of acts, and humility the most praiseworthy of attributes.—Our sufficiency is God, and what an excellent keeper of trust is He!

King Bahman's Words of Wisdom

King Bahman was fascinated by the beauties of speech; by it he selected and because of it he chose his confidants and companions. So he brought together the learned men of his time and the knowledgable people who were famous through their wisdom and understanding. Then he said to them:

'I have brought you together for an important task on which I have reflected, and for things that I should like to know, and I shall ask you about them. So each of you men shall exercise his judgment to the utmost degree of his mind and understanding with no haste nor rushing to the answer without reflection. Inform me about the loftiest things and the things that best remove[1] the lowliness of the lowly which no ancient has ever mentioned.' They agreed that it was righteousness and knowledge, for these two truly enhance the nobility of the noble and place slaves in the seat of kings. The king said: 'This is the most important thing in the world and in religion when it is supported by the intellect, for the building [stands] through its foundation, because the foundation is understanding, its support is solid opinion, there is no solid opinion without being acquainted with knowledge, and there is no foundation for knowledge save by the intellect.'

They then said: 'The divisions of things are manifold: some are protectors and some are protected. The protected is property, and the protector is the intellect. Some can be taken away and some are preserved. What is taken away is property and what is preserved is the intellect. So, the intellect protects you and you protect property. Property cannot be protected from theft and fraud, from the tyranny of the ruler and many other dangers that rush upon it. Nothing of this, however affects the intellect and nothing can overwhelm it, no usurper can take it away by force, and no ruse of an envious man can harm it. Furthermore, the intelligent man lives by his intelligence when he is denied property, but the ignorant one cannot [even] live by his property. This is so, because he who does not live by his intelligence is deprived of knowledge of the difference between the good and

1. I prefer to read *arfaʿihā* instead of *arfaʿihī*.

the bad and [deprived of] insight into the results of that which is suitable and permitted and that which is not suitable and not permitted. There is no good in the life of someone who misses these qualities, especially the kings. For they are in greater need of these things, since they are the governors and the leaders, and the other people follow; so they are in greater need of keeping themselves in order, for the subjects are in a healthy state when they (i.e., the kings) are in a healthy state, and people's corruption happens through their corruption. So there is no strength for the subjects except through [the strength of] the patron, no strength for the body except through the head, no strength for the king except through awe, and there is no awe before the kings except through justice. Also, the need of proper conduct (*adab*) and the manly virtue (*muruwwah*) for the intellect is like the need of the body for nourishment and the need of the land for cultivation and water. The various ways of proper conduct and manly virtue need the intellect, but the intellect does not need them. The intellect is pointed out by the great benefits that the intellect shows in avoiding sins. And happiness is connected with the intellect, for whoever is endowed with good intellect it will lead him to the means for obtaining happiness, and for him who is granted happiness no goal remains that he could strive for, because happiness is the goal of everything that one strives for.'

Then the leader of the people said: 'A sign of the intellect is that man is seen as guarding himself from himself and his circumspection from his impetuosity, and he tames the recalcitrant camel of desire so that he makes it subservient to the intellect. For intellect and desire come in turns, they alternate in overcoming this soul [of ours] in its agreement and opposition, for the intellect is for it a worry and desire is a time for rest for it. That is so because desire brings to it the passions and the pleasures, and intellect restrains it from those, except for that which is permitted and is suitable, and it guards it from the consequences. But the soul hurries more toward that which is near to desire and is most unhappy about everything that weighs heavy on it.'

THE HEALTH OF THE SOUL: ITS PRESERVATION AND ITS RESTORATION; THE DISEASES OF THE SOUL

From *Tahdhīb al-akhlāq* (The Refinement of Character)

Reprinted from the Sixth Discourse, *The Refinement of Character* (Tahdhīb al-akhlāq), tr. C. K. Zurayk (Beirut, 1966), pp. 157–209.

With God's aid and support, we will discuss in this discourse the cure of the diseases which affect the soul of man and their remedies as well as the factors and causes which produce them and from which they originate. For skilled physicians do not attempt to treat a bodily disease until they diagnose it and know its origin and cause. Then they seek to counteract it by remedies which oppose it, beginning with dieting and light medicines and ending in some cases with the use of distasteful foods and unpleasant medicines and in others with amputation and cauterization.[1]

Now, as the soul is a divine, incorporeal faculty, and as it is, at the same time, used for a particular constitution and tied to it physically and divinely in such a way that neither of them can be separated from the other except by the will of the Creator (mighty and exalted is He!), you must realize that each one of them [i.e., the soul and the constitution] is dependent upon the other, changing when it changes, becoming healthy when it is healthy, and ill when it is ill. This we can observe directly and clearly from their activities which appear to us, for just as we can see the man who is ill in his body—especially when the origin of his illness is in one of the two noble parts [of the body], namely, the brain or the heart—undergoing a change of intellect and an illness of soul whereby he repudiates his mind, thought, and imagination, and other noble faculties of his soul (he himself being aware of all of this), so also we can observe the man who is ill in his soul, whether with anger, grief, passionate love, or agitated desires, undergoing a change in the form of his body whereby he shakes, trembles, turns pale or red, becomes emaciated or fat, and the form of his body is affected by the various [other] changes which can be perceived by the senses.

Thus, we must inquire into the origin of the diseases of our souls. If it lies in the soul itself—as is the case when we think of evil things and ponder over them, or have a sense of fear, or are frightened by accidental or expected occurrences or by agitated

1. The view that vices are diseases of the soul, that these diseases should be subject to treatment as are the diseases of the body, and that their treatment and remedy are by appropriate means of moral education—this view is common in Muslim ethical writings and among Muslim mystics. See al-Ghazzālī, *Iḥyā' 'ulūm al-dīn* (4 vols., Cairo, 1352), vol. 3, pp. 52 ff. The influence of Miskawayh's *Tahdhīb* is evident in this part of the *Iḥyā'* (Third Quarter: 'Rub' al-Muhlikāt', 'The Quarter on the Destructive [Vices]'), and particularly in the Second Book containing the above-mentioned reference: 'Kitāb Riyāḍat al-Nafs wa-Tahdhīb al-Akhlāq wa Mu'ālajat Amrāḍ al-Qalb' ('The Book on the Training of the Soul, the Refinement of Character, and the Treatment of the Diseases of the Heart'), vol. 3, pp. 42 ff.

passions—we should try to remedy these diseases in the way which is appropriate to them. But if, on the other hand, their origin lies in the [physical] constitution or in the senses—as in the case of the lassitude which results from a feebleness of the heat of the heart combined with laziness and luxurious living, or of passionate love which starts with gazing [at the object of one's love] together with idleness and leisure—then we should attempt to remedy it in the way which is appropriate to these diseases.

The Preservation of the Health of the Soul

Moreover, as the medicine of bodies is divided primarily into two parts, the first to preserve health if it is present and the second to restore it if it is absent, so also we should divide the medicine of souls in this same way, trying to restore their health if it is missing and proceeding to preserve it if it is already there. So we say:

When the soul is good and virtuous, loving the acquisition of virtues and desirous of attaining them and longing for the true sciences and for sound knowledge, then its possessor should associate with those who are akin to him and seek those who resemble him, and should not enjoy the presence of others or sit in their company. He should be very careful lest he associate with the wicked and the defective among the frivolous or among those who display enjoyment of disgraceful pleasures and commitment of vile deeds and boast of them and indulge in them. Let him not listen to these people's tales with interest, nor recite their poetry with approbation, nor sit in their company with delight; for sitting once in their company, or listening to one of their tales, or reciting one verse of their poetry would attach to the soul such dirt and filth as would not be washed away except with the passage of a long time and with difficult treatments. It could be the cause of the corruption of [even] the virtuous and experienced man and the seduction of the discerning knower and might lead to their infatuation—to say nothing of the youth who is growing up and the student seeking guidance. The cause of all of this is that the love of physical pleasures and of bodily relaxations is inborn in man on account of his imperfections. We are inclined to them and we covet them by our primitive nature and our original disposition, and it is only by means of reason's restraint that we keep ourselves from them, stopping at the limits which reason prescribes to us and contenting ourselves with what is necessary.

The exceptions and stipulations which I noted at the beginning of this discussion were mentioned for the following reason: Association with one's friends, whose conditions I described in the preceding discourse and with whom, and through whom, I judged that complete happiness is attainable, cannot be successful without friendliness and intimacy. This involves necessarily pleasant fun, agreeable conversation, the delightful exchange of jokes, and the pursuit of pleasures permitted by the Law and determined by reason without going beyond these pleasures to excessive indulgence, or, on the other hand, scorning them and abstaining from them. For to be carried to one of the extremes would be called—if the extreme is excess—frivolity, depravity, dissoluteness, and other blameworthy qualities; if the extreme is deficiency, it would be stupidity, sternness, peevishness, and similar qualities which are also blameworthy. The mean between these two extremes is the graceful person who is distinguished by cheerfulness, pleasant disposition, and good companionship. However, it is as difficult to achieve the mean in this case as it is with the other virtues.

Another obligation incumbent on the person who seeks to preserve the health of his soul is to apply himself to a duty relating to the theoretical part [of knowledge] as well as to the practical—a duty, which he should not, under any circumstances, be allowed to neglect, so that it may serve the soul as physical exercise is pursued to preserve the health of the body. Physicians ascribe great importance to exercise in the preservation of the health of the body, and the physicians of the soul attribute even greater importance to it in the preservation of the health of the soul. For when the soul ceases to speculate and loses the power of thought and of deep searching for meanings, it becomes dull, stupid, and devoid of the substance of all good. If it becomes accustomed to laziness, shuns reflection, and chooses to remain idle, it draws near to destruction, because, by this idleness, it casts off its particular form and returns to the rank of beasts. This, indeed, is the relapse of character. May God protect us against it!

If the youth who is growing up accustoms himself, from the start of his life, to intellectual exercise and pursues the four mathematical sciences,[1] he will become accustomed to truthfulness and will be able to bear the burdens of reflection and speculation. He will delight in the truth, his character will shun falsehood, and his ear will abhor lying. When he reaches his prime and proceeds to study philosophy, he will retain the same disposition as he goes through it and will absorb from it what should be kept in store. Nothing in philosophy will seem strange to him, nor will he need to toil hard to understand its secrets or extract its hidden treasures. Thus, he will achieve rapidly the happiness which we have described. Further, should the one who is seeking to preserve this health [of the soul] become unique and eminent in knowledge, then let not his pride in what he has achieved cause him to cease to seek beyond, for knowledge has no limit, and above every man of knowledge there is One who knows. Let him not be too lazy to review what he has learned and perfected by studying it [further], for forgetfulness is the bane of learning. Let him remember the words of Ḥasan al-Baṣrī[2] (may God grant him

1. *'Al-ta'ālīm al-arba'ah'*. See al-Tahānawī, *Kashshāf iṣṭilāḥāt al-funūn* (2 parts, Calcutta, 1862), p. 1066. The four mathematical sciences are: geometry, arithmetic, music, and astronomy. See Ibn Khaldūn, *al-Muqaddimah* (Beirut, 1900), pp. 478–479.

2. One of the greatest intellectual and religious figures of the first century of Islam (110/728). An authoritative transmitter of tradition, jurist, scholar, and teacher, he was known and revered for his ascetic piety and exerted a deep influence on the rise of Muslim theology, mysticism, and other intellectual and religious movements in Islam. Numerous pious sayings, such as the one quoted by Miskawayh, are ascribed to him and are often reported in Muslim writings.

mercy!): 'Curb ye these souls, for they are inquisitive, and polish them, for they quickly become rusty.' And let it be known to you that these words, though short, are full of meaning and, at the same time, they are eloquent and fulfil the condition stipulated by rhetoric.

Again, let the one who is seeking to preserve the health of his soul realize that, by so doing, he is indeed preserving noble blessings which are bestowed upon it, great treasures which are laid up in it, and splendid garments which are cast on it. Let him realize also that, if one possesses such sublime blessings within himself and is not obliged to seek them from outside, or to pay money to others for their sake, or to endure hardship and burdensome troubles in their pursuit—if such a person then shuns and neglects them to the point of shedding them off and becoming devoid of them, he, indeed, will deserve blame for his action, will show poor judgment, and will prove to be neither wise nor successful. [The seeker of this health should realize this fact] all the more as he observes how the seekers of external goods venture on far and perilous journeys, travel frightful and rugged roads, and expose themselves to all kinds of dangers and possibilities of destruction by beasts of prey and wicked aggressors. In most cases, even after undergoing all these horrors, such people fail and they may suffer excessive repentance and crippling sorrows which stifle their breath and sever the members of their body. And even if they attain one of their desires, this is inevitably lost quickly or is exposed to loss and holds no hope of endurance, since it is external. What is external to us cannot be secure against the innumerable accidents which affect it; and, at the same time, its owner is in a state of intense fear, constant anxiety, and weariness of body and of soul, trying to keep what can in no way be kept and to watch over something where watchfulness is of no avail.

If the seeker of these external things is a ruler or the companion of a ruler, these dangers are multiplied many times for him because of his great involvement and what he suffers from those who oppose and envy him, both far and near, as well as because of the vast provisions which he needs in order to win over his associates and those next to them and to cajole both his friends and his enemies. Yet in spite of all this, he is blamed and accused of being slow [to give]; he is reproached and charged with falling short [of what is expected of him]. All his relatives and connections are constantly asking more from him, but there is no way to satisfy one of them—to say nothing of all. Reports keep reaching him about those who are closest to him, such as his children, his womenfolk, and others among his retinue and attendants—reports which fill him with anger and fury. Their mutual jealousies being what they are, he cannot feel himself secure from their side against the enemies writing to them or the envious conspiring with them. Moreover, the more helpers and supporters he has, the more they add to his worries and bring him troubles which he has not experienced before. People consider him a rich man, and yet he is the poorest among them; they envy him, and yet he is the one who envies most.

For how could he not be poor when poverty is, by definition, the excess of need? Those who have the greatest need are the poorest of people, while the richest are those whose need is least.

This is why we have concluded—and rightly so—that God (exalted is He!) is the richest of the rich, for He is in need of nothing, and that the greatest of kings are the poorest of people, because of the many things they need. Abū Bakr al-Ṣiddīq (may God be pleased with him!) was right when he said in one of his sermons: 'Kings are the most wretched people in both this world and the next.' Describing them further, he said: 'When a king assumes kingship, God makes him indifferent to what he has and desirous of what others have. He shortens the term of his life and fills his heart with anxiety. For the king begrudges the little and is embittered by plenty. He is bored by easy life, and splendour ceases to have attraction for him. He does not learn by example, nor has he confidence in [anybody's] trustworthiness. Like the counterfeit coin or the illusory mirage, he is gay on the surface but unhappy inside. And after his soul has passed away, and the years of his life have been exhausted, and his shadow has been effaced, then God (exalted is He!) will call him to account and will be severe in reckoning and sparing in pardon. Indeed, kings are the ones who deserve mercy!'[1]

This, then, is the condition of the king if he gets a firm hold on his rule and does not neglect any part of it. I have heard the greatest among the kings whom I have known asking to have these words [of Abū-Bakr] repeated to him and then weeping in grief because of their agreement with what was in his heart and their true reflection of his state and condition. He who sees the outside [of the life] of kings: their thrones, their beds, their ornaments, and their furniture; and who beholds kings in processions surrounded by, and standing in the midst of, throngs [of retinue], with horses, carriages, slaves, attendants, chamberlains, and servants ready at their disposal—he who sees this is possibly struck with awe and imagines that kings are happy with what he takes to be theirs. No! By Him who has created them and saved us from their preoccupations! In such circumstances, kings forget indeed what the stranger sees to be theirs and are lost in thoughts which occur and recur to them regarding the needs which we have described. We ourselves have experienced this condition in the little that we possess, and it has led us to an understanding of [the condition of] plenty which we have described. It may be that some of those who attain to [a position of] kingship or rule are happy for a very short time in the beginning, until they become established in [this position] and look [at it] with open eyes, but after this stage, all that they

1. See the texts of this sermon in al-Jāḥiẓ, *al-Bayān wa'l-tabyīn*, ed. 'Abd al-Salām Muḥammad Hārūn (Cairo, 1948–50), vol. 2, pp. 43–44; Ibn Qutaybah, *'Uyūn al-akhbār*, ed. Dār al-Kutūb al-Miṣriyyah (Cairo, 1925–30), vol. 2, p. 233; and Ibn-'Abd-Rabbihi, *al-'Iqd al-Farīd*, ed. A. Amīn, A. al-Zayn, and I. al-Ibyārī (Cairo, 1940–53), vol. 4, pp. 59–60. There are slight variants among these texts and the text in the *Tahdhīb*. The only noteworthy one is in the last sentence, where the three above-mentioned texts have: '*al-fuqarā*' ' ('the poor'), instead of '*al-mulūk*' ('the kings').

possess becomes as a matter of course to them and they are neither delighted in it nor mindful of it. They then look beyond to what they do not possess, and, even if they come to own the [whole] world with all that it includes, they still long for another world, or their aspiration rises towards gaining the eternal life and the true kingship, with the result that they become weary of all that they have achieved and have been able to attain. For [the king] to maintain the things of this world is extremely difficult on account of the [predisposition to] dissolution and annihilation in the nature of those things and because of what the king is obliged to do, as described above, and the large sums of money which he needs in order to pay the soldiers attached to him and the attendants in his service, as well as the reserves and treasures which he must lay in store against misfortunes and accidents from which one cannot be safe. This, then, is the state of those who seek blessings which are external to us.

As for those blessings which are in ourselves, they exist with us and in us. They do not quit us, because they are the gift of God the Creator (mighty and exalted is He!). He has commanded us to put them to use and to rise higher in their scale. If we follow His commandment, these blessings will yield us [other] blessings in succession, and we will rise from one grade to another until they lead us to the eternal bliss which we have described previously. Here is that true kingship, which does not pass away, and that eternal and pure happiness, which does not change. Who is it, then, who suffers a worse deal or a more obvious fall than he who loses precious and lasting gems which are with him and at his disposal and seeks base and perishable unessentials which are neither with him nor at his disposal? Even if he happens to obtain the latter, they will not remain in his possession or be left with him, for it is inevitable that either they will be separated from him or he from them.

This is why we have said that the person who has been sufficiently provided for and who has gained a moderate share of external happiness should not be engaged in the superfluities of life because they are endless and lead their seeker to endless perils. We have explained to you previously what sufficiency and moderation are. We have also explained that the true purpose sought through them is the treatment of one's pains and the avoidance of falling victim to them, and not enjoyment and the pursuit of pleasure. For, when one treats hunger and thirst—both of which are incidental diseases and pains—one should not seek the body's pleasure but, rather, he should seek its health, and he will get the pleasure eventually. But he who, through treatment, seeks pleasure and not health, will neither obtain health nor keep such pleasure.

As for the man who is not sufficiently provided [with external goods] and who has to toil and worry to obtain sufficiency, he should not go beyond moderation and the extent of his need so as to be obliged to exert constant toil and relentless care and risk the danger of being exposed to dishonourable gains and the various kinds of perils and calamities. Rather, he should conduct himself gracefully in their pursuit, as does the one who realizes their worthlessness and the fact that they are necessary for him [only] because of his deficiency, and who thus seeks them just as the other animals seek their necessities. For when the intelligent man considers the conditions of animals, he finds that some of them feed upon dead carcasses or upon dung and excrement and yet are happy and delighted in the food they get and do not feel any aversion to it. They do not turn away from it as do the other animals of opposite nature; instead, they turn away from the food of the latter which is quite the opposite of their food in cleanliness. Take, for instance, the scarab and the black beetle and contrast them with the bee. They run away from fragrant odours and clean food, whereas the bee seeks them and is delighted in them. It follows, then, that to each animal there is a food appropriate to it; and each is satisfied with what sustains its existence and life, desires it, and is delighted in it.

It is in this light that we should look upon our food. We should put it in the same class as the toilet which we are forced to visit in order to excrete what we were so anxious to get. We should not set the two far apart because both of them are necessities. We should have recourse to them only as such and not worry our heads in choosing and enjoying them, nor waste our lives preparing for them and endeavouring to secure them, nor, on the other hand, fail to provide for our needs of them. If we prefer the one to the other and deem it appropriate to seek what goes into our bodies and inappropriate to seek what they excrete, the reason is that the first is a nourishment which agrees with us and takes the place of the decomposed parts of our bodies. And as we do not feel alienation from, or aversion to, our bodies and do not find them filthy, so also we are not averse to what we take to meet their loss and to replace it. The second [the excrement], on the other hand, is the residue of that food and the part which nature ejects after taking its need of it, that is, [after assimilating] what it reduces into pure blood and distributes to the different organs through the veins, and discarding the dregs which it does not need and which are extremely different and distant from our own constitution. Because of this difference and opposition we feel alienated from [this residue] and averse to it, but we are forced to eject, remove, and discharge it by means of the organ with which we are endowed and which we use for this purpose, so that its place may be taken by what will come after it and go through the same process.

Another requirement which should be observed by whoever is anxious to preserve the health of his soul is to refrain from stirring his concupiscent and irascible faculties by reminding himself of what he obtained from them and of the pleasure which he has thus experienced through them. He should rather leave them alone until they are stirred by themselves. I mean by this that a person may remember the pleasures he has had from the satisfaction of his passions and their delightfulness or the grades he has achieved of the honour and glory of authority, and may consequently desire these things. But once he desires them he moves towards them; and when he does so he comes to regard them as ends, and thus finds himself drawn to use his [power of] reflection and to employ his rational faculty to help him attain those ends. This is like the one who arouses beasts of prey and excites wild, rapacious animals and then seeks to appease them and to be delivered from them. The intelligent man does not choose to be in such a condition. This is rather the conduct of fools who do not distinguish between good and evil, or between right and wrong. This is why he [who is anxious to preserve the health of his soul] should not remind himself of the actions of these concupiscent and irascible faculties, lest he desire them and seek them. Let him, instead, leave them alone, for they will be aroused by themselves, they will be excited when necessary, and they will seek what the body needs. You [the reader of this book] will find in the stimulus of nature what will save you the trouble of stimulating these two faculties by your thought, reflection, and discernment. Your thought and discernment will then be used in satisfying their need and in assessing the freedom that you should give them to ensure what is necessary and requisite for our bodies to preserve their health. This is the way to execute the will of God (exalted is He!) and to carry out His plan, for He (exalted and sanctified is He!) has endowed us with these two faculties, only in order that we use them when we need them and not to become their servants and slaves. Thus, anyone who puts the rational faculty in the service of its own slaves violates God's commandment, transgresses the limits which He has set, and reverses His guidance and design. For our Creator (mighty and exalted is He!) has provided us with these faculties by His plan and design, and no justice could be nobler or superior to that of His provision and design. Anyone who opposes it [His justice] or deviates from it commits the greatest wrong and injustice towards his own self.

Furthermore, he who wishes to preserve the health of his soul should pay minute attention to of all his acts and plans in the execution of which he uses the organs of his body and soul, lest he use them by force of a previous habit which diverges from his judgment and reflection. How often it happens that a person sets out to do something which varies from his previous resolution and decision! Whoever finds himself in this position should fix for himself penalties to counteract such misdeeds. If [for instance] he suspects himself of seeking some kind of harmful food, or failing to adhere to a self-imposed diet, or eating unwholesome fruits or pastries, he should penalize himself by fasting and should only break his fast by taking the lightest and the smallest amount of food. If he is able to suffer hunger, let him do so and be more strict in his diet even though he may not need such strictness. In reproaching his soul, he may address it as follows: 'You intended to take what is useful to you but you took, instead, what is harmful. Such is the conduct of whoever is devoid of reason. One would think that many animals are better than you, because none of them seeks what is pleasurable and then takes what is painful. Hold now yourself, therefore, [ready] for the penalty.'

Likewise, if he [who wishes to preserve the health of his soul] suspects himself of being aroused to an anger for which there is no reason, or which is directed against an innocent person, or which exceeds what is proper for himself, then let him react by exposing himself to a person who is insolent and whom he knows to be obscene and let him suffer to endure that person ['s abuse]; or let him humble himself before someone whom he knows to be good but towards whom he had not acted humbly before; or let him impose upon himself a certain amount of money to give away as alms and make this a vow which he should never fail to execute.

Also, if he suspects in himself a certain laziness or neglect of any of his interests, let him punish himself by engaging in some hard labour, or a long prayer, or certain good works which entail toil and fatigue. In brief, let him impose upon himself certain definite prescriptions which he should consider as duties and punishments that admit of no infringement or compromise, whenever he suspects himself of violating his reason or transgressing its command. Let him be wary at all times of involving himself in any vice, or of helping a friend in it, or of violating what is right. Let him not consider as slight any of the small faults which he commits, nor try to excuse himself for them, because this would lead him to serious ones. Whoever is accustomed in his childhood and youth to controlling himself instead of surrendering to his passions, to being magnanimous when his anger is aroused, to checking his tongue, and to enduring his companions will bear lightly what others, who have not gone through this training, find burdensome. As evidence of this, we find that slaves and their like, whenever they have the misfortune of living under masters who revile them and insult their honour, become used to enduring easily what they hear until it ceases to affect them. Even when they hear a gross unpleasantness, they laugh among themselves without affectation and proceed with their work meekly, cheerfully, and without being perturbed, whereas previously [before living under such masters] they used to be ill-natured, irritable, and unwilling to endure [insult], or to refrain from reacting and from avenging themselves with words and seeking to quench their anger by fighting. The same is true of us if we accustom ourselves to virtue, avoid vice, and refrain from repaying and retaliating [the injuries of] vicious people and from inflicting revenge on them.

Furthermore, he who is anxious to preserve the health of his soul should follow the example of those kings who are known for their prudence, for they prepare themselves for enemies with equipment, war material, and means of defence while they can still do so in ample time and with the possibility of looking ahead. If they were to neglect this until they fell prey to dangers and were overtaken by adversities, they would be overwhelmed and unable to use their craftiness or good judgment. It is on this basis that we should establish our means in preparing for such enemies as greed, anger, and all that removes us from the virtues which we pursue. This preparation consists in accustoming ourselves to being patient where patience is necessary, to forgiving those whom we should forgive, to abstaining from wicked desires, and to mastering these vices before they rage, for otherwise the task would be very difficult if not utterly impossible.

Moreover, he who desires to preserve the health of his soul should search very diligently for his own defects. He should not be satisfied with what Galen said on the subject. In his work known as *Man's Understanding of His Own Defects,*[1] he said: Inasmuch as every man loves himself, he is not able to discover his faults, or to see them though they may be apparent. In this same book, Galen advised the person who wishes to become free from defects to look for a perfect and virtuous friend. After a long period of intimacy, he should tell that friend that he will trust the sincerity of his affection only if he tells him the truth about his defects so that he may avoid them. He should take his pledge in this regard and should not be satisfied if this friend tells him that he does not discern in him any defect whatsoever. Rather, he should approach his friend and contest what he says, telling him that he accuses him of betrayal. Let him ask his friend again and urge him. If this friend still declines to tell him of any of his defects, let him show his resentment gently and his reproach openly and pursue further his request from him with insistence. If the friend still refrains, he should persist a little more. When this friend [finally] tells him of some of the defects which he has found in him, let him not show on his face or in his words any antipathy or distress. On the contrary, let him look at his friend with a cheerful face and show pleasure in what he has brought forth to him and called to his attention, and let him thank him as the days go by and in times of intimacy, so as to make it easy for the friend to tell him of similar defects. Then let him remedy that defect until its trace is removed and its shadow is effaced. [If you do this,] then he who guides you to your defect will be convinced that you are proceeding to improve your soul and endeavouring to remedy your disease and, consequently, he will not refrain from coming back to you and giving you advice.

But this, which Galen prescribed, is wanting and non-existent, and there is no hope of securing it. In this situation, any enemy might be more useful than a friend, for he would not be diffident of us in showing our defects; he might even go beyond the defects which he knows to tell falsehoods and lies in their regard. In this way, not only our attention would be called from the enemies' side to many of our defects, but we would even go further to impute to our souls that of which they are innocent.

Galen has another treatise in which he states that good people derive benefit from their enemies.[2] This is true, and nobody disagrees with him on it because of what we have mentioned.

---

1. See *supra*, Second Discourse, n. 2. There are slight variants in the title. Both Miskawayh and Ibn Abī Uṣaybiʿah have '*Taʿarruf*' ('Understanding', 'Acquainting oneself'), whereas Ibn al-Nadīm has: '*Taʿrīf*' ('Causing to understand', 'Acquainting').

2. See also *supra*, Second Discourse, n. 2. There are here also variants in this title: In *Ṭabaqāt al-aṭibbā'*, it includes '*qad*' ('may' benefit). Max Meyerhof, p. 700: *That the Best People Take Advantage of their Enemies.*

As for the view of Abū Yūsuf Ya'qūb ibn Isḥāq al-Kindī[1] on this subject, it is expressed in the following [passage] which I relate in his own words: 'The seeker of virtue should look at the images of all his acquaintances as if these images were to him mirrors in which he can see the image of each one of these acquaintances as each of them undergoes the pains which produce misdeeds. In this way, he will not fail to notice any of his own misdeeds, for he will be looking for the misdeeds of others. Whenever he sees a misdeed in someone, he will blame himself for it as if he had committed it and will reproach himself exceedingly on its account. At the end of every day and night, he will review all his actions so that none of them will escape his attention. For it is disgraceful for us to strive to preserve those things which we have [in fact] expended, such as base stones and extinct ashes[2] which are alien to us and whose loss will not hurt us a bit on any day, while [on the other hand] we fail to preserve what we expend of our essences, whose abundance assures our existence and whose diminution brings our annihilation. Let us, therefore, whenever we come upon a defect in our deeds, reprove our souls severely for it and impose upon them a punishment which we should prescribe and never lose sight of. If we review the acts of others and find a misdeed among them, let us reproach ourselves also for it, for the soul will then be loath to commit misdeeds and will get accustomed to deeds which are good. Misdeeds will thus remain constantly in our minds and we will not forget them; their memory will not be effaced [even] by the passage of a long time. We should follow the same behaviour in regard to good deeds in order that we may hasten to [perform] them and not miss [performing] any of them.'

Kindī said [further]: 'We should not be content to become like notebooks and books, which convey to others the meanings of wisdom while remaining themselves devoid of such meanings, or like the whetstone which sharpens [other instruments] but does not itself cut. Rather, let us be like the sun which benefits the moon. Whenever the sun shines on the moon, it causes it to shine out of the emanation of its light and exerts its effect on it exactly in that way which makes it resemble itself, though not so radiant. The same should be true of us if we transmit virtues to others.' This, which al-Kindī said on the subject, is more meaningful than what was said by his predecessors.[3]

1. On the ethical treatises ascribed to al-Kindī, the first Arab philosopher (*c.* 260/873), see Richard J. McCarthy, *al-Taṣānīf al-mansūbah ilā faylasūf al-'arab* (Baghdad, 1962), Index.

2. This passage is not very clear. I presume that by 'stones and ashes' al-Kindī means the remnants that are left from the destruction of buildings. The use of the word: 'expended' ('*anfaqnāhu*', paralleling '*nunfiqahu*' further on in the sentence) adds to the obscurity of the passage.

3. Cf., on this subject: man's understanding of his defects, al-Ghazzālī, *Iḥyā' 'ulūm al-dīn* (Cairo, 1352), vol. 3, pp. 55–56.

Discussion of the Restoration of Health to the Soul When Health is Missing

This discussion deals with the treatment of the diseases of the soul. We begin—with the aid of God (exalted is He!)—by mentioning the superior genera of these diseases, then by treating the most serious and harmful among them, one after another. So we say: The superior genera of these diseases are the opposites of the four virtues which we have enumerated in the beginning of this work. Now, since the virtues are definite means [between extremes] and existing essences, they may be sought, pursued, and attained by activity, effort, and diligence. On the other hand, the other points which are not means are indefinite, do not have existing essences, and exist *qua* accident rather than *qua* essence. For instance, the circle has only one centre. This centre is a single point which has an existence of its own that can be sought and pointed out. If we do not locate it through our senses, or cannot point it out, we are yet able to deduce it and to demonstrate that it is the centre to the exclusion of any other point. On the other hand, the points which are not centres are infinite in number and do not exist in essence. Their existence is merely a matter of assumption, and they do not possess any concrete individual essence of their own. Thus, they are not sought, nor can they be deduced, for they are unknown and are diffused throughout the whole area of the circle. As for the two extremes which we call opposites, they are definite existents because they are the two ends of a definite straight line and each is at the furthest distance from the other. For instance, if we draw a straight line from the centre of a circle to the circumference, its two ends will thus be definite: the one is the centre, the other the extremity of the line at the circumference. Here again, the two ends are at the furthest distance each from the other. A similar example from the domain of the senses is that of white and black. The one is the opposite of the other, both are definite and existent, and they stand at the furthest distance each from the other, but the means that lie between them are infinite in number, and so also are the colours. The extremes of virtue, however, being more than one, cannot be called opposites, for a thing has only one opposite. We cannot find anything that has several opposites, for only two opposites can lie at the furthest distance each from the other.

A single virtue may have more than one extreme. If we imagine, for instance, the virtue as a centre, and draw from this centre a straight line ending at a certain point, we can also draw in the other opposite side another line as a straight continuation of the first and ending at another point. These two points will be opposites to the centre which we have assumed to be a virtue, but one of them will represent immoderation and excess, the other want and deficiency. Having understood this, let us note that every virtue has two definite extremes which can be indicated and innumerable means between them which cannot be indicated. However, there is only one real mean, and it is this which we have called virtue.

Furthermore, let us note that, in accordance with this exposition, we consider the genera of vices to be eight, because they are twice the number of the four virtues which we discussed before. They are: recklessness and cowardice, the two extremes of the mean which is courage; profligacy and frigidity, the two extremes of the mean which is temperance; ignorance and stupidity, the two extremes of the mean which is wisdom; and [finally] tyranny and servility—in other words, inflicting injustice and suffering injustice—the two extremes of the mean which is justice. These, then, are the superior genera of diseases, which stand in opposition to the virtues that represent the health of the soul. Under these genera, there are species beyond limit.

Anger: Its Causes and Treatment

We begin by discussing recklessness and cowardice[1] which are the two extremes of courage—itself a virtue of the soul and [a constituent of] its health. So we say: Their cause and origin is the irascible soul. Thus, all three of them [recklessness, courage, and cowardice] are related to anger. Anger is, in reality, an agitation of the soul as a result of which the blood of the heart boils in a passion for vengeance. If this agitation is violent, it kindles and inflames the fire of anger, the heart's blood boils more intensely, and the arteries and the brain become filled with a dark and turbulent smoke which impairs the state of the mind and weakens its activity. In this condition, a man becomes, as the philosophers have said, like a cave ablaze and completely full of fire, and thus chocked with flames and smoke, with the blaze rising from it as well as the sound called 'the voice of fire' [*waḥy al-nār*]. Such a fire is hard to control and impossible to extinguish, and anything which one brings near to it for the purpose of extinguishing it becomes a cause of its extension and material for its intensification. For this reason, the [angry] man becomes blind to reason and deaf to advice; on the contrary, advice becomes, in such a condition, a cause for the stimulation of anger and fuel for inflammation and flaring up, and there is no hope for such a person.

People differ in this respect according to their temperaments. If one's temperament is hot-dry, his condition is almost like that of sulphur which bursts into flame when even a weak spark is brought near to it. The contrary is true of those whose temperament is opposed to this one. But this difference is only at the beginning and when anger is growing. When it blazes, however, the condition of the one becomes almost akin to that of the other. You can conceive this by comparing the degree of inflammability of the dry firewood with that of the moist. Imagine also the rapid

1. Of these eight superior genera of vices, Miskawayh proposes to limit himself to two only: recklessness and cowardice, which are the two extremes of the virtue of courage, and which, like courage, originate in the irascible faculty. In fact, Miskawayh does not deal with these two vices as with the dispositions and the 'diseases' of the irascible faculty which produce these vices: anger on the one hand, and fear on the other. The discussion of fear leads to that of grief. Cf., on anger, al-Ghazzālī, *op. cit.*, vol. 3, pp. 143–152.

and intense inflammability of sulphur and naphtha and come down therefrom to the intermediate greases until you end with friction. For although friction is usually a weak producer of fire, yet it may become so effective as to set on fire a huge jungle or a closely entangled thicket. Another example is that of the clouds which are composed of the two vapours and yet, through friction, they produce between them blazing fires and shoot down thunderbolts whose flame no material can withstand. Such thunderbolts leave anything they touch reduced to ashes, even though it be a bare mountain or a hard rock.

Socrates said: 'I have more hope for a ship in the midst of raging winds, with waves slashing at its sides and hurling it into the deep troughs wherein there are big rocks, than for a man inflamed with anger. For in the case of a ship in this condition, its sailors take care of it and save it by various devices, while an enraged soul is beyond saving by any device whatsoever. This is because any attempt to calm anger, whether by supplication, advice, or submission, ends by becoming so much more firewood to inflame it and increase its intensity.'

The causes that produce anger are: vanity, boastfulness, bickering, importunity, jesting, self-conceit, derision, perfidy, wrongfulness, and the seeking of things which bring fame and for which people compete and envy one another. The culmination of all these causes of anger is the desire for revenge; all of them lead to it. Among the consequences of anger are: repentance, expectation of retaliatory punishment sooner or later, change in temperament, and quickening of pain. For anger is temporary madness and may even lead to death by stifling the heat of the heart or to serious diseases which cause death. It results also in one becoming the object of dislike to his friends, of malicious joy to his enemies, and of ridicule to those who are envious or vicious.

Now, each one of these causes has a remedy which one may attempt [and then pursue] until it is completely uprooted. When we proceed to sever and remove these causes, we weaken the power of anger, cut off its substance, and protect ourselves against its consequences so that, should it befall us in some form, we would be amenable to reason and would abide by its rules. The virtue associated with anger—namely, courage—would appear, and any venture which we may then undertake would be in the right way and place, in the right measure, and against the right person.

As for vanity, when we come to define it, [we find that] it is, in fact, a false belief in one's self whereby that self is held to belong to a rank which it does not deserve. But he who knows his own self should be aware of the many vices and defects which blemish it, and [should realize] that virtuousness is divided among men and that no one can attain perfection without the virtues of others. Consequently, when one's virtues depend upon others, it is one's duty not to be vain.

The same is true of boastfulness, for it consists in taking pride in things which are external to us. But he who takes pride in that which is external to him is doing so in regard to things which he does not possess. For how can one possess what is subject at every hour and every moment to evils and to destruction, and of which we are not sure at any time whatsoever. The most correct and the truest of parables is that told by God (mighty and exalted is He!) when He said: 'And set forth to them as a similitude: two men, on one of whom We bestowed two gardens of vines', up to the words: 'Then began he to wring his hands for what he had spent on it, as it was falling down upon its trellises.' Said He further (exalted is He!): 'And set forth to them the similitude of the present life: It is as water which We send down from Heaven; the earth's vegetation mingles with it, and it then becometh chaff which the winds scatter. Verily, God hath power over everything.'[1] The Qur'ān is full of such parables, and so also are the traditions reported from the Prophet (may peace be upon him!). If one boasts of his descent, the most that he can claim—assuming that he is truthful—is that his father was virtuous. But suppose that that virtuous [father] comes and says: 'This virtuousness which you claim is my own. I lay claim to it all, leaving nothing to you. What then do you possess of it, which is not found in others?' The son would be unable to answer and would be reduced to silence. Many genuine traditions in this sense are reported from the Apostle of God (may the prayer and peace of God be upon Him!). One such tradition is the one in which he said (may peace be upon Him!): 'Do not come to me with your pedigrees, but with your deeds', or words with the same purport.[2] It is related of a slave, who belonged to a certain philosopher, that, when one of the chiefs of his time boasted of his superiority to him, he said: 'If you boast of your superiority to me because of your horse, the beauty and liveliness are the horse's and not your own; if you take pride in your clothes and your outfit, the beauty is theirs and not yours; and if you brag of your ancestors, they were the meritorious people and not you. Thus, if the merits and the virtues are outside of yourself and you are divested of them, and [if] we have returned them to their owners (in fact, they have not been really taken away from them, so they do not have to be returned to them)—then who would you be?' It is also related that a certain philosopher called on a man of affluence and wealth, who had amassed ornaments and boasted of his abundant money and means. Feeling the need to spit, this philosopher cleared his throat, turned in the house right and left, and then spat right in the face of the owner of the house. When he was rebuked for his action, he said: 'I looked around the house and all that was in it, and I could not find there anything uglier than the man himself, so I spat at him.' This is the lot of those who are devoid of virtues of their own and boast of things which are outside of themselves.

As for bickering and importunity, we have shown in the preceding discourse[3] how disgraceful they are and how much dissension, discord, and mutual hate they cause among friends.

1. Sūrah XVIII (*al-Kahf*: The Cave) 32, 42, 45.
2. I have not been able to trace this tradition in the authoritative collections.
3. *Supra*, Fifth Discourse, p. 146.

Jesting is laudable so long as it is moderate. The Apostle of God (may the prayer and peace of God be upon him!) used to jest, but never said anything that was not true. The Prince of Believers[1] talked often jestingly, so that someone criticized him, saying: 'If only he were not given to jesting!' But it is hard to keep jesting within a moderate measure, and most people begin but do not know where to stop, so they overstep the limit and endeavour to outdo their friends until their jesting becomes a cause of estrangement, rousing a latent anger and sowing a lasting hate. It is for this reason that we have reckoned it among the causes [of anger]. Thus, whoever does not know its right limit should avoid it. Let him remind himself of what has been said: 'Many a difficult situation is brought about by play.' And again: 'Sometimes a war begins as jesting.' Jesting may also create dissension which it is then unable to remedy.

Self-conceit is similar to vanity. The difference between the two is that the vain man deceives himself in what he thinks of himself, while the self-conceited is haughty towards other people but does not deceive himself. However, the remedy of the latter is exactly the same as that of the former, namely, by making him realize that intelligent men consider what he boasts of to be petty, and they attach no importance to it. This is so because of its low value and its trivial share of happiness, because it is changing, ephemeral, and of doubtful permanence, and because wealth, furniture, and other worldly goods may be found among the depraved and the foolish, while wisdom is found only among the wise.

Derision is practised by buffoons and clowns and those who do not care what they suffer in return since they have accepted to endure such suffering and even many times as much. Thus, the one who is in this category laughs and feels satisfied in the face of the different forms of scorn which befall him. Indeed, he earns his living by subjecting himself to humiliation and abasement. By beginning to ridicule others slightly, he exposes himself to greater ridicule in order to arouse the laughter of others and to receive a little of their favour. The free and virtuous man is in a far different position, for he regards himself and his honour too highly to expose them to insolent people; nor would he sell them for all the treasures of kings, much less for what is petty and trivial.

Perfidy has many aspects. I mean that it may be employed in respect to wealth, reputation, womenfolk, or affection. Whichever of these many aspects it takes; it is decried by every tongue and considered disgraceful by everyone. The listener loathes to have it mentioned before him and no man, no matter how small is his share of humanity, will admit to it. It is present only among a single race of slaves who are avoided by people and disliked by the other types of slaves. For loyalty—this is the opposite of perfidy—is found among the Greek, the Ethiopian, and the Nubian races. In fact, we have seen more good loyalty displayed by slaves than by many of those who call themselves free. Whoever knows the meanness

1. ʿAlī ibn Abī Ṭālib. See *supra*, Fourth Discourse, n.5.

which the word 'perfidy' implies, and the aversion which intelligent people feel to it, and whoever understands its true meaning, will not practise it, especially if he is endowed with a good nature or has read what we have presented earlier in this work and cultivated it, and reached in his reading the present point.

Wrongfulness is causing others to suffer injustice. Anger arises in defiance of it and in a passion for revenge. We have already discussed both the inflicting of injustice and the suffering of injustice and have described the condition of each of them. Let us not, therefore, when we are wronged, hasten to take our revenge before we have considered the wrong carefully, and let us beware lest the harm that the revenge would bring us be more serious than the bearing of that wrong. To consider and to take heed in this way is to follow the counsel of reason. It is the essence of magnanimity.

As for the seeking of those things which bring fame and for which people compete with one another, it is an error which is committed by kings and great men as well as by ordinary people. For when a king has in his treasury a highly valuable object or a precious jewel, he is thereby exposing himself to the grief which he would suffer if he lost it. Such things cannot escape evils because of the nature of the world—I mean the world of generation and corruption—in which things are subject to change and transformation, and what is acquired and treasured up is liable to corruption. If the king lost a rare treasure, he would look like a bereaved person who had suffered the loss of a dear one. His need of something comparable to it, but which he would be unable to find, would become evident, and both friend and foe would know of his grief and distress. It is told of a certain king that he received a dome-shaped piece of crystal of amazing clarity and purity which was also extremely well cut. Its maker had carved out from its surface columns and figures and had repeatedly risked [breaking] it in his attempt to refine the engravings, letters, and concaves that ran among the figures and the foliage. When it came into the king's possession, his amazement and his admiration of it were immense. He ordered it to be kept in his private treasury. But before long it suffered the kind of damage which usually affects such objects. When the news reached the king, he showed such sorrow and distress that he was unable to conduct his business, or to attend to his tasks, or to hold court for his soldiers and retinue. People exerted themselves to find something similar to it, but were unsuccessful. As for the king himself, the incapacity which he thus revealed and his inability to attain his object served to double his distress and sorrow.

Turning now to ordinary people, we find that, whenever one of them treasures up a costly object or a precious jewel or acquires a sprightly mount or anything of the kind, he may be asked by someone, whose request he cannot refuse, to hand it over to him. Should he keep it from him and hold on to it, he would expose himself and his prosperity to ruin, and, on the other hand, should he give it up, he would cause himself unnecessary grief and anguish.

Precious stones, such as rubies and the like for which people vie with one another, while they may be free from internal corruption, cannot be secure against external evils such as theft and various forms of cheating. When a king amasses them, he derives little benefit from them when he needs them, and they may become useless to him all at once. For, if he should need them, they would prove to be of no help to him in the immediate situation and the pressing necessity. Indeed, we have ourselves observed how the greatest of the kings of our time, when he needed his precious stones after all his money had been expended and his treasures and castles exhausted, he could not find any person who was able to pay their price, or anything approaching it. All that he got from them was the disgrace [which resulted from the revelation] that he was in need of his subjects for part of their value and that he was unable to obtain a small or a large fraction of their price. In the meantime, these gems were being offered cheaply and circulated among brokers, merchants, and the common people, who admired them but could not afford what they were worth. Furthermore, even if someone could afford the price of some of them, he would not dare to offer it for fear that he would later be pursued, discovered, and dispossessed of them. This, then, is the fate of such treasures when possessed by kings and others. When it comes to merchants who are in this trade, they may live in a favourable time, with peace among the chiefs and security in the land, but their goods would still be in little demand since they are saleable only to those kings who are secure, who are not troubled by any misfortune, who have long enjoyed affluence, and who have accumulated more wealth than can be hoarded in treasures and castles. Those kings are deceived by good fortune, and thus fall prey to such illusions [as we have mentioned] and end in that state against which we have given warnings.

These, then, are the causes of anger and the diseases which result from it. We have mentioned their remedies and warned against their causes and against being affected by them. He who has known justice and cultivated it as we have written in the preceding parts will find it easy to remedy this disease, because it is a form of injustice and immoderation. Thus, we should not call it by names which imply praise. I mean by this that some people call this form of injustice—that is unjustified anger—manliness and firmness and treat it as if it were courage, a name which implies praise in the true sense of the word. But what a great difference there is between the two forms of conduct! For the possessor of the trait which we have condemned commits many bad acts in which he wrongs first himself, then his friends, and, one after another, the nearest of those with whom he deals, and finally his slaves, servants, and womenfolk. He is to them as a whip of torture, neither forgiving any of their faults, nor showing mercy at any tear they shed, even though they may be innocent of any offence and may have committed no crime or evil. On the contrary, he accuses them unjustly and is aroused at the least cause that may give him a chance at them. He goes so far as to attack them with his tongue and hands, while they, on their part, offer no resistance and dare not repulse him, but rather submit to him and confess offences which they did not commit in order to escape his mischief and appease his anger. Yet he keeps on in his own course, restraining neither his hands nor his tongue. He may even proceed to apply the same treatment to irrational animals and to inanimate utensils. A man of this evil character may fall upon a donkey or a pack animal, a pigeon or a bird, and beat and injure it, or he may bite a lock which proves too difficult [to open], or he may break vessels which do not conform to his wishes. This sort of bad character is known among many ill-bred people who vent their anger against clothing, glassware, ironware, and other objects.

Kings that belong to this category become enraged against rains and winds, and the air if it blows contrary to their whims or the pen if it does not comply with their desires; they curse the former and break the latter. One of the early kings used to be furious at the sea if a ship was delayed because of the sea's agitation and the tossing of its waves, even going so far as to threaten to cast the mountains into it and fill it up with them. And in our times, one insolent person used to get angry at the moon and curse it, and he satirized it in a famous poem because he was annoyed by it whenever it shone during his sleep. All such deeds are disgraceful, and some of them are, in addition, funny and expose one to ridicule. How can these, therefore, be praised as indicating manliness, strength, and the soul's nobility and might, when they are deserving of blame and exposure rather than of praise? And how much might and strength do they embody when we find them more prevalent among women than among men and more among the sick and weak than among the healthy and sturdy, and when we observe that boys are more quick to anger and irritation than men and the old more so than the young?

We also find the vice of anger accompanying that of greed, for the greedy man who does not obtain what he desires becomes angry and irritated against those of his women, servants, or other intimates who prepare his food and drink. The same is also true of the miser, who, when he loses any of his possessions, is immediately roused to anger against his friends and companions and accuses his trustworthy servants and subordinates. The only results that this class of people derive from their [bad] character are loss of friends and good counsellors, speedy regret, and painful rebuke. Such traits cannot lead to any happiness or joy. Their possessor is always sad and depressed, troubled in his life, and discontented with his situation. This places him in the condition of the unhappy man who evokes compassion.

The courageous and self-respecting man, on the other hand, is he who overcomes his anger by magnanimity, who is able to discern and consider what comes suddenly upon him, and who is not roused by any of the causes which provoke anger until he has reflected and considered how, upon whom, and in what measure to take his revenge, or how and whom to pardon and condone, and for which offence. It is related of King Alexander that he was informed of a friend who was criticizing and disparaging him. 'Why not impose upon him, O king!', said one of his counsellors, 'a punishment that will ruin him?' His answer was: 'But, after punishing him, how deeply engaged he will be in slandering me and looking for my defects! For then he will talk more freely and will find more sympathy among people.' On another occasion, one of his enemies, who had gained power, rebelled against him and caused much havoc in his territories. This person was brought into his presence and was pardoned by him. 'If I were you', said one of those in his company, 'I would have killed him'. 'Since I am not you', retorted Alexander, 'I will not kill him'.

We have now mentioned most the causes of anger and indicated the ways of treating them and putting an end to them. Anger is the most serious of the diseases of the soul. If one proceeds early to put an end to its cause, he will then have no fear that it will take hold of him. Whatever anger will then arise in him will be easy to remedy and quick to vanish, as it will have no material to allow it to flare and continue to burn and no cause to inflame and kindle it. [The faculty of] reflection will have a chance to ponder and to deliberate on the virtue of magnanimity, as well as to reward, in case that is right, or to ignore, in case that is the way of prudence.

Fear: Its Causes and Remedy

The treatment of this disease of the soul [anger] is followed by the treatment of cowardice which is the other extreme of the health of the soul. Now, since each of two opposites can be known from the other, and since we have come to know one of the extremes—which we have defined as a strong and violent agitation of the soul the result of which is the boiling of the blood of the heart in a passion for revenge—it follows that we thereby know its opposite. I mean [by this] the other extreme which is a quiescence of the soul when it should be agitated and an absence of the passion for revenge. This is the cause of cowardice and faintness. It results in humiliation and an unfortunate life, in being at the mercy of the low classes as well as of one's relatives, children, and those with whom one has dealings, and in a lack of steadiness and patience in situations where steadiness is required. It is also the cause of laziness and of the love of ease which are the causes of all vice. Among its consequences are: subservience to everyone, acceptance of every humiliation or wrong, enduring all sorts of scandal affecting one's self, one's relatives, or one's possessions, hearing every form of vile and offensive insult and calumny, enduring every type of injustice from all those with whom one deals, and an inability to disdain what is disdained by free men.

The remedy of these causes and consequences can be effected through their opposites, that is through the awakening of the soul which suffers from such a disease, by shaking and agitating it. For the irascible faculty cannot be so completely lacking in a person that it has to be brought to him from another place. The fact is, rather, that in such a case this faculty is weaker than it should be and resembles a fire which has nearly gone out but which has still enough left to be affected by fanning and blowing. If it is stirred in a suitable way, it will inevitably be animated and will revive the burning and the blazing which are in its nature. It is said of one of those who were engaged in philosophy that he used to look deliberately for dangerous places and put himself in them, and to induce himself to take grave risks by trying to confront them. He used to go out on the sea when it was disturbed and agitated so that he could train his soul to be steadfast in dangerous situations, to rouse its quiescent [irascible] faculty whenever such rousing was needed, and to deliver it from the vice of laziness and its consequences. It would not hurt a person who is affected with such a disease to engage in some quarrels, and to expose himself to abuse and to the antagonism of those from whose danger he is safe. In this way, he could approach the virtue which is a mean between the two vices, namely, courage, which is the desired health of the soul. When he achieves it and comes to feel it in himself, he should cease and stop without going any further lest he pass to the other side [that of anger] whose remedy we have taught you.

Now, since excessive and unjustified fear is one of the diseases of the soul, and since it is related to the same [irascible] faculty, it is necessary for us to mention it and to note its causes and remedy. So we say: Fear is caused by either the anticipation of an evil or the expectation of a danger.[1] Anticipation and expectation relate only to those events which will take place in the future. And those events may be either serious or trivial, and either necessary or contingent. Contingent events may be caused either by us or by other people. None of these [above-mentioned] categories should be feared by the intelligent man. Concerning contingent events, they generally may or may not take place. One should not, therefore, count on their taking place, become apprehensive about them, or anticipate the evil of the suffering which they might cause, since they have not yet occurred and they may [very well] not occur. The poet was right when he said:

'When seized by fear, say to thy heart: Be comforted; most fears are false.'

Such, then, is the condition of those [fearful things] which is due to external causes. We have told you that such things do not belong to the category of the necessary which must definitely take place. Consequently, fear of the evil which such things bring should be relative to the possibility of their occurrence. And, indeed, life is agreeable and happy only with good trust and strong hope and the abandonment of worry about any evil which may not occur. As for those fearful things which are caused by our own bad choice and by what we inflict on ourselves, we should guard against them by avoiding offences and crimes whose consequences we dread and by refraining from venturing on any action from whose danger we

1. *N.E.* 1115a 9.

cannot be safe. For a person who acts in this way forgets that the contingent either may or may not take place. When he perpetrates an offence or commits a crime, he presumes that it will either remain hidden and undisclosed or, if the contrary is the case, that it will be disregarded, or that no harm will ensue from it. It seems, then, that such a person, like the former one whose fear is of the first kind [i.e., from outside causes], considers the contingent as necessary. But while this one feels safe particularly from what is dangerous, the former [on the contrary] is afraid particularly of what is safe. I mean by this that, since the contingent is half-way between the necessary and the impossible, it is, as it were, like an object which has two sides, the one adjoining the necessary, the other adjoining the impossible. For instance, in the [straight] line ACB: A represents the necessary, B the impossible and C the contingent. The contingent is at an equal distance from both A and B, one side of it extending towards A, the other towards B. When its future has become past, we should cease calling it the contingent and it will have moved either to the side of the necessary or to that of the impossible. However, so long as it is the contingent, one should not reckon it either on this side or on that, but should rather attribute to it its own appropriate nature, that is, that it may move either here or there. This is why the philosopher said: 'The aspects of contingent things are [revealed] in their consequences.'

Concerning the fear of things that are necessary, such as old age and its concomitants, [we say that] the remedy is to realize that if a man desires a long life he also certainly desires [to reach] old age and anticipates it as something inevitable. Old age is accompanied by a diminution of the innate heat and of the original moistness which accompanies it, by the predominance of their opposites: coldness and dryness, and by the weakening of all the principal organs. This is followed by reduction of movement, fading of energy, enfeeblement of the organs of digestion, falling off of the grinding organs, and abatement of the faculties that regulate life, that is, those of attraction, discharge, withholding, and nutrition, as well as the other accompanying constituents of life. Diseases and pains are nothing other than these things. To them should be added the death of one's beloved and the loss of those who are dear to him. He who, in the beginning of his life, anticipates these things and observes their requirements will not fear them, but will rather expect them and look forward to them. Others will wish that they be granted to him and he himself will solicit them from God (exalted is He!) in prayers and when he is in mosques and shrines.

Fear of Death: Its Causes and Remedy

So much for a summary discussion of fear in general.[1] Now, as the most serious fear which affects man is the fear of death, and as this fear is not only prevalent but

1. Cf., *Risālah fī dafʿ al-ghamm min al-mawt* in M. A. F. Mehren, ed. and tr., *Traités mystiques*

also more intense and far-reaching than any other kind of fear, it is necessary that we discuss it fully. So we say: Fear of death befalls only the person who does not know what death really is; or who is not aware of the ultimate destiny of his soul; or who believes that when his body dissolves and decomposes his essence thereby dissolves and his soul decomposes to the point of annihilation and effacement, and that—as is believed by those who are ignorant of the immortality of the soul and of the life to come—the world will continue to exist after him and he himself will not exist in it; or who thinks that death involves a great pain other than the pain of these diseases which may precede it, or lead to it, or be the cause of its occurrence; or who believes that a punishment will befall him after death; or who is puzzled, not knowing what he will face after he dies; or [finally] who is grieved because of the money and possessions which he will leave behind.

All of these are false beliefs and devoid of truth. To the one who is ignorant about death and does not know what it really is, we explain that death is nothing more than the soul's abandonment of the use of one's tools, namely, the organs which, when taken as a whole, are called a body, just as an artisan abandons the use of his own tools. [We explain also] that the soul is an incorporeal substance, and not an accident, and that it is not subject to corruption. To understand this explanation, one needs to have gone through certain sciences which precede it; it is demonstrated and thoroughly explained [elsewhere] in its proper place. Whoever looks for it and strives to grasp it will not find his goal hard to attain. And he who is content with my statement in the beginning of this work and is satisfied with it will know that this substance [the soul] is unlike the substance of the body and that it differs from it completely in its essence, properties, actions, and effects. When it leaves the body, in the manner we have described and according to the condition we have laid down, it achieves the eternal life which is proper to it, becomes cleansed from the impurity of nature, and experiences complete happiness. There is absolutely no way for it to perish or to be annihilated. For, a substance does not perish *qua* substance, nor can its essence be nullified. Only accidents, properties,

d'Aboû Alī al-Hosain b. Abdallāh b. Sīnā au d'Avicenne, IIIième Fasc. (Leiden, 1894), pp. 49–57 (trans. pp. 28–33). Mehren edited this treatise from two Mss., one in London and the other in Leningrad, both of which ascribe it to Ibn Sīnā. This treatise is identical (with some variations) with this section of the *Tahdhīb*, pp. 185–192. Mehren noted this identity, but considered that this section of the *Tahdhīb* is copied from Ibn Sīnā's treatise, without any mention of the original author (Ibid., p. 49, n.a; p. 28, n. 1).

In 1908, Louis Cheikho published the same text, *Al-Machreq*, XI (1908), pp. 839–844, from a Ms. in the Bibliothèque Nationale, which did not give the author's name. Aḥmad Tīmūr Pāshā called Cheikho's attention to the identity between this text and that published by Mehren. See *Al-Machreq*, XI (1908), pp. 958–961, where Cheikho concluded that the author was probably Miskawayh. He republished it with indications of the variants between the Mehren edition and the *Tahdhīb* (Cairo, 1298) in *Maqālāt falsafiyyah qadīmah li-baʿḍ mashāhīr falāsifat al-ʿarab* (Beirut, 1911), pp. 103–114. It is evident that this text was taken out of the *Tahdhīb* and wrongly ascribed to Ibn Sīnā, and not the other way around, as Mehren thought.

and the proportions and relations which exist between the substance and bodies are nullified by their opposites. But the substance itself has no opposite; and when anything is corrupted, its corruption is due to its opposite. You may understand this easily from the first principles of logic even before you reach its proofs. And if you observe a bodily substance—which is base as compared with that noble substance [the soul]—and examine its condition, you will find that it does not perish nor pass away *qua* substance, but that some parts of it are transformed into others and, in this way, its properties and accidents disappear gradually. The substance itself, however, remains and cannot, in any way, be annihilated or nullified. Take for instance, water; when it is transformed into vapour or air, or, similarly, when air is transformed into water or fire, the accidents and properties of the substance disappear, but the substance *qua* substance remains and cannot, in any way, be annihilated. If this is the case with the bodily substance which is subject to transformation and change, how can we imagine that the spiritual substance will perish and be annihilated, when it is not subject to transformation or change in itself, but receives rather its own perfections and the completions of its forms?

Proceeding to the person who fears death because he does not know the ultimate destiny of his soul, or because he believes that, when his body dissolves and decomposes, his essence is thereby dissolved and his soul nullified, or because he is ignorant of the immortality of the soul and the nature of the life to come—such a person does not, in reality, fear death but is only ignorant of what he should know. Ignorance, then, is what makes him afraid. And it is this ignorance which impelled the philosophers to seek knowledge, to work hard for it, to give up bodily pleasures and comforts for its sake, to choose toil and night work in its stead, and to hold that the comfort by which one is relieved from ignorance is real comfort while real hardship is that which is caused by ignorance—because ignorance is a chronic disease of the soul and recovery from it brings to the soul salvation, eternal rest, and everlasting pleasure. When the philosophers became certain of that, reflected on it, grasped its truth, and attained the spirit and the comfort embodied in it, nothing in the world was too hard for them. They came to despise all that the mass of the people honours: property, wealth, sensual pleasures, and all the other desires which lead to them. For such things are unstable and transient; they soon vanish and pass away; they cause great worries when they are achieved and great pains when lost. Thus, the philosophers sought only as much of such things as are necessary to life and did not care for the superfluities which have all the defects that I have mentioned as well as those that I have not. Such things are at the same time endless, for, in seeking them, if one attains a certain end; his soul still yearns for another end without stopping at any limit or terminating at any time. Death is indeed this condition itself, and not what he [the type of person who fears death out of ignorance] fears. To covet this condition is to covet the ephemeral, and to be preoccupied with it is to be preoccupied with what is false. For this reason, the philosophers affirmed that death is of two kinds: the voluntary and the natural, and that life also is of the same two kinds. By voluntary death, they meant the suppression of desires and their abandonment and by natural death the separation of the soul from the body. Voluntary life was to them what man seeks in this world of such things as food, drinks, and desires, while natural life was to them the eternal existence of the soul in everlasting bliss through one's acquisition of the true sciences and his purification from ignorance. Thus Plato advised the student of philosophy by telling him: 'Die by will, and you will live by nature.'[1]

But he who fears man's natural death fears what he should really wish for, because this death is the realization of what is implied in the definition of man, namely, that he is a living being, rational, and mortal. By death, he becomes complete and perfect and attains his highest plane. He who knows that every thing is composed of its definition, that its definition is composed of its genus and its differentia, and that the genus of man is the living being and his two differentia are the rational and the mortal—such a person will realize that man will be resolved into his genus and his differentia, since every composite must inevitably be resolved into that of which it is composed. Who, then, is more ignorant than the one who is afraid of his own completion, and who is more miserable than the one who supposes that he is annihilated by living and that he becomes incomplete by being complete? For when one who is incomplete is afraid of becoming complete, he thereby proves himself to be extremely ignorant. The intelligent man should, therefore, shrink from incompletion and find comfort in being complete. He should seek everything that could make him complete and perfect, that could ennoble him and raise his rank, and that could free him in such a way as to make him safe from falling into captivity rather than tighten his fetters and add to his complexity and entanglement. He should also trust in the fact that when the noble and divine substance is delivered from the thick and corporeal one, in purity and clarity rather than in mixture and turbidity, that substance attains happiness, returns to its heavenly abode, becomes near to its Creator, wins the proximity of the Lord of the universe, associates with its kindred and fellows among the good spirits, and escapes from what is contrary and foreign to it. It follows, then, that the soul, which at the time of its separation from the body still yearns and cares for it and is afraid to leave it, is extremely miserable and at the utmost distance from its own essence and substance, following a course which is furthest removed from its own abode, and seeking security for that which can never be secure.

As for the one who believes that death involves a great pain other than the pain of the diseases which may have preceded and caused it, the remedy is to

1. See Franz Rosenthal, 'On the Knowledge of Plato's Philosophy in the Islamic World', *Islamic Culture*, 14 (1940), p. 409.

demonstrate to him that this is a false belief since pain belongs to the living being only, and a living being is one that is subject to the effect of the soul. A body which is not subject to this effect does not suffer or feel. Consequently, death, which is the separation of the soul from the body, does not involve any pain because the body suffers and feels only by virtue of the effect of the soul on it, but, when it becomes merely a body and devoid of this effect, it neither feels nor suffers pain. It is evident, therefore, that death is a condition of the body which it does not feel or suffer because this condition involves the loss of that by which the body felt and suffered.

To the one who is afraid of death because of the punishment with which he feels threatened after it, we must explain that he is not, in fact, afraid of death but of the punishment. Now, such punishment is suffered only by something that will still be living after the body has perished. And whoever acknowledges that something survives the body, acknowledges also necessarily that he has committed offences and bad deeds for which he deserves punishment. At the same time, he acknowledges that there is a Ruler who is just and who punishes for bad deeds and does not punish for good ones. [It can be seen, then, that] such a person is, in fact, afraid of his own offences and not of death. If one fears punishments for an offence, his duty is to guard against it and to avoid it. Earlier, we have clearly shown that the bad deeds which are called offences originate from bad dispositions. Bad dispositions belong to the soul, and are the vices which we have enumerated and whose opposite virtues we have made known to you. Consequently, he who fears death in this way and for this reason is ignorant of what he should fear and afraid of what has no effect and should not be feared. The remedy for ignorance is knowledge. It is, therefore, wisdom that releases us from these pains and these false suppositions, which are the consequences of ignorance. And, indeed, God will lead to what is good!

In the same way, we address the person who is afraid of death because he does not know what he will face after he dies, for this is again the case of an ignorant person who is afraid because of his ignorance. The remedy is for him to learn so he will know and have faith. For whoever believes in a certain state for his soul after death, and yet does not know what that state is, is confessing his ignorance. And the remedy for ignorance is knowledge. He who has knowledge is confident; he who is confident knows the way to happiness and thus follows it; and he who follows a straight path to a worthy goal attains it inevitably. Such confidence, which is born of knowledge, is certitude. It is the state of the man who reflects deeply on his religion and holds fast to his philosophy, and whose rank and dignity we have already described to you in the course of this work.

[Finally,] he who claims that he does not fear death but is grieved because of the relatives, descendants, wealth, and property which he will leave behind, and who regrets the delights and desires of this world which he will miss—such a person must be told clearly by us that grief is the anticipation of a pain or an evil and that such grief brings no benefit whatsoever. We shall discuss the remedy of grief in a special section reserved for it, since in this section we are dealing only with the pain of fear and its remedy. We have treated this subject in an adequate and convincing manner, but in order to explain and clarify it further we say: Man is one of the generables. Philosophical views have made it clear that every generable is inevitably corruptible. Thus, he who wishes not to suffer corruption also necessarily wishes not to be, and he who wishes not to be also necessarily wishes for his own corruption. It is as if he wishes [both] to suffer corruption and not to suffer corruption, to exist and not to exist. This is impossible and would not occur to the mind of an intelligent person.

Furthermore, had our predecessors and ancestors not passed away, we could not have come into existence. If it were possible for man to live forever, our predecessors would have continued to live. But if this had happened and our predecessors, given their reproductiveness, had not died, the earth would not be large enough to contain them. You will see the truth of this statement from the following: Let us suppose that a person who was alive four hundred years ago were still alive at this time. Let him be one of the famous personalities so that his descendants can be found and recognized. Take, for instance, ʿAlī ibn Abī Ṭālib (may peace be upon him!) and suppose that he had had children and children's children and that they had continued to reproduce in this fashion without any one of them passing away; how many of them would there have been at the present time? You would be able to find more than ten million of them. Indeed, in spite of the deaths and the devastating massacres which these descendants have suffered, more than two hundred thousand of them have survived. Now, if you were to make the same calculation for everyone who lived in that age on the surface of the earth, east and west, [you would find that] you would not be able to determine their multiplicity or to reckon their number. If then you surveyed the surface of the earth, [you would find also that] it is limited and its area defined, and you would realize that, in that event, the earth would not be spacious enough to hold all of these people even if they were standing and crowded together, much less if they were seated or engaged in activities. There would be left neither more place for construction, nor ground for cultivation, nor the possibility for one to walk or move about—to say nothing of other activities. And this is only in a short period of time. What would happen then if the time were extended and people kept reproducing at the same rate? Such, then, is the state of ignorance and stupidity of those who desire the eternity of this life and abhor death, and who imagine that eternity is possible or desirable! It is, therefore, evident that consummate wisdom as well as the justice established by divine planning are the right course which we should not shun and from which we should not deviate, and that this also represents the very extreme of generosity, beyond which there is no further end for the persistent seeker or the one who covets benefit. To fear it is to fear the justice of the Creator and His wisdom—or, indeed, His generosity and munificence.

It has become now quite evident that death is not an evil, as the mass of the people supposes, but that the evil, indeed, is the fear of death and that whoever is afraid of death is ignorant of it and of his own self. It has also become evident from our preceding discussion that the reality of death is the separation of the soul from the body and that this separation is not a corruption of the soul but only the corruption of the composite. As for the substance of the soul, which forms the essence, core, and quintessence of man, it is immortal and, being incorporeal, it is not subject to the attributes of bodies which we mentioned a little earlier. Nor is this substance subject to any of the accidents of bodies: it is not crowded in space, for it has no need of space, nor does it seek any permanence in time, for it can dispense with time. The senses and the bodies have imparted to this substance certain perfection. But having achieved this perfection through them, if it was then liberated from them, it would pass to its noble world which is near to its Creator and Maker (exalted and sanctified is He!). We have already, in our preceding discussion of this subject, explained this perfection which it acquires in the sensible world and shown you the way to it. We have noted that it is the extreme happiness which man can attain, and we have also informed you of its opposite which is man's extreme misery. But, along with this, we have explained the different grades of happiness, as well as the ranks of the righteous and their share of the favour of God (mighty and exalted is He!) and of His Paradise, this being the lasting abode. Similarly, we have described to you the ranks of the opposites of the righteous [and their share of] God's wrath and their downward stages in Hell, this being the abyss where there is no rest. We solicit God's good help in what will bring us nigh unto Him. Generous is He indeed, munificent, compassionate, and merciful!

The Remedy of Grief

Grief is a suffering of the soul occasioned by the loss of a dear one or the failure to fulfil a desire. Its cause is concern for material acquisitions, covetousness of bodily desires, and sorrow for what one loses or misses of these things. But a person is grieved and distressed at the loss of what is dear to him or at his failure to attain his desires, only if he believes that the coveted worldly things which he acquires can endure and remain stable for him, and that all that he seeks of the worldly things which he misses will inevitably be achieved and possessed by him. If, however, he is fair to himself and realizes that everything in the world of generation and corruption is neither enduring nor stable and that the only stable and enduring things are those which belong to the world of the intellect, then he will not crave the impossible or endeavour to get it. And when he ceases to crave it, he will also cease to be grieved if he loses what he desires or if he fails to secure what he wishes in this world. He will direct his efforts to ends that are pure and limit his attention to the seeking of permanent goods only. He will discard all that is not by nature stable and enduring. When he obtains any one of these goods, he will immediately put it in its proper place and take only as much of it as is necessary to remove the pains which we have enumerated, such as hunger, nakedness, and similar exigencies. He will not try to treasure up these things, or to seek to accumulate them or to show them off and boast of them. He will not entertain the hope of amassing them, nor will he long for them. If he loses them, he will not regret them, nor care about them. Whoever accepts this advice will feel confident rather than distressed, joyous rather than grieved, and happy rather than miserable. But he who does not accept it and who does not treat himself in this way will continue to be in constant distress and unabating grief. For such a person cannot at all times be immune from the failure to fulfil a desire or from the loss of something that is dear to him. Such failure and loss are bound to take place in this world of ours, it being a world of generation and corruption. And whoever expects what is subject to generation and corruption not to be generated and not to be corrupted is expecting the impossible; and he who expects the impossible is always disappointed, and the disappointed man is always grieved, and he who is grieved is miserable.

On the other hand, he who acquires by good practice the feeling of being satisfied with all that he finds and of not being grieved at anything he loses will always be joyful and happy. Should one doubt that such a feeling could be possible or helpful, let him consider the feelings of people in regard to the aims which they seek and the lives which they lead, and observe how people differ in such matters according to the intensity of these feelings. This consideration will reveal to him clearly and openly the joy of people in their own lives—no matter how different those lives may be—and the contentment of those who practice different crafts in their various occupations. Let him note this carefully in one class after another among the common people: he will not fail to observe the joy of the merchant in his trade, of the soldier in his courage, of the gambler in his gambling, of the swindler in his swindling, and of the effeminate in his effeminacy. Each one of these people comes to think that anyone who is not in the same condition as he and who thus misses its joy is certainly duped, and that anyone who is ignorant of that condition and thus deprived of its pleasures is a fool indeed. This is only because each group feels strongly that its own course is the right one and because it becomes attached to that course by long practice. Now, if the seeker of virtue stays attached to his particular course, if his feeling [that it is the right course] becomes strong, and if his judgment remains sound and his practice is prolonged, he will be more entitled to joy than all those classes of men who stray in the darkness of their ignorance. Indeed, his share of the lasting bliss will be greater because he is right and they are wrong, he is certain and they are uncertain, he is sane and they are ill, he is happy and they are miserable, he is God's friend and they are His enemies. And God (exalted is He!) has said: 'Verily, God's friends—no fear shall be on them, nor shall they be put to grief.'[1]

Al-Kindī's Remarks on Grief

In his work called *The Repelling of Griefs* [*Dafʿ al-aḥzān*],[2] al-Kindī made the following remarks which show you clearly that grief is brought forth by man and imposed on himself and is not a natural thing:

'If a person who has lost a property or who seeks an object without finding it, and is grieved in consequence, considers his grief philosophically; if he realizes that the causes of this grief are not necessary; and if he realizes also that many people who do not possess such property instead of being grieved are, on the contrary, joyful and happy—if such a person does this, he will undoubtedly come to know that grief is neither necessary nor natural and that he who is grieved and brings this accident upon himself will inevitably be comforted and will return to his natural state. Indeed, we have observed people who were strongly afflicted by the loss of children, friends, or some who were dear to them or loved by them, and who after a while returned to the state of joy, laughter, and happiness and regained the condition of those who have never been distressed. The same is true of the one who is deprived of his money, his estate, and all the desirable possessions which man may acquire and whose loss would bring him disappointment and grief. Such a person is finally consoled, his grief fades away, and he inevitably regains his cheerfulness and happiness. Therefore, if the intelligent man reflects on the conditions of people when they are in grief and on the causes of grief, he will know that he is not the particular victim of a strange misfortune, that he is not distinguished from others by a singular distress, that the ultimate end of his misfortune is consolation, and that grief is an accidental disease which resembles the other evils. He will thus not subject himself to an evil accident, nor get an acquired disease—I mean a disease which man brings upon himself and which is not natural.'

1. Sūrah X (*Yūnus*: Jonah), 62.

2. See Ibn al-Nadīm, *al-Fihrist*, ed. G. Flügel (Leipzig, 1871–72), vol. 1, p. 260. This treatise is mentioned, under varying titles, by Saʿīd al-Andalusī, al-Qifṭī, and Ibn Abī Uṣaybiʿah. See Richard J. McCarthy, *al-Taṣānīf al-mansubah ilā faylasūf al-ʿarab* (Baghdad, 1962), p. 31, no. 171, and p. 65, no. 17. It was published with an introduction by H. Ritter and R. Walzer, 'Studi su al-Kindī II, Uno scritto morale inedito di al-Kindī', *Memorie della Reale Academia Nazionale dei Lincei*, Ser. VI, vol. 8, Fasc. 1 (Rome, 1938), pp. 1–38. See also Franz Rosenthal's review in *Orientalia*, 9 (1940), pp. 182–191.

'Such a person should remember what we have mentioned previously about the man who is presented with a rare [and fragrant] object on condition that he smell and enjoy it and then return it for others to smell and enjoy as well, but who covets it and thinks it is bestowed upon him permanently, so that when it is taken away from him, he is grieved, disappointed, and angered. This is the condition of the man who has lost his reason and who craves the impossible. It is the condition of the envious man, because he desires to monopolize the goods without sharing them with others; and envy is the worst of diseases and the most horrid of evils. That is why the philosophers said: Whoever desires evil to befall his enemies is a lover of evil, and the lover of evil is a wicked man. More wicked is he who desires evil to befall those who are not his enemies, and still worse is he who wishes no good to come to his friends. He who wishes to deprive his friends of the goods is wishing them evil.'

'The consequence of these evils is that one becomes grieved at the goods which people obtain and envies them on account of what they attain of them. It matters not whether these goods are, or are not, among our acquisitions and possessions, for all of them are common to mankind as a whole. God has entrusted them to His creatures, and it is His right to withdraw these entrusted goods at any time and through whatever person He wishes. It is not a disgrace for us nor a shame to return these goods. On the contrary, it is both a shame and a disgrace to be grieved when they are withdrawn from us. It also represents ingratitude, because the least appreciation that we owe to anyone who lends us something is to return it to him willingly and to respond to him with alacrity when he wants it back. Especially should this be the case when the lender leaves with us the best of what he has lent us and takes back the meanest.'

Al-Kindī said [further]: 'By the best and noblest, I mean that part which no hand can reach, and which no one else can share with us, that is, the soul, the intellect, and the virtues which are granted to us as a gift which will never be taken back or withdrawn.' He said also: 'If as justice demands, God withdraws the smaller and meaner part, He leaves with us the greater and better part, and if we were to grieve for everything we lose, we would be in permanent sorrow. The intelligent man should not, therefore, think of harmful and painful things, and, since the loss of property is a cause of grief, he should acquire as little of it as possible. It is said of Socrates that when he was asked about the cause of his liveliness and lack of sorrow, he said: "I do not acquire the things whose loss would put me to grief."'

We have discussed the genera of the diseases which affect the soul, indicated their treatments, and pointed out their remedies. Now, the intelligent man, who cares for his soul and who endeavours to rid it of its pains and to save it from its perils, should not find it hard to examine the diseases which fall under these genera as species and individuals, to cure his soul of them, and to treat them with their opposite remedies. Then the help of God (mighty and exalted is He!) should be solicited to ensure success. For success is coupled with diligence: neither can be achieved without the other.

This is the end of *The Book of Purification Concerning the Refinement of the Soul*. Praise be unto God, at the beginning and at the end. May His blessings be upon His Prophet Muḥammad and his family, and may His salutations of peace be abundant!

14

Bahmanyār Ibn Marzbān

Abu'l-Ḥasan Bahmanyār ibn Marzbān Kīyā, who hailed from Āzarbāyjān, was the most famous of Ibn Sīnā's students. Little, however, is known of his life except that he was a young man when Ibn Sīnā discovered him and asked his father to have the gifted young student study with him. We also know that he died thirty years after Ibn Sīnā—that is, in 458/1066. As for his religious affiliation, it is known that he came from a Zoroastrian background. Some have believed that he converted to Sunni Islam and others to Shiʿism, while a number of scholars consider him to have remained a Zoroastrian. His discussions of Divine Unity (*tawḥīd*) point, however, to a thoroughly Islamic perspective.

Bahmanyār spent many years studying with Ibn Sīnā and carried out much discussion with his teacher concerning difficult philosophical issues. These discussions are reflected in Bahmanyār's works, which are in reality a continuation of Islamic Peripatetic philosophy and valuable commentaries upon the work of Ibn Sīnā. But this does not mean that Bahmanyār simply repeated Ibn Sīnā's philosophy. There are certain issues, such as the consideration of the substance (*jawhar*) of a genus as the highest substance and 'proof of the ladder' (*al-burhān al-sullamī*), where one sees differences between him and Ibn Sīnā. Bahmanyār seems to have been most influenced by Ibn Sīnā's Neoplatonic views of creation through emanation and the uncaused and necessary nature of God. Regarding the identity of the soul in the afterlife, he seems to have taken a different view from Ibn Sīnā. The soul, Bahmanyār maintains, will undergo a change through death but remains similar to its previous status.

The most important work of Bahmanyār is the *Kitāb al-taḥṣīl* (The Book of Exposition), which summarizes Peripatetic philosophy as exposed by Ibn Sīnā in his *al-Shifā'* and *al-Najāh*. This work, whose order is based on Ibn Sīnā's *Dānish-nāmah-yi ʿalā'ī*, *al-Shifā'*, and *al-Najāh*, is considered by some as one of the best texts for the teaching of the philosophy of the school of Ibn Sīnā. Historians refer to other works by Bahmanyār that seem to have been lost. Among these are *Kitāb al-bahjah fī manṭiq wa'l-ṭabī'ī wa'l-ilāhī* (Treatise of Splendour on Logic, Natural Philosophy and Metaphysics), *Kitāb al-rutbah fi'l-manṭiq* (Treatise on the Ranks in Logic), *and Kitāb al-zīnah fi'l-manṭiq* (Treatise on the Ornament of Logic).

By and large, however, Bahmanyār's thoughts are a continuation of Ibn Sīnā, and his works provide precious keys for unravelling many difficult aspects of the philosophy of his teacher.

The following translation reproduces Bahmanyār's introduction and brief summary of the *Book of Exposition*, as well as the section dealing with fundamentals in the descending hierarchy of being through the intellects, souls, and bodies of the celestial spheres to the sublunary world of generation and corruption. The final portion of this section is devoted to the problem of the origin of evil in the corporeal world. Bahmanyār labels this section 'Discussion of the Heavens and the World', referring thus to the standard Arabic title of Aristotle's *On the Heavens.* In his introduction, Bahmanyār indicates that the subjects treated are also in part those of the Alpha Minor of the *Metaphysics* (on Aristotle's four causes) and the (pseudo-Aristotelian) *Theology* (epitome of the *Enneads* of Plotinus).

The known manuscripts of the *Kitāb al-taḥṣīl* display considerable textual variations, to the point of suggesting multiple recenscions of the work from the author's hand, and the edition relied on for this translation is far from definitive. In particular, of the four parts of the 'Discussion of the Heavens and the World', the second and third are manifestly variants of the same text. A full translation of the third part has been given—the fuller of the two—noting variants from the second part in the notes. There seems to be no evidence that this section originally contained more than three parts (although some original text may be missing), and the parts have been renumbered accordingly.

M. Aminrazavi

AUTHOR'S FOREWORD
From *Kitāb al-taḥṣīl* (The Book of Exposition)

Translated for this volume by Everett K. Rowson, from Bahmanyār's *Kitāb al-taḥṣīl*, ed. M. Muṭahharī (Tehran, 1970), pp. 1–3, 631–662.

Introduction

In the Name of God, the Merciful, the Compassionate

To God be praise commensurate with His exalted position and His overflowing beneficence, and His blessings on His Prophet, his family and his companions.[1]

After this invocation, Bahmanyār [b.] al-Marzbān says:

In this epistle, addressed to my maternal uncle Abū Manṣūr Bahrām b. Khurshīd ibn Īzadyār, I present a critical exposition of the essentials[2] of wisdom as refined by al-Shaykh al-Ra'īs Abū 'Alī al-Ḥusayn ibn 'Abdallāh ibn Sīnā (God have mercy on him). For its organization I have taken the *'Alā'ī Wisdom* as my model, but for treating the subject matter comprehensively I have relied on all of his works in general, as well as my own discussions with him. I have also supplemented it with secondary conclusions which I have confirmed through my own investigation, and which serve here as primary postulates; you can be guided to these secondary conclusions through your own investigation into his books.

This book is divided into three books.

Book I is on logic. It has three sections. Section I has three chapters. Chapter 1 explains the intention of the *Isagoge*. Chapter 2 explains the intention of the *Categories*. Chapter 3 explains the intention of the *On Interpretation*. Section II has one chapter, on the *Prior Analytics*. Section III has two chapters, treating the points covered in the *Posterior Analytics*.

Book II is on the basic premises required in all the sciences. This is the science which is called 'metaphysics'. It has six sections.

Book III is concerned with the existents themselves, and has two sections. Section I is concerned with indicating the existent which has no reason or cause; it includes an explanation of the intention of the *Theology* and the section (of the *Metaphysics*) called *Alpha Minor*. It has one chapter. Section II treats caused existents, and has four chapters. Chapter 1 is concerned with the basic premises required in physical questions; it includes an explanation of the intention of the *Physics*. Chapter 2 is concerned with knowledge of the celestial bodies, their souls, their intellects, and their circumstances in general; it includes an explanation of

1. pp. 1–3.
2. Reading *lubāb* for text *kitāb*; see D. Gutas, *Avicenna and the Aristotelian Tradition* (Leiden, 1988), p. 111, n. 17.

the intention of the *On the Heavens*, as well as parts of *Alpha Minor* and the *Theology*.[1] Chapter 3 is concerned with knowledge of the physical elements and of those compounds which are close to them, and with explaining the intention of the *On Generation and Corruption* and of the *Meteorology*. Chapter 4 is concerned with the science of the soul and its survival, and with the circumstances of the Hereafter.

The way to learn from this book is to begin first with the *ʿAlāʾī Wisdom*, learning from it logic in particular, and only then to progress on to this book, so that he who seeks knowledge may acquire what he seeks, in a shorter time than it would take to memorize the *Ḥamāsa*,[2] God willing and assisting.

Now, what is sought in the sciences of wisdom is knowledge of the existents. An existent may be existent without a reason (*sabab*)[3] or with one. The Existent which has no reason must, in Its reality, be One in every way; It must be neither a body nor a power in a body; Its quiddity (*māhiyyah*) must be identical to Its being (*anniyyah*); Its knowledge of Itself must be Its existence, and Its knowledge of (other) existents must be among Its concomitants (*lawāzim*); Its will, power, and life must be themselves Its knowledge, and all that must belong to It in itself (*bi'l-dhāt*); and Its knowledge must be an unchanging and imperishable knowledge, not a knowledge that is passively acquired but rather an active knowledge. It is efficient cause (*al-fāʿil*) and final cause (*al-ghāyah*) together. Further elaboration on what is specific to this Existent follows below.

The existent which has a reason is not required, in itself, to be one in every way, although it is one in a different manner, which we will further determine at an appropriate point. Observation and syllogistic argument (*qiyās*) indicate that this existent is multiple; it includes both what is body and what is not body; that which is not body is either accident or substance; the substance which is not body is intellect, soul, form, or matter.

Bodies are multiple. Some of these are celestial bodies, which are multiple, their number being indicated by astronomical observation. Others are elemental bodies, which are indicated by a kind of syllogistic argument to be four in number. Others are bodies compounded of these elements; there is no way of enumerating these, by either syllogistic argument or sense perception, because they are a result of celestial motions that cannot be determined with precision. Only those that can be hunted down by sense perception and to which direct observation can attain can be grasped; they include clouds, meteors, and winds, minerals, plants, and animals and the like. All of these collectively have an order and arrangement, as well as varying circumstances, some of which can be evaluated as good and others as bad.

1. This is the section translated below.

2. That is, the celebrated poetic anthology by Abū Tammām (d. 231–2/845–6); see *EI2*, s. v. Abū Tammām.

3. Bahmanyār generally uses *sabab* ('reason') for proximate or subsidiary cause, and *ʿillah* ('cause') for remote or primary cause; but he is not always consistent.

Intellects are also multiple.

Of souls some are celestial, some vegetable, some animal, and some human. The human soul survives after this body and has certain circumstances in its Hereafter.

This science concerns itself with these ideas.

Part One of the *On the Heavens*, that is, of Book III, Section II, Chapter 2 of *The Book of the Exposition*:[1]

That the first body which delimits the dimensions is the heaven; that all other bodies subsequent to it are in motion from it and to it; on the characteristics of the first body; and that a celestial body cannot be a cause for the existence of another body beneath it.

It has already been stated that body in general cannot be a cause for body. This part is now devoted specifically to the celestial body to the exclusion of any other. It has been shown that natural motions are three: that which is in motion away from the centre, that which is in motion toward the centre, and that which is in motion about the centre. That which is in motion from the centre is not (specifically) that whose motion is from the centre itself, nor is that which is in motion toward the centre (specifically) that whose motion must absolutely terminate at the centre itself. Nor is that which is in motion about the centre (specifically) that whose centre is a precise central point for it, for even if the latter is not a precise central point for it but lies inside (its orbit) it will be in motion about it, since it is in motion around it in a certain fashion.[2]

That which is naturally in motion toward the centre is what is called 'heavy', and the heavy in an absolute sense is that which sinks beneath all (other) bodies. That which is in motion away from the centre is what is called 'light', and the light in an absolute sense is what floats above all (other) natural bodies. The heavy in a relative sense is that which is in motion along most of the distance extending between the two limits of rectilinear motion, (moving) toward the centre but not reaching it; it may, however, occur that it moves away from the centre, an example being water which moves from the location of fire toward the centre without reaching the very centre itself, since when it reaches the location of earth it naturally moves away from it to float on top of it. This applies correspondingly to the light in a relative sense.[3]

This being the case, then whatever behaves such that when it is not in its natural location it moves in one of the two directions, due to a natural inclination in it,

1. pp. 634–640.

2. From 'It has been shown', this paragraph is an abridgement of Ibn Sīnā, *al-Shifā'*, *Ṭabī'iyyāt*, ed. M. Qassem (Cairo, n. d.), 2, 2, p. 6f.

3. This paragraph is an abridgement, omitting certain elaborations, of *al-Shifā'*, *Ṭabī'iyyāt*, 2, 2, p. 7f.

is either light or heavy. If the 'inclination' of a natural body is taken to mean 'in act', then when bodies are in their natural places they are neither heavy nor light in act.[1]

As for the body which is naturally in circular motion, it is neither light nor heavy—not in the sense of being deprived of the two extremes and thus occupying the middle (between them), but in the sense of being deprived (of both categories) absolutely.[2]

Now given that it is impossible for there to be rectilinear motion without the existence of direction, nor for there to be direction without something encompassing (it) by nature, nor for there to be something encompassing (it) by nature without the existence of that which is circular and in voluntary motion; and given further that naturally rectilinear (motion) exists, then circular (motion) also exists, and the bodies which have in their nature a circular inclination—whether they be many or one—are a genus differing naturally from bodies with natural rectilinear motion. They can, however, have a multiplicity of species.[3]

Now, it cannot elude your observation that natural upward motion is directed toward the heaven and natural downward motion is directed toward the earth. But were the earth occupying the position of that which encompasses (the universe), then you could direct your line of sight so as to produce chords cutting arcs of the earth which would pass by the heaven without striking it, just as you can (in fact) do with the heaven (and the earth, respectively); furthermore, the earth would have no principle of rectilinear motion, and it would not accept forcible motion. But since the conclusions are not true, the premise must be false; and since one of the two must necessarily occupy the position of that which encompasses, then it is the heaven which is the body occupying the position of that which encompasses (and) which moves with circular motion, and it is the simple body which is anterior to all (other) bodies, and it is not in its nature to move rectilinearly. The circular motion of fire, on the other hand, is accidental motion.[4]

Since the heaven is a finite simple body, then, its natural shape must necessarily be spherical, and this natural shape of it must exist; for if, on the contrary, there existed some unnatural shape for it, the existence for it of this unnatural shape would mean that its body accepted the cessation of its natural shape, through extension and rectilinear moving, in short, by force. But whatever can be moved by force can move rectilinearly; and were this the case, then rectilinear motion would be in the

---

1. This paragraph is an abridgement, omitting certain elaborations, of *al-Shifā'*, *Ṭabī'iyyāt*, 2, 2, p. 7f.

2. This is a rephrasing of *al-Shifā'*, *Ṭabī'iyyāt*, 2, 2, p. 9. Bahmanyār omits Ibn Sīnā's following discussion establishing the correspondence between simple bodies and simple (rectilinear or circular) motions.

3. This reproduces, with variants, *al-Shifā'*, *Ṭabī'iyyāt*, 2, 2, p. 12. Bahmanyār omits the following discussion and refutation of a number of objections.

4. This recasts *al-Shifā'*, *Ṭabī'iyyāt*, 2, 3, p. 16; the following argument about fire is omitted.

nature of the celestial sphere. Therefore, the existing shape of the celestial sphere must be circular, encompassed by circular surfaces.

Furthermore, the body which moves by nature away from it and toward it must move with an equivalent inclination, while being itself simple and requiring a circular shape and delimiting a circular place; and thus this body must also be circular. In short, these bodies are spheres, one nested inside the other, or behave as spheres, constituting altogether a single sphere. How could it be otherwise, when both (their) inclination to the encompassing and their flight from it toward the centre are equivalent and an equivalent centering necessitates a circular shape, as does an equivalent circular congruity? In short, the simple natural bodies must have simple shapes, that is, circular ones.[1]

Now you have learned that the body which delimits the dimensions and which has no principle of rectilinear motion by nature is not such that it can be breached. You have also learned that the body in which there is no principle of rectilinear motion is not generated, that what is not generated is not corrupted, and that the body which has no contrary is not subject to generation. But since there is no contrary to circular motion, then the nature from which this motion emerges also has no contrary, and it is thus not subject to generation. Rather, it moves by way of arousing desire, as the beloved moves the lover. The matter of the celestial spherical form, then, must be set aside for (*mawqūfa ʿalā*) this form, and this celestial matter cannot be shared between this form and any other form. It does not have the power to accept another form, for otherwise it would be possible for there to exist in it another form for it, and that form could not exist along with the form of the celestial sphere, and thus the reason for the matter's accepting the form of the celestial sphere could cease to operate, with the result that this body would accept generation and corruption. But this consequence is absurd, since were it to accept generation and corruption it would also accept rectilinear motion; and any body which accepts rectilinear motion cannot delimit the dimensions or produce and preserve eternal[2] motion.

It being clear that it does not accept generation and corruption, neither does it accept growth; for that which accepts growth also naturally accepts generation. From this it is clear that it does not accept transformations leading to change in its nature, as water for instance, accepts heat which leads to its loss of watery form.[3]

Nor can a celestial body be a cause of another celestial body (for several reasons). First, because it is a compound of matter and form, and you have learned that every body has a reason which is not a body. Second, because the form of a

1. These two paragraphs précis *al-Shifāʾ*, *Ṭabīʿiyyāt*, 2, 3, pp. 19–21, omitting a discussion of the shape of the sublunary world and a refutation (on the basis of the impossibility of a vacuum) of the possibility of ovoid or lenticular celestial bodies, as well as a subsequent discussion of the four sublunary elements.

2. *Sarmadiyyah*; some MSS read *mustadīrah*, 'circular'.

3. These two paragraphs are a very succinct summary of *al-Shifāʾ*, *Ṭabīʿiyyāt*, 2, 4, pp. 26–34.

body, as you have learned, acts by positioning (*waḍʿ*)[1] and with the intermediation of matter; but then it would be necessary that the matter be in reality a cause for the existence of the other body, which is absurd. Furthermore, what comes forth from a body does so (only) after the body has been individuated, since a general (unindividuated) body cannot exist; but the individuation of a body is, as you have learned, by means of positioning, and in that case the positioning would share in the body's producing another body; but if a celestial body were positioned (*mawḍūʿ*) by another body, then it would be preceded (temporally) by (another) body, whereas the celestial bodies are (in fact) the first bodies, and ungenerated, as you have learned. And furthermore, if a celestial body were a cause for another celestial body, given that—as we have shown—every body acts by its positioning and after having achieved perfection as an individual existent, then the first body would necessarily be individuated in something (spatially) delimited (*maḥwī*) which (could only be) the vacuum, which is absurd. And furthermore, it would thus be a reason for the extinction of that vacuum by the bringing into existence of the body which filled it; but the existence of a vacuum is absurd in itself, and the absurd has no cause. But this absurdity will not be necessitated so long as we posit the existence of two bodies simultaneously, due to some other reason, for in that case the two bodies will exist simultaneously in nature or time, and their possibility will be simultaneous, and thus there will be no priority to the delimiter (*ḥāwī*) in either its possibility or its existence over the delimited. (The latter would require) that the possibility of the delimited be posterior to (that of) the delimiter; but the existence of the delimited after the existence of the delimiter would be possible only due to (some) cause, whereas possibility does not have a cause. Thus this delimiter will not be a cause of the possibility of the delimited, (in which case) it would be necessary for this prior delimiter to be individualized in a vacuum. Rather, it is necessary that its individuation be in something delimited which is a body, (in which case) both of them have an external reason—as is the case with matter and form.

Part Two of the *On the Heavens,* that is, of Book III, Section II, Chapter 2 of *The Book of the Exposition:*[2]

Establishment of active intellects, and indication of their number; establishment of celestial souls and the final cause (ghāyah) *toward which the spheres progress in*

1. According to a previous discussion (505f.), 'positioning' or 'position' (*waḍʿ*, Gk. *keisthai*) is the only one of the nine categories that 'is individuated in itself so as to preclude participation' (by more than one individual), and is thus identified as the 'individuator' (*mushakhkhiṣ*).

2. pp. 641–646 and 647–663. The redactor of the MS used by the editor as his basis for this section notes here that he found two different versions of this part, and decided to include them both sequentially, labelling them Parts Two and Three; the editor's other MSS reflect variants on this procedure. The different versions are here combined, following the text of the editor's 'Part Three', with parallels and variants from 'Part Two' indicated in the notes. The correct order of

their motions; establishment of the elemental bodies; and that the corporeal world is one.[1]

You have learned that from the First Existent there can come into existence, first of all, only something essentially unitary. We do, however, see multiple bodies, souls, and accidents. Let us consider, then, how it is possible for this multiplicity to exist. We say: This thing which is essentially unitary will be either matter, accident, corporeal form, or intelligible form. Clearly, however, matter and accidents cannot be a reason for anything subsequent to them. But this is equally impossible for corporeal form, whether it be a nature or a soul, the proof being as follows: What comes forth from these forms does so only after their coming into existence; their existence subsists in matter; thus the coming forth of what comes forth from them must be with the participation of matter, and matter will then be a reason for the existence of what is subsequent to matter; but that is absurd, since the existence of matter is in itself potential and it can only receive, and thus cannot be a cause for the existence of anything. You have already learned that a sphere cannot be the cause for the existence of another sphere below it, as was shown by another, specific argument.[2] Furthermore, if one were to deem possible the coming forth of an act from a form of this sort without matter, then the existence of the form would not be material. Necessarily, then, this thing which is essentially unitary will be an intelligible form.

This intellect cannot fail to have three characteristics (*ṣifāt*), which are either its constituents (*muqawwimāt*) or its necessary consequents (*lawāzim*): it is essentially a possible quiddity; it has existence emanated on it from the First; and it must certainly intellect the First, since its being caused[3] is one of its essential accidents. Other than this tripleness, it possesses no multiplicity at all. Therefore, the existence of multiplicity will be dependent on this aforementioned tripleness: two of the three will be a cause for the existence of the matter of the first body and that of its form or soul, and one of them will be a reason for the existence of another intellect, since it is not possible for there to come forth from that one more than one. Thus, (at this stage,) there cannot exist another body (other than the first). But bodies are many. So the rule for the second intellect, in being a reason for the existence of the second globe (*kurah*), will be just like that of the first intellect—and so on, until the number of the celestial globes is completed. The number of intellects will thus equal the number of celestial globes.[4]

---

individual paragraphs is not always clear, and there is a strong possibility that some sections of Bahmanyār's original chapter have been lost entirely.

1. So the editor's 'Part Three' (p. 641). The heading for 'Part Two' (p. 633) reads: On the final cause (*ghāyah*) and on celestial motion; establishment of active intellects and celestial souls; establishment of the elemental bodies; and that the corporeal world is one.

2. See the last paragraph of Part One above.

3. *Ma'lūl*. Variants: 'intelligized' (*ma'qūl*) and 'known' (*ma'lūm*).

4. For parallels, see *al-Shifā', Ilāhiyyāt*, ed. S. Dunyā et al. (Cairo, 1960), 406f.

The world of nature must necessarily have an intellect; otherwise it could not exist, since the existence of simple bodies, as you have learned, can only be through the intermediation of intellects. Were it not that matter is shared by the four elements and the mixtures made up of them, it would be necessary to assign to every species (of matter) an intellect, these intellects being a reason for bodies just as motion is a reason for temporal coming to be. And if you consider the matter carefully, you will see that these globes (?)[1] are final causes for the celestial motions, in the sense that they move by way of arousing desire.

Having established the celestial souls, let us now discuss their circumstances. We say: Celestial motions are by will, the reason being as follows: You have learned that motions are either natural, compelled, accidental, or voluntary. You have also learned that natural motions occur to a body only when it has gone outside its natural precinct or its natural condition—such as water when heated or water when shot upwards; but when a body attains its natural place it does not move, for otherwise (this place) would not be natural for it. But if circular motion were natural, then it would be possible for that body to come to rest; and if one posits such a state of rest for that body then one must put an end to time, motion, and temporal coming to be. But putting an end to time can only be accomplished by establishing a 'before' and 'after'; these, however, belong to time; putting an end to time, then, could only be done by (paradoxically) establishing it. It is clearly impossible, then, for this motion to lead to a state of rest. But any motion which does not lead to a state of rest is not natural. Thus, this motion is not natural.

Another proof: A spherical body (in rotation) moves from a place to precisely the same place, and from a point to precisely the same point. Nature cannot require that (something) seek something and yet flee from the same thing. This is rather the province of volition (*ikhtiyār*) alone, since nature is a single thing and what it requires is also one. Thus, this motion is not natural. And *a fortiori* it cannot be compelled or accidental. By elimination it will be voluntary.[2]

Every voluntary (*ikhtiyāriyyah*) motion has a willing mover; every willing mover must necessarily be preceded by a conception (*taṣawwur*). Every conception will be either universal or particular; but from the universal there will not come forth a particular motion, and in general there will not come forth from a universal conception a particular act; but celestial motions are particular, and they therefore come forth from successive particular conceptions.[3]

1. *Kurāt*: one would expect *'uqūl*, 'intellects'.

2. This first section of 'Part Three' has no parallel in 'Part Two'. For parallels in Ibn Sīnā, see *al-Shifā'*, *Ilāhiyyāt*, 382.

3. This paragraph is paralleled in Part Two as follows: Is has become clear that celestial motion is by will (*irādiyyah*); every motion by will has a willing (*murīd*) mover; every willing mover's moving is preceded by desire; and every desire is preceded by a conception; thus circular motion is preceded by a conception. Every conception will be either universal or particular; from the universal there will not come forth a particular motion; celestial motions are particular; every

It is further known that the separated intelligibles cannot seek motions, since the separated intelligible is something actual in every way, while the seeker of motion is thereby necessarily seeking something which it does not have and therefore must have some aspect (*maʿnā*) which is potential, and will according be, necessarily, corporeal.

Another proof: If one should posit as the cause of this motion something intelligible, motion would be impossible, since the intelligible is fixed and the fixed will not be a cause for change in that which changes. But if one posits the fixed as a cause for motion, then necessarily none of the parts of the motion could cease to exist, and this would be rest, not motion.[1] In the same way,[2] a nature cannot be a cause for motion, nature being something fixed; a motion can come forth from nature only if nature has successive states, such as proximity and remoteness from the natural place, so that each case of proximity or remoteness would differ from the others.

Returning to our main argument, we say: Every successive particular conception must certainly come to be, and this coming to be will have a cause. This cause must be either the soul in which this conception comes into being—which is absurd, since that which has something potentially, as with conception here, cannot be what brings itself into actuality with regard to that thing (this being the basis for our learning that every body in motion has a mover)—or its cause will be one of the celestial bodies, or a soul (of one of them). But these bodies are finite, and the rule for both these souls and bodies is the same. And as for the elemental bodies, they are posterior to motion.

Therefore, the provider of these successive conceptions is the same as the provider of these souls; for although these conceptions are among the necessary consequents of these souls, their provider is the provider of (the souls) of which they are necessary consequents, since the reason for the necessary consequent is identical to the reason for that to which it is a necessary consequent, albeit through the intermediation of the latter. Thus the provider of these conceptions will be either the First or those intellects.[3]

---

particular comes to be; therefore (celestial motions) come forth from successive particular conceptions, and every successive particular conception comes to be.

1. See Ibn Sīnā, *al-Najāh* (Cairo, 1912), pp. 109, 258.

2. Reading, with one MS, *ka-dhālika* for *li-dhālika*, 'thus'.

3. In Part Two, the preceding discussions appear as follows: But for every particular conception that comes to be, that which conceptualizes with regard to it emerges from potential to act. Everything in which something emerges from potential to act has a reason that brings it out from potential to act; every reason that brings something out from potential to act is an incorporeal separable entity. (All) this you (already) know.

The point to be made specifically here is that (this entity), were it a body, would be either celestial or elemental. But elemental bodies exist posterior to motion, and celestial bodies do not in themselves in any way bring out from potential to act with regard to anything. Therefore the celestial circular motion has a separable principle, a corporeal power that conceptualizes the particulars, a desiring power, and a moving power.

Now you know that this motion is perpetual, while the act of powers of the corporeal is finite. Necessarily, then, there must be there some fixed conception from which the successive conceptions branch off—an analogous situation being that if you resolve to travel to a given land that resolution is fixed while successive resolutions and choices branch off from it. Therefore, the provider of these conceptions is itself a cause of their fixedness, continuity, and persistence; and the relation of each conception to its predecessor will be like that of conclusions to premises. Every prior conception will function as a premise to a subsequent conception, which will be a conclusion for it.

The final cause of these motions must necessarily be a perfection. But it is absurd that what is sought by these spheres in their motions be the lower world, since if the lower world provided them with perfection they would (in effect) be providing themselves with perfection. Rather, their quest must be that their perfections be preserved, and from this quest ensue these conceptions, from which ensue spatial motions, that is, changes in their locations—just as natural bodies seek through motions to preserve their perfections, and from this seeking ensues rest in their places and their natural states. From these celestial motions, then, ensues the order of the lower world—not that this is intentionally sought, but rather, just as sexual intercourse is followed by procreation, although what is sought in sexual intercourse is erotic pleasure, so their conceptions and motions are necessarily entailed by the final cause (*min ḍarūrat al-ghāyah*) according to the first aspect (*ʿala'l-wajh al-awwal*) of the two aspects of necessary entailment, while the order of the world is necessarily entailed according to the second aspect.

And you must know that their souls are their natures, unlike the case with our souls, which come upon bodies whose natures are different from them.[1]

---

1. Only loosely parallel to the above paragraphs in the discussion in Part Two:

Now all that emerges from potential to act with regard to something strives for perfection by means of it; all that strives for perfection by means of something is seeking perfection in it; every perfection is pleasurable and in it is rest; therefore the spheres seek by means of motion only to attain to their perfection. But it is impossible that their perfection lie in what comes forth from them of the order of the lower world; otherwise, the effect would be perfecting the cause and the cause would thus be a reason for its own perfection.

It is clear, then, from all this, that what is sought is their attaining their perfection; from this quest ensue conceptions, from which ensue pleasure and rest, from which ensue motions and changes in location, from which ensues in turn the order of the lower world. By 'the lower world' I do not mean the four elements, but something else; for conceptions, motions, and changes in location are necessarily entailed by the final cause (*min ḍarūrat al-ghāyah*) according to the first aspect (*ʿal'l- wajh al-awwal*) (of necessary entailment) that we have mentioned, while the order of the world is necessarily entailed by the final cause according to the second aspect we have mentioned. If what were sought by motion were the ensuing order of the lower world, the spheres would be perfecting themselves and bringing out themselves in (their) perfections from potential to act. It is this way with everything in motion: it seeks a perfection, from which ensues motion and other things.

Now these conceptions may be a cause for what exists in the lower world without the

Now let us establish the elemental bodies. We say: You have learned that no spatial motion can exist except with a fixed body. This fixed body cannot be beyond the celestial sphere, since every body has in it a principle of motion, either rectilinear or circular; with the circular there is no spatial (motion), while the rectilinear will be within the body which delimits the dimensions; thus it is necessary that this body be contained within the celestial sphere. But this body, albeit at rest, has in it a principle of motion, in the sense that were it to separate from its natural place it would move to it in rectilinear fashion; and this body must be at rest in its place naturally, for if it were compelled to be in it spatial motion could not exist for it. Furthermore, this encompassed (*ḥāshī*) body cannot be in a single state; for the state of that part of it which adjoins the celestial sphere must differ, due to the motion[1] of the celestial sphere, from that of the part which is remote from it.[2]

Human beings have no way of establishing the number of these simple bodies encompassed by the celestial sphere on the basis of the celestial motions. Rather, the way to determine their number and the number of their compounds and the mixtures which come to be from them is by means of observation, just as the number of the celestial bodies is itself known by observation.

We will speak further about how they[3] are subject to generation and corruption. Since generation and corruption are matters which come to be, their causes will necessarily also come to be, and thus these causes will necessarily be motion, so that coming to be may be possible, as you have learned. Therefore, their coming to be is dependent on the circular motion (of the spheres); as for the existence of their forms, that is due to the form-providing reason that we have established previously.

Let us now offer some further elucidation of this. We say: These bodies accept generation and corruption, so there must be matter shared among them.[4] For if they did not have shared matter, coming to be could not occur, since every coming to be is preceded by matter, and if coming to be were in need of a preceding matter

---

intermediation of motion, or they may be a cause for that with the intermediation of motion but nevertheless naturally, since what its nature requires is no different from what its soul requires, its nature being identical to its soul.

1. Reading, with one MS, *li-ḥarakat* for text *ka-ḥarakat*.

2. This paragraph appears in Part Two with only minor variations in wording, but is followed immediately by the following stray pericope, whose proper location is unclear: ... and their intellects must necessarily be intellects in act, not material intellects; so each of them will have an object of intellection and an object of imagination which are fixed, and which are followed, by way of consequence, by the objects of intellection and imagination which are the reason for partial motion; and thus the soul will be prepared for every object of intellection which is followed by an object of imagination, just as with us it is prepared by means of premises for conclusions and by means of conclusions for further conclusions.

3. *Wa-sanatakallam annahā*; other MSS read *wa-sataʿlam annahā*, 'and you will learn that they', *wa-sanukallim*, 'and we will address (you)', and *wa-sayuʿlam annahā*, 'and it will be learned that they'.

4. The previous two paragraphs and this sentence appear more or less identically in Part Two. From this point the MSS diverge, and the order of subsections becomes uncertain.

which itself came to be, that matter would also be in need of a preceding matter, and so on *ad infinitum*, which is absurd.[1]

The cause of the matter must therefore be a single cause. But the cause providing the various forms cannot be due to the matter itself,[2] since matter[3] is prepared to accept all the forms. There must then be reasons which tip the scales (in favour of a given form), and those reasons will undoubtedly be such as come to be; so their causes must be something changeable, but while changeable also constant; and this is characteristic of circular motion. Matter exists, then, by way of forms, not by itself; otherwise, when one of these forms ceased to exist it would necessarily follow that the matter also ceased to exist, since matter cannot perdure without form. The form must therefore have a partner in maintaining the matter, so that one matter is handed on as the forms pass in succession over it. This partner is the separated (intellect), which provides the forms by way of the will of one willing, since we have already shown that a body cannot be a cause of existence.

As for how motion prepares matter (to receive a form), an example would be its bringing fire near water so that the latter would lose the cold opposed to the fiery form and the matter thus be prepared, with the loss of the obstacle, for the fiery form; the fiery form would then come to be in it, provided by the Giver of Forms … .[4]

… Rather,[5] matter is prepared to accept one form rather than another, in a complete way, due to a preparer; and that preparer must be opposed to the preceding form. But even if we posit the forms as mutually opposed, while their existence occurs instantaneously, they must have qualities that ensue from them and which accept greater and lesser degrees of intensity. Thus the matter's being prepared to receive that (new) form must be gradual, so that the quality which removes the (old) form[6] may exist; and the fact that the preparedness is gradual with regard to the (coming into) existence of the form is one of the subcategories (*aqsām*) of what is necessarily entailed by the final cause. And if the forms are not essentially opposed, but only opposed by reason of their qualities, then *a fortiori* will the preparedness of the matter be gradual.[7] An example of this in actuality would be the heat which belongs to air: the matter of water cannot be prepared for the existence of this heat in it unless its preparedness to accept (the form of) water should cease; necessarily,

1. This sentence appears in this form at p. 653 n. 8; variants, lacking the last two phrases, appear on p. 644f., and p. 654.

2. Or: the matter considered apart from the forms (*li-mujarrad al-māddah*).

3. Inserting *fa-inna'l-māddah* with one MS.

4. These two paragraphs appear at both p. 653f. and p. 644 n. 6.

5. This paragraph (p. 654f. 645f.) seems to be an alternative continuation after the sentence (two paragraphs above) beginning 'For if they did not have shared matter …'

6. *Hattā yaṣiḥḥa wujūd al-kayfiyyāt al-rafiʿah li'l-ṣūrah*; for *al-rafiʿah* one MS reads *al-muwāfiqah* ('so that the quality compatible with the (new) form may exist').

7. Reading, for *kaistiʿdād al-māddah shay'an baʿd shay' yūjab*, *fa-istiʿdād al-māddah shay'an baʿd shay' awjab*.

then, if this heat arrives the form of water ceases and the form of air comes to be in the matter.

Now since you have learned that the body which delimits the dimensions cannot be essentially multiple, since if the thing which is one were multiple in itself[1] there could exist no 'one' from it; and you have also learned that this body cannot be divided or accept any breaching so as to become multiple by way of cutting up (*qaṭ'*); and you have further learned that every body which is multiple must be preceded by a body in circular motion, so that its multiplicity may be due to that motion; then, all this being the case, there cannot exist a plurality of bodies which delimit the dimensions, and thus there can exist neither a plurality of centres nor a plurality of worlds.

(Furthermore,) we have already shown that outside the celestial sphere there is neither vacuum nor plenum; and it is clear that there is no matter which is not enformed with a form. Therefore, the form of the world (*ṣūrat al-ʿālimiyyah*) is characterized (*makhṣūṣah*) by a single matter from which are made up an aggregate of things confined within a single world, and thus the existence of a plurality of worlds is outside the realm of possibility.[2]

The unity of existence must be actual (*bi'l-fiʿl*), not hypothetical.[3] Thus it has unity of existence actually and multiplicity of existence of parts potentially. Everything posterior to the First must have a possibility that is one actually and multiple potentially, and an existence that is one actually and multiple potentially. This unity is a unity of order or something of that sort.[4]

Part Three[5] of the *On the Heavens*, that is, of Book III, Section II, Chapter 2 of *The Book of the Exposition*:[6]

How evil enters into divine determination (*qaḍā'*), and indication of the order (*niẓām*) of the world.

You have learned from our discussion of the essentially necessary Existent that this order is the true order, there being none superior to it or more perfect than it. You have also learned that the active intellects are necessary consequents to

1. Text *li-annahū huwa*; read *bi-annahū huwa*?
2. These two paragraphs appear in virtually identical form in Part Two.
3. Reading *bi'l-farḍ*, as in Part Two (p. 645), rather than *bi'l-ʿaraḍ* ('by accident') with Part Three (p. 655).
4. This paragraph appears in the same form in Part Two; but a variant version in one MS (p. 645 n. 2) reads: The unity of existence must be actual, not hypothetical. Indeed, everything posterior to the First is one with a unity of order, or such, actually and not hypothetically, and multiple potentially, not actually. Thus everything posterior to the First is characterized by a unity of existence and a multiplicity of existents which are, relative to the All, potential, while the All has one possibility actually as well as multiple possibilities actually.
5. Text: Part Four.
6. Pp. 657–663.

(*lāzama ʿan*) and an inevitable product of (*min muqtaḍā*) the Absolute Good; that the spheres come forth from It as well, imitating It in their motions by accepting that model;[1] and that the order of these things which come to be below the spheres is dependent on the motions of the spheres, which are the most superior motions, so that this order existing in the world of nature must also be in the most perfect and most superior state possible, there being no order more perfect than it; and that nothing occurs among the existents by chance, but rather all is either natural in itself—like the motion downward of a stone—or natural in relation to the All even if not natural in relation to itself—like the existence of fingers as an instrument for acquisition;[2] and that willing is something that comes to be, and everything that comes to be has infinite reasons—as you have learned—so that it will also be dependent on the motion which can have infinite existence—specifically, the continuous, perpetual motion which is the motion of the celestial sphere; and that motion comes forth from the First, so that our willing must also, in consequence, be dependent on the essentially necessary Existent, and It be its reason.

To the question 'Do we have power (*qudrah*) to act or not?' we reply: We do have power to act in relation to single (acts), but in relation to the whole we have no power except (to do) the foreordained (*muqaddar*).

As for the existence of different sorts of evil in this world, and how it enters into divine determination, I have this to say: It is known that possible quiddities have no reason for themselves and for their being possible; nor is there a reason for their needing a cause of their existence; nor is there a cause for the mutual exclusivity of existence between contraries; nor is there a cause for the perishability of every generated thing; nor is there a cause for the possible's falling short of the existence of the essentially necessary Existent and its inferiority to It in rank; nor is there a cause for fire's burning, nor for the receiving of burning by that which burns—since all of these belong to the constituents of quiddities and the nature of the basic elements, or to their necessary consequences.

There are other such (causeless) things, such as the fact that some of the final causes of some existents may be injurious or destructive to some other existents, as for example the final cause of the irascible power is injurious to the intellect while being good in relation to the concupiscent power. But you have already learned in what has preceded about the consequences necessarily entailed by final causes (*al-ḍarūrāt allatī talzam al-ghāyāt*).

Anything whose existence is in the greatest degree of perfection, and has nothing potential in it, can have no evil attached to it. For evil is a lack of existence, or a lack

1. Reading *bi-taqabbul dhālikaʾl-mithāl* for text *munqaliba bi-dhālika fa-taqbalu dhālikaʾl-mithāl*, with the variant (in two MSS) *sa-taqbalu dhālika biʾl-mithāl*. The correct reading remains uncertain.

2. *lil-iktisāb*; variant: *liʾl-insān*, 'for man'.

of perfection of existence, and all that (will obtain only) where there is something potential. But inferiority to the rank of the First varies in degree among the quiddities; (for instance,) the inferiority of the earth to Its rank is greater than that of the sun to Its rank. All this is due to the difference among quiddities in themselves. Were the inferiority to be equivalent among all quiddities, the quiddities would all be one. And just as the quiddities of genera vary in this respect, so too do the quiddities of the individuals under the genera.

Know that while there is great evil in the world of nature, it is not preponderant.[1] Furthermore, while the conceptions[2] of the necessary consequents of all final causes, and what ensues (from them) necessarily, are an evil in relation to some things, (that evil) nevertheless is not lacking in some good, (as) is known from their being necessary consequents[3] of the Absolute Good. The good is determined (*maqḍī*) in itself, the evil is determined by accident; but everything determined is foreordained.[4] By saying 'by accident' we mean that if we bring it into relation to what our own benefits depend upon then it is by accident; otherwise, deeming everything as good and deeming everything as foreordained amounts to the same thing, since it is all willed by the First. For you know that the final cause for all that exists from It is It Itself, so all things have (ultimately) a single relation to It.

Furthermore, it is not the case that if something is evil in relation to one thing it is evil in the order of the All; on the contrary, it may be good in relation to the order of the world. Therefore, there is no evil in relation to the All, and everything determined is foreordained. In short, every individual, and every genus, even if imperfect in relation to another individual or genus, is in itself perfect. And injustice, even if evil, is in relation to the irascible power good.

One cannot say that it would have been possible for the First Regulator (*mudabbir*) to bring into existence pure good innocent of evil.[5] For while this is necessary for absolute existence, it is not necessary for a given existence or another. For He has brought into existence both that for which it is possible to exist like that (i.e., as pure good) and that for which it is possible to exist (only) without being free of some evil. If there did not exist what is not free from some evil, evil would then be greater; for[6] the existence of this pattern (*namaṭ*) (of the world as it in fact is) does not lack good, and the evil which is in it corresponds only to the non-existence which is mixed therein, whereas if it were all nonexistent, there being no existence at all, that would be more truly evil. And if all things existed innocent of evil, and (thus) in a single state with a single character, then all the quiddities would be one.

---

1. See the parallel passage in *al-Shifā'*, *Ilāhiyyāt*, p. 422.
2. *Taṣawwurāt*. One MS reads *taṣawwar anna*, '(you should) conceive (of the fact) that'; perhaps to be emended to *taḍarrurāt*, 'harms'.
3. Reading, with one MS, *luzūmihā* for text *lawāzimihā*.
4. This sentence paraphrases *al-Najāh*, p. 289.
5. For a parallel passage, see *al-Shifā'*, *Ilāhiyyāt*, p. 418.
6. Reading *fa-inna*, with three MSS, for text *fa-idhan*.

But since the matter of natural bodies is prepared for one form after another, due to external reasons, their forms are by necessity opposed, so that by reason of them there may possibly come to be action and passion on the part of bodies and thus come to be a mixture from which ensue acts of generation, and with this mixture minerals may reach the stage where they merit becoming alive. But a necessary consequence of opposition is inevitably corruption (*fasād*).

You have learned that every matter has been given what it merits of form and perfection, and that some matters are more imperfect than others by reason of the preparers, which are infinite. Now if there exists some genus that is corruptive to man, despite its being perfect in itself, it will be considered evil only by someone who thinks that the creation of the world was for the sake of man. But you have learned that that is not the case.

Now since these bodies are subject to generation and corruption, and there was no avoiding their coming into mutual contact so that mixing could occur, a necessary consequence of that was that some should corrupt others. For example, when fire comes in contact with a person's garment it burns it; it would be absurd for fire to be fire and the garment a garment and for contact to occur without the garment being burned. And it would be absurd for the fire not to come in contact with the garment in accordance with those motions which have been established for you as being the most superior sorts of motions. Therefore, such evil as this must be a necessary consequence of the final cause. And those things that are (thus) necessarily entailed are, in relation to the All, willed, even if they are accidental. But you have learned that this order is noble, superior, and perfect. It was not possible for these entailments not to be part of this order, for were they not, this order would not be this order.

In summary, it would be absurd for something to be based on motion and then for what is required by all (the different) motions in it to be a single thing; rather, what is required by one motion must differ from what is required by another, so that if what is required by the first is in conformity (with something) what is required by the second is not. It follows that there must necessarily exist things identified as evil in this order, despite its being entirely goodness, wisdom, and order; and it would have been no part of wisdom for this creation, with the evil it entails, not to be created, for the reasons we have already stated.

But there is also another sort of evil: if man is to exist, his mutually opposed powers inevitably must exist as well, these powers being among man's essential accidents. Furthermore, it was not possible for these powers to be in mutual balance, no one of them predominating over another, since otherwise individuals would all be identical.

You have learned the reason for death, and that it is not the final cause for man's existence. That a man should be mortal has no cause, for the heat which leads to the corruption of man's substance is one of the essentials or necessary consequents of bodies, and such a thing has no cause; rather, it is the First which is a cause for his perduring for a time which is the most perfect amount of time for him to perdure, this being known from Providence. Every lifetime is natural in relation to the All, although not natural absolutely. In sum, all evils are so in comparison and relation to single individuals; but in relation to the All there is no evil.

Now prayers and thoughts that occur to a person are among the foreordained things, but without intellection of the one who prays there would be no intellection that he is praying. Thereupon, if the thing prayed for is something not prevented by the order of good—that is, the order of the world—(its) existence ensues. Now you have learned that everything conceived by the First whose existence is possible comes necessarily into existence; so the one who prays or has a fancy (*wahm*) will be one of the reasons for the First's conceptualization of his prayer or fancy, in a certain respect, and thus his prayer will be, in a certain respect, a reason for the existence of what he prays for. Just as, so long as there is no conceptualization of the form of Zayd, there will be no conceptualization of his being a secretary, so that Zayd's existence is one of the reasons for Zayd's being a secretary, so also Zayd will be one of the reasons for the First's conceptualization of his prayer, and his prayer will be one of the reasons for what he prays for.

So it is also with regulatory measures (*tadbīrāt*). For these will be efficacious only if they befit the order of the world; if they contradict that order they do not occur.

It is clear that these states are necessary in relation to the All, and good, and that everything other than the Creator must necessarily contain evil and imperfection. You know that it is not a matter of intention that the spheres follow this order; rather, the very coming forth of these things from the First *is* the order, and thus from it ensues everything in the most perfect possible order.

Part IV

Early Islamic Philosophy: The Independent Philosophers

Introduction

The focal point of Islamic philosophy is a tradition whose various manifestations are diverse intellectual and philosophical schools, not individual views. It is the centrality of the tradition that dominates the intellectual life of individual philosophers, as opposed to modern Western philosophy in which this equation is reversed. Despite the predominance of the traditional perspective in Islamic philosophy, however, there are a few figures who do not belong to any of the established schools and can be considered to be independent philosophers. This is not to say that they were beyond the pale of religion and its intellectual dimension, but that they should be regarded as philosophers in their own right who left an indelible mark on the Islamic intellectual tradition in Persia.

Among such figures, the most important are Muḥammad Zakariyyā' Rāzī, Abū Rayḥān Bīrūnī, and the celebrated philosopher-poet 'Umar Khayyām. Rāzī has made major contributions to the philosophy of science, and although much of his work has not survived, we know that he criticized Plato and Aristotle and that he was influenced by pre-Islamic Persian philosophical thought. This influence, to which Nāṣir-i Khusraw alludes, may have come from his mysterious teacher, Īrānshahrī. Rāzī, who advocated use of the empirical method in scientific experiments, also lived a 'philosophic life', as expounded in his work *On the Philosophic Life*.

Bīrūnī, who was also interested in the teachings of Rāzī, as well as pre-Islamic Persia, is a significant figure in the philosophy of science and comparative religion. While his scientific observations and debates with such figures as Ibn Sīnā are of utmost significance, Bīrūnī's keen interest in Indian philosophical thought and comparative religion makes him a unique figure in the annals of the Islamic sciences. He is in fact considered to be one of the founders of the discipline of comparative religion in the Islamic intellectual tradition.

Finally, there is 'Umar Khayyām, the most famous Persian poet in the West, whose philosophical and, to some extent scientific, thought has remained largely unknown. Khayyām was not only a poet but first and foremost a philosopher, scientist, and gnostic (*ʿārif*). Perhaps it was the rendition of his beautiful quatrains into English that overshadowed his philosophical writings, or it may have been the fact that Khayyām wrote so little that he was never considered a serious philosopher. However, it should be noted that what he did write is significant and is an indication of his philosophical perspective—an insight which is imperative for a better understanding of his quatrains. Without this philosophy Khayyām could be interpreted erroneously as an agnostic hedonist, a view that in fact is held by many today.

In Part 4 of this volume the intellectual thoughts of these three scientist-philosophers are presented. The selections clearly show how philosophical thought, even outside of well-established schools of philosophy, is still generally within the contours of the Persian intellectual tradition.

S. H. Nasr

15

Abū Bakr Muḥammad Zakariyyā' Rāzī

Rāzī, known in the West as Rhazes, was born in Rayy, a city near today's Tehran in 240/854 and he died in 320/932. He was an undisputed master of medicine and alchemy, and was one of the first people to attribute medical problems to chemical, spiritual, and psychological imbalances in the patient, as well as biological causes. Most of his traditional biographers have emphasized his major contributions to various branches of science, in particular medicine and alchemy.

Rāzī studied philosophy with Abū Zayd Balkhī and medicine with 'Alī ibn Rabban Ṭabarī. Much has been said about his philosophical views by later commentators, and he was, in general, severely criticized by many for having left the bounds of religious orthodoxy. For example, Qāḍī Sa'īd al-Andalusī, in his *Ṭabaqāt al-umam*, accuses Rāzī of being shallow and not having understood the goal of *kalām*. Even Maimonides, in his *Guide for the Perplexed*, indicates that Rāzī had a book entitled *Ilāhiyyāt* in which he had 'demonstrated his ignorance'. Among the other eminent figures who attacked Rāzī are the Ismaili philosopher Abū Ḥātam Rāzī, who wrote two books to refute Rāzī's views on theodicy, prophecy, and miracles; and Nāṣir-i Khusraw. Shahrastānī, however, indicates that such accusations should be doubted since they were made by Ismailis, who had been severely attacked by Muḥammad ibn Zakariyyā' Rāzī.

It appears that Rāzī wrote about 220 works ranging from comprehensive volumes on medicine to short treatises on science and philosophy. Among his major works on philosophy, most have been lost and only fragments of them survive. It is therefore difficult to elaborate upon Rāzī's philosophical views with precision. We do know that he was an independent philosopher who did not belong to any of the major philosophical schools, such as the *mashshā'ī* or Ismaili. What is known of the content of his thought can be summarized as follows:

1. Rāzī considered alchemy to be an integral part of philosophy and held the view that a true philosopher is he who also knows alchemy. Furthermore, he

maintained that such philosophers as Plato, Aristotle, and Galen had known and practised alchemy. This view reflects the wedding of philosophy and alchemy in Hermeticism and in later schools of alchemy. Rāzī was, however, the first person to take a step in transforming alchemy into chemistry by denying the symbolic significance of alchemical substances and elements.

2. Rāzī had a well-developed theory of motion contrary to Aristotle's, who maintained that motion requires a mover. Rāzī had argued that a being with physical existence inherently and intrinsically possesses motion, but this movement is not necessarily observable. Another interpretation of this idea, which resembles Leibnitz's view of motion, was later propagated by Mullā Ṣadrā, a view known as trans-substantial motion.
3. Rāzī is said to have believed in five eternal principles: God, Universal Soul, absolute matter, absolute space, and absolute time. He believed that existing objects are reducible to individual particles, which themselves are indivisible. He believed in a form of atomism that once again resembles Leibniz's theory of monads.
4. Perhaps the most controversial idea of Rāzī was his view on theodicy. He maintained that the presence of evil in the world exceeds that of the good and therefore this world is not the best of all possible worlds. Whether Rāzī actually propagated such an idea is, however, subject to debate, since our knowledge of this aspect of his thought is based on fragments of sayings and the titles of his works.
5. Rāzī believed that the power of intellect/reason (*ʿaql*) is sufficient to reach the truth and the person who possesses this power—that is, the philosopher—has no need of revelation but can reach the knowledge of God by himself. It was this denial of the necessity of prophecy that was severely criticized by Ismaili philosophers such as Abū Ḥātam Rāzī.
6. Finally, Rāzī considered worldly desires as obstacles that can curtail the power of reasoning and the possibility of intellection, and therefore he believed that the true philosopher must overcome such desires as part of living a philosophic life. Rāzī regarded intellection and reasoning in the Greek sense with high esteem as a divine gift. His frequent references to the Greek philosophers are testament to his reverence for figures whom he regarded as 'masters of the proper use of reasoning'; and yet Rāzī did not consider himself to be subservient to them, but thought of himself as the equal of Plato and Aristotle.

Rāzī seems to have exercised little philosophical influence during later centuries, although he did pose certain questions that incited great theological and philosophical debates, as seen in the rebuttals of Abū Ḥātam Rāzī. Rāzī's greatest influence was in the field of the sciences, as attested by Bīrūnī's exceptional interest in his works. During later centuries of Persian history, Rāzī continued to be revered particularly as a physician and alchemist, who in reality had converted alchemy to chemistry as a result of his rejection of *ta'wīl* understood in the sense of reaching the symbolic and inner meaning of external realities.

In this chapter there is provided the complete text of two famous works of Rāzī, *al-Ṭibb al-rūḥānī* (The Spiritual Physick) and *al-Sīrat al-falsafiyyah* (The Philosophic Life). In the first work Rāzī discusses the place of reason and praises it as a divine gift. He also considers how passion can be restricted through the proper use of reason. Rāzī describes the goal of this book as the 'reformation of the soul's character'. In his *Philosophic Life*, Rāzī turns to the Greeks and in particular to Socrates as a model for living a philosophic life.

M. Aminrazavi

OF THE EXCELLENCE AND PRAISE OF REASON
From *al-Ṭibb al-rūḥānī* (The Spiritual Physick)

Reprinted from A. J. Arberry, tr,. *The Spiritual Physick of Rhazes*, (London, 1950), pp. 21–103.

The Creator (Exalted be His Name) gave and bestowed upon us Reason to the end that we might thereby attain and achieve every advantage, that lies within the nature of such as us to attain and achieve, in this world and the next. It is God's greatest blessing to us, and there is nothing that surpasses it in procuring our advantage and profit. By Reason we are preferred above the irrational beasts, so that we rule over them and manage them, subjecting and controlling them in ways profitable alike to us and them. By Reason we reach all that raises us up, and sweetens and beautifies our life, and through it we obtain our purpose and desire. For by Reason we have comprehended the manufacture and use of ships, so that we have reached unto distant lands divided from us by the seas; by it we have achieved medicine with its many uses to the body, and all the other arts that yield us profit. By Reason we have comprehended matters obscure and remote, things that were secret and hidden from us; by it we have learned the shape of the earth and the sky, the dimension of the sun, moon and other stars, their distances and motions; by it we have achieved even the knowledge of the Almighty, our Creator, the most majestic of all that we have sought to reach and our most profitable attainment. In short, Reason is the thing without which our state would be the state of wild beasts, of children and lunatics; it is the thing whereby we picture our intellectual acts before they become manifest to the senses, so that we see them exactly as though we had sensed them, then we represent these pictures in our sensual acts so that they correspond exactly with what we have represented and imagined.

Since this is its words and place, its value and significance, it behooves us not to bring it down from its high rank or in any way to degrade it, neither to make it the governed seeing that it is the governor, or the controlled seeing that it is the controller, or the subject seeing that it is the sovereign; rather must we consult it in all matters, respecting it and relying upon it always, conducting our affairs as it dictates and bringing them to a stop when it so commands. We must not give Passion the mastery over it, for Passion is the blemish of Reason, clouding it and diverting it from its proper path and right purpose, preventing the reasonable man from finding the true guidance and the ultimate salvation of all his affairs. Nay, but we must discipline and subject our Passion, driving and compelling it to obey the every dictate of Reason. If we do thus, our Reason will become absolutely clear and will illuminate us with all its light, bringing us to the achievement of all that we desire to attain; and we shall be happy in God's free gift and grace of it.

Of Suppressing and Restraining the Passion, with a Summary of the Views of Plato the Philosopher

Now following on this we will proceed to speak about Spiritual Physick, the goal of which is the reformation of the soul's character; and we propose to be extremely concise, going straight forward to deal with those points, principles and ideas which are the foundations of this entire object. We state that our intention in prefixing our views on Reason and Passion was because we considered this to be as it were the starting-point of our whole purpose; we shall now follow it up with a discussion of the most important and loftiest fundamentals of this matter.

The loftiest and most important of these fundamentals, and the most helpful in reaching our object in the present book, is the suppression of passion, the opposing of natural inclinations in most circumstances, and the gradual training of the soul to that end. For, this is the first point of superiority of man over the beasts—I mean the faculty of will, and the release of action after deliberation. This is because the beasts are undisciplined, and do whatever their natural inclinations dictate, acting without restraint or deliberation. You will not find that any undisciplined animal will refrain from defecating, or from seizing upon its food whenever it is there at hand and it feels the need of it, in the way you find a man leaving that on one side and compelling his inclinations to obedience at the dictate of various intellectual ideas; on the contrary, the beasts act exactly as their instincts urge, without restraint or conscious choice.

This degree of superiority over the beasts, in the way of reining the natural impulses, belongs pretty well to the majority of men, even if it be as a result of training and education. It is general and universal, and may readily be observed on all hands, and in fact every child is accustomed to it and is brought up accordingly; the point requires no labouring. At the same time there is a great difference and a wide range of variety between the different peoples in this respect. However, to reach the highest summit of this virtue attainable by human nature is scarcely open to any but the supreme philosopher; such a man must be accounted as superior to the common run of humanity, as mankind as a whole excels the beasts in reining the natural instincts and controlling the passion. From this we realize that whosoever desires to adorn himself with this ornament, and to perfect this virtue in his soul, is upon a hard and difficult quest; he needs to acclimatize himself to controlling and opposing and wrestling with his passion. And because there is a great difference and a wide range of variety between men as regards their temperaments, the acquisition of certain virtues rather than others and the getting rid of certain vices rather than others will prove a harder or an easier task for some men rather than the rest.

Now I will begin by mentioning how this virtue may be acquired—I mean the suppression and opposing of the passion—seeing that it is the loftiest and most important of these virtues and its position relative to this entire purpose is similar to that of the element which immediately succeeds the origin.

Passion and instinct are always inciting and urging and pressing us to follow after present pleasures and to choose them without reflection or deliberation upon the possible consequence, even though this may involve pain hereafter and prevent us from attaining a pleasure many times greater than that immediately experienced. This is because they, our passion and instinct, see nothing else but the actual state in which they happen to be, and only seek to get rid of the pain that hurts them at that very moment. In this way a child suffering from ophthalmia will rub its eyes and eat dates and play in the sun. It therefore behooves the intelligent man to restrain and suppress his passion and instinct, and not to let them have their way except after careful and prudent consideration of what they may bring in their train; he will represent this to himself and weigh the matter accurately, and then he will follow the course of greater advantage. This he will do, lest he should suffer pain where he supposed he would experience pleasure, and lose where he thought he would gain. If in the course of such representation and balancing he should be seized by any doubt, he will not give his appetite free play, but will continue to restrain and suppress it; for he cannot be sure that in gratifying his appetite he will not involve himself in evil consequences very many times more painful and distressing than the labour of resolutely suppressing it. Prudence clearly dictates that he should deny such a lust. Again, if the two discomforts—that of suppression and that consequent upon gratification—seem exactly balanced, he will still continue to suppress his appetite; for the immediate bitterness is easier and simpler to taste than that which he must inevitably expect to swallow in the great majority of cases.

Nor is this enough. He ought further to suppress his passion in many circumstances even when he foresees no disagreeable consequence of indulgence, and that in order to train and discipline his soul to endure and become accustomed to such denial (for then it will be far less difficult to do so when the consequences are bad), as much as to prevent his lusts getting control of him and dominating him. The lusts in any case have sufficient hold, in the ordinary way of nature and human disposition, without needing to be reinforced by habit as well, so that a man will find himself in a situation where he cannot resist them at all.

You must know also that those who persistently indulge and gratify their appetites ultimately reach a stage where they no longer have any enjoyment of them, and still are unable to give them up. For instance, those who are forever having intercourse with women, or drinking, or listening to music—though these are the strongest and deepest-rooted of all the lusts—do not enjoy these indulgences so much as men who do not incessantly gratify them; for these passions become for them exactly the same as any other passion with other men—that is to say, they become commonplace and habitual. Nevertheless it is not within their power to leave off these pursuits because they have turned into something of the nature of a necessity of life for them, instead of being a luxury and a relish. They are in consequence affected adversely in their religious life as well as their mundane situation, so that they are compelled to employ all kinds of shifts, and to acquire money by risking their lives and precipitating themselves into any sort of danger. In the end they find they are miserable where they expected to be happy, that they are sorrowful where they expected to rejoice, that they are pained where they expected to experience pleasure. So what difference is there between them and the man who deliberately sets out to destroy himself? They are exactly like animals duped by the bait laid for them in the snares; when they arrive in the trap, they neither obtain what they had been duped with nor are they able to escape from what they have fallen into.

This then will suffice as to the amount the appetites should be suppressed: they may only be indulged where it is known that the consequence will not involve a man in pain and temporal loss equivalent to the pleasure thereby obtained—much less discomfort superior to and exceeding the pleasure that is momentarily experienced. This is the view and assertion and recommendation even of those philosophers who have not considered the soul to have an independent existence, but to decay and perish with the body in which it is lodged. As for those who hold that the soul has an individual identity of its own, and that it uses the body as it would an instrument or an implement, not perishing simultaneously with it, they rise far, far beyond the mere reining of the instincts, and combating and opposing the passions. They despise and revile exceedingly those who allow themselves to be led by and who incline after their lower nature, considering them to be no better than beasts. They believe that by following and indulging their passion, by inclining after and loving their appetites, by regretting anything they may miss, and inflicting pain on animals in order to secure and satisfy their lusts, these men will experience, after the soul has left the body, pain and regret and sorrow for the evil consequences of their actions alike abundant and prolonged.

These philosophers can put forward the very physique of man to prove that he is not equipped to occupy himself with pleasures and lusts, seeing how deficient he is in this respect compared with the irrational animals, but rather to use his powers of thought and deliberation. For a single wild beast experiences more pleasure in eating and having intercourse than a multitude of men can possibly achieve; while as for its capacity for casting care and thought aside, and enjoying life simply and wholly, that is a state of affairs no man can ever rival. This is because that is the animal's entire be-all and end-all; we may observe that a beast at the very moment of its slaughter will still go on eating and drinking with complete absorption. They further argue that if the gratification of the appetites and the indulgence of the calls of nature had been the nobler part, man would never have been made so deficient in this respect or been more meanly endowed than the animals. The very fact that man is so deficient—in spite of his being the noblest of mortal animals—in his share of these things, whereas he possesses such an ample portion of deliberation and reflection, is enough to teach us that it is nobler to utilize and improve the reason, and not to be slave and lackey of the calls of nature.

Moreover, they say, if the advantage lay in gratifying carnal pleasure and lust, the creature furnished by nature to that end would be nobler than that not so equipped. By such a standard the bull and the ass would be superior not only to man, but also to the immortal beings, and to God Himself, Who is without carnal pleasure and lust.

It may be (they go on) that certain undisciplined men unused to reflect and deliberate upon such matters will not agree with us that the beasts enjoy greater pleasure than men. Those who argue thus may quote against us such an instance as that of a king who, having triumphed over an opposing foe, thenceforward sits at his amusement, and summons together and displays all his pomp and circumstance, so that he achieves the ultimate limit of what a man may reach. 'What', they ask, 'is the pleasure of a beast in comparison with the pleasure of such man? Can so great a pleasure be measured or related with any other?' Those who speak in this fashion should realize that the perfection or imperfection of such pleasures must not be judged by comparing one pleasure with another, but in relation to the need felt for such a pleasure. Consider the case of a man who requires 1,000 dīnārs to put his affairs in order: if he is given 999, that will not completely restore his position for him. On the other hand suppose a man needs a single dīnār: his situation will be perfectly amended by obtaining that one dīnār. Yet the former has been given many times more than the latter, and still his state is not completely restored. When a beast has enjoyed full satisfaction of the call of its instincts, its pleasure therein is perfect and complete; it feels no pain or hurt at missing a still greater gratification because such an idea never occurs to its mind at all. Yet in any case the beast always experiences the superior pleasure; for there is no man who can ever attain all his hopes and desires, since his soul being endowed with the faculties of reflection, deliberation, and imagination of what he yet lacks, and it being in its nature always to consider that the state enjoyed by another is bound to be superior, never under any circumstances is it free from yearning and gazing after what it does not itself possess, and from being fearful and anxious lest it lose what it has possessed; its pleasure and desire are therefore always in a state of imperfect realization. If any man should possess half the world, his soul would still wrestle with him to acquire the remainder, and would be anxious and fearful of losing hold of as much as it has already gotten; and if he possessed the entire world, nevertheless he would yearn for perpetual well-being and immortality, and his soul would gaze after the knowledge of all the mysteries of heaven and earth. One day, as I have heard tell, someone spoke in the presence of a great-souled king of the splendid and immortal joys of Paradise, whereupon the king remarked, 'Such bliss seems to me wholly bitter and wearisome, when I reflect that if I were granted it, I should be in the position of one on whom a favour and a kindness had been conferred.' How could such a man ever know perfect pleasure and enjoyment of his lot? And who is there that rejoices within himself, save only the beasts and those who live like beasts?

So the poet says:

Can any man be truly blest,
Save him immortally possessed
Of fortune, who has scarce a care
And never goes to bed with fear?

This sect of philosophers soar beyond the mere reining and opposing of passion, even beyond the contempt and mortification thereof, unto a matter exceedingly sublime. They partake of a bare subsistence of food and drink; they acquire not wealth or lands or houses; and some advance so far in this opinion that they go apart from other men, and withdraw into waste places. Such are the arguments they put forward in support of their views regarding the things that are present and seen. As for their reasonings about the state of the soul after it has left the body, to speak of this would take us far beyond the scope of the present book, alike in loftiness, length and breadth: in loftiness, because this involves research into the nature of the soul, the purpose of its association with and separation from the body, and its state after it has gone out of it; in length, because each of these several branches of research requires its own interpretation and explanation, to an extent many times the discourse contained in this book; and in breadth, because the purpose of such researches is the salvation of the soul after it has left the body, though it is true that the discourse involves a major consideration of the reformation of character. Still, there will be no harm in giving a very brief account of these matters, without however involving ourselves in an argument for or against their opinions; what we have particularly in view are those ideas which we think will assist and enable us to fulfil the purpose of our present book.

Plato, the chief and greatest of the philosophers, held that there are three souls in every man. The first he called the rational and divine soul, the second the choleric and animal, and the third the vegetative, incremental and appetitive soul. The animal and vegetative souls were created for the sake of the rational soul. The vegetative soul was made in order to feed the body, which is as it were the instrument and implement of the rational soul; for the body is not of an eternal, indissoluble substance, but its substance is fluid and soluble, and every soluble object only survives by leaving behind it something to replace that element which is dissolved. The choleric soul's function is to be of assistance to the rational soul in suppressing the appetitive soul and in preventing it from preoccupying the rational soul with its manifold desires so that it is incapable of using its reason. If the rational soul employed its reason completely, this would mean that it would be delivered from the body in which it is enmeshed. These two souls—the vegetative and the choleric—possess in Plato's view no special substance that survives the corruption of the body, such as that which belongs to the rational soul. On the contrary one of them, the choleric, is the entire temperament of the heart, while the other, the appetitive, is the entire temperament of the liver. As for the temperament of the brain, this he said is the first instrument and implement used by the rational soul.

Man is fed and derives his increase and growth from the liver, his heat and pulse-movement from the heart, his sensation, voluntary movement, imagination, thought and memory from the brain. It is not the case that this is part of its peculiar property and temperament; it belongs rather to the essence dwelling within it and using it after the manner of an instrument or implement. However, it is the most intimate of all the instruments and implements associated with this agent.

Plato taught that men should labour by means of corporeal physick (which is the well-known variety) as well as spiritual physick (which is persuasion through arguments and proofs) to equilibrate the actions of the several souls so that they may neither fail nor exceed what is desired of them. Failure in the vegetative soul consists in not supplying food, growth and increase of the quantity and quality required by the whole body; its excess is when it surpasses and transgresses that limit so that the body is furnished with an abundance beyond its needs, and plunges into all kinds of pleasures and desires. Failure in the choleric soul consists in not having the fervour, pride and courage to enable it to rein and vanquish the appetitive soul at such times as it feels desire, so as to come between it and its desires; its excess is when it is possessed of so much arrogance and love of domination that it seeks to overcome all other men and the entire animal kingdom, and has no other ambition but supremacy and domination—such a state of soul as affected Alexander the Great. Failure in the rational soul is recognized when it does not occur to it to wonder and marvel at this world of ours, to mediate upon it with interest, curiosity and a passionate desire to discover all that it contains, and above all to investigate the body in which it dwells and its form and fate after death. Truly, if a man does not wonder and marvel at our world, if he is not moved to astonishment at its form, and if his soul does not gaze after the knowledge of all that it contains, if he is not concerned or interested to discover what his state will be after death, his portion of reason is that of the beasts—nay, of bats and fishes and worthless things that never think or reflect. Excess in the rational soul is proved when a man is so swayed and overmastered by the consideration of such things as these that the appetitive soul cannot obtain the food and sleep and so forth to keep the body fit, or in sufficient quantity to maintain the temperament of the brain in a healthy state. Such a man is forever seeking and probing and striving to the utmost of his powers, supposing that he will attain and realize these matters in a shorter time than that which is absolutely necessary for their achievement. The result is that the temperament of the whole body is upset, so that he falls prey to depression and melancholia, and he misses his entire quest through supposing that he could quickly master it.

Plato held that the period which has been appointed for the survival of this dissoluble and corruptible body, in a state the rational soul can make use of to procure the needs of its salvation after it leaves the body—the period that is from the time a man is born until he grows old and withers—is adequate for the fulfilment of every man, even the stupidest; provided he never gives up thinking and speculating and gazing after the matters we have mentioned as proper to the rational soul, and provided he despises this body and the physical world altogether, and loathes and detests it, being aware that the sentient soul, so long as it is attached to any part of it, continues to pass through states deleterious and painful because generation and corruption are forever succeeding each other in the body; provided further that he does not hate but rather yearns to depart out of the body and to be liberated from it. He believed that when the time comes for the sentient soul to leave the body in which it is lodged, if it has acquired and believed firmly in these ideas it will pass immediately into its own world, and will not desire to be attached to any particle of the body thereafter; it will remain living and reasoning eternally, free from pain, and rejoicing in its place of abode. For life and reason belong to it of its own essence; freedom from pain will be the consequence of its removal from generation and corruption; it will rejoice in its own world and place of abiding because it has been liberated from association with the body and existence in the physical world. But if the soul leaves the body without having acquired these ideas and without having recognized the true nature of the physical world, but rather still yearning after it and eager to exist therein, it will not leave its present dwelling-place but will continue to be linked with some portion of it; it will not cease—because of the succession of generation and corruption within the body in which it is lodged—to suffer continual and reduplicated pains, and cares multitudinous and afflicting.

Such in brief are the views of Plato, and of Socrates the Divine Hermit before him.

Besides all this, there is neither any purely mundane view whatsoever that does not necessitate some reining of passion and appetite, or that gives them free head and rope altogether. To rein and suppress the passion is an obligation according to every opinion, in the view of every reasoning man, and according to every religion. Therefore let the reasoning man observe these ideals with the eye of his reason, and keep them before his attention and in his mind; and even if he should not achieve the highest rank and level of this order described in the present book, let him at least cling hold of the meanest level. That is the view of those who advocate the reining of the passion to the extent that will not involve mundane loss in this present life; for if he tastes some bitterness and unpleasantness at the beginning of his career through reining and suppressing his passion, this will presently be followed by a consequent sweetness and a pleasure in which he may rejoice with great joy and gladness; while the labour he endures in wrestling with his passion and suppressing his appetites will grow easier by habit, especially if this be effected gradually—by accustoming himself to the discipline and leading on his soul gently, first to deny trifling appetites and to forgo a little of its desires at the requirement of reason and judgment, and then to seek after further discipline until it becomes associated with his character and habit. In this way his appetitive soul will become submissive and will grow accustomed to being subject to his rational soul. So the process will continue to develop; and the discipline will be reinforced by the joy he has in the results yielded by this reining of his passion, and the profit he has of his judgment and reason and of controlling his affairs by them; by the praise men lavish upon him, and their evident desire to emulate his achievement.

Summary Prolegomena to the Detailed Account of Each of the Evil Dispositions of the Soul

Now that we have laid level the foundations for that part of our discourse which is to follow, and have mentioned the most important principles as constituting an adequate capital and reserve on which to draw, we will proceed to describe the various evil dispositions of the soul, and the gentle means of reforming them, to serve as an analogy and an example for what we have not attempted to set forth. We shall withal endeavour to be as brief and concise as possible in speaking of these vices; for we have already established the chief cause and principal reason, from which we shall derive and on which we shall build all the divers treatments necessary for the reformation of any particular evil characteristic. Indeed, if we should not single out even one of these for special consideration, but leave them all aside without any individual mention, ample resources would be available for putting them to right by keeping in mind and holding fast to our first principle. For all these dispositions are the result of obeying the call of passion and yielding to the persuasion of the appetite: to rein and guard these twains will effectively prevent being seized and moulded by them. But in any case we intend to state as much on this subject as we consider needful and necessary to assist in fulfilling the purpose of our present book. And God be our help in this.

Of the Virtuous Life

The life which has been followed by all the great philosophers of the past may be described in a few words: it consists in treating all men justly. Thereafter it means acting nobly towards them, with a proper continence, compassion, universal benevolence, and an endeavour to secure the advantage of all men; save only those who have embarked upon a career of injustice and oppression, or who labour to overthrow the constitution, practising those things which good government prohibits—disorder, mischief and corruption.

Now many men are constrained by their evil laws and systems to live a life of wrongdoing; such are the followers of Daisān,[1] the Red Khurramīs,[2] and others

1. An early heresiarch.
2. A branch of the Kurramī sect, heretics of the ninth century.

who hold it lawful to act deceitfully and treacherously towards their opponents; or the Manicheans with their refusal to give water or food to those who do not share their opinions or to treat them medically when they are ill, who abstain from killing snakes, scorpions and suchlike noisome creatures which cannot possibly be expected to be of use or to be turned to any profitable purpose whatsoever, and who decline to purify themselves with water. Many men, I say, are of this persuasion and do various things, some of which result in mischief to the community as a whole, while some are hurtful to the practitioner himself. Such men cannot be won from their evil manner of life, except by serious discourse on opinions and doctrines; and that discussion far transcends the scope and purpose of this book.

There is nothing left for us to say on this subject, therefore, further than to recall the kind of life which, when strictly followed, will secure a man from the hurt of his fellows, and will earn him their love. So we assert that if a man cleaves to justice and continence, and allows himself but rarely to quarrel and contend with his fellows, he will in the main be safe from them. If to this he adds goodness and benevolence and mercy in his dealings with others, he will win their love. These two attributes are the reward of the virtuous life; and what we have said is sufficient for our purpose in this book.

Of the Fear of Death

This disposition cannot be expelled from the soul entirely, except it be satisfied that it will pass after death into a state more salutary to it than its present. Now this is a topic which calls for an extremely long discussion, if it be sought by way of logical demonstration and not mere report; and there is no possibility of such a discussion, especially in this book, because as we have said before its content exceeds the content of this alike in loftiness, breadth and length. For it would need a consideration of all the religions and sects which believe and require that man will have a certain estate after death, and passing verdict thereafter in favour of those which are true and against those which are false. It is no secret that the purport of this matter is very difficult, and needs and must have a long discussion. We shall therefore put this aside, and turn our attention to satisfying those who hold and believe that the soul perishes with the corruption of the body; for as long as a man continues to fear death he will turn away from reason to follow after passion.

Man, according to these, will after death be affected by no pain whatsoever; for pain is a sensation, and sensation is a property only of the living being, who during the state of his life is plunged and saturated in pain. Now the state in which there is no pain is obviously more salutary than the state in which pain exists; death is therefore more salutary to man than life.

THE BOOK OF THE PHILOSOPHIC LIFE
al-Sīrat al-falsafiyyah

Translated by Charles Butterworth from al-Rāzī, *Kitāb al-sirat al-falsafiyyah*, in Muḥammad ibn Zakariyyā' Rāzī, *Rasā'il falsafiyyah*, ed. P. Kraus (Tehran, 1964), pp. 703–713.[1] First published in *Interpretation*, 20:3 (1993), pp. 227–236.

[I. Introduction]

1. Abū Bakr Muḥammad ibn Zakariyyā' al-Rāzī, may God join gladness and repose to his spirit, said: When people of speculation, discernment, and attainment saw that we were engaging with people and becoming involved with the means of making a living, they criticized us and found fault with us claiming that we were turning away from the life of philosophers, especially the life led by our leader, Socrates. Of him it is related that he did not call upon kings but made light of them when they called upon him, did not eat pleasant food, did not wear fine clothing, did not build, did not acquire, did not beget, did not eat flesh, did not drink wine, and did not attend festivities. Instead, he confined himself to eating vegetables, wrapping himself in a ragged garment, and lodging in a cask in the desert. Moreover, he did not practice dissimulation either with the common people or with those in authority. Instead, he confronted them with what was truth according to him in the most explicit and clearest utterances. We, however, are the opposite of that.

2. Then they said, among the evils of this life that our leader Socrates led is that it goes against the course of nature and provision for cultivation and begetting and leads to the ruination of the world and the perdition of people and their destruction.

3. We shall respond to them concerning whatever of that is in us, God willing.

[II. The Philosophic Life]

[A. The Reasons For Socrates' Earlier Life]

4. Thus, we say that they speak the truth in what they relate and mention about Socrates. That was part of him. However, they ignore other things and refrain from mentioning them so intent are they on forcing a proof against us. That is, these matters they relate about Socrates did pertain to him at the very outset and for a long period of his life. Then he turned away from many of them so that he died having had daughters, fought the enemy, attended sessions of festivities, eaten good things

1. The numbers in square brackets refer to the pages of the Kraus edition.

except for flesh, and drunk a little intoxicating beverage. That is known and related among those who are concerned about inquiring into the reports about this man.

5. Indeed, he was the way [100] he was at the very outset because of his great amazement over philosophy, his love for it, his desire to devote to it the time otherwise dedicated to passions and pleasures, his nature being inclined to it rather than to that, and his making light of and looking down on those who did not view philosophy in the way it deserves and who preferred what was baser than it. Without a doubt, at the start of stirring and ardent matters, one prefers turning to them, being excessive in loving them and pursuing them, and hating those opposed to them until, when he penetrates them deeply and the matters become firmly settled in him, the excessiveness about them declines and he returns to moderation. As it is said in the adage; 'there is a pleasure to every new thing'. So this was the condition of Socrates during that period of his life. And what was related of him with respect to these matters is more widespread and numerous because they are more curious, astonishing, and remote than the conditions of people. People are enamoured about spreading the curious, unusual report and shunning the familiar and habitual.

6. We are not, therefore, opposed to the praiseworthy aspect of Socrates' life, even though we fall short of him greatly and acknowledge our deficiency in practising the just life, suppressing desires, loving knowledge, and aspiring to it. Our difference with Socrates, then, is not about quality of life but about quantity. We are not inferior if we acknowledge our failing with respect to him, for that is the truth; and acknowledging the truth is more noble and virtuous. So this is what we say about this topic.

[B. Austerity Versus Profligacy]

7. With respect to what they criticize in [the first of] Socrates' two lives, we say: what is truly blameworthy there also is the quantity, not the quality. For it is clear, as we have explained in our book *On Spiritual Medicine*, that abandoning oneself to passions and preferring them is not most virtuous and most noble. Rather, it is taking each need to the extent that is indispensable or to the extent that does not bring about a pain that surpasses the pleasure thereby obtained.

8. And Socrates did turn back from what was excessive in it, that which is truly blameworthy and leads to the ruination of the world and the perdition of people, for he did come back and beget, war against [101] the enemy, and attend sessions of festivities. Anyone who does that leaves off rushing into the ruination of this world and perdition of the people. It is not necessary that not to be like that is to be mired in the passions. And we, even if we do not deserve the name of philosophy in comparison to Socrates, surely deserve its name in comparison to non-philosophic people.

[C. Principles of the Philosophic Life]

9. Since this has come forth with respect to the issue, let us complete the argument about the philosophic life so that the lovers of knowledge and those who prefer it may profit from it. So we say: we need to support the matter concerning the goal we are intent upon in this treatise on fundamentals whose explanation has been set forth in other books that are to be consulted to make easier what is in this treatise. Among them are our book *On Divine Science*, our book *On Spiritual Medicine*, our book *On Blaming those Characterized as Philosophers who Occupy Themselves with what is Superfluous in Geometry*, and our book characterized as *The Glory of the Art of Alchemy*, but above all our book characterized as *The Spiritual Medicine*. Indeed, it is indispensable for bringing to completion the goal of this treatise and the fundamentals upon which we build the branches of the philosophic life—which we take here and set forth in an abridged form. They are:

I. We will have a praiseworthy or blameworthy state after death according to our life during the time our souls are in our bodies.

II. The most virtuous matter for which we were created and towards which we are moved is not getting bodily pleasures, but the acquisition of knowledge and the practice of justice; through these two comes about our deliverance from this world of ours to the world in which there is neither death nor pain.

III. Nature and desire call us to prefer present pleasure, whereas intellect frequently calls us to leave present pleasures aside for matters that are to be preferred.

IV. Our Master, from whom we hope for reward and fear punishment, looking over us and having compassion for us, does not want us to cause pain; detesting injustice and ignorance on our part, He loves for us to be knowledgeable and just; indeed, this [102] Master punishes the one among us who causes pain and who deserves to be pained according to what he deserves.

V. We ought not to endure a pain in the hope of getting a pleasure that the pain itself surpasses in quantity and quality.

VI. The Creator, may He be magnified and glorified, has bestowed upon us the particular things of which we have need, like tilling, weaving, and similar things of which the world and subsistence are constituted.

10. Let them [i.e., these principles] be accorded us, then, so that we may build upon them.

[D. About Pleasure]

11. So we say: if the pleasures and pains of this world are interrupted when life is interrupted whereas the pleasures of the world in which there is no death are always uninterrupted and unlimited, he is deceived who would purchase a transitory,

interrupted, limited pleasure for one that is eternal, lasting, uninterrupted, and unlimited. Since the matter is such, it follows necessarily that we ought not to seek a pleasure which to acquire we will undoubtedly perpetrate something that prevents us from deliverance to the world of the soul or that forces upon us in this world a pain that is greater and more severe in quantity and quality than the pleasure we prefer. Any pleasures apart from that are permitted to us.

12. The philosophic man may, however, leave aside many of these permitted pleasures in order to condition and habituate his soul so that—as we have mentioned in the *Book of the Spiritual Medicine*—it will be more comfortable and easier for him in case of necessity. For habit, as the ancients mention, is second nature making the hard easy and the strange familiar—either with respect to matters of the soul or bodily matters. As we see that couriers are stronger at walking, soldiers bolder at war, and so on, there is no obscurity about habits facilitating matters that were difficult and hard before habituation.

13. Even though this argument—I mean, what we have mentioned about the extent of restricted pleasure—is abbreviated and summary, many particular matters are subsumed under it—as we have explained in the *Book of the Spiritual Medicine*. [103] For if the fundamental we have set down—namely, that the intelligent man ought not to yield to a pleasure when he fears it will entail a pain surpassing the pain he acquires in putting up with forsaking pleasure and stifling passion—is sound and true in itself or is so postulated, then it necessarily follows that: even if we were in such a condition as to possess the whole earth for the length of our life by perpetrating upon people what does not please God, such that we would be prevented by Him from acquiring eternal good and abiding grace, we ought not to do or prefer it. Again, if we were sure or almost sure that by eating something like a plate of fresh dates we would get an opthalmia for ten days, we ought not to prefer eating them. This is the case with respect to the particular instances falling between the two examples we have mentioned, despite the one being great and the other petty in relation. Each of the particular instances is petty in relation to the greater and big in relation to the more petty. Because of the multitude of particular instances falling under this general rule, it is not possible to make the argument exhaustive.

14. Since what we wanted to explain has been explained with respect to this topic, we are intent upon explaining another one of our goals that follows upon this goal.

[E. About Pain]

15. So we say: from the fundamental we have set down to the effect that our Lord and Master is concerned about us, looks over us, and has compassion for us it follows also that He detests pain befalling us. Any pain befalling us that is not by our

enterprise or choices but pertains to nature is thus due to a necessity and occurred inevitably. It results therefrom that we ought not to cause pain to any sensible being unless it deserves such pain or unless by means of that pain we spare the creature a more intense one. [104] Under this maxim, as well, there fall many details: all the sorts of wrongs, the pleasure kings take in hunting animals, and the excess to which people go in exerting tame animals when they use them. Now all of that must be according to an intelligent and just intent, rule, method, and doctrine—one that is not exceeded nor deviated from.

16. Pain occurs when one hopes to push away a greater one by means of it, as when the surgeon lances [an abscess]; cauterizes a gangrenous limb; and makes [the sick person] drink bitter, repugnant medication and forego pleasant food from fear of great, painful sicknesses. Again, tame animals are to be exerted with [considerate] intent and without violence, except in instances when necessity calls for violence and reason and justice require it—as in spurring a horse in seeking to save oneself from the enemy. For justice then requires spurring and injuring if it is hoped thereby to save a human being, especially if he is a good, learned man or one of great value in a way that confers well-being on most people. For the value of such a man and his remaining in this world is better for his people than the horse remaining. Again, when two men happen to be in a waterless desert and one of the men has enough water that he is able to save himself but not his companion, in such a case the one of the two who confers more well-being to the people is to be preferred. So this is the analogy for these and similar kinds of cases.

17. Hunting, pursuing, exterminating, and annihilating ought to be engaged in with respect to animals that lead a complete life only by means of flesh—such as lions, tigers, wolves, and the like—as well as with those which cause major harm without there being any hope of profiting from them or need to use them—like vipers, scorpions, and so on. So this is the analogy for these kinds of cases.

18. It is permissible to destroy these animals only from two perspectives. One is that when they are not destroyed, they destroy many animals. [105] This is a feature particularly characteristic of these animals, I mean those that live only by flesh. The other [perspective] is that souls are delivered from the bodies of no animals except for the body of human beings. Since this is the case, the delivering of souls like these from their bodies is like a bringing along and facilitating to [ultimate] deliverance.

19. Since both perspectives apply to those that live only by flesh, they must be exterminated so far as possible. Indeed, that brings about a lessening of animals being pained and a hope that their souls will enter into more suitable bodies. Vipers, scorpions, wasps, and so on have in common that they cause pain to animals and are not suitable to be used by man the way tame animals are used and put to work. Therefore it is permissible to annihilate and exterminate them.

20. Animals that are put to work and that live from grass must not be exterminated and annihilated. Rather, they are to be worked gently as we have mentioned and, as much as possible, used sparingly for food and bred sparingly lest they become so numerous that it is necessary to slaughter them in great numbers. That, however, is to be done with intent and according to need. Were it not that there is no hope of a soul in any but a human body being delivered, the judgment of reason would not give rein to their being slaughtered at all. Now those who engage in philosophy have disagreed about this matter. Some of them are of the opinion that man is to nourish himself by means of flesh, and others are not of that opinion. Socrates was among those who did not permit it.

21. The judgment of intellect and justice being that man is not to cause pain to others, it follows that he is not to cause pain to himself either. Many matters forbidden by the judgment of intellect also come under this maxim, such as what the Hindus do in approaching God by burning their bodies and throwing them upon sharp pieces of iron and such as the Manicheans cutting off their testicles when they desire sexual intercourse, emaciating themselves through hunger and thirst, and soiling themselves by abstaining from water or using urine in place of it. Also entering into this classification, though far inferior, is what Christians do [106] in pursuing monastic life and withdrawing to hermitages as well as many Muslims staying permanently in mosques, renouncing earnings, and restricting themselves to a modicum of repugnant food and to irritating and coarse clothing. Indeed, all of that is an iniquity towards themselves and causes them pain that does not push away a preponderant pain.

22. And Socrates had led a life like this in his early years, but he renounced it in later years as we mentioned before. There is a great diversity among people with respect to this classification not to be gone into here. Yet it is unavoidable that we say something approximating it by way of illustration.

[F. Upper And Lower Limits]

23. Thus we say: people differ with respect to their conditions. Some are raised in comfort and others in misery. Desires make a greater demand upon the souls of some—as with those who are enamoured of women, wine, love of rule, and matters such as that with respect to which great diversity occurs among people. Thus the pain that befalls them in suppressing their desires differs greatly in accordance with the difference in their conditions. The skin of one born of kings and brought up in their comfort will not endure coarse clothing nor will his stomach tolerate repugnant food in the way the one born of common people will. Rather, he will be severely pained from that. Similarly, those accustomed to having a certain kind of pleasure will be pained when prevented from having it; and the inconvenience will be multiplied for them and be more extensive and sharper than for one not accustomed to that pleasure.

24. Because of that it is not possible to charge everyone in the same way; rather, it is to differ in accordance with the difference in their conditions. Thus, the philosophically minded children of kings are not charged with adhering to the food, drink, and other staples of life that the children of the common people are charged with unless it is done gradually when necessity calls for it.

25. However, the limit it is not possible to go beyond is that they abstain from anything pleasant that can be attained only [107] by perpetrating iniquity and murder and, in general, from everything that antagonizes God and must not be done according to the judgment of intellect and justice. What is apart from that is allowed them. So this is the upper limit, I mean, with respect to giving oneself over to enjoyment.

26. The lower limit—I mean, with respect to being ascetic and restricting oneself—is for a human being to eat what does not harm him or make him sick and not to reach beyond to what excessively pleases him or what he desires so that he becomes intent upon pleasure and desire rather than upon satisfying his hunger. And for him to wear what his skin endures without suffering and not to have a propensity for sumptuous, colourful clothing. And for him to dwell in what shelters him from excessive heat and cold and not to reach beyond to magnificent, splendid, colourfully adorned, and highly decorated dwellings unless he have such an abundance of wealth that it is possible for him to extend it to such matters without iniquity, transgression, or self-exertion in acquisition. Therefore those born of poor fathers and brought up in shabby circumstances excel in this instance. For, restricting oneself and being ascetic is easier for those like this, just as it was easier for Socrates than for Plato to restrict himself and be ascetic.

27. What falls between these two limits is allowed. The one who practises that does not go outside of the title of philosopher; rather, it is permissible for him to be so entitled. Nonetheless, it is preferable to have a propensity for the lower limit more than for the higher limit. Virtuous souls, even if they are companions to bodies raised in comfort, gradually bring their bodies towards the lower limit.

28. Yet to go beyond the lower limit is to go outside of philosophy, somewhat in the way we have mentioned with respect to the conditions of the Hindus, Manicheans, monks, and hermits. It is to go outside the just life and to antagonize God, may He be exalted, by causing pain to souls needlessly and warrants [108] being placed outside the title of philosophy. The situation is similar with respect to going beyond the higher limit. We beseech God—the Endower of intellect, the Dispeller of grief, and the Remover of anxiety—to give us success, direct us, and assist us in doing what is most favourable to Him and in bringing us closest to Him.

[G. The Philosophic Life in Sum]

29. In sum, I say: Since the Creator, may He be glorified and magnified, is a knower who is not ignorant and a doer of justice who does no injustice; and since He is unqualified knowledge, justice, and compassion; and since He is a creator and master to us, whereas we are slaves and vassals to Him; and since the slaves most beloved of their owners are those who most adhere to their ways of life and are most in accordance with their traditions; the slaves closest to God, may He be magnified and glorified, are those who are most learned, most just, most compassionate, and most kindly. This whole speech is what is meant by the statement of all philosophers: "Philosophy is making oneself similar to God, may He be glorified and magnified, to the extent possible for a human being." And this is the sum of the philosophic life. A detailed statement of it is what is in the *Book of the Spiritual Medicine*. For there we have mentioned how to rid the soul of bad moral habits and the extent to which someone aspiring to be philosophic ought to concern himself with gaining a livelihood, acquisition, expenditure, and seeking ranks of rulership.

[III. Self-Justification]

30. Since we have explained what we wanted to explain with respect to this topic, we will return and explain what pertains to us. And we will mention those who defame us and will mention that even until this day we have not lived a life—due to success granted by God and to His assistance—such that we deserve to be excluded from being designated 'philosopher'. That is because the one who deserves to have the title of philosophy stripped from him is the one who falls short in both parts of philosophy—I mean, knowledge and practice—through ignorance of what the philosopher is supposed to know or leading a life the philosopher is not supposed to lead. Yet we—due to God's praise, grace, granted success, and guidance—are free from any of that.

31. Now with respect to the classification of knowledge, if we had only the power to compose a book like this that would prevent us from having the title of philosophy stripped away. In addition, there are our books like *On Demonstration*, *On Divine Science*, [109] *On Spiritual Medicine*, and our book *On an Introduction to Physical Science*, which is designated as *Lecture on Nature*. And there are our treatises like *On Time, Place, Matter, Eternity, and Vacuum*, *On the Form of the World*, *On the Reason for the Earth arising in the Middle of the [Heavenly] Sphere*, *On the Reason the [Heavenly] Sphere has Circular Movement*, and our treatises *On Composition* and *On Body having its own Motion and this Motion being Known*. And there are our books pertaining to the soul, our books pertaining to matter, and our books about medicine like *The Mansūrī Book*, our *Book to those whom the Physician does not Visit*, our *Book about Existing Drugs*, the one designated as *Royal Medicine*,

and the book designated as *The Summary.* With respect to the latter, none of the people of the kingdom has surpassed me nor has anyone yet followed along in my steps or copied me. And there are our books about the art of wisdom, which is alchemy according to the common people. In sum, up to the moment of my doing this treatise, nearly two hundred books, treatises, and pamphlets have issued forth from me in the physical and metaphysical branches of philosophy.

32. With respect to mathematics, I acknowledge that I have looked into them only to the extent that was indispensable for me. That I have not consumed my time in trying to master them is deliberate on my part and not due to incapacity for them. For those who so wish, I have set forth my excuses to the effect that what I have done is correct and not what those designated as philosophers do who consume their lives busying themselves with the details of geometry.

33. If what I have reached with respect to knowledge is not what is reached by the one deserving to be called a philosopher, then I would like to know who such a one would be in this epoch of ours.

34. Now with respect to the practical part, I have not in my life—due to God's assistance and granting of success—reached beyond the two limits that I defined. Nor has there appeared anything from my actions such that it deserves to be said that my life is not a philosophic life. For I have not kept company with the ruler as a bearer of arms or as one entrusted with his affairs. Rather, I have kept company with him as one engaged in medicine and a convivial having free rein over two matters: when he was sick, to cure him [110] and to improve the condition of his body; and when his body was healthy, to entertain him and to advise him—God knows that of me—about everything I hoped would be of sound benefit for him and for his flock.

35. It has not appeared that I have avidity for amassing money and spending it nor for disputing with people, quarrelling with them, or being iniquitous to them. Rather it is known that I am the opposite of all that and have an aversion to claiming many of my rights.

36. With respect to the way I eat, drink, and engage in festivities, those who have frequently observed me in such activities surely know that I do not reach any point of excess. It is the same with the rest of what can be observed of my conduct with respect to clothing, mounts, and male and female servants.

37. With respect to my love of knowledge, my avid desire for it, and my striving for it, it is known among those who have been my companions and have observed me that from the time of my youth until this moment I have never ceased being eagerly devoted to it. It is such that should I chance upon a book I have not read or a man I have not sounded out, I do not pay attention to any concern whatever—even if that is of major harm to me—until I have gone through the book and learned what the man is about. My patience and striving are such that in a single year I have written, in a script like that used on amulets, more than twenty thousand pages.

In working on the large *Summary*, I spent fifteen years working night and day so weakening my eyesight and ruining the muscles in my hand that at this moment I am prevented from reading and writing. Though my situation is thus, I exert myself as much as I can not to abandon them and always have recourse to someone to read and write for me.

[IV. Conclusion]

38. Thus if according to these people the extent of my practice with respect to these matters brings me down from the rank of philosophy and the goal of following the philosophic life according to them is other than what we have described, then let them set it before us either in clear speech or in writing. Thus we may accept it from them, if they bring forth a superior knowledge; or we may refute them if we establish that there is a mistake or deficiency in it.

39. Let me, out of indulgence towards them grant that I fall short with respect to the practical part. Still, what can they possibly say with respect to the theoretical part? If they have [111] found me to be deficient with respect to it, let them tell me what they have to say about that so that we may look into it and afterwards concede that they are right or refute their error. And if they have not found me to be deficient with respect to the theoretical part, the most appropriate thing is for them to take advantage of my knowledge and not to pay attention to my life. Then they will be doing something like what the poet says:

Put into practice my learning,
For if I fall short in my doing,
To your advantage is my learning,
And of no harm my short falling.

40. This is what I wanted to set down in this treatise. To the Endower of intellect, praises without end—as He deserves and merits. And may God bless His chosen male servants and His good female servants.

41. *The Book of the Philosophic Life* is completed. To God, May He be exalted, praise in every circumstance, always, perpetually, and eternally.

16

Abū Rayḥān Bīrūnī

Abū Rayḥān Muḥammad ibn Aḥmad Bīrūnī, one of the greatest Islamic scientists and one of the most universal figures of Islamic thought, was born outside the city of Khwārazm in 362/973. He received his early education, especially in mathematics, in that city and later travelled throughout the realms of the Samanids. In 408/1017, Maḥmūd of Ghaznah captured Khwārazm and took Bīrūnī with him as a member of his court, where he became court astronomer and astrologer. Bīrūnī also accompanied Maḥmūd on his famous campaign in India, where he found the opportunity to study Sanskrit, Hinduism, and Indian culture, as well as the sciences of that land. Returning to Ghaznah, Bīrūnī wrote his most famous work *Taḥqīq mā li'l-Hind* (India) in 422/1031. He spent the rest of his days in Ghaznah, serving Maḥmūd's son Mas'ūd and continuing to write until his death in 442/1051.

A precise scientist, a meticulous scholar, and an independent philosopher and thinker, Bīrūnī produced some of the greatest works in Islamic science, such as his astronomical masterpiece *al-Qānūn al-mas'ūdī* (The Mas'ūdic Canon), and also major historical works such as *India* and *al-Āthār al-bāqiyah* (The Chronology of Ancient Nations). He wrote definitive pieces in mathematics, astronomy, geography, metallurgy, and pharmacology, as well as the first works on astronomy and astrology in Persian, the *Kitāb al-tafhīm* (Elements of Astrology).

Although known primarily as a scientist, Bīrūnī was also the founder of the discipline of comparative religion, as shown in his incomparable *India*. He was also a philosopher, but his philosophical ideas are scattered throughout his extensive works, and except for *al-As'ilah wa'l-ajwibah* (Questions and Answers) exchanged with Ibn Sīnā, none is devoted solely to philosophy.

A work of his, the *Kitāb al-shāmil* (The Book of General Knowledge), which is said to have contained his philosophical views, is lost. In his catalogue of the works of Muḥammad ibn Zakariyyā' Rāzī, Bīrūnī shows his great interest in Rāzī's works; at the same time, he reveals his opposition to certain of Rāzī's philosophical views, such as the latter's espousal of particular Manichean theses.

Bīrūnī was a devout Muslim who approached the study of both science and philosophy from the Quranic worldview while revealing remarkable logical acumen and a keen sense of observation. However, he displayed a nondenominational attitude, as seen by the ring which he wore one side of which had an inscription revered by the Sunnis and the other an inscription with Shiʿi colour. Bīrūnī's critical faculties are fully displayed in *al-As'ilah wa'l-ajwibah*, the series of questions and answers exchanged between him and Ibn Sīnā. This work, which marks a peak of intellectual exchange in Islamic history, is an unparalleled critique of Aristotelian natural philosophy. Likewise, his *India* not only is a remarkably objective description of religious currents in India but also contains many passages of philosophical importance as far as Bīrūnī's own thoughts are concerned.

Moreover, many of Bīrūnī's scientific works contain segments dealing with the philosophy of nature and methodology of the sciences, the latter which is itself a philosophical question. In this domain, Bīrūnī made major philosophical contributions. He rejected the eternity of the world and accepted creation *ex-nihilo*. For him, nature was not simply matter, but possessed creative power. He saw in nature the design of the Ultimate Designer who has created a world in which there is no deficiency. In discovering the significance of this design—that is, the study of the functioning of nature and its meaning—Bīrūnī not only advocated observation and experimentation but also appealed to revelation as contained in Sacred Scripture. He was thus to have a lasting effect not only upon branches of later Islamic science but also on the Islamic philosophy of nature.

This chapter presents a portion of Bīrūnī's *India* that is a fine example of comparative religion and comparative philosophy in Islam. Bīrūnī uses Hindu, Greek, Zoroastrian, and Sufi textual support for his interpretations of some central philosophical concepts. He begins with a reflection on the nature of God, and often in a dialectical manner reminiscent of Plato's dialogues, he provides us with an insight into the Hindu view of God, the nature of liberation, *mokśa*, and the nine commandments of the Hindu religion. His elaborations on the Hindu school of Sāṃkhya and the parallels he draws with Sufism are of much importance in the realm of comparative philosophy.

The single most important philosophical work of Bīrūnī is the *As'ilah wa'l-ajwibah* (Questions and Answers), an exchange between him and Ibn Sīnā concerning Peripatetic natural philosophy. We have included here several chapters of this exchange that cover a variety of topics. In Part I, the correspondence between al-Bīrūnī and Ibn Sīnā offers a criticism of Aristotelian natural philosophy, of *De Caelo*, and discusses such topics as levity and gravity, heavenly bodies, circular motion and celestial bodies in the Islamic scientific tradition. In Part II, criticism of Aristotle's reliance on the views of the ancients, his notion of six directions of space and the continuity and discontinuity of physical bodies are offered. In Part III, the shape of the heavens, criticism of Aristotle's reasoning for the spherical motion of the heavens, sublunar physics and the theory of transformation of elements are presented.

S. H. Nasr

THE BELIEF OF THE HINDUS IN GOD

From *Taḥqīq mā li'l-Hind* (India)

Reprinted from *Alberuni's India*, tr. E. C. Sachau (Lahore, 1962), vol. 1, pp. 32–39, 89–131.

The belief of educated and uneducated people differs in every nation; for the former strive to conceive abstract ideas and to define general principles, whilst the latter do not pass beyond the apprehension of the senses, and are content with derived rules, without caring for details, especially in questions of religion and law, regarding which opinions and interests are divided.

The Hindus believe with regard to God that he is one, eternal, without beginning and end, acting by free-will, almighty, all-wise, living, giving life, ruling, preserving; one who in his sovereignty is unique, beyond all likeness and unlikeness, and that he does not resemble anything nor does anything resemble him. In order to illustrate this we shall produce some extracts from their literature, lest the reader should think that our account is nothing but hearsay.

In the book of *Patanjali* the pupil asks:

'Who is the worshipped one, by the worship of whom blessing is obtained?'

The master says:

'It is he who, being eternal and unique, does not for his part stand in need of any human action for which he might give as a recompense either a blissful repose, which is hoped and longed for, or a troubled existence, which is feared and dreaded. He is unattainable to thought, being sublime beyond all unlikeness which is abhorrent and all likeness which is sympathetic. He by his essence knows from all eternity. *Knowledge*, in the human sense of the term, has as its object that which was *unknown* before whilst *not knowing* does not at any time or in any condition apply to God.'

Further the pupil speaks:

'Do you attribute to him other qualities besides those you have mentioned?'

The master says:

'He is height, absolute in the idea, not in *space*, for he is sublime beyond all existence *in any space*. He is the pure absolute good, longed for by every created being. He is the knowledge free from the defilement of forgetfulness and not-knowing.'

The pupil speaks:

'Do you attribute to him speech or not?'

The master says:

'As he knows, he no doubt also speaks.'

The pupil asks:

'If he *speaks* because he *knows*, what, then, is the difference between him and the *knowing* sages who have *spoken* of their *knowing*?'

The master says:

'The difference between them is time, for they have learned in time and spoken in time, after having been not-knowing and not-speaking. By speech they have transferred their knowledge to others. Therefore their speaking and acquiring knowledge take place in time. And as divine matters have no connection with time, God is *knowing, speaking* from eternity. It was he who spoke to Brahman, and to others of the first beings in different ways. On the one he bestowed a book; for the other he opened a door, a means of communicating with him; a third one he inspired so that he obtained by cogitation what God bestowed upon him.'

The pupil asks:

'Whence has he this knowing?'

The master answers:

'His knowing is the same from all eternity, for ever and ever. As he has never been not-knowing, he is *knowing* of himself, having never acquired any knowledge which he did not possess before. He speaks in the Veda which he sent down upon Brahman:

"*Praise and celebrate him who has spoken the Veda, and was before the Veda.*"'

The pupil asks:

'How do you worship him to whom the perception of the senses cannot attain?'

The master says:

'His name proves his existence, for where there is a report there must be something to which it refers, and where there is a name there must be something which is named. He is hidden to the senses and unperceivable by them. However, the soul perceives him, and thought comprehends his qualities. This meditation is identical with worshipping him exclusively, and by practising it uninterruptedly beatitude is obtained.'

In this way the Hindus express themselves in this very famous book.

The following passage is taken from the book *Gita*, a part of the book *Bharata*, from the conversation between Vasudeva and Arjuna:

'I am the universe, without a beginning by being born, or without an end by dying. I do not aim by whatever I do at any recompense. I do not specially belong to one class of beings to the exclusion of others, as if I were the friend of one and the enemy of others. I have given to each one in my creation what is sufficient for him in all his functions. Therefore whoever knows me in this capacity, and tries to become similar to me by keeping desire apart from his action, his fetters will be loosened, and he will easily be saved and freed.'

This passage reminds one of the definitions of philosophy as *the striving to become as much as possible similar to God*.

Further, Vasudeva speaks in the same book:

'It is desire which causes most men to take refuge with God for their wants. But if you examine their case closely, you will find that they are very far from having an accurate knowledge of him; for God is not apparent to every one, so that he might perceive him with his senses. Therefore they do not know him. Some of them do not pass beyond what their senses perceive; some pass beyond this, but stop at the knowledge of the *laws of nature*, without learning that above them there is one who did not give birth nor was born, the essence of whose being has not been comprehended by the knowledge of any one, while *his* knowledge comprehends everything.'

The Hindus differ among themselves as to the definition of what is *action*. Some who make God the source of action consider him as the universal cause; for as the existence of the *agents* derives from him, he is the cause of their action, and in consequence it is his own action coming into existence through their intermediation. Others do not derive action from God, but from other sources, considering them as the *particular causes* which in the last instance—according to eternal observation—produce the action in question.

In the book *Samkhya* the devotee speaks: 'Has there been a difference of opinion about *action* and the *agent*, or not?'

The sage speaks: 'Some people say that the soul is not alive and the matter not living; that God, who is self-sufficing, is he who unites them and separates them from each other; that therefore in reality he himself is the *agent*. *Action* proceeds from him in such a way that he causes both the soul and the matter to move, like as that which is living and powerful moves that which is dead and weak.

'Others say that the union of *action* and the *agent* is effected by nature, and that such is the usual process in everything that increases and decreases.

'Others say the agent is the soul, because in the Veda it is said, "Every being comes from Purusha." According to others, the agent is time, for the world is tied to time as a sheep is tied to a strong cord, so that its motion depends upon whether the cord is drawn tight or slackened. Still others say that action is nothing but a recompense for something which has been done before.

'All these opinions are wrong. The truth is, that action entirely belongs to matter, for matter binds the soul, causes it to wander about in different shapes, and then sets it free. Therefore matter is the agent, all that belongs to matter helps it to accomplish action. But the soul is not an agent, because it is devoid of the different faculties.'

This is what educated people believe about God. They call him *isvara*, i.e., self-sufficing, beneficent, who gives without receiving. They consider the unity of God as absolute, but that everything beside God which may appear as a unity is really a plurality of things. The existence of God they consider as a real existence, because everything that exists exists through him. It is not impossible to think that the existing beings are *not* and that he *is*, but it is impossible to think that he *is not* and that they *are*.

If we now pass from the ideas of the educated people among the Hindus to those of the common people, we must first state that they present a great variety. Some of them are simply abominable, but similar errors also occur in other religions. Nay, even in Islam we must decidedly disapprove, e.g., of the anthropomorphic doctrines, the teachings of the Jabriyyah sect, the prohibition of the discussion of religious topics, and such like. Every religious sentence destined for the people at large must be carefully worded, as the following example shows. Some Hindu scholar calls God *a point*, meaning to say thereby that the qualities of bodies do not apply to him. Now some uneducated man reads this and imagines, God is as small as *a point*, and he does not find out what the word *point* in this sentence was really intended to express. He will not even stop with this offensive comparison, but will describe God as much larger, and will say, 'He is twelve fingers long and ten fingers broad.' Praise be to God, who is far above measure and number! Further, if an uneducated man hears what we have mentioned, that God comprehends the universe so that nothing is concealed from him, he will at once imagine that this comprehending is effected by means of eyesight; that eyesight is only possible by means of an eye, and that two eyes are better than only one; and in consequence he will describe God as having a thousand eyes meaning to describe his omniscience.

Similar hideous fictions are sometimes met with among the Hindus, especially among those castes who are not allowed to occupy themselves with science, of whom we shall speak hereafter.

On the Nature of Liberation from the World, and on the Path leading Thereto

If the soul is bound up with the world, and its being bound up has a certain cause, it cannot be liberated from this bond save by the opposite of this identical cause. Now according to the Hindus, as we have already explained the reason of the bond is *ignorance*, and therefore it can only be liberated by *knowledge*, by comprehending all things in such a way as to define them both in general and in particular, rendering superfluous any kind of deduction and removing all doubts. For the soul distinguishing between things (τά όντα) by means of definitions, recognizes its own self, and recognizes at the same time that it is its noble lot to last for ever, and that it is the vulgar lot of matter to change and to perish in all kinds of shapes. Then it dispenses with matter, and perceives that that which it held to be good and delightful is in reality bad and painful. In this manner it attains real knowledge and turns away from being arrayed in matter. Thereby action ceases, and both matter and soul become free by separating from each other.

The author of the book of *Patanjali* says: 'The concentration of thought on the unity of God induces man to notice something besides that with which he is occupied. He who wants God, wants the good for the whole creation without a single exception for any reason whatever; but he who occupies himself exclusively with his own self, will for its benefit neither inhale, breathe, nor exhale it (*svasa* and *prasvasa*). When a man attains to this degree, his spiritual power prevails over his bodily power, and then he is gifted with the faculty of doing eight different things by which detachment is realized; for a man can only dispense with that which he is able to do, not with that which is outside his grasp. These eight things are:

1. The faculty in man of making his body so thin that it becomes invisible to the eyes.
2. The faculty of making the body so light that it is indifferent to him whether he treads on thorns or mud or sand.
3. The faculty of making his body so big that it appears in a terrifying miraculous shape.
4. The faculty of realizing every wish.
5. The faculty of knowing whatever he wishes.
6. The faculty of becoming the ruler of whatever religious community he desires.
7. That those over whom he rules are humble and obedient to him.
8. That all distances between a man and any far-away place vanish.'

The terms of the Sufi as to the *knowing* being and his attaining the *stage of knowledge* come to the same effect, for they maintain that he has two souls—an eternal one, not exposed to change and alteration, by which he knows that which is hidden, the transcendental world, and performs wonders; and another, a human soul, which is liable to being changed and being born. From these and similar views the doctrines of the Christians do not much differ.

The Hindus say: 'If a man has the faculty to perform these things, he can dispense with them, and will reach the goal by degrees, passing through several stages:

1. The knowledge of things, as to their names and qualities and distinctions, which, however, does not yet afford the knowledge of definitions.
2. Such a knowledge of things as proceeds as far as the definitions by which particulars are classed under the category of universals, but regarding which a man must still practise distinction.
3. This distinction (*viveka*) disappears, and man comprehends things at once as a whole, but within *time*.
4. This kind of knowledge is raised above *time*, and he who has it can dispense with names and epithets, which are only instruments of human imperfection. In this stage the *intellectus* and the *intelligens* unite with the *intellectum*, so as to be one and the same thing.'

This is what *Patanjali* says about the knowledge which liberates the soul. In Sanskrit they call its liberation *Moksha*—i.e., *the end*. By the same term they call the last contact of the eclipsed and eclipsing bodies, or their separation in both lunar and solar eclipses, because it is *the end* of the eclipse, the moment when the two luminaries which were in contact with each other separate.

According to the Hindus, the organs of the senses have been made for acquiring knowledge, and the pleasure which they afford has been created to stimulate people to research and investigation, as the pleasure which eating and drinking afford to the taste has been created to preserve the individual by means of nourishment. So the pleasure of *coitus* serves to preserve the species by giving birth to new individuals. If there were not special pleasure in these two functions, man and animals would not practise them for these purposes.

In the book *Gita* we read: 'Man is created for the purpose of *knowing*; and because *knowing* is always the same, man has been gifted with the same organs. If man were created for the purpose of *acting*, his organs would be *different*, as actions are *different* in consequence of the difference of the *three primary forces*. However, bodily nature is bent upon *acting* on account of its essential opposition to *knowing*. Besides, it wishes to invest action with *pleasures* which in reality are *pains*. But knowledge is such as to leave this nature behind itself prostrated on the earth like an opponent, and removes all darkness from the soul as an eclipse or clouds are removed from the sun.'

This resembles the opinion of Socrates, who thinks that the soul 'being with the body, and wishing to inquire into something, then is deceived by the body. But by cogitations something of its desires becomes clear to it. Therefore, its cogitation takes place in that time when it is not disturbed by anything like hearing, seeing, or by any pain or pleasure, when it is quite by itself, and has as much as possible quitted the body and its companionship. In particular, the soul of the philosopher scorns the body, and wishes to be separate from it.'

'If we in this our life did not make use of the body, nor had anything in common with it except in cases of necessity, if we were not inoculated with its nature, but were perfectly free from it, we should come near *knowledge* by getting rest from the ignorance of the body, and we should become pure by knowing ourselves as far as God would permit us. And it is only right to acknowledge that this is the truth.'

Now we return and continue our quotation from the book *Gita*.

'Likewise the other organs of the senses serve for acquiring knowledge. The *knowing person* rejoices in turning them to and fro on the field of knowledge, so that they are his spies. The apprehension of the senses is different according to time. The *senses* which serve the heart perceive only that which is present. The heart reflects over that which is present and remembers also the past. The *nature* takes hold of the present, claims it for itself in the past, and prepares to wrestle with it in future. The *reason* understands the nature of a thing, no regard being had of time or date, since past and future are the same for it. Its nearest helpers are *reflection* and *nature*; the most distant are the five senses. When the *senses* bring before reflection some particular object of knowledge, *reflection* cleans it from the errors of the functions of the senses, and hands it over to reason. Thereupon reason makes universal what was before particular, and communicates it to the *soul*. Thus the soul comes to know it.'

Further, the Hindus think that a man becomes *knowing* in one of three ways:

1. By being inspired, not in a certain course of time, but at once, at birth, and in the cradle, as, e.g. the sage Kapila, for he was born knowing and wise.
2. By being inspired after a certain time, like the children of Brahman, for they were inspired when they came of age.
3. By learning, and after a certain course of time, like all men who learn when their mind ripens.

Liberation through knowledge can only be obtained by abstaining from *evil.* The branches of evil are many, but we may classify them as *cupidity*, *wrath*, and *ignorance*. If the roots are cut the branches will wither. And here we have first to consider the rule of the two forces of *cupidity* and *wrath*, which are the greatest and most pernicious enemies of man, deluding him by the pleasure of eating and the delight of revenge, whilst in reality they are much more likely to lead him into pains and crimes. They make a man similar to the wild beasts and the cattle, nay, even to the demons and devils.

Next we have to consider that man must prefer the reasoning force of mind, by which he becomes similar to the highest angels, to the forces of cupidity and wrath; and, lastly, that he must turn away from the actions of the world. He cannot, however, *give up* these actions unless he does away with their causes, which are his lust and ambition. Thereby the second of the *three primary forces* is cut away. However, the abstaining *from action* takes place in two different ways:

1. By laziness, procrastination, and ignorance according to the *third force*. This mode is not desirable, for it will lead to a blamable end.
2. By judicious selection and by preferring that which is better to that which is good, which way leads to a laudable end.

The abstaining from actions is rendered perfect in this way, that a man quits anything that might occupy him and shuts himself up against it. Thereby he will be enabled to restrain his senses from extraneous objects to such a degree that he does not any more know that there exists anything besides himself, and be enabled to stop all motions, and even the breathing. It is evident that a greedy man strains to effect his object, the man who strains becomes tired, and the tired man pants; so the panting is the result of greediness. If this greediness is removed, the breathing becomes like the breathing of a being living at the bottom of the sea, that does not want breath; and then the heart quietly rests on one thing, viz. the search for liberation and for arriving at the absolute unity.

In the book *Gita* we read: 'How is a man to obtain liberation who disperses his heart and does not concentrate it alone upon God, who does not exclusively direct his action towards him? But if a man turns away his cogitation from all other things and concentrates it upon the One, the light of his heart will be steady like the light of a lamp filled with clean oil, standing in a corner where no wind makes it flicker, and he will be occupied in such a degree as not to perceive anything that gives pain, like heat or cold, knowing that everything besides the One, *the Truth*, is a vain phantom.'

In the same book we read: 'Pain and pleasure have no effect on the real world, just as the continuous flow of the streams to the ocean does not affect its water. How could anybody ascend this mountain pass save him who has conquered *cupidity* and *wrath* and rendered them inert?'

On account of what we have explained it is necessary that cogitation should be continuous, not in any way to be defined by number; for a number always denotes *repeated times*, and repeated times presuppose a break in the cogitation occurring between two consecutive times. This would interrupt the continuity, and would prevent cogitation becoming united with the object of cogitation. And this is not the object kept in view, which is, on the contrary, *the continuity of cogitation*.

This goal is attained either in a *single shape*, i.e., a single stage of metempsychosis, or *in several shapes*, in this way, that a man perpetually practises virtuous behaviour and accustoms the soul thereto, so that this virtuous behaviour becomes to it a nature and an essential quality.

Virtuous behaviour is that which is described by the religious law. Its principal laws, from which they derive many secondary ones, may be summed up in the following nine rules:

1. A man shall not kill.
2. Nor lie.
3. Nor steal.
4. Nor whore.
5. Nor hoard up treasures.
6. He is perpetually to practise holiness and purity.
7. He is to perform the prescribed fasting without an interruption and to dress poorly.
8. He is to hold fast to the adoration of God with praise and thanks.
9. He is always to have in mind the word *om*, the word of creation, without pronouncing it.

The injunction to abstain from killing as regards animals (No. 1) is only a special part of the general order to *abstain from doing anything hurtful*. Under this head falls also the robbing of another man's goods (No. 3), and the telling of lies (No. 2), not to mention the foulness and baseness of so doing.

The abstaining from hoarding up (No. 5) means that a man is to give up toil and fatigue; that he who seeks the bounty of God feels sure that he is provided for; and that, starting from the base slavery of material life, we may, by the noble liberty of cogitation, attain eternal bliss.

Practising purity (No. 6) implies that a man knows the filth of the body, and that he feels called upon to hate it, and to love cleanness of soul. Tormenting oneself by poor dress (No. 7) means that a man should reduce the body, allay its feverish desires, and sharpen its senses. Pythagoras once said to a man who took great care to keep his body in a flourishing condition and to allow it everything it desired, 'Thou art not lazy in building thy prison and making thy fetter as strong as possible.'

The holding fast to meditation on God and the angels means a kind of familiar intercourse with them. The book *Samkhya* says: 'Man cannot go beyond anything in the wake of which he marches, it being a scope to him (i.e., thus engrossing his thoughts and detaining him from meditation on God).' The book *Gita* says: 'All that which is the object of a man's continuous meditating and bearing in mind is stamped upon him, so that he even unconsciously is guided by it. Since, now, the time of health is the time of remembering what we love, the soul on leaving the body is united with that object which we love, and is changed into it.'

However, the reader must not believe that it is only the union of the soul with any forms of life that perish and return into existence that is perfect *liberation*, for the same book, *Gita*, says: 'He who knows when dying that God is everything, and that from him everything proceeds, *is liberated*, though his degree be lower than that of the saints.'

The same book says: 'Seek deliverance from this world by abstaining from any connection with its follies, by having sincere intentions in all actions and when making offerings by fire to God, without any desire for reward and recompense; further, by keeping aloof from mankind.' The real meaning of all this is that you should not prefer one because he is your friend to another because he is your enemy, and that you should beware of negligence in sleeping when others are awake, and in waking when others are asleep; for this, too, is a kind of being *absent* from them, though outwardly you are *present* with them. Further: Seek deliverance by guarding soul from soul, for the soul is an enemy if it be addicted to lusts; but what an excellent friend it is when it is *chaste*!'

Socrates, caring little for his impending death and being glad at the prospect of coming to his Lord, said: 'My degree must not be considered by any one of you lower than that of the swan', of which people say that it is the bird of Apollo, the sun, and that it therefore knows what is hidden; that is, when feeling that it will soon die, sings more and more melodies from joy at the prospect of coming to its Lord. 'At least my joy at my prospect of coming to the object of my adoration must not be less than the joy of this bird.'

For similar reasons the Sufi defines *love* as being engrossed by the creature to the exclusion of God.

In the book of *Patanjali* we read: 'We divide the path of liberation into three parts:

'I. *The practical one* (*kriya-yoga*): a process of habituating the senses in a gentle way to detach themselves from the external world, and to concentrate themselves upon the internal one, so that they exclusively occupy themselves with God. This is in general the path of him who does not desire anything save what is sufficient to sustain life.'

In the book *Vishnu-Dharma* we read: 'The king Parikisha, of the family of Bhrigu, asked Satanika, the head of an assembly of sages, who stayed with him, for the explanation of some notion regarding the deity, and by way of answer the sage communicated what *he* had heard from Saunaka, Saunaka from Usanas, and Usanas from Brahman, as follows: 'God is without first and without last; he has not been born from anything, and he has not borne anything save that of which it is impossible to say that it is *He*, and just as impossible to say that it is *Not-he*. How should I be able to ponder on the absolute good which is an outflow of his benevolence, and of the absolute bad which is a product of his wrath; and how could I know him so as to worship him as is his due, save by turning away from the world in general and by occupying myself exclusively with him, by perpetually cogitating on him?'

'It was objected to him: 'Man is weak and his life is a trifling matter. He can hardly bring himself to abstain from the necessities of life, and this prevents him from walking on the path of liberation. If we were living in the *first* age of mankind, when life extended to thousands of years, and when the world was good because of the non-existence of evil, we might hope that that which is necessary on this path should be done. But since we live in the *last* age, what, according to your opinion, is there in this revolving world that might protect him against the floods of the ocean and save him from drowning?'

'Thereupon Brahman spoke: 'Man wants nourishment, shelter, and clothing. Therefore in *them* there is no harm to him. But happiness is only to be found in abstaining from things besides them, from superfluous and fatiguing actions. Worship God, him alone, and venerate him; approach him in the place of worship with presents like perfumes and flowers; praise him and attach your heart to him so that it never leaves him. Give alms to the Brahmans and to others, and vow to God vows—special ones, like the abstaining from meat; general ones, like fasting. Vow to him animals which you must not hold to be something different from yourselves, so as to feel entitled to kill them. Know that he is everything. Therefore, whatever you do, let it be for his sake; and if you enjoy anything of the vanities of the world, do not forget him in your intentions. If you aim at the fear of God and the faculty of worshipping him, thereby you will obtain liberation, not by anything else."

The book *Gita* says: 'He who mortifies his lust does not go beyond the necessary wants; and he who is content with that which is sufficient for the sustaining of life will not be ashamed nor be despised.'

The same book says: 'If man is not without wants as regards the demands of human nature, if he wants nourishment to appease thereby the heat of hunger and exhaustion, sleep in order to meet the injurious influences of fatiguing motions and a couch to rest upon, let the latter be clean and smooth, everywhere equally high above the ground and sufficiently large that he may stretch out his body upon it. Let him have a place of temperate climate, not hurtful by cold nor by heat, and where he is safe against the approach of reptiles. All this helps him to sharpen the functions of his heart, that he may without any interruption concentrate his cogitation on the unity. For all things besides the necessities of life in the way of eating and clothing are pleasures of a kind which, in reality, are disguised pains. To acquiesce in them is impossible, and would end in the gravest inconvenience. There is pleasure only to him who kills the two intolerable enemies, *lust* and *wrath*, already during his life and not when he dies, who derives his rest and bliss from within, not from without; and who, in the final result, is able altogether to dispense with his senses.'

Vasudeva spoke to Arjuna: 'If you want the absolute good, take care of the nine doors of thy body, and know what is going in and out through them. Constrain thy heart from dispersing its thoughts, and quiet thy soul by thinking of the upper membrane of the child's brain, which is first soft, and then is closed and becomes strong, so that it would seem that there were no more need of it. Do not take perception of the senses for anything but the nature immanent in their organs, and therefore beware of following it.'

II. The second part of the path of liberation is renunciation (the *via omissionis*), based on the knowledge of the evil which exists in the changing things of creation and their vanishing shapes. In consequence the heart shuns them, the longing for them ceases, and a man is raised above the *three primary forces* which are the cause of actions and of their diversity. For he who accurately understands the affairs of the world knows that the good ones among them are evil in reality, and that the bliss which they afford changes in the course of recompense into pains. Therefore he avoids everything which might aggravate his condition of being entangled in the world, and which might result in making him stay in the world for a still longer period.

The book *Gita* says: 'Men err in what is ordered and what is forbidden. They do not know how to distinguish between good and evil in actions. Therefore, giving up acting altogether and keeping aloof from it, this is *the* action.'

The same book says: 'The purity of knowledge is high above the purity of all other things, for by knowledge ignorance is rooted out and certainty is gained in exchange for doubt, which is a means of torture, for there is no rest for him who doubts.'

It is evident from this that the first part of the path of liberation is instrumental to the second one.

III. The third part of the path of liberation which is to be considered as instrumental to the preceding two is *worship*, for this purpose, that God should help a man to obtain liberation, and deign to consider him worthy of such a shape of existence in the metempsychosis in which he may effect his progress towards beatitude.

The author of the book *Gita* distributes the duties of worship among the *body*, the *voice*, and the *heart*.

What the *body* has to do is fasting, prayer, the fulfilment of the law, the service towards the angels and the sages among the Brahmans, keeping clean the body, keeping aloof from killing under all circumstances, and never looking at another man's wife and other property.

What the *voice* has to do is the reciting of the holy texts, praising God, always to speak the truth, to address people mildly, to guide them, and to order them to do good.

What the *heart* has to do is to have straight, honest intentions, to avoid haughtiness, always to be patient, to keep your senses under control, and to have a cheerful mind.

The author (Patanjali) adds to the three parts of the path of liberation a fourth one of an illusory nature, called *Rasayana*, consisting of alchemistic tricks with various drugs, intended to realize things which by nature are impossible. We shall speak of these things afterwards (*vide* Chap. xvii). They have no other relation to the theory of *Moksha* but this, that also in the tricks of Rasayana everything depends upon the intention, the well-understood determination to carry them out, this determination resting on the firm belief in them, and resulting in the endeavour to realize them.

According to the Hindus, liberation is union with God; for they describe God as a being who can dispense with hoping for a recompense or with fearing opposition, unattainable to thought, because he is sublime beyond all unlikeness which is abhorrent and all likeness which is sympathetic, knowing himself not by a knowledge which comes to him like an accident, regarding something which had not in every phase before been known to him. And this same description the Hindus apply to *the liberated one*, for he is equal to God in all these things except in the matter of beginning, since he has not existed from all eternity, and except this, that before liberation he existed in *the world of entanglement*, knowing the objects of knowledge only by a phantasmagoric kind of knowing which he had acquired by absolute exertion, whilst the object of his knowing is still covered, as it were, by a veil. On the contrary, in the world of liberation all veils are lifted, all covers taken off, and obstacles removed. There the being is absolutely knowing, not desirous of learning anything unknown, separated from the soiled perceptions of the senses, united with the everlasting ideas. Therefore in the end of the book of *Patanjali*, after the pupil has asked about the nature of liberation, the master says: 'If you wish, say, Liberation is the cessation of the functions of *the three forces*, and their returning to that home whence they had come. Or if you wish, say, It is the return of the soul as a *knowing* being into its own nature.'

The two men, pupil and master, disagree regarding him who has arrived at the stage of liberation. The anchorite asks in the book of *Samkhya*, 'Why does not *death* take place when *action* ceases?' The sage replies, 'Because the cause of the separation is a certain condition of the soul whilst the spirit is still in the body. Soul and body are separated by a natural condition which severs their union. Frequently when the cause of an effect has already ceased or disappeared, the effect itself still goes on for a certain time, slackening, and by and by decreasing, till in the end it ceases totally; e.g., the silk-weaver drives round his wheel with his mallet until it whirls round rapidly, then he leaves it; however, it does not stand still, though the mallet that drove it round has been removed; the motion of the wheel decreases by little and little, and finally it ceases. It is the same case with the body. After the action of the body has ceased, its effect is still lasting until it arrives, through the various stages of motion and of rest, at the cessation of physical force and of the effect which had originated from preceding causes. Thus liberation is finished when the body has been completely prostrated.'

In the book of *Patanjali* there is a passage which expresses similar ideas. Speaking of a man who restrains his senses and organs of perception, as the turtle draws in its limbs when it is afraid, he says that 'he is not fettered, because the fetter has been loosened, and he is not liberated, because his body is still with him.'

There is, however, another passage in the same book which does not agree with the theory of liberation as expounded above. He says: 'The bodies are the snares of the souls for the purpose of acquiring recompense. He who arrives at the stage of liberation has acquired, in his actual form of existence, the recompense for all the doings of the past. Then he ceases to labour to acquire a title to a recompense in the future. He frees himself from the snare; he can dispense with the particular form of his existence, and moves in it quite freely without being ensnared by it. He has even the faculty of moving wherever he likes, and if he like, he might rise above the face of death. For the thick, cohesive bodies cannot oppose an obstacle to his *form* of existence (as, e.g., a mountain could not prevent him from passing through). How then, could his body oppose an obstacle to his soul?'

Similar views are also met with among the Sufi. Some Sufi author relates the following story: 'A company of Sufis came down unto us, and sat down at some distance from us. Then one of them rose, prayed, and on having finished his prayer, turned towards me and spoke: "O master, do you know here a place fit for us *to die* on?" Now I thought he meant *sleeping*, and so I pointed out to him a place. The man went there, threw himself on the back of his head, and remained motionless. Now I rose, went to him and shook him, but lo! he was already cold.'

The Sufi explains the Quranic verse, 'We have made room for him on earth' (Sūra 18, 83), in this way: 'If he wishes, the earth rolls itself up for him; if he wishes, he can walk on the water and in the air, which offer him sufficient resistance so as to enable him to walk, whilst the mountains do not offer him any resistance when he wants to pass through them.'

We next speak of those who, notwithstanding their greatest exertions, do not reach the stage of liberation. There are several classes of them. The book *Samkhya* says: 'He who enters upon the world with a virtuous character, who is liberal with what he possesses of the goods of the world, is recompensed in it in this way, that he obtains the fulfilment of his wishes and desires, that he moves about in the world in happiness, happy in body and soul and in all other conditions of life. For in reality good fortune is a recompense for former deeds, done either in the same shape or in some preceding shape. Whoso lives in this world piously but without knowledge will be raised and be rewarded, but not be liberated, because the means of attaining it are wanting in his case. Whoso is content and acquiesces in possessing the faculty of practising the above-mentioned eight commandments (*sic, vide*), whoso glories in them is successful by means of them, and believes that *they* are liberation, will remain in the same stage.'

The following is a parable characterizing those who vie with each other in the progress through the various stages of knowledge: A man is travelling together with his pupils for some business or other towards the end of the night. Then there appears something standing erect before them on the road, the nature of which it is impossible to recognize on account of the darkness of night. The man turns towards his pupils, and asks them, one after the other, what it is? The first says: 'I do not know what it is.' The second says: 'I do not know, and I have no means of learning what it is.' The third says: 'It is useless to examine what it is, for the rising of the day will reveal it. If it is something terrible, it will disappear at daybreak; if it is something else, the nature of the thing will anyhow be clear to us.' Now, none of them had attained to knowledge, the first, because he was ignorant; the second, because he was incapable, and had no means of knowing; the third, because he was indolent and acquiesced in his ignorance.

The fourth pupil, however, did not give an answer. He stood still, and then he went on in the direction of the object. On coming near, he found that it was pumpkins on which there lay a tangled mass of something. Now he knew that a living man, endowed with free will, does not stand still in his place until such a tangled mass is formed on his head, and he recognized at once that it was a lifeless object standing erect. Further, he could not be sure if it was not a hidden place for some dunghill. So he went quite close to it, struck against it with his foot till it fell to the ground. Thus all doubt having been removed, he returned to his master and gave him the exact account. In such a way the master obtained the knowledge through the intermediation of his pupils.

With regard to similar views of the ancient Greeks we can quote Ammonius, who relates the following as a sentence of Pythagoras: 'Let your desire and exertion in this world be directed towards the union with *the First Cause*, which is the cause of the cause of your existence that you may endure forever. You will be saved from destruction and from being wiped out; you will go to the world of the true sense, of the true joy, of the true glory, in everlasting joy and pleasures.'

Further, Pythagoras says: 'How can you hope for the state of detachment as long as you are clad in bodies? And how will you obtain liberation as long as you are incarcerated in them?'

Ammonius relates: 'Empedocles and his successors as far as Heracles (*sic*) think that the soiled souls always remain commingled with the world until they ask the universal soul for help. The universal soul intercedes for it with the *Intelligence*, the latter with the Creator. The Creator affords something of his light to Intelligence; Intelligence affords something of it to the universal soul, which is immanent in this world. Now the soul wishes to be enlightened by Intelligence, until at last the individual soul recognizes the universal soul, unites with it, and is attached to its world. But this is a process over which many ages must pass. Then the soul comes to a region where there is neither place nor time, nor anything of that which is in the world, like transient fatigue or joy.'

Socrates says: 'The soul on leaving space wanders to the holiness (*τύ καθαρόν*) which lives for ever and exists eternally, being related to it. It becomes like holiness in duration, because it is by means of something like contact able to receive impressions from holiness. This, its susceptibility to impressions, is called *Intelligence*.'

Further, Socrates says: 'The soul is very similar to the divine substance which does not die nor dissolve, and is the only *intelligible* which lasts for ever; the body is the contrary of it. When soul and body unite, nature orders body to serve, the soul to rule; but when they separate, the soul goes to another place than that to which the body goes. There it is happy with things that are suitable to it; it reposes from being circumscribed in space, rests from folly, impatience, love, fear, and other human evils, on this condition, that it had always been pure and hated the body. If, however, it has sullied itself by connivance with the body, by serving and loving it so that the body was subservient to its lusts and desires, in this case it does not experience anything more real than the species of bodily things (*τύ σωμάτοεεδές*) and the contact with them.'

Proclus says: 'The body in which the rational soul dwells has received the figure of a globe, like the ether and its individual beings. The body in which both the rational and the irrational souls dwell has received an erect figure like man. The body in which only the irrational soul dwells has received a figure erect and curved at the same time, like that of the irrational animals. The body in which there is neither the one nor the other, in which there is nothing but the nourishing power, has received an erect figure, but it is at the same time curved and turned upside down, so that the head is planted in the earth, as is the case with the plants. The latter direction being the contrary to that of man, man is a heavenly tree, the root of which is directed toward its home, i.e. heaven, whilst the root of vegetables is directed towards *their* home, i.e., the earth.'

The Hindus hold similar views about nature. Arjuna asks, 'What is Brahman like in this world?' Whereupon Vasudeva answers, 'Imagine him like an *Asvattha* tree.' This is a huge precious tree, well known among them, standing upside down, the roots being above, the branches below. If it has ample nourishment, it becomes quite enormous; the branches spread far, cling to the soil, and creep into it. Roots and branches above and below resemble each other to such a degree that it is difficult to say which is which.

'Brahman is the upper roots of this tree, its trunk is the Veda, its branches are the different doctrines and schools, its leaves are the different modes of interpretation; its nourishment comes from *the three forces*; the tree becomes strong and compact through the senses. The intelligent being has no other keen desire but that of felling this tree, i.e., abstaining from the world and its vanities. When he has succeeded in felling it, he wishes to settle in the place where it has grown, a place in which there is no returning in a further stage of metempsychosis. When he obtains this, he leaves behind himself all the pains of heat and cold, and coming from the light of sun and moon and common fires, he attains to the divine lights.'

The doctrine of *Patanjali* is akin to that of the Sufi regarding being occupied in meditation on *the Truth* (i.e., God), for they say, 'As long as you point to something, you are not a *monist*, but when *the Truth* seizes upon the object of your pointing and annihilates it, then there is no longer an indicating person nor an object indicated.'

There are some passages in their system which show that they believe in the pantheistic union; e.g., one of them, being asked what is *the Truth* (God), gave the following answer: 'How should I not know the being which is *I* in essence and *Not-I* in space? If I return once more into existence, thereby I am separated from him; and if I am neglected (i.e., not born anew and sent into the world), thereby I become light and become accustomed to the *union*' (*sic*).

Abū Bakr al-Shiblī says: 'Cast off all, and you will attain to us completely. Then you will exist; but you will not report about us to others as long as your doing is like ours.'

Abū Yazīd al-Basṭāmī once being asked how he had attained *his* stage in Sufism, answered: 'I cast off my own self as a serpent casts off its skin. Then I considered my own self and found that *I* was *He*', i.e., God.

The Sufi explain the Quranic passage (Sūra 2, 68), '*Then we spoke: Beat him with a part of her*', in the following manner: 'The order to kill that which is dead in order to give life to it indicates that the heart does not become alive by the lights of knowledge unless the body be killed by ascetic practice to such a degree that it does not any more exist as a reality, but only in a formal way, whilst your heart is a reality on which no object of the formal world has any influence.'

Further they say: 'Between man and God there are a thousand stages of light and darkness. Men exert themselves to pass through darkness to light, and when they have attained to the stations of light, there is no return for them.'

On the Different Classes of Created Beings, and on Their Names

The subject of this chapter is very difficult to study and understand accurately, since we Muslims look at it from without, and the Hindus themselves do not work it out to scientific perfection. As we, however, want it for the further progress of this treatise, we shall communicate all we have heard of it until the date of the present book. And first we give an extract from the book *Samkhya.*

'The anchorite spoke: "How many classes and species are there of living bodies?"

'The sage replied: "There are three classes of them—the spiritual ones in the height, men in the middle, and animals in the depth. Their species are fourteen in number, eight of which belong to the spiritual beings: Brahman, Indra, Prajapati, Saumya, Gandharva, Yaksha, Rakshasa, and Pisaca. Five species are those of the animals—cattle, wild beasts, birds, creeping things, and *growing things*, i.e., the trees. And, lastly, *one* species is represented by man."'

The author of the same book has in another part of it given the following enumeration with different names: 'Brahman, Indra, Prajapati, Gandharva, Yaksha, Rakshasa, Pitaras, Pisaca.'

The Hindus are people who rarely preserve one and the same order of things, and in their enumeration of things there is much that is arbitrary. They use or invent numbers of names, and who is to hinder or to control them?

In the book *Gita*, Vasudeva says: 'When the *first* of the *three primary forces* prevails, it particularly applies itself to developing the intellect, purifying the senses, and producing *action* for the angels. Blissful rest is one of the consequences of this force, and liberation one of its results.

'When the *second* force prevails, it particularly applies itself to developing cupidity. It will lead to fatigue, and induce to actions for the Yaksha and Rakshasa. In this case the recompense will be according to the action.

'If the *third* force prevails, it particularly applies itself to developing ignorance, and making people easily beguiled by their own wishes. Finally, it produces wakefulness, carelessness, laziness, procrastination in fulfilling duties, and sleeping too long. If man acts, he acts for the classes of the Bhuta and Pisaca, the devils, for the Preta who carry the spirits in the air, not in paradise and not in hell. Lastly, this force will lead to punishment; man will be lowered from the stage of humanity, and will be changed into animals and plants.'

In another place the same author says: 'Belief and virtue are in the Deva among the spiritual beings. Therefore that man who resembles them believes in God, clings to him, and longs for him. Unbelief and vice are in the demons called Asura and Rakshasa. That man who resembles them does not believe in God nor attend to his commandments. He tries to make the world godless, and is occupied with things which are harmful in this world and in the world beyond, and are of no use.'

If we now combine these statements with each other, it will be evident that there is some confusion both in the names and in their order. According to the most popular view of the majority of the Hindus, there are the following eight classes of *spiritual* beings:

1. The *Deva*, or angels, to whom the north belongs. They specially belong to the Hindus. People say that Zoroaster made enemies of the Shamaniyya or Buddhists by calling the devils by the name of the class of angels which *they* consider the highest, i.e., *Deva*. And this usage has been transmitted from Magian times down to the Persian language of our days.
2. *Daitya'danava*, the demons who live in the south. To them everybody belongs who opposes the religion of the Hindus and persecutes the cows. Notwithstanding the near relationship which exists between them and the Deva, there is, as Hindus maintain, no end of quarrelling and fighting among them.
3. *Gandharva*, the musicians and singers who make music before the Deva. Their harlots are called Apsaras.
4. *Yaksha*, the treasurers or guardians of the Deva.
5. *Rakshasa*, demons of ugly and deformed shapes.
6. *Kinnara*, having human shapes but horses' heads, being the contrary of the centaurs of the Greek, of whom the lower half has the shape of a horse, the upper half that of a man. The latter figure is that of the Zodiacal sign of Arcitenens.
7. *Naga*, beings in the shape of serpents.
8. *Vidyadhara*, demon-sorcerers, who exercise a certain witchcraft, but not such a one as to produce permanent results.

If we consider this series of beings, we find the angelic power at the upper end and the demoniac at the lower, and between them there is much interblending. The qualities of these beings are different, inasmuch as they have attained this stage of life in the course of metempsychosis by *action*, and actions are different on account of the *three primary forces*. They live very long, since they have entirely stripped off the bodies, since they are free from all exertion, and are able to do things which are impossible to man. They serve man in whatever he desires, and are near him in cases of need.

However, we can learn from the extract from *Samkhya* that this view is not correct. For Brahman, Indra, and Prajapati are not names of species, but of individuals. Brahman and Prajapati very nearly mean the same, but they bear different names on account of some quality or other. Indra is the ruler of the worlds. Besides, Vasudevae numerates the Yaksha and Rakshasa together in one and the same class of demons, whilst the Puranas represent the Yaksha as guardian angels and the servants of guardian-angels.

After all this, we declare that the spiritual beings which we have mentioned are one category, who have attained their present stage of existence by action during the time when they were human beings. They have left their bodies behind them, for bodies are weights which impair the power and shorten the duration of life. Their qualities and conditions are different, in the same measure as one or other of the *three primary forces* prevails over them. The first force is peculiar to the Deva, or angels who live in quietness and bliss. The predominant faculty of their mind is the comprehending of an idea *without matter*, as it is the predominant faculty of the mind of man to comprehend the idea *in matter*.

The *third force* is peculiar to the Pisaca and Bhuta, whilst the second is peculiar to the classes between them.

The Hindus say that the number of Deva is thirty-three *koti* or *crore*, of which eleven belong to Mahadeva. Therefore this number is one of his surnames, and his name itself (Mahadeva) points in this direction. The sum of the number of angels just mentioned would be 330,000,000.

Further, they represent the Deva as eating and drinking, cohabiting, living and dying, since they exist within matter, though in the most subtle and most simple kind of it, and since they have attained this by action, not by knowledge. The book *Patanjali* relates that Nandikesvara offered many sacrifices to Mahadeva, and was in consequence transferred into paradise in his human shape; that Indra, the ruler, had intercourse with the wife of Nahusha the Brahmin, and therefore was changed into a serpent by way of punishment.

After the Deva comes the class of the *Pitaras*, the deceased ancestors, and after them the *Bhuta*, human beings who have attached themselves to the *spiritual beings* (Deva), and stand in the middle between them and mankind. He who holds this degree, but without being free from the body, is called either *Rishi* or *Siddha* or *Muni*, and these differ among themselves according to their qualities. *Siddha* is he who has attained by his action the faculty to do in the world whatever he likes, but who does not aspire further, and does not exert himself on the path leading to liberation. He may ascend to the degree of a Rishi. If a Brahmin attains this degree, he is called *Brahmarshi*; if the Kshatriya attains it, he is called *Rajarshi*. It is not possible for the lower classes to attain this degree. Rishis are the sages who, though they are only human beings, excel the angels on account of their knowledge. Therefore the angels learn from them, and above them there is none but Brahman.

After the Brahmarshi and Rajarshi come those classes of the populace which exist also among us, the castes, to whom we shall devote a separate chapter.

All these latter beings are ranged under matter. Now, as regards the notion of that which is above matter, we say that the ιύλη is the middle between matter and the spiritual divine ideas that are above matter, and that the *three primary forces* exist in the ϋλη dynamically (ἐν δυνάμει). So the ϋλη, with all that is comprehended in it, is a bridge from above to below.

Any life which circulates in the ϋλη under the exclusive influence of the *First Cause* is called *Brahman*, *Prajapati*, and by many other names which occur in their religious law and tradition. It is identical with nature in so far as it is active, for all bringing into existence, the creation of the world also, is attributed by them to Brahman.

Any life which circulates in the ὕλη under the influence of the *second force* is called *Narayana* in the tradition of the Hindus, which means nature in so far as it has reached the end of its action, and is now striving to preserve that which has been produced. Thus Narayana strives so to arrange the world that it should endure.

Any life which circulates in the ὕλη under the influence of the *third force* is called *Mahadeva* and *Samkara*, but his best-known name is *Rudra*. His work is destruction and annihilation, like nature in the last stages of activity, when its power slackens.

These three beings bear different names, as they circulate through the various degrees to above and below, and accordingly their actions are different.

But prior to all these beings there is one source whence everything is derived, and in this unity they comprehend all three things, no more separating one from the other. This unity they call *Vishnu*, a name which more properly designates the *middle force*; but sometimes they do not even make a distinction between this *middle force* and the *first cause* (i.e. they make Narayana the *causa causarum*).

Here there is an analogy between Hindus and Christians, as the latter distinguish between the Three *Persons* and give them separate names, Father, Son, and Holy Ghost, but unite them into one substance.

This is what clearly results from a careful examination of the Hindu doctrines. Of their traditional accounts, which are full of silly notions, we shall speak hereafter in the course of our explanation. You must not wonder if the Hindus, in their stories about the class of the Deva, whom we have explained as *angels*, allow them all sorts of things, unreasonable in themselves, some perhaps not objectionable, others decidedly objectionable, both of which the theologians of Islam would declare to be incompatible with the dignity and nature of angels.

If you compare these traditions with those of the Greeks regarding their own religion, you will cease to find the Hindu system strange. We have already mentioned that they called the angels gods. Now consider their stories about Zeus, and you will understand the truth of our remark. As for anthropomorphisms and traits of animal life which they attribute to him, we give the following tradition: 'When he was born, his father wanted to devour him; but his mother took a stone, wrapped rags round it, and gave him the stone to swallow, whereupon he went away.' This is also mentioned by Galenus in his *Book of Speeches*, where he relates that Philo had in an enigmatical way described the preparation of the λώνειον φάρμακον in a poem of his by the following words:

'Take red hair, diffusing sweet odour, the offering to the gods,
And of man's blood weigh weights of the number of the mental faculties.'

The poet means *five* pounds of saffron, because the senses are *five*. The weights of the other ingredients of the mixture he describes in similar enigmatic terms, of which Galenus gives a commentary. In the same poem occurs the following verse:

'And of the pseudonymous root which has grown in the district in which Zeus was born.'

To which Galenus adds: 'This is *Andropogon Nardus*, which *bears a false name*, because it is called *an ear* of corn, although it is not an ear, but a root. The poet prescribes that it should be Cretan, because the mythologists relate that Zeus was born on the mountain Δικταίον in Creta, where his mother concealed him from his father Koronos, that he should not devour him as he had devoured others.'

Besides, well-known story-books tell that he married certain women one after the other, cohabited with others, doing violence to them and not marrying them; among them Europa, the daughter of Phoenix, who was taken from him by Asterios, king of Crete. Afterwards she gave birth to two children from him, Minos and Rhadamanthus. This happened long before the Israelites left the desert and entered Palestine.

Another tradition is that he died in Crete, and was buried there at the time of Samson the Israelite, being 780 years of age; that he was called *Zeus* when he had become old, after he had formerly been called *Dios*; and that the first who gave him this name was Cecrops, the first king of Athens. It was common to all of them to indulge in their lusts without any restraint, and to favour the business of the pander; and so far they were not unlike Zoroaster and King Gushtāsp when they desired to consolidate the realm and the rule (*sic*).

Chroniclers maintain that Cecrops and his successors are the source of all the vices among the Athenians, meaning thereby such things as occur in the story of Alexander, *viz.* that Nectanebus, king of Egypt, after having fled before Artaxerxes the Black and hiding in the capital of Macedonia, occupied himself with astrology and soothsaying; that he beguiled Olympias, the wife of King Philip, who was absent. He cunningly contrived to cohabit with her, showing himself to her in the figure of the god Ammon, as a serpent with two heads like rams' heads. So she became pregnant with Alexander. Philip, on returning, was about to disclaim the paternity, but then he dreamt that it was the child of the god Ammon. Thereupon he recognized the child as his, and spoke, 'Man cannot oppose the gods.' The combination of the stars had shown to Nectanebus that he would die at the hands of his *son*. When then he died at the hands of Alexander from a wound in the neck, he recognized that he was his (Alexander's) father.

The tradition of the Greeks is full of similar things. We shall relate similar subjects when speaking of the marriages of the Hindus.

Now we return to our subject. Regarding that part of the nature of Zeus which has no connection with humanity, the Greeks say that he is Jupiter, the son of Saturn; for Saturn alone is eternal, not having been born, according to the philosophers of the Academy, as Galenus says in the *Book of Deduction*. This is sufficiently proved by the book of Aratos on the φαινόμενα, for he begins with the praise of Zeus:

'We, mankind, do not leave him, nor can we do without him;
Of him the roads are full,
And the meeting-places of men.
He is mild towards them;
He produces for them what they wish, and incites them to work.
Reminding them of the necessities of life,
He indicates to them the times favourable
For digging and ploughing for a good growth,
Who has raised the signs and stars in heaven.
Therefore we humiliate ourselves before him first and last.'

And then he praises the spiritual beings (the Muses). If you compare Greek theology with that of the Hindus, you will find that Brahman is described in the same way as Zeus by Aratos.

The author of the commentary on the φαινόμενα of Aratos maintains that he deviated from the custom of the poets of his time in beginning with the gods; that it was his intention to speak of the celestial sphere. Further, he makes reflections on the origin of Asclepius, like Galenus, and says: 'We should like to know which Zeus Aratos meant, the mystical or the physical one. For the poet Krates called the celestial sphere *Zeus*, and likewise Homer says: "As pieces of snow are cut off from *Zeus*."'

Aratos calls the ether and the air *Zeus* in the passage: 'The roads and the meeting-places are full of him, and we all must inhale him.'

Therefore the philosophers of the Stoa maintain that Zeus is the spirit which is dispersed in the ὕλη and similar to our souls, i.e. the nature which rules every natural body. The author supposes that he is mild, since he is the cause of the good; therefore he is right in maintaining that he has not only created men, but also the gods.

QUESTIONS AND ANSWERS
From *al-As'ilah wa'l-ajwibah*

Reprinted from *al-As'ilah wa'l-ajwibah,* tr. Rafik Berjak and Muzaffar Iqbal as 'Ibn Sīnā–al-Bīrūnī Correspondence', *Islam and Science*, 49 (June, 2003), pp. 1–14.[1]

In the name of Allah the Most Merciful the Most Compassionate

1. The Grand Master, Abū ʿAlī al-Ḥusayn Abū ʿAbdallāh Ibn Sīnā—may Allah grant him mercy—said, All Praise is for Allah, the Sustainer of the worlds, He suffices and He is the best Disposer of affairs, the Granter of victory, the Supporter. And Allah's blessings be upon our master Muḥammad and upon his family and all his companions, and now to begin:

2. This letter is in response to the questions sent to him by Abū Rayḥān al-Bīrūnī from Khwārazm. May Allah surround you with all you wish for, and may He grant you all you hope for and bestow on you happiness in this life, and hereafter, and save you from all you dislike in both lives. You requested—may Allah prolong your safety—a clarification about matters some of which you consider worthy to be traced back to Aristotle, of which he spoke in his book, *al-Samā' wa'l-ʿālam* (3) and some of which you have found to be problematic. I began to explain and clarify these briefly and concisely, but some pressing matters inhibited me from elaborating on each topic as it deserves. Further, the sending of the response to you was delayed, awaiting al-Maʿsūmi's dispatch of the letter to you. Now, I would restate your questions in your own words, and then follow each question with a brief answer.

3. The first question: You asked—may Allah keep you happy—why Aristotle asserted that the heavenly bodies have neither levity nor gravity and why did he deny absence of motion from and to the centre. We can assume that since the heaven is among the heaviest bodies—and that is an assumption, not a certainty—it does not require a movement to the centre because of a universal law that applies to all its parts judged as similar. If every part had a natural movement toward the centre, and the parts were all connected, then it would result in a cessation (*wuqūf*) [of

1. For a detailed note on 'questions and answers' as a technique used extensively in the Islamic intellectual tradition, see H. Daiber, 'Masā'il wa-Adjwiba', *EI2*, vol. 6, pp. 636–639, where Daiber mentions that 'the oldest Islamic question-answer literature endeavours to solve philological and textual problems.' He cites the correspondence between Ibn Sīnā and al-Bīrūnī on the basis of 1974 Turkish edition of the correspondence, Ulken, ed., *Ibn Sīnā risaleleri,* vol. 2, pp. 2–9; M. Türker, ed., *Beyruni'ye armagan* (Ankara, 1974), pp. 103–112. Daiber also cites numerous other examples of correspondence literature. It is also relevant to note that at the time when this correspondence took place, the technique of *reductio ad absurdum* used by Ibn Sīnā in his response to al-Bīrūnī had already become a refined tool in this literature.

all motion] at the centre. Likewise, we can assume that the heaven is among the lightest of all bodies, this would not necessitate (i) a movement from the centre until its parts have separated and (ii) the existence of a vacuum outside the heaven. And if the nonexistence of a vacuum outside the heaven is an established fact, then the heaven will be a composite body like fire. [And you also say] that the circular movement of the heaven, though possible, might not be natural like the natural movement of the planets to the east [which] is countered by a necessary and forceful movement to the west. If it is said that this movement is not countered because there is no contradiction between the circular movements and there is no dispute about their directions, then it is just deception and argument for the sake of argument, because it cannot be imagined that one thing has two natural movements, one to the east and one to the west. And this is nothing but a semantic dispute with agreement on the meaning, because you cannot name the movement toward the west as opposite of the movement to the east. And this is a given; even if we do not agree on the semantics, let us deal with the meaning.

4. The answer: May Allah keep you happy, you have saved me the trouble of proving that heaven has neither levity nor gravity, because in your prelude you have accepted that there is no place above heaven to where it can move, and it cannot, likewise, move below because all its parts are connected. I say it is also not possible for it to move down, nor is there a natural place below it to where it can move, and even if it were separated—and we can make the assumption that it is separated—it would result in the movement of all the elements from their natural positions and this is not permissible, neither by the divine nor by the natural laws. And that would also establish a vacuum which is not permissible in the natural laws. Therefore, heaven does not have a natural position below or above to which it can move in actuality (*bi'l-fi'l*) or in being, neither is it in the realm of possibility (*bi'l-imkān*) or imagination (*bi'l-wahm*) because that would lead to unacceptable impossibilities we have mentioned, I mean the movement of all the elements from their natural positions or the existence of a vacuum.

5. There is nothing more absurd than what cannot be proved to exist either by actuality or by possibility or imagination. If we accept this, it follows that heaven does not have a natural position, either at the top or at the bottom. But every body has a natural position. And to this, we add a minor term and that is our saying: 'heaven is a body', and hence, it will follow from the first kind of syllogism (*shakl*) that heaven has a natural position. And if we could transfer the conclusion to the disjunctive positional syllogism, we could then say: its natural position is above or below or where it is. And if we hypothesize the negation of its being either above or below, we could say: it is neither up nor down; hence the conclusion is: it is where it is.

6. Everything in its natural position is neither dense nor light in actuality and since heaven is in its natural position, it is, therefore, neither light nor dense in

actuality. The proof of this is that whatever is in its natural position and is light, will be moved upward because it is light and its natural position is upward but it cannot be said that whatever is light, is in its natural position in actuality because this will contradict what I have just said: it will be 'in its natural position' as well as 'not in its natural position' at the same time; and that is self-contradictory. And likewise for the dense. Because the dense is what naturally moves downwards and its natural position is down because anything that moves naturally, its movement takes it toward its natural position. And from the first premise, it is clear that the thing in its natural position is not dense in actuality, so when we add the results of the two premises, the sum of this will be that whatever is in its natural position, is neither dense nor light in actuality. And it was established in the second minor term that the heaven is truly in its natural position, therefore, the correct logical conclusion is that the heaven is neither light nor dense in actuality and it is not so potentially (*bi'l-quwwa*) or contingently.

7. The proof of this is that the light and dense in *potentia* can be so in two situations: (i) It can be so either as a whole, like the parts of the fixed elements in their natural position, so if they were neither dense nor light in actuality, then they are so potentially, for the possibility of their movement by a compulsory motion which can cause them to move from and to their natural position either by an ascending or descending natural movement; and (ii) by considering the parts as opposed to the whole in the fixed elements. These parts are neither light nor dense in their totalities, because if it would move upward, some of the parts would move downward because they are spherical in their shapes and have many dimensions, but indeed, the levity and density are in their parts, so if the heaven is light or heavy potentially, that is in its totality—and we have proved that by nature, the upward or downward movement of the heaven is negated (*maslūb*) to its totality, and to prove that we depended on some of your premises. So it was made clear to us that heaven in its totality is neither light nor dense. And I say that it is neither heavy nor light potentially in its parts because the levity and the density of the heavy and the light parts appear in their natural movement to their natural position. And the parts which are moving to their natural position move in two cases: (i) they might be moving from their natural position by force [in which case] they would move back to their natural position by nature or (ii) they are being created and moving to their natural position like the fire that emerges from the oil and is moving up. It is not possible for a part of the heaven to move from its natural position by force because that requires an outside mover, a corporeal or non-corporeal mover that is not from itself.

8. The non-corporeal movers, like what the philosophers call nature and the active intellect (*al-'aql al-fa''āl*), and the First Cause (*al-'illat al-'ūlā*), are not supposed to create forced movement (*ḥarakah qasriyyah*); as for nature, it is self-evident, and as for the intellect and the First Cause, their inability [to do so] is left to the Divine

knowledge. As for the physical cause, it should be, if possible, one of the [four] elements or composed of them because there is no corporeal body other than these five—the four simple elements and [the fifth being] their combination.

9. And every body that moves by itself and not by accident, moves when it is touched by an active mover. And this has been explained in detail in the first chapter in the book of Generation and Corruption (*Kitāb al-kawn wa'l-fasād*). Thus, it is not possible for a part of the heaven to move without being touched by the mover during its movement toward it either by force (*bi'l-qasr*), or by nature (*bi'l-ṭabʿ*). The outside mover that moves it by force has to be connected to another mover, which in turn, has to be connected to the first mover of all. And if it was moving by nature, it will be either the non-composite fire or a combination in which the fire-parts are dominant. The non-composite fire does not affect the heaven because it engulfs it from all sides and the impact of bodies on bodies is by touch and there is no part in the heaven which is more passive than the other, unless one of the parts is weaker in its nature. However, the weakness of the substance does not come from itself but through an outside factor.

10. Thus, the question now returns to the beginning, to that of a compound mover in which the fire-part is dominant. It will not have impact until it reaches the sphere of the heaven and when it reaches the airy zone, then it will turn into pure fire and burst into a flame as seen in the case of comets. And if it is too slow to reach that transforming stage, it would not touch the heaven, [it may be so] because in it are dense parts, earthly and others, which have gravity. Thus, it is not possible for anything to touch the heaven except pure fire. It is possible for pure or non-pure fire—and the compound is not pure fire—and for the one that is not pure fire it is possible for it to be in the neighborhood of the three elements but it is not possible for it to touch the heaven by nature.

11. As for the other elements, it is not possible for them to touch the heaven in their totality because they do not move in their totality from their natural position, neither in their compound form nor in their parts, thus, they cannot have any impact on the heaven for they are unable to touch it because when they reach the ether (*al-athīr*), they will burn and turn into fire and the fire does not touch heaven, as we have proved. But ether changes and disjoins everything that occurs in its [realm] because it is hot in actuality and one of the properties of the hotness in actuality is that it brings together similar genera and separates dissimilar genera—it is the separator of dissimilar and gatherer of similar genera. And when the fire takes over a body that is being affected by it, if it were a compound body made from different parts, the fire will return it to its nature; this shows that [the body] did not change into something that is contrary to its essence by mixing with the affective element. As for the cold, it is not like this. And there is no doubt that the hot is most effective and powerful of all things; and the thing that is in its natural position, strengthens its genus; and the whole

is stronger than its parts. So what do you think of something that is hot in its natural position and is whole, and allows a part to enter into its sphere and does not produce any effect [on this part], neither changes it back to its nature, nor separates it, if it were compound?

12. From these premises, it is clear that it is not possible for any part or compound from the elements to reach the heaven. Since they do not reach it, they do not touch it, and if they do not touch it, they do not produce any effect on it. None of the parts or the compounds has any effect on parts of the heaven and if nothing is able to affect it, other than it, from whole or parts, simple or compound bodies, it is not going to be affected and moved potentially by itself. And if we would set aside our premise—and that is our saying, 'and it is not possible [for the heaven] to be affected by anything other than by itself', which is true—the result is our saying: 'it is not possible that it will be affected and moved by force'; and this is also true. So the heaven is neither light nor dense potentially, neither as a whole nor in its parts. And we have proved that it is not so in actuality. It is neither light nor dense, in general or absolutely. And that is what we wanted to clarify. But you can call the heaven light from the perspective in which people call a floating body, on top of another body, lighter than the latter by nature. So, from this perspective, it is possible that the heaven is the lightest of all things.

13. Now, as to your saying that the circular motion [of the heaven] is natural to it, and your saying, 'if it is said that this is not accidentally' et cetera, there is no one among the scholars who has proven the natural circular motion of the heaven, who has ascertained what you have said. I would have explained the reasons, had it not been a separate issue, taking too long [to explain].

14. As for your demonstration that the movement of the stars and the planets is opposite, it is not so. It is only different. Because the opposite movements are opposite in the directions and the ends, and if it was not that the high is opposite of low, then we would not have said that the movement from the centre is the opposite of the movement to the centre; and this has been explained in detail in the fifth chapter of *Kitāb al-samāʿ al-ṭabīʿī*. As for the directions of the two circular motions and their ends, they are, in our assumption, positional, not natural. Because in nature, there is no end to the circular movement of the heaven, hence it is not opposite; hence the two different circular motions are not opposite and this is what we wanted to clarify.

Part II[1]

15. The second question: Why did Aristotle consider the views of the ancients and predecessors concerning the heavens and their finding [the celestial bodies] to be just as he found them to be, a strong argument for the immutability and

1. *Islam and Science*, 1 (December, 2003), p.253.

perpetuity of the heavens? Anyone who is not stubborn and does not insist on falsehood would agree that this is not a known [fact]. We do not know more [about the celestial bodies] than what has been reported by the people of the Book as well as by Indians and other nations like them, appears to be false upon investigation. This is because of the continuous changes [which occur] on the surface of earth, [changes] that occur in increments or all at once. Likewise, the obvious alterations in the state of mountains since antiquity are proof of events resulting in changes.

16. The answer: You should know that [Aristotle] did not give [the views of the ancients] as evidence; it was only something that came by way of speech which he mentioned in two places. [Further], the case of mountains does not apply to the celestial sphere; even if nations witnessed mountains preserved in their totality, [this observation] does not disclose changes resulting from the action of the elements on their different parts, some of which are collapsing and folding upon one another, and some of which are altering their shapes and undergoing other changes beyond these—changes which have been mentioned by Plato in his book *fī Siyāsat* as well as in other books. It is as if you have taken this objection from John Philoponos, who was opposed to Aristotle, simply because he himself was a Christian. However, whoever reads his commentary on generation and corruption and his other books would find that he agrees with Aristotle on this issue. Or [you may have derived your arguments] from Muḥammad ibn Zakariyyā' al-Rāzī, who meddles in metaphysics and exceeds his competence. He should have remained confined to surgery and to urine and stool testing—indeed he exposed himself and showed his ignorance in these matters. And you should also know that when Aristotle said 'the universe has no beginning' he did not mean that the universe did not have a Creator; rather, he intended to exalt and protect the Creator from the charge of inaction, but this is not the place to discuss this.

17. And as for your saying, 'anyone who is not stubborn and who does not insist on falsehood': this is an ugly and rude insult—either you comprehended the saying of Aristotle in this matter or you did not. If you did not, your belittling of someone who said something beyond your grasp is inappropriate. And if you did understand, your comprehension of the meaning should have prevented you from dragging in this quarrel; for your pursuit of what your intelligence prevents you from pursuing is inappropriate.

18. The third question: Why do [Aristotle] and others say that there are only six directions in space? Their example is that of the cube, for which the six directions have parallels. If we add to these six tangent cubes, so that when the spaces are all filled in there will be 27 cubes, which will all be touching the first cube from angles and sides. And if the directions did not exceed that number, from which direction are these cubes touching the first cube when these directions do not exist in the sphere?

19. The answer: The directions of any body are not parallel to its surface, but are rather hypothetical directions. The six directions that the philosophers meant are parallel to the extremities of the three dimensions of the body: the length, the width and the depth. In the third essay of his *Kitāb al-samāʿ al-ṭabīʿī*, wherein Aristotle discussed infinity, he argued that since a body is limited, it is necessary that its length, width and depth also be limited and that each one of these have two extremities, their total being six. What parallels them is also six. So that which is parallel to the extremity of length is next to the centre of the world in which its length ends, in the direction of the centre, being below, while its opposite is above. And there is no name for the four remaining directions of a body, though that is only for living bodies. The direction of the extremity of the width in a living body, from which its movement arises is called the right, while its opposite is called the left. And the direction that parallels the extremities of the depth of the living body is the one toward which the vision of the body is directed, and it is called front while its opposite is known as behind. These are the six necessary directions in every body.

20. Your denial of the six directions of the sphere is incorrect. If the sphere were a body, it should have length, width and depth, they all being limited with two extremities. The total thus being six. The directions parallel to these six extremities are also six. When the premise is right, all conclusions are right, and the conclusion here is that the sphere has six directions. So how is it then possible that the six directions of a body are parallel to its surface while it is known that the sphere has directions from its sides that are different in observation? The direction of the north pole is not the direction of the east or the west nor that of the south pole and likewise all other directions, and the same holds true for their correspondents. And if the surface of the sphere is one, then there is no one single direction, neither in the demonstrative proof—as we clarified—nor hypothetically, as it is necessary for the body to have directions parallel to the surface. It is possible for angular bodies to have directions parallel to their surfaces, because their surfaces are straight by their position and view but not by their structure. So what really accompanies a body physically apart from their directions is what parallels its three extremities, and that is what the philosophers meant.

21. The fourth question: Why did Aristotle oppose the position of the atomists—though their stance that a body is divisible *ad infinitum* is absurd—in that if two bodies are moving in the same direction, one ahead of the other, they will be unable to overtake one another, even if the velocity of the first is less? Take, for instance, the example of the sun and the moon. If there were a certain distance between them and if both moved [in the same direction] but the sun travelling a shorter distance than the moon in the same amount of time, and if this continued *ad infinitum* we would see the moon overtaking the sun. The atomists are also opposed to other things well known to engineers. And what I just mentioned about

those who oppose the atomists is also very absurd, so how can we get rid of both [of these groups]?

22. The Answer: Firstly, it is not possible that a continuous thing that has no body, no surface, no length, no movement, no time, be composed of indivisible atoms. I mean a body without two dimensions and a middle upon which it is centred. Aristotle has explained it in the sixth chapter of *Kitāb samʿ al-kiyān* with strong logical and credible proofs; he has raised this objection himself and has provided an answer. But you should know that the saying of Aristotle that the body is divisible *ad infinitum* did not mean that it is actually divisible [but only potentially so]; it means [instead] that every atom in it has a middle and two dimensions. Some of these atoms are divisible into two parts adjacent to the two dimensions and the middle; these are the parts that are divisible in actuality. While other parts, even if they have a middle and a place to divide, are too small to be actually divisible; [hence] these parts are divisible [only] potentially and in themselves.

23. My objection should silence those who say that the body is divisible actually, but the one who says that some parts of the body are divisible in actuality and some parts are divisible only potentially is correct, because movement brings finite division of the congruent parts, though this is not actual division. So, this is the way leading to these two absurd notions, coming from both sides. And whatever Aristotle has said in response to this matter has been interpreted by interpreters only for the sake of argument and for finding fault with others. If it were not for my preference to avoid unnecessarily lengthening the matter, I would have mentioned all that, but whatever follows after already hitting the mark is sheer wastefulness and excessiveness.

24. The Fifth Question: Why did Aristotle oppose the possibility of the existence of another world, outside our world, made up of a different nature? We did not know the natures and the four elements until our existence here [in this world], much like the one born blind who, if he did not hear people mentioning vision, would not be able to imagine the process of vision by himself and would not be able to recognize colours. [We also cannot grasp] a world that has the same characteristics as this world but is moving in directions different than those of this world, if both these worlds are separated from each other by a barrier (*barzakh*). An example of this can be demonstrated by a hill on the surface of the earth defined by three points, A, B and C; A and C being close to the surface of the earth as compared to B. Naturally, water will flow from B to A or to C; and these are two opposite movements to a known point.

25. The Answer: This question is not mentioned in Aristotle's book, *al-Samāʾ wa'l-ʿālam*, as a denial of the existence of worlds other than this [world] because he did not address the case of those who claim the existence of worlds unlike this; he [only] responded to those who claimed the existence of worlds with skies, earths, and elements similar to this world in kind (*nawʿ*) and nature (*ṭabʿ*), with

dissimilarity in character. And he supported this denial with the argument that 'our reference to the world and the sky without specifying and without mentioning the elements is more general than our reference to a specific world or to this world from this part from this element.' Thus the existence of other worlds beyond this one world specified by the elements is possible.

26. The possibility of eternal things is a necessity (*wājib*), thus the existence of many worlds is *wājib*. The existence of other worlds other than this world is a necessity; some people considered them limited and others unlimited, and all of them have proved their points. The Philosopher has refuted this argument in his *Kitāb al-samā' wa'l-'ālam* and he has made it clear that the existence of many worlds is not possible. Other philosophers said that the elements of the other worlds are not different than those of this world but indeed, they have the same nature. The Master said that if the elements of many worlds are not different from each other in nature and the things that depend on nature, [then] they depend on the direction of their natural movement and the elements of many worlds depend on their natural positions. So, if they were found in different positions over one another, they would be stationary in these positions by force. And whatever happens by force, follows whatever happens by nature. It is known that [elements] were initially all together in one unit and they then separated and [hence] those who consider them to be different eternally end up with the impossibility of dealing with a situation in which they are eternally different and not different eternally and that is an impossible contradiction. And whatever comes by force necessarily vanishes and the thing returns to its original nature. So, those separated worlds will meet again though philosophers claim that they will never meet again, [hence we have a situation in which] they will meet and, on the other hand, they will not meet eternally. And this is [again] an impossible contradiction.

27. There is no doubt that whatever happens by force has a cause. And these bodies are not supposed to force each other from their natural positions or to move to meet in unnatural positions, because we have already established that forcing bodies are forcing each other to move until they end up with a body moving by nature. And if there were a body that was moving by force to an unnatural position, such as the elements of the worlds, it is necessary that another body would move in that direction by nature. There is also no body except that composed from these elements, because we have made it clear that there is nothing here that has a position by nature, so if we consider that what moves by nature to its natural position is other than those present in their places naturally, that would be a contradiction. Hence, there is no other body except for these since there is no other body different than these. We will further clarify the correctness of this later. So, the result of the previously mentioned antithesis is that none of these bodies force each other toward the movement of that direction, because none of them is moving to that direction by nature or otherwise. This is so because it has

no forceful physical or non-physical cause because causes which are not bodies, like the things which the philosophers call 'nature', 'Intellect' (*ʿaql*) and the 'First Cause' (*al-ʿillat al-ʾūlā*) do not change order to disorder; their job is to transform disorder into order or to hold the order in place, hence there is no automatic physical or non-physical cause to do this.

28. As for the accidental causes, such as chance, even if their aims are secondary, their causes are fixed by themselves—and whoever wants to clarify that should see the second article in the Philosopher's book, *Fī samʿ al-kiyān* or our commentary on the first article in Metaphysics. We say that these have accidental causes while they also have natural causes. If we exempt the second premise, the logical result will lead to nullification of the first premise, and that is to say that there is no accidental or causal cause. People agree that it is impossible for a thing to be in this condition, and this is common sense. If books were not already full of refutations of this, I would have refuted it. And if a thing does not have an essential or an accidental cause, it would be impossible for it to exist without a cause. So, the existence of other worlds like this one is impossible, and this is what we wanted to clarify [in the first place].

29. I want to explain that the existence of a body other than these bodies is not possible in movement or characteristics because movement, by logical necessity, is either in a straight line or is circular. Assuming there is no vacuum, the moving bodies would be touching each other by necessity. Now, the linear movement is either toward the centre or intersecting the centre in its straight path, and is either coming from the two sides or is parallel to them. By nature, however, it is not permitted that the movement should be from one end to the opposite end or in relation to it. And all of this has been explained in Aristotle's books, particularly in the fifth article of the book *Kitāb al-samāʿ al-ṭabīʿī* and in its commentaries as well as in some of our own works.

30. From this we understand that the natural movements are finite in all bodies, either from the centre or to the centre. And as for the sensory characteristics, it is not possible for the number of these to exceed nineteen, as the Philosopher has explained in the third article of his *Kitāb al-nafs* and [has been explained] in the commentaries of Themistius and Alexander [of Aphrodisias] and others. Were it not for the length, I would have elaborated on this issue further but I just wanted to briefly mention it.

31. So, I say if nature does not give the higher kind the elements of the lesser kind, it will not be able to enter the second kind from the second category. The example of this is the body, the first of the lowest kind. If nature did not give it all the characteristic qualities of bodies, it would not be able to bring it up to the second higher kind by relation, that being the plant kingdom. And if all plant qualities—such as the ability to nourish and to grow and to procure—were not present in this kind, nature would not be able to take it to the next higher

kind, which is the animal stage and the characteristics of the animal stage are divided into sense and intentional movement. So if this lower kind did not get all the cognitive senses (*ḥiss al-mudrakah*) to sense all things, the animal kind would not be able to develop to the speaking kind (*al-nawʿ al-nuṭqī*). Nature has, however, created in those who are born (*mawālīd*), a speaking element. It is, thus, necessary that it gave them all sensory powers (*al-quwwa al-ḥissiyyah*), and it followed these things with the speaking powers. So if the speaking kind has all sensory cognitive powers, then the speaking kind is aware of all the sensory things. Hence, there is no sensory thing except what the speaking kind can realize. There are no qualities but the sixteen that are sensed by themselves and three that are sensed accidentally, these being movement, rest and figure. There is no body that has any qualities except these. So, there is no other world opposite to this world with similar physical qualities. However, were there many worlds, they should be similar to this one, and we have already explained that there is no world similar to this one. So, to conclude, there is only one world and that is what we had wanted to clarify.

32. Know that if there were another way to discuss this issue, it would necessarily lead to an endless discourse, and that would harm science in a sense and would play into the hands of sophists. And their cure is not in this medicine but in other medications, and for this we seek Allah's help.

Part III[1]

(33) The Sixth Question: [Aristotle] has mentioned in Book II that [the shape of the heaven is of necessity spherical because] the oval and the lenticular shapes would require space and void whereas the sphere does not, but the matter is not so. In fact, the oval [shape] is generated by the rotation of ellipse around its major axis, and the lenticular by its rotation around its minor axis. As there is no difference concerning the rotation around the axes by which they are generated, therefore none of what Aristotle mentions would occur and only the essential attributes of the spheres would follow necessarily. If the axis of rotation of the oval is its major axis and if the axis of rotation of the lenticular is its minor axis, they would revolve like the sphere, without needing an empty space. This could happen, however, if the axis of [rotation of] the oval is its minor axis and the axis of [rotation of] the lenticular is its major axis. In spite of this, it is possible that the oval can rotate around its minor axis and the lenticular around its major axis, both moving consecutively without needing an empty space, like the movement of bodies inside the celestial sphere, according to the opinion of most people. And I am not saying this with the belief that the celestial sphere is not spherical, but oval or lenticular; I have tried hard to refute this theory but I am amazed at the reasons offered by the man of logic.

1. *Islam and Science*, 2 (Summer, 2004), p. 57.

(34) The Answer: Yes—may Allah lengthen your life—your objection to Aristotle is sound and I have clarified this matter in some of my writings. Every commentator [of Aristotle] has offered apologies for his views. What comes to my mind now is what Themistius has said in his commentary on *Kitāb al-samāʾ*, [that is], that the Philosopher's views should be interpreted in the best possible way. So we say that no void whatsoever would result from the circular movement of the sphere, whereas this is possible in the case of the oval and lenticular shapes. Despite this apology, he still denounces Aristotle's view, for it is possible to prove that the shape of the heavens is not oval or lenticular with arguments—some of which are natural proofs and others which are mathematical. And since you have a mastery of mathematics and live in a region where [numerous] experts in geometry reside, there is no need for me to go into further details.

(35) Nonetheless, your assertion that no void would occur from the movement of the oval and lenticular shapes, as you have observed from the moving bodies within the celestial sphere, is not the same as [the other saying], because in the celestial sphere there are, vis-à-vis the moving bodies, other moving bodies touching them consecutively. As for the heavens, if they were lenticular and moved, but not around the minor axis, or if they were oval and moved, but not around the major axis, then a void would necessarily occur because there is no body beyond the heavens that would be touched by the body of the heavens during the movement, as is the case for the bodies within the heavens.

(36) The Seventh Question: When [Aristotle] mentioned directions, he established that the right is the starting point for the motion of every planet; he then reversed the matter, for he said that the motion in the sky is from the east because that is the right side; and the reverse is not permissible, thus leading to a circular argument.

(37) The Answer: The Philosopher did not assert that the motion of the heavens is from the east because the east is right. What he asserted was that the east is the right side because motion appears from the east. The movement of animals appears from the right and, for him, the moving heavens are [like] an animal; thus it necessitated that the east is the right of the heavens. It is impossible for a rational person to embark upon the task of proving that the heavens move from the east because there is no doubt about that; it has been always the case that the heavens move from the east. However the Philosopher wanted to clarify the nature of [what is meant by] the right of the heavens after he had asserted what is the right direction for the heavens with reasoning.

(38) The Eighth Question: [Aristotle] claimed that when planets move, the air that touches the planets is heated because heat comes as a result of motion and coldness is a result of rest. So when the heavens move quickly, the air being touched becomes hot, eventually becoming fire, known as Ether. The faster the motion, the stronger and more intense the heating. It is very clear that the

fastest motion of the heavens occurs at the equator and when it approaches the two poles, the motion slows down. Let us assume that the heaven is A, B, C, D and the two poles are AB and the equator CD; the hottest points would be EF and these are the farthest points because here the motion is the fastest. Then, the motion slows down toward the two poles. The heat will gradually decrease until it disappears at the two poles. The fire image is presented here by the outer shape and the air image by the inner shape. This is what should occur according to the agreement of the ancients who agreed that the shape of the fire is spherical and so is that of air. [1]

(39) The Answer: According to most philosophers, the fire is not brought into being by the motion of the heavens but it is an independent element; it has its own sphere and a natural position of its own, like any other element. What you have said is nothing but the beliefs of those who considered the four elements to be [only] one, two or three, like Thales, who considered them to be water; or Heraclitus, who considered them to be fire; or Diogenes, who considered them to be a substance between water and air; and Anaximander, who considered them to be air. Each one of them considers other bodies—as well as the generated accidents—as the accidents that appear in those bodies according to how they are shaped and do not consider that they are derived from another body. And Anaximander says—what you have mentioned—namely that the first element is air; when it is affected by cold, it becomes water and when it is heated by the motion of the heavens, it becomes fire or ether. However, Aristotle did not consider any of the four elements to be coming into existence from another element and the same is true for their parts. This objection [you raise], then, does not apply to Aristotle or to whoever said the same thing, which is the right and wise saying. As for the shape you drew, it is not supposed to be like that. The two nooks, E and F, that you drew, only apply to the condition you described. But the figure to prove your point has a problem, and it is that the curve AE should meet the curve EB roundly, without nooks between the points. And so should be the case with the two curves AF and FB.[2]

(40) The Ninth Question: If [it is in the nature of] heat [to] rise from its centre, how is it that the heat of the sun reaches us? Are rays bodies, accidents, or something else?

(41) The Answer: You must know that heat does not leave its centre because heat is motionless, except in the case of accidental motion, when it is inside a moving body, like a motionless person inside a moving ship. And you must also know that the heat of the sun does not come to us by descending down from the sun for the following reasons: firstly, heat does not move by itself; secondly, there is no hot body that descends from above and heats what is down below, neither does heat come

1. Figure is omitted.
2. Figure is omitted.

down from the sun by accidents; third, the sun is not even hot because heat that is being created here is not descending from above for the three reasons already mentioned. [Rather], heat occurs here from the reflection of light and air is heated by this process as can be observed in the [experiment of] burning mirrors. And you must know that the rays are not bodies—for if they were bodies there would be two bodies in one place, [and by that] I mean the air and the rays—but attributes of a transparent body. Aristotle has defined it in Book II of *Kitāb al-nafs* (*On the Soul*) and in Book I of *Kitāb al-ḥiss* (*Sense and Sensibilia*). According to him, light is the perfection of transparency and is in itself transparent.

(42) The Tenth Question: What causes transformation of elements into each other? Is it the result of their proximity or intermingling or some other process? Let us take the example of air and water: when water transforms into air, does it become air in reality, or is it because its particles spread out until they become invisible to the sight so that one cannot see these separate particles?

(43) The Answer: The transformation of elements into one another does not occur the way you mentioned. Water does not transform into air by the separation and the spread of its particles in the air until they disappear from the sight; rather, the water particles take off their watery image and put on an airy image. For more details, one can see the commentaries on *Kitāb al-kawn wa'l-fasād* and *Kitāb al-āthār al-ʿulwiyyah* and Book III of *Kitāb al-samā'*. But here I clarify this case according to their methods and the following logical example that they used to prove their sayings.

(44) Increase in the mass of bodies can be explained by means of an example: [Suppose], we took a flask filled with water, sealed it tightly and exposed it to intense heat. The water particles in the flask would expand and crack the flask because their volume increased when they transformed into air. This happened either because of the spread of the space between the water particles, or not because of the spread of particles. But the void is impossible; therefore it is necessary that the latter is true. [Thus] the reason for transformation [of water into air] is not the spread of its particles, but the acceptance of another image by its atoms.

(45) If it would be said that air or something else entered the flask and increased its volume, we would say that is impossible because a full container cannot accept another body inside it until it is emptied of the first occupant, and the water cannot leave the flask because it is tightly sealed and there is no way out. I observed a little flask. We tightly sealed it and put it in a kiln. It did not take long before it cracked and everything that was in it exploded into the fire. And it is known that nothing mixed with the particles of the water that were inside the flask that could cause a change, because, firstly, the fire was not inside the flask and, secondly, it did not enter it because there was no way into the flask. It is, therefore, obvious that this transformation occurred through a change in the air and fire natures of [air

and fire] and not through the spread of parts. I have provided an example which supports Aristotle's views on generation and change as parts of nature; and this suffices, for further elaboration would demand tenuous efforts. Many objections could arise in this matter and if you encounter any, please convey your questions and I would explain to you, God willing.

(46) These are the answers to the ten questions arising from the *Kitāb al-samā'* of Aristotle; now we will answer the other questions by the permission of Allah the Exalted.

17

ʿUmar Khayyām

Abu'l-Fatḥ ʿUmar ibn Ibrāhīm Khayyām was born in 439/1048 in Nayshāpūr, a great centre of learning at the time. Not much is known about his teachers, but he considered himself intellectually to be a student of Ibn Sīnā and is regarded to be the most important philosopher between Ibn Sīnā and Suhrawardī. Malik Shāh Saljūqī was a patron of Khayyām, and he commissioned Khayyām to reform the calendar, an endeavour which led to the completion of what is known as the *taqwīm-i jalālī* in 471/1078. Khayyām met with several great masters of learning, such as Abū Ḥāmid Ghazzālī, who is said to have studied mathematics with Khayyām, according to Zamakhsharī. Khayyām also knew Abu'l-ʿAlā' al-Maʿarrī, the prominent Arab poet.

ʿUmar Khayyām has gained fame for his *Rubāʿiyyāt* or *Quatrains*, but in his own time he was known as a metaphysician, mathematician, astronomer, scientist, and Sufi. It was for the latter that he was attacked by some exoteric jurists, to the point that he decided to perform the pilgrimage as a testimony to his faith. Khayyām wrote very little and unfortunately much of what he did write has been lost; however, what remains includes short treatises on existence, theodicy, generation and corruption, and necessity and contradiction, as well as works on physics, mathematics, arithmetic, algebra, and research on Euclid's axioms.

Following his journey to Mecca, Khayyām died at 517/1131 in his birthplace. Bayhaqī describes the last day of Khayyām's life as follows:

> Ḥakim was studying the *Ilāhiyyāt* of *Shifā'* and once he came to the section on unity and multiplicity, stopped in order to pray and utter his last words. His companions gathered and he [Khayyām] announced his last will and testament and performed his noon prayer. He neither ate nor drank again until he performed his night prayer. He bowed and placed his forehead on the ground and said: 'O God, I know Thee in as much as my ability allows, forgive me for I know Thy way is the way towards Thee', and then died.

This chapter includes two of 'Umar Khayyām's treatises. The first, written in Arabic, deals with free will and determinism; the second, written in Persian, treats the subject of existence and its relationship to universals.

M. Aminrazavi

THE NECESSITY OF CONTRADICTION, FREE WILL AND DETERMINISM

From *Ḍarūrat al-taḍādd fi'l-ʿālam wa'l-jabr wa'l-baqā'*

Reprinted from 'Ḍarūrat al-taḍādd fi'l-ʿālam wa'l-jabr wa'l-baqā'', tr. M. W. Rahman in Swami Govinda Tirtha, *The Nectar of Grace: Omar Khayyām's Life and Works* (Allahabad, 1941), pp. 104–110.[1]

I

If the necessity of contradiction is contingent being, it must have a cause and this causal series comes to an end with the Necessary Being. If, on the other hand, this necessity is self-existing, then there are other necessary beings besides God; but it is argued that the Necessary Being is One, and not many, in all respects. Now if we accept the first alternative, it follows that the Necessary Being is its cause and the inventor. But it is an established fact that evil cannot emanate from such a Being. The rejoinder to all this reasoning is:

The attributes of things are of two kinds—the essential and the accidental. The former is an attribute which is essential for a conception of that object, so much so that we cannot conceive that object without first conceiving that attribute. The attribute of animality in man is an example of such an attribute. This attribute always precedes the object having that attribute, or in other words it is its cause and not its effect, as an animal in relation to a man. In general it can be said that all the constituent parts of a term are essential attributes. The latter kind of attribute is just the opposite of the former. It is quite possible to conceive an object without first conceiving the accidental attributes. This attribute, again is not the cause of the object, and neither does it precede in the order of existence or nature.

The accidental attribute is again divided into two classes. It is inseparable, as man's ability to think or to wonder or to laugh, or it is separable. The separable accidental attributes are either separable in imagination only, as the blackness of a crow, or both in imagination and reality, as man's being a writer or a peasant. These are the primary classes of attribution.

Then the necessary attributes of the existing objects can again be, primarily and intellectually, divided into two classes: (1) Their necessity is dependent upon the necessity of some other attribute, which is, as it were, its cause, as man's being a laughing animal is dependent on his being a wondering animal. This wonder in its turn depends upon some other attribute. This ultimate attribute is either (*a*)

1 For a complete new translation of this work see M. Aminrazavi, *The Wine of Wisdom: The Life, Poetry and Philosophy of Omar Khayyam* (Oxford, 2007), pp. 293–299.

inseparable or (*b*) separable. But a separable attribute cannot be the cause of an inseparable attribute. This means that this ultimate attribute is necessarily inseparable. Now in this causal series the causes succeed each other, continuously *ad infinitum*, which has been shown to be impossible, or they move in a circle, i.e., the effect is the cause of its own cause. This is also obviously impossible, or again this series ends with a cause which has no cause. Such a cause or the attribute becomes the self-existing attribute for that object, for example, man's ability to think. Thus it is clear that some attributes are self-existing for an object. After this preamble we return to our theme.

Existence or being is a relative term, which can be used to designate two meanings. *'Alā sabīl al-tashkīk*: (1) Being in reality. This is existence *par excellence* according to the general opinion. (2) Subjective Existence, e.g., the sensory, the imaginary, the fanciful and the intellectual concepts, which exist in mind alone. Now this second meaning is exactly the same as the first meaning, for the knowledge and conceivable meanings, in so far as they are knowable and conceivable, are found in reality, and the knowing self is a real thing among other real things and it is clear that an attribute that is found in one of the real things is also found in all the other real things, save that sometimes the example, the scheme and the outlines of a knowable and conceivable thing, does not exist in a real thing, for instance, the conception of man. This is because the meanings of man exist in mind, and also in real things, for the mind is one of the real things. But in so far as man has mental existence his example, scheme or outline does not exist in the real thing. This is the main difference between the two forms of existences. From all this it should be clear that their difference is necessary (*aḥaqq*) and fundamental and the precedence and the succession, which is known as (*tashkīk*) is not in the sense of (*ishtirāk*). This problem is undoubtedly very subtle and deep, but it does not require much of elucidation, as Mr. So and So is not ignorant of it.

It is said that the attribute of animality exists in man, as the quality of the sum of all the three angles of a triangle is equal to two right angles in a triangle. Here by existence we do not mean existence in reality, but only a mental existence. This is because it is not possible to conceive a man without first conceiving that he is an animal. The meaning animal is necessary for the meaning man. Similarly oneness is necessary for three-ness, for the latter cannot be conceived save by the help of oneness. Now if a thing cannot be conceived without conceiving someone out of the many attributes, then this attribute becomes necessary for that thing. In other words, that thing does not possess that attribute on account of some cause. It is self-existing for that thing. Thus oneness is self-existing for three-ness, as is animality for man. In general it can be said that the essential attributes are self-existing in relation to the things having those attributes.

Out of these self-existing attributes some are such on account of the precedence of some other attribute which is self-existing for that attribute, and other's self-existence does not depend upon the precedence of some other attribute. All the inseparable and the necessary attributes are self-existing in relation to the objects possessing them in this very sense. Out of this, some are necessary on account of the necessity of some other antecedent, and some are necessary not because of the something else but because of the thing possessing that attribute. All this argument is exactly the same as we have put forward a few lines back.

Now if oneness is a necessary and self-existing attribute of three-ness, it cannot, by its very nature, be present in reality, save that it be self-existing in those real things, or be a contingent in an object, for its resultant is one thing and the resulting real thing is another thing. Sometimes the attributes not existing in the real things exist in mind and intellect for the things that have no real existence. So we are not justified in saying that they exist in reality. Someone for example says that the void is a natural and extended dimension, in which the bodies extend, and move from one position to another. Now these attributes of the void exist in the intellect and the void exists in, and is conceived by, the intellect, but is non-existent in reality. The attributes of things exist in the mind and the intellect in the first instance. They are not obtained from outside.

Now about real existence. Whenever it is said that such and such an attribute has a necessary existence in such and such a thing, what is meant is that it exists in the mind and the intellect, and not in reality. Similarly whenever it is said that the existence of such and such an attribute is dependent upon the existence of some other attribute, what is meant is existence in mind and the intellect. We have already explained the difference between the two, whatever the attribute. The real existence is quite different from the existence of a thing for a thing, the difference being from the point of view of *tashkīk*. This has already been explained.

It has been argued that the necessarily existing real thing is one in all respects and attributes, and that it is the cause of the existence of all the real things. It has already been known that existence in mind is the same as existence in reality from the point of view of *tashkīk*. So that the Supreme Being is the cause of all the existing objects. The non-existence and its causes are obvious to Mr. So and So, hence I do not like to dilate upon it.

From all this it should be clear that when it is said that oneness exists necessarily for three-ness, what is meant is that it is so not on account of some other cause, and is not due to the act of some other actor. Similar is the case with all other essential and necessary attributes. It is quite possible that an essential and necessary attribute might become the cause of some other essential and necessary attribute, and thus lead to an essential or necessary attribute for which there is no cause. Thus this essential attribute becomes the cause in some sense. This judgment, however, does not negate the proposition that the necessary being is one in all the respects, for here existence means existence in reality and as has already been shown, the necessary real thing is one. This existence is extraneous to the thing. It does not depend upon existence in reality or in mind. In general all the things existing in reality are contingent and naught else, except the necessity of the One Being.

After this introduction we take up the analysis of the general problem. The contingent beings have emanated from the Holy Being according to a definite order and arrangement. Out of these beings there are some which are necessarily contradictory. Their contradiction, in other words, is not the result of the action of some actor, so that whenever that being is found, the contradiction is also necessarily found, and wherever the contradiction is formed, non-existence is also necessarily formed. Again whenever non-existence is found, evil is also necessarily found. It is quite correct to say that the Necessary Being created blackness or heat, thereby creating the contradiction, for if A is the cause of B, and B is the cause of C, A is necessarily the cause of C. But here we are led to a particular purpose, *viz.*, the Necessary Being created blackness. This necessarily is creating contradiction. But there is no doubt about the fact that the Necessary Being created this contradiction in the real things not by its own nature but by accident. He did not create blackness as a contradictory to whiteness but as a nature existing contingently. All natures existing contingently are made necessary by the Necessary Being, for existence itself is a good, and not an evil. But blackness is a nature, which is necessarily contradictory to something else. So whoever created blackness on account of its being a contingent existence created the contradiction accidentally. Hence the evil cannot, in any way, be attributed to the creator of blackness, for the primary purpose of the Eternal Being was the creation of the primary and good, but this particular form of species of Good cannot possibly be free from evil and non-existence. It follows from all this that we can attribute Evil to Him only accidentally and it is evident that we are discussing the essentials and not the accidents.

Here another question crops up: Why did He create a thing, which He knew would be necessarily accompanied by non-existence and Evil? The answer is: Take Blackness for instance, in it there are a thousand goods and only one Evil. To abstain from a thousand goods for the sake of a single evil is itself a great evil, for the proportion of the good of blackness to its evil as one found in the creation of God is accidental and not essential. It is also evident that the evil according to the first Wisdom was very little, and that qualificatively or quantitatively it does not compare with Good.

II

Turn we now to the second question: Out of the two views—the free will and the determinism—which is nearer truth? Apparently the determinist is on the right path, but in reality he talks nonsense, for sometimes he is very far from the truth.

Some people say that duration (*baqā'*) is an attribute of a thing additional to its other attributes. How far are they correct?

Now duration is naught but the continued existence of a thing for a particular period of time. This means that duration is an existence, which includes length of time, so that existence is more general than duration. Hence we can say that the difference between the two is that of the general and the particular. What strikes one as wonderful is that the thinkers who admit that in relation to reality the existence and the existing thing are one and the same, although they are different as mental concepts, are led astray when dealing with duration. But the following argument of the dialectician always leads him to impossibilities. He is asked: Is there anything here having the attribute of duration? If he says yes there is, our rejoinder is: as if what you say is right it does not endure here, so what is that thing which creates the existing things, and, as you believe perpetuates it through succession and creation in recurring moments in spite of the fact that the existence of the recurring moments has been disproved. Anyhow for the sake of peace we grant it. If on the other hand, they say that this creator through succession does not endure, they are faced with the worst kind of impossibility.

If they reply that there is a thing here which endures, we say that this enduring thing endures on account of a duration which is additional to its own self. Now this duration will either endure, or it will not. If it endures, it will endure on account of the duration, and this duration, again, on account of other duration, and so on. But all this is impossible. If, on the other hand, the duration does not endure, how can the enduring thing endure? This means that the duration, on account of which that thing endures, itself does not endure. This is also impossible.

These dialecticians, in fact, commit the fallacy of asserting that the enduring thing endures on account of the continuous and contiguous durations in recurring moments, and hence they require an explanation, which is quite simple. We ask them: What is the meaning of those recurring durations? If they have any meanings, the enduring things will endure meanings should adhere. It is necessary that those meanings should adhere to the enduring thing for some time thereby qualifying the enduring thing with this attribute. If it is not so, duration and the enduring thing have no meaning. If they are two bipartite existences, it is clear that existence and duration are one and the same. Duration is nothing but the perpetuation of existence, or the existing thing having the attribute of existence, for a period of time. It is possible for the absolute existence to be in a moment of time, but it is not possible for duration to be except in a period of time.

UNIVERSALS OF EXISTENCE
Kulliyyāt-i wujūd

Reprinted from 'Kulliyyāt-i wujūd', tr. M. W. Rahman in Swami Govinda Tirtha, *The Nectar of Grace: Omar Khayyām's Life and Works* (Allahabad, 1941), pp. 124–128.[1]

[*First Section*] (1). Know that whatever exists, save the Godhood, is one Genus (*jins*), and that is an Essence (*jawhar*). Essence is of two kinds: Body (*jism*) and Spirit (*basīṭ*). Of the words which stand for the 'Universal', the first word is Essence and when you differentiate it into two, one word is the Body and the other the Spirit. The Universal Existences have no other names than these three, namely, the Essence, the Body and the Spirit, because save Godhood Existence is this much only. One kind of the universal is separable and the other inseparable. The separable is the Body and the inseparable the Spirit. The separable and the inseparable are antagonistic in status. The Spirit (*basīṭ*) in view of the difference in gradation is of two universal kinds one is called Intellect (*'aql*) and the other Mind (*nafs*). Each of these have ten states. The Cosmic Mind has no limit as to its individual parts. The first is the Creator's Intellect, which is the first effect of the Necessary Existence and the primary cause of Existences thereunder, and ordainer of Cosmic Existences. The Second Intellect is the ordainer of the Highest Sphere, the third of Sphere of Spheres, the fourth of Saturn's Sphere, the fifth of Jupiter's Sphere, the sixth of the Sphere of Mars, the seventh of Sun's Sphere, the eighth of the Sphere of Venus, the ninth of Mercury's Sphere and the tenth of Moon's Sphere. Each of these Intellects has also its Mind, because there cannot be an Intellect without a Mind, nor a Mind without an Intellect. These Intellects and Minds which are the ordainers of the Spheres each move the celestial orbs pertaining to their sphere. The Mind acts as a Lover and the Intellect as the Beloved. Because the Intellect is higher in status and nobler than the Mind, hence it is nearer to the necessary existence.

(2). It must be understood, we say, that the Mind moves Ether like a Lover and Intelligence moves the Mind as a Beloved, because the Mind simulates and tries to penetrate into Intellect, and as a result of the Mind's endeavours to fulfil its longings for the Intellect, motions in Ether are evinced. These motions impart numbers to parts of Ether. Number is a Universal, the complete number is Infinite as a Universal; because a finite number is only a part, since it may be either odd or even, if odd, it is exceeded by even and even by odd, odd and even are parts of the number. Hence it rightly follows that no Universal has a limit and the Whole Number (Infinite) is doubtless among the Universals.

1 For a complete new translation of this work see M. Aminrazavi, *The Wine of Wisdom: The Life, Poetry and Philosophy of Omar Khayyam* (Oxford, 2007), pp. 303–310.

Now be it known that Universal existences which are perpetual, being the effects of the Necessary Existence are first the Creative Intellect, then the Cosmic Mind and then the Cosmic Body. The Body is of three kinds: Ether, Elements and Creations. Each of these admits subdivision and their parts come into being and cease to be without an end. The Ether and Stars have no creation or destruction as regards the parts. Thereunder come the Elements, Fire, Air, Water, Earth and then the Creations, *viz.*, the Mineral, the Vegetable and the Animal. Among the Genus of Animal is Man, but he is the final kind and being rational, superior to other animals.

The sequence of Beings is like the sequence of the letters of the Alphabet, each letter being derived from the one previous to it. Alif is not derived from any other letter and is the first cause of all letters of the alphabet, because it has no precedent but has a subsequent. Hence if any one asks us the question as to what the least number is, we shall reply 'Two', since 'One' is no number; because a number must have a precedent and a subsequent. Thus they say one into one is one, one into two is two, one into three is three, and so on. But two into two is four because one precedes two and three succeeds it, three and one make four. The same is the case with all numbers. Hence Necessary Existence is one *not as a Number* because one is no number, as it has no precedent; but the Necessary Existence is One as being the Primal Cause. The effect thereof is the Intellect, and effect of Intellect the Mind, the effect of Mind the Ether, the effects of Ether the Elements, the effect of Elements the creatures, and each of these are the causes of what comes as an effect under them. That which is an effect is undoubtedly the cause of another. This is called a causal chain. A man is rightly a man if he understands the causal chain and knows that the above-mentioned are only medial entities, and because the Ether, the Elements and creations are the causes and effects of his existence, but not of his Genus, as he hails from Lord Almighty!

Now that we have found the noblest thing in Intellect and Mind in the end, we know that the beginning also was the same. The man who knows the beginning and the end understands rightly that his individual Intellect and Mind are of the same Genus as the cosmic Intellect and cosmic Mind and these other entities are alien from him, and he an alien to them. Hence he should endeavour to attain his Genus, so that he may not remain far apart from his kindred souls; because perdition is a static condition. We know that a Body has no relation to the Spirit (*basīṭ*); and the Man's Self is in reality a Spirit; incapable of subdivision and the Body is capable of subdivision. Body is thus defined: it has length, breadth and thickness and other incidences, such as lines and surfaces which can be laid thereon. The Spirit (*basīṭ*) is thus defined: it has no dimensions such as length, breadth, etc.; it understands all things, and is capable of recording impressions of knowledge; it is neither a point, nor a line, nor a body, nor has any other incidences, such as the why, the how, the whose, the where, the when, shape, qualities, activity or passivity. On the other hand, Man's soul as an Essence is this: it records the impressions of knowledge. Now, knowledge is incidental and an incidental cannot stand on an incidental but on its Essence. Really the Man's soul is not a bodily Essence, because body is divisible and the soul understands the divisibility, and is not divisible; what is divisible cannot understand the divisibility. Hence this Essence (Man's self) should be kept pure from the qualities of the bodies. By qualities is meant the consequence of proximity which it has with the bodies—a proximity which it should not have lest it lead to its destruction. (God knows!).

[*Second Section*] (3). Know that the Intellect (*'aql*) is busy with its Mind (*nafs*) in understanding the objects and the Mind needs the Intellect for knowing reality of the objects. The benefit and advantage is attached to the Mind. Hence the Mind always resembles the Intellect. The proof of this is that no Mind ever envies the Intellect at the time of understanding, because the Mind counts its ability more than that of the Intellect at the time of understanding. But its ability to understand is only discursive and by no means definite. This semblance of the Mind with the Intellect is in its very nature, the effects of it become evident in the feelings (*maḥsūsāt*). Hence the Mind, which is higher than the body, is not without egotism, and whatever be the condition of the body, it is not free from egotism. Body is composed of Matter and Form, and has conditions. Its condition is given by the Mind in the Universals, and in the individuals by the bodily cause to its effect. And what we say here about the details requires explanation. Thus the Cosmic Mind imparts mind to the individual, Ether imparts Elements to the creation and to Man who is a part of the creation. Conditions in Man's constitution are given by the Mind, the Ether, the Elements and creations. Hence the egotism of Man is greater than of those other things.

(4). Know that the ancients have not pondered on the individuals because the individuals come and go and are transitory. The ancients have dealt with the Universals because the Universals remain, and knowledge founded on them is durable. Whoever knows the Universals will necessarily understand the individuals.

Know now the Universals are of five kinds; Genus (*jins*), Species (*naw'*), Kind (*faṣl*) Specific Difference (*khāṣṣah*), Incidence (*'araḍ*). Each of these is a universal by itself. Thus Genus is a universal comprising many universals. Thus Body and Essence (*jawhar*) are each themselves universal comprising many individuals. Essence (*jawhar*) is a word implying all knowable objects, save Godhood. Essence is of two kinds, with a name and nameless. That which has a name is of two kinds, animate and inanimate. The animate is of two kinds, the rational and irrational. Now the Genus is found, i.e., the rational animal, because to its species there is no other superior. The other species are intermediate. The intermediate species are only kinds to the species above them and Genus to the kinds below them. When they are 'kinds', they are parts of their universal. Hence each of them is a whole as well as a part. Thus, Essence is a Genus to its species and its species are Animate and Inanimate, the Animate is a Genus to its specie and its species are Rational and Irrational. Now Essence is a Universal, so that every Genus that exists is its part. The '*Kind*' is a universal which has the power of separating a Genus from Genus and Species from Species. Thus, Animal is a word comprising Rational and Irrational. Rational and Irrational are the kinds by which Man is distinguished, because it is rationality which can distinguish a Man from other animals. Similarly for other things.

Special Quality is an incidence which cannot be separated from its Essence either by imagination or by reason; for example wetness from water, heat from fire, dryness from earth, fineness from air and so on.

The Incidences (*aʿrāḍ*) are generally of nine kinds, Quality, Quantity, Relation, Place, Time, Position, Propriety, Activity, and Passivity.

(5). The actions which emanate from Man are of two kinds: the Present (*ḥāl*) means the movement or repose produced in a man as result of a change or emotion or desire. These are of two kinds: agreeable and disagreeable; for example, anger and malice are both disagreeable; affection and love are both agreeable. Whatever comes and soon disappears is present action (*ḥāl*), whatever remains for a longer time is habitual (*malikah*). Thus one reads a book and remembers it for a long time. These agreeable and disagreeable qualities remain in Man. But when they disappear, they become also incidental and have no relation to the nobility of Man … .

We should know that whatever one can think of, is one of the three kinds: Necessary, Possible and Impossible. The necessary thing is one that cannot but exist. The Possible is that which may or may not exist … . 'Non-existent' is merely a word in the imagination of folk. Whatever exists necessarily is, the Lord: His name be praised! Whatever has a possible existence are all beings (excepting the Lord). The Impossible cannot exist at all!

(6). Know that Existences are of two kinds: the necessary and that is Lord Almighty, and other possible existences, i.e., the Essence which is free from all incidents and the Incidental which is never free from incidents. The Essence is of two kinds: Body and non-Body. Some bodies are homogeneous in formation. Their effects are different, some are hot, some cold, some vegetable, some mineral. The effects of heterogeneous bodies are mixed … .

Philosophers call these effects Properties. Thus a magnet attracts iron, and fire has the power of producing a hundred thousand sparks from a single spark without diminution in the fire. Fire is visible and consequently has lost its wonder, otherwise the atom of fire is the most wonderful of all. Anyhow, a man does not think fire wonderful and knows that fire has the power of ignition and heat, similarly, he should think that in the Body of the Magnet there is a power which acts in attracting iron. Whoever knows this will solve many cases.

Select Bibliography

Abbreviations

BSOAS	*Bulletin of the School of Oriental and African Studies*
EI2	*The Encyclopaedia of Islam*, New edition
EIR	*Encyclopaedia Iranica*
IJMES	*International Journal of Middle East Studies*
JRAS	*Journal of the Royal Asiatic Society*

Primary Sources

al-ʿĀmirī, Abu'l-Ḥasan. *al-Amad ʿala'l-abad* (*A Muslim Philosopher on the Soul and its Fate: al-ʿĀmirī's* Kitāb al-Amad ʿala'l-abad), ed. and tr. E. K. Rowson. New Haven, CT, 1988.

__ *al-Iʿlām bi-manāqib al-Islām*, ed. A. A. Ghorab. Cairo, 1967.

al-Andalusī, S. *Ṭabaqāt al-umam*. Najaf, 1967.

Bahmanyār b. Marzbān. *Fī marātib al-mawjūdāt*, ed. and tr. S. Poper, in *Behmenjār Ben El-Marzubān, der persische Aristoteliker aus Avicenna's Schule: Zwei metaphysische Abhandlungen von ihm arabisch und deutsch mit Anmerkungen*. Leipzig, 1851, pp. 17–28 (trans. pp. 24–47).

___ *Fī mawḍūʿ ʿilm mā baʿd al-ṭabīʿah* (*On the Subject of the Science of Metaphysics*), ed. and tr. S. Poper. Cairo, 1329/1911.

___ *Kitāb al-taḥṣīl*, ed. M. Muṭahharī. Tehran, 1349 Sh./1970. Partial Russian trans., A. V. Sagadeev in *Kniga Pervaya. Perevods arabskogo vodnaya stat'ya i kommentarii*. Baku, 1983.

Bayhaqī, Ẓahīr al-Dīn ʿAlī. *Tā'rīkh ḥukamā' al-Islām*. Damascus, 1972.

___ *Tatimmah ṣiwān al-ḥikmah*. Lahore, 1351/1935.

al-Bīrūnī, Abū Rayḥān. *Kitāb al-āthār al-bāqiyah ʿan al-qurūn al-khāliyah*, ed. E. C. Sachau. Leipzig, 1878.

___ *The Chronology of Ancient Nations*, tr. E. C. Sachau. New York, 1984.

___*Épître de Beruni contenant le repertoire des ouvrages de Muhammad Zakariyya al-Razi*, ed. and tr. P. Kraus. Paris, 1936.

___ *Fī taḥqīq mā li'l-Hind*, ed. E. C. Sachau. Leipzig, 1925.

___ *Kitāb al-jamāhir fī ma'rifat al-jawāhir*, ed. E. Krenkow. Hyderabad, 1936.

___ *al-Qanūn al-mas'ūdī*. Hyderabad, 1334/1915.

___ *Das Vorwort zur Drogenkunde des Berūnī*, tr. with preface by M. Meyerhof. Berlin, 1932.

al-Fārābī, Abū Naṣr. *al-Fārābī's Commentary and Short Treatise on Aristotle's 'De interpretatione'*, ed. and tr. F. W. Zimmermann. Oxford, 1981.

___ *al-Fārābī on the Perfect State: Abū Naṣr al-Fārābī's* Mabādi' ārā' ahl al-madīnah al- fāḍilah, ed. and tr. R. Walzer. Oxford, 1985.

___ *al-Fārābī's Philosophy of Plato and Aristotle*, tr. M. Mahdi. New York, 1962.

___ *Alfarabius compendium legum Platonis*. Vol. 3, *Plato Arabus*, ed. and tr. F. Gabrieli. London, 1951.

___(Alfarabius) *De Platonis Philosophia*, ed. and tr. F. Rosenthal and R. Walzer. London, 1943.

___ *Deux ouvrages inédits sur la rhétorique*, ed. and tr. Jacques Langhade and Mario Grignaschi. Beirut, 1971.

___ *Deux traités philosophiques*, tr. D. Mallet. Damascus, 1989.

___ *Kitāb al-burhān*, ed. M. Fakhry. Beirut, 1987.

___ *Kitāb al-jam' bayn ra'yay al-ḥakīmayn, Aflāṭūn al-ilāhī wa-Arisṭū*, ed. A. N. Nādir. Beirut, 1960.

___ 'Le traité d'al-Fārābī sur les buts de la métaphysique d'Aristote', tr. T. A. Druart. *Bulletin de Philosophie médiévale*, 24 (1982), pp. 38–43.

___ 'The Letter Concerning the Intellect', tr. A. Hyman, in A. Hyman and J. J. Walsh, ed., *Philosophy in the Middle Ages: The Christian, Islamic and Jewish Traditions*. 2nd ed., Indianapolis, MI, 1973, pp. 215–221.

Ḥājjī Khalīfah. *Kashf al-ẓunūn*. Istanbul, 1310/1892.

Ibn Abī Uṣaybi'ah. *'Uyūn al-anbā'*. Beirut, 1915; 2nd ed. 1965.

Ibn al-Athīr, 'Izz al-Dīn 'Alī. *al-Kāmil fi'l-tā'rīkh*. Beirut, 1386/1966.

Ibn Ḥazm, Abū Muḥammad 'Alī. *Faḍā'il al-Andalus wa ahluhā*. Beirut, 1968.

Ibn Khallikān, Abu'l-'Abbās Aḥmad. *Wafayāt al-a'yān*. Beirut, 1969–1971.

Ibn al-Nadīm, Muḥammad b. Isḥāq. *al-Fihrist*, tr. B. Dodge. New York, 1970.

Ibn al-Qifṭī. *Tā'rīkh al-ḥukamā'*. Delhi, 1903.

Ibn Sīnā. *Avicenna's De Anima*, ed. F. Rahman. London, 1959.

___ *Avicenna's Psychology*, tr. F. Rahman. London, 1952.

___ *A Treatise on the Canon of Medicine of Avicenna Incorporating a Translation of the First Book*, tr. O. C. Gruner. London, 1930.

___ *Dānish-nāmah-yi 'alā'ī*, ed. M. Mu'īn. Tehran, 1331 Sh./1952. French trans. M. Achéna and H. Massé as *Le Livre de science*. Paris, 1955–1958.

___ *Remarks and Admonitions, Part One: Logic*, tr. Sh. Inati. Toronto, 1984.

___ *al-Ishārāt wa'l-tanbīhāt*, ed. S. Dunyā. Cairo, 1957–1960.

___ *Le Livre des directives et remarques*: Kitāb al-ishārat wa'l-tanbīhāt, tr. A. M. Goichon. Beirut, 1951.

___ 'Le poème de l'âme', tr. H. Massé. *La Revue du Caire*, 27 (1951), pp. 7–9.

___ *Poème de la medicine-urǧūza fi'l-ṭibb*, ed. and tr. A. Jahier and H. Noureddine. Paris, 1956.
___ *al-Qaṣīdat al-ʿayniyyah* (*Ode on the Soul*), tr. A. J. Arberry in G. M. Wickens, *Avicenna, Scientist and Philosopher: A Millenary Symposium*. London, 1952.
___ '*Risālah fi'l-ʿishq*', tr. E. L. Fackenheim. *Medieval Studies*, 7 (1945), pp. 208–228.
___ *al-Shifā': al-Ilāhiyyāt*, ed. G. Anawati and S. Zāyid. Cairo, 1960.
Juzjānī, Abū ʿUbayd. *Sīrat al-Shaykh al-Ra'īs*, ed. and tr. W. E. Gohlman as *The Life of Ibn Sīnā: A Critical Edition and Annotated Translation*. Albany, NY, 1974.
Khwānsārī, Muḥammad Bāqir. *Rawḍāt al-jannāt*. Tehran, 1341 Sh./1962.
al-Masʿūdī, Abu'l-Ḥasan ʿAlī. *al-Tanbīh wa'l-ishrāf*. Cairo, 1960.
Miskawayh, Abū ʿAlī Aḥmad. *An Unpublished Treatise of Miskawayh on Justice* or *Risālah fī māhiyyat al-ʿadl li-Miskawayh* ed. M. Khan. Leiden, 1964.
___ *al-Ḥikmat al-khālidah: Jāwidān khirad*, ed. ʿA. Badawī. Tehran, 1358 Sh./1979.
___ *Tajārib al-umam*, ed. A. Emāmī. Tehran, 1366 Sh./1987.
___ *The Refinement of Character* (Tahdhīb al-akhlāq), ed. and tr. C. K. Zurayk. Beirut, 1967.
Nāṣir-i Khusraw. *Zād al-musāfirīn*. ed. M. Badl al-Raḥmān. Berlin, 1341/1923.
Niẓām al-Mulk. *Siyāsat-nāmah*. Tehran, 1369 Sh./1990.
Niẓāmī ʿArūḍī. *Chahār-maqālah*, ed. M. Qazwīnī and M. Muʿīn. 3rd ed. Tehran, 1333 Sh./1954.
Rāzī, Abū Bakr Muḥammad Zakariyyā'. 'Extracts of a Correspondence between Abū Ḥātim al-Rāzī (from his *Aʿlām al-nubuwwa*) and Zakariyyā' Rāzī', tr. F. Brion in *Bulletin de Philosophie médiévale*, 28 (1986), pp. 134–162.
___ *La Physiognomie arabe et le* Kitāb al-firāsa *de Fakhr al-Dīn al-Rāzī*, ed. P. Gauthner. Paris, 1939.
___ *Kitāb al-sīrat al-falsafiyah* (*Rhazes on the Philosophic Life*), French tr., P. Kraus, 'Rāziānā I', *Orientalia*, 4 (1935), pp. 300–334; rev. ed. in *Abi Bakr Moḥammadi filii Zachariae Raghensis (Razis), Opera Philosophica*, ed. P. Kraus. Paris-Cairo, 1939, pp. 99–111.
___ *al-Sīrat al-falsafiyyah* (*The Philosophical Life*), tr. A. J. Arberry. Tehran, 1964.
___ *The Spiritual Physick of Rhazes*, tr. A. J. Arberry. London, 1950.
___ *Traité sur le calcul, les reins et la vessie*, tr. P. de Köning. Leiden, 1896.
Shahrazūrī, Shams al-Dīn Muḥammad. *Nuzhat al-arwāḥ*. Alexandria, 1993.
Tabrīzī, M. ʿA. *Rayḥānat al-adab*. Tehran, 1332 Sh./1953.
Tawḥīdī, Abū Ḥayyān. *al-Imtāʿ wa'l-mu'ānasa*. Cairo 1939–44.
Ṭūqān, Q. H. *Turāth al-ʿarab al-ʿilmī*. Cairo, 1963.
Yāqūt al-Ḥamawī, Shihāb al-Dīn. *Muʿjam al-udabā'*. Cairo, 1936.

Secondary Sources

Abed, S. B. *Aristotelian Logic and the Arabic Language in Alfārābī*. Albany, NY, 1991.
Abū Rayyān, M. A. 'La critique de la philosophie d'Avicenna par Abu'l-Barakāt al-Baghdādī', *Bulletin of the Faculty of Arts*: University of Egypt, 7 (1958), pp. 17–60.

Afnan, S. M. *Avicenna, His Life and Works*. London, 1958.

Aḥmad, N. 'Some Less Known Writings of 'Umar Khayyām', *Oriental College Magazine*, 35 (1959), pp. 1–24.

Aḥmad, Z. 'Al-Bīrūnī, His Life and His Works', *Islamic Culture*, 5 (1931), pp. 343–351.

Allard, M. 'Un philosophe théologien: Muḥammad b. Yūsuf al-'Āmirī', *Revue de l'Histoire des Religions*, 187 (1975), pp. 57–69.

Alonso, M. A. 'Ibn Sīnā y sus primera influencias en el Mundo Latino', *Revista del Instituto Egypcio de Estudios Islamicos*, 1 (1953), p. 36–57.

___ 'La "al-anniya" de Avicenna y el problema de la esencia y existencia', *Pensamiento*, 14 (1958), pp. 311–346.

Amedroz, H. F. 'Note on the Historian', in L. Caetani, ed., *The Tajārib al-umam or History of Ibn Miskawayh*, reproduction in facsimile from the Aya Sofiya Ms. in Constantinople, vol. 1, pp. xvii–xxvii.

Amid, A. M. *Essai sur la psychologie d'Avicenne*. Geneva, 1940.

Aminrazavi, M. 'Īrānshahrī: Life and Views on Time and Space', *Islamic Studies*, 31 (1992), pp. 479–486.

___ *Suhrawardi and the School of Illumination*. Richmond, UK, 1997.

___ *The Wine of Wisdom: The Life, Poetry and Philosophy of Omar Khayyam*. Oxford, 2005.

Anawati, G. C. *Essai de bibliographie avicennienne*. Cairo, 1950.

___ 'La destinée de l'homme dans la philosophie d'Avicenne. L'Homme et son destin'. *Actes du ler Congrès International de Philosophie Médievale*. Louvain, 1955, pp. 257–266.

___ *Études de philosophie musulmane*. Paris, 1974.

___ and L. Gardet. *Introduction à la theologie musulmane*. Paris, 1948.

Ansari, A. H. *The Ethical Philosophy of Miskawayh*. Aligarh, 1964.

___ 'Miskawayh's Conception of God, the Universe and Man', *Islamic Culture*, 37 (1963), pp. 131–144.

Archibald, R. C. 'Notes on 'Omar Khayyām (1050–1122) and Recent Discoveries', *Pi Mu Epsilon Journal*, 1 (1953), pp. 350–358.

Arkoun, M. 'Deux épîtres de Miskawayh', *Bulletin d'Études Orientales*, 17 (1961), pp. 7–74.

___ 'À propos d'une édition récente du *Kitāb tahdhīb al-akhlāq*', *Arabica*, 9 (1962), pp. 61–73.

___ 'Texts inédits de Miskawayh', *Annales Islamologiques*, 5 (1963), pp. 181–205.

___ 'Notes et documents Miskawayh: de l'intellect et de l'intelligible', *Arabica*, 11 (1964), pp. 80–87.

___ *Contribution à l'étude de l'humanisme arabe au ive/xe siècle*. Paris, 1970.

___ 'Logocentrisme et vérité religieuse dans la pensée islamique d'après *al-I'lām bi-manāqib al-Islām* d'al-'Āmirī', *Studia Islamica*, 35 (1972), pp. 5–52.

Arnaldez, R. *Conception et pratique de la science chez Avicenne et Bīrūnī*. Karachi, 1973.

___ 'La science 'arabe à travers l'oeuvre de Bīrūnī', *Lumières arabes sur l'occident mediéval* (1978), pp. 41–54.

Azkai, P. *Kārnāmah-yi Bīrūnī (Essai bibliographique) d'après Bīrūnī et Boilot*. Tehran, 1973.

Badawī, ʿA. *Mubāḥathāt*, in *Arisṭū ʿind al-ʿarab*. Cairo, 1947.

___ 'Miskawayh', in M. M. Sharīf, ed., *A History of Muslim Philosophy*. Wiesbaden, 1963, vol. 1, pp. 469–479.

___*Taʿlīqāt*. Cairo, 1973.

Bāmdād, M. *Sharḥ-i ḥāl-i rijāl-i Īrān*. Tehran, 1347–1350 Sh./1968–1971.

Bausani, A. 'Al-Bīrūnī, un genio del x secolo', *Islam: Storia e Civiltà*, 4 (1985), pp. 5–15.

___ 'Some Considerations of Three Problems of the Anti-Aristotelian Controversy between al-Bīrūnī and Ibn Sīnā', *Akten Kongresse für Arabistik*, 7 (1974, 1976), pp. 74–85.

Beale, Th. W. *An Oriental Biographical Dictionary*, rev. ed. Henry G. Keene. London, 1894.

Beveridge, H. "Omar Khayyām', *JRAS*, 1 (1909), pp. 124–125.

Bhat, B. *Abū ʿAlī Miskawayh: A Study of His Historical and Social Thought*. New Delhi, 1953; 2nd ed., 1991.

Biesterfeldt, H. 'Abu'l-Ḥasan al-ʿĀmirī und die Wissenschaften', *Zeitschrift der deutschen Morgenlandischen Gesellschaft*, Supplement II, 1: XIX. Wiesbaden, 1977.

Boilot, D. J. 'L'oeuvre d'al-Bīrūnī. Essai bibliographique', *Institut Dominicain d'Études Orientales du Caire, Mélanges*, 2 (1955), pp. 161–256.

Bowen, H. "Umar Khayyām and a Relative of Niẓām al-Mulk', *BSOAS*, 6 (1930), pp. 274–275.

Bolotnikov, A. 'Omar Khayyām (filosof-poet-matematick)', *Na rubezhe vostoka*, 1 (1930), pp. 97–18; 2, pp. 93–111.

Boyce, M. *A History of Zoroastrianism*. Leiden, 1982.

___ *Textual Sources for the Study of Zoroastrianism*. Manchester, 1984.

Boyle, A. "Umar Khayyām: Astronomer, Mathematician and Poet', *Bulletin of the John Rylands Library*, 52 (1969), pp. 30–45.

Brockelmann, C. *Geschichte der arabischen Literatur*. Weimar, 1898–1902; 2nd ed., Leiden, 1943–1949; *Supplement*, 1937–1942.

Browne, E. G. *A Literary History of Persia*. London and Cambridge, 1902–1904.

Cahen, C. *Introduction à l'histoire du monde musulman médiéval: VIIe–XVe siècle*. Paris, 1982.

Carra de Vaux. *Avicenne*. Paris, 1939.

___ *Lexique de la langue philosophique d'Ibn Sīnā*. Paris, 1939.

___ *La Philosophie d'Avicenne et son influence en Europe médiévale*. Paris, 1944.

Corbin, H. *Avicenne et le récit visionnaire*. Paris, 1954. English trans., *Avicenna and the Visionary Recital*, tr. William R. Trask. New York, 1960.

___ with S. H. Nasr and O. Yahya. *Histoire de la philosophie islamique I: Des origines jusqu'à la mort d'Averroës (1198)*. Paris, 1964.

___ *En Islam iranien: Aspects spirituels et philosophiques*. Paris, 1971–1972.

___ *Spiritual Body and Celestial Earth: From Mazdean Iran to Shīʿite Iran*, tr. N. Pearson. Princeton, NJ, 1977.

___ *History of Islamic Philosophy*, tr. L. Sherrard. London, 1993.
Chahine, O. E. *Ontologie et théologie chez Avicenne*. Paris, 1956.
Chelkowski, P. J., ed. *The Scholar and the Saint. Studies in Commemoration of Abū Rayḥān al-Bīrūnī and Jalāl al-Dīn al-Rūmī*. New York, 1975.
Cruz Hernández, M. *La metafisica de Avicenna*. Granada, 1949.
___ 'La distincion Avicenniana de la esencia y la existencia y su interpretacion en filosofia occidental', *Homenaje a Millàs Vallicrosa*, 2 (1956), pp. 351–374.
___ 'La nocion de "ser" en Avicenne', *Pensamiento*, 15 (1959), pp. 83–98.
___ *Historia del pensamiento en el mundo islámico*; vol. 1: *Desde los origenes hasta el siglo XII*. Madrid, 1981.
Csillik, B. "Umar Khayyām miscellanea', *Acta Orientalia (Acad. ssi. hungariea)*, 10 (1960), pp. 59–77.
Daiber, H. 'Bahmanyār Kīā', in *EIR*, vol. 3, pp. 501–503.
___ *Bibliography of Islamic Philosophy*. 2 vols. Leiden, 1999.
D'alverny, M. T. 'Notes sur les traductions mediévales d'Avicenne', *Archives d'Histoire Doctrinale et Littéraire du Moyen Âge*, 27 (1952), pp. 337–358.
Dānish-Pazhūh, M. T. *Fihrist-i kitābhā-yi ihdā'ī-yi Sayyid Muḥammad Mishkāt*. Tehran, 1354 Sh./1975.
De Boer, T. J. *The History of Philosophy in Islam*, tr. E. R. Jones. New York, 1967.
___ 'Ethics and Morality (Muslim)', in *Encyclopedia of Religion and Ethics*. New York, 1980, vol. 5, pp. 507b–508.
Donaldson, D. M. *Studies in Muslim Ethics*. London, 1953.
Druart, Th. A. 'al-Fārābī and Emanationism', in John F. Wippel, ed., *Studies in Medieval Philosophy*. Washington, DC, 1987.
Duchesne-Guillemin, Jacques. *La Religion de l'Iran ancien*. Paris, 1962.
Encyclopaedia Iranica. London-Boston, 1982—.
Encyclopaedia of Iran and Islam. Tehran, 1976–1982.
Encyclopaedia of Islam, first edition. Leiden and London, 1913–1938.
Encyclopaedia of Islam. New ed., Leiden and London, 1960–2006.
Ergin, O. *Ibni Sīnā Bibliografyasi*. Istanbul, 1956.
Fāḍil, A. 'The Fame of 'Umar Khayyām (Between Science and Literature)', *Muslim World*, 50 (1960), pp. 269–268.
Fakhry, M. 'The Platonism of Miskawayh and its Implication for his Ethics', *Studia Islamica*, 42 (1973), pp. 39–57.
___ 'al-Bīrūnī and Greek Philosophy—An Essay in Philosophical Erudition', in *Al-Bīrūnī Commemoration Volume*. Karachi, 1979, pp. 344–349.
___ *A History of Islamic Philosophy*. New York, 1983.
___ *Ethical Theories in Islam*. Leiden, 1991.
Gai, B. M. "Omar Khayyām—Poet and Philosopher', *Indo-Iranica*, 8, 3 (1955), pp. 37–48.
Galindo Aguilar, E. 'Anthropologie et cosmogonie chez Avicenne', *Institut des Belles-lettres Arabes Revue*, 87 (1959), pp. 287–323.
Galston, M. *Politics and Excellence: The Political Philosophy of al-Fārābī*. Princeton, NJ, 1990.

Gardet, L. *La Pensée religieuse d'Avicenne (Ibn Sīnā)*. Paris, 1951.

___ *La Connaissance mystique chez Ibn Sina et ses présupposés philosophiques*. Paris, 1952.

___ 'En honneur du millénaire d'Avicenne', *La Revue Thomiste*, 51 (1951), pp. 333–345.

___ 'L'Étude de la philosophie arabe et son rôle dans l'interprétation de la scholastique', *Proceedings of the Sixth International Congress of Philosophy*. Cambridge, 1926; New York, 1927, pp. 592–596.

Gardner, Iain, ed. *The Kephalaia of the Teacher: The Edited Coptic Manichaean Texts in Translation with Commentary*. Leiden, 1995.

Gilson, E. 'Les sources greco-arabes de l'augustinisme avicennisant', *Archives d'Histoire Doctrinale et Littéraire du Moyen Âge*, 4 (1929), pp. 5–149.

Goichon, A. M. *La Distinction de l'essence et de l'existence d'après Ibn Sīnā*. Paris, 1937.

___ *Lexique de la langue philosophique d'Ibn Sīnā*.Paris, 1938.

___ *Vocabulaires comparés d'Aristote et d'Ibn Sina*. Paris, 1939.

___ *La Philosophie d'Avicenne et son includence en Europe médiévale*. Paris, 1951.

___ 'La théorie des formes chez Avicenne', *Congresso Internazionale di Filosofia*, 9 (1958), pp. 131–138.

___ *La Philosophie d'Avicenne et son influence en Europe médiévale*. Paris, 1944.

Goodman, L. E. 'Rāzī's Myth of the Fall of the Soul: Its Function in his Philosophy', in G. Hourani, ed., *Essays on Islamic Philosophy and Science*. Albany, NY, 1975, pp. 25–40.

___ 'The Epicurean Ethic of Muḥammad ibn Zakariyā' al-Rāzī', *Studia Islamica*, 34 (1971), pp. 5–26.

___ 'Rāzī's Psychology', *Philosophical Forum*, 4 (1972), pp. 26–48.

___ *Avicenna*. London, 1992.

___ 'al-Rāzī, Abū Bakr Muḥammad', *EI2*, vol. 8, pp. 474–477.

Gutas, D. *Avicenna and the Aristotelian Tradition*. Leiden, 1988.

Ḥalabī, 'A. A. *Tārikh-i falsafah dar Īrān wa jahān-i islāmī*. Tehran, 1373 Sh./1994.

Heinen, A. 'Al-Bīrūnī and Al-Haytham: A Comparative Study of Scientific Method', *Al-Bīrūnī Commemoration Volume*. Karachi, 1979, pp. 501–513.

Holmyard, E. J. and Mandeville, D. C., tr. *Avicennae de congelatione et conlutinatione lapidum, being Sections of the Kitab al-Shifa. The Latin and Arabic Texts edited with an English Translation of the latter with critical notes*. Paris, 1927.

Horton, M. *Die spekulative und positive Theologie des Islam*. Leipzig, 1912.

Inati, Shams. *A Study of Ibn Sīnā's Mysticism*. Albany, NY, 1996.

Iqbal, M. *The Development of Metaphysics in Persia*. Lahore, 1934.

Iskandar, A. Z. 'The Medical Bibliography of al-Rāzī', in G. Hourani, ed., *Essays on Islamic Philosophy and Science*. Albany, NY, 1975, pp. 41–46.

Izzat, A. A. *Trois recherches philosophiques*. Cairo, 1947.

Jackson, A. V. W. *From Constantinople to the Home of 'Omar Khayyām*. New York, 1911.

Janssens, J. *An Annotated Bibliography on Ibn Sīnā* (1979–1989). Leuven, 1991.

Kabīr, Aḥmad Khān. 'A Select Bibliography of Writings on al-Fārābī in English', *Muslim World Book Review*, 13 (1993), pp. 56–61.

Karam, Y. 'La vie spirituelle d'après Avicenne', *La Revue du Caire*, 27 (1951), pp. 44–55.

Khan, M. S. *Studies in Miskawayh's Contemporary History*. Ann Arbor, MI, 1980.

Kraemer, J. L. *Philosophy in the Renaissance of Islam: Abū Sulaymān al-Sijistānī and his Circle*. Leiden, 1986.

___ *Humanism in the Renaissance of Islam: The Cultural Revival During the Buyid Age*. Leiden, 1993.

Kraus, P. *Abī Moḥammadi filii Zachariae Raghensis (Razis) opera philosophica fragmentaque quae supersunt*. Cairo, 1939; repr., Beirut, 1973.

Lacroix, M. C. 'Education et instruction selon Abu'l-Ḥasan al-ʿĀmirī: Présentation et traduction d'un extrait du *Kitāb al-saʿāda wa'l-isʿād*', *Revue Philosophique de Louvain*, 87 (1989), pp. 165–214.

Leaman, O. 'Ibn Miskawayh', in S. H. Nasr and O. Leaman, ed., *History of Islamic Philosophy*. London, 1996, pp. 252–257.

Ley, H. *Avicenna*. Berlin, 1953.

Lobato, A. *Ysanato Tomas en la teoria del conocimiento*. Granada, 1957.

Madkour, M. *L'Organon d' Aristote dans le monde arabe*. Paris, 1943.

___ 'Le traité des categories du Shifā'', *Mélanges Institut Dominicain d'Études Orientales*, 5 (1958), pp. 253–278.

___ 'Avicenne et l'alchimie', *La Revue du Caire*, 27 (1951), pp. 120–129.

___ 'al-Fārābī', in M. M. Sharif, ed., *A History of Muslim Philosophy*. Wiesbaden, 1963, vol. 2, pp. 450–468.

Mahdavi, Y. *Bibliographie d'Ibn Sīnā*. Tehran, 1332 Sh. /1953.

Mahdi, M. 'Alfārābī', in L. Strauss and J. Cropsey, ed., *History of Political Philosophy*. Chicago, IL, 1987.

___ 'al-Fārābī's Imperfect State', *Journal of the American Oriental Society*, 110 (1990), pp. 691–726.

Mahdihassan, S. 'Interpreting al-Bīrūnī's Observations on Indian Alchemy', *Al-Bīrūnī Commemoration Volume*. Karachi, 1979, pp. 524–529.

Margoliouth, S. *Lectures on Arabic Historians*. Calcutta, 1930.

Massignon, L. 'La philosophie orientale d'Ibn Sīnā et son alphabet philosophique', *Memorial Avicenne*, 4 (1954), pp. 1–18.

___ 'Avicenne et les influences orientales', *La Revue du Caire*, 27 (1951), pp. 10–12.

Meyerhof, M. 'The Philosophy of the Physician al-Rāzī'. *Islamic Culture*, 15 (1941), pp. 45–58.

___ 'Thirty-three Clinical Observations by Rhazes', *Isis*, 23 (1935), pp. 321–356.

Mīnuvī, M. 'Az khazā'in-i Ṭurkiyyah', *Majalla-yi dānishkadah-yi adabiyyāt-i dānishgāh-i Tehrān*, 4 (1954), p. 75.

Mohaghegh, M. 'Notes on the "Spiritual Physick" of al-Rāzī', *Studia Islamica*, 26 (1967), pp. 5–22.

___ *Fīlsūf-i Rayy*. Tehran, 1349 Sh./1970.

___ ed. and tr., *Fihrist-i kitābhā-yi Rāzī*. Tehran, 1352 Sh./1973.

Muṭahharī, M. *Khadamāt-i mutaqābil-i Īrān wa Islām*. Tehran, 1353 Sh./1974.

Naficy, S. *Bibliographie des principaux travaux européens sur Avicenne*. Tehran, 1333 Sh./1954.

Nallino, A. 'Filosofia "orientale" od "illuminativa' d'Avicenna"', *Rivista degli Studi Orientali*, 10 (1925), pp. 367–433.

Nasr, S. H. 'Cosmologies of Aristotle and Ibn Sīnā', *Pakistan Philosophical Journal*, 3 (1960), pp. 13–28.

___ *al-Bīrūnī: An Annotated Bibliography*. Tehran, 1973.

___ *Abū Rayḥān Bīrūnī, Scientist and Scholar Extraordinary*. Tehran, 1973.

___ *Three Muslim Sages*. New York, 1976.

___ 'From the Alchemy of Jābir to the Chemistry of Rāzī', in Nasr, ed., *Islamic Life and Thought*. Albany, NY, 1981, pp. 120–123.

___ *Science and Civilization in Islam*. New York, 1992.

___ *An Introduction to Islamic Cosmological Doctrine*. Albany, NY, 1993.

___ *The Islamic Intellectual Tradition in Persia*, ed. M. Aminrazavi. London, 1996.

___ 'Why Fārābī was called the Second Teacher?', tr. and ed. M. Aminrazavi in S. H. Nasr, *The Islamic Intellectual Tradition in Persia*. London, 1996.

___ *Islamic Philosophy from its Origins to the Present*. Albany, NY, 2006.

___ and O. Leaman, ed., *History of Islamic Philosophy*. London, 1996.

Netton, I. *Allāh Transcendent*. New York, 1989.

___ *al-Fārābī and his School*. London, 1992.

Nyberg, H. S. *Hilfsbuch des Pehlevi*. Uppsala, 1928–31.

Partaw, A. *Andīshahā-yi falsafī-yi Īrānī*. Tehran, 1363 Sh./1984.

Partington, J. R. 'The Chemistry of Rāzī', *Ambix*, 1 (1938), p. 193.

Pearson, J. D. *Index Islamicus, 1906–1955*. Cambridge, 1958; *Supplement*, 1962, and later volumes.

Pines, S. *Beiträge zur islamischen Atomenlehre*. Berlin, 1938.

___ 'La "philosophie orientale" d'Avicenne et sa polemique contre les Bagdadiens', *Archives d'Histoire Doctrinale et Littéraire du Moyen Âge*, 27 (1952), pp. 5–37.

___ 'Rāzī critique de Galien', *Actes du Septième Congrès International d'Histoire des Sciences*, 8 (1953), pp. 480–487.

Pūr-Dāvūd, I. *Farhang-i Īrān-i bāstān*. Tehran, 1330 Sh./1951.

Qurbānī, A. *Bīrūnī-nāmah*. Tehran, 1353 Sh./1974.

___ 'al-Rāzī', in *Dictionary of Scientific Biography*. New York, 1981.

Rankking, G. S. A. 'The Life of Rhazes', *International Congress of Medicine* (1914), pp. 237–268.

Rempis, C. H. *Beiträge zur Khayyām-Forschung*. Leipzig, 1937.

Rescher, N. *al-Fārābī: An Annotated Bibliography*. Pittsburg, 1962.

Ritter, H. 'Al-Bīrūnī's Übersetzung des Yoga-Sutra des Patañjali', *Oriens*, 9 (1956), pp. 165–200.

Rosenfeld, B. A. 'O matematicheskikh rabotakh 'Umara Khaiyama', *Uchenye Zapiski Azerbaidzanskogo Univ.*, 9 (1957), pp. 3–22.

___ and A. P. Yushkevich. *'Umar Khayyām*. Moscow, 1965.

Rosenthal, F. 'State and Religion According to Abu'l-Ḥasan al-'Āmirī', *Islamic Quarterly*,

3 (1956), pp. 42–42.
___ *A History of Muslim Historiography*. Leiden, 1968.
Ross, E. D. "Umar Khayyām', *BSOAS*, 4 (1926–28), pp. 433–439.
___ and H. A. R. Gibb. 'The Earliest Account of 'Umar Khayyām', *BSOAS*, 5 (1928–30), pp. 467–473.
Rothfeld, O. *'Umar Khayyām and His Age*. Bombay, 1922.
Ṣadūqī Suhā, M. *Ḥukamā wa 'urafā-yi muta'akhkhirīn-i Ṣadr al-muta'allihīn*. Tehran, 1359 Sh./1980.
Ṣafā, Dh., ed. *Avicenna Commemoration Volume*. Tehran, 1334–37 Sh./1954–58.
___ 'Barkhī az naẓarhā-yi falsafī-yi Abū Rayḥān wa mukhtaṣarī dar munāqishāt-i 'ilmi-yi ū wa Ibn-i Sīnā', *Indo-Iranica*, 5 (1952), pp. 5–12.
___ *al-Bīrūnī, ses oeuvres et ses pensées*. Tehran, 1973.
Sa'īd, H. M., ed. *al-Bīrūnī Commemoration Volume*. Karachi, 1979.
Sa'īd, Kh. *The Bibliography of al-Bīrūnī*, tr. A. Ḥabībī. Tehran, 1973.
Salet, P. *'Umar Khayyām, savant et philosophe*. Paris, 1927.
Saliba, Dj. *Étude sur la métaphysique d'Avicenne*. Paris, 1926.
Sarton, G. *Introduction to the History of Science*, vol. 1. Baltimore, MD, 1927.
Sauvaget, J. *Introduction à l'histoire de l'orient musulman: Elements de bibliographie*. Paris, 1946.
___ *Introduction to the History of the Muslim East: A Bibliographical Guide*, ed. and tr. C. Cahen. Berkeley, CA, 1965.
Schoy, C. 'Original Studien aus al-Bīrūnī's al-Qānūn al-Mas'ūdī', *Isis*, 5 (1923), pp. 51–74.
Sezgin, F. *Geschichte der arabischen Schrifttums*. Leiden, 1967–.
Sharif, M., ed. *History of Islamic Philosophy*. Wiesbaden, 1963–1966.
Shayegan, Y. *Avicenna on Time*. Ph.D. diss., Harvard University, 1986.
Siassi, A. A. *La Psychologie d'Avicenne et ses analogues dans la psychologie moderne*. Tehran, 1954.
___ *Le Livre du millénaire d'Avicenne*. Tehran, 1956.
Siddiqi, B. H. 'Ibn Miskawayh's Theory of History', *Iqbāl*, 12 (1963), pp. 71–80.
Spies, O. 'Der deutsch Beitrag zur Erforschung Avicennas', in *Avicenna Commemoration Volume*. Calcutta, 1956.
Storey, W. E. *'Umar Khayyām as a Mathematician*. Boston, MA, 1918.
Storey, C. A. *Persian Literature: A Bio-bibliographical Survey*. London, 1927. Persian tr. Y. Āriyānpūr. Tehran, 1362 Sh./1983.
Strauss, L 'Fārābī's Plato', in *Louis Ginsberg Jubilee Volume*. New York, 1945, pp. 357–393.
Suter, H. and E. Wiedemann. 'Über al-Bīrūnī und seine Schriften', *Beiträge zur Geschichte der Naturwissenschaften. Sitzungsberichten der physikalisch-medizinischen Sozietät in Erlangen*. Erlangen, 1902–1929, pp. 1–69.
Thabit al-Fandi, M. 'Dieu et le monde: Leurs rapports d'après Avicenne', *Bulletin of the Faculty of Arts, University of Egypt*, 11 (1958), Arabic sect., pp. 159–180.
Troilo, E. 'Lineamento e interpretazione del sistema filosofico di Avicenne', *Atti d. Ac-*

cad. dei Lincei, Memorie, Classe di scienze morali storiche e filologiche. Rome, 1956, pp. 397–446.

Vadet, J. C. *Le souvenir de l'ancienne perse chez le philosophe Abu'l-Ḥasan al-ʿĀmirī*. Paris, 1983.

Vajda, G. 'Les notes d'Avicenne sur la "théologie d'Aristote"', *La Revue Thomiste*, 51 (1951), pp. 346–406.

Validi Togan, A. Z. 'Bīrūnī's Picture of the World', *Memoirs of the Archaeological Survey of India*, 53 (1937–1938), pp. 90–104.

von Horten, M., tr. *Die Metaphysik Avicennas. Metaphysik: Enthaltend die Metaphysik, Theologie, Kosmologie und Ethik*. New York and Halle, 1907.

von Mehren, A. F. *Traités mystiques d'Abou 'Alī al-Hosain b. 'Abdallāh b. Sīnā ou d'Avicenne; texte arabe avec l'explication en français*. Leiden, 1889–1891.

___ 'L'allégoire mystique Ḥay ben Yaqzān', *Le Muséon*, 5 (1885), pp. 411–426.

___ 'La philosophie d'Avicenne', *Le Muséon*, 1 (1883), pp. 89–409, 506–522.

___ 'Vues théosophiques d'Avicenne', *Le Muséon*, 4 (1885), pp. 594–599; 5 (1886), pp. 52–67.

Walzer, R. 'al-Fārābī's Theory of Prophecy and Divination', in R. Walzer, ed., *Greek into Arabic: Essay on Islamic Philosophy*. Oxford, 1962, pp. 206–219.

____ 'al-Fārābī', *EI2*, vol. 2, pp. 778–781.

West, E. W., tr. *Pahlavi Texts*. Oxford, 1880–97.

Widengren, G. *Die Religionen Irans*. Stuttgart, 1965.

Wilczynski, J. Z. 'On the Presumed Darwinism of al-Bīrūnī Eight Hundred Years before Darwin', *Isis*, 50 (1959), pp. 459–466.

Yushkevich, A. P. ''Umar Khayyām (1040–1123)', *Materiali po istorii progressivnoy obshetvenno filosofskoy misli v Uzbekistane* (1957), pp. 199–210.

Yūsuf ʿAlī, A. 'Al-Bīrūnī's India', *Islamic Culture*, 1 (1927), pp. 31–35, 223–230, 473–487.

Zaehner, R. C. *Zurvan, A Zoroastrian Dilemma*. Oxford, 1955.

Index

Aaron 200
Abū Bakr al-Ṣiddīq 360
Abū Ḥanīfa 204
Abū ʿAlī al-Khāzin *see* Miskawayh
Achaemenian dynasty 2
adab 344, 355
Adam 81, 193, 198, 240
Adharbādh 337–338
ʿAḍud al-Dawlah 217, 242
Āfrāsyāb 84
Aghrāḍ mā baʿd al-ṭabīʿah of Fārābī 135
Aharman *see* Ahriman
Ahriman (Aharman) 17, 19, 20, 23, 27, 28, 29, 30, 32, 48, 51, 55–63, 68–70, 80, 81, 82, 83, 84, 86, 88, 89, 90, 91, 94, 96, 101
Ahunavar (*Yathâ ahû vairyô*) 19, 29, 31, 57, 69
Ahura Mazda (Aûharmazd, Ohrmazd) 14, 15, 16–26, 27–34, 35, 36, 37, 40, 41, 44, 45, 47, 51, 53–55, 55–63, 64–66, 68–71, 73, 74–76, 80, 82, 83, 86, 88, 89, 90, 91, 93, 96, 102
Ahuras 54
Airyaman 63, 72
Akhlāq-i jalālī of Dawānī 324
Akhlāq-i muḥtashamī of Ṭūsī 324
Akhlāq-i Nāṣirī of Ṭūsī 324
Akôman 20, 31, 33, 58, 61, 63
ʿAlāʾ al-Dawlah 243, 244, 247
alchemy 186, 411, 412, 413, 432
Alexander the Great (Dhuʾl-Qarnayn) 84, 159, 160, 210, 374–375, 420, 457
Alexander of Aphrodisias 127, 217, 229, 468
algebra 474
ʿAlī b. Abī Ṭālib, Imam 5, 93, 193, 202, 206, 382
ʿAlī al-Riḍā, Imam 5
al-Amad ʿalaʾl-abad of ʿĀmirī 180, 181, 207–215
Amahraspands 14, 31, 58, 59, 60, 73, 78, 82, 85, 86, 90, 92
Amesha Spentas (*ameshôspendân*) 22, 64
ʿĀmilī, Bahāʾ al-Dīn 5, 8
ʿĀmirī, Abuʾl-Ḥasan 5, 180–181, 182–206, 207–215
Ammon 457
Ammonius 450, 451
Analytica Posteriora of Aristotle 136, 137–155
Anaximander 471
al-Andalusī, Qāḍī Saʿīd 180, 181, 207
Angra Mainyu 14, 66
anthropomorphism 440, 456
Anūshīrwān 324, 345–354
Apostle of God *see* Muḥammad the Prophet
ʿaql see intellect
Arabs 5, 6, 84, 130, 326
Arabic (language) 2, 3, 4, 8, 127, 130, 134,

135, 216, 243, 244, 245, 319, 323, 335, 385, 474
Aramaic (language) 106
Archimedes 210
Ardashīr I (Ardašir) 84, 106
Aries 80, 241
Aristotle, Aristotelianism 2, 6, 127, 134, 135, 136, 147, 155–163 *passim*, 181, 182, 210, 211, 214–215, 216, 217, 225, 226, 231, 238, 245, 260, 321, 324, 389, 390, 409, 412, 435, 436, 459–472 *passim*
arithmetic 187, 188, 268, 474
Arjuna 438–439, 447, 451–452
ascetics, asceticism 105, 107, 303-304, 307, 333, 358, 430
Asclepius 197, 458
al-Asfār al-arba'ah of Mullā Ṣadrā 180
Ash'arism 6, 9
Āshtiyānī, Jalāl al-Dīn 9
al-As'ilah wa'l-ajwibah of Bīrūnī 434, 435, 459–472
al-Āthār al-bāqiyah of Bīrūnī 434
anger 368–375
Athenians 127, 457
atomism 412
astrology 86, 434, 457
astronomy 187, 188, 211, 225, 268, 434
Aûharmazd *see* Ahura Mazda
Averroes *see* Ibn Rushd
Avesta, Avestan 13, 46, 75, 84, 85, 86, 94, 102
Avicenna *see* Ibn Sīnā
Āzarbāyjān 388

Baghdad school of philosophy 216
Bahman, King 10, 354–355
Bahmanyār *see* Marzbān, ibn Bahmanyār
Bahrām, King 106, 324
al-Balkhī, Abū Zayd 3, 211, 411
al-Baṣrī, Ḥasan 358
al-Basṭāmī, Abū Yazīd 452
Bāṭinīs (Bāṭinīya) 182, 209 *see also* Ismailis
Bayhaqī, Ẓahīr al-Dīn 'Alī 474
al-Bayt al-Muqaddas 312
Bharata 438
Bhuta 453, 455
Bidāyat al-ḥikmah of 'Allāmah Ṭabāṭabā'ī 3
Bīrūnī, Abū Rayḥān 6, 106, 130, 131, 409, 412, 434–436, 437–458, 459–472
Book of God *see* Qur'ān
Brahmans 438, 443, 446, 451, 452, 453, 454, 455, 456, 458
Brahmarshi 455
Bretheren of Purity *see* Ikhwān al-Ṣafā'
Buddha, Buddhists 105, 106, 454
Bukhārā 243
Bundahišn 2, 15–26
burhān see demonstration
Buyid dynasty 243, 323
Būzarjumihr 324, 341–344
Byzantium, Byzantines 1, 339, 341

Cancer 80, 82, 241
Capricorn 241
cause[s] 148–150, 166, 230, 251, 256, 261, 268, 269, 284, 467–468, 476–477, 482 *see also* final cause
Celestial Jerusalem 312
celestial bodies , 392, 394, 395
celestial sphere[s] 21, 25, 189, 213, 223, 319, 389, 394, 399, 400, 402, 403, 406, 458, 463–473 *passim*, 469, 470 *see also* heavenly bodies
certainty 137–140
Chinvat Bridge 15, 60, 64, 67
Christianity, Christians 2, 14, 105, 116, 121, 134, 180, 216, 236, 237, 238, 245, 429, 441, 456, 464
contingency, the contingent 75–76, 138, 250–251; 466, 478, 479; contingent beings 247, 476; contingent existence 212, 245, 479; contingent events 376–377
Corbin, Henry 9, 246, 247

corporeal world 13, 14, 188, 389, 396
cosmic body 482
cosmic history 108
cosmic mind 481, 482, 483
cosmogony 2
cosmology 14, 245
creation 14, 16, 17, 18, 20, 21, 24, 26, 27, 28, 29, 30, 31, 32, 33, 35, 36, 37, 38, 42, 47, 55, 56, 57, 58, 59, 60, 61, 63, 69, 70, 72, 73, 74, 75, 76, 79, 80, 85, 86, 107, 113, 132, 187, 188, 212, 215, 232, 242, 246, 254, 256, 260, 269–276, 289, 388, 405, 435, 438, 440, 444, 447, 456, 479, 480, 482, 483; immediate creation 273
creation stories 14
Creator 31, 34, 58, 59, 64, 73, 75, 76, 79, 80, 86, 155, 187, 194, 196, 197, 211, 212–215, 224, 238, 255, 269, 356, 363, 380, 383, 406, 414, 426, 431, 451, 464, 481
Creta, Cretans 457
Ctesiphon 105

Dādistān-i Dīnīk 14, 35–43, 64–66
Daena 65
Daevas 54; Aeshma Daeva 14
Daf' al-aḥzān of al-Kindī 385–387
Dahāk the Arab (Ẓaḥḥāk) 84
daimons 319
Daisān 422
Dānish-nāmah-yi 'alā'ī of Ibn Sīnā 244, 245, 246, 247–268, 388
Ḍarūrat al-taḍādd fi'l-'ālam wa'l-jabr wa'l-baqā' of 'Umar Khayyām 476–480
David 209
Dawānī, Jalāl al-Dīn 324
Dayṣāniyyah 130
De Anima of Aristotle 163
De Caelo of Aristotle 238, 435
definitions 150–155
Democritus 210
demons 15, 18, 19, 23, 24, 25, 26, 28, 29, 30, 32, 37, 42, 49, 64, 81, 83, 84, 85, 90, 91, 92, 94, 98, 99, 100, 102, 317, 318, 443, 453, 454
demonstration[s] 140–144, 148–150
Dēnkard (*Dēnkart*) 2, 14, 15, 73–76, 88–102
determinism 181, 474, 475, 476–480
Deva 453, 454, 455, 456
devs 56, 57, 58, 59, 60, 61, 68
Dhu'l-Qarnayn *see* Alexander
Dhūbān 334, 335, 336
Dīnā-i Maīnog-i Khirad 14, 44–52
discursive philosophy 181, 217
divine unity *see* unity of God
divine wisdom 232, 233, 287
Diogenes 210, 471
Dios 457
dreams 263–264
dualism 2, 123
duration 76, 132, 133, 298, 299, 312, 451, 480

Egypt, Egyptians 134, 209, 457
Ekesaite Mughtasilist cult 105
emanation 76, 135, 175, 212, 217, 277, 283, 289, 366, 388
Empedocles 2, 181, 209, 212–213, 451
elements, the 82, 85, 189, 217, 218–221, 223, 240, 260, 397, 462–463, 464, 466, 467–468, 471, 482, 483
enlightenment 233
Enneads of Plotinus 127, 135, 389
Epiphany 320
eschatology 15
ethics 2, 128, 129, 134, 159, 180, 323, 324
Ethiopian 372
Euclid 210, 474
Europa 457
evil 2, 13, 14, 15, 16, 23, 28, 30, 31, 36, 38, 40, 42, 54, 70, 74, 82, 84, 85, 86, 89, 90, 91, 93, 94, 96, 98, 99, 100, 102, 104, 110, 111, 120, 122, 171, 172, 176, 182, 194, 208, 215, 246, 258, 260, 278–288,

389, 402–406, 412, 422, 423, 443, 446, 447, 476, 479; evil spirit 18–20, 23–26 *passim*, 56–58, 60, 63, 81
existence[s] 212, 235, 237, 238, 245, 250, 269–276, 277–278, 280, 284, 286, 287-288, 289, 296–302 *passim*, 391, 396, 401, 402, 403-404, 406, 439, 474, 475, 477–479, 481–484; necessary existence 247–260, 481, 482; nonexistence 250, 254, 269, 270, 271, 272, 273, 275, 276, 279, 284, 295–299 *passim*, 460; Universal Existences 481
existent[s] 15, 77, 128, 132, 139, 156, 157, 164, 165, 166, 167, 168, 170, 173, 174, 178, 179, 212, 224, 225, 230, 232, 233, 235, 237, 238, 239, 241, 245, 247, 251, 252, 261, 269, 274, 289, 297, 298, 299, 301, 327, 367, 390, 391, 395, 396, 403; contingent existent 245; First Existent 164–166, 196, 396; necessary existent 402–403; nonexistent 78, 269, 276, 279, 280, 297, 298, 299, 404, 478, 484

faculty[ies] 83, 92, 168, 171–176 *passim*, 184, 223, 224, 233–235, 238, 240, 248, 254, 257, 258, 259, 261, 262–266 *passim*, 278, 304, 306, 320, 324, 356, 362, 363, 368, 376, 377, 415, 418, 435, 439, 440, 441, 446, 449, 450, 455, 457
Faḍl ibn Sahl 334
fahlawiyyūn (Pahlavis), philosophy of 2
falsafah 3, 4, 6, 9
Fārābī, Abū Naṣr 5, 127, 128, 129, 134–136, 137–155, 156–179, 180, 181, 228
Farīdūn (Frêdûn) 36, 84
Fāṭimids 6
al-Fawz al-akbar of Miskawayh 323
fear 375–377; of death 377–383, 423
Fi'l-ʿaql of Fārābī 135
final cause 148, 153, 180, 227, 229, 391, 395–396, 399, 401, 403, 404, 405–406
First Agent 237, 238, 239
First Being 260
First Cause 136, 164–171, 173, 174, 224, 225, 228, 230, 232, 237, 450, 455, 456, 461, 468
First Existent 164, 165, 396
First Intellect *see* intellect
First Mover 217, 224, 225–232, 262
First Providence 290, 311
First Principle 239
First Truth 214, 258, 305, 308
al-Fihrist of Ibn Nadīm 134
Fī iḥṣāʾ al-ʿulūm of Fārābī 135
filius Vigilantis 312
fiqh see jurisprudence 203, 345
Flood of Noah 323
fravāhar (*fravahr*, *fravahar*) 15, 59, 61, 83, 85
free will 181, 437, 450, 475, 476, 476–480

Gabriel, Angel 201
Galen 210, 227, 228, 323, 365, 366, 412, 456–457, 458
Galenus *see* Galen
Gathas 2, 13, 14, 65
Gâyômard (Gayōmart, Gayomard) 24, 25, 33, 34, 36, 37, 41, 59, 61, 62, 63, 72, 81, 82
Gemini 21, 80, 241
genera 145, 147, 153, 154, 155, 367, 368, 387, 404, 462
generation 270, 405, 473
generation and corruption/world of generation and corruption (*ʿālam al-kawn wa'l-fasād*) 225, 234, 235, 239, 337, 372, 383, 384, 389, 394, 400, 405, 421, 464
genus 144, 145–147, 149, 153–155, 165, 174, 311, 380, 388, 393, 404–405, 462–463, 481, 482, 483, 484
geography 434
geometry 187, 209, 210, 211, 268, 282, 288, 432, 470
Ghazna 434
al-Ghazzālī, Abū Ḥāmid Muḥammad 6,

7, 128, 324, 474
Gita 438, 442, 443, 445, 446, 447, 448, 453
gnostics, gnosticism 8, 105, 410
Good Religion *see* Zoroastrianism
grammar 193, 216
Greater Bundahišn 14, 27–34, 55–63
Greater Persia 14
Greece, Greeks 1, 2, 5, 6, 13, 76, 106, 127, 135, 181, 209, 210, 217, 321, 322, 323, 324, 372, 412, 435, 454, 458
grief 89, 278, 285, 329, 338, 349, 356, 372, 382, 383–387
Guide for the Perplexed of Maimonides 411
Gundīshāpūr 106
Guštāsp, King 84

Hadhokht Nask 14, 15, 64, 66
ḥāl (state[s]) 250, 252, 258, 259, 260, 261, 264, 265
Hamadān 243, 244
Hamadānī 7
Ḥanbalites 202, 204
happiness 108–109, 170, 188, 190, 213, 257–259, 260–261, 290, 342, 347, 355, 357, 358, 361, 371, 374, 378, 380, 381, 383, 446, 459
Ḥasan ibn Sahl 334, 335, 336
Ḥashwiyyah 186, 190
Ḥayy ibn Yaqẓān of Ibn Sīnā 245–246
heaven 15, 42, 69, 80, 85, 86, 100, 118, 213, 228, 229, 319, 329, 392, 393, 418, 451
heavens, the 78, 109, 188, 197, 217, 235, 249, 255, 277, 316, 317, 389, 392–402, 436, 459–463, 464, 469, 470–473
heavenly bodies 173, 218, 220, 234–235, 239, 241, 459, 262, 435, 459 *see also* celestial spheres
Hegel 216
hell 26, 42, 48, 49, 57, 61, 62, 63, 68, 69, 75, 80, 82, 83, 85, 86, 89, 94, 95, 100, 383, 453
Heracles 451
Heraclitus 471
heresy, heretics 30, 74, 97, 102, 201, 202, 204, 211, 212, 422
Hermes 197
Hermeticism 412
ḥikmat see wisdom
al-ḥikmat al-ʿamaliyyah 129
al-ḥikmat al-ishrāq 7, 245
Ḥikmat al-ishrāq of Suhrawardī 7
al-Ḥikmat al-khālidah or *Jāwīdān-khirad* of Miskawayh 323, 324, 326–355
al-ḥikmat al-khusrawāniyyah 2
Ḥikmat al-mashriqiyyah of Ibn Sīnā 321
al-ḥikmat al-mashriqiyyah 244, 245
al-ḥikmat al-mutaʿāliyah 9
al-ḥikmat al-naẓariyyah 129
Hinduism, Hindus 105, 130, 429, 430, 434, 435, 437–458
Hipparchus 149
Hippocrates 210
Homer 210, 458
Hurmuz, King 106
Hormazyār 79–87
human species 232–242
Hūshang 326–333, 336 (*Aushahnaj*); Hôshâng 36
Hûshêdar 36, 51

Ibn Abī Uṣaybiʿah 134
Ibn al-Sarrāj 134
Ibn ʿArabī 7
Ibn Bishr Mattā 134
Ibn Khallikān 134
Ibn Marzbān *see* Marzbān
Ibn Nadīm 106, 134
Ibn Rushd (Averroes) 128
Ibn Sīnā, Abū ʿAlī al-Ḥusayn ibn ʿAbdallāh (Avicenna) 3, 4, 5, 6, 7, 127, 128, 129, 135, 180, 181, 243–246, 248–268, 269–276, 277–288, 289–302, 303–311, 312–320, 321–322, 388, 389, 390, 392, 409, 434, 435, 459, 474

Ibn Turkah Iṣfahānī 9
Ikhwān al-Ṣafā' (Bretheren of Purity) 3, 216
Ilāhiyyāt of Ibn Sīnā *see Metaphysics*
al-I'lām bi-manāqib al-Islām of 'Āmirī' 180, 181, 182–206
'ilm see knowledge
imagination 174, 225, 233, 234, 253–254, 261–266 *passim*, 268, 269, 287, 306, 309, 356, 418, 420, 460, 484
Imāmiyyah 202, 204
Imams 5, 177
'Imrān al-Ṣābī 5
India, Indians 2, 4, 6, 105, 106, 135, 197, 324, 326, 432–458 *passim*
Indra 453, 454, 455
infinite, the 17, 27, 30, 75, 77, 78
infinite being 276
infinite time 25, 27, 29, 75, 76
infinity 15, 75, 76, 144, 168, 269, 275, 465
intellect 38, 77, 78, 155, 166–169, 174–176, 180, 84, 185, 187, 189, 192–193, 194–196, 200, 203–204, 205, 206, 210, 212, 214, 222, 232, 233, 237–239, 241, 258–259, 260, 261–262, 266, 267, 269, 273, 276, 284, 330, 333, 338, 339, 348, 350, 353, 354, 355, 355–356, 383, 386, 391, 396–397, 401, 403, 412, 426, 429, 430, 433, 453, 461, 468, 478, 481, 482–483; Acquired Intellect 175; Active Intellect 174, 175, 178, 179, 267, 461; Agent Intellect 261–262, 267; Creative Intellect 482; Creator's Intellect 481; First Intellect 169; Passive Intellect 174–175; prophetic intellect 181; Second Intellect 481
intellection 127, 400, 406, 412
intuition 217, 267, 322
Īrānshahr 335
Īrānshahrī, Abu'l-'Abbās 130–131, 132–133, 409
Iraq 3, 334
'irfānī wisdom 9
Iṣfahān 3, 7, 8, 243, 244, 323
al-Ishārāt wa'l-tanbīhāt of Ibn Sīnā 128, 245, 246, 265–276, 289–292, 303–311
ishrāqī thought *see* School of Illumination
Islamic philosophy 4–5, 6
Ismailis 2, 180, 411 *see also* Bāṭinīs
Israelites 209, 457
Istiṭālat al-fahm of al-Jāḥiẓ 326

Jabriyyah 440
Jacobites 236
al-Jāḥiẓ, Abū 'Uthmān 326, 334
Jamšīd 84
Jāwīdān-khirad see al-Ḥikmat al-khālidah
Jawzjānī, Abū 'Ubayd 243
Ja'far al-Ṣādiq, Imam 5
Jesus 1, 105, 109, 110, 111, 116, 122, 236
Jilwah, Mīrzā Abu'l-Ḥasan 128
John Philoponus 217
John the Grammarian 214
Judaism, Jews 14, 180, 201, 216, 245
Jupiter (Ohrmazd) 83, 241, 457, 480
jurisprudence, jurisprudents 15, 185, 193, 199, 202, 203, 204, 205, 206, 345
Jurjān (Jurgan, Gurgan) 195, 243
Juwaynī, Imām al-Ḥaramayn 6
Juzjānī Abū 'Ubayd 243

kalām 6, 7, 8 *see also* theology
Kardar 106
Kāshānī, Afḍal al-Dīn 4, 180, 324
Kāshānī, Mullā Muḥsin Fayḍ 8, 324
Kay Xusrau (Kaî-Khûsrôî) 51, 84
Kephalaia 107, 108–123
Khayyām, 'Umar b. Ibrāhīm 6, 409, 410, 474–475, 476–480, 481–484
Khiṣr ibn 'Alī 335
Khurāsān 3, 5, 134, 180, 334
Khwārazm 434
al-Kindī, Abū Ya'qūb 3, 5, 127, 130, 211, 366, 385–386
Kirmānī, Ḥamīd al-Dīn 6
Kisrā Qubādh 339–344

Kitāb-i athīr of Īrānshahrī 132
Kitāb al-bahjah fī manṭiq wa'l-ṭabīʿī wa'l-ilāhī of Bahmanyār 389
Kitāb al-burhān of Fārābī 135, 137
Kitāb al-ḥiss of Aristotle 472
Kitāb al-ḥurūf of Fārābī 135
Kitāb-i jalīl of Īrānshahrī 132
Kitāb al-jamʿ bayn ra'yay al-ḥakīmayn, Aflāṭūn al-ilāhī wa Arasṭū of Fārābī 135, 136, 155–163
Kitāb al-mūsīqā al-kabīr of Fārābī 135
Kitāb al-samā' wa'l ʿālam of Aristotle 467
Kitāb al-samāʿ al-ṭabīʿī of Aristotle 462, 463, 465, 468, 470, 473
Kitāb al-shāmil of Bīrūnī 434
Kitāb al-shifā' of Ibn Sīnā 244, 292–302, 322
Kitāb al-tafhīm of Bīrūnī 434
Kitāb al-taḥṣīl of Bahmanyār 388, 389, 390
Kitāb al-tajrīd of Naṣīr al-Dīn Ṭūsī 9
Kitāb al-zīnah fi'l-manṭiq of Bahmanyār 389
knower 249, 250, 251, 252, 260, 303–311, 357, 431
knowledge 77–78, 161, 162–163, 185, 248–249, 251–253, 254–256, 260, 327; certain knowledge 142, 161, 162 *see also* wisdom
Koronos 457
Kramer, Joel 217
Krates 458
Kulliyyāt-i wujūd of ʿUmar Khayyām 481–484

L'Anthologie de la littérature persane of Dh. Ṣafā 1
Leibnitz 324, 412
Leo 80, 24
liberation 435, 441, 443, 445, 446, 447, 448, 449, 450, 451, 453, 455
Libra 241
logic 157, 216, 226, 244, 268, 299, 321–322, 379, 389, 390, 391
Luqmān 209

al-Maʿarrī, Abu'l-ʿAlā' 474
Mabādī āra' ahl-madīnat al-fāḍilah of Fārābī 134, 136, 164–179
al-Mabda' wa'l-maʿād of Ibn Sīnā 244
Macedonia, Macedonians 84, 457
Madā'in (Seleucia-Ctesiphon) 334
Magians 79, 454
magic 186, 316, 338
Maḥmūd of Ghaznah 243, 244, 434
Maimonides 411
al-Ma'mūn 334–336
Mani 105–107, 108, 112, 113, 116, 119, 121, 122
Manichaeism, Manicheans 2, 103, 105–107, 108–123, 130, 423, 429, 430, 435
Mannāniyyah 130
Manṭiq al-mashriqiyyīn of Ibn Sīnā 245, 246, 321–322
Manūskihar 35
Mars (Bahrām) 83, 241, 480
Marzbān, ibn Bahmanyār 14, 388–389, 390–406
mashshā'ī philosophy *see* Peripatetic philosophy
mathematicians 185, 187, 189
mathematics 209, 244, 358, 432, 434, 474
Mazda *see* Ahura Mazda
Mazdaeans, Mazdaean 2, 216
Mazdayasnians 16, 20, 27, 31, 75
Ma'mūn 334, 335, 336
Mecca 474
mechanics 187, 189
medicine 86, 189, 211, 243, 244, 245, 268, 323, 347, 357, 411, 414, 431, 432, 469
megalopsychos 176
Melkites 236
Mercury (Tīr) 83, 241, 481
metallurgy 434
Metaphysics of Aristotle 127, 135, 217,

225–232, 390, 468
Metaphysics (*Ilāhiyyāt*) of Ibn Sīnā 190, 246, 247–268, 277–288, 411, 474 *see also al-Shifā'*
metaphysics 2, 134, 135, 157, 164, 210, 230, 244, 247, 323, 390, 432, 464
Michael 201
Middle Persian (language) 106
miracles 266–267
Mīr Dāmād 7, 8, 128
Mīr Findiriskī 8
Miskawayh, Abū 'Alī Aḥmad 129, 323–325, 326–355, 356–387
Mithra 64
monasticism 429
Moses 200
motion, principle of 217, 218, 226, 227, 231, 400
Mount Qāf 315
Muḥammad, the Prophet 189, 192, 200, 201, 203, 207, 268, 326, 336, 370, 371, 387, 390
Muḥammirah 130
Mullā Ṣadrā 4, 7, 8, 128, 180, 217, 245, 412
Muṣannafāt of Sijistānī 218–242
music 134, 135, 268, 416, 454
Mu'ādh ibn Jabal 203
Mu'āwiya 197
Muḥammirah 130
mutakallimūn see theologians
Mu'tazilites 3, 6, 186

nafs see soul
Nahj al-balāghah of 'Alī b. Abī Ṭālib 5
al-Najāt of Ibn Sīnā 244, 280, 282, 388, 389, 404
Narayana 456
natural bodies 218–219, 392, 394, 399, 405 *see also* supernal bodies
natural philosophy 6, 225, 226, 244, 435
Nāṣir-i Khusraw 3, 6, 130–131, 132, 245, 409, 411
Nayshāpūr 130, 474
al-Naẓẓām 203
Necessary Being 245, 246, 476, 479
necessary consequents 396, 398, 402, 404, 405
Nectanebus 457
Neoplatonism, Neoplatonists 127, 130, 131, 135, 181, 216, 245, 324, 388
Nestorians 236
Nichomachean Ethics of Aristotle 324
Nihāyat al-ḥikmah of 'Allāmah Ṭabāṭabā'ī 3
Nubians 371

occult sciences 216
occultation 188, 320
Ohrmazd *see* Ahura Mazda
Olympias 457
On the Heavens of Aristotle 389, 391, 392, 395, 402
ontology 135, 245
oriental philosophy 246, 321
oriental wisdom *see al-ḥikmat al-mashriqiyyah*
Ottomans 4

Pahlavi (language) 2, 15, 16, 35, 44, 49, 79, 323
Palestine 1, 457
Parmenides 2
Parthians 13
Patanjali 437, 440, 441, 445, 448, 449, 452, 455
Pāzand 84; language 86
Peripatetic philosophy, Peripatetics 5, 6, 7, 8, 127–129, 135, 180, 244, 245, 321, 388, 411, 435
Persia, Persians 1–10 *passim*, 13, 14, 15, 105, 106, 107, 128, 130, 131, 134, 135, 180, 243, 245–246, 323, 324, 326, 334, 337–338, 340, 409, 410, 412
Persian (language) 1–10 *passim*, 106, 130, 242, 244, 245, 246, 324, 336, 434, 454, 470

Phaedo of Plato 161, 163, 181, 214
pharmacology 434
Philip, King 457
Philoponos, John 464
Phoenix 457
physics 157, 158, 209, 210, 436, 474
Physics (*Physica*) of Aristotle 217, 225, 226
Physics (*Ṭabīʿiyyāt*) of Ibn Sīnā 246, 261–268, 292–302, 390 *see also al-Shifāʾ*
physiognomy 312–313
Plato 135, 136, 155–163 *passim*, 181, 209, 210, 211, 214–215, 323, 380, 409, 412, 415, 419, 420, 421, 430, 435, 464
Platonic Academy 1
Plotinus 1, 127, 135, 389
politics 128, 159–160
polytheism, polytheists 209, 210
Pope, Arthur Upham 1
Porphyry 324
Posterior Analytics of Aristotle 161, 162, 163, 390
potentiality 73, 76, 143, 154, 162, 215, 237, 278, 280, 297, 302
Prior Analytics of Aristotle 161, 390
predetermination, divine 277
predicates 140, 143, 262; essential 144–145
Primal Being 235
Primal Cause 282
Primal Principle 229, 230, 238, 240
privation 168, 279–286, 288, 300
Proclus 214, 451
proof of the ladder (*al-burhān al-sullamī*), 388
prophecy 177, 209, 323, 411, 412
proposition[s] 144, 207, 267, 299, 478
prosody 190–191, 193
providence 246, 254, 272, 277, 289, 311, 406
psychology 181, 245, 252, 323, 324
Pythagoras, Pythagorean philosophy 2, 181, 209, 213, 215, 445, 450, 451

Qajar dynasty, Qajars 8, 9
al-Qānūn fi'l-ṭibb of Ibn Sīnā 244
al-Qānūn al-masʿūdī of Bīrūnī 434
quiddity 156, 157, 245, 247, 256, 274, 391, 396, 403, 404
Qūnawī, Ṣadr al-Dīn 7
Qurʾān 5, 128, 130, 200, 203, 209, 211, 243, 256, 315, 370

al-Radd ʿalā saysān al-mannānī of Rāzī 130
Rajarshi 455
Rayy 180, 243, 323, 411
Rāzī, Abū Ḥātam 6, 411, 412, 414
Rāzī, Fakhr al-Dīn 7, 128
Rāzī, Muḥammad Zakariyyāʾ (Rhazez) 6, 130, 132, 133, 210, 409, 411–413, 414–423, 424–433, 434, 435, 464
reason 412, 413, 414–423, 428, 429, 442 *see also* intellect
Red Khurramīs 422
religious sciences 180, 181, 185, 187, 189, 190, 192–206, 209
Republic of Plato 136
resurrection 14, 15, 19, 20, 29, 36, 37, 51, 55, 57, 62, 75, 79, 84, 85, 86, 100, 128, 211
revelation 3, 17, 36, 105, 139, 175, 181, 194, 198, 205, 268, 304, 373, 412, 435
Rhazes *see* Rāzī, Muḥammad Zakariyyāʾ
Risālat al-ṭayr of Ibn Sīnā 245
Rishi 455
Romans 1, 84, 105, 106
Rubaʿiyyat of ʿUmar Khayyām 474

al-Saʿādah waʾl-isʿād of ʿĀmirī 180
Sabaeanism, Sabaeians 180, 216
Safavids 4, 7, 8–9
sages 45, 88, 99, 135, 155–165 *passim*, 185, 186, 192, 197, 200, 210, 211, 312, 437, 446, 448
Sagittarius 21, 241
Salāmān and Absāl 303
Salāmān wa Absāl of Ibn Sīnā 245

Saljūqī, Malik Shāh 474
al-Samā' wa'l-'ālam of Aristotle 466
Samanid dynasty 243, 434
Sāṃkhya, school of 435
Samkhya 439, 445, 449, 450, 453, 454
Samson 457
Sanskrit 2, 434, 441
Sarakhsī, Aḥmad ibn Ṭayyib 3, 5
Sasanid dynasty, Sasanians 13, 15, 67, 84, 181, 324
Saturn (Kēvān) 83, 241, 457, 458, 481
School of Illumination 2, 7, 8, 245
School of Iṣfahān 3, 7, 8
School of Khurāsān 5–6
School of Shīrāz 8
sciences, classification of 135, 142–143, 185–192
Second Teacher (*al-mu'allim al-thānī*) *see* Fārābī
Seljūq dynasty 6
sensus communis 265–266
Shāh Walīallāh of Delhi 4
al-Shahrastānī 128, 411
Shahrazūrī, Muḥammad 7, 134
Shāpūr I 106
Shāpūrgān of Mani 106
Sharī'ah 180
al-Shaykh al-Ra'īs 243, 390 *see* Ibn Sīnā
al-Shifā' of Ibn Sīnā 128, 246, 261–268, 277–288, 292–302, 388, 390
Shīrāzī, Quṭb al-Dīn 4, 7, 8, 245
Shi'i Islam, Shi'is 7, 8, 9, 129, 236, 323, 435 *see also* Imāmiyyah, Twelvers
Siddha 455
Sijistānī, Abū Sulaymān Muḥammad ibn Ṭāhir 5, 216–217, 218–242, 323
Sijistānī, Abū Ya'qūb 6
Šikand Gumānī Vazār 14, 15, 77–78
Simplicius 127
al-Ṣīrāfī 180
al-Sīrat al-falsafiyyah of Rāzī 413, 424–433
Sīstān 13
Ṣiwān al-ḥikmah of Sijistānī 216
al-Sīyāsat al-madaniyyah of Fārābī 135
Socrates 161, 181, 209, 213, 215, 369, 387, 413, 421, 424–425, 429, 430, 442, 445, 451
Solomon, King 209
sophisticates 194–195
soul 15, 24, 38, 41, 45,–51 *passim*, 54, 55, 59, 60, 62, 64–66, 67–68, 77–79 *passim*, 83, 85, 86, 88, 89–102 *passim*, 110–119 *passim*, 127, 135, 138, 139, 140, 141, 153, 155, 158, 159, 161–163, 218–224, 229, 233, 237, 238, 239, 241, 248, 249, 253, 259, 261–263, 265, 267–268, 282, 285, 288, 290, 302, 304, 306, 307–308, 309, 310, 311. 324–325, 327, 328, 331, 332, 333, 340, 346, 349, 350, 351, 355, 356–387, 388–389, 391, 392, 395, 396, 397, 398, 399, 412–423 *passim*, 426, 427, 428, 429, 430, 431, 439, 440–442 *passim*, 444–451 *passim*, 458, 482, 483; animal 309, 419; appetitive 419, 420, 422; choleric 419, 420; knowledge of (*'ilm al-nafs*) 249; rational 419–422; universal 412, 451; vegetative 419, 420
Spain 3, 128
Spring of Life 315
St. Augustine 106
Stagirite school 127
Statesman of Plato 214
Stoics 127, 324
Sufism, Sufis 7, 324, 326, 435, 441, 445, 449, 452, 474
Suhrawardī 2, 4, 7, 8, 128, 245, 474
Sunna 200, 202, 203, 204
Sunni Islam, Sunnis 7, 8, 388, 435
supernal bodies 218–225 *see also* natural bodies
Survey of Persian Art of Arthur Upham Pope 1
syllogism 138, 140, 142–143, 144, 150, 157, 161, 163, 191, 255, 460
Syria 134, 209
Syriac (language) 2, 116, 236

Ṭabaqāt al-aṭibbā' of Ibn Abī Uṣaybiʿah 134
Ṭabaqāt al-umam of Qāḍī Saʿīd al-Andalusī 411
al-Ṭabarī, ʿAlī ibn Rabban 411
Ṭabīʿiyyāt of Ibn Sīnā 249, 258, 259, 261–268
Tabrīzī, Mullā Rajab ʿAlī 128
Tahdhīb al-akhlāq of Miskawayh 323, 324, 356–387
Taḥqīq mā li'l-Hind of Bīrūnī 434, 437–458
Taḥṣīl al-saʿādah of Fārābī 135
Tajārib al-umam of Miskawayh 323
tāj-nāmah literature 2, 181
Tā'rīkh al-ḥukamā' of Shahrazūrī 134
tawḥīd see unity, of God
al-Tawḥīdī, Abū Ḥayyān 216
Thales 471
Themistius 127, 324, 468, 470
theodicy 2, 14, 277, 289, 411, 412, 474
theologians 7, 13, 128, 185, 190, 199, 201, 204, 236, 456
theology 6, 7, 8, 181, 190, 191, 193, 199, 201, 202, 205, 411
Theophrastus 2
Thomas the Apostle 106
al-Ṭibb al-rūḥānī of Rāzī 413, 414–423, 426, 427, 431
Timaeus of Plato 214, 215
time 15, 17, 29, 30, 31, 57, 59, 69, 70, 73, 74–75, 76, 77, 80, 81, 82, 100, 131, 132, 133, 168, 246, 292–302, 439, 441
Tūrān 106
Tūrān-Shāh 106
Ṭūsī, Khwājah Naṣīr al-Dīn 4, 7, 8, 128, 129, 245, 324
Twelvers 4 *see also* Imāmīyyah, Ismailis, Shiʿism

ʿulūm-i ḥikmat 268
ʿUmar b. al-Khaṭṭāb 201
unity of God 213, 232, 327, 388, 435, 440 *s*
Ūthūlūjiyā ('Theology') of Aristotle 127
Valerian 106
Vasudeva 438–439, 447, 450–451, 453, 454
Veda 438–439, 452
Vendidad 14, 64–66
Venus (Nāhīd) 83, 241, 481
Virgo 21, 80
Vishnu 446, 456
Vishnu-Dharma 446
Vohûman (Vohu Manah) 19, 20, 39, 40, 64

Wafayāt al-Aʿyān of Ibn Khallikān 134
wahm see imagination
al-Wāqidī 334
wisdom 167, 210–211, 213, 215, 237, 256–257, 268
wisdom literature (*andarz*) 15

Yaḥyā ibn ʿAdī 134, 216
Yasna 53–54
Yezdigird 79
Yemen 203
Yūḥannā ibn Haylān 134

Zād al-musāfirīn of Nāṣir-i Khusraw 131, 132–133
Ẓaḥḥāk *see* Dahāk
Zamakhsharī 474
Zand 8, 55, 84, 86, 102
Zand-âkâs 16
Zarqān 130
Zātspram 15, 68–73
Zeus 456–458
zodiac 80, 83, 241
Zoroaster (Zarathushtra, Zarathustra, Zardusht, Zartušt) 1, 13, 40, 62, 64, 66, 71, 71–73, 79, 79–87, 84, 84–87, 95, 95–102, 105, 105–106, 454, 457, 457–458
Zoroastrianism, Zoroastrians 1–2, 13–15, 16–102 *passim*, 105, 106, 130, 180, 323, 324, 326, 388, 435
Zurvān 27, 68, 70, 73, 77, 79